M000110704

Additional Praise for *Good Derivatives*

"This book by Dr. Richard Sandor powerfully reminds us that the well-being of any economy is directly related to its ability to be innovative. Sandor, with his inventive mind, has himself helped to create new markets that have not only strengthened our economy but have also given us new ways to achieve important environmental and social goals. From his example, we learn that the creator of new markets must excel not only as an innovative thinker, but also as an effective advocate and teacher to policy makers and the general public. His life story demonstrates what one talented and committed person can accomplish in a free society."

—David L. Boren, President, The University of Oklahoma, Longest-Serving Chair of the U.S. Senate Select Committee on Intelligence

"A fascinating story from a most eloquent storyteller. A must read for anyone interested in the complex relationship between financial innovation and low-carbon economic growth."

—Christiana Figueres, Executive Secretary of the United Nations Framework Convention on Climate Change (UNFCCC)

"The evolution of derivatives is a fascinating tale and no one tells it better than 'Doc' Sandor, one of the most dynamic intellects this industry has ever seen. Starting with his early days of creating electronic trading at the University of California, Berkeley, and ranging through his leading role in the creation of financial futures and the development of a global market for emission credits, Richard spins a wonderful story that is difficult to put down. I recommend this book to anyone who is curious about capital markets and the power of innovation to transform the world."

—John M. Damgard, President, Futures Industry Association

"Richard Sandor quotes Schopenhauer's comment that all important truths go through stages when they are ridiculed and then opposed. Today even the existence of climate change is ridiculed by some, and serious action to cap the gases that cause it is forcefully opposed by others. Richard's account of how the tools of modern financial markets can be turned to environmental use reminds us that there is a way forward, and the truth, founded on the laws of economics, that the environment can be saved if it can be commoditized will become regarded as self-evident."

—Henry Derwent, President/CEO, International Emissions Trading Association

"At a time when markets around the world are struggling to find secure footings, Richard Sandor, through an artfully crafted story of his career, reminds us that financial innovation isn't all bad and that risk entails, well, risk. Writing for both the financially literate as well as the challenged, Sandor has recapped a career that blazed new paths in financial exchanges in a readable and informative way. Not only does *Good Derivatives* show how derivative and financial innovations can create market value, but in the book Sandor demonstrates how careful planning, perseverance, and understanding the climate in which you operate are the keys to success. An important read for today's policy makers."

—Christine Todd Whitman, Former Governor, State of New Jersey

Good Derivatives

A Story of Financial and Environmental Innovation

Richard L. Sandor

John Wiley & Sons, Inc.

Published by John Wiley & Sons, Inc., Hoboken, New Jersey.
Published simultaneously in Canada.

For general information on our other products and services or for technical support, please contact our Customer Care Department within the United States at (800) 762-2974, outside the United States at (317) 572-3993 or fax (317) 572-4002.

Wiley also publishes its books in a variety of electronic formats. Some content that appears in print may not be available in electronic books. For more information about Wiley products, visit our web site at www.wiley.com.

Library of Congress Cataloging-in-Publication Data:

Sandor, Richard L.
Good derivatives : a story of financial and environmental innovation / Richard Sandor.
p. cm.
Includes bibliographical references and index.
ISBN 978-0-470-94973-3 (hardback); ISBN 978-1-118-18528-5 (ebk);
ISBN 978-1-118-18529-2 (ebk); ISBN 978-1-118-18530-8 (ebk)
1. Financial services industry—Technological innovations. 2. New products.
3. Green marketing I. Title.
HG173.S256 2012
332.64'57—dc23 2011043305

Printed in the United States of America
10 9 8 7 6 5 4 3 2 1

Dedicated to My Family

From top left (clockwise): My granddaughter, Justine Sandor Ludden; Ellen and I at People's Park, Berkeley; my grandson, Elijah Sandor Ludden; my grandson, Caleb Sandor Taub; my daughter, Penya Sandor and her husband, Eric Taub; my daughter, Julie Sandor and her husband, Jack Ludden; my parents, Henry R. Sandor and Luba Mirner Sandor; my brother, Frank (left) and I, at ages 18 and 13; my grandson, Oscar Sandor Taub at a chess tournament in Atlanta; Charlie Finley and I; (center) Ellen and I on our wedding day. I was 21 years old; (center insert) Ellen and I today.

Contents

Foreword

There are some books that change our way of looking at a subject. Dr. Richard Sandor's book is one of them.

Our modern life, with all its comfort, convenience, and freedom unimaginable to early generations, depends critically on the smooth, joint working of an intricate web of interconnecting markets, from fairs and supermarkets to commodity exchanges and financial futures. In most cases, these markets appear to work so effortlessly that many of us take their existence and operation for granted. But they are human creations.

In this book, Dr. Richard Sandor presents a personal account of how new derivative markets have come to be invented over the past few decades, a time of explosive growth of financial instruments, most of which we still poorly understand today. It is an engaging and informative tale of how markets are created.

Although economists claim to study the working of the market, in modern economics, exchange takes place without any specification of its institutional setting. When economists say that the market works, what usually comes to their mind is a diagram in which the demand schedule intersects the supply schedule, giving rise to the equilibrium point at which the price and quantity are mutually determined. The demand and supply schedules, which Alfred Marshall referred to as the two blades of the price scissors, are theoretical constructions. While we cannot conduct economic reasoning without certain basic concepts and some relevant theories, economic reasoning cannot be all and only about a theoretical world and detached from the real economy. Unfortunately, modern economics for the most part has become a theory-driven subject. I have referred to this kind of economics as *blackboard economics*. Economics professors can proudly and conveniently teach it to students in the classroom without obliging themselves and their students to investigate how the real economy works.

But the diagram of demand and supply schedules is too detached from reality to inform students and their professors about how the markets actually operate in the economy. In the first place, the markets do not exist automatically. When economists discuss the choice between the pricing mechanism and administrative ordering, they usually assume that the two choices are readily available, not so different from the situation in which a consumer decides which car to purchase, a Toyota or General Motors. But as Dr. Sandor shows, the creation of markets is a lengthy struggle, full of surprises and uncertainties. Dr. Sandor details the endless meetings and exhausting negotiations that he held with other entrepreneurs, lawyers, and financiers, as well as government officials and regulatory agents in the process of creating those markets. This account opens a window to the complex reality of market making in the real world. It brings to light what is really involved when economists say that the market mechanism is used in resource allocation.

Markets are social institutions that exist to reduce the cost of carrying out exchange transactions and thus facilitate exchange and the division of labor. An important source of such costs in creating new markets is convincing the potential beneficiaries as well as the regulators of the economic value of the exchange that will be facilitated by the new markets. While it is obvious that a grain market benefits both consumers and farmers, it requires far more effort and ingenuity to convince the public of the value of a market for carbon dioxide emission rights, a market for climate exchanges, or a market for interest rate futures. Early research by Dr. Sandor in the late 1960s to implement an all-electronic, demutualized exchange did not advance despite being ahead of its time both conceptually and technologically but it eventually became the prevalent model in the exchange sector. The creation of new markets is frequently complicated and sometimes even thwarted by ideological enmity, political resistance, fear of uncertainty, or mere ignorance.

As Dr. Sandor illustrates well in this book, the creation of markets is always a social enterprise. It requires the collective actions of many individuals, organizations, and government agents. As in all collective efforts, human relations matter. The market does not and cannot reduce flesh and blood people with distinct identities into machine-like atomistic agents. Market participants certainly calculate and reason; but they remain social animals. The operation of the market also requires complicated rules and structures, which in turn requires concerted efforts and planning. Rules and norms are frequently needed. Many such rules and norms are self-enforced. But the state is often involved in enacting rules and providing credible third-party enforcement. All of this is discussed in Dr. Sandor's book.

I first met Richard Sandor many years ago when I was editor of the *Journal of Law and Economics* at the University of Chicago Law School. He submitted a paper on the development of a plywood futures contract. It was a most interesting article and I was very happy to publish it. Dr. Sandor was upset that the market failed because it did not attract enough customers to cover the costs. It did not upset me at all. On the contrary, it showed how difficult it was to create and maintain markets. In the years since then, Dr. Sandor has turned himself from an academic economist into a full-time entrepreneur, a market maker. In this book, he recounts how his study of economics at the University of Minnesota got him interested in economics problems in the real world. I hope this book will get more economists to leave their studies and look into the real world, without changing their careers.

RONALD COASE

Preface

> The path of least resistance and least trouble is a mental rut already made. It requires troublesome work to undertake the alternation of old beliefs.
>
> —*John Dewey*

I've always loved stories. It really doesn't matter whether I'm listening to other people's stories or telling my own. The best are always personal. This is my story. It's an economist's tale, but it isn't dismal. It's a story about invention and innovation. It's about high hopes and determination. It's about the exhilaration of initiating change. It's also about dealing with frustration and failure. Both, after all, are inevitable in any saga on transformation. This is also a story about the spirit of Chicago, a true American city that embraced innovation and was the stage for much of my work. It is a story that spans five decades of inventive activity and institutional building in the commodity markets that saw Chicago's LaSalle Street transform from a grain trading hub to a pioneer in financial and environmental markets. I decided to commit this fuller story to paper on June 26, 2009.

That night at 6:15 P.M., my wife, Ellen, and I attended a formal banquet hosted by Ernst & Young at the Hilton in Chicago, honoring "Entrepreneurs of the Year" in the Upper Midwest. As we sat in the hotel bar just prior to entering the ballroom for the event, Ellen's cell phone rang. It was our daughter, Penya. Ellen listened, then turned to me with a big smile and loudly said, "It passed!"

What Ellen was referring to was the American Clean Energy and Security Act (ACES). It was a historical event for both the United States and the world. Following numerous unsuccessful attempts, the U.S. House of Representatives had passed a bill that required the country to reduce greenhouse gases contributing to global warming. It was legislation I strongly supported.

President Obama articulated three goals during the days following his inauguration: revitalize the economy, enhance U.S. military security, and develop new domestic energy sources while mitigating climate change. In my view, ACES facilitated the achievement of all three goals. First, green entrepreneurship and green jobs would help revitalize the economy. Second, the substitution of renewable energy for imported fossil fuels would begin the path toward energy independence and thus military security. Lastly, ACES would reduce energy usage, increase domestic supply, and combat global warming.

For me personally, the passage of ACES was a milestone in a long journey. The road that began at the Earth Summit in Rio de Janeiro in 1992 led me on a path toward creating financial products to reduce environmental pollution, and ultimately toward my involvement in creating the Chicago Climate Exchange. That night, I was elated that the United States was taking a leadership role in solving the most important environmental objective of our time. It was a moment of personal vindication.

We were seated next to Sadhu Johnston, one of the judges for the evening and chief environmental adviser to Chicago mayor Richard M. Daley. I mentioned to Sadhu that the evening was momentous for yet another reason: it was the eve of our forty-sixth wedding anniversary.

The event was staged like the Academy Awards, with eight award categories ranging from financial services to technology. Chairmen and CEOs from both public and private companies dotted the stage. A one-minute video on each nominee was broadcast onto two large screens. Terry Duffy and Craig Donahue from the Chicago Mercantile

Exchange were the first winners, awarded for having transformed a mutual floor trading exchange into the largest publicly traded electronic futures exchange in the United States. I had served numerous terms on the board of directors of both the Chicago Board of Trade and the Chicago Mercantile Exchange, and knew both men well. I was delighted to see them recognized for their achievements.

About three-fourths of the way into the ceremony, Sadhu leaned over to tell me that I was next. He told me the video was four minutes long, not the one-minute version reserved for other categories. He joked that there was more to say about me. Personally, I suspected that the longer length was more due to a new interest in sustainability and not my work, per se. The video began with my first job as an assistant professor at the University of California at Berkeley. The photograph of a young man with very long sideburns was a bit comical and reflected the tastes of the 1960s. The nostalgia had begun. The video proceeded to describe my role as the principal architect of interest rate futures and the universal recognition afforded to me as the "father of financial futures."[1] My work in emissions trading came next, along with the role of markets in combating and virtually eradicating the acid rain problem in the United States. It concluded with highlights from the history of the Chicago Climate Exchange and its efforts to deal with global warming in the United States, Europe, China, and other parts of the world.

The award set my mind whirling with images of the people who had shaped and influenced my life. The award didn't just signify individual achievement, as inventive activity was often collaborative and I had the good fortune of living in the right time and being in the right place. That evening, I resolved to write this book.

This is a story of financial innovation. For the most part, innovation is respected and valued. Yet as I record my own story, there is a cloud over financial innovation. As America continues its struggle to regain its economic footing, financial innovation has been widely blamed for causing the 2008 global financial meltdown. Critics are not always well versed in economics and finance. But even sophisticated observers share this view. During the financial crisis, Chairman of the Federal Reserve Bank, Paul A. Volcker, remarked that the only valuable

---

[1]Resolution by the City of Chicago, honoring Richard L. Sandor, August 12, 1992.

financial innovation in the past twenty years has been the automatic teller machine. He went on to say, "I wish someone would give me one shred of neutral evidence that financial innovation leads to economic growth. One shred of evidence."[2]

I believe that there is more than one shred of evidence. It may have gone unnoticed since much of the positive financial innovation of the past four decades emanated not from Wall Street, but from LaSalle Street—home to the Chicago Board of Trade, the Chicago Mercantile Exchange, and the Chicago Board Options Exchange. The Chicago exchanges, traditionally the trading arena of agricultural products, revolutionized global finance by developing and popularizing financial futures and options.

Perhaps it was their comfort with the concept of managing risk that made Chicago exchanges more willing to experiment with new financial instruments. Perhaps it was the notion of being second, and wanting to unseat the guy at the top, that has left the leaders of these exchanges hungry to try new approaches. This is not to say that the business transacted on these exchanges was small. In 1970, Chicago was flexing its big shoulders. That year's annual report of the Chicago Board of Trade proclaimed:

> The year 1970 might well be recorded in CBT annals as the "year of the markets." Trading activity at the Board set an all-time record as more than 8.1 million contracts were traded during the year. This was 500,000 more than the previous record of 7.6 million contracts, set in 1966. The estimated dollar volume of these contracts soared to $73.3 billion, an increase of 96 percent over year-earlier levels. During July, August, and September, our estimated dollar volume exceeded that of the NYSE; a fact worthy of particular note, since the NYSE continues to be the only financial institution in the world larger than ours.[3]

---

[2] *Wall Street Journal's* Future of Finance Initiative, December 8, 2009, http://blogs.wsj.com/marketbeat/2009/12/08/volcker-praises-the-atm-blasts-finance-execs-experts/.

[3] *Annual Report*, Chicago Board of Trade, 1970.

Still, Chicago commodities exchanges were always seen as niche markets, the province of agricultural regulators and of interest to far fewer people than the Dow Jones Industrial Average or the New York Stock Exchange.

But it was the Chicago Board Options Exchange, and not the Big Board in New York, that provided a home for trading in stock options in 1973. In 1975, it was the Chicago Board of Trade that introduced interest rate futures. This allowed financial institutions to hedge or cushion their risk against interest rate swings. Similarly, stock index futures originated in Kansas City and were commercialized by the Chicago Mercantile Exchange. The same pattern applies to currency futures.

So while Volcker's discomfort with financial innovation may have been understandable, his nihilistic attitude stunned me. Innovation has helped make the American economy what it is. The economist Robert Solow won a Nobel Prize in Economics for demonstrating more than 40 years ago that the well-being of an economy is tied, in part, to its ability to innovate. More than 30 years ago, Kenneth Arrow, another Nobel laureate in economics, observed that financial innovations, such as the limited liability corporation and double entry bookkeeping, may have been just as important to economic development as technological innovations like the steam engine or semiconductor. Yet such financial innovations are often overlooked for at least three reasons. First, they are intangible and may be difficult to understand by laypeople. Second, they tend to be wholesale, that is, they are not part of the retail mass market. And third, until recently, they were not patentable and their benefits accrued only to first movers.

In the late 1970s and early 1980s, while Volcker was battling a pronounced upsurge in inflation and interest rates, Chicago's new interest rate futures contracts undoubtedly helped banks and other financial institutions protect themselves as interest rates shot up. While some of the risky strategies that firms like Lehman Brothers used in the hopes of making giant profits were clearly rash and ill informed—within the firm and externally—such examples should in no way stand as a blanket indictment against financial innovation. Documentaries like *The Inside Job* criticized financial maneuvering for causing the 2008 financial crisis, but failed to properly distinguish between markets that are transparent and regulated and over-the-counter markets that are opaque and unregulated.

One of my goals in writing this book is to shed more light on the process of financial innovation, and the careful thought that went into the innovations that I helped shape in Chicago. This book provides a description of my early life, starting with my childhood in Brooklyn as the son and grandson of immigrants. I move on to my graduate studies in Minnesota, and through my stint as a young professor in Berkeley. Next is my failed attempt at starting a totally electronic exchange in the 1960s, and my migration to the fast-paced commodities markets in Chicago. From there, I move on to the innovations themselves: mortgage interest rate futures contracts, Treasury bond futures, options on Treasury bond futures, Treasury note futures, environmental derivatives, and the birth of the Chicago Climate Exchange. Every innovation has its own unique story. Throughout my book, I try to explain how each new financial product came about, its intended purpose, and the economic, political, and financial ramifications. Technical explanations are provided for those interested in gaining a more in-depth understanding of these products. I also emphasize the importance of selling an idea, having discovered early on that simply creating a new product is not enough. New financial products are sold, not bought.

Good Derivatives, those listed on regulated exchanges, create value for society and prevent systemic breakdown of financial institutions and capital markets. These markets create value by providing a mechanism for corporations and financial institutions to hedge against price risks in commodities, stocks, and bonds. They also allow us to discover market-based forecasts of future prices. The transparency of futures prices on regulated exchanges results in lower transaction costs for the purchase or sale of commodities, stocks, and bonds for the spot, or immediate delivery market.

Good Derivatives are financial innovations that are created and can't be assumed to exist. Economists generally imagine, conjure, or assume the existence of markets. Furthermore, they often assume that markets function efficiently. While these assumptions may be effective for teaching and developing theories, they overlook a critical part of economics: the creation of the market themselves. In reality, establishing a viable market involves a great deal of hard work, expense, and marketing to potential users. It involves building layers of institutional capacity that can support and nurture young markets. It involves getting the right combination of new legislation, regulation, and compliance to ensure trust in the markets, exchanges, and/or standardized contracts.

I believe that the recent collapses of financial institutions and the banking system could have been avoided if financial innovation—be it CDSs,[4] subprime mortgages, or CDOs—had followed the path of innovations described in this book. This is a story about good derivatives that were created in the past 40 years. There were no regulated and transparent futures and options exchanges that required a bailout by governments during the great recession. Good derivatives performed flawlessly.

The value of financial innovation can only be realized if the costs of establishing and operating a market do not exceed the benefits. Markets that minimize transaction costs are designed to do so. They too do not simply exist. Ronald Coase, a Nobel Prize–winning economist, taught us that if we view economics through this lens, we can come closer to understanding the nature of organizations and markets.

This is a story about good derivatives that were created in the last 40 years. It is my hope that it will be useful to financial innovators, regulators, and policy makers in America and around the world. This is also a story about the future. I hope it will be of value in predicting new geographies and new financial innovations that occur in the next 40 years.

Richard Sandor
September 21, 2011
Wrigley Building, Chicago, Illinois

---

[4]A credit default swap (CDS) is a swap designed to transfer the credit exposure of fixed income products between parties.

Acknowledgments

As I pen these acknowledgments, I want to foremost thank the man who urged me to write this book and advised me to just tell the story. Ronald Coase has personally inspired and mentored me for the past four decades. My gratitude toward him cannot be described. I have been visiting Professor Coase for many years, before and during the time this book was being written. We often discussed the book over lunch and he gave me invaluable advice. He possessed the clarity common to great teachers. When I finished the first half of the book, I nervously handed him the manuscript like a student completing an exam. I came back two weeks later and asked him what he thought of it. After complimenting me on my achievement, he added, in a soft English accent, "It's one damn thing after another." His words meant a lot to me. I was finally telling the story he asked me to tell. The process of financial innovation was—and is—one damn thing after another. And I wouldn't have it any other way.

I have long since discovered the flaws of human memory. Thankfully, there were many friends who helped me recount the events captured in this book. Natalie Persky, Tom Cushing, Mike Walsh, Mike MacGregor, Rob McAndrew, Rohan Ma, Jeff Huang, Fran Kenck, and Kathy Lynn Minervino-Myers all delivered colorful personal accounts of what took place in the past decade. Neil Eckert, Helene Crook, Peter Koster, Sara Stahl, and Albert DeHaan generously shared their memories of the creation of the European Climate Exchange with me. Tony Chiarenza, Joe Cole, and Ed Berko's recollections of the 1990s helped me convey the exciting possibilities of insurance derivatives during that time. Ricardo Cordero provided me with an accurate history of electronic trading in Europe that was also rich in astute personal observations. Al Swimmer, Jay Feuerstein, Norman Mains, and Rick Ferina all related their experiences of the 1980s to me. Their conversation was enthralling, and I regret that not all of it could be incorporated into this book. My former colleagues, Chris Andersen, Peter Ackerman, and Syl Schefler, also shared stories about how capital markets helped finance entrepreneurs in the 1980s. Lou Margolis described the birth of indexing in the equity markets while Jay Pomrenze helped me understand how early adopters used financial futures. Michael Spencer, a former colleague and now the CEO of ICAP, the world's premier interdealer broker, gave me invaluable insight into that sector of the business. Michael has always been a good friend and supportive of my efforts. Philip McBride Johnson inspired me with an adventurous account of how he crafted the language that enabled the birth of financial futures. Jon Goldstein, my friend of almost five decades, recapped the wonderful memories of our years at the University of Minnesota. Many thanks to my brother, Frank, my nephew, David, and my cousins, Ruth and Jocelyn, who reminded me of many stories of our family and childhood.

I also tapped the knowledge of members of Chicago's futures community. I am thankful to Bill Brodsky, Jack Sandner, Rick Kilcollin, Scott Gordon, Tom Donovan, Larry Rosenberg, Frank Jones, Lee Stern, David Goldberg, Joe Gressel, Pat Hennessy, Don Wilson, and Nathan Laurell. Galen Burghardt revived memories of the early seminars we conducted to educate users of financial futures. Ken Raisler gave me an expert's insights into the regulatory process in the futures industry. A special thanks to John Lothian, who provides a valuable service of disseminating news and commentary on the futures industry from Chicago to the world. His support over the years has been important to me. My friend and mentor, Les Rosenthal, was, as always, a source of inspiration and fond memories.

Without the advice and dedication of investment bankers Paul Hodges and Jim Durkin, we would have never been able to finance the largest carbon market in the world today. Neil Woodford, an early and committed believer in our concept, deserves the same if not greater credit. They are the unsung heroes of European emissions trading.

As with any book that deals with finance, reliable data and facts are critical. For their promptness and patience with my requests I am grateful to Gil Avidar, Chris Bartlett, Greg Busler, Nicole Cook, John Fyfe, Tom Gibson, Steve McComb, Dan Scarbrough, and Andy Totman. Will Acworth and Toby Taylor at the Futures Industry Association were terrific. Thank you to Charlie Carey and Lindsay Phillips at the Chicago Mercantile Exchange, the Intercontinental Exchange, and the Joyce Foundation for kindly sharing and allowing us to use many important materials in this book.

Eric Chow, Alice Xie, and Kwangun Lee meticulously organized the daunting pile of information files we've accumulated over a decade and did research. Fang-Yu Liang, and Daphne Yin performed excellent research and were exemplary as editors. They were all seamlessly managed by Rafael Marques. In fact, I couldn't have written this book without his help. His feedback and editorial contribution to the entire manuscript were crucial. Thanks also to my colleagues, Murali Kanakasabai and Nathan Clark, for reading, editing, and harshly critiquing the manuscript. I cherish Nathan's sometimes near-brutal honesty and embrace Murali's vigor for always challenging me intellectually. Both were crucial to the integrity of the end product. A special thanks to my assistants, Mary Ann White and Melanie Rakovic, who were invaluable throughout this process.

I also need to thank Karen Arenson, Victoria Rowan, Margery Mandell, Emily Lambert, and Andrew Szanton for their help in the early chapters and the advice they gave me on writing. Dan Yergin gave me an invaluable piece of advice: to start the story at a point where my comfort level was high. It didn't have to be at the beginning. He was given this advice by one of his mentors, and it served him well. It served me well, too.

A special thanks to Joyce Gladstone Silver and Martin Greenberg for keeping memories of P.S. 99 and Midwood High School vivid and alive.

This is a unique book—a hybrid of a memoir and a financial and economics text. At times, the two themes complemented one another, and at times, they conflicted. This was a source of constant challenge for me. Fortunately I relied on some of my trusted friends and former colleagues to review parts of the manuscript. I am grateful to Paula DiPerna, Carole Brookins, Sylvie Bouriaux, Keith and Arlene Bronstein, Chris Culp, and Ning Wang. Their insights, edits, suggestions, and criticisms were priceless. As friends, they went above and beyond what I asked of them. I would also like to thank John Beasley, who gave me a terrific suggestion for one of the chapter titles on the Chicago Climate Exchange.

I am grateful to my executive editor, Kevin Commins at John Wiley & Sons, for approaching me with the proposal to write a book about my work as an inventor of "good derivatives." Other members of the Wiley team, like Meg Freeborn and Melissa Lopez, were also instrumental in guiding me through the manuscript production process.

As with any other book, the acknowledgment section has often been, and should be, a place to express one's true feelings of gratitude toward one's family. My daughter Penya advised me to write the book I would like to read. My daughter Julie told me to write it as if I was teaching, and Ellen, an artist at heart, prodded me to "follow my instincts." She patiently read and re-read each draft and her comments were uniquely valuable. Ellen is a loving and very wise woman. I owe her thanks not only for this book, but for a lifetime. Ellen, my daughters, their husbands, Jack Ludden and Eric Taub, and my grandchildren, Elijah Sandor Ludden, Justine Sandor Ludden, Caleb Sandor Taub, and Oscar Sandor Taub, always did, and still do, provide me with all that one would want from a family. I offer a heartfelt thank you to each and every one of them.

Chapter 1

The Early Years

America is another name for opportunity.

—*Ralph Waldo Emerson*

I grew up in Brooklyn, New York, in the 1940s and 1950s, with a father who loved vaudeville and movies, and a mother whose memories of her wealthy upbringing in Europe dominated our home.

The House of Sandor and Mirner

My father, Henry R. Sandor, was dark-haired, olive-skinned, and heavy-set. A pharmacist by day, Henry worked six days a week from 10 in the morning until 10 at night, and came home well after I went to bed. The summer of 1950, when I was almost nine, he taught me how to make ice cream sodas and malted milkshakes at his store in Brighton Beach. The store was often filled with my father's friends from show business, and I loved going to work every day. He measured his ingredients with precision as he ground medicines in his mortar and pestle, readying them to be put into capsules. It was wonderful watching him. A side effect from my summer job was a gain of 10 pounds, and it wasn't until my junior year in college that I stopped being overweight. My father used to say that I had personality, and that it was almost as important as brains when it came to success. I felt his love and respect.

My father often told stories about his own father and grandfather. His father, Maurice Sandor, was a dapper and handsome man. He was going to be hung for anarchy at the ripe old age of 16 for conspiring with Leon Trotsky to overthrow the Czar. Maurice's father, however, was the chief engineer for the Trans-Siberian Railroad, and through political connections at the court of the Czar, was able to arrange to have him leave for America that very day. Trotsky wrote letters to my grandfather, asking him to return to Russia, and came to the pharmacy to play chess when he visited New York. We never really knew what was fact or fable. Maurice, according to Ellis Island records, did not, in fact, sail to this country in steerage. He spoke no English when he landed in New York, survived by selling apples on Hester Street, and within 10 years earned a pharmacy degree from Columbia University and an MD degree from New York University. Before long, Dr. Maurice Sandor owned and ran a drugstore and practiced medicine. He met Frances Diamond, my grandmother, on the Atlantic crossing. Frances came from a family of performers—her cousin, Selma Diamond, was a comedienne.

While my father profoundly respected education and spoke proudly of his father's degrees, he was more of a Bohemian than an intellectual. He had two particular quirks. I have the fondest memories of the different hats he would wear on whim, ranging from berets to fedoras. He also had a passion for cars. Most cars on our streets were Buicks or Chevrolets, but not ours. Henry drove foreign cars—mostly Jaguars and Volvos. There was an occasional American car like the Nash Rambler.

Known as "Broadway Hank," my father was a quiet person unless he was standing before an audience. He had a giant personality when he performed. An entertainer at heart, he loved stand-up comedy, singing, and playing the guitar. He received an offer to play in a big band in the 1920s but had to turn it down. His father had died at an early age, and he had to help raise and support his brother and sisters. He worked as a pharmacist to accomplish this and put his career as an entertainer on hold. His brother worked side by side with him at the drugstore. Two of his sisters went to Hunter College and became teachers, while his youngest sister became a housewife. My father's brothers and sisters led typical middle class lives, working hard and placing a strong emphasis on education. The next generation of Sandors, following my father's generation, produced two doctors, three dentists, one psychologist, one economist, and a teacher.

My memories of growing up were not dominated by my father's profession, but more by the Bohemian lives of the people who traipsed through our house from time to time. I remember the first time I saw my father entertain. My brother, Frank, and I hid behind a chair in our house as Broadway Hank charmed everybody at the party with his humor and songs. My mother kept on coming out with food, and my piano teacher played the piano and they all sang late into the night. Her father was the lead violinist in the Moscow Symphony, and she herself was an attractive woman with a sassy attitude—there were often many allusions to sex in the adults' conversions that I heard but never understood. I fell asleep that night to the sounds of song and laughter.

I loved Sundays. It was the only day of the week my father was home. He slept late and woke up to a sumptuous breakfast prepared by my mother. Sunday was also a day of rituals. We would all jump into a car and drive to Manhattan. We went to double features in one of the many movie theatres in and around Times Square. One memorable Sunday, we went to the RKO Palace for a double feature with 10 acts of vaudeville between two movies. Another wonderful memory is attending my first Broadway show starring Paul Muni, a famous movie actor of the day and a friend of my father's. Paul captivated audiences in *Scarface* and *The Story of Louis Pasteur.* I felt a surge of pride that there, standing on stage, was my father's friend. After movies, we frequented Chinatown. Henry had a great nose for restaurants and a small joint, Hong Fat Company at 69 Mott Street, became our regular stop. Unlike the many chop suey restaurants that dotted Brooklyn, that one was actually authentic.

On other Sundays, we frequented a Chinese restaurant owned by my father's friend Tom Kwan. The restaurant was on the second floor of a two-story building. We sat in the kitchen for hours and watched Tom at work, tasting the pork and duck as he cut the meat and prepared the dishes with amazing precision. He often barked commands in Chinese to his Alaskan husky, whereupon the dog sat down or trotted away. It turned out that the dog understood not only Chinese, but also English. I was awed by that bilingual dog. I wondered, "How could a dog understand Chinese?"

My father first got to know Tom during the Roaring Twenties. Broadway Hank was performing in a speakeasy when Tom, a regular, stopped by one night wearing a lot of gold jewelry. My father noticed some local gangsters eyeing Tom, so he offered to store Tom's valuables until the next time he came back. Tom did this without any sign of distrust or suspicion. My father also had him keep a small amount of cash handy, in case Tom needed to placate any thieves. Sure enough, Tom was mugged as he left. My father returned his valuables the next day and from then on, Tom visited our house every couple of years at some unexpected time during the Christmas season with bags of Chinese sausages, pork, and duck in tow. He sometimes even brought a large wok to cook food. I sat for hours watching him cook. The meal always ended with a big Christmas fruitcake.

At some point, Tom stopped showing up—in fact, he didn't come for three consecutive years. He had always kept his personal life to himself, and my dad never knew where to contact him. I asked my father why we hadn't seen him. My father said in a matter-of-fact way, "Tom always comes. He must have died." It turned out that Tom had closed his restaurant and retired. Those wonderful days spent in Tom's company taught me a lot about Chinese culture and loyalty—something that would prove invaluable later in life during my visits to China.

On the opposite side of Tom's restaurant was Nathan's Famous—the largest seller of hot dogs and hamburgers in Coney Island and a big threat to the smaller hot dog vendors. According to my father, competitors once spread word that Nathan's food was unsafe. To recover his business, Nathan went to the local hospital and announced that any doctor or nurse who came in uniform would get a free meal. When locals and tourists saw so many white-uniformed professionals eating there, they stopped paying attention to the rumors of a dirty restaurant with unsafe food. The importance of perception and promotion was a life lesson that stayed with me.

Just as my father was the patriarch of his family, my mother was the matriarch of her family. My mother, Luba Mirner Sandor, was born in Poland in a city that ultimately became Russian. Luba was a petite, shapely brunette quick to smile. Her father, David, had changed his name from Berenson to Mirner for some unknown reason, and then migrated to Antwerp, Belgium, to become a successful diamond merchant. Family lore was that he was a cousin to Bernard Berenson, the preeminent art critic. I personally never knew what was fact or fancy. David Mirner became a member of the Diamond Bourse. He was recognized in Belgium for his charity and was reportedly one of the great chess players in the country. He lost his fortune investing in a diamond mine in South Africa and from his frequent visits to Monte Carlo. He and my grandmother, Penya Mirner, along with my mother, her sister, and two brothers, came to the United States penniless. My mother's sister had Tourette's syndrome and could not work. Her brothers got married and were partners in a dry-cleaning business together. Education was a critical part of the Mirner family's values. The third generation of Mirners became chemists, musicians, and teachers.

All of the Mirners seemed to have settled into normal middle-class lives when things changed. My uncle Joe fell in love with a neighbor's wife and left home. He moved into my room shortly after my brother moved into our basement apartment. My dreams of finally having my own room were dashed. Joe was an elegant dresser and articulate man with a small moustache, whose dress and demeanor reflected his European upbringing. To avoid World War I, David Mirner moved the family to London. All the children were sent to boarding school there and in Switzerland. Joe's life in boarding school in England had left him adept at the art of conversation, and he was a wonderful companion. He also had a great sense of humor. His companion was a stylish woman many years his junior. Joe lived with us for a short time, only to have a fatal heart attack shortly after moving in with his companion.

My uncle Charlie, a kind man with boundless empathy for others, was the next to move into my room. He later dated Uncle Joe's companion, in what others would at best call an odd set of circumstances.

My mother, Luba, had absorbed all that a privileged lifestyle enabled. She was a woman of boundless energy, fluent in five languages. While my father was not talkative when not performing, my mother was naturally outgoing and gregarious. She was filled with strong beliefs and passionate about every activity she participated in. According to my brother and me, she was "America's Sweetheart." My mother shared her father's business skills and later in life became manager of a chain of women's clothing stores. Although frustrated by not being afforded the opportunity to go into business and somewhat bitter about not receiving the things in life she thought she richly deserved, she gradually came to terms with the circumstances and genuinely enjoyed life.

Five years older than me, my brother, Frank, had been difficult as a child with learning disabilities, so Luba hadn't wanted any more children. As she later told me, "You were unplanned." We didn't know it at the time, but he was dyslexic. Frank was much too old to be a companion to me, and my mother was always helping him work through his learning challenges. As a result, she was often not available for me. Frank was deeply loved and grew up as a generous human always concerned with others. He had a red Radio Flyer wagon that he was happy to give up when he learned that the war effort required iron—certainly an incredible sacrifice for an eight-year-old child. I understood his nobility but sorely missed that wagon. Frank went to medical school and later became a hematologist. He was and is a caregiver.

Given my father's work schedule, my mother's justifiable attentiveness toward my brother, and the age difference between Frank and me, I grew up often feeling alone in my own home. My mother's eyes lit up whenever my brother walked into a room. They never lit up for me, but I was determined to make that different outside of our home. For as long as I can remember, friends became an important part of my life. By the time I was six years old, my mother began giving me an allowance of 25 cents per week. I would use 15 cents for a movie and candy, and my mother often asked me about the movie when I came back. She and the neighbors used to listen attentively as I faithfully described the plot and the characters. Their positive feedback only increased my desire to see more movies and tell people about them. This was further enhanced by the Sunday ritual of my father taking us out to movies. Movies were not only entertainment, but became a means to learn about life. I came to enjoy them as much as I did reading.

Bobby Fischer and My Days at School

Friendship helped combat the isolation I felt on most days. Public School 99 ("P.S. 99") provided all that I needed in kindergarten through third grade. School was easy, and I had plenty of friends. My world was shattered when my mother announced that we had bought a house and were moving. I began fourth grade at a new school with a great deal of apprehension. I soon learned that I had been put in class 4-5, which in those days meant that I would be among the slowest students in the fourth grade as well as those who were troubled and had behavioral problems. 4-1 was reserved for the brightest students. As the year went by, I was forced to get along with classmates who were very different from those in my earlier grades, which actually turned out to be a wonderful learning experience. After several months, the teacher recognized how quickly I was learning and responded accordingly. She started to treat me more like an assistant than a student, and I helped her prepare lesson plans and pointed out how she could reach some of the other students. Teaching thrilled me. In some ways, these days turned out to be some of the happiest days of my childhood. At the end of the year, my teacher told me that I had "made her year" and recommended that I be transferred to 5-1. I came back later on to see her as I grew up, and it always thrilled us both to speak about my year there.

Meanwhile, I made friends with Robert Friedman, who was a year younger than me. We played stickball, softball, and cards together and ultimately taught ourselves how to play chess, another driver in my life. We met Raymond Sussman, who lived in the neighborhood. He easily beat both of us in chess. His father, Dr. Harold Sussman, a nationally ranked player and dentist from Brooklyn who played in the Manhattan Chess Club, taught us strategies such as sacrificing pieces for positions known as gambits and how to think about chess in terms of opening, middle, and end games. He emphasized the importance of controlling the central four squares on the board, a life lesson for business and politics.

One day, out of nowhere, a boy a year or two our junior passionately pleaded to be included in Dr. Sussman's classes. His name was Bobby Fischer. We played blitz chess—one second per move—and initially Bobby was rattled. He went away and came back more polished and in each game became harder to beat. The last time we played together, he came back to play in a tournament organized by Dr. Sussman. Robert had eliminated him in an early round, and we were faced off for the final match. I won a closely contested game. The next thing we heard from Dr. Sussman was that Bobby had been studying chess from five in the morning until school began and then from the time school ended until he went to sleep. He wanted a rematch with both of us. We declined. And that's how Robert Friedman and I managed to have a lifetime winning record against the one and only Bobby Fischer.

Fifth grade was harder. I was the new kid in class and had to make a new set of friends. As the next two years went by, I became bored and often misbehaved. My sixth-grade teacher was a martinet and berated me in public for my behavior until I became silent and refused to answer any of her questions. Eventually, she found a solution by assigning me to the principal's office to prepare tests and outlines for teachers. I learned how to type, a skill that proved invaluable, and relished the hours outside the classroom. Before long, I went to junior high at yet another new school. The experiences, feelings, and challenges resembled those I had gone through in grade school.

A friend of my father's found a job for my brother as a counselor in a summer camp in the Berkshire Mountains and I was sent along as a camper. As it turned out, one of my classmates from junior high school had poisoned the well for me and made it hard for me to make friends. I was miserable and wanted to go home after the first week. My parents told me that I had to stay.

To escape reality, I often listened to an old radio with static. The static annoyed the other campers and in an effort to placate them, I one day started screaming at the radio and shaking it. My fellow campers started to laugh as I went through a 10-minute routine about how bad the radio was and ultimately smashed it on the floor, creating an uproar of laughter. It was the beginning of my role as the camp comedian, and I became adept at finding humor wherever it existed. We had variety nights when I was urged by all to do a standup routine for 15 minutes. Years of watching my father finally gave me a chance to learn how to deal with an audience. I was a good mimic, and while I had experimented with humor sporadically with friends, I had never performed onstage. Yet it all came together, and from then on I became accustomed to providing comic relief to campers and counselors alike. I did my standup routine for the next three years and at one time actually thought it might become my career. I was not the only comic at Camp Pontiac. Another camp comedian, Larry Brezner, and I spent time together sharing jokes. We lost touch over the years but I had fond memories of him. He later went on to Hollywood and co-produced the original version of the film *Arthur* and *Good Morning, Vietnam.*

After my first summer at camp, I advanced to the ninth grade at a new high school. My breakthrough with comedy at camp helped me win new friends even though I was short, fat, and at 14, a year younger than other sophomores. Midwood High School, also attended by Woody Allen, became a dream come true. I was elected president of the student council, which consisted of the presidents of the junior and senior classes. I loved the student government, although I ran for mayor and lost. I naively thought that good ideas and effective communication were all that was required, and didn't realize until too late that politics also required alliances and organization. Those days prepared me for a life that would often revolve around election politics at exchanges.

Classwork was moderately challenging, and I did reasonably well while maintaining an active social life. In fact, my parents constantly prodded me to do better. They thought me lazy as I spent most of my time with friends or in front of the television. While I frequented movies and played poker on weekends, Frank worked endlessly to overcome his learning challenges and set the standard for dedication and hard work. He performed well and followed my father and grandfather to study pharmacy at Columbia. My father wanted him to enter the pharmacy business but soon realized that it did not really suit him. Frank went on to study art and obtained a master's degree at New York University, all in preparation for medical school.

Discovering Economics in Brooklyn

By the time I had to attend college, my family's resources had already been depleted on Frank's education. I had the choice of going to Columbia to study pharmacy or one of the free public universities in New York City. At 16, I was deemed too young to go to college and live away from home. I didn't want to be a pharmacist, so my best choice came down to either the City College of New York, which had a reputation as the Harvard of New York City colleges, or Brooklyn College, another highly rated City college. I hated the 90-minute commute it took to reach CCNY by bus and subway, and ended up enrolling at Brooklyn College.

Like many college freshmen, I had no direction or focus. My highest priority was to find a group of friends and begin dating. I pledged Tao Alpha Omega, a local fraternity whose members liked to party and gamble. I loved the card games and trips to the racetracks. To meet women and endear myself to my newfound fraternity brothers, I organized a campus-wide beauty contest. *Esquire* was a popular magazine of the time and I called the girls in the pageant Esquire girls. Aside from being a hit, the pageants taught me how to organize an event, attract an audience, and the potency of being a convener. Classes were of secondary importance to me. I enrolled in a number of different liberal arts and science classes, trying to find a subject that ignited my passions. My grades were barely passing, as parties and gambling occupied most of my time.

Ellen Simon, a smart and pretty coed on campus, had a quirky and adventurous side to her. Like many women of her generation, she was preparing to be a teacher. Her mother was a social worker and her father was a history teacher who became the owner of a small business to better support his family. Ellen grew up sharing many of her parents' values—she was always a caregiver and a cheerleader for others. Like my father, Ellen loved to perform and possessed the heart and soul of an artist. She read voraciously about politics, contemporary culture, fashion, and art, all blind spots for me. In this respect, she was my eyes and ears into that world. Her art reflected her enthusiasm for all that was new as well as the clear and intelligent way she saw the world. Ellen thought in pictures while I thought in words, making us complementary.

Simply put, I was smitten with her. Ellen ignited my passions and ambitions after our first dance. We dated and fell in love. Although

I had dated before, I had never known what intimacy was. With Ellen, I could share my most secret thoughts, dreams, and fears. Ellen's grandfather, a deeply religious man, often said, "She was born under a special star," and she was. Ellen was responsible, hardworking, and passively ambitious, holding her ambitions and leadership skills in check for many years in order to help me advance mine. Because of her, I came to take my studies more seriously. She demanded it for herself and for me. Together, we shared a vision for a life that was different from that of our contemporaries. I realized that my academic success was necessary to achieve this dream.

Ellen's younger brother, Jeff, was only 11 years old when I met him. Ellen's father, Julius "Julie" Simon, died of an embolism in his early fifties and her mother, Mattie, had to raise him. Jeff became like a younger brother to me. He was bright, sensitive, and a competitive runner. Jeff went on to get a PhD with a specialty in terrorism well before it had the relevance it does today. It always puts a smile on my face when he appears on television to comment on some recent event. I helped raise him and am very proud of the man he has become.

Ellen had taken an economics course from a young professor, T. Bruce Birkenhead, and somehow knew that I should meet and study with him. Having done his master's thesis on the economics of the British sports car industry, Bruce was not your typical theocratical economist. Bruce and I had common interests, as my father at this point was in his Jaguar car phase. Bruce's PhD thesis had been on the economics of Broadway, another common interest. He made economics come alive, and made me realize that it was possible to bridge the gap between theory and practice. I decided to major in economics. Bruce told me that economics was the queen of the social sciences and encouraged me to go on to graduate school. He thought it would open up a whole new world to me. He was right. Finally, I had found something to be passionate about, and college academics became enjoyable. I got straight A's from then on and went on to win a prize from the department when I graduated.

Graduate school was the next step, a large departure from the expectations of my parents and my fellow students who were focusing on professional careers like medicine, dentistry, or law. Seeking

Bruce's advice, I applied to all of the leading economics departments around the country, as well as the London School of Economics. The University of Minnesota was not an obvious choice for somebody born and bred in Brooklyn, New York. However, Bruce pointed out that its economics department was ranked sixth in the country, and also had Walter Heller as a member of the faculty. Heller was then the head of the Council of Economic Advisers under President Kennedy. Economics had at the time attained a certain sort of glamour because it was embraced by the young and handsome president as a solid part of the New Frontier.[1] It was no longer a dismal science, and had begun to attract serious followers, even among college students.

Among the schools I was accepted into, the London School of Economics was my school of choice. Unfortunately, there was no financial aid for the first year. Ellen and I had become engaged, and wanted to get married at the end of my first year of graduate school. We had had some tumultuous years while dating. I had been the bad boy, rarely attending classes and either gambling or going to movies, according to her friends and family. While I had started to do well and wanted to become an economist, she still allegedly would have been better off marrying a professional. We broke up in the summer of 1961, after her sophomore year and my junior year. She ended up in Europe while I hitchhiked across the United States. After a separation of six long months, we got back together during one Christmas break.

The decision was not difficult. When it came down to it, the University of Minnesota offered me the most financial aid and provided the opportunity for us to get married. We had a plan: I would spend the first year there alone while she finished her studies and began teaching. She would then find a teaching job here in Minnesota, when I started my second year of graduate school. We would get married in June 1963.

---

[1]The term New Frontier was coined by John F. Kennedy in 1960 to describe the program of his new administration. What was notable about the New Frontier was its advocacy of economics as a means of pushing the nation forward.

Bruce was not only a mentor but a friend. He arranged for me to teach at Brooklyn College the summer following my first year of graduate school. He went away that summer to manage a theater at Hyannis Port, and subletted his apartment to Ellen and me.

On to Minnesota

In September 1962, shortly after my twenty-first birthday, I boarded an airplane for the Twin Cities. My friends warmly joked that I needed a visa. I had never lived on my own, and decided to live in an international residence hall. It was completely different from attending a college in New York, which had been filled with commuters, which was not to say that the college experience in New York City had not been interesting. On the contrary, it had not only been filled with campus life, but had also given me the opportunity to take advantage of the city's great museums, theaters, and cultural events. These were the years of the beatniks,[2] and college life was inseparable from regular trips to Greenwich Village. Fine dining and ethnic food knew no boundaries in New York City. Saturday nights were spent in some of the city's best restaurants. I had a particularly good run at poker in college, which allowed us to visit a different restaurant almost every night during college breaks.

The University of Minnesota was a typical Big Ten school and had a completely different college culture from what I was used to. I met a lot of local students, and spent the first year going to football, basketball, and hockey games. Beer and pizza were the standard fare. I typically got up late in the mornings, went to classes, and taught, before hitting a bar called the Mixers with other graduate students. I made friends with students from diverse international backgrounds, as well as from across the United States.

One of them was Jon Goldstein, a lifelong friend who urged me to focus on environmental issues back during our days together in

---

[2]Beatnik was a media stereotype of the 1950s and early 1960s that caricaturized the Beat Generation literary movement and violent film images. The term was coined by journalist Herb Caen in "Pocketful of Notes," SFGate.com Archive, April 2, 1958.

Minnesota, and continued to prod me for more than 40 years afterward. His advice would have a profound impact on my life and career.

After my first quarter of intermediate micro- and macroeconomic theory, I began to explore what the economics department had to offer. I took a microeconomic theory course from Leo Hurwicz, whose formulation of mechanism design challenged Adam Smith's basic formulation of the invisible hand. Hurwicz saw that Smith's model of perfect competition, which harnessed individual self-interest to optimize the allocation of scarce resources, did not really work. Markets were not always competitive, not to mention that people were not perfectly informed and could use private information to further self-interests. What Hurwicz tried to do was to design institutions—or mechanisms—that provided incentives for people to achieve social objectives. I was struck by Hurwicz's willingness to take on one of the gods and foundational tenets of the economics profession, and by his efforts to come up with a creative alternative.

In Hurwicz's course, I also came across the writings of Ronald Coase, then a lesser-known economist at the University of Chicago. At the time, I was impressed by the utter clarity with which he used pure, succinct prose to explain complex topics such as the theory of the firm, and found his style a refreshing change from the mathematical equations that were engulfing economics.

Ellen joined me in Minnesota as I started my second year, and began teaching fifth graders at a public school near our home. She helped support me throughout graduate school, putting her own desire to go on to graduate school on hold. She was a wonderful teacher and was widely praised in the school newspaper when we left the Twin Cities. We returned to New York for the summer of 1964 where I taught introductory economics at NYU and Ellen studied art. We met after our classes in Greenwich Village and visited many art galleries. It was during this time that we began collecting affordable lithographs.

Back in Minnesota, I added a minor in statistics and studied econometrics in addition to my majors in public finance and international trade. My real passion, however, became the economics of innovation. My interest took root in a graduate seminar on the economics of research and development taught by Jacob Schmookler, which exposed me to the relationship between invention and economic growth. A book by Professor Schmookler, *Invention and Economic Growth*, published in 1966[3] became the classic explanation of technological progress. Until then, economists had generally assumed that inventive activity was exogenous, or not subject to the forces of supply and demand. As a result of Schmookler's work, invention came to be viewed as endogenous, an activity responsive to incentives or demand.

The concept of innovation had fascinated me for many years. As a child, I loved hunting through my father's pharmacology library for tales of how ancient civilizations had developed cures for certain ailments. I also loved Paul de Kruif's book *Microbe Hunters*, which told of the quests of modern scientists like Louis Pasteur and Marie Curie. In economics, I found parallels in the descriptions of modern technological inventions like the transistor, the photocopy machine, and the Sidewinder missile, including details about the challenges that had to be overcome for these products to succeed. A British economist, John Jewkes, co-author of *Source of Invention*,[4] was a favorite author of mine. I decided to write my doctoral dissertation on the economics of inventive activity. The topic was not in vogue in the economics profession, but fascinated me nonetheless. Throughout this process, Professor Schmookler encouraged and advised me.

Before I could start on my dissertation, I needed to pass a preliminary oral examination. I returned to New York to prepare. Fortunately, I had kept meticulous notes for all of my courses, as well as summaries for the written examinations in theory, public finance, and international trade. I then narrowed those summaries down further to focus on the highlights. This process of funneling complex ideas into their simplest forms would later serve me well in my career. Unnerved by the prospect of the two-hour examination that would determine my future, I came down with a severe case of shingles. Nonetheless, I took the exam in the early fall of 1965 and passed. The committee directed me to take more mathematics. "Real analysis" helped nurture my inductive

[3]Jacob Schmookler, *Invention and Economic Growth* (Cambridge, MA: Harvard University Press, 1966).

[4]John Jewkes, David Sawers, and Richard Stillerman, *Source of Invention: A Study of the Causes and Consequences of Industrial Innovation through the Inventions of the Nineteenth and Twentieth Centuries* (New York: St. Martin's Press, 1958).

reasoning, while the quantitative methods in economics turned out to be a course I was later asked to teach.

In my dissertation, "Size of Firm, Economies of Scale in Research and Development and the Use of Patented Inventions,"[5] I explored the sources of inventive activity in industrial corporations and the commercial value of patented inventions. I hypothesized that investments in different projects by a company were tantamount to investments in a diversified portfolio of stocks of the sort described by Harry Markowitz, a finance professor at the University of California at San Diego and a pioneer of modern portfolio theory. If companies viewed their investments in various research and development projects as a portfolio of investments, it was reasonable for them to use fewer of their patented inventions. They only needed one or two successful inventions to achieve large payoffs.

I designed a survey to test my hypothesis and sent it to 365 companies. The research was expensive, but I managed to secure a grant from the National Science Foundation. The data I collected confirmed my hypothesis and found that large firms, which had larger, more diverse R&D portfolios, used smaller portions of their patents. This led to diminished output from non-R&D employees due to less communication and joint inventive activity between R&D and non-R&D staff. In addition, it led to less research geared toward specific firm needs. I later realized that my study of the value of patented inventions was really an attempt to standardize inventive activity. I managed to get a couple of articles about my research accepted into academic journals such as *The Copyright and Trademark Journal*[6] and *The Journal of Business*.[7] R&D diversification taught me another lesson I would use in my future career as financial innovator.

---

[5]Richard L. Sandor, "Size of Firm, Economies of Scale in Research and Development and the Use of Patented Inventions" (PhD diss., University of Minnesota, 1967).

[6]Richard L. Sandor, "A Note on the Commercial Value of Patented Inventions," *The Patent, Trademark and Copyright Journal of Research and Education*, 1970.

[7]Richard L. Sandor, "Some Empirical Findings on the Legal Costs of Patenting," *Journal of Business* (University of Chicago, 1972).

Berkeley Beckons

I began to search for an academic job. Every year, the American Economic Association held a meeting in January, where economists presented their research and job candidates interviewed for possible positions. I attended the 1966 AEA meeting, having applied for a post in applied economics at the University of California at Berkeley's School of Business. David Alhadeff, a Berkeley professor, spoke with me about the department, his research, and my dissertation. In his own soft-spoken way, David epitomized all that was professorial. Some academics focused only on the teaching and research of economics, while David's interests were more catholic. At the end of the conversation, David said encouragingly, "You remind me of my nephew. I know you'd like him." I enjoyed the interview and felt at ease, and thought I had a good shot at a job there. Ellen and I grew excited at the prospect of moving to San Francisco. I soon learned, however, that a fellow graduate student had been invited to Berkeley to give a lecture, while I had still heard nothing since my interview. Other job prospects were not as exciting, and Ellen and I resigned ourselves to spending another year in Minnesota.

Then, one morning, I received a letter from Berkeley offering me a job as an acting assistant professor at the business school. I would be paid $8,600 per year and have a "step two" appointment, meaning a higher salary, with "acting" to be removed from the title once I successfully completed my dissertation. It was a prestigious job at a world-class university in a city that was the definition of change in America. I rushed to Ellen's school, and asked the principal if she could be called out of the classroom. We were ecstatic. The irony was that my supplementary mathematical training had been part of the reason I was hired. The first course I taught was for graduate students who needed sufficient mathematics to complete the program and obtain their MBA or PhD degrees.

While I continued my dissertation research, Ellen traveled to Berkeley to find us an apartment and begin a new job. I followed later with my classmate. He had strongly recommended me for the job and I believed he was instrumental in my getting the offer. Together, we climbed into the 1966 Toyota that Ellen and I had just bought. 1966 was the first year that Toyota began selling cars in the United States. Exotic cars still fascinated me, and I thought it would be fun to own one of these supposedly lower quality Japanese imports. We made the journey in a day-and-a-half, and the car performed flawlessly.

Minneapolis and St. Paul were Midwestern cities with values that reflected the post–World War II period in America. In contrast, San Francisco and the neighboring town of Berkeley across the Bay represented America's frontier, the cutting edge of the free speech movement, the drug scene, and just about every other aspect of the country's 1960s counterculture.

We rented an apartment a block away from the storied Telegraph Avenue and less than a 10-minute walk to my office on campus. The streets were filled with a mix of students and other young people who had simply come to live in the hip university town and hang out. Long-haired men and braless women advocated for social and political change in Sproul Plaza, the heart of Berkeley's campus. A typical day found me walking up Telegraph Avenue and through the campus courtyard, lined with booths espousing everything from free love to protests against the war in Vietnam. They all had their own tables and their own literature: civil rights, women's rights, sexual freedom, anti–Vietnam War, pro-drugs. Even in the business school, there were hints of change. Dogs romped in the fountain, and long-haired hippies rallied against the "fascists" in the Alameda County Police Department. Students came to class high on marijuana and brought their dogs for company; their mood and demeanor reflected the time and place. Sometimes I felt the dogs were listening more than the students. The climate on the Berkeley campus reflected the enormous structural change that was occurring in the domestic and international arenas.

Another type of change was occurring across the Bay. South of San Francisco, Stanford University had spawned a flurry of new technology companies. In 1971, the southern San Francisco Bay area became known as Silicon Valley for the principal ingredient, silicon, used in semiconductor chips, which had become one of the area's hot industries, alongside computers.

This environment of frenetic change was a delicious cocktail for me. Although I looked more business school than hippie, I felt at home with these social and political outsiders. I wore a tweed sports jacket with leather elbow patches. It was a little out of place but seemed compatible with my vision of an academic. At the same time, the high-tech companies provided a laboratory and classroom to learn about the inventive process—and to invest in stocks. There was a bull market at the time, so it was hard not to do well.

In June 1967, I returned to Minnesota to defend my thesis, and was granted my doctorate in July. I did not return to Minneapolis for graduation, which seemed anti-climactic. It was the Summer of Love in San Francisco, after all, the summer when journalist Herb Caen popularized the term *hippie*.[8]

Now that I had my doctorate, I faced a different type of pressure. Earning tenure required the publication of articles in well-regarded professional journals. Teaching quality was secondary. I would have to mine my thesis and try to write three or four articles that would be accepted in journals. Like many universities, Berkeley had a seven-year up or out policy. I would either be granted tenure within that time, or have to leave.

Another pressure came from my growing family. Ellen, who had started a job as an elementary school teacher, became pregnant in November 1967. We bought a house in the Berkeley Hills and prepared for the birth of our first child. Ellen gave me the lump sum she received from a retirement fund when she retired to buy the car of my dreams—a 1966 Austin Healey 3000, painted British racing green. I donned leather racing gloves for the short trip to work. Our first daughter, Julie Sarah Sandor, was born on August 10, 1968. All of the women we had grown up with had given birth in hospitals with painkillers, while we went with natural childbirth. It was Berkeley in the Sixties, and Ellen had started to become involved in the women's movement. My misgivings about natural childbirth were wrong. Words fail to describe the sense of wonderment and elation when watching your own child being born. Julie looked like Ellen. I remember how cheerful she was and her adorable laugh. She was a pretty and good-natured baby, well balanced even at three years old. One day, a colleague came to work with me on some research. Julie strolled into the room and started asking some intelligent questions. After about 10 minutes of back and forth, my colleague affectionately said to her, "Julie, would you marry me someday?" Without batting an eye, she explained, "Fred, we can't do that because you are much too old for me." She is a great observer and always makes me laugh.

---

[8]Herb Caen, "Small Thoughts at Large," SFGate.com Archive, June 25, 1967.

I had been on the Berkeley faculty for two years, but was still only 26. I took another position teaching "Price Theory and Resource Allocation" to graduate students in the Department of Engineering–Economic Systems and Operations Research at Stanford University. I needed the additional income to support my family, and the class provided me with the opportunity to meet with executives of companies located in Silicon Valley on my weekly trips to Palo Alto. I also used the money to invest in the stock market, which became a lifelong hobby.

My interest in the stock market helped cement a friendship with a new Berkeley colleague, Fred Arditti. Fred was very smart, had a great sense of humor, and shared my passion for movies. He also had a practical and intellectual interest in the stock market. When I described my own interest and my penchant for risk, he suggested that I trade commodities and pointed me to the literature. I started reading academic and practical articles about trading in commodity futures contracts, which fascinated me. I began trading.

Concerned with the ticking tenure clock and the pressure to publish, I reviewed the work I had done for my dissertation, refreshed myself on new developments in my field, and began searching for new ideas. Since I had always learned from teaching, I proposed teaching a new graduate seminar titled "Industrial Research and Technological Change." To prepare, I reviewed my seminar with Jacob Schmookler and read all of the new literature on the economics of technological change that had been published since I had completed my thesis.

Ellen helped me transform the room next to the furnace in our small Berkeley home into a personal office. Every night at about eight or nine o'clock, I went into the office and turned on the television. With the images and sounds of old movies in the background, I read journal articles and books while making notes for the class. After about three months of work in "the cave," I emerged with a course outline, a reading list of 18 articles and books, and over 60 pages of handwritten notes.

The course covered the definition and measurement of technological change, the microeconomics of technological change, the management and planning of research and development, the role of the public sector in technological change, and the impact of taxation and regulation. Rather than relying solely on academic work, I scheduled field trips to Silicon

Valley so the students could listen to real inventors speak. The highlight for many of us was a visit to the research and development facilities of Hewlett-Packard, where we were given presentations by scientists and the management team. Bill Hewlett, the co-founder himself, even personally addressed the class. What I saw exhilarated me and stirred my own appetite to become an inventor and entrepreneur. I didn't know it at the time, but the preparation and teaching behind the course would be great preparation for my future career as a financial innovator.

Chapter 2

Trying to Change the World

Launching an Electronic Futures Market

For the times they are a-changin'.

—Bob Dylan, 1964[1]

As a college student, I used my understanding of odds and knowledge of chess to play poker and bet on horses. I applied these same skills again while studying statistics and economic game theory. Moving on as a college professor, much of my time was spent trading stocks and commodities. For me, this was a variant of what I had been doing all along in college and graduate school—taking probability, statistics, and risk-taking to a new level. To the outside world—where speculation and academic economics were just a paradox—this

[1]Bob Dylan, "The Times They Are A'Changin'." Copyright © 1963, 1964 by Warner Bros. Inc.; renewed 1991, 1992 by Special Rider Music.

must have seemed unusual. Thankfully, it was not so among professional economists. In fact, many of us were in awe of John Maynard Keynes, who was both a legendary economist and a successful speculator in currencies.[2]

It was the beginning of 1968, and I was increasingly convinced that the rise of computers could revolutionize commodities trading, and provide much better trading tools. Using computers to quickly analyze statistical trends might prove invaluable, as a short response time posed a huge advantage in a volatile market. As a stock trader and a student of computer science, I keenly followed these developments. I also followed the use of computers in stock and commodity exchange operations. While there was limited adoption for clearing and electronic trading, no major institution had a fully electronic trading platform. Computers and their use on organized markets were still in their infancy.[3]

I began gathering data and building statistical models to forecast prices. I told David Ware, my commodities broker, about my ambitions and further needs for data. Dave was an uncommon commodity broker both in looks and demeanor. He was slight-framed, wiry, and had the look of a conservative New England lawyer or banker. Dave was aware of my fascination with using computers as a trading tool.

He was a member of the Commodity Club of San Francisco, a diverse group of agribusiness companies and commodity brokers. He

---

[2]Keynes ran an early precursor of a hedge fund in the early 1930s. As the bursar of the Cambridge University King's College, he managed two investment funds, one of which invested in the then-emerging market for U.S. stocks, as well as commodity futures and foreign currencies. See J. H. Chua and R. S. Woodward, "The Investment Wizardry of J. M. Keynes," *Financial Analysts Journal* 39, no. 3 (May–June 1983): 35–37.

[3]For most of the 1960s, computers were not yet used to consummate transactions or transmit information. Some from the exchange community saw the potential, but most viewed it as a threat to their jobs. In 1967 Alan Kay created AutEx, the first automated exchange. In 1969, NASD and NYSE began launching their own systems. In 1971, NASD debuted NASDAQ with a computer bulletin board but did not yet connect buyers and sellers.

told me that the club was considering launching an electronic and for-profit commodity exchange to trade coconut oil futures.

I thought this was a great idea, and it occurred to me that the members of the club were onto something I hadn't thought much about—an electronic exchange. It was obvious that an electronic exchange could improve access for existing participants, along with new speculators and hedgers. It was a transformational way to reduce transaction costs.

But there was a problem. Electronic for-profit exchanges represented a double departure from established norms. Exchanges had always been highly political organizations that operated not to maximize profit but to provide specific benefits to their members. So while going electronic was breaking one barrier, going for-profit was breaking another.

Since there were no existing exchanges in San Francisco, it was also hard to attract local speculators to serve as market makers. Without people to buy and sell throughout the trading day, we had little hope for success.

Once the idea was planted there in my head, however, I couldn't just give up. I met with some key members of the club in the new Bank of America headquarters in San Francisco. The skyscraper was a metaphor for the power and presence of the bank. It had a black sculpture near the entrance that looked like a two-ton piece of coal. The local joke was that it was the artist's concept of a banker's heart.

There were four key members, each with different motivations for supporting Project CCARP. The first wanted to earn commissions from commodity brokerage, the second wanted to increase his agricultural lending business, the third wanted to hedge coconut oil, and the fourth saw this as an opportunity to become CEO of an exchange and make a name for himself in the financial world. A for-profit electronic exchange was the key to meeting everyone's desires and hopes. The challenge was to turn these seemingly diverse goals into reality.

That first meeting helped me draft a proposal for a two-phase research project at Berkeley. I named the project the California Commodity Advisory Research Project (CCARP).

Phase I of CCARP examined the feasibility of an electronic for-profit exchange model. The question was, could we computerize the mechanics of floor trading? To find out, I would have to study the Chicago Board of Trade (CBOT) and the Chicago Mercantile Exchange (CME), the two largest exchanges in Chicago.

I also had to make sure that I understood all of the functions performed by the exchange before I could help properly design the new for-profit organization. We hired a technical consultant, Barry Sacks, to help determine whether computer technology was advanced enough to accommodate an electronic exchange. A man with an agreeable personality, Barry was an assistant professor in electrical engineering and computer sciences at Berkeley. whom I had befriended after he audited my seminar on inventive activity. We agreed to assemble a software team in Phase II—but only if the feasibility study suggested that we move forward.

Mid-1969 was a time of significant change. In July, the world saw us put a man on the moon and bring him back. In September, the first ATM was installed at Rockville center, New York. All the while, the Vietnam War was going on in the background. Berkeley witnessed riots over a student and community effort to commandeer a piece of university land and turn it into a "People's Park" a few blocks from my office. Times were changing for me personally as well. CCARP was established on September 1, 1969. Berkeley had generously agreed to house our project within the Institute of Business and Economic Research at the School of Business.

I was becoming better at identifying good investments and trading opportunities. But distracted by my research on the proposal, I stopped paying enough attention to my trading and lost a pile of money. Stung by my recent financial losses, I stopped trading. I had already given up on the thought that I could both pursue an electronic exchange and write career-building academic journal articles that were expected of ambitious young Berkeley faculty.

I focused my attention fiercely on researching two questions. First, what functions did exchanges perform? And what kind of exchange could maximize profits for shareholders and minimize transaction costs for users?

The exchange publications and rulebooks I read taught me very little I didn't already know. And the histories of the Chicago Board of

Trade[4] and the Chicago Mercantile Exchange were only slightly more helpful. There were no for-profit electronic exchanges anywhere in the world at the time, and none of the written material out there was going to do me much good.

I always believed that to really learn something, you had to teach it to someone else. So I began teaching Barry Sacks and my three research assistants about exchanges. I simplified the ideas but not by too much. And as I fielded their questions and honed my presentation, I began to understand an exchange as a system.

The main functions of organized exchanges were threefold. The first was contract standardization. This involved specifying the grade, quantity, delivery location, and other characteristics of the commodity. In doing so, all options for specificity were given to the sellers, as they held the key to the supply. Standardization allowed the sellers to choose what they were selling and the buyers to understand the range of what could be delivered.

The next function of an exchange was to assemble buyers and sellers in a central marketplace, the trading floor or "the pit." The trading floor represented the soul of the exchange where members physically met to conduct transactions. Floor traders traded as principals on their own accounts, while floor brokers represented customers. The trading pit reduced the time required for a buyer to meet a seller and vice versa, increasing market liquidity. Gathering many buyers and sellers in one place created competition that drove the bid-offer spread—the wholesale retail spread—down to a minimum. This resulted in lower transaction costs.

A customer with a buy or sell order typically communicated with his brokerage firm. The order was then passed on to a floor clerk, where a runner physically took the order to the floor broker in the trading pit. The floor broker's role was to execute the order as per the customer's request. Once executed, that information was again given to the runner who communicated it back to the brokerage firm, which informed the customer.

Both standardization and the use of a central marketplace lowered transaction costs, leaving both buyers and sellers better off.

---

[4]Charles Henry Taylor, *History of the Board of Trade of the City of Chicago* (Chicago: R. O. Law, 1917).

The Benefits of Standardization, a Central Market, and Clearing

To better understand the enormous reduction in transaction costs made possible by exchanges and their clearinghouses, consider the alternative scenario in which all trades are conducted over the counter. A would have to go through considerable trouble to find B. At best, this could be a simple Internet search. At worst, this could involve going from door to door. Then, the two parties need to negotiate a price. In the absence of exchanges, price information may not be as readily available—something we often take for granted. Legal costs are also incurred as a legal contract will need to be drafted to ensure that both parties will perform. Since A has no way to know that B would be creditworthy throughout the duration of the contract, A needs to perform tedious, time-consuming due diligence, which may range from anything including B's financial statements and credit ratings to previous lawsuits filed against B. B has to do the same for A. All this work is required just for a single transaction. As more market players get involved, the piles of information required become increasingly formidable, as do the transaction costs.

Now imagine that there are three parties who want to trade with each other. Each party has to conduct due diligence on two other parties. The result is six files for three parties. Similarly, there are 12 files needed for four parties, 20 files needed for five parties, and so on. As more and more counterparties are added, the resulting due diligence files exponentially increase. One cannot begin to imagine the amount of work required when there are a hundred or more buyers and sellers.[5]

[5]Galen Burghardt, an Adjunct Professor of Finance at the University of Chicago, used this type of example in a course he taught at the university.

An exchange reduced counterparty risk through clearing, further minimizing transaction costs. The heart of the exchange was its clearinghouse. The clearing function involved the exchange providing guarantees for trades by acting as counterparty for each and every transaction.

In other words, the clearinghouse became a seller to every buyer and a buyer to every seller. To support this guarantee, the clearinghouse set membership standards, operated a margining system to mitigate the credit risk of counterparties, monitored daily positions, and maintained a guarantee fund on which it could draw in the event of default.

The Clearing Concept Simplified

The concept of a clearinghouse can be best understood through a ledger. Suppose there are three futures commission merchants (FCMs)—A, B, and C—who will trade on behalf of customers 1, 2, and 3. Suppose also that there are three trading days and that the contract being traded is gold, which trades at $1,000 per ounce. Customer 1 wants to buy 100 ounces of gold from Customer 2, which is equal to a contract value of $100,000 (100 oz. × $1,000/oz.), deliverable in December 2011. Figure 2.1 demonstrates day one in the activity in the accounts of the FCMs, who are acting on behalf of their respective customers throughout the three trading days.

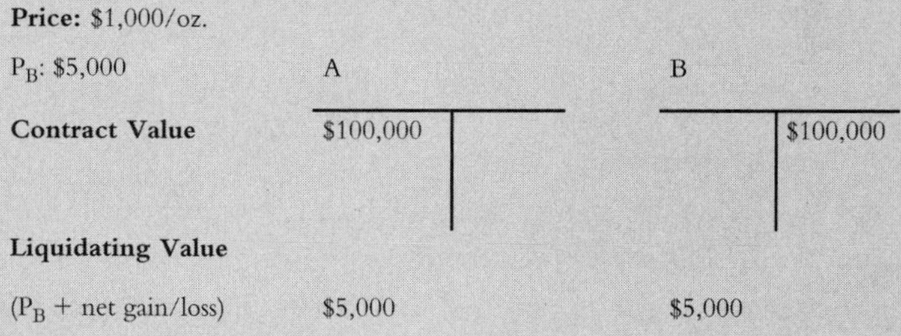

Figure 2.1 Day One

The only way that the clearinghouse is able to absorb the credit risk of both counterparties is for each of them to put up

(continued)

The Clearing Concept Simplified (*Continued*)

an initial margin at the time of trading. This is similar to a performance bond (P_B)—a guarantee against the failure of the other party to meet obligations specified in the contract. In this case, this amount is $5,000, 5 percent of the contract value.

At the end of each business day, each open position on the exchange is marked to market and compared with the day's closing price. If the position is in profit, the margin account will be credited with the profit. Similarly, if the position has made a loss, the margin account will be debited by that amount. To illustrate, on Day 2, the price of gold went up to $1,010 per ounce—see Figure 2.2.

Price: $1,010/oz.

P_B: $5,000	A		B	
Contract Value	$100,000			$100,000
Gain/Loss	+$1,000			−$1,000
Liquidating Value				
(P_B + net gain/loss)	$6,000		$4,000	

Figure 2.2 Day Two

Since the price of gold went up by $10 ($1,010 – $1,000), the clearinghouse credits A's margin account by $1,000 ($10/oz. × 100 oz.) and debit B's margin account by $1,000. All accounts must be cleared at the end of each trading day. Through a mark-to-market process, the clearinghouse is able to reduce its customers' credit exposures to one day's movement in prices because the cash has been deducted from Firm B and moved to Firm A.

On Day 3 (Figure 2.3), the price of gold increases to $1,030. To prevent further losses, B now will exit its position. It does so by buying 100 ounces of gold at $1,030. A new seller, C, enters

The Clearing Concept Simplified (*Continued*)

Price: $1,030/oz.

P_B: $5,000	A		B		C	
Contract Value	$100,000			$100,000		$103,000
Gain/Loss	+$3,000		$103,000	−$3,000		0
Liquidating Value						
(P_B + net gain/loss)	$8,000		$2,000		$5,000	

Figure 2.3 Day Three

the market and sells to A. At the end of the day, all trades are again cleared.

Herein lies the beauty of a clearing system—the seller does not have to go through delivery. In fact, the seller can liquidate his position by assuming an equal and opposite futures position. The removal of counterparty risk, made possible by the clearinghouse, allows both parties to net off trades against each other, that is, you can buy 100 contracts from A and then sell 1,000 contracts to B, and your net position will still be zero.

The offset provision is critical to both buyers and short sellers. Historically, the purchase of commodities in the spot market was relatively easy, so the advantage of futures as a substitute was not as important as the advantages to short sellers—who sold futures they didn't own, in the hopes of buying them back at a lower price. Shorting physical commodities, or stocks and bonds, has higher transaction costs than short selling in the futures market. In a spot market, an entity would have to borrow the commodity from a third party in order to sell short. This introduces additional transaction costs, as there are fees associated with borrowing. These borrowing fees could increase dramatically when the commodity or bond is in scarce supply. Furthermore, the borrower may not be creditworthy enough to borrow, and there is always the remote possibility that the cost of buying back the short could increase significantly. The old adage, "He who sells what isn't his'n buys it back or goes to prison," reflects the precarious position of short

(*continued*)

The Clearing Concept Simplified (*Continued*)

sellers. This problem is easily solved, however, by the offset feature of futures contracts, which dramatically reduces the transaction costs associated with short selling.

Not only do margins protect customers from daily variations in prices, they also act as a sort of equalizer—any bank can deal with any other bank or individual in the market, whatever their credit standing, as long as they can put up the initial margin. Each party knows that once the trade is matched and cleared, their only counterparty risk is to the clearinghouse. Firms with small amounts of capital become equals of firms with large amounts of capital.

The buyer and seller of a futures contract each deposited initial margins. Their open positions were marked-to-market at the end of the day, and daily variation margin was deposited to further reduce credit exposure. If the seller wanted to eliminate their delivery obligation, they could purchase a contract to offset this obligation. An offset was simply an equal and opposite position. This was a critical part of the financial engineering that made the system extremely cost-effective compared to over-the-counter markets where positions could not be easily liquidated.

Exchanges also facilitated delivery. This ensured that the standards specified in the futures contract, such as grade and location, were met. When I told people at a cocktail party that I traded futures, their reaction was almost inevitable. One person said, "I heard about a guy who bought wheat futures and one day got 5,000 bushels of wheat delivered to the front door of his house." But nothing like that ever happened. Typically, a customer notified the clearing firm that it would deliver evidence of ownership of the physical commodity such as wheat, as required by the contract. The clearinghouse then notified the weighing and inspecting department of delivery of the commodity, and informed the buyer of the upcoming delivery. The weighing or inspecting department made periodic visits to the grain elevator and took small samples of the commodity to make sure that it met standards. Delivery was accomplished through a warehouse receipt, the only physical sign of ownership required. The owner of the grain receipt then picked a time for the grain to be unloaded and put on a railcar or barge. The contract specifications assured that standards were satisfied upon delivery.

Additionally, exchanges published and distributed prices and volumes, audited and investigated members, and conducted marketing and educational outreach. Information disseminated in this public marketplace to individuals, firms and regulators benefited both the public and private sectors. Anyone interested in seeing the prices could call members of the exchange or locate the daily high, low, and close in financial newspapers or local papers.

In summary, not only did exchanges reduce search costs, eliminate unnecessary legal costs, and insulate customers against counterparty risks, but also enforced certain regulations on member firms and preserved the financial integrity of executing purchases and sales of commodities. Ultimately, in a centralized exchange model, all transactions were consummated in a fair and equitable manner.

Figure 2.4 is a schematic that describes the architecture of commodity exchanges in 1969. The system is activated by a decision to buy or sell by a speculator or hedger, or a customer's intention to deliver. Orders from speculators and hedgers are sent to members of the exchange. These orders are transmitted to the trading floor to be matched in the pit, a name evocative of the unique architecture of trading floors at the Chicago Board of Trade.[6] The diagram also contains a unit labeled floor traders. After a trade is consummated by either a broker or a principal (speculator or hedger) trading for their own account, it is recorded on an order or trading card. Trading cards and orders are input into the computers of the clearing members, who provide the information to the clearinghouse.

To achieve the functions of standardization, aggregating buyers and sellers in a central marketplace and clearing, traditional exchanges used a governance structure that was mutually owned and member dominated. Member owners elected a board of directors, and were

[6]The Chicago Board of Trade building held polygonal pits with steps climbing to a height of four or five feet and then descending by 10 feet. Due to this architecture, they became known as trading pits.

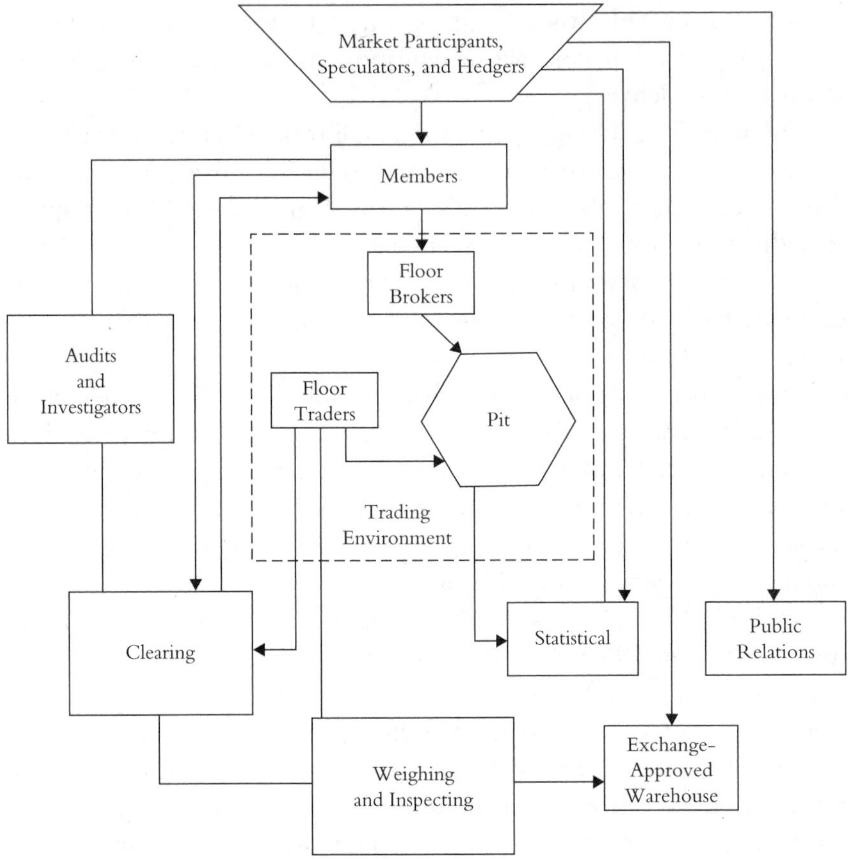

Figure 2.4 The Layout of the Chicago Board of Trade Floor

appointed by the board to committees which helped to operate the exchanges. Exchanges put the authority in the hands of the committees, and gave responsibility to professional managers. The professional staff of the exchange also operated the trading floor, maintained price dissemination, recorded and cleared trades, and helped with conflict resolution.

What if the trading floor was in cyberspace? Furthermore, what if all of these transactions took place in a for-profit exchange? A for-profit electronic exchange might allow for all of these functions to be performed at lower costs. As intriguing as this notion was, such a cyberspace had yet to be uncovered.

A Different Structure for a Different Kind of Exchange

An electronic platform would eliminate the trading floor and the infrastructure necessary for the functions mentioned above, which included everything from the runners to the price reporters and the traders in the pits. Instead, the new electronic exchange would rely heavily on a central IT department for its operations. We therefore placed great responsibility on the computer and information services department. This emphasis was drastically different from any other exchange in the world at the time. Most notably, about one third of the exchange staff was allocated to the IT department. With an electronic platform, an exchange could have more buyers and sellers and more frequent trading at any given time.

In the for-profit model, the board of directors of the new exchange would play no operational role. Instead, it would work almost exclusively on setting policy. Exchange members themselves would play an integral part in the market-making aspect of electronic trading. Member committees would complement the professional staff of the exchange. The committees would have no line authority. The professional staff made the final decisions. The members of the committees would instead be appointed by the president of the exchange, subject to the approval of his board.

Realizing the important role of floor traders in keeping transaction costs low and providing liquidity, we felt that these market makers deserved to play a role on our committees, either as policy counselors, market makers, or both. This move not only honored their work but served the exchange by helping to align market makers' incentives with the overall interests of the exchange.

However, details about what went on in the trading pit and how liquidity was actually created remained a mystery to me. I had to go to Chicago to find out.

Chicago—My Kind of Town

In late 1969, I decided to go to the two major Chicago exchanges, watch them in action, and talk to some traders in person.

David Ware arranged for me to meet some of the top traders and their agents on the floor of the Chicago Mercantile Exchange. He also introduced me to Robert "Bob" Martin, a former chairman of the Chicago Board of Trade, through whom I met traders on the CBOT floor. Bob was a large man with a quick smile. When we first spoke he said, "Past chairmen are a dime a dozen" before introducing me to the traders who would teach me the business. My network was expanding.

At the Chicago Mercantile Exchange, Dave introduced me to an independent broker who showed me around the trading floor. The markets had already been open for hours when I arrived but, luckily for me, they were at a late-morning lull. The broker showed me how orders were taken from the Teletype to the pit. Then Larry Rosenberg, a successful young trader, patiently explained the various actors in the pit and some of the basics of the business. Larry later owned a plane and would have been the envy of all of my fraternity brothers. He went on to become chairman at the CME. He gave me a trader's account of the CME's recent history.

In 1958 after a price cornering scandal, the U.S. Congress had banned futures trading in onions—but some years later, the CME had launched a comeback with a wildly successful futures market in frozen pork bellies. I learned from my visit that the CME wisely published all sorts of data throughout the month, giving traders a lot to speculate on. I loved an audacious ad campaign that the CME used many years later that lampooned a fictitious Moscow Mercantile Exchange.[7] I left the CME thinking: "We can do this! We can design an electronic exchange."

It was time to go to the Chicago Board of Trade. Bob Martin had written me letters of introduction to Henry Shatkin. I went first to Shatkin & Company, a firm whose customers were floor traders on the exchange, and catered to professional traders only. Henry "Hank" Shatkin told me all about the floor-trading business, and how firms like his financed the seats of new members in order to cultivate customers.

Hank and I hit it off, and he invited me to his home in a tony North Shore suburb after work. The house was beautiful but not ostentatious. Hank was no less skeptical than the others I had met regarding

[7]Cohen & Greenbaum, "How Come There's No Moscow Mercantile Exchange?" Ad for Chicago Mercantile Exchange, *Fortune Magazine*, October 1974.

the idea that electronic trading could become a reality. But he was fascinated by the idea of a for-profit exchange and did everything he could to help me. We talked deep into the evening, and he generously lent me his own car to drive back into the city on that cold, blustery Chicago night.

By 9:00 the next morning, I was sitting in the CBOT visitors' gallery, eager to witness the famous open outcry system of trading.

I was going to get to watch traders in soybeans, a highly volatile futures market. I had been fascinated with soybean and soybean oil trading ever since the great Salad Oil Swindle of 1962.[8] That was the year a Bronx-born crook named Tino De Angelis cornered the market on soybean oil, and then was found to have loaded his soybean oil tank cars with water. By the time the scandal caught up with him, De Angelis had bilked 51 banks, leaving him in personal bankruptcy and causing Allied Crude Vegetable Oil Refining Corporation to default, with American Express to cover the bad loans. De Angelis had generated $175 million in faked soybean oil—huge money in 1962, roughly $1.31 billion today.

The world's biggest and oldest futures exchange, the CBOT was housed in a great old building on West Jackson Boulevard, and was famous for trading in wheat, corn, and soybean futures. The lobby of the building was filled with art deco fixtures, and the elevator doors had pewter squares decorated with shocks of wheat. The CBOT had a marvelous trading floor about five stories high overlooking LaSalle Street. The building had been completed in 1929, just prior to the stock market crash that would have rendered the opulence impossible. The wall inside the trading floor had a multi-story painting of Ceres, the Roman goddess of grain and agriculture. By 9:15, the room had begun to fill. The trading floor had many pits, and price reporters took their positions in raised stations at each pit.

In the middle of the floor, traders gathered to resolve any disputes from the day before about price or quantity. I had heard of this process, but its crucial importance was only just dawning on me. An equitable system required yesterday's errors to be resolved before

---

[8]Norman C. Miller, *The Great Salad Oil Swindle* (Baltimore, MD: Penguin Books, 1965).

the opening of every new day's trading. I was struck by how many different small groups were negotiating at that hour. The sociologist in me was fascinated but, as a businessman I saw a very inefficient system, ripe for overhaul.

Here and there, traders on the floor began drifting into the pits. By 9:25, several hundred men were jammed shoulder to shoulder. When the opening bell rang at 9:30, it was suddenly pandemonium on the entire floor.

Everywhere I looked, men were signaling with their hands waving wildly. I couldn't interpret the apparent pandemonium but my adrenaline was flowing. What I saw so closely resembled a form of performance art that it reminded me of my own brief moments as a stand-up comedian. If all this were to be done electronically through a computer, it would be like a comic performance with little to no audience. It struck me then that it was just as important to design a system that could energize the traders who sat in front of a screen. I quickly dismissed the thought, however, and went on watching the frenzied activity in the pit.

My eyes moved from the soybean pit to an electric board that showed the opening price, high price, low price, and last three prices. The prices were moving so fast, the wall board couldn't keep up.

After a thrilling half-hour in the gallery, I moved to the floor and spoke to market reporters, price reporters, and public relations people. Bob Martin also introduced me to Lee Stern. Lee B. Stern, Ltd. turned out to be a boutique FCM with a customer base that included grain merchants and professional speculators. Lee himself was renowned for his trading skill, both in and out of the pits. In order to carry some of the large positions of its customers, Lee and other small FCM clearing members needed capital and risk management skills. These local firms complemented the large FCMs such as Merrill Lynch in facilitating order flow from commercial customers and professional speculators.

Having spent my childhood in a household that operated a small pharmacy and after earning a modest income in academia, I was amazed that a futures trader in the brokerage industry could be this successful. In his beautifully appointed office, Lee explained to me the sign language of the pit. A trader's palms turned inward, as if gathering grain, meant buy. Palms turned outward meant sell. Fingers parallel to the ground signaled price, fingers straight up and down signaled quantity. Speaking quickly, Lee told me how words, facial expressions, and body language all came into play. To the initiated, every word or small gesture meant something. I leaned forward in my chair, trying to follow. When the conversation turned to automatic trading, Lee was skeptical about an electronic exchange.

Bob Martin suggested that I meet two other traders. We met at a small, dimly lit restaurant called Brokers Inn, across the street from the CBOT. One was a big man who could have been a character right out of Damon Runyon's short stories on Broadway in New York City during the Prohibition era. The other was more introverted and a real student of markets. Together they explained to me the difference between trading corn and trading soybeans. One of the traders was also a farmer and knew that the corn yields were three times that of soybeans. When prices didn't reflect that difference, he bought corn and sold soybeans. He expected farmers to plant crops that were more profitable. They often didn't.

Both men ate oversized steaks that night, smothered in ketchup. They were big men with big appetites, and by the end of the meal I began to get a much better feel for the psychology of traders on the floor.

At that time, the markets were dominated by grain merchants and speculators on the floor. I learned that floor brokers were critical to the traders. They occupied the same position in the pit every day and were surrounded by speculators. It was like a chessboard with the pieces set up at the opening. However, instead of pieces that moved, it was the prices that moved. The dynamic among the market makers, speculators, grain merchants, and floor brokers determined price. The process was being demystified.

As I checked out of my hotel, and took the long plane ride home, I found myself upbeat. The greatest lesson I had learned in Chicago was that the current system spent enormous resources running the trading floor. I knew that an electronic trading system could reduce errors, cut costs, attract more traders into the system and provide much greater transparency of the deals made.

There remained two challenges. First, could we configure existing computer technology to replicate order entry and the matching of buyers and sellers? That meant creating a communication network to carry various messages in hard copy, including order messages, market updates, and confirmed trades.

And second, could we cost-effectively invest in and operate the hardware and software for trading? This required understanding exactly what kind of information floor traders needed to make their decisions. To do so, I had to visit yet more exchanges so I could observe and interview more traders. Thankfully, I enjoyed this process. After all, I was getting closer to achieving this goal of mine, about which so many men I respected were highly skeptical.

I remember getting off the plane and coming home to Ellen. As I spoke animatedly to her about the trip, she looked at me and said, "One day, we're going to live in Chicago." My wife was a prophet, but in 1970, all that was in the future.

Structuring the Exchange

The pressing problem of the moment was that I had to design a systems flow chart for an electronic exchange. The design needed to describe the order entry and matching functions in order to electronically replicate the process that was in place for existing functions. Figure 2.5 illustrates the final flow chart in the report. Designing the system felt, in some ways, like simultaneously playing a number of chess games while blindfolded. Each game was separate, but you had to keep all of them in your mind at once. The fatigue at the end of the day was familiar and reminded me of those eight-hour chess sessions at Dr. Sussman's house.

The essential element of the system was an editor-member communication network that could carry several types of messages in hard copy. These included messages for placing orders, retransforming orders for error control, transmitting fundamental information, communicating market updates, and confirming trades.

Another element of the system included displaying information on a cathode ray tube. Information on the screen was intended to simulate the environment that a floor trader was used to seeing on the wall boards. Again, I reminded myself that the screen had to be designed to

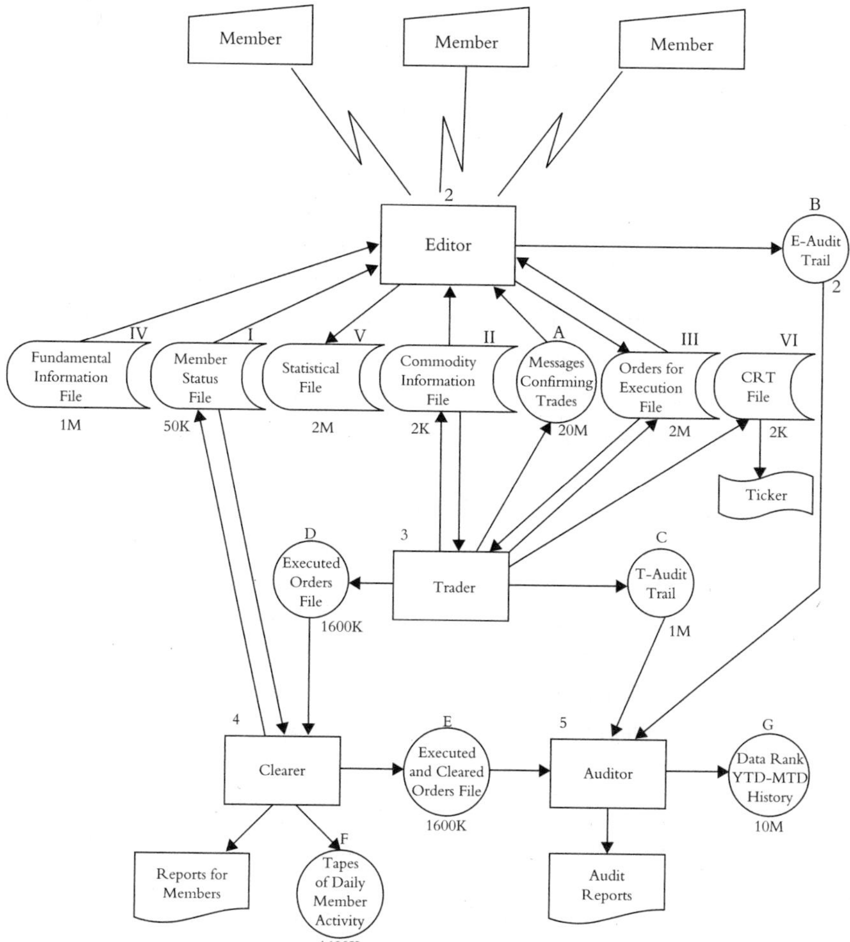

Figure 2.5 The Preliminary Design for an Electronic Market for the Pacific Commodities Exchange

Source: Project CCARP, Interim Report, "Preliminary Design for an Electronic Market for the Pacific Commodities Exchange," April 1, 1970.

energize the trader, given the loss of the performance aspect of floor trading. In this, I was inspired by the design of a chessboard. I made an additional visit to existing exchanges in order to more closely identify the type of information used by floor traders in decision making. This second trip permitted me to better understand both the nature of the matching algorithm and the clearing function of trading.

We also had to design a screen. Floor traders had information concerning a bid or offer, as well as a notion of the quantities available at respective prices. In the exchanges I visited, the last trades were available on either electronic devices or, for commodities with low volume and less continuous trading, a blackboard. Floor traders could easily observe a short-term trend by observing the last three prices. An electronic platform would be able to record both price and volume on a continuous basis. The ability to record price changes and display them on a screen would provide traders with a precise record of price changes so that they would not have to rely solely on their own informed guesses. Fundamental information on the underlying commodity would also be available on screen, rather than posted on exchange walls. Posting open interest on a continuous basis would provide traders more information during the trading day.[9] All of this additional information theoretically compensated for the liquidity that could be lost amid the transition from open outcry to electronic markets.

The report went on to note that floor traders relied on observing other members' physical movements to determine what their positions were and whether they would be buyers or sellers. This would be absent in an electronic exchange. We recognized that it also helped to provide additional information on the breakdown between hedging and speculating activity regularly during the trading day in order to compensate for some loss of liquidity due to the absence of face-to-face trading.

One advantage of electronic trading was that access to the market could be achieved over a wider geographic area. It took a while for me to learn about the sources of speculation. When data on speculation emerged, the results were surprisingly obvious. People who speculated on frozen concentrated orange juice futures tended to live in areas where oranges were grown. Similarly, people who speculated on grain futures tended to live in the Midwest. This was intuitive as speculators were more familiar with their local economies, and thus the commodities indigenous to them. The advent of electronic trading changed this localized

[9]Project CCARP, Interim Report, "Preliminary Design for an Electronic Market for the Pacific Commodities Exchange," (April 1, 1970): 42.

trading pattern. Initially, telecommunication devices would be established in the San Francisco Bay area and complemented by a national network that would subsequently include Chicago, Los Angeles, and New York. These offices could also be used to market the exchanges and provide space for housing professional traders as well as stations for systems experimentation.

Another critical aspect of the system would incorporate response time. Markets were often volatile. If an order was placed, given the drawn-out response time, participants could not immediately check the price or the quantity bought and sold. This hurt market liquidity and generated higher transaction costs. By churning out market information by the second, electronic trading would allow hedgers and arbitrageurs to simultaneously purchase in the spot or forward market and sell futures, thereby resolving the issue.

The electronic system contained six different programs. A pretrading program would perform various functions related to initializing values such as volume and the removal of expiring contracts. Three programs would perform on the post-trading day, related to closing, clearing, and auditing. The first related to receiving orders, the second to obtaining quotations, and the third related to confirming trades.

We designed an automated order entry and a system that matched buyer and seller. The system would serve as an information system for the exchange, as well as distribute information to the public and to regulators. To this end, information for each of the departments would be kept and stored on files. The necessary data needed to make their decisions would be made available to traders on a regular basis. For example, the clearing association would have all of its activities fully automated, and the computer output would effectively reduce operational costs.

Specifications for the various file sizes and requirements of the system represented another challenge. Total volume estimates were based on the activity and open interest of pork bellies—the most active commodity traded in 1969. The distribution of trading throughout the day was obtained by observing the patterns for several different commodities. There was a striking similarity in the distribution of files for all commodities. To hone our computer system, we gave a group of FCMs a confidential survey in which they were asked to provide the ratio of orders, confirmations, and straddles[10] in various futures markets, including wheat, soybean oil, cattle, and pork bellies.

For the technical phase of the project, we had to select hardware and software that best mimicked the conceptual system flow chart. Our selection was based on considerations to response time, system reliability, and control against order entry errors. As the CCARP team solicited proposals from General Electric and IBM and went through their cost estimates, it became clear how much more cheaply our system could run than the open outcry system. I was elated. Even in a worst-case scenario, with one successful contract and an annual volume of 175,000 contracts, we would be profitable by the third year.

When it came to deciding what contracts to trade, we recommended coconut oil futures, to be followed by palm oil, and then iced broilers. We believed each of these commodities could be standardized, and continued volatility in prices warranted a futures market.

Strangely enough, the evolution of commodity regulation required commodities to be regulated but not the futures exchanges themselves. Because our product of choice—coconut oil—was a regulated commodity, we needed the Commodity Exchange Authority (CEA) within the U.S. Department of Agriculture to provide approval to electronic trading. We therefore tailored the bylaws of our exchange to the requirements of the CEA.

Talking to Regulators

In early 1970, I went to Washington, DC, to visit with Alex Caldwell, the head of the CEA, and several other USDA economists. Though they were cautious about saying so publicly, Caldwell and the others quietly welcomed us to apply as a contract market in coconut oil futures. They were interested in anything that could improve the ability to monitor markets, and a computerized system seemed to provide just that.

---

[10] "An option position consisting of the purchase of put and call options having the same expiration date and strike price"—CFTC Glossary.

All the while, protests against the war in Vietnam were raging on college campuses. Eleven soldiers had been indicted for their part in the My Lai massacre. The Beatles had broken up, students were getting ready to celebrate the first Earth Day, and legislators were unveiling what would become the Clean Air Act of 1970. Our concept was extremely radical at the time. The world's first general microprocessor, the Intel 4004, would not come out until two years later in 1971. The C programming language would be developed in early 1973. It would be almost four years before Steve Jobs and Steve Wozniak developed the personal computer in a garage in Los Altos, California in 1975. It took another 25 years before the popularization of the Internet.

With only one month before our deadline, six of us worked feverishly on finishing our interim report. Barry Sacks evaluated the proposals from vendors while our research assistants each did their part.

Finally, after hundreds of cups of coffee and a few sleepless nights, we finished our report and delivered it to our supporters in early April of 1970. It was 132 pages long. We thought we had anticipated every skeptic and answered every question,

I celebrated with my team that afternoon in my office—one of my researchers was a Mormon and going out for beer was inappropriate. I went home and celebrated with Ellen all over again. In just seven months, with a mere $15,000—roughly equivalent to $87,000 in 2011[10]—we had created a blueprint for an electronic futures exchange that would run as a for-profit company. The world of commodity exchanges would never be the same. At 27 years old, I had changed the world. Or so I thought.

The Dream Is Dashed

David Ware gave me the first reaction to the report. He admired it but had questions. It was typical Dave and didn't bother me. I valued his thoroughness and honesty. I then called the man who was leading the effort at the Commodity Club. He appeared to be interested in moving to the next phase. One of the appendixes contained a proposal for Phase II, which called for finalizing hardware and software configurations, recommending a vendor, and developing specifications for the first contract. A target completion date for the next phase was set for mid-September that same year on a $41,525 budget. We would study other potential contracts that were oriented to the western part of the United States, including cattle and rice. Even though previous iced broilers contracts had failed, we were still optimistic that a successful contract could emerge from a careful study of those failures.

I met with the whole group on April 22, which was Earth Day and also Ellen's birthday. I thought of the gathering as a celebratory dinner until I saw the group had brought its attorney along and still had questions about our report. Though they had directed their attorney to draft a formal contract, the questions from the group suggested basic misgivings, even from their leader. But I had worked too hard for weeks, and brushed off these storm warnings. I was an optimist at heart.

Over the next several weeks, I negotiated the terms of Phase II with the lawyer. I fantasized about heading an independent technology company that would provide software for the exchange and invent innovative new products.

And then one day the attorney called and told me, in a monotonous voice as if he were mundanely cleaning off his desk on a Friday afternoon, that the group had decided an electronic exchange was too risky. The lawyer suggested, instead, a for-profit exchange on the old, open outcry model.

I jumped off the phone with the lawyer and began calling the principals separately. I was still under the delusion that I could change all their minds with technology. Maybe they didn't understand the report. Maybe they just didn't realize that great change was in the air all over America.

I had underestimated how risk-averse these men were. One by one, each politely told me my concept was too risky. As they bid me goodbye, I put the telephone receiver back in its cradle. I was devastated.

Soon, other gloomy thoughts started to crowd my mind. I was 27 years old and had been on the Berkeley faculty almost three years without a single publication in an academic journal. I was like the lead character in Mike Nichols's movie *The Graduate*, worried about my future. Unless I could stage a quick comeback, I wasn't going to get tenure. The old childhood fears about being lazy and failing to reach my potential came back to haunt me.

Chapter 3

The Berkeley Years

> The thing the sixties did was to show us the possibilities and the responsibility that we all had. It wasn't the answer. It just gave us a glimpse of the possibility.
>
> —*John Lennon*

The failure of Project CCARP only increased my determination to learn more about futures markets. I continued to write academically about industrial inventive activity as a means to procure tenure, but my heart wasn't fully in it. Coincidentally, some of my research would serve as a natural segue into understanding and practicing financial innovation. I had always wanted to invent, and the futures industry was changing. It had become ripe for new ideas, and the seeds of inventive activity were beginning to flower.

A New Direction

As I sought to expand my understanding of the industry and how new futures contracts were developed, it occurred to me to teach a course on futures markets. Two fortuitous opportunities led me to propose this to the dean at Berkeley.

Although Project CCARP was dead, the network and reputation I had built during its life had some unintended consequences. Gerry Taylor, a publisher at the humor magazine *National Lampoon*, had been organizing annual conferences run by *Institutional Investor* for equity investors. He was convinced that he could create a comparable event for futures traders. Gerry sought to include academics in his event alongside senators, industry leaders, and CEOs, and was given my name by some traders in Chicago. He was intrigued by my work in computerized trading models and on Project CCARP.

Gerry came to my office at Barrows Hall one day to discuss his plans to put together his conference for the futures industry. He was a tall man, was nattily dressed, and had a terrific sense of humor. Gerry was married to Mary Travers of the folk band Peter, Paul, and Mary. A willowy woman with sleek blond hair, his wife reflected the activist liberal mood of Greenwich Village in the '50s and '60s. I reveled at Gerry's stories about working at *National Lampoon*, and we shared many stories about our New York origins. He invited me to speak at the conference he was organizing. I accepted, even though it wasn't clear that he could pull it off.

I was buoyed by my personal life that summer. Ellen was pregnant and we were expecting at the end of September. This time, it was me prodding Ellen to start classes in natural childbirth. My second daughter, Penya Lauren Sandor, a fair-haired baby, was born on September 24, 1970. Ellen was in labor for only two hours before Penya came into the world. The lightning speed at which she was delivered was a metaphor for her life. Penya was and is adventurous, resourceful, and perceptive. By the time she was 18 months old, Penya was watching *Sesame Street* with her sister, reading numbers, deciphering words, and counting in English and Spanish. Like her sister, she was always quick to defend those who were attacked due to their disadvantages. When Penya was in grade school, she witnessed a teacher yelling at a fellow student who had difficulty reading. She audibly told the student that the teacher was stupid and insensitive—the exact words she used were less pleasant. Ellen received a call to meet the school principal to discuss Penya's behavior. After she learned what our daughter had said, Ellen proclaimed that Penya's description was accurate, and challenged the group to differ. No one did, and that was the end of that. Penya's perceptiveness and creativity with words revealed that she would become a published poet.

Gerry's idea about a commodities conference became a reality. I went to New York to attend the 1970 International Commodities Conference just after Penya was born.[1] I had never seen anything like it. From the exquisitely plated hors d'oeuvres to the gleaming ballroom in which the event was held, Gerry spared no expense.

Unfortunately, the event wasn't a financial success. There were almost as many speakers as attendees. Nevertheless, the conference was an opportunity for me to further my knowledge of the industry and to meet its leaders. Speaking on a panel titled, "Will Computers Take Over Futures Markets?" I now knew there was life after Project CCARP after all. My ideas on using computers to forecast prices were better received than my views on electronic exchanges. Although some in the audience encouraged me to pursue the latter, others argued that the vested interests in the industry were opposed to being replaced by computers. I realized that without support from industry or a large grant, it was futile to continue my research. In 1970, the concept of a fully automated futures exchange was dead on arrival. It was simply ahead of its time, and the only way it could happen was if a new exchange was interested in starting from scratch, which was unlikely.

Soon, I received an invitation to speak at another conference, organized by the New York Coffee and Sugar Exchange (NYCSE). "The Changing Complexion of Commodity Trading"[2] attracted about 50 faculty and student attendees from 40 different colleges and universities. The NYCSE president delivered welcoming remarks. Unlike the International Commodities Conference, it was held in a more humble room at the exchange itself.

---

[1]Attendees included Senator Robert Dole of Kansas and Senator George McGovern of South Dakota; industry CEOs such as Henry Hall Wilson, the new president of the Chicago Board of Trade; Dwayne Andreas, the CEO of Archer Daniels Midland; Hendrik Houthakker of the Council of Economic Advisers and former professor at Harvard University.

[2]Seminar/70, "Commodity Futures Market and the College Curriculum," conducted by New York Coffee and Sugar Exchange, Inc. "The Changing Complexion of Commodity Trading" by Richard L. Sandor, October 22, 1970.

The conference program had two themes: university course curriculums on commodity trading, and new directions in futures trading. I described what was going on in futures trading at the Berkeley Graduate School of Business Administration.[3] For the most part, the study of futures trading was confined to departments of agricultural economics. A small number of graduate courses in MBA programs featured brief discussions on futures markets, including a course on agribusiness taught at Harvard Business School. At Berkeley, I encouraged my students to conduct individually supervised research on futures markets in satisfaction of their MBA degrees. Examples included studies on futures trading in frozen concentrated orange juice, cattle, and broilers, as well as our previous feasibility study and bylaws for the Pacific Commodities Exchange.[4]

After the conference, I became convinced that business schools should offer courses on futures markets.

The other part of my presentation was devoted to the use of computers in price forecasting. Instead of sticking with arcane charting, I focused on mathematical forecasting models based on fundamental analysis, as well as computerized forecasting models based on price and volume statistics. The infancy of computers was matched by the nascency of forecasting models. I suggested that widely used academic tools, such as econometrics and simulation, could be applied to price forecasting and I stated that these models would not only be applicable to speculators, but also be used by agribusiness companies for hedging purposes.

I left New York knowing that I was about to make the unalterable decision to enter the world of futures trading. It promised to be a life-changing experience. It was a little frightening to leave behind

---

[3]This was renamed the Haas School of Business in 1989.

[4]"An Analysis of Futures Trading in Frozen Concentrated Orange Juice as an Investment Opportunity," "Application of Fundamental and Technical Analysis to Cattle Futures," "The Broiler Industry in Futures Trading: An Overview," "The Pacific Commodity Exchange Feasibility Study," and "By-Laws of the Pacific Commodities Exchange." Quoted in Richard L. Sandor, "The Changing Complexion of Commodity Trading," U.C. Berkeley, October 22, 1970.

everything—my research on patent life and R&D, as well as articles I had written on these subjects—to focus on the study of futures.

At the beginning of 1971, I developed an outline and readings list for a proposed course on futures exchanges and trading. The preparation was exhilarating. I read histories of exchanges,[5] futures pricing theories, and everything available regarding the invention of new contracts.[6] The course was approved and was the first of its kind in a school of business administration. The course included not only history and theory, but also an impressive list of guest speakers, including practitioners like the head of agricultural lending at the Bank of America, the administrator of the Commodity Exchange Authority (CEA), and Warren Lebeck, executive vice president and secretary of the CBOT.

After one particular class, Warren and I walked through Sproul Plaza together. Warren was a former Navy officer who dressed immaculately at all times—a distinct contrast with the student body and faculty on campus. He was made somewhat uncomfortable by the hippies and dogs that roamed Berkeley's campus. He said, "I like stories about rebels. The movie *Love Story* is one of my favorites, but that's a lot different from these guys."

The experience with CCARP had taught me the power of the press. I had been quoted in *The Financial Times* and *The Journal of Commerce*, and this public visibility gave me both exposure and access to industry leaders. I persuaded a reporter from *The San Francisco Chronicle* to write an article on the course. I clipped the article and sent copies of it to the guest speakers along with a thank-you note.

---

[5]Charles H. Taylor, *History of the Board of Trade of the City of Chicago* (Chicago: R. O. Law, 1917).

[6]H. S. Irwin, *Evolution of Futures Trading* (Madison, WI: Mimir Publishers, 1954), Appendix I; H. Houthakker, "The Scope and Limits of Futures Trading," in *The Allocation of Economic Resources*, ed. Moses Abramovitz et al. (Stanford, CA: Stanford University Press, 1959), 134–159; H. Houthakker, "Can Speculators Forecast Prices?" *Review of Economics and Statistics* 39, no. 2 (May 1957): 143–151; H. Houthakker, "Systematic and Random Elements in Short-Term Price Movements," *American Economic Review* 51 (1961): 164–172.

Ultimately, it was a combination of the futures course, Project CCARP, research on financial innovation, press coverage, speaking engagements, and finally, a casual conversation with one of the other guest speakers, that opened up a life-changing opportunity for me in Chicago.

Plywood Futures—Learning How Others Create a Good Derivative

Between 1960 and 1970, the volume on U.S. exchanges had more than tripled. One-third of that growth came from new commodities. In 1969, the CBOT had launched a futures contract in plywood, and by 1970, the exchange had traded more than 47,000 contracts. This had created a new arena for futures markets, namely, that of fully processed industrial commodities. I suspected that a case study on the evolution of commodities would be exciting and might even be worthy of publication.

I called Warren to ask if the CBOT would cooperate with a case study of the research and development of the plywood futures contract. Warren's response was both positive and enthusiastic. Desperate to be published, I made a cold call to Ronald Coase, editor of *The Journal of Law and Economics*, to see if the journal was interested in an article on financial innovation. I remember sitting in my office in Barrows Hall and hearing a crisp English accent saying, "This is Ronald Coase returning your call." I explained the case study I was planning and asked if he was interested in seeing it when it was completed, but was careful not to ask about publication. He was especially intrigued because the plywood futures study was a practical example of theoretical economics.

Studying the research and development activities conducted on exchanges helped me transition from inventive activity in the industrial sector to inventive activity in finance. I learned that the CBOT's New Products Committee had considered launching a futures market in plywood back in 1961. The idea lay dormant for some time due to the lack of price volatility. In 1967, plywood cash prices had risen from under $70 at the beginning of the year to about $95 during the summer months, retreating to a little over $70 toward the end of the year—representing an unusual amount of price volatility. By mid-1968, prices had rebounded to approximately $100.

The volatility in plywood prices had set the stage for a futures contract, and the exchange hired a forestry graduate to conduct some economic research. His first assignment was to conduct a feasibility study on a lumber or plywood futures contract. The study was quite extensive, describing the lumber and plywood industries while hypothesizing a futures contract for both. It was clear that both could be standardized. Using figures on concentration of product, size of wholesalers, and institutional relationships in the industry, the study concluded that the industry was competitive. Production of both commodities was also sizable.

Furthermore, as a result of supply and demand, prices continued to be volatile throughout 1967 and 1968. The study's description of the industry implied that a high-volume, liquid spot market existed, although the forestry graduate did not seem to have looked for this specifically.

The study went on to specify the salient features of a futures contract in plywood, which included grade, delivery points, and pricing. Other salient features, such as the location of delivery, changed as a result of feedback from both producers and users of plywood. They also changed as a result of market makers and speculators.

The final contract was not designed in a vacuum, but benefited from the continuous input of potential buyers and sellers throughout the inventive process.

The inventive process of the plywood futures contract, from its inception to the initiation of trading, took approximately 17 months. Almost seven years had gone by since the New Products Committee had first begun its investigation into plywood futures. The biggest challenge was determining the right location for delivery, one of the most important features of a commodity futures contract. Grain futures contracts at the time specified delivery at grain elevators in Chicago. Since the city had historically been a center for the buying and selling of grain, both buyers and sellers would be able to make or take delivery at a convenient location. Furthermore, the local market was representative of grain prices nationally. The first draft of the futures contract called for delivery in Chicago. This proved to be a mistake.

The original contract in plywood called for mills to deliver a shipping certificate, a promise by the issuer to deliver to the buyer the quantity and quality of plywood specified in the contract. The contract price would be settled using the freight-on-board mill convention (dubbed *FOB mill*), through which plywood was loaded on to a carrier at the mill without incurring any additional cost to the buyer. There were a limited number of mills that were eligible to make delivery. As a result of the small number of mills, prices on the futures market were artificially high relative to the national market. Hedges were therefore ineffective, calling for a modification of the original contract. The new contract provided for unrestricted mill delivery and also permitted warehouses in certain newly designated areas to qualify as delivery points. The changes resulted in the elimination of artificial scarcity. The solution was so simple that it was amazing that no one had thought of it before. The contract subsequently became more representative of national prices.

The case study gave me an understanding of how a new futures contract was developed. First, the market had to be large enough to warrant a futures market. Second, there had to be a sufficient number of buyers and sellers for the standardized product. Third and finally, there had to be volatility of prices and a concomitant need and desire by industry to hedge. If all these characteristics were satisfied, the staff of the exchange proceeded to draft an initial contract. The staff then took in comments and input from plywood manufacturers and distributors, as well as the member committee charged with developing the new product. Once there was consensus by the industry and member committee, the contract was launched. If necessary, the contract was redesigned based on market experience.

The entire activity was characterized by interactions among professional exchange staff, exchange members, and advisory groups who were commercial users of the market. My research for the article on plywood futures gave me insight into how to design a futures contract. I was ready for what was about to happen.

Grain Markets and Mortgages

In the 1960s, I shared a bullpen with Albert H. "Hank" Schaaf and other Berkeley faculty. Hank was an expert in real estate economics and we often discussed the changes in the world around us. At the time, the rise in interest rates in 1966 and 1969 was having a particularly strong effect on the California real estate market. The state was in a high-growth stage of development, and capital was needed to finance the growing demand for housing. I kept on bouncing between trading futures and discussing mortgage finance. Combining my interest in the housing markets with hands-on experience trading futures led me to an interesting solution to the California housing problem—mortgage interest rate futures. The prospects of solving the problem of the interest rate risk in California was exciting. I had to let this go, however, in order to work on Project CCARP. I was only speculating about an idea and didn't have any interest in pursuing it at the time.

The idea later took on a life of its own. While teaching a course on futures markets at the Berkeley Graduate School of Business Administration, I was struck by the similarity between the business flows in the grain and mortgage markets. Farmers grew wheat and sold it to grain merchants that operated storage facilities known as elevators.[7] Local merchants took temporary ownership of the commodity, and then sold it to larger elevators in major markets known as terminal electors. Eventually, the grain was sold to food processors.

In many ways, the mortgage market functioned in the same manner as the grain market: the borrower was the farmer, the mortgage banker was the local grain elevator (even the terminology was the same—elevators "originated" grain just like mortgage bankers "originated" mortgages), the investment banks were the terminal grain elevators, and savings and loans associations (S&Ls) and pension funds were the food processing companies. The convergence of a number of factors—the increase of interest rates, the long tradition of futures contracts in the grain market, the state of real estate finance, and the

[7]Grain elevator store grain and prepare it for eventual shipment.

surge in mortgage rates—made the potential for a mortgage interest rate futures contract obvious. The origins of the idea of a futures market in interest rates lay in the work of W. R. Hicks. Although he did not explicitly state the need for such a market, it could be easily inferred from his pioneering work.[8]

The conception of mortgage interest rate futures faced three challenges. First, a standardized mortgage instrument needed to be created. Second, there had to be a real or perceived interest rate risk to generate demand from hedgers. In other words, interest rates had to be volatile. Third, the legal and regulatory environment needed to be conducive to allowing an exchange to launch a futures contract based on that instrument.

Major structural economic changes typically precede the development of new markets. The invention of any new product is ultimately a response to latent demand or overt demand. Accordingly, the latent demand for new markets in the financial sector typically follows a period of major structural economic change. To the dispassionate observer, the period from 1960 to 1975 represented one such period. The stage was set by Kennedy-Johnson deficit spending, an unpopular, socially disruptive war in Vietnam, President Nixon going off the gold standard, and the OPEC oil embargo. All of these led to an increase in inflation and interest rates.

California and the rest of the nation suffered from a spike in interest rates in 1966 and another in 1969, as federal deficits had begun to take their toll. In addition, there was a special set of problems for faster-growing western states: a rapidly rising population was sparking a burst in housing starts, which was the number of residential building construction projects that began each month. Local S&Ls, however, had insufficient capital to satisfy the growing demand for mortgages. To fill the funding gap, rates on deposits had to be higher than in the savings banks in the Northeast. Of course, the higher costs of procuring funds forced banks to raise mortgage rates. Deposit rates could even go higher in order to attract capital. A better solution

[8]W. R. Hicks, *Value and Capital: An Inquiry into Some Fundamental Principles of Economic Theory* (Oxford: Clarendon Press, 1939).

was to create a transparent and liquid secondary market in which S&Ls in the high-growth areas of the West could sell to translate what they created, the proceeds from which could then be used to relend to new borrowers. To make this possible, a hedging mechanism was desirable to reduce the risk of owning mortgages while they were being originated for resale, thereby transferring risk from hedger to speculator. All of my studying, research, and teaching made me more confident about the value proposition.

Structural economic changes that result in the need for capital and risk-shifting mechanisms typically drive the standardization of products, regardless of whether the products are tangible commodities or financial assets. Here again, the grains market provides a useful paradigm. In the mid-nineteenth century, the American westward expansion and the growing demand in Europe for imports from the United States led to the development of standards for measuring and grading grains set by the CBOT. The standards allowed market participants around the world to buy and sell grain futures with confidence because everyone agreed on the exact nature of the underlying commodity should they wish to take or give delivery. In short, standardization is a necessary condition for financial innovation in the development of new markets—a major theme that will occur throughout this story.

Mortgage Interest Rate Futures—Creating Good Derivatives

As the 1960s drew to a close, three men from the savings and loan industry would change the capital markets in the United States: an academic-turned-regulator and central banker, a real estate developer-turned-CEO of a government-sponsored enterprise, and the CEO of a financial institution. Over the next decade, Preston Martin, Thomas Bomar, and Anthony Frank played unique roles in the invention of financial futures. Preston, Tom, and Tony significantly modified existing financial institutions and created new ones.

Preston Martin was a professor at the University of Southern California. He was subsequently appointed the regulator of California's savings and loan industry, and in 1969 was appointed the chairman of the Federal Home Loan Bank Board (FHLBB) by President Nixon. It was at the FHLBB that he strongly advocated for the development of a futures market in mortgages.[9]

Thomas "Tom" Bomar was the first CEO of the Federal Home Loan Mortgage Corporation. His objective was to create a secondary market and for the Federal Home Loan Mortgage Corporation (FHLMC), nicknamed Freddie Mac, to be a temporary holder of mortgages. He also promoted the idea of interest rate risk management for depository institutions through the use of variable rate mortgages and interest rate futures. Tom went on to become chairman of the Federal Home Loan Bank and took a leadership role in providing the regulatory authority for savings and loan institutions (S&Ls) to hedge against adverse interest rate movements. Tom was a creative businessman who used his practical skills as a public servant. In retrospect, if Tom's philosophy had been adhered to, I believe the failure of government-sponsored enterprises such as the Federal National Mortgage Association (FNMA), nicknamed Fannie Mae, might never have occurred. Tom embraced change and innovation, but valued careful regulatory oversight.

I learned about the interest rate risk facing Freddie Mac from Preston Martin in the spring of 1971. He helped arrange a meeting with Thomas Bomar to discuss how a futures market in interest rates could be designed to manage Freddie Mac's interest rate risk. Tom had a laser-like focus and a propensity to laugh. Having reviewed all recent literature on the subject and fortified by my own research on plywood contracts, I was confident that interest rate volatility was going to become a permanent part of the U.S. economic landscape. The big challenge lay in translating heterogeneous mortgages into a homogeneous pool. Simply put, mortgages had to be standardized before a futures contract could be written.

If grain standards could be developed with features such as protein and infestation requirements as early as the 1850s, then the same could certainly be done with mortgages. If we could standardize mortgages

---

[9]Preston Martin, "A Futures Market in Your Future?" *Federal Home Loan Bank Board Journal* (October 1972), 1–4.

with features like percentage down payment and the ratio of household income relative to mortgage payments, a market could be created. I summed up the need for standardization by saying, "If you could grade it, you could trade it." Tom laughed and I knew that this was the beginning of a long friendship. What I needed was a large portfolio of mortgages that could be statistically analyzed. Tom advised me to call Anthony Frank and give him a heads up. The vistas seemed unending as I drove my Austin Healy across the San Francisco–Oakland Bay Bridge for my first meeting at Tony's headquarters at Citizens Federal on Market Street in San Francisco. It was the summer of 1971 and I was looking forward to doing research during my break from teaching. This was a unique opportunity to combine my interest in futures and the need to get published in academic journals.

Citizens Federal was an industry leader that greatly affected its fellow thrift institutions. As its CEO, Anthony "Tony" Frank had led the first transformation of an S&L mutual organization to a stock-owned company. Tony was unafraid of taking positions that were unpopular in the industry and led the thrift industry efforts to embrace new financial innovations that would mitigate its risk. Tony did not fit the mold of a traditional banker. He went on to become postmaster general of the United States in 1998, and even put Elvis Presley on a postage stamp.

As I walked into Tony's office, a tall, athletic man with a big smile extended his hand and welcomed me. Conversation flowed easily and I knew almost immediately that he would help. Tony asked one of his associates to help me access a portfolio of 18,000 conventional loans to find a representative sample. I returned to Berkeley and immediately contacted Hank Schaaf, the head of the Center for Real Estate and Urban Economics, to see if the center would give me a grant to support the study. I knew Hank was always interested in finding new ways to make the center nationally preeminent while advancing real estate finance at the same time.

From an academic point of view, we needed to gain some understanding of mortgage risk premiums based on the size of loans as well as borrower characteristics before mortgages could be standardized. Although there had been prior research conducted on the subject, this was the first study to analyze the risk premiums of a particular institution. Aggregated data might not have yielded the same results, and I could perhaps shed some light on this important subject. I had to craft the proposal in a way that would fit into the literature and therefore be promising for publication in an academic journal. Admittedly, my real motive was to see if mortgages could be standardized enough to create a futures market. Nevertheless, this idea was too novel at the time and, in order to secure the funding, I had no choice but to frame my objectives in this manner. I did, however, share this long-term goal with Hank.

Massaging the data was a serious challenge, especially because not all paperwork associated with new mortgages had yet been computerized at that time. A sample of 556 loans were drawn from the 4,907 originated loans, but only loans that had all the required data were included in the sample. Statistically speaking, these loans were representative of the entire portfolio. We broke down mortgage characteristics according to the effective mortgage rate, loan-to-appraisal ratio, loan amount, and term in months. The loans were distinguished by neighborhood ratings and property condition ratings, both with five ratings from poor to excellent. We included four borrower characteristics: net worth, housing-to-income ratio, loan amount to net worth ratio, and secondary financing.[10] The study took quite some time to complete and publish, but yielded some interesting and statistically significant results because it expanded on previous research on mortgage standardization by including borrower, property, and neighborhood characteristics.[11] While the study proved academically interesting, it turned out to be a blow to my long-term goal of mortgage grading. Conventional mortgages could not be standardized because every house and every borrower were different.

As Louis Pasteur once said, "Chance favors the prepared mind."[12] I was sitting in my office in 666 Barrows Hall (the office number

[10]A second mortgage is a loan secured by the home owner's equity in a property that already been mortgaged.

[11]Richard L. Sandor and Howard B. Sosin, "The Determinants of Mortgage Risk Premiums: A Case Study of the Portfolio of a Savings and Loan Association," *Journal of Business* 48, no. 1 (January 1975): 27–38.

[12]Louis Pasteur, Lecture, University of Lille, December 7, 1854.

was the butt of a lot of jokes related to my work on futures), reading *The Wall Street Journal* in late 1971, when I saw an ad by First Boston advertising its role in the new Ginnie Mae (GNMA) market. I had been following the creation of the security but until then dismissed it as a solution to standardization because the market was too small and was of less interest to the S&L industry. If a leading investment bank was advertising, however, it must have meant that the market was growing and that there was perhaps enough supply to warrant a futures market. I called the number in the ad to ask for a brochure. I was connected to a helpful GNMA salesman who not only got me a brochure but personally delivered it to my office two weeks later. We spent about an hour together and then went to lunch on Telegraph Avenue. It seemed that he, like most Americans, had the images of hippies and antiwar protests burned into his mind from the media. He soon supplied me with GNMA data and introduced me to a GNMA trader at the desk. There began the story of the introduction of the first financial futures, all done on notes taken in a Chinese restaurant on Telegraph Avenue.

Chicago Calls

I received some surprising news in the fall of 1971. The Chicago Board of Trade had hired an executive search firm to head up a new planning department. The existing planning department had been working on establishing what would become the Chicago Board Options Exchange (CBOE), and the entire department were leaving the CBOT in order to manage the CBOE. There was a need to develop a new department from scratch, and my name had surfaced during the executive search.

I had no idea about this when the phone rang. "This is Warren Lebeck," the caller said. "Remember when we spoke after I lectured at your class in Berkeley? I asked you if you'd ever leave the academic world, and you said, 'Only if the chief economist post at a major financial institution opened up.' Well, it's opened up now." He proceeded to ask me if I was interested in becoming the head of the new Department of Economic Research and Planning at the CBOT.

I told him that this was the opportunity of a lifetime and it was a great honor to be considered for the position. I was ecstatic.

Unbeknownst to me, I gained another endorsement from the CBOT management team. The director of education had flown to Berkeley to ask me to write a booklet on speculation, the purpose of which was to create well-versed speculators and educate traders on the supply and demand dynamics in the grain markets.[13] The director had done his due diligence on my credentials and gave a ringing endorsement to Warren.

Warren wanted me to come to Chicago as soon as possible, hoping that I could get an early lead in the search. Ellen and I flew to Chicago in early 1972. I met with Henry Hall Wilson first, a charming Southerner. Henry had served President Kennedy in the White House as liaison to the House of Representatives, and exemplified the President's New Frontier team. He was convinced that a research and development department was needed to modernize the exchange and professionalize its staff.

I explained to Henry the vision of the agricultural exchange and continuing his push for new futures products. Henry had been a large supporter of CBOE, and mortgage interest rates and reinsurance futures fascinated him. Phil Johnson, an attorney with Kirkland and Ellis, also sat in on the meeting to provide legal counsel to the CBOT. Phil served as more of a consigliere for Henry and the small management team. Henry relied on him for much more than legal insight, valuing his opinion on almost all matters. Next, I spoke to Henry about Walter Heller, a professor at the University of Minnesota. Walter was the chairman of the Council of Economic Advisors under President Kennedy and, like Henry, was also part of the New Frontier. This proved to be an icebreaker.

It was a grueling day, though the numerous meetings with other members from the board of directors appeared to go well. But then, of course, I had also mistakenly thought that the presentation for the CCARP report had gone well.

---

[13]Richard L. Sandor, "Speculating in Futures," Chicago Board of Trade, 1973.

In between meetings, Henry, Phil, and I met Ellen for lunch at the Union League Club. A small problem arose when Henry told me that Ellen would have to go through the woman's entrance on the side door in order to meet us in the lobby. This spelled trouble. Ellen had been the founding member of the Berkeley chapter of the National Organization for Women in the 1960s. In the end, she entered the lobby through the front entrance and in doing so, became one of the first women to walk into the club's entrance unaccompanied by a man.

Shortly after, we flew back to Berkeley where I waited to hear from the exchange. As advised by some colleagues, I had planned a sabbatical year. A prestigious position such as chief economist at the Chicago Board of Trade would surely favor the case for my tenure. My desire was to return to the academic world once I had established the new department at the CBOT—a dilemma that I would have explain to Warren. Although my heart was set on moving to Chicago, I had alternatives if the offer was not made.

I received an offer letter two weeks later outlining my responsibilities at the exchange and reflecting the vision I had for the department. It included developing new products, revising existing contracts and long-term strategic plans, serving as chief economist, and being a spokesperson on these matters for the exchange.

Now came the tough part. I explained to Warren and Henry that I wanted to have the option to return to Berkeley at the end of the first year. It could kill the deal, but I wanted to give it a try. In return, I promised to build a fully functional research and planning department within a year, and swore that I would not leave until this was accomplished. Berkeley too was prepared to move forward with the understanding that I would be taking a sabbatical.

I told my colleagues about the offer, and went home to celebrate. Ellen and I took the kids to our favorite Chinese restaurant. The kids had their usual *guō tiē*, which Julie chewed and Penny gummed. I had never felt more relaxed than during that day and the several months thereafter. It was like being between jobs. I had mentally left behind my position on the faculty and had no full-time responsibilities yet at the exchange.

I signed my employment contract in May 1972 without the advice of an attorney, as I couldn't really afford one. The contract specifically said that any new products I developed would be the property of the exchange. Furthermore, I was forbidden to write about my work until years after it was done. This was consistent with what I knew about professional inventors and scientists at industrial companies, and I was unfazed. We agreed that I would begin consulting immediately and start full time as vice president and chief economist on July 1, 1972. This was the high point of my life to date and I was brimming with excitement.

Chapter 4

The Chicago Board of Trade Years

The Commodity Futures Contract

Architecture starts when you carefully put two bricks together. There it begins.

—*Mies van der Rohe*

My new job was the crowning achievement of all I had been working on for the past 10 years. But I was also apprehensive, having left the comforts of academia for the uncertainties of the business world. I had no idea about the unprecedented changes that were going to take place in the agricultural markets.

Ellen and I settled down in an old brownstone apartment in the Lincoln Park neighborhood of Chicago. The neighborhood was in transition and yuppies were buying and remodeling the buildings. I vividly remember the very first drive to work on July 1, 1972. As the taxi drove south on LaSalle Street, I could see the CBOT building at the foot of the street. When completed in 1930, it had been the tallest building in the city of Chicago.

My first tasks were to staff the department, change existing contracts to reflect the current economic situation, and develop new contracts. We recruited a diverse group of individuals whose competencies spanned agriculture, economics, and finance. They hailed from all parts of the world: the United States, England, Israel, and India. The employees of the exchange joked about the little United Nations contingency in our department. It was like being in graduate school again. Warren suggested that I consider hiring a secretary who had been with the exchange for some time. I agreed to have lunch with Marilyn Grace. The lunch was carefully orchestrated so as to include two other exchange officials. Warren acted as the matchmaker. After about five minutes, I found myself falling into an hour-long conversation with Marilyn, with little regard to the others at the table. Marilyn was an elegant brunette who was good-natured and loved to laugh. She immediately won my favor. By the end of lunch, there was an implicit understanding that she was going to work as my executive secretary. In fact, Marilyn worked with me for the next 28 years and became a family friend too.

Henry Hall Wilson, president of the CBOT, called the office when I first started and said, "Rich, please join us for the Director's meeting pre-board luncheon today." I could hardly contain my emotions. This was an honor reserved for the senior executives. In his attempt to modernize the exchange, Henry had built a group of highly qualified directors to expand the profile of the exchange and provide expertise from diverse industries. Past and current directors included individuals with national and international renown such as Milton Eisenhower,[1] Charlie Schultze,[2] and James Roche.[3] It was very unusual for a commodity exchange in the late sixties and early seventies to have board members of that prominence. It would set an example to other exchanges for the foreseeable future.

[1]Milton Stover Eisenhower had been the president of Kansas State University, Pennsylvania State University, and John Hopkins.

[2]Charles L. Schultze was chairman of the United States Council of Economic Advisers during the Carter Administration.

[3]James M. Roche was the chairman, CEO, and president of General Motors Corp.

An adroit politician, Henry held lunch for the independent directors before the scheduled board meeting in order to inform them of important issues and discuss the agenda in a more casual setting, thereby reducing tensions that may arise in the actual meetings. The lunches took place at a private club. The club itself was filled with many of the most important business leaders in the city, and Henry seemed to know everyone. As he passed by each table, he shook hands with each person and said, with a charming Southern drawl, "How y'all doing?" Henry then threw in smoothly, "These are the most controversial issues on today's agenda and I would like you to *remembah* them." Henry never asked for their votes directly. Nevertheless, by the end of lunch, the independent directors and management team knew where he stood on the issues.

As we moved on to the scheduled board meeting, I noticed the hallway on the sixth floor leading to the boardroom was steeped in tradition. Rows of sepia-toned photographs of chairmen of the exchange since 1848—the founding year—hung on the walls. The boardroom itself was magnificent—a paneled art deco space lit by wall lamps whose glass shades were etched with shocks of wheat. The atmosphere lent a certain grandeur to the board meetings that were held there. The directors sat at an oval-shaped, dark wooden table that accommodated 20 or more members. The staff of the exchange sat behind the directors. I sat quietly in a chair against the wall next to Phil Johnson. Henry graciously introduced me to the board and said, "Rich, describe the department you are building to the directors." I responded with some brief comments about what we would be doing. Henry took pride in having a chief economist at the board meeting, and I was proud to be there. Through these meetings, I learned valuable lessons on how to interact with the board of directors that would serve me well in the future.

I left my very first lunch and board meeting and proudly wondered, "How in the world did I ever get here?" But I was also worried about doing a good job.

Mentors and Leaders

I struck up a good relationship with James "Jim" Roche from the Board of Directors, and arranged to visit him.

The door to Jim's office in the GM building in New York was without handles and opened automatically, my first experience with the top echelon of corporate America. At the time, GM was the largest corporation in the world. I learned about what gave rise to the success of the company in the years following World War II. Jim had started as a car salesman managing a dealership in the Carolinas, an experience which had made him customer-oriented. Although it would be difficult to replicate his emphasis on customers, I found it a good model to follow for the exchange. After all, the exchange was dominated by the local market makers. The CBOT model had kept its advantage only because of the imagination and entrepreneurship provided by its floor traders and brokers. The mutual nature of the organization made it impossible to provide financial incentives to FCMs and commercial members. I knew it would be different in a for-profit exchange. Out of curiosity, I asked Jim what it felt like to be the most powerful industrialist in the world and have no bosses. His response was memorable, "Everybody has a boss. Customers, dealers, and the stockholders are all my bosses." These words would always stay with me.

I met with CEOs of major FCMs to help me do my job. Donald Regan, a direct and confrontational man, was the Chairman and CEO of Merrill Lynch. The first words he spoke were, "Why am I paying so much to the floor brokers on your exchange?" I countered by asking him how much the specialists make on the floor of the NYSE. I compared the system of specialists with the system of competitive market-makers at the commodities exchanges and concluded that the system on futures exchanges was more efficient and beneficial to the public.[4] "Do you support their role as monopolists in market making?" I countered. The muscles in Don's face relaxed and in a noticeably friendlier tone, he said "You have made some important points." I believe that the strength of my convictions based on my academic training gave me the right to be argumentative about the value of

[4]The Chicago Board Options Exchange (CBOE), which was established by the CBOT in 1973 and began with a system of competitive market makers. In today's world, the nature of electronic communication networks (ECN) and algorithmic trading results in a market that is similar to one with competitive specialists.

commodities exchanges, and Don seemed to respect that. He later sent me a copy of *Confusion de Confusiones*.[5] The oldest book ever written on the stock exchange business, it provided an account of the Amsterdam Stock Exchange and trading in the Dutch East India Company shares in the 1600s. Don would became Secretary of the Treasury and Chief of Staff to President Ronald Reagan.

It was necessary for me to fully understand agribusiness and the role of the CBOT in that sector of the economy. I toured soybean crushers, wheat millers, and even bakers. The insights and knowledge I gained from these on-site experiences enabled me to speak first-hand at the meetings of the various product committees at the exchange, be it wheat or soybeans. I finally began to develop a firmer grasp of domestic and international grain trade. It would have been difficult to write a commodity futures contract or understand the irrationality of some of its features without seeing first how the agriculture industry was structured. These experiences helped me redesign futures contracts so they created value for the buyers and sellers and produced a transparent and representative price for the domestic and international grain trade. There hadn't been any soybean or wheat farms in Brooklyn. For people who grew up in New York, the outdoors was either parks or, as Woody Allen famously said, the spaces between buildings. Trading had given me only a cursory overview of agriculture. These meetings made me a student again, and I loved it.

The Executive Vice President of Central Soya was on the board of directors of the CBOT. He was a generous man and offered to show me his firm's elevators and soybean crushing facilities. I flew back with him on a corporate plane to Indianapolis, Indiana, and he spent the next morning explaining how the firm operated. First, he showed me the machines that crushed the soybeans. The physical act of crushing the soybeans released soybean oil, which was not only an ingredient in mayonnaise and margarine but also had industrial uses. Once the oil had been crushed out of the soybeans, the resulting meal was used as feed for cattle and hogs. He added, "These are the Dark Ages." Most

[5]Joseph de la Vega, *Confusion de Confusiones*, Publication Number 13 of the Kress Library of Business and Economics, 1688 (Cambridge, MA: Harvard University Printing Office, 1957).

of the machines used to literally crush soybeans had been replaced by a chemical process that separated the soybean meal from the soybean oil. I had seen "an industrial antique," and it put the agricultural processing industry in perspective.

The rest of the day was spent with other executives in the company learning about sales and marketing. I flew back to Chicago and told Ellen about the trip. She patiently listened to my lecture on soybean processing and once again prophetically said, "I don't think we're going back to Berkeley."

Some of my experiences with the executives of grain merchants were not as good as others. One particular meeting I had with the CEO of one of the multinational grain exporters in New York stood out in my memory. The office was located in Manhattan and was very posh. The CEO was aloof and the meeting lasted only a short 10 minutes. I struggled afterward to understand the coolness of the CEO and the brevity of the meeting. When I returned to Chicago, the pit broker of the CEO told me with a smile, "You should have never called him by his first name. That's the last time you will ever see him." The broker was right. I learned a valuable lesson. The ease and familiarity with which Midwesterners conducted business was just out of place, if not downright disrespectful, for many international grain merchants.

A minor event ended up profoundly changing my work. I had completed the article I was writing in Berkeley, "Innovation by an Exchange: A Case Study of the Development of the Plywood Futures Contract,"[6] and was awaiting an acceptance or rejection from the editor of *The Journal of Law and Economics*, Ronald Coase. A rejection would have been a personal blow to me as a young economist. I received a letter back from Professor Coase who thought the paper needed some additional work. Once satisfactorily revised, however, it would be accepted for publication. I was elated. The letter provided some academic ratification of my new career.

The paper was published in April 1973. I called Professor Coase to thank him for publishing my article, and extended an invitation to the

[6]Richard L. Sandor, "Innovation by an Exchange: A Case Study of the Development of the Plywood Futures Contract," *Journal of Law and Economics* 16, no. 1 (April 1973): 119–136.

floor of the exchange, which he readily accepted. Professor Coase had never been on the floor of the exchange before, and asked me questions about each and every detail. He was struck that so many transactions could take place with a simple nod or shout. I explained to him that in all the frenzy, some trades were bound not to match. Traders could be mistaken about the size of the trade, whether it was a buy or sell, or even about the identity of the counterparty. Unmatched trades were called out trades, to be reconciled by floor brokers on the exchange before the opening. If out trades could not be reconciled, they would be arbitrated by a committee of exchange members. If a trader had a reputation for not honoring trades, his bids and offers would no longer be recognized by other members in the trading pit. He then asked, "What is the role of lawyers?" I replied, "They have no role in dispute resolution." The Illinois legislature passed a law in 1859 dictating that certain types of member disputes be settled by the exchange and treated outside the judicial system. The notion that the exchange had self-regulated for well over a hundred years said something about the ability of markets to regulate themselves. Professor Coase was impressed by the efficiency of this quasi-legal system and recommended that I write an article about it. Unfortunately, I never wrote on the topic. It might have provided insight into dispute resolution in other businesses.

Having caught a glimpse of Professor Coase's interest in the efficiency of the dispute process, I further explained that not only were disputes resolved without lawyers, contracts themselves were drafted by exchange members and staff. The contracts were very simple and needed to be unambiguous. The process had evolved over time such that the actual drafting of the contract was easily done by adapting the terms for a new commodity into a standard boilerplate of rules and regulations. No lawyers were involved in drafting, despite the exorbitant dollar amount of the commercial transactions on these contracts. Lawyers were only involved in assuring that the rules and regulations were consistent with the rulebook of the exchange. The value of contract standardization and its impact on reducing transaction costs was inevitable. Once again, Professor Coase suggested that I write an article on this and encouraged me to conduct more research about this process at other exchanges. The last topic we discussed was my idea for interest rate futures. Professor Coase prodded me to pursue it and to keep him informed of my progress. This provided all the encouragement I needed.

Professor Coase had never taken a single course in economics. He spent several years in the United States on a fellowship, listening keenly to people in industry and learning about the operations of companies. From these conversations, he wrote "The Nature of the Firm" in 1937 to explain why companies existed.[7] According him, the existence of firms had everything to do with "transaction costs." While the article was theoretical, it contained no mathematics. Qualitative reasoning was his methodology. The theory cultivated in this article would later be used to explain the rise of the Internet. The paper was not given great praise initially, and later gave Professor Coase only limited renown within the economics profession. In fact, he would have to wait 54 years before he was awarded the Nobel Prize in Economics for that work and a subsequent article entitled "The Problem of Social Cost."[8] Professor Coase was one of the key men in the field of law and economics. An outsider that profoundly changed the field of economics, his convictions were inspiring to those of us who had the opportunity to be mentored by him. Teachers can have a profound effect on those who attempt transformational change. I never heard him say a discouraging word about a new idea. He was the epitome of a teacher and reminded me of Robert Donat in the great English film, *Goodbye Mr. Chips*.

The year ended on a wonderful note. Don Jacobs, dean of the Kellogg School of Management, offered me a position to teach at Northwestern University. I accepted and created a futures and options course which began in 1974.[9] The first course on futures and options at Kellogg, it would become a permanent part of the curriculum in the finance department and was widely imitated at other academic institutions.

---

[7]R. H. Coase, "The Nature of the Firm," *Economica* 16, no. 4 (1937): 386–405.

[8]R. H. Coase, "The Problem of Social Cost," *Journal of Law and Economics* 3 (1960): 1–44.

[9]Title of course at Kellogg in 1974, "The Economics of Organized Futures and Options Markets."

Trading with the Soviets

As my own world changed, so did the real world. The decade of high deficits and the continued expenditures of the war in Vietnam had begun to take their toll. Bretton Woods[10] was abandoned, and on August 15, 1971, the Nixon administration removed the United States from the gold standard. The dollar was weakening and monetary supply was growing. Inflation was rearing its ugly head. Not surprisingly, the prime rate—the interest rate that commercial banks charge their most creditworthy borrowers—continued to rise.

Several other decisions by the administration helped foster the coming change. The Soviet Union had decided to upgrade the diet of its citizens, which involved increasing its animal herds and relying more on imported grains. The Nixon administration removed the requirements that grain exporters had to obtain licenses to export and 50 percent of all shipping had to take place on American vessels, a move that promoted U.S. grain exports. Weather patterns were also changing, setting the stage for a new dynamic in the commodities markets that exacerbated inflationary pressures. Furthermore, wheat production in the Soviet Union dropped dramatically in the crop year ending in June 1972, and the Soviet Union was forced to buy close to 450 million bushels from the United States, a purchase that totaled $700 million—more than the total U.S. commercial wheat export for the previous year. To put the magnitude of the purchase further into perspective, the sales were more than 80 percent of the wheat used for domestic food during that same period.[11] All of this, of course, put upward pressures on grain prices. It was also a catalyst that ignited an idea for my first try at a new futures contract.

At the time, the grain trade was dominated by five major private companies: Cargill, Continental, Louis Dreyfus, Bunge, and Andre.

[10]The Bretton Woods system was an international monetary regime where foreign exchange rates were fixed by the central banks of signatory nations. This fell apart in 1971.

[11]Clifton B. Luttrell, "The Russian Wheat Deal—Hindsight vs. Foresight." Review from the Federal Reserve Bank of St. Louis, October 1973, 2–9.

A newcomer, Cook Industries, was a family-owned cotton business run by a small grain merchant named Edward "Ned" Cook. Ned would later tell me the story of his part in Cook Industries' first transaction with the Soviet Union.[12]

The Soviets typically arranged to buy grain on the weekends. One Saturday in 1972, Ned received a call to meet the team of Soviet purchasers in New York City. Together, they began drinking vodka early in the evening, ate dinner, and continued drinking until about 4 A.M. before they called it a night. Shortly after Ned arrived back in his hotel room, the phone rang. The liaison for the delegation said, "Please meet us at 7 A.M. to discuss some business." Ned was a Southern gentleman whose toleration for alcohol was helped by his large size and a practiced Memphis tradition. Nevertheless, he told me they had outdone him. He took a small chair, put it in the shower and stayed there for the next two hours. He followed with a pot of coffee, got dressed, and went to the meeting ready and able to negotiate with the Russians.

There were approximately 10 people on their team as fresh and ready as Ned was. Ned told me that very moment he knew he had a deal. When I asked him why, he responded quickly with a broad smile, "It didn't take 10 Russians to say no." Ned surmised that they were having ongoing conversations with the other major firms. He left the meeting and immediately called his company to arrange for vessels to ship the grain. He decided to cover his own needs, but also to buy as much additional shipping as he could purchase. If he controlled the freight from the Gulf of Mexico, he could resell it when increased demand from other grain companies appeared as a result of their sales of grain to Russia. He did well—managing to land a contract to supply 600,000 tons of grain and 1,000,000 tons of soybeans to the Soviet Union in July and August of 1972. He did even better on the resale of the vessel charters, establishing himself as a major player in the years to come.[13] I learned a vital lesson from Ned. Always think about second and third round effects in markets.

---

[12]Philippe Chalmin, *Traders and Merchants: Panorama of International Commodity Trading* (Chur, Switzerland: Harwood Academic Publishers, 1987).

[13]"Annual Crop Summary." Crop Reporting Board, SRS, USDA, January 1973, p. A-6.

An Explosion in Grain Prices

Each day, there was talk about the Russian purchase of wheat. I ran into another new employee, Carole Brookins, who reported on markets by gathering information on the floor before the exchange made such information available to other members and the public. She had worked in the municipal bond business and knew finance. We immediately hit it off. Carole and I would remain friends for close to 40 years, and would work together in the future on my biggest challenge as a financial innovator. One day, Carole and I both noted that the usual harvest selling in the wheat market was not causing a drop in prices—as normally occurred—but rather, prices were actually rallying by the end of the summer. We both agreed something important was happening. The markets were telling us something that we didn't know. Unknown to us, a whole new environment was emerging. The year would be dominated by extraordinary weather events, a political shock felt internationally, and a domestic economy that would continue to reel from deficits and a weak dollar.

Heavy rains in the spring of 1973 delayed the planting of corn and soybeans, followed by a very hot summer that hurt corn yields.[14] Russian and Chinese crops failed, and an early frost interfered with the harvest. To make matters worse, the OPEC oil embargo occurred in October 1973. This was followed by another weather event. 1972 to 1973 was an El Niño year, and waters off the coast of Peru changed temperatures. As a result, the number of anchovies running off the coast dramatically waned. This was important because anchovies were used as feed for live animals such as cattle, and were necessary to supplement other feed grains such as corn and soybean meal. In 1973, all agricultural commodities traded at record levels per bushel—corn at $2.68 and wheat at $4.78. Even the smallest food and feed grain oats traded at a record price of $1.20 per bushel. Nixon introduced price controls on June 13, 1973, but America's agricultural lobbies were too strong. On August 6, wheat prices reached a historical high of $4 a bushel, and wheat prices

[14]Corn yield is a statistic that gives the amount of corn harvested per unit of land, for example, metric ton per hectare.

reached $5 a bushel on August 15.[15] Only plywood was affected by the price controls, pushed down to $100 in September from $130 per sheet in June.[16]

Iron Men in Wooden Pits

I made a practice of going down to the trading floor every day. Up close and personal, speculators and their styles were very different. There was nothing more exciting to me than the soybean pit in 1973. It was performance art at its best. It kept me apprised of current events and I enjoyed watching prices being determined. I relished my conversations with Keith Bronstein during those lulls in the market that regularly occurred during the middle of the trading day.

A nephew of Lee Stern, Keith was a brilliant independent broker and trader who represented a generation of market makers that embraced change. He subsequently joined Tradelink, a major worldwide provider of liquidity that was also a commodity trading advisor. Keith traded as many as 75 different positions in stocks, commodities, and currencies after he left the trading floor, and was a self-taught economist that could match any of the formally trained professionals I knew of. Keith possessed the hand-eye coordination that was critical for brokers, and was knowledgeable about the underlying supply and demand conditions that determined long-term prices. I loved running new ideas by Keith, and he always provided me with valuable counsel. Keith became a lifelong friend and a liquidity provider in every new market that I pioneered—both successes and failures.

I sometimes went to the top of the soybean pit to talk to a blind trader who had a seeing-eye dog that knew him by his distinctive cologne. As a child, I had known a dog that was bilingual, and now I knew one that was a market maker. After meeting the trader, I always

---

[15]Jerry W. Markham, "Financial Turmoil," in *A Financial History of the United States* (Armonk, NY: M. E. Sharpe, 2002), 42.

[16]Mills D. Quinn, "Some Lessons of Price Controls in 1971–1973." *The Bell Journal of Economics* 6, no. 1, RAND Corporation, Spring 1975: 22, Fig. 3.

took visitors to the soybean pit to illustrate the range of abilities that market makers and speculators embraced. The trader relied on the sound of the other traders to sense market direction. I always joked that the trader got all winning trades and the dog got the losers.

The idea of sound and markets got hammered home in another incident. I was on the floor one day when a Playboy bunny sashayed from the visitor's gallery on to the catwalk overlooking the trading floor. The traders in the wheat pit were the first to notice her and started shouting. The uproar filled the trading floor and the people in the other pits started buying. I smiled and thought that the price of beans and corn for one brief moment were driven by that attractive woman. It also made me think about how we might incorporate sound into electronic trading. Bull markets sound different than bear markets. I never pursued this but still think it could generate additional liquidity.

Dave Goldberg was a "scalp spreader" in the wheat pit. I met him shortly after joining the exchange. Dave and his brother owned a clearing firm called Goldberg Brothers that specialized in clearing locals. They were clearing members of the Chicago Board Options Exchange from inception. They were both typical floor traders and entrepreneurs. Dave and I became lifelong friends and we spent a lot of time talking on the exchange floor when the markets were quiet. David Goldberg was a total contrast to the image of a commodity trader. He was conservative and never celebrated his success. As a matter of fact, he was always afraid of financial disaster. He always reminded me, "This is a very tough business and could end tomorrow." It was great advice and served me well for years to come.

The same year I was playing defense, I also learned some important lessons related to the press and congressional reactions to political and economic events. On one of my trips to Washington, I was charged with educating congressional staffers and the press on the fundamental causes of the increase in agricultural commodity prices.

Looking back, the best lesson I had ever received on the value of speculation was from Abba Lerner, a member of the economics department at Berkeley and a devout socialist. He told me that food prices in Spain had increased dramatically during the 1930s. Speculators were blamed for the price increase. Francisco Franco, Spain's dictator at the time, determined a need for action and held a meeting for speculators in a square in Madrid. Upon their arrival, he had every one of them shot. His actions had the intended consequence. Buffer stocks of grain owned by the late speculators were sold, and food prices fell. There were unintended consequences that Franco missed, however. A drought followed, and because there were no buffer stocks of grain, famine ensued.

The most persuasive evidence I used was the commitment of trader statistics published by the Commodity Exchange Authority (CEA), which required large hedgers and speculators to report their positions. A preliminary analysis showed what was intuitively obvious to anybody in the business: long positions were dominated by hedgers and exporters who were buying to satisfy foreign and domestic demand, while short positions were dominated by speculators. In fact, by selling or shorting the market as it rose, speculators exerted downward pressure on prices.

At the end of the day, I called my boss and proudly said, "The meeting in Washington was terrific! We had made our point."

I was completely mistaken. An article appeared shortly thereafter blaming speculators at the CBOT for the increase in food prices. I learned that the most sincere efforts could fall on deaf ears if they interfered with a bias on some particular issue. I had seen this in Berkeley, watching the broadcast media focus on a small group of students who were protesting some political or social action and sensationalize it as widespread in their reports. I also learned that there had to be scapegoats when everything went wrong. The speculation business was one such victim. Another was the futures industry. The latter would be the spark that ignited legislative efforts to create a full-blown federal regulatory agency, as opposed to only a subagency of the USDA. You know you're important in the United States financial sector when you get your own regulatory commission.

The Gulf Wheat Futures Contract

1973 was also a year of offense at the CBOT. That year, I wrote an internal memorandum advocating a contract that came to be known as the Gulf wheat contract. The prevailing wheat market was not particularly homogeneous. There were three major types of wheat: hard red winter wheat used for bread; soft red winter wheat used for cookies and cake; and spring wheat used for pasta. Of the three, hard red wheat was the largest crop, and the one that was being exported. However, the CBOT wheat contract had been written in a way that favored the delivery of soft red winter wheat.

The Kansas City Board of Trade (KCBT) traded the hard red wheat contract, and the Minneapolis Grain Exchange (MGE) traded the spring wheat contract. It seemed obvious that the CBOT should have a futures contract exclusively based on the grade of wheat that was both the largest domestic crop and reflected the type of wheat most traded internationally. I drafted the initial terms of the Gulf wheat contract and brought it to the wheat committee, which approved it, as did the board of directors after some minor changes. While there were concerns that the new contract would cannibalize the CBOT's existing soft red winter wheat contract, we argued that this was more desirable than being cannibalized by a similar contract originating from Kansas City. I made a trip to Kansas to persuade the grain dealers to adopt a "regular for delivery" policy.[17] We signed up enough elevators to get approval from the CEA to launch the contract.

I was in the middle of a meeting with an executive of a local grain merchant when his secretary said there was an important call from my office. I took the call with a great deal of apprehension—I was never called out of meetings unless there was a real problem. I picked up the telephone and Marilyn said, "I am so sorry to tell you, but your father has just died." I said, "Get me on the first plane back to Chicago." I excused myself from the meeting, went back to my hotel, and cried.

Frank and I went down to Miami to grieve with my mother. Broadway Hank was cremated and his ashes scattered in the ocean. Those were his wishes. I was glum but we managed to joke about his last words.

---

[17]The CBOT must approve of a firm as "regular for delivery" before they can issue shipping certificates. The approved firm will become the source of all delivery instruments for their shipping stations. See Scott H. Irwin, Philip Garcia, Darrel L. Good, and Eugene L. Kunda, "Spreads and Non-Convergence in CBOT Corn, Soybean, and Wheat Futures: Are Index Funds to Blame?," *Applied Economic Perspectives and Policy*, November 2009.

I had seen him about two weeks earlier after his leg had been amputated from complications arising from diabetes. At the time, I had leaned over his hospital bed, kissed him on the cheek, and with tears in my eyes said, "Dad, I'm so sorry." He looked up at me with his characteristic smile and joked, "From now on, call me Lefty." We all broke into laughter. He was unstoppable. After a few days, I returned to Chicago.

The Gulf wheat contract started trading shortly. It was hard to be upbeat but the start of trading buoyed my spirits. Since the CBOT did not substitute the new contract for the old contract, they traded side-by-side.[18]

There were only two significant traders for the Gulf wheat contract. One large grain merchant and one market maker. It was evident after a very short time that the contract would be a complete and utter failure. Launched in April 1974, it became moribund within eight months after only a dismal 1,455 contracts were traded.

The world seemed very bleak at the time. I had just lost my father and my first try at financial innovation was a complete and utter failure. I took it more seriously than did the members of the exchange. Traders kept my spirits up and encouraged me. One jokingly asked me how the contract was faring many years after it died. Their good nature and sense of humor minimized my anguish over the failure. Open interest at the KCBT was sticky and would have been impossible to move even if there had been a liquid related contract trading at the same exchange. Large grain merchants would rather use a market that was liquid and provided imperfect hedges than participate in a new and illiquid market. The smaller participants would continue to use the KCBT. They knew their hedge would be perfect because they could always deliver their grain on the exchange.

Contract Improvement—The Brooklyn Farmer in Iowa

The aftermath of the volatile grain markets resulted in modifications to the contract specifications and the exchange's procedures. The parlance

[18]Traded simultaneously and in the same pit.

of technological change made frequent use of the terms basic patents and improvement patents. These terms mean exactly what they appear to mean. The first windshield wiper, for example, had to be operated manually with a lever. Modifications, such as the addition of different speeds, constituted improvements. In this case, there were two improvements implemented that were worth noting: the addition of alternative delivery points in the grain contracts and the institution of variable price limits.

Ever since I had been involved with the CBOT, farmers and elevators throughout the country wanted to have multiple delivery points for the agricultural futures contracts. For example, the wheat contract specified that only grain elevators in Chicago would be regular for delivery, that is, the delivery of warehouse receipts in satisfaction of the futures contract would have to be from Chicago-based grain elevators. If a hedger owned or needed grain in Chicago, the hedge could be perfected by taking or making delivery. The technical term was that such hedgers were "in position." If a grain elevator owned corn in Iowa and hedged in Chicago, they were termed "out of position" hedgers and faced basis risk. One should think of hedging as the purchase of price insurance. If a farmer in Iowa purchased price insurance on Chicago prices, there was a risk that prices in Iowa could drop more than the prices in Chicago. If prices fell more in the local area than the area of the insurance policy, the insurance policy would fail to cover all of the farmer's losses. That potential difference was known as basis risk.

The Relationship between Futures Prices and Spot Prices

In an ideal world, the price of grain in Iowa should be equivalent to its futures price minus the cost of handling and the cost of transporting the grain to an elevator in Chicago. For example, if the futures contract at the end of November is $3.40 a bushel, and it costs $0.10 to unload the grain elevator in Iowa, transport the grain, and reload in an elevator in Chicago that is regular for delivery, the local price should be $3.30. The grain elevator would then be indifferent to delivering grain in satisfaction of its short position or buying the contract back and selling it locally at $3.30.

The real world differs. Local prices might be lower than $3.30 for a variety of reasons, including lack of transportation or an unusually large amount of local supply that needs to be sold because of the seller's cash requirements. If the hedge is placed at $3.50, then the $0.10 decline to $3.40 would be accompanied by a decline of $0.10 in local prices in a perfect world. The farmer or grain elevator could then buy in the futures contract at $3.40 and receive a $0.10 gain on his hedge. He or she would sell the grain in the local market at $3.30. This would be $0.10 lower than when the hedge was initiated. The $0.10 profit in the futures contract would exactly offset the $0.10 lower price in the local market. The difference in price on the CBOT futures price and the local price is known as the basis. Continuing this example, if the local price fell to $3.35, there would be a $0.15 loss on the sale of the grain in the spot market and only a $0.10 gain on the futures contract. The hedge would not work perfectly. There would be a loss due to a basis change. If local prices were $3.35, there would be a $0.10 gain in the futures position and only a $0.05 loss in the spot market. In that case, the farmer or grain elevator operator would realize a basis gain of $0.05 and final proceeds of $3.35 per bushel.

Some economists, most notably Keynes, argue that futures prices usually trade below the present spot prices. In economics lingo, this is called *backwardation*. This is because the futures contract price needs to compensate for the risk taken by the asset holder. This risk premium causes the actual price upon expiry to be lower than the futures contract price. The opposite of this is called a *contango*, which generally occurs for nonperishable commodities such as gold, which have a cost of carry such as warehousing fees, interest forgone, and income forgone from the leasing commodity.

There is one other subtle point to be made. If the cost of storing the grain locally is higher than the costs of storing the grain in Chicago, then there should be over time a gain arising from the basis risk. Conversely, if the cost of storing grain locally is lower than the cost of storing grain in Chicago, then there should be a loss arising over time from the basis risk. Basis gains or losses can also arise because the grain being hedged is a different grade from that traditionally delivered on the exchange. In any event, the CBOT can be used as a reference for pricing grain any place in the world. For example, the price in Rotterdam should theoretically be the CBOT price plus shipping and handling to that port.

Another point is that hedgers are really speculating on the basis.[19] The basis provides a price signal that drives capital formation. For example, if there are significant supplies in a certain geographical area but no storage facilities there, local prices might be priced below the costs of transporting the grain to another region or Chicago. In that case, a grain company should build grain elevators there, whereupon the company would reap normal profits from storage, as well as significant basis gains on its hedge. Rail or other transportation improvements might then follow in order to accommodate new grain elevators. Understanding this is important for two reasons: it explains the changes in contract specifications that we will discuss next, and more importantly, the very characteristics of the basis risks that increase liquidity in the grain markets would have to synthetically be developed for financial instruments for which there are neither handling nor transportation charges.

While in theory multiple delivery points would be beneficial for the short hedger, it would in fact result in lower prices, or equivalently, higher transaction costs. This was due to the fact that buyers of grain who wanted to take delivery would be uncertain as to the location. They would be uncertain with regards to transportation, and therefore the price they would be willing to pay would assume that delivery would occur in the most undesirable location for them. This was a nuanced but important point.

I met with a group of farmers and grain elevator operators in Des Moines to explain this conundrum in the early fall of 1972. Who would have *thunk* it? The world's largest grain exchange being represented by a Brooklyn-bred Berkeley professor on sabbatical, explaining grain trading to Iowa farmers. I was silently amused at the irony of the situation.

The crowd was pretty hostile. Max Naylor, a farmer from Greene County, Iowa, was clearly the unofficial leader. Hearing what he would later describe as an Eastern accent, he politely said, "Dr. Sandor,

---

[19]Holbrook Working, "Hedging Reconsidered," *Journal of Farm Economics* 35, no. 4 (November 1953): 544–561.

where are you from?" I replied, "Brooklyn, New York." He said, "Do they have any farms in Brooklyn?" I said, "Yes." He looked puzzled, and I went on to say, "There was a farm in Canarsie not too far from Brooklyn. We would go there from time to time to see if we could steal an ear of corn." Laughter followed, and the tension levels in the crowd dropped quickly. Max asked good-naturedly, "Have you had any real experience in farming?" I responded, "No, but I would happily be your free-hired hand during planting and harvesting if you like." The rest of the meeting went smoothly after that.

And that was how I ended up on a tractor in Greene County, Iowa, in 1973. Max had previously taught farming in Brazil under a USDA grant, and came to also serve as a board member of a local bank and the Federal Reserve Bank in Chicago. Max was no ordinary farmer. He kept meticulous records of every field he had and religiously checked his drainage tiles, fertilizer levels, and measured any adjustments to changes in yield. His farm yielded almost 10 to 20 bushels per acre more than the county average, and exceeded the average yield of the state. Indeed, there was no substitute for practical knowledge for a researcher and teacher, and my educational experience on a tractor would help me write my first multiple delivery grain contracts.

Record-level grain prices were putting pressure on the CBOT to have multiple delivery points. Prices in rural areas sometimes didn't increase as much as Chicago because of local supply and demand conditions. Some erroneously thought that the solution was to change the contracts in Chicago and allow for delivery of grain throughout the United States. They didn't understand that the uncertainty imposed on the buyer would reduce demand and therefore have the unintended consequence of lowering prices significantly. The answer was to add delivery points as a safety valve only. The grain trade had changed in 1972 and 1973 because of increases in international trade. We had to avoid shortages in Chicago given its limited storage space. The result of short squeezes in Chicago would cause huge basis losses if the futures prices increased dramatically and if local prices increased only mildly. The dilemma was to find a solution that would increase supply but not cause buyer uncertainty. The answer was to add delivery points in Toledo at a low enough discount to Chicago so that delivery would only occur when the futures price became dramatically higher than the local price in Toledo. We added St. Louis as a further precaution. The alternative delivery points would simply add supply only if prices in the local Chicago market did not reflect the national level of supply and demand.

One last point on improvement innovations. In 1972, the significant volatility in the spot markets required committees to convene from time to time in order to adjust daily trading limits and change margin requirements. To institute a rule-based system, I suggested we automatically raise the limits if they were hit in three different contract months. If trades reached the wider limit and stayed there a second day, the limit would automatically go to 200 percent of the original limit. The system of variable price limits worked well and is still in use today. In contrast, limits of any kind were an anathema on U.S. stock exchanges. Only after the crash of 1987 were they put in place in securities trading. They were called "circuit breakers" but applied only to moves in indexes.

The Gold Futures Contract

At the end of 1974, the Ford administration removed the ban on U.S. citizens owning gold. The ban had occurred during the Depression and was a measure prompted by the belief that it would improve economic conditions. Removing the link between the dollar and gold allowed the federal government to pursue an easier monetary and fiscal policy. If the reason had ever been valid, it certainly was no longer relevant. This meant that futures trading in gold could commence at the end of the year. I worked with the precious metals committee to draw up the contract specifications. Like everybody else, I was sure that futures trading in gold would be successful. It seemed obvious that gold prices would be determined in the United States, and the London "fix"[20] ultimately became irrelevant.

Since the international trade was dominated by kilo bars, I thought that the CBOT should have a three-kilo contract rather than an even

[20]"Fix" or gold fixing is the practice of setting the price of gold twice a day. London acted as a benchmark for gold prices before gold futures started trading. See J. Orlin Grabbe, "The Gold Market," *Laissez Faire City Times* 2, no. 16.

100 ounces. The committee was convinced that the preciseness of the contract would eliminate the uncertainty associated with a 100-ounce contract with a variance of 5 percent above or below that amount. The convention in the silver market was a 5,000-ounce deliverable in five bars from 1,000 to 1,100 ounces per bar. If the contract closed at high prices, the seller would deliver the heavier bars and in a declining market shorts would deliver lighter bars. This created liquidity for firms that arbitraged in the spot and futures markets. While the precise nature of the proposed contract would eliminate this liquidity, the committee believed that this would be more than compensated by being the world standard. The CBOT would ultimately settle on a three-kilo contract while the Comex and the CME would keep the silver convention and trade 100-ounce bars. Some members of the committee wanted risk-free arbitrage, thinking that some buyers would pay more or less than prices quoted in the spot market. But nobody came to the party.

The three-kilo gold contract died almost as soon as it was launched. The CME contract persisted for a while, but it was the Comex contract that prevailed. Comex already had a successful silver contract and traders could easily speculate on the difference in the prices of silver and gold, that is, they could simultaneously buy silver and sell gold, and vice versa. However, this was not the main reason for the firm's success. The Comex's customers and members were part of the bullion trade and were tied into the exchange through various internal procedures and investments they had made as members. In a sense, it wasn't too much different from retail shopping. Most people would rather buy a new product from a familiar store than to buy the same product at a new store. This was by no means a new phenomenon. The tendency for exchanges to trade in clusters of new products was already there. The CBOT was the leader in grains, the CME in meats, and the New York Coffee, Sugar and Cocoa Exchange in tropical commodities. First-mover advantages implied a competitive edge for new products as well as the introduction of new related products. From this failure, I learned that futures contracts should not be precise and perfectly replicate the spot market. They need to have different set of characteristics to create liquidity and serve their primary purpose of hedging and price discovery. That imprecision, or spin, is what is called "putting English in the contract."

In the meantime, I continued to teach at Northwestern as a Martin C. Remer Distinguished Professor of Finance, participated in the International Commodities conferences, and further extended my network. However, there were already two strikes against me—the Gulf wheat futures contract and the kilo gold futures contract. Metaphorically, I had begun the architecture for two new markets and couldn't get any further than "putting two bricks together." I desperately needed a winner. I thought about mortgage interest futures—an idea I never abandoned. All of my dreams now depended on its success.

Chapter 5

The Chicago Board of Trade Years

Financial Futures Contract

Yes, we're boys, always playing with tongue or with pen and I sometimes have asked, "Shall we ever be men?"

—*The Boys,* Oliver Wendell Holmes, 1859

I stepped into Warren Lebeck's small office in May 1972 and noticed that it was as fastidious as the man himself. I was joining the exchange as a consultant, just two months prior to my appointment as chief economist. The purpose of the meeting was to brief Warren on the potential of interest rate futures. He surprised me by announcing, "I rented a conference room in the Palmer House and we're going over there to draft the first GNMA futures contract." Given my limited knowledge of the process, I was terrified by the prospect of having to write the contract on the spot.

A large oak table covered in emerald-green cloth awaited us in the modest-sized conference room. I took out a folder that contained my notes of interviews with mortgage bankers, savings and loan executives, and Government National Mortgage Association Mortgage-Backed Securities (GNMA MBS) market data, while Warren brought out the rules and regulations from the CBOT. Meticulous as ever, he had also brought along a pair of scissors and Scotch tape. When I asked him what they were for, he answered, "To copy and paste from the rulebook."

A GNMA is a mortgage-backed security that is collateralized by mortgages guaranteed by two agencies of the U.S. government. These mortgages are pooled into one security. The agency guarantees the timely payment of interest in the event the underlying mortgages go into default. The GNMA has a fixed interest rate. Each month, the owner of the GNMA receives a fixed payment of both principal and interest. Although the life of the mortgage is originally 30 years, the life of the security is significantly shorter because of prepayments. Very few people stay in the same house for 30 years.

At the time, the securities were traded as if the principal would be paid at the end of 12 years. As with bonds, the price of GNMAs was inversely related to interest rates. Since borrowers had to pay a fixed interest rate when interest rates rose and were higher than that fixed payment, investors had to be compensated by paying a lower price. Our challenge was to write a futures contract based on the hybrid security.

How GNMAs Work

GNMA mortgage- backed securities are bonds where the borrower—a homeowner—pays interest and a portion of the loan back on a monthly basis.

Understanding Bonds
A bond is a financial instrument issued by a government or corporation. The issuer or borrower promises to pay the lender or investor a stated rate of interest on the amount originally borrowed.

Understanding Bonds (*Continued*)

For example, a bond with a face value of $1,000,000 with a stated interest rate of 8 percent requires the borrower to pay $40,000 every six months, or $80,000 annually, and $1,000,000 at the end of the loan period. A bond is generally quoted as a percentage of its face value. In our example, a bond quoted at 100 points is priced at $1,000,000, or 100 percent of $1,000,000. Similarly, a bond quoted at 98 points is priced at $980,000, or 98 percent of $1,000,000. Price movements are often quoted in 1/8 fractions—a convention probably based on the Spanish convention of dividing a piece of gold into eight pieces.[1] Parenthetically, the same convention also explains the origin of calling $0.25 a quarter. Price movement fractions are further divided into 1/32nds.

Bonds are obligations of 11 to 30 years. Notes are between one and 10 years, and bills are one year or below. Bills are issued at a price below face value and carry an implied rather than explicitly stated interest rate. For example, a one-year bill might be issued at $970,000, and at the end of the year, the borrower gives the lender $1,000,000 at maturity. The difference of $30,000 is interest.

A 30-year bond with an 8 percent coupon pays interest of $40,000 twice a year. If interest rates drop to 4 percent, then a new issue of $1,000,000 will have to make two payments of $20,000 per year to be competitive with current rates. An investor has two alternatives. She can buy the new issue that yields $40,000 per million dollars invested, or buy the existing bond which yields $80,000 per million dollars. The choice is obvious: buy the outstanding bond. Faced with this opportunity, everyone bids higher for the outstanding bond until the amount of interest received per million dollars is about the same for the new issue and the existing outstanding bond. There is thus an inverse relationship between the price of the bond and interest rates.

[1]"NYSE's Conversion to the Decimal System," *Wall Street Journal*, June 6, 1997, C1.

GNMA mortgage-backed securities are bonds where the borrower—a homeowner—pays interest and a portion of the loan back on a monthly basis. Unlike a conventional bond, the homeowner can prepay the loan if the house is sold, or refinance if interest rates move lower, such that the term is uncertain. GNMAs therefore must have higher interest rates than government securities of the same maturity in order to attract lenders, that is, investors. If interest rates move lower, the life of the mortgage-backed security could be weeks or months. This makes mortgage-backed securities that are priced above par even riskier.

A hedge is when you take equal and opposite positions in the spot and the futures markets to protect yourself from losses arising from volatile prices. For example, if a farmer has sold corn futures contracts and owns corn, he has an opposite position in the spot and futures markets. He is long in the spot market because he owns the corn, and short in the futures market because he sold futures contracts. If the price falls for his crop, the farmer will make less than he anticipated when he sells his corn for cash. However, the loss will be offset, or at least minimized, when he buys back his futures contracts at a lower price.

Managing Interest Rate Risk through Hedging

In the case of GNMAs, one insures against interest rate fluctuations by locking in the price of the security. Since GNMAs, like bonds, are priced inversely with interest rates, GNMA futures can be used to hedge interest rate risk. Interest rate fluctuations in GNMA securities often follow those in the 10-year Treasury note market.

The following example comes from the educational materials I prepared for the Exchange. In June a mortgage banker makes a commitment to close a $1 million mortgage pool in September. At that point, he is exposed to any changes in interest rates. A mortgage banker hedges that risk by selling GNMA futures. If interest rates have risen, the value of the mortgage pool decreases. If the pool has been hedged, then the mortgage interest futures contract declines and the banker can buy back this contract and make a profit, mitigating his losses in the spot market.

Managing Interest Rate Risk through Hedging (*Continued*)

Table 5.1 Hedging Example with GNMA Futures Contracts

Spot Market	Futures Market
June 1	**June 1**
Makes commitments for $1 million mortgage pool, based on current GNMA coupon of 8 percent ("GNMA 8s"), spot price of 99–24*	Sells 10 December GNMA contracts at prevailing market price of 99–00
Current yield 7.989 percent	Yield of 8.092 percent
September 15	**September 15**
Sells $1 million of GNMA 8s to investors at market price of 92–24	Buys back 10 December contracts at prevailing market price of 92–00
Current yield 8.992 percent	Yield of 9.105 percent
Loss: $70,000	**Gains: $70,000**

*All prices are quoted in points and 32nds. For example, 99–24 means 99 and 24/32. Commissions and transaction costs have not been included.

Using specific prices and simplified timelines, Table 5.1 provides a hedging example.[2]

Of course, interest rates could have declined, in which case the mortgage banker would have experienced a loss in the futures market approximately equal to his gain in the spot market. This is termed a short hedge.

The market also offers an opportunity for hedgers to purchase futures contracts in order to lock-in a price for a transaction they plan to make in the spot market at a later time. This is termed a long hedge. The mechanics of the long hedge are the palindrome of the short hedge.

Although the possibility of making or taking delivery is available to hedgers, this is seldom done in futures markets. Futures markets are primarily used for price protection as discussed, and most contracts are offset before expiration.

---

[2]GNMA Mortgage Interest Rate Futures, Chicago Board of Trade, 1975.

Drafting GNMA Futures

Warren opened the rulebook and turned to the rules and regulations that enabled the exchange to trade in wheat. Due to the similarity between grain and GNMA trading, I recommended that we use the wheat contract as a paradigm.

The first draft of the GNMA mortgage interest rate futures contract required the seller to deliver a $250,000 face amount of 6.5 percent GNMAs with a 4.0 percent tolerance, that is, $240,000 to $260,000. To further standardize the contract, the issue date of GNMAs was set no later than 45 days prior to the delivery date and no earlier than two years prior to the delivery date. The notional amount of $250,000 made the daily price movements similar, by design, to those of the grains. GNMA futures had to compete for speculative capital. Performance bonds or margins were based on daily price movements, or volatility. We set the interest rate based on the current rate of newly issued GNMAs. All specifications allowed flexibility to the short seller and a minimum degree of uncertainty for the buyer. The tradition of futures contracts was to give the seller more flexibility since they controlled the supply.

The minimum price increment or tick size was established at 0.01 percent of par or $25 per contract. The grain contract had a price increment of 1/8 of a cent, or $12.50 per contract. The tick size of the GNMA contract was designed to be larger than that of the grain contract so as to attract market makers—if market makers could buy at the bid price and sell at the offer price, they would make $25.00 per contract. However, this price increment was still much smaller than in the spot market where the bid-offer spread was a full point. Therefore, transaction costs would be lower on futures contracts if we could attract liquidity. The trading limit was set at 0.5 percent of par above or below the previous day's settlement price, or $1,250 per contract. This limit was consistent with the limit for the grains, which was set at $0.10. No position limit was established, and trading hours and delivery moments were to be specified later.

We managed to finish our first drafting by the end of the day, but I knew there was a lot more to do. The idea of GNMA futures had been born almost six years prior to the initial draft. I anticipated an additional 12 months of research to finalize the contract, and thought it would require a research budget totaling less than $100,000. I was wrong. It took another three and a half years, 23 or so more drafts, countless staffers, a new federal law, the creation of a regulatory agency, and approximately $250,000 in research and development costs. The final contract represented the input of hundreds of meetings of the formal advisory board—consisting of dealers, savings and loan associations (S&Ls), and government agencies—that had been created by the exchange to provide outside input into the contract design. The application to the Commodity Futures Trading Commission (CFTC) described the economic purpose and value of the market and included several letters from chairmen and CEOs of the biggest S&Ls, the former chairman of Freddie Mac, and the president of GNMA.

What follows is not just the story of how that contract evolved, but how an act of Congress and a new federal regulatory agency changed the face of capital markets in the United States and globally. It was my debut in designing the first successful contract, and the birth of financial futures.

Selling the Concept to Financial Institutions

By the end of 1972, we had settled into a wonderful personal life in Chicago, and I loved my work. Ellen went back to school to pursue an MFA in sculpture at the School of the Art Institute of Chicago. I was happy to help her and enjoyed the role reversal.

The grain markets were active, and interest rates were beginning to be volatile. The commercial banks and S&Ls in New York and Chicago, however, were not receptive to the idea of interest rate futures.

I tried to build industry support for interest rate futures while premarketing the contract. At the time, depository institutions had little or no interest in managing interest rate risk. The field of asset and liability management had not even been born. Needless to say, a Berkeley professor on sabbatical with a Midwest commodity exchange was not an ideal set of credentials in New York City. An executive at a major commercial bank in New York told me, "interest rates don't fluctuate and there's no need to hedge." The executives at savings banks and S&Ls also shared this view. One executive simply left it at, "What are you smoking?" I tried to explain that while interest rates hadn't fluctuated in the recent past, the stability in rates was a historical anomaly. It was evident to me that the ongoing fluxes in the social and political world were just the first of drastic changes to come. Financial change continued with large deficits and an unpopular war. I had taught the first baby boomers, and the impact of their generation was just beginning to become apparent to those of us in academia. I dismissed the criticisms and was determined as ever to move forward.

The financial community in California was totally different. Throughout the State, I continued to draw significant support from institutions associated with the real estate finance sector. I met with Eli Broad of Kaufman and Broad,[3] a forceful man with mild manners who was always honest about his capabilities. He was highly focused and listened intently as I pitched the idea that builders could use GNMA interest rate futures to manage interest rate risk during the construction of houses. He agreed to serve on an advisory board that I was forming in hopes to engage as much support from industry as possible. A blue ribbon advisory group would not only serve as an imprimatur but would also bring its participating companies into the new market. My conversation with Eli drifted to other topics, and we managed to break the ice with our shared interest in art and education.

I next met with Stuart "Stu" Davis, the CEO and chairman of Great Western Financial, a savings and loan association based in California. Stu represented a new breed of Western bankers who were refreshingly different from their staid counterparts in New York and New England. A bachelor who had dated some of Hollywood's famous stars, he personified the glamorous part of Los Angeles power. I didn't expect Stu to support my idea but was interested in his input. Thankfully, he was fascinated with all that was new, and later invited me to have dinner with him at his elegant home in Beverly Hills. I had never been to a more opulent home and grounds. The interior was furnished with Chinese antiques, and the grounds were manicured with a small bridge over a running stream. Stu later invited Ellen and me to spend time with him and actress Debbie Reynolds, his girlfriend at the time. I was in awe of

[3]Kaufman and Broad is a U.S. homebuilding company.

her vast talent, yet it surprised me how demure she was in the face of this important businessman. She alluded to his financial success and power several times. It was a lesson for me about how stardom didn't necessarily trump financial success and power.

In retrospect, I realized that the first users of GNMA futures often shared similar traits. They were young risk takers and outsiders who challenged mainstream thinking. Most were from Chicago and the Western part of the United States. What stood out the most, however, was the fact that they were all blank slates. Without preconceived notions, they were eager to learn, experiment, and innovate. It was no surprise, therefore, that one man became the first Postmaster General of the U.S. who introduced a pop icon on the stamp; another became the CEO of Blackrock, the largest fixed income manager in the world; and yet another, then a mortgage banker, became the chairman of the Federal National Mortgage Corporation. Many other young Chicago traders who bought the first GNMA permits also went on to become successful entrepreneurs, starting their own proprietary trading firms or hedge funds.

Although there were naysayers, I gained a lot of traction for the idea during my trips to Los Angeles, San Francisco, Texas, Arizona, and Colorado. These hubs of financial institutions became first movers in the GNMA futures market. Separately, Preston Martin had just published an article in the FHLBB journal, and another economist followed with an article a month later.[4] We were gaining traction.

Inflation was stirring and volumes were picking up. Mortgage interest rates continued their upward movement. The issuance of GNMA mortgage-backed securities climbed, and a forward market began to emerge. I continued to build relationships that I hoped would lead to the creation of a prestigious advisory group.

The prime rate had reached record levels in 1973, and any arguments about the lack of volatility in interest rates were rendered invalid. This, coupled with the bull market in grains, led me to ask the dean at Berkeley for an extension on my sabbatical. I reasoned that the experience I was receiving at the exchange, along with the industry's gradual acceptance of the idea of financial futures, would be

---

[4]Preston Martin, "A Futures Market in Your Future?" *Federal Home Loan Bank Board Journal*, October 1972.

of benefit both to the university and to me. I was apprehensive about the dean's reaction but luckily, he was very understanding and granted me another year of sabbatical. The dean I reminded me that university rules limited sabbaticals to two years. If I didn't return the next year, I would have to resign. I had already fulfilled my promises to the exchange and felt that I now had options. My position on the chessboard seemed excellent.

Enabling Legislation and Regulation for GNMA Futures

During my interview with Henry Wilson, I had expressed my excitement about applying the academic ideas I had entertained for years to real markets. One of these ideas was for interest rate futures, and another was a tool for hedging against hurricanes and tornados. Henry and Philip Johnson, the CBOT's young outside counsel from Kirkland and Ellis, were big supporters of both mortgage interest rate futures and event-based catastrophe futures. While I believed in portfolio diversification in R&D, the time was ripe for interest rate futures.

Trading in agricultural commodities at the time was regulated by the Commodity Exchange Authority (CEA) of the U.S. Department of Agriculture. Futures markets were generally associated with agribusiness and metals trading firms, as well as a limited number of professional and public speculators. The combination of federal regulation and self regulation worked well, and was generally irrelevant to the majority of legislators in Washington until 1972.

Henry met with CEA officials in February 1973. The CEA called the meeting to discuss the regulation of futures on exempt commodities. The CEA believed it was important to extend federal regulation beyond its prevailing boundaries. Until that point, the CEA regulated products, but not the exchanges themselves. As regulation emerged over concerns about food, wheat was on the list of regulated futures contracts, while silver was not. A graduate of Yale Law School, Phil was politically savvy and an expert in commodity law. Phil was generally quiet and smoked a pipe. When he did speak, however, Henry listened. Phil believed that the definition of a "commodity" could be expanded to include all current and new products that were traded as futures. This required changing the nature of jurisdiction from its orientation toward products to one oriented toward futures exchanges. The CEA also had to have exclusive jurisdiction, and its status as a subagency had to be elevated to that of a fully independent regulatory agency. Commodities were eventually defined as anything "tangible or intangible"[5] for future delivery.

Tracing the Definition of a Commodity

At the start of the twentieth century, the definition of a commodity from which a spot market could evolve into a futures market was widely accepted as one comprised of standardized, bulk, and storable commodities. Futures markets were dominated by agricultural produce and metals at the time, following the birth of the Chicago Board of Trade in 1848 with standardized futures contracts introduced in 1865. The latter part of the twentieth century witnessed a significant broadening in the definition of commodity. New innovations in the form of soybean oil, soybean meal, and frozen concentrated orange juice suggested the elimination of "primary" from the commodity definition. In the mid-1960s, futures markets in live cattle and hogs eliminated the necessity for storability.

The introduction of currency futures in 1970 extended the definition of commodity to a medium of exchange and eliminated the prerequisite of "bulk" commodities. In 1974, the Commodity Futures Trading Commission Act was passed. By defining a commodity as anything tangible or intangible, it enabled the introduction of financial futures, that is, interest rate and stock index

(continued)

[5]Section 1a(4) in the Commodity Futures Trading Commission Act in 1974 included the following phrase: "and all other goods and articles except onions, . . . all services, rights and interest in which contract for future delivery are presently or in the future dealt in. . . ." This broadened the definition of a commodity to include tangible and intangibles. As mentioned before, onions were banned in 1958, so they were excluded from the list of commodities. See Philip M. Johnson and Thomas L. Hazen, *Derivatives Regulation* (New York: Aspen Publishers, 2004).

Tracing the Definition of a Commodity (*Continued*)

futures. The Act also facilitated the introduction of event-based and property rights futures markets, which included catastrophe futures and emissions trading.

The most recent definition of commodity by the CFTC includes a wide class of primary and secondary products, services, rights, interests, and events. The bulk of trading activity today is comprised of new product innovations that deviate from the original definition to what we now know as commodity.

By the end of March 1973, Phil had drafted language allowing mortgages to be included in the definition of a commodity. Henry received approval from the board of directors to proceed. The new language met resistance from exchanges that traded exempt commodities, such as the New York Coffee, Sugar and Cocoa Exchange. Henry wanted the senior management to keep everything confidential until the right moment arose for us to alert the CME of our intentions and bring the exchange in as an ally. I was told to prepare a paper on GNMA futures for the Secretary of Agriculture. The CEO of Central Soya accompanied Warren and me to Washington to make our introduction. The secretary was receptive to the idea, and later had his staff work with me.

"The best laid schemes of mice and men gang aft agley"[6] could not have been more accurate. Things went astray when volatility dominated the agricultural markets for the rest of the year. I had been in touch with Preston Martin, who continued to push for mortgage futures. The FHLBB backed a bill titled the Mortgage Futures Act of 1973, introduced at the end of that year. The act had little prospect of passing, but a new regulatory path was opening.

Inflation in the 1970s changed the existing regulatory framework. Inflation started with grain prices, while the first Arab oil embargo exacerbated the situation. Inflation and interest rates continued to soar.

[6]"But Mousie, thou art no thy lane,/In proving foresight may be vain:/The best-laid schemes o' mice an' men/Gang aft agley,/An' lea'e us nought but grief an' pain,/For promis'd joy!" —Robert Burns, 1785.

As food prices soared, many in Congress discovered the futures industry. When you have a fever, the knee-jerk reaction is to break the thermometer. In this case, the fever was high prices and the thermometer was the futures market. While the criticism was unfounded, it was clear that the time was ripe for redefining the regulatory structure of futures markets. We could no longer quietly create this new regulatory framework. Instead of the exchange pushing for this new regulatory power, it was now being demanded by Congress.

Once the enabling legal and regulatory framework became likely, we had to design further drafts of the GNMA futures contract. The CBOT's new products committee had still not convened, despite having existed for two years. Launching any new product required the committee chairman to take a leadership role. Elected to the board of directors at the end of 1973, Leslie "Les" Rosenthal energized the membership and became a leading advocate for GNMA futures.

Les shared my vision about financial futures and I was thrilled when he was named chairman of the financial instruments committee by the incoming CBOT chairman. We called it the "financial instruments" committee because it was evocative without being specific. The name ensured that the committee would be able to continue innovating and extending the political franchise given to it by the board of directors. Les appointed a savvy group of market makers and two futures commission merchants (FCMs) to the new products committee. There were no representatives from commercial or investment banks on the committee because there were no exchange members from this sector aside from Continental Illinois, the CBOT's banker.[7]

Les called a meeting shortly after the committees were appointed. We held our meeting in the very small room adjacent to the board of directors' room. The meeting had two purposes: to describe the GNMA market and its potential, and to present the second draft of a proposed futures contract. At that point, there could be no dispute about interest rate volatility and the need to hedge. The members immediately sensed the market-making and brokerage opportunities

[7]Continental Illinois was a member but not involved in any active way. Its membership stemmed from its position as the exchange's banker.

for this new product. I realized that this was the beginning of an internal marketing program for the membership.

We had come a long way since the first draft of the GNMA futures contract at the Palmer House. The second draft provided minimum price increments of $0.01, or $10.00 per contract. The daily price limits remained at half a point, and position limits of the 300 contracts and the physical delivery remained unchanged. The draft also reflected changes that had occurred over the last two years. Interest rates had risen, and the current coupon—the interest rate for the 30-year mortgage—was now 8 percent. We recommended this to be the standard rate. The contract also provided for other coupons to be deliverable on a yield maintenance basis. The tradition in the spot market was to price these GNMA mortgage-backed securities as if the underlying mortgages had a 12-year life.

Transparent Markets—Greetings from the Grim Reaper

GNMAs were the stepchild of bonds, which were in turn the stepchild of stocks. The business of GNMA trading and salesmanship generally attracted outsiders since it was new. This called for new dealers and people with foresight. Those who were already successful in stocks and bonds were unlikely to move into this new area. I thought it would be easier to convince these new people of the value of interest rate futures.

Energized by Les and the committee, I made more frequent trips to California and my first trip to New York to call on GNMA dealers. Bob Martin, former chairman of the exchange, introduced me to mortgage brokers and GNMA dealers in New York; neither was enthusiastic about the idea of GNMA futures. This was understandable given the nature of OTC transactions. Mortgage brokers and GNMA dealers were reaping profits by being opaque and making markets 1/2 to 1 point wide. On the other hand, we were proposing trades at much smaller increments in a transparent, regulated market. I might as well have said, "I'm here from Chicago to narrow your spreads and reduce your profits." Going to a single broker in an opaque market was equivalent to not shopping around.

Recognizing that they would be among the last to support the concept, I turned my attention to their customers, which included mortgage bankers, S&Ls, and pension funds. The hope was that dealers would change their minds if their customers expressed interest in GNMA futures. Although this didn't happen, I was still able to gain intellectual support from economists at investment banks who recognized the importance of GNMA futures in managing interest rate risk when inflation soared.

I sought out one investment bank's economist, expecting support. He was candid and said he wouldn't support interest rate futures. Surprised, I asked him why. I never forgot his thoughtful response. He said, "I think this is a great idea but it will help make it easier to live with the significant inflation that this country faces. I believe anything that makes it easier to live with inflation is not good for the country." His idea had merit and was something I thought about for a long time.

Everything started to fall into place in 1974. I had to ensure that any legislation coming out of Congress would enable GNMA futures, and finish the contract design. I worked closely with Phil Johnson. We were on a clear path to seeing interest rate futures become a reality. It was at that time that I finally decided to stay in Chicago and give up my full-time academic career. I had too much vested in the birth of financial futures. I called the dean at Berkeley and some of my friends on the faculty and told them about my decision. They were supportive. To keep my options open, I also called Don Jacobs, the dean at Northwestern University's Kellogg School of Management and a friend. I told him about my decision to remain in Chicago, and proposed that Kellogg offer a new course in futures and options. Don agreed. With my decision set in stone, I proceeded to throw myself into the work on the enabling legislation for GNMA futures.

Phil and I went to Washington to meet the staff member assigned to the drafting of the legislation. I learned an important lesson. While acts of Congress typically have the names of legislation and sponsors attached to them, i.e. the Financial Reform Act of 2010 is also referred to as Dodd-Frank—the names of the chairmen of the Senate and House committees that originated the legislation, it was really the staff members who drafted the legislation. The details of the legislation, determined by the staff of the House and Senate agriculture committees, were critical.

We were told that support from other parts of the government or the private sector could bolster the drafters' confidence. I swung into action. Preston Martin and Tom Bomar were apprised of the new legislation and were very supportive. Preston enlisted the help of the U.S. Savings and Loan League, which held enormous political clout as the voice of almost 6,000 S&Ls throughout the country. In 1973, Tom assumed the role of chairman of the Federal Home Loan Bank Board, and supported the bill politically.

Les was selfless throughout the entire process. Most people in Chicago in the exchange community wanted credit, but Les was result-driven and uninterested in the spotlight. Since there was no bottom line in mutual or not-for-profit organizations, leaders were often driven by the desire for personal publicity and renown. Les preferred being behind the scenes. I called him "El Sinistro." He was like a character out of one of Clint Eastwood's spaghetti westerns: a quiet Mexican sitting under a huge sombrero and wrapped in a serape. It was a façade. If he lifted his head and took off the serape, you would find a rifle in his lap and two crisscrossed belts of bullets around his chest. He spoke only at the most propitious moments and judiciously used his weapons and ammunition.

While the bill was originated in the House, the Senate subsequently drafted its own bill. I had worked assiduously from the outset to build a network of individuals who championed the idea, and was reaping the fruits of my labor.

Sometimes chance played a very important role. When I was working on the plywood paper years earlier, I made a cold call to the U.S. Senate agriculture committee that was productive in an unforeseen way and very embarrassing in another. I was sitting in my office in Barrows Hall on a typical rainy winter day, taking a break from my research on plywood. Partly out of impulse and curiosity, I called the main line for the Senate agriculture committee to see what data it had on forest products. Imagine my shock when the telephone was answered by Senator Herman Talmadge (D-GA), then the sitting chairman of the agriculture committee, himself. At that time, I had never spoken with a senator, much less expected one to pick up the line directly. Unprepared, it took what seemed like an eternity to gather my thoughts and explain the purpose of the call. I told him what I was doing and we had a short but pleasant conversation about new directions in the futures industry. I remember him gently telling me that his committee was concerned with food and fiber, not forestry. He politely gave me the number for the Interior Committee, which could help me with the information I needed—and asked me to call him if I needed further assistance. After the conversation, I felt ridiculous about my own ignorance and made a mental note to do my homework next time. I called Senator Talmadge again nine months later, but with a very different request.

Gerry Taylor, who had organized the first International Commodities Conference, was in a tight spot. While the second conference proved to be a great industry event, it was a financial train wreck. Gerry was forced to sell the rights to the conference to New York University (NYU), and recommended to them that they speak to me about becoming the conference moderator.

The commodity markets were on fire in 1973. NYU asked me to design the program and moderate the conference. I thought Herman Talmadge would be a great keynote speaker, and extended an invitation to him. We became better acquainted during the conference and I complained to him about the growing role of government. His advice was, "You can't have more people riding on the wagon than pulling it." Unfortunately, it has since grown to become even more of a concern today than it was then.

I made several trips to make sure that Herman Talmadge and his chief of staff understood the issues concerning the CBOT, and they expressed support in giving exclusive jurisdiction to a new regulatory commission with oversight over the futures industry. Nine months after the conference, Senator Talmadge and his chief of staff forever changed the futures industry. On October 19, 1974, the Commodity Futures Trading Commission Act was passed and signed by President Ford. For Senator Talmadge, exclusive jurisdiction extended the powers of his committee into the financial arena. He left a legacy but few remember him for it. The story of how this happened combines the legal savvy of two young lawyers, Phil Johnson and Mike McLeod, and the leadership of a veteran politician, Senator Talmadge. The House version of the commodity futures bill allowed the SEC to assert its jurisdiction over securities-related futures. Phil's challenge was to find a new definition of a commodity that covered securities futures without using the word "securities." Eventually, intangibles such as securities, were subsumed under the language "all rights and interests." Phil's other challenge was to ensure CFTC's exclusive jurisdiction over financial futures, such as the GNMA futures contract, without eliminating SEC from the bill, which would have resulted in a political storm. To achieve this, Phil inserted the phrase "except as hereinabove provided" just above the SEC language. That single phrase, plus the extended definition of a commodity to include "intangibles," made good derivatives possible. A friend later joked that Phil's tombstone should read "Except as Hereinabove Provided." These three men, in their different roles, created a trillion-dollar industry worldwide.

The passage of the Act not only demonstrated the strength of individual power, but the CBOT's familiarity with the machinations of federal policy. Due to its long history and role in agriculture, the CBOT enjoyed longstanding relationships with the House and Senate agricultural committees. The additional support from the Federal Home Loan Bank Board, Freddie Mac, S&Ls, mortgage bankers, builders, and GNMA itself made mortgage interest rate futures inevitable.

The CFTC became operational in the spring of 1975, with oversight from the House and Senate agriculture committees. The GNMA mortgage interest rate futures contract was the first contract submitted to the new commission.

As a result of this legislation, the industry was also able to trade a wide variety of financial instruments while remaining under the exclusive jurisdiction of the CFTC. The enabling legislation and the regulatory framework facilitated the global imitation of interest rate futures. In the ensuing years, the Chicago markets redefined themselves into financial powerhouses, becoming major players in the interest rate, equity, and foreign exchange markets.

The GNMA Contract: Simple in Concept, Complex in Detail

The biggest challenge we faced in designing the GNMA market was designing a contract that was not a replica of the spot and forward markets in order to facilitate hedging and avoid the possibility of having two different regulators.

I spent a good part of the rest of the year conducting additional research on the contract and working with Les and the committee. Some decisions were easier than others.

The tick size was established at 1/32 or $31.25 per contract. We changed the tick size to accommodate the needs of mortgage bankers, dealers, and S&Ls. This was larger than that of the grain markets, providing better opportunities for market makers. It was also significantly lower than the spot and forward markets, thereby making the futures contract less inexpensive for hedgers if we attracted sufficient liquidity.

Choosing contract months proved to be more of an art than a science. For example, the wheat harvest began in June, so a July contract was created to reflect the newly harvested wheat. May was the last month of the crop year, so there was also a May contract. The exchange filled the intervening months with other contracts. Since there wasn't a comparable planting and harvesting cycle for GNMAs, we expediently listed quarterly contracts which coincided with quarterly reports from financial institutions. This was a departure from the forward market, which were traded monthly.

Trading hours were a challenge, as we wanted to attract market makers from other pits. The grain markets opened at 9:30 A.M. and closed at 1:15 P.M. The committee knew that local traders were unlikely to leave their profitable trading in the wheat and soybean pits to enter the GNMA pit. We had to somehow attract liquidity at the opening and closing of the GNMA market. If we opened or closed trading at the same time as the grain markets, there would be little attention given to the mortgage interest rate futures market. We decided to open at 8:35 A.M. and close at 2:00 P.M.—the period between 8:35 and 9:30 A.M. attracted liquidity from grain traders before grain markets opened, and the period from 1:15 to 2:00 P.M. could attract local traders who drifted into the pit before leaving the floor. We eventually opened much earlier to further extend the trading day.

The contract size was $1 million in the forward market, and this was what the dealers wanted for the futures market. We wanted to broaden the market to maximize liquidity. To compete with other contracts, we chose a contract size of $100,000. This was roughly equivalent to the volatility in a 5,000 bushel grain contract. The margins would be the same and we could compete for the speculative business.

The contract grade in the spot and forward market was the current coupon. At the time we were writing the contract, it was 8 percent. The forward market required the delivery of the current coupon if rates changed. Here is where we radically departed from the conventions in the spot and forward contract. We wanted to increase the deliverable supply to avert price distortions. Once again, the research staff and the committee turned to grain contracts for a solution. In grains, delivery called for one particular grade. However, at the option of the seller, and at fixed differentials established by the exchange, other grades could be delivered. This procedure was adopted in the GNMA contract. We standardized the GNMA contracts so that the only characteristics that mattered were price and coupon. Specifically, it was decided that the $100,000 market value of GNMAs had to be delivered under the assumption that the interest rate was 8 percent.[8]

Thus, more than $100,000 of 6.5 percent (for example, $112,123.30) and less than $100,000 of 9 percent (for example, $93,167.70) could be delivered. The design of the contract maximized deliverable supply, thereby averting a temporary spike in price due to an artificially induced shortage. Clearly, a short would choose the coupon whose market value deviated most from the payment he was to receive, which was deemed the settlement price. He or she would deliver the cheapest GNMA, just as in the grain trade where people delivered the grade with the most distorted price. The cheapest-to-deliver concept was imitated throughout the world. In summary, the GNMA futures contract, like the agricultural contract, gave sellers the option to deliver any grade at any location that was within the contract standards. Buyers assumed they would receive the cheapest grain at the worst location. Buyers in the GNMA contract assumed they would receive the cheapest GNMAs. We referred to this practice as the cheapest to deliver (CTD). This concept was extended from agriculture to financial commodities like GNMAs, Treasury bonds, and Treasury notes.

There were other challenges. GNMAs had a unique characteristic of being wasting assets. That is, mortgage payments by individuals represented both interest payment and repayment of the principal, whereby

---

[8]Richard L. Sandor and Howard B. Sosin, "The Determinants of Mortgage Risk Premiums: A Case Study of the Portfolio of a Savings and Loan Association," *Journal of Business* 16, no. 1 (January 1975).

Yield Maintenance and Cheapest to Deliver

Let's say a bond has a principal amount of 100 with an 8 percent coupon rate. Accordingly, a 4 percent coupon would now require 200—twice the principal amount—to yield the same interest payments and therefore would have a conversion factor of 2. A 16 percent coupon would require only 50—half the principal—to provide the same interest payments, so its conversion factor would be 0.50. Because all three bonds yield $40,000 in semiannual interest payments, you are indifferent to investing in any one of them.[9]

Extending the case to the GNMA contract, say you have the choice to invest in either an 8 percent GNMA with a principal amount of $100,000 or a 9 percent GNMA with a principal amount of $93,167.70. You should be indifferent. Even though the face value of the 9 percent is less than that of the 8 percent GNMA, its higher interest rate will compensate the buyer with higher coupon payments such that the two GNMAs share the same nominal value. Table 5.2 is a complete table of yield maintenance, illustrating all of the outstanding coupons that were deliverable on a yield maintenance basis.

Certain derivative products provide contract holders the right to deliver different grades of underlying stocks, bonds, or commodities at specific delivery or expiry points. Because investors always want to deliver the cheapest available underlying, the price of derivatives will always factor the cheapest to deliver product.

The bond that is cheapest to deliver on a particular date is the bond with the least value expressed as:

$$\text{Quoted GNMA price} - (\text{Settlement price} \times \text{Conversion factor})$$

[9]The conversion factors have been simplified here for purposes of explanation. In reality, they may differ once you take into account the discounted value of interest payments.

(*continued*)

Yield Maintenance and Cheapest to Deliver (*Continued*)

Table 5.2 GNMAs with Nominal Value Equivalent to $100,000 Principal Balance of GNMAs with an 8.00 Percent Coupon[10]

GNMA Interest Rate	Amount Equivalent to $100,000 Principal Balance of GNMAs
6.50%	$112,123.30
7.00%	$107,816.70
7.25%	$105,820.10
7.50%	$103,806.20
7.75%	$101,867.50
8.00%	$100,000.00
8.25%	$ 98,219.80
8.50%	$ 96,501.80
9.00%	$ 93,167.70

Example:

Stated Interest Rate	Conversion Factor	Settlement Price	Market Price
8%	1.000000	101.00	99.00
9%	1.073422[11]	101.00	105.00

Assume the futures settlement price is 101.00

Cheapest to deliver is also the bond that results in the greatest gain upon delivery. Gains from delivery:

8% Bond: 101.00 × 1.000000 – 99 = 2.00
9% Bond: 101.00 × 1.073422 – 105 = 3.41

The short in the hypothetical example will deliver the 9 percent coupon. It is the cheapest to deliver and therefore gives the short the highest profit.

[10]"Regulations Relating to Futures Trading in Mortgage Backed Certificates Guaranteed by Government National Mortgage Association." Chicago Board of Trade, September 16, 1975, 697.

[11]The conversion ratio is simply the reciprocal of conversion amount. 100,000 divided by 93,167.70 is equal to 1.073422.

the holder of a GNMA received both interest and principal monthly, hence the term *pass-through* attached to GNMAs. Prepayments were also passed through to the holders of the GNMA. Thus a $100,000 face value of a GNMA would waste away over time. It was entirely possible that the $100,000 face value of a GNMA received as delivery on one futures contract (for example, the March contract) would not be deliverable on a subsequent short contract (for example, the June contract). If half of the mortgages in the underlying pool were prepaid, then the remaining $50,000 was below the minimum amount that could be delivered.

The wasting issue implied that a speculator or spreader who took delivery on a GNMA futures contract would not be able to redeliver the commodity and would be forced to liquidate an odd lot[12] in the spot market. The spot market could well be one in which he had neither expertise nor credit arrangements. In this case, he or she would be at a disadvantage compared to regular traders in the spot market, and risk being a distressed seller. All else held constant, the wasting problem would be expected to reduce market liquidity and participation. The bid-offer spreads of GNMA futures would reflect the risk associated with this wastage, and would be larger than that of nonwasting commodities.

The problem of balancing the interests of the longs and the shorts, and the interests of commercial traders and floor traders, was not a new one. At the CBOT, the issue was particularly important in the development of both soybean meal and plywood futures contracts. I was well aware of the issue because of my original research on plywood and my later work on the Gulf wheat contract. The delivery of plywood was accomplished by issuing shipping certificates that represented a call on production. For grains, delivery took the form of a warehouse receipt instead of grain delivered by truck to one's door.[13] A due bill gave the long trader a call on GNMAs but did not force the long to take delivery of the underlying commodity unless he wanted to. However, another problem developed.

In the case of plywood, the commodity did not have to be produced until the certificate was exercised, which in fact implied that

[12]An odd lot is a quantity of a security less than the security's default unit of trading. The typical trading unit in the GNMA was $1 million. A new contract size of $100,000 would be considered an odd lot.

[13]The Ginnie Mae due bill grew out of this heritage, as a combination of a warehouse receipt and a shipping certificate.

production would not occur until a fixed time interval thereafter. However, the short side or seller of a GNMA contract making delivery typically had the underlying GNMAs. Unlike the case of grains where the long had to pay storage costs to store the commodity, GNMAs when stored paid out interest and principal. The due bill had to pay the long for the use of her funds—this was conceptually similar to the stream of interest payments that the holder of a bond is entitled to.

All of these considerations resulted in a preliminary structure for due bills, a new mode of GNMA delivery. The long would pay the settlement price for the due bill, with all other discrepancies settled through the daily mark-to-market procedure of the exchange.[14] The due bill could be collateralized with GNMAs. The short would be charged with the responsibility of maintaining the collateral (that is, increasing it when wastage occurred). At any time in the future, the long would have the right to tender the due bill and receive the underlying GNMAs.[15] In the interim between delivery and tendering, she would receive $667 per month, equal to the monthly interest payment from an 8 percent perpetuity. It was simply a pass-through from the creator of the due bill to the owner of the due bill. This posed an obstacle.

The long could now take delivery of the due bill, carry it until the next delivery month, and redeliver it. All wasting was removed. However, the wasting risk now resided with the short. True, he was probably better equipped to handle it than the long, but he still would not take on unnecessary risk without compensation. That is, what incentive was there for a short to create a due bill? To handle this problem, the interest rate on the perpetuity was reduced from 8 to 7.62 percent ($635 per month). The differential was a reward for bearing wasting risk and could be viewed as a servicing fee. In fact, the magnitude of the servicing fee was set to be consistent with the servicing fee paid to mortgage bankers that serviced the mortgages underlying the GNMA pool.

---

[14]Mark-to-market, also known as fair value accounting, adjusts the value of assets and liabilities to reflect the current market price.

[15]When a warehouse receipt is tendered to a grain elevator, it is a request for the physical grain in storage to be unloaded to a rail car, barge, or ship.

Due bill delivery made its way into the final draft of the GNMA contract. It was complicated and cumbersome. To the extent that these difficulties were symmetrical, however, it was fair to both the long and the short, and could have contributed to the success of the contract.

We held a meeting of dealers, mortgage bankers, and S&Ls to review the contract, chaired by Les. We explained cheapest to deliver and contract size, and emphasized that a futures contract should not be a duplicate of a forward contract. Despite our best efforts, we still met resistance.

There was one last challenge. The GNMA mortgage-backed security was just that—a security. As such, we were concerned that the Securities and Exchange Commission would want to participate in the regulation of the market. Most members of the exchange were not registered to deal in securities, and there would be significant costs for having to register and undergo dual regulation. This increased the transaction costs for users of the contract, which could permanently impair liquidity. The term *due bill* had been carefully chosen to refute any misconceptions about the GNMA being a security. Since due bill was considered confusing to some, we renamed it to collateralized depository receipt. The actual design of the instrument, and its subsequent modifications to facilitate trading, fortuitously prevented the perception that it was the GNMAs themselves that were being traded. The design of this delivery receipt had astutely differentiated the contract itself from the underlying GNMAs. This was similar to modern instruments like collateralized debt obligations (CDOs), with two major exceptions. First, the delivery instrument was collateralized with the obligations of a U.S. government agency. Second, the delivery instrument was created under the auspice of a federally regulated exchange.

Liquidity is critical to the success of a contract and does not exist a priori, so it must be created. We decided that additional floor memberships were necessary to provide speculative interest in the contract because some FCMs did not encourage their customers to speculate in new contracts. To provide market makers in the pit, the exchange issued trading permits. We wanted to issue new special seats but Les was convinced it would be a hard sell to the membership—they were expensive due to their equity component. Members who wanted to sponsor new traders often didn't want to pay the expense of buying a seat on the exchange, which was priced as high as $125,000 in 1973, roughly equivalent to $638,000 in today's dollars. How could we invite people to trade on the floor without memberships? Thankfully, my work on Project CCARP had taught me that it was possible to unbundle membership by separating ownership from trading privileges. I proposed creating permits, which, unlike membership seats, had neither equity nor rights to vote. This allowed permit owners to trade in the pit at a cheaper price than buying membership seats.

Attracting buyers became relatively easy. The fees for a permit were $5,000 for the first six months, and $5,000 for the next six months at $1,500 per quarter. The permits had a finite life of three years. I personally promoted the permit program at Northwestern University, framing it as a new opportunity. I proclaimed, "For all of you who missed getting in on the CBOE, this is your second chance! Interest rate futures could become the biggest and most important futures market in the world!" One of the attendees said that he could survive on $31.25 per contract as a market maker. He had no overhead—his lunch was prepackaged noodle soup. Many of the men and women in that room played a pivotal role as liquidity providers in GNMAs and the other financial futures contracts launched at the exchange. We sold 37 permits, comparable to the number of traders in some of the smaller active pits.

The First Financial Good Derivative—GNMA Mortgage Interest Rate Futures

We finalized the contract on one winter day in 1975. The financial instruments committee meeting was scheduled for 1:30 P.M. in the boardroom at the CBOT. The objective was to complete the terms of the first interest rate futures contract in the world. The members of the exchange represented a great collage of the neighborhoods of Chicago—a great mix of street kids. Many were of humble origins, but despite their practical bent, all had a real respect for education. Unlike most investment bankers, they were self-made individuals without the prestige of MBA degrees.

People began drifting in from the hallway next to the boardroom right after the grain markets closed at 1:15 P.M. Eleven men participated in the meeting. They were dressed in business suits and brightly colored trading jackets. Ties were loosened and yellow badges with trading acronyms hung unevenly from their left jacket pockets. They were in that room that day because inflation had generated interest rate volatility and, as a result, a new form of regulation of the futures industry. Those 11 men would emerge from that meeting with a completed first draft of the first interest rate futures contract. They were aware that this was a departure from existing markets, but did not realize at the time just how much it would come to mean. Later, one of the members would say, "It was a seminal event in modern financial history."

The idea that futures trading could be extended to interest rates was completely radical, and there was no blueprint to guide us. Nevertheless, that final meeting of the committee eased through the size of the contract, minimum price movements, daily price limits, and the maximum long or short position that could be held by a market participant. The deliverable grade and delivery instrument proved to pose the biggest challenge.

We had been at it for over three hours. It was getting late, and enthusiasm was starting to wane. There is a well-worn expression in many places, including Chicago that says, "If you don't like the weather, just wait five minutes." Light snow that afternoon had unexpectedly turned into a blizzard. Excitement mounted as these men realized that they had to stay in the city that night. It reminded me of a time in college, when a late afternoon poker game had been extended to an all-night event because of a snowstorm. The members of the committee were just man-sized college boys, playing with a new idea instead of toys or cards.

I was one of the 11 men. I had no prior experience in creating a successful contract. As a matter of fact, the first contracts that I had worked on had been unambiguous failures. As chief economist of the exchange, I had to change the existing grain contracts to allow for delivery of the commodity at multiple locations. This was necessary in order to have a larger amount of deliverable supply and avoid manipulation. I learned a lot from the exercise. Those experiences of failure and success, coupled with my knowledge of the history of futures markets, provided me insight into the complexity of the product development process. As an academic, the article I had written on the terms of a futures contract in plywood[16] had given me some important insights into the art of drafting a new contract.

Economists had never really developed a body of work on the supply and demand for markets. A significant number of textbooks and academic articles assumed a default market for a good or service like widgets, then proceeded to teach or do research on properties of those markets. This assumed away the reasons markets exist in the first place, and the role of financial innovation in creating the markets. This had been how I first learned economics.

My experience in producing failures like the gold and Gulf wheat contracts, paired with some knowledge of Chicago exchange folklore, provided all the skills that were necessary to design that first interest rate futures contract. Likewise, the other 10 men also didn't have any real experience. They did, however, share my vision of how important these markets would become one day once the volatility of interest rates had grown apparent and experts had ratified my belief. They were also guided by an invaluable set of experiences as financial practitioners, which provided a knowledge base more powerful than any economic theory. This was about economics in the real world, not the ivory tower.

Contracts without Lawyers

Although the research department had provided the committee with a significant amount of information about the GNMA market, there were no dealer representatives on the committee. There were no lawyers present either. Futures contracts were simply a set of rules and regulations, and new futures contracts were just modifications to the existing rulebook. Drafting them was, once again, more art than science; it required the ability to take complex ideas and concepts and turn them into simple solutions. The simplicity stemmed from standardization. Contingencies were covered under the general rules and regulations of the exchange, and didn't have to be dealt with whenever a new contract

[16]Richard L. Sandor, "Innovation by an Exchange: A Case Study of the Development of the Plywood Futures Contract," *Journal of Law and Economics* 16, no. 1 (April 1973).

was written. The futures contract included only the commercial terms, leaving everything else for the exchange rulebook to explain.

The committee finally finished the deliverable grade and the delivery instrument, late in the day. It was about 7:30 P.M. when the meeting finally ended. The position limits on the contract were raised to 600 contracts in 1979 because GNMA issuance had reached a new high. Eventually, all position limits were eliminated when issuance reached $20.60 billion in 1980. The importance of position limits persists, largely given their role in preventing price distortions due to limited supply. In the wake of the 2008 financial crisis, position limits have spurred debate in both the Senate and the CFTC as a matter of congressional legislation over oil speculation.[17]

We finished the final draft on that wintery day in 1975, and submitted it to the CFTC for approval in April of the following year. The new act required all new futures contracts to meet an economic purpose test.[18] Personally, I thought that the success of a futures contract was *prima facie* evidence that the contract had fulfilled its economic purpose. The CBOT research department prepared a report rationalizing the economic purpose of the GNMA mortgage interest rate futures contract. The nascent CFTC was predominantly staffed by the former CEA personnel who, despite their lack of expertise in capital markets, were enthusiastic and willing to learn. I spent some time traveling to Washington to educate them. The CFTC's legacy was illustrated when I was literally asked, in a form, whether there was enough storage space in Chicago for the GNMAs. Smiling, I wrote that it was a financial instrument and all that was needed was a place to store the CDRs. Traditionally, futures markets benefits were based on providing a medium for hedging and price discovery—allowing market participants to learn the prices of the commodity in the future—and an alternative place of purchasing or selling the commodity. The value of the markets was created by the fact that it was

[17]The Sanders bill would increase margin requirements for speculative trading in crude oil and heating oil to 25 percent. "U.S. Senate Bill Would Force CFTC to Act on Position Limits," *Reuters*, June 2, 2011.

[18]The economic purpose test has since been eliminated in the Commodity Futures Modernization Act of 2000.

cost-effective to hedge. Similarly, price discovery would have large spillover benefits in the related spot markets. For one, it would cut the search costs associated with determining the value of a commodity, thereby reducing the difference between wholesale and retail prices. In effect, transaction costs would be driven lower by an order of magnitude. Fortunately, the CFTC had hired an economist to opine on the concept. His report was favorable and gave approval to launch the new contract.

Her Name was Ginnie Mae

I spoke with Les about a large marketing campaign. In a radical departure from CBOT policy, the committee asked for a separate marketing budget. Budgets for new products were generally limited, though the CME had somewhat broken the barrier with its own ads on the nonexistent "Moscow Mercantile Exchange" and "Peking Duck Exchange." I had never really been into popular culture and its potency, typically relying on Ellen to keep me up to speed on what was happening in the world. This time, I learned about popular culture and the power of the press in a different way. The CBOT board approved our budget and published booklets, bought advertising space, and hired a full-time employee to market interest rate futures. We even held a "beauty contest" to choose among the advertising agencies bidding for work on the ad campaign.

Unfortunately, the recommendations presented by the ad agency felt uninspired. I had an idea. We should have ads with a pretty cartoon faced girl named Ginnie Mae—the personification of GNMA—winking and smiling with her name sitting under her face. The ad marketing campaign was controversial and at odds with the staid manner of the exchange. Luckily, both Les and the committee found the idea terrific, and immediately had the ad agency to draw up the new ad. The board of directors approved the ad. Following the launch of the new contract, buttons were handed out to the members to pin on their trading jackets. They were given to the press and to the financial community too.

I thought we were set to go when another challenge emerged. Whenever people responded to the ad requesting educational material, they were simply sent material by the exchange. The members of the committee wanted the names of the respondents to solicit the business. The exchange had been steadfast in its refusal to give out the respondents' names, but the committee managed to have that policy changed as well.

The CFTC approved the contract on October 1, 1975. I was sitting in my office at the CBOT at the time, and felt like I was on top of the world. We chose October 20, a Monday, to ring the opening bell and launch the contract. This was untraditional. New contracts were typically launched on Fridays, so that any problems could be resolved over the weekend. The Mortgage Bankers Association was holding its annual meeting on Monday, so the opening would attract attention. Despite the objection from the exchange staff, this decision prevailed.

The phone rang on Friday morning and it was Les. The CBOT had been contacted by the SEC with the threat of injunction to stop trading on Monday. GNMAs were securities. Phil Johnson persuaded the SEC to wait until Tuesday to discuss the matter. I grew worried, and my excitement about Monday quickly dissipated. It was a power grab by the SEC. Commodity trading had already faced the prospect of falling under federal regulation, but we had won that battle by obtaining exclusive jurisdiction through the legislation that created the CFTC. Some of the members at the exchange suspected that the SEC's power grab was being supported by some of the GNMA dealers.

We opened trading on Monday and did a very respectable 871 contracts—equivalent to $87,100,000—even while facing the possibility that all trades could be nullified. On Tuesday, Phil and the exchange officers met with the SEC and convinced them that they had no case. Phil was a hero. Ultimately, the painstaking care we had taken to navigate the legislative process and design the delivery instrument won the day. We had carefully designed our product with due CDRs, which were more in line with the definition of a commodity than a security. The irony of this legacy is that to this day, the oversight of the futures industry is vested in the Senate Agriculture Committee in spite of the fact that nearly 80 percent of the volume is in financial instruments.[19] Agriculture only constitutes 8.66 percent of the volume. The fact that oversight remains with the agriculture committee is appropriate because the purpose of securities markets is very different from that of futures commodities. The competitive battle for regulatory turf would persist for the next 35 years, and continues to this day.

The Economic Benefits of GNMA Futures

When the futures markets began, the bid-offer spread of the current coupon was 1/2 to 3/4 point and the others had a bid-offer spread of up to 1 point. Shortly after trading began, the current coupon began trading 1/4, 1/8, and 1/32 increments. The gains in the reduction of transaction costs in the primary issuances of GNMAs and the secondary market inure to the benefit of the borrower, lender, and final investor in some way. We leave the actual split of the benefits to be determined by academic studies.

The following example is designed to illustrate the societal gains from introduction of the GNMA futures through increased market efficiency in risk sharing, transparency, and reduced information asymmetry.[20] Assuming a home value in the United States of $260,300, the future value of average savings for a home owner in the United States is estimated to be $5,959.27.

Additional value is created by the reduction of the spreads in the spot and forward markets. The transparency in the futures markets drove the spreads to 1/32 there too. In 2010, the reduced transaction costs translated to $269,843,750 in savings in the primary market, and $9,343,750,000 in savings in the secondary market. These benefits would go to recipients such as pension funds, mutual funds,

---

[19] Summing up the interest rate futures, equity index futures, foreign currency/index futures, and individual equity index futures in 2010 gives us 75.8 percent of the total number of contracts traded in the United States in 2010 ("Volume of Futures and Options Trading on U.S. Exchanges," Futures Industry Association).

[20] This savings calculation is based on bid-offer spreads. A second approach to savings is presented in the book's concluding chapter.

Savings Provided through the GNMA Futures Market

Consider a 30-year fixed mortgage loan for a $1,000,000 at an interest rate of 5.00 percent with good credit scores. The monthly principal and interest for this loan is estimated to be $5,368. Examination of the bid-ask spreads of the GNMA contracts suggest a narrowing of the spreads by half a percentage point (0.50 percent) as a result of market efficiencies. This gain suggests that the mortgage lender can now finance the same loan for only $995,000, the difference being the dollar value ($5,000) from half point reduction in the original loan amount. The estimated monthly mortgage principal and interest payment for the $995,000 loan at 5.00 percent is $5,341. The overall dollar value of this gain is estimated to be ($5,368 – $5,341) $26.84 monthly or $322 per year. Over the course of the mortgage, the future value of this saving is estimated to be $22,797.

Estimating the same computation for an average home owner in the United States,[21] the future value of the average savings is estimated to be $5,959.27. See Table 5.3 for an example of savings gained through market efficiencies from the GNMA contract.

Table 5.3 Example of Savings through Market Efficiencies from the GNMA Futures Contract

Loan Amount ($)	Term (yr)	Interest Rate (%)	Monthly Interest and Principal
Case 1: Loan Analysis for $1 Million Mortgage			
$1,000,000	30-Fixed	5.00%	$ 5,368
$ 995,000	30-Fixed	5.00%	$ 5,341
		Monthly Savings	$ 27
		Annual Savings	$ 322.08
		FV over 30 yrs.	$22,796.73
Case 2: Loan Analysis for $260K Average U.S. Home Value			
$ 260,300	30-Fixed	5.00%	$ 1,397.35
$ 258,999	30-Fixed	5.00%	$ 1,390.36
		Monthly Savings	$ 7
		Annual Savings	$ 83.88
		FV over 30 yrs.	$ 5,959.27

[21] Average home value in the United States was estimated to be $260,300.

and insurance companies and dealers as they rebalanced portfolios and inventory.

The concepts that the committee had agreed upon eventually altered the nature of not only futures markets, but also global capital markets. We eleven men (see Appendix C for the list of committee members) had participated in a creative process that was to be repeated again and again, in a more concentrated timeframe at the CBOT, and at other exchanges in the U.S. and abroad. That process—financial innovation—lies at the core of this story.

Moving On

I was very excited about the prospects for the contract, but was faced with the need to make a critical career decision. The economic purpose test provided more than ample opportunity for me to stay with the exchange and become a career economist. My publications and part-time position at Northwestern University also provided a small insurance policy that kept me in the academic world. My post as chief economist at the world-renowned futures exchange increased my speaking and writing opportunities, which helped my public profile. This resulted in some very attractive offers from International Paper, J. Aron and Co., and Continental Grain. Alternatively, I could try my hand at becoming a broker and be part of helping the markets succeed. I went to Les and sought his advice. He told me candidly that the glamour and exposure of working at the exchange would eventually wear off and its politics would sap my energy, while these other opportunities could offer me the same ego gratification. Working at the exchange as a staff member was analogous to working in Washington, DC, and having to serve two political parties. I was there for the economics, not the politics.

I decided to take a big risk after the GNMA contract was launched. I was 33 years old—not 21—had two children and a small negative net worth. Time was running out, as I had missed a dozen years of working in the private, for-profit sector. I was scared about leaving my secure position, but the bleak picture of waking up one day to financial troubles while my children were in college frightened me even more.

I took a position of vice president with ContiCommodity, and started a new unit called ContiFinancial devoted to servicing commercial users of the new market. Even if the contract was a success, I was fearful that all my work would leave me as nothing more than a commodity broker.

Chapter 6

Educating Users and Building the Market

Education is not the filling of a pail, but the lighting of a fire.

—*William Butler Yeats*

On October 22, 1975, I started a whole new career as vice president of the ContiFinancial division of ContiCommodity Services, Inc. It was a difficult adjustment. I went from being the chief economist of the world's largest futures exchange to a commodity futures salesman in a small brokerage company. It was also my first job with a for-profit company. My loyal secretary and I were the only employees at the start. The early days were tough because the division was losing money.

Although the mortgage interest rates contract was now listed for trading, the market still needed a constant stream of buyers and sellers to be successful. My network of S&Ls, mortgage bankers, and dealers provided me with a solid base of potential clients.

Just before I started my new post, Freddie Mac had opened an account with ContiFinancial and hedged $5 million of mortgages that it held in inventory. They sold 50 futures contracts. Fixed commissions were being phased out, but were for the time being still $60 round turns per contract.[1] The hedge generated $3,000 in commissions. Today, because of competition, that same commission would be $1.00 or less. My payout was 40 percent of $1,500, or $600. I foolishly figured that this level of business would become business as usual, only to later suffer through many days for hedging and speculating when I did no business at all. It was my worst scenario—no more researching or inventing of new financial products, and a job as a low-paid salesman unable to adequately support my family.

Adapting at Conti

My new routine at Conti was simple. I checked into the office and read the news before heading down to the CBOT trading floor. There was a sense of camaraderie between the people manning the booths and the GNMA permit holders in the pit. We were all in this experiment together. There were plenty of highs and lows during the early days. On days when there was no volume, everybody was glum. GNMA mortgage interest rates didn't move with grain prices, which isolated those of us trading the new contract. On busy days, I felt thrilled about our own business but remained concerned about how the folks in the pit were faring. The GNMA permit holders were thinly capitalized, and we needed them around. They came from diverse backgrounds; many were friends or relatives of members who had bought permits and hoped to get their relatives onto the floor at lower costs. Other permit holders were there because we marketed and advertised the program. We managed to attract both men and women as market makers who went on to become successful traders on the exchange despite their total lack of experience. Les predicted, "Some of these guys will be cannon fodder, and some will really make it." The most successful traders possessed athleticism, excellent hand-eye coordination, street

[1]A round turn denotes a completed transaction, that is, the purchase and sale of a contract.

smarts, and a love of competition. Not everyone had these attributes. Strict discipline was needed to survive. The trading floor was a place for prudent risk taking, not gambling.

Once the market closed for the day, I returned to the office and continued to call potential customers, making cold calls, and following up on leads. Calls to the East stopped at 4 P.M. CST, those to the Midwest at about 5 P.M., and calls to California at about 6 P.M or even 7 P.M. It was arduous talking 8 to 10 hours a day and I often came home with a hoarse voice. Emotionally, it was painful to see little or no interest in this new financial product. Ninety percent of the calls were fruitless. Nevertheless, I forged ahead, believing that if I built a large enough pipeline of potential users, and even a small number became clients, my business would grow.

After two months in the business, my financial situation was stark. I was relieved when Les called me one day with some good news. "I just got out of the board meeting where bonuses were being awarded," he said. "The board of directors wasn't going to give you the two-week bonus because you left before the end of the year. I immediately put a stop to that. They are not only still going to give you the Christmas bonus, but are going to prorate it."

That small bonus was used to pay off my credit cards and buy gifts for family and friends. We transferred Julie from the Latin School of Chicago to Ogden, a public elementary school. The switch helped remove a financial burden, and we were fortunate that Julie and her sister, Penya, came to love the new school. They later returned and proudly graduated from the Latin School. Ellen finished her MFA at the Art Institute of Chicago, and so that expense came to an end. Every bit helped during those difficult times, and we somehow managed to survive the transition. Years of living as an academic had habituated us to a lifestyle of inexpensive restaurants and entertainment. Although Ellen was always supportive, I still felt the pressure of being the sole provider for my family.

Ellen, my children, and our new circle of friends, faculty and students from the School of the Art Institute, provided an escape from the tedium of the business world. But it was also the beginning of an exciting lifelong friendship that came to have a profound impact on me personally.

Travels with Charlie O. Finley

We moved into Lake Point Tower, a condominium overlooking the Chicago River and Lake Michigan, in the fall of 1974. Ever since Ellen told me she had seen Charlie O. Finley in the building elevator, I had been hoping for a serendipitous encounter. On my way to the market in the building one evening, I saw Charlie. He wasn't hard to recognize, wearing his familiar Kelley Green sport jacket and a hat to cover his balding head. He was the owner of the Oakland Athletics baseball team. They had just won the World Series for the third time in a row. Charlie was an innovator and a risk taker. This was the man who had introduced color uniforms to baseball, who gave the players on his team bonuses if they all wore mustaches, and ensured that they had magical nicknames that were familiar to every baseball fan. "Catfish" Hunter and "Blue Moon" Odom were my favorites. He introduced designated hitters into American League baseball in 1973. He followed by proposing that the league introduce pinch runners to speed up the game. Unfortunately, he failed to persuade other owners that this new type of player was a good idea, just as he had failed to persuade them to adopt a rule of three balls and two strikes before a batter was put on base or struck out (it remained at four balls and three strikes), and to use orange-colored baseballs.

I eagerly introduced myself and told Charlie that I had been following him and his team ever since I lived in the Bay Area. "I love everything you've done to promote the Oakland A's, and can't believe you owned both a professional basketball team and a professional hockey team," I gushed. Charlie invited me out for a drink. He became a lifelong friend and a father figure to me. Together, we had more fun than is describable. The lessons he taught me about salesmanship and public relations had a profound impact on my life.

My new position at ContiFinancial required me to become an effective salesman. I learned a lot about salesmanship from Charlie Finley. Over the years, I watched him charm individuals and crowds and promote his baseball team until his death 20 years later. He was always at home with people whether they were young or old, conventional or unconventional.

Of all the things that Charlie taught me, the most valuable was how to ask for help. I vividly recall the time we were stuck in traffic together on our way to the Indianapolis 500. As the owner of the Oakland A's, Charlie could not afford to be late to the opening. He stuck his head out the car window and asked a policeman to clear a path for us through thousands of people converging on the raceway. "My name is Charlie Finley," he said, "Can you help me get to the race? I need to be there when it starts." I was surprised by the policeman's acquiescence. Noticing my surprise, Charlie said to me, "Always ask for help. People like to be helpful." Charlie loved practical jokes and was shameless. He then said to the policeman, "This is my girlfriend Farah Fawcett Majors." The funny part was that his girlfriend wasn't actually Farah, the movie star—she only looked like her. From then on, I became less hesitant in asking for help. I got the same message from Les, who often said, "Stop being an academician. Learn how to ask people for their business."

Charlie was a great salesman who had made a fortune selling insurance. He had thought up the idea of a group medical insurance policy while suffering from tuberculosis. The policy was the first of its kind. His illness led him to believe that if he could get physicians to join, it could open the way to a lot of business for other groups. He successfully sold the idea of group insurance to the American Medical Association. His prior experience selling life insurance to doctors one at a time ultimately helped him sell the new group policy. Doctors were very hard to reach, much less sell insurance to, because they always had a continuous stream of patients. None of them wanted to talk about insurance during their busy hours at work. Instead of giving in to frustration, Charlie used a practical joke to win their attention, something he was famous for. When dialing in, he stopped saying he was calling about insurance. Instead, he said in a serious voice, "Nurse, tell the doctor that there's a man on the phone who wants to talk to him. And tell him it's about his wife." Not knowing what to think, the doctors immediately picked up the phone. Charlie then proceeded to say, "Doctor, your wife would be much happier if you told her you had a lot of life insurance." The doctors were usually so relieved to hear this that they agreed to see him, and Charlie shamelessly laughed with them about his prank. At the end of the day, Charlie taught me that a good sense of humor was important for salesmanship. I even used some of his stories and lines.

Charlie always made me laugh. He once said to me, "Richard, ask me about the worst love affair I've ever had." I dutifully replied, "Charlie, tell me about the worst love affair you've ever had." He responded with a guileless smile on his face, "It was great." He meant it too.

Because of Charlie, my career as a salesman of financial futures was filled with a willingness to ask for help and a readiness to embrace good humor. I had relied too much on my academic credentials and knowledge of the business. I must have appeared supercilious. That changed. I still possessed my own sense of humor, thanks to my love of standup comedy at summer camp. I often joked to my customers that my daughters were getting rickets and eating paint off the wall, and that's why I needed the business. It always got a good laugh, but I was only half kidding. Although it was my in-depth knowledge of the GNMA contract's details and risk-free ways to arbitrage that attracted clients, it was my soft skills that managed to pull in dealers who were on the fence about hedging. Most of them agreed to meet with me because they knew they would have a fun time.

Finding Early Adopters

There were a number of steps I had to take before actually receiving an order from a client to buy or sell. Getting an account opened was the first step. This required answering questions about the financial status of ContiCommodity, discussing how the clearing corporation worked, and explaining contract details. Lawyers often reviewed the account forms and unnecessarily slowed down the opening of the account. Sometimes their modifications made sense, other times they didn't. It was a tedious process not only because it spelled out the obligations of the company and the brokerage firm, but also because lawyers were clueless about futures contracts. Once an account was open, I informed clients of price movements and any trading opportunities. All FCMs and their customers' men solicited their business in this manner throughout the day, whether from the floor of the exchange or from their offices in brokerage firms. Brokerage firms in different cities were beginning to hire salesmen who specialized in financial futures. They sat side by side with the other commodity brokers.

There was an active spot market and forward market for GNMAs before and after the futures contract was launched. Dealers provided bids and offers to potential sellers and buyers. Mortgage bankers used this market to sell GNMAs that would be originated in the coming months. Investors used the market to buy GNMAs with cash they expected to receive in the coming months.

The forward prices were generated by calculating the profits or losses from owning the GNMAs until the forward date. Theoretically, the price of a forward should be equal to its fair value, which is the spot price plus the interest earned less the cost of financing. For example, if the current price was 100, the interest rate was 8 percent, and the cost of financing was 4 percent per year, the one year forward price would be 96. Using similar reasoning, the three-month forward would be 99, the six-month forward would be 98, and the nine-month forward would be 97. The price difference between the three-month and six-month forward reflects the interest rate earned and the cost of financing of the GNMAs for that 90-day period.

The fair value of futures contracts was determined in very much the same manner. However, there were some fundamental differences between the two, and I took great pains when working at the exchange to help others differentiate between forward and futures contracts. Futures contracts are standardized contracts traded and cleared on regulated exchanges. Forward contracts are not standardized. They are tailored to the needs of the buyer and seller and rely on the financial integrity of the counterparties to honor their agreements. Thus, futures and forward prices were not necessarily the same. When the futures price was above the forward price futures, or above fair value, they were referred to as *rich*. When futures prices were below forward prices, or below fair value, then they were referred to as *cheap*. Arbitrage opportunities are created when futures prices are not trading at fair value.

My job was to make the dealers and financial institutions aware of price movements, as many were not following the market on a moment-by-moment basis. Futures markets were new, and most traders only followed the spot and forward markets. Knowing this, I always checked on the forward market when I reported futures prices in Chicago. If the futures were rich or cheap I pointed out the arbitrage opportunities to the dealers, some of whom were not calculating those numbers on their own. This also informed them of the best place to buy or sell based on their market viewpoint. If futures were expensive then they should buy the forwards or spot, and if they were cheap then they should buy the futures instead.

If the futures were cheap, there were three opportunities. First, a dealer could arbitrage by buying the futures contract and selling the forward market. Second, she could use the futures as the cheapest way to get long. Third, she could buy the futures and take delivery.

The individuals on trading desks differed vastly in their styles and talents. Some were great students of the market, and some had an uncanny sense for market directions. Jay Pomrenze was one of the biggest users of the GNMA futures market. He had been trained as a rabbi but went on to graduate with an MBA from New York University before joining Bankers Trust. He approached the market like the Talmudic scholar he was. When studying the details of the GNMA futures contract, Jay found a small window—he realized that the contract provisions, which extended the June delivery period into early July, allowed him to take a delivery in the forward market and redeliver on the futures contract, while reaping a profit. The June futures contract could be delivered against the July forward contract. He bought July forward 9 percent coupons and sold the futures contract with a guaranteed profit of one point. Since bonds were typically sold in round lots of $1 million, this translated into a profit of $10,000. It was risk-free arbitrage.

Other early adopters included a trader at Kuhn, Loeb, and Company, one of the small but influential investment banks of its day. He had a great knack for hedging the firm's purchases or sales, as well as for trading the firm's account. When he thought prices would rise, he bought futures as the cheapest way to get long.

A West Coast fund manager used to buy the futures when it was cheap, take delivery of the CDRs, and hold them. He liked the fact that there were perpetuities. These market players never asked for the underlying GNMAs.

Arbitrages could also occur if futures were expensive. It was possible to buy the cheapest-to-deliver GNMA, finance it, and sell the futures for a profit. Typically the forward and futures prices would converge prior to delivery and the dealer could sell the GNMAs and buy the futures contract to reap a profit. On some occasions, the profit was possible only by making delivery. Some of my customers picked us because of our ability to finance the purchase of GNMAs while they were packaging them for delivery. Dealers also used the market to get short if the prices were higher than in the forward market.

The Relationship between Prices in Different Months

As explained earlier, the futures prices in different periods reflect the cost of financing the underlying commodity. Termed *calendar spreads* in the futures markets, they fascinated me ever since a conversation I had with a prominent member of the exchange. I was on the floor of the exchange with him when he pointed out that the prices in different months of the soybean market implied an interest rate much higher than the prime rate. "How could that exist?" I asked. He responded that his clients couldn't borrow at prime, and that the spreads were implying what the real interest rate was. The grain spreads were indeed quantifying the real interest rates for us. This taught me to look at the relationship between different contract months for financial futures. Since forward and futures prices were determined on the basis of short- and long-term interest rates, the difference between calendar months reflected real interest rates. I pointed out calendar spread opportunities to my clients whenever the future prices in different months did not accurately reflect the relationship between the cost of financing and the yield on GNMAs.

Another type of arbitrage was created by the timing of the delivery process. In the grain markets, trading closed at 1:30 P.M. and customers had until 4:00 P.M. to notify the FCM that they would deliver. The two-hour gap ensured adequate time for paperwork that had to be completed. The same convention was adopted by other financial instruments. There was one big difference. The spot market in GNMAs and bonds moved as a result of economic news and political events between 2:00 and 4:00 P.M. If the market fell, the shorts signaled their intent to deliver. It was effectively a free two-hour option to sell.

While market participants thought the loophole was intelligent design, it was one that was never thought through—an accident of history.

When explaining the concept of risk-free arbitrage to customers, I got a glimpse of an interesting correlation between the size and influence of the dealer and the level of enthusiasm displayed. The first movers in the GNMA futures market were usually small dealers characterized by the absence of a franchise. These small dealers generally had more to gain from transparent markets with clear price signals and were therefore more interested in the opportunities provided by the GNMA futures market.

The biggest dealers didn't care about the new market. In fact, none of the biggest GNMA dealers were first adopters. Large dealers profited from opaque prices, and only came to use the market once profit opportunities enabled by the increase in futures liquidity exceeded those provided by the opaque status quo market. Only later did they realize that it was better to make a 1/8 or even 1/32 of a point from a very large inventory, rather than 1/2 a point from a small inventory. The big dealers liked markets with limited competition, while the small dealers were more interested in price transparency and opportunities to profit from the new market. They had no franchise to protect. The futures market democratized the spot market and helped dispel the existing monopoly of information. The spot markets were not regulated and there was no requirement to publicly list prices. After the introduction of financial futures, most became better off, even the large dealers.

As the futures market matured, arbitrage profits were reduced and transaction costs decreased due to the increased liquidity. In a short period of time, the futures markets caused the bid-offer spread in the dealer market to narrow to an 1/8 of a point. They later narrowed to 1/32. Good derivatives were making it cheaper to transact in the spot and forward markets. The market gradually evolved from one based on arbitrage to a liquid, efficient market that provided low transaction costs of hedging, one of our original objectives in forming this market.

The transaction costs were driven so low in fact, that it started to make economic sense for some large dealers to sell markets which were cheap, or buy futures which were expensive.

Disseminating Prices

When a new futures contract started, newspapers didn't publish its prices, volume, and open interest. We placed paid advertisements in local newspapers like the *Chicago Sun-Times* and the *Wall Street Journal.* When the open interest reached 5,000 contracts, the press then carried the prices without having to be paid. Live futures prices were provided by information vendors and brokerage firms were charged for each unit that was provided. Unfortunately, there was little desktop real estate in the dealer community and it was rather costly.

I had to make a big effort on behalf of the exchange to these providers to carry GNMA futures prices. The first data vendor was Telerate Systems. They offered real-time data through live markets. Telerate experienced some initial opposition by dealers. To help mitigate the opposition, I suggested that the founder expand his market by showing live futures markets. He spotted the opportunity, and his firm consequently began carrying GNMA futures prices. Bloomberg later became a fellow provider of prices and analytics in the interest rate futures markets. While live data was given out initially for free, it eventually became a large source of revenue for exchanges as participation broadened.

The Gordian Knot of Building a New Market

In the first couple of years at ContiFinancial, I continued to build a small but well-balanced business of mortgage bankers, S&Ls, smaller GNMA dealers, and trading firms. My colleagues on the GNMA committee who were FCMs took a similar approach. Other FCMs began to solicit customer business once they saw the volume grow, and we managed to attract some new dealers who understood the futures market. Henry Jarecki, with whom I had worked on gold futures, launched a firm to originate and trade GNMAs. So did Cantor Fitzgerald, which specialized in short-term interest rates and whose traders used Treasury bill futures.

Bernie Cantor, the firm's founder, became a big client of mine. Bernie was heavy-set and steely eyed, with an unmistakable air of intensity. I had an easy rapport with Bernie since we had both grown up in New York and came from humble means. He had grown up in the Bronx, and used to sell hot dogs at Yankee Stadium. I first met Bernie in his Los Angeles office after speaking with some of his traders, and I was stunned by what I saw. He had about a dozen Rodin sculptures, either erected on pedestals or standing on the floor. The walls were embellished with original letters from Rodin and photographs of the sculptures. I had never seen art presented this way, and it influenced my own art collection in the years to come. Bernie had first seen Rodin's sculptures while stationed as a soldier in France, and had become obsessed with his work ever since. He eventually built the largest collection of Rodin's work in the world.[2] Bernie did not buy art as a status symbol but as a means to experience the joys of discovery—this could be inferred from the fact that he enjoyed purchasing artwork that was not particularly fashionable or expensive.

Shortly after we met, Bernie urged me to start collecting serious art. Up until that point, Ellen and I had collected some folk art and inexpensive but fine-quality lithographs. We had very little money but decided to spend whatever we had on our first sculpture, "The Man with the Broken Nose," considered by many to be Rodin's seminal work. From then on, art and business became inseparable.

Ellen's advisor, Jim Zanzi, suggested we collect photographs. This consequently became a lifelong obsession for Ellen and me. Zanzi, as he was known, was a fantastic teacher who taught us about photography and outsider art. Collecting photographs came naturally to me because of my passion for movies. The black-and-white movies I had watched as a child had left some subliminal images. When we started collecting photography, it was not yet considered fine art by many—admittedly, this contrarian aspect appealed to me as well.

Although I was no longer employed by the CBOT, Conti-Commodity had bought and delegated an exchange membership to me and I became a member of the CBOT financial instruments committee.

---

[2]Today, a large part of his collection can be seen at New York's Metropolitan Museum of Art and at Stanford University.

The committee continued to make marketing decisions and develop new contracts.

In 1976, I turned my energy to developing a new contract, which eventually became the most widely traded contract in the world. It was imitated in Europe and Asia and provided me an opportunity to expand my vistas internationally.

Chapter 7

Treasury Bond and Note Futures

Spanning the Yield Curve

To everything there is a season, a time for every purpose under the sun.

—*Ecclesiastes, 3:1*

I talked to Les about my vision to create a family of interest rate futures products that spanned the yield curve. There was a real sense of urgency, as we knew the Chicago Mercantile Exchange was attempting to gain a foothold in the interest rate market. Mike Weinberg, the CME's chairman, had indicated that the exchange had no interest in mortgage interest rate futures because it posed too many problems.[1] CME was terrific at executing ideas developed by others, such as of currency futures. I was relieved that the CME had decided not to compete with the CBOT.

[1]"Mortgage Futures Market Planned," *Chicago Today*, September 28, 1972, 76.

Mark Powers, the CME's chief economist, came up with the idea of a futures contract on Treasury bills.[2] The CME submitted an application to the CFTC in the fall of 1975, and launched a contract in March of 1976.

Brokers and traders were easily able to determine if the futures contract was cheap or expensive by looking at the relationship between the spot 90-day T-bill and the spot six-month T-bill. If futures were cheap, then there were arbitrage opportunities. Cheap futures also provided the most cost-effective way to go long, and the best way to invest anticipated cash flows three months from now. The user bought the futures and took delivery. If T-bill futures were expensive, then it also provided arbitrage opportunities, the best way for traders to go short and a place to sell T-bills. It was a mirror image of the GNMAs.

Determining the Fair Value of Treasury Bills

The fair value of Treasury bill futures was determined in a similar way to GNMAs, although there was no formal forward market for T-bills. The 90-day forward T-bill rate can be derived from the spot rates for a 90-day T-bill and a six-month T-bill. For example, if the spot rate for a 90-day T-bill were 3 percent and the spot rate for a six-month T-bill were 5 percent, then the implied forward rate for a 90-day bill three months from now was 4 percent. This can be viewed another way. If an investor earns 4 percent over six months, the investment yields 3 percent for the first 90 days—since that is the three-month rate—and 5 percent for the next 90 days. This is equivalent to earning 4 percent over six months. In our example, if the three-month T-bill futures were below or above 5 percent, then futures were cheap or expensive.

When T-bill futures were cheap, arbitrageurs could go long on 90-day T-bills in the spot market, and go long on 90-day T-Bills

[2]Larry Rosenberg and Mark Powers confirmed this to me in a recent conversation.

Determining the Fair Value of Treasury Bills (*Continued*)

in the futures market, while simultaneously shorting a six-month T-bill in the spot market. Borrowing a six month T-bill and selling it is equivalent to borrowing money for six months. Purchasing a 90-day T-bill in the spot market and a 90-day T-bill in the futures market is equivalent to investing for six months. Obviously, if an arbitrageur can borrow at one rate and lend at a higher rate, there are significant profits to be made. One does not have to be an arbitrageur to take advantage of the anomaly. Investors who owned six-month T-bills were better off by selling them in the spot month and buying 90-day T-bills and 90-day T-bill futures.

Initial liquidity was created by market makers in the pit, arbitrageurs, and brokers who called dealers. ContiFinancial established a desk on the CME floor, so we could recommend trades to dealers and alert them to price changes. Proprietary trading firms emerged after 90-day T-bill futures were launched.

When Treasury bill futures first began trading at the CME in 1976, Morton Lane, an employee of the Treasury department at the World Bank, was asked to do a report on the new market from the cash management point of view. He completed the report and subsequently decided to leave the bank to join J. F. Eckstein & Co., a big player in the Treasury futures market. Morton was able to both arbitrage as principal and develop customer business. The spreads were wide in the spot market. Futures were traded in basis points while the spot market traded in increments of four to eight basis points. The transparency of the futures market and the arbitrage opportunities it enabled helped to narrow the spreads in the spot market. It was a repeat of what had happened in the GNMA futures and spot markets.

I was having a conversation with John Eckstein, the quick-witted CEO of J. F. Eckstein & Co., when a man entered the room wearing a light-blue seersucker suit. It was a huge departure from the standard pinstripe suits and red ties that investment bankers wore in New York. John suspected he was from the Midwest and described him as wearing a "half Cleveland." "Then what's a full Cleveland?" I asked, laughing. "A Sears leisure suit and white shoes," he said. John was joking about the difference between New Yorkers and Midwesterners. When all was said and done, it was the half Clevelands and the full Clevelands—not the pinstripes—who were typically the first movers in futures markets.

J. F. Eckstein & Co. had arbitraged the spot market against the new one-year Treasury bill futures introduced by the CME in 1997. It was a small firm that didn't have enough capital to support the size of its positions. Ironically, it was the lack of cash to fund the margin calls, rather than its strategy, that forced the firm to liquidate its positions. To retain its positions, the firm ended up turning its arbitrages over to Discount Corporation, a major dealer in Treasury bills, and Salomon Brothers. This was the reason why large dealers began using the T-bill futures market.

The competition with the CME was beneficial to the CBOT. It increased the credibility of interest rate futures and added marketing heft to what the CBOT was doing. I had mixed feelings about this. As a businessman, it provided me with a chance to earn commissions in a new market. Alternatively, I viewed the CME as a competitor because of my love and loyalty toward the CBOT. The exchanges would spend the next 30 years competing in the new products space like dueling banjos. In the end, however, everyone benefited from the fierce competition.

We had the choice to start a second contract that focused on either short-term or long-term interest rates. I made the case that we should focus on the long end of the interest rate markets. It was a bigger market and the CME didn't have an advantage in that sector. The customer bases for Treasury bills and long-term Treasury bonds were very different. Investment and commercial banks had large trading floors, and the trading desks of GNMA securities traders and Treasury securities traders were often near one another. The GNMA traders were guided by price movements in the 10-year Treasury note and the 30-year Treasury bond. Because of their price relationship, the 30-year Treasury bond traders were aware of GNMA interest rate futures. Discount houses, which traded in Treasury bills, generally did not trade long-term interest rates. I believed that the long-term Treasury bond was more volatile and would clearly attract the most hedging and speculation. It was a new market, and the exchange had to take a risk in hopes that it would continue to grow.

There had been a long history of challenges leading up to the Treasury bond futures contract. In 1918, a ceiling of 4.25 percent had been set on Treasury bonds by the U.S. government. By definition, this ceiling limited volatility, which reduced the need to hedge. From about 1965 onward, this ceiling amounted to a complete prohibition on the government issuing bonds. This changed in 1971. Legislation was passed that permitted the Treasury to issue up to $10 billion in bonds that were not subject to this ceiling. On May 8, 1975, the Treasury department auctioned the 8.25 percent of 2005. The size of the auction was $1.8 billion. Less than nine months later, the Treasury reopened the issue and auctioned another $700 million.[3] This $10 billion limit was raised to $12 billion in March 1976. Finally, there was sufficient existing supply and a strong enough promise of future auctions to start a futures market. It was still risky for the CBOT, however, because the market was barely two years old.

I told Charlie about my idea for Treasury bond futures. Although he didn't follow financial markets, he had always encouraged me to invent and initiate change. He believed in me just as my father had. Perhaps I would not have been so bold had Charlie not encouraged me.

Another mentor spurred me on as well. Les shared my excitement for the idea of a Treasury bond futures contract and had the new financial instruments committee create a special subcommittee to design the contract. I was appointed subcommittee chair. The financial instruments committee had already begun to attract interest from many exchange members, and Les and I identified a handful of members to work on the contract. Every complex of futures contracts had one contract that stood out as the most volatile and important. In the grain and oilseed markets, it was soybeans. In the meat markets, it was

---

[3]David P. Simon, "The Treasury's Experiment with Single-Price Auctions in the Mid-1970s: Winner's or Taxpayer's Curse?" *Review of Economics and Statistics* 76, no. 4 (November 1994): 754–760.

live cattle. I believed there was potential for Treasury bond futures to become the king of all interest rate futures.

The subcommittee met throughout 1976. The contract was essentially a replica of the GNMA contract, but with fewer technical challenges. Mortgages have monthly payments of principal and interest. Treasury bonds have interest payments twice a year, with the entire principal paid at maturity. The size of the futures contract was established at $100,000 and the minimum price increment at 1/32. The daily price limits were set at 3/4 of a point (24/32) above or below the previous day's settlement price, with position limits at 32nds of one point, and the minimum price change set at 1/32.[4] The daily price limits allowed for a maximum gain or loss of $750 per contract. As with the grains, they were designed to limit volatility and allow clearing members time to collect additional margins.

Trading a Notional Bond

The specifications for deliverable grade and delivery instrument posed the biggest challenges. The committee strongly felt that the coupon should be the same as it had been for the GNMA contract—8 percent. The problem was that there was no existing long-term bond with an 8 percent coupon. We improvised and created an instrument that did not exist in the cash market. We planned to simply trade a notional 8 percent 20-year bond, while all other bonds could be delivered on a yield maintenance basis—a term borrowed from the mortgage market. In simple terms, yield maintenance meant that bonds with different coupons would have the same amount of interest paid to the investor.

Using the same convention in Treasury bonds, the contract specified that the seller, at his option, could deliver any bond that had a 15-year minimum term on a yield maintenance calculation. The yield curve was fairly flat from 15 to 30 years, and that was why we chose this cut-off point. This was once again called the cheapest-to-deliver.

---

[4]Richard L. Sandor, "Commercial Paper and Treasury Bonds: More Interest Rate Futures Innovations and How They'll Work," *Commodities* (October 1977), 22–69.

Bonds were in certificate form, paper at the time, and we held on to this convention in our contract. We approved banks as "regular for delivery" if their vaults were deemed safe.

To the uninitiated, the design of the contract appeared almost surreal. We had created a fictional bond as a proxy for the long-term bond market, and a delivery mechanism that provided for a vault receipt collateralized by bonds that met the contract standards. What became the most successful contract in the futures industry was in fact based on a bond that didn't exist and required shorts to deliver collateralized vault receipts. The economic value was derived from the hedging, price discovery, and transparency. The second drove down costs in the spot market. We chose to keep the contract's vault receipts due to conventions in the futures markets. We were also still concerned that dual regulation by the CFTC and the SEC could drive up transaction costs. The CFTC was still a young agency with little political clout.

The exchange wrote a short letter on September 14, 1977, accompanied by documents advocating economic purpose, requesting that the CBOT be designated as a contract market for trading in contracts for the future delivery of Treasury bonds.[5] The CFTC came back insisting that the conversion factor be changed on a quarterly basis, rather than be held constant. I received a call from the CBOT research department with the news. They were concerned but I brushed it off, convinced that this was just the CFTC's way of ensuring more accuracy. Frankly, I thought the new requirement only complicated what should have been a simple concept, and increased the educational effort required. I was wrong. Without intending to, these quarterly changes actually created liquidity because they created early arbitrage opportunities for those who developed software to determine the cheapest to deliver. The changes were subsequently submitted to the subcommittee, and we had little choice but to accept them. Overall, these changes were good and helped the market develop.

---

[5]"Application for Designation as a Contract Market in Treasury Bonds," Chicago Board of Trade submission to the CFTC, September 14, 1976.

I had kept my original promise to Henry Wilson at the CBOT. The department that had started when I first arrived in Chicago now included a staff of 10. Succession planning had paid off. John Harding took over when I left as head of the department, and Tom Coleman was the lead researcher for the Treasury bond interest rate futures contract. Both worked on translating the committee-approved features of the contract into exchange regulations, and on writing the feasibility study for the CFTC. I continued to stop by the department's office from time to time. It gave me a chance to see my former colleagues and to discuss the design of the contract. Staff researchers at the exchange played a vital role in the inventive process.

As with the case of GNMAs, we gained support for the contract from many of the smaller primary dealers in government bonds, but not from the large ones. The last thing that large dealers wanted was a transparent market. There were also continuous objections to the contract size, the minimum price increment, and the synthetic nature of our instrument coupled with yield maintenance. Dealers wanted a million-dollar futures contract that reflected only the current coupon. The subcommittee and the full committee both agreed to weather all objections to the design. Les had already brought our design recommendations to the full board, which accepted them unanimously. We had the success of the GNMA contract as proof of concept and had shown that we could create opportunities for the members of the exchange. As Les used to say, "Rich designs contracts that give everybody a way to make money." I felt good about that.

The financial instruments committee recommended to the board of directors that the CBOT sell 100 new financial instruments memberships at $30,000 each. The GNMA permits had a limited life of three years. Just as grain traders were unlikely to move to the GNMA pit, GNMA permit holders were unlikely to move from the GNMA pit. They all had access to other pits but were doing well as pit brokers and market makers. The committee also recommended that GNMA permit holders be given the option of purchasing memberships at only $25,000 each. It was the equitable thing to do because they had helped build the market and had already paid for their permits. Exchange members had to be convinced that the value of their seats would not be diluted. After a considerable amount of debate at the board, the idea was voted on and passed. We were ready to launch the contract.

The contract design was completed by the committee and approved by the CFTC on August 2, 1977, and began trading on August 18, 1977. The initial price was $102.08, the highest price for years to come. This was a time of inflationary pressure building in the economy. The first auction of the new 7-7/8 of 2007 witnessed the first use of the market by some bond dealers. It was dubbed the "James Bond"—in recognition of the bond's coupon and maturity, 2-"007"—a name that also had some personal significance. Ian Fleming had written a number of books on James Bond, or Agent 007, a fictional character who worked for the British secret service. I had enjoyed all of these books and watched their movie adaptations while in graduate school. They provided an entertaining diversion from the self-imposed discipline of not having a television.

Marketing Treasury Bond Futures

Bankers Trust was one of the early users of both the GNMA and Treasury bond futures markets. It had been a traditional money center bank focused on corporate lending. A trader who eventually rose to become its CEO built up the bank's market-making in the GNMA, T-bond, note, and bill markets. Jay Pomrenze, an acolyte of the CEO, had great insight and was very positive about the design of the Treasury bond contract, just as he had been about the original GNMA contract. Bankers Trust traders understood the nuances of the contract, and once again became my biggest client.

Despite the support provided by Jay and other talented individuals, we met our fair share of resistance. My pitch for the contract at the Bond Dealers Association, arranged by Jay's boss, was poorly received by the large primary dealers in government bonds. As expected, they wanted to protect their franchise and maintain opaque markets.

Then something happened in 1977 that brightened the prospects for the contract. The U.S. Treasury auctioned the 7-5/8 percent of 2007, and held three more auctions of the same bond. The long-term bond had become a regular part of the department's debt management policy, essentially as loans to the government used to help pay for government projects. These auctions had two effects. They increased the supply of long-term bonds, thereby removing any concerns about shortness in supply, and provided a means to hedge. Aside from being sold in auctions through the primary market, Treasury bonds could also be purchased through a broker in the secondary market. Smaller dealers hedged the bonds that they bought in auctions. Second, the auctions provided transparent evidence of market sentiment before an auction. Despite these positive signs, the Treasury bond futures contract still met resistance from the big dealers. Once again, it was the smaller dealers that dominated the contract in its early days.

A few lessons could be drawn from the GNMA futures contract. The GNMA futures contract owed its success to its lower transaction costs compared to the spot or forward markets. Initial liquidity arose from market makers in the pit, other exchange members, arbitrageurs, and small dealers. They traded because of the difference in transaction costs in the spot and futures markets, which created arbitrage opportunities. Spreads in the dealer market were reduced to 1/32 by 1977. It is worth reiterating that bringing buyers and sellers into a central marketplace increased competition, reducing the bid-ask spread. Oftentimes, the buyer could not even participate in the spot or forward market without a significant balance sheet, as dealers had to assume some credit risk. However, the buyer could pay more than fair value for the futures contract, which was cheaper than buying in the spot or forward market. The arbitrageur could then provide the liquidity to the futures market by buying in the spot or forward market, thereby guaranteeing a spread. Increasing the number of new participants and expanding the volume of trading left everyone better off. Once again, volume was driven by the futures contract being expensive or cheap relative to the spot market. The market could be thought of as a beehive, where many different bees with distinct talents and jobs were all committed to one end.

The economic value of the Treasury bond futures also mimicked that of the GNMA futures markets. This contract facilitated hedging and price discovery. It occasionally provided a vehicle to make and take delivery of Treasury bonds. The spillover benefits associated with transparency were enormous. The bid-offer spread was 1/4 point for the current or on-the-run bond when the contract started. The outstanding bonds, or off-the-run bonds, had spreads of 1/2 a point if not more. The futures contract on Treasury bonds drove the spreads in the primary market and secondary market down to 1/32. Both the borrowers and the investors were made better off. The effect of the cheapest-to-deliver was to make the off-the-run bonds trade closer in yield to the on-the-run bonds, increasing the liquidity of the former. This notional 20-year bond drove the commoditization of bonds in the spot market.

This good derivative has only been modified once in its 34 years of seamless operation. There has been absolutely no systemic risk at any time in its history, in spite of interest rate volatility. It is the oldest stock and bond future in the world.

Educating Users

Another decisive factor in the success of GNMA futures, often overlooked, was the immense educational effort involved. The same was true for Treasury bond futures. Once again, there was a Gordian knot in this new market. Potential participants typically waited to see liquidity before they entered, thereby paradoxically stalling the creation of liquidity. In order to cut through this knot, it was crucial for exchanges to create the right infrastructure for these new markets. Educating users of Treasury bond futures required the joint effort of academic institutions, funding entities, trade associations, advisory groups, banks, clearing corporations, legal institutions, and exchanges. The importance of academic institutions and nongovernmental organizations in jumpstarting the market could not be emphasized enough. Academics gave the concept credibility and also alerted students to new careers.

Equally, if not more importantly, specific orders had to be generated on a moment-by-moment basis. Salesmen, whether upstairs or on the floor, did so throughout the trading day, thereby generating liquidity.

The reason buyers and sellers put orders in the market was often because the futures contracts were rich or cheap. The bond contract was often priced above or below fair value. Sometimes it was priced below fair value, which invited risk-free arbitrage. Arbitrageurs were as critical as day traders in the pit and position traders who were members of the exchange. Members of the public that bought and sold stocks the same day were called day traders, not to be confused with professionals on the floor of the exchange.

To create liquidity in the Treasury bond futures market, we followed the same process as with GNMAs. The CBOT's exchange committees now served a dual purpose: to provide input into the design of the Treasury bond futures contract, and to provide liquidity to the contract in its early days. They solicited professional speculators on the floor of the exchange to become their customers. They also solicited the business of nonmember hedgers and public speculators, and became market makers.

Markets should not be assumed to exist. Markets are created, and liquidity must be built. Listing a contract is only the first step. A professional research department, coupled with external advisers and an exchange-based committee, must produce both the contract and the initial and ongoing liquidity. This process was repeated for all of the financial futures developed at the exchange.

Legal challenges of launching a new contract were daunting. Another challenge was developing the accounting treatment for hedging within financial institutions. The CBOT encouraged and often participated in educational conferences held for hedgers, accountants, and lawyers, as it was absolutely necessary to educate them about these new instruments. Lawyers for commercial and investment banks, in particular, had little knowledge of new account agreements required by brokers, and had limited knowledge about the roles of brokers and exchanges. Similarly, accountants were unaware of how gains or losses on futures contracts should be treated. Financial futures as a new invention were not readily understood. The CBOT extended its outreach to academics and students. Table 7.1 illustrates an example of the number of outreach activities we participated in, and the extent of our efforts.

Table 7.1 Treasury Bond Futures Education and Outreach

Outreach Event	Date	Type
Financial instrument course on the economic factors affecting the T-bond market at the Chicago Board of Trade	January 1979	Educating users
Western Finance Association, Ramada Inn, San Francisco	January 1979	Potential users' trade associations and groups
San Francisco Commodity Club	February 2, 1979	Potential users, thought leaders outreach
Treasurer's Group (treasurers and CFOs of major U.S. corporations)	February 27, 1979	Potential users and hedgers
Association of Primary Dealers in U.S. Government Securities, Florida	March 1979	Potential users' trade associations and groups
Securities Industry Association Regional Firms Conference, Chicago	March 1979	Potential users' trade associations and groups
Public Securities Association, Second Annual Forum	June 1979	Potential users' trade associations and groups
Mortgage-backed futures market, the CBT Experience, University of British Columbia	June 1979	Academic outreach abroad
CBOT Financial Instrument User Seminar: "How a commercial bank uses the futures markets"	August 1979	Educating users
Financial and Futures Conference sponsored by *BusinessWeek* and *Securities Week*, New York City	October 1979	Public outreach, educating potential users, educating the media
Alaska State Pension Fund Board, Juneau	October 5, 1979	User education and public sector outreach
Commodities and Financial Futures Conference, Shoreham Americana Hotel, Washington, DC (Federal Bar Association and Commerce Clearing House, Inc.)	October 31, 1979–November 2, 1979	User education

(*continued*)

Table 7.1 (*Continued*)

Outreach Event	Date	Type
Columbia University Grad School of Business, Futures Markets and Commodities Pricing "Financial Futures" course	November 2, 1979	Academic outreach
Bond Quant Group, Manufacturer's Hanover Bank	January 1980	Internal presentation to a user (bank)
"History, Growth, and Usage of Financial Futures" seminar, Columbia Business School	March 1980	Academic outreach
Mortgage Bankers Association, First Annual Single Family Marketing Clinic, New Orleans	May 1980	User outreach
"How to Capitalize on the 250 Billion Dollar Financial Futures Market," Marriott's Essex House, New York City	May 1980	User outreach and public education
Second Financial Futures Conference, sponsored by *Business Week* and *Securities Week*	June 1980	Public outreach, educating potential users, educating the media
Annual Meeting of the American Agricultural Economics Association, University of Illinois*	July 1980	Academic outreach
Internal presentation to Harris Bank on financial futures	August 12, 1980	Internal presentation to a user (bank)
Business Week Editorial Board	October 1980	Educating the press
Mortgage Bankers Association, 67th Annual Conference	October 1980	Educating potential users
CBOT Interest Rate Futures Seminar—education to banking industry on how to use interest rate futures	November 20, 1980	Educating potential users
Options Conference, Salomon Bros. Center for the Study of Financial Institutions, New York University	January 1982	Educating potential users

Table 7.1 (*Continued*)

Outreach Event	Date	Type
1982 Bonds Seminar, The Fixed Income Society of New York	February 1982	Educating users
Ontario Securities Commission Hearing on the Toronto Stock Exchange Futures Contract	April 1982	Educating regulators and policy makers
Berkeley Program in Finance, "Applications of the Theory of the Term Structure of Interest Rates"	September 1982	Academic outreach
"Financial Futures, Options, and Stock Indexes Futures Markets" Seminar—Financial Analysts Federation, Palmer House, Chicago	October 1982	Educating potential users

*Howard B. Sosin and Richard L. Sandor, "The Determinants of Mortgage Risk Premiums: A Case Study of the Portfolio of a Savings and Loan Association," *Journal of Business* 48, no. 1 (1975): 27–38.

Inspired by the success of the International Commodities Conference, I advocated a more intensive program of seminars on financial futures at New York University. This not only deepened the educational push but also helped me identify potential clients. Fred Arditti, my friend and former colleague at U.C. Berkeley, taught this seminar with me for a number of years. Fred later became chief economist at the CME and helped design the Eurodollar and the S&P futures contract. It was poetic justice. He had recommended futures trading to me, and I had played some small role in helping him build professional standing in the futures community.

By 1977, business was getting somewhat better. My customers were trading daily. My first new hire at ContiFinancial was a researcher from Great Western Financial, who wrote newsletters and helped identify arbitrage opportunities between the spot and futures markets. Moreover, many CBOT employees saw no long-term opportunities at the mutual organization, and left to join ContiFinancial and other member firms. The not-for-profit nature of the exchange thus had the side effect of providing a breeding ground for the industry and for me.

At Conti, I hired traders at banks who were trained as economists. We hired a few people who had no experience whatsoever, including two smart and natural saleswomen who were members of the Ogden PTA, a renowned public school peppered with children of diplomats. The brother of one of my colleagues started as a runner and worked his way up the organization. He was a natural salesman. All in all, we had an eclectic, young group of highly motivated people who embraced new ideas. They all liked to compete and hated to lose. Since the field was new, nobody had any experience.

One night during the 1976 baseball season, I received a call from Charlie at 11:00. The Oakland A's were playing at home and he wanted me to listen to the game. He called the broadcasting booth and said, "This is Charlie Finley, let me speak to Hammer." Although he would later grow up to become a famous American rap artist, M.C. Hammer was still a teenager at the time. Charlie had first befriended Hammer outside the stadium in Oakland while he was singing and dancing. Charlie had invited him to sit in his box, and had an Oakland A's hat made for him with "VP" stitched on the front of the cap. Charlie told everyone that Hammer was a Vice President of the Oakland A's. Early on in the game when they were watching, a runner went on base. Charlie asked Hammer, "Do you think we should put a pinch runner in?" "Yes, Mr. Finley." Charlie said, "Go down to the dugout and tell the manager to put in the designated runner." Hammer did as told, and sure enough, a pinch runner was announced. Back at his apartment in Lake Point Tower, Charlie was managing the game remotely and I spent the whole night watching Hammer do play-by-play announcements of the game and giving Charlie advice. This made me smile but also taught me a very important lesson: hire young people with little or no experience, and pay attention to their advice if you trust them. I always hired people with Charlie's advice in mind.

New Interest Rate Contracts

While I continued to develop my business at ContiFinancial for the next two years, I worked on writing a futures contract on commercial paper—short-term promissory notes issued by major corporations. It was an attempt to compete with the CME's Treasury bill contract and capture a foothold in the short-term interest rate (STIR) market. The commercial paper contract died upon arrival because there had been very little secondary trading in the market and very few dealers. It failed because of all these reasons. From this, I learned an important lesson. To the extent that dealers carried inventories and experienced losses when a market declined, it was they who most often hedged. In turn, they attracted speculators. The result was a successful futures contract. This applied to both grain and bond markets.

Secondly, it was especially difficult to interest corporate hedgers because they incurred an opportunity cost if they failed to hedge. Granted, this opportunity cost was not a real cost, but if they hedged and short-term interest rates moved lower, they could incur real losses that had to be explained to the CEO and possibly the board of directors. Unlike with Treasury bills, there were very few dealers in commercial paper. Even though nongovernmental or corporate short-term rates often diverged from Treasury bill rates, the existing liquidity at the CME was large enough to accommodate any cross-hedging.[6] Third, an imperfect hedge in a liquid market is better than a perfect hedge in an illiquid market. The commercial paper contract failed because of all three reasons.

Separately, the volume continued to grow in Treasury bond futures as interest rates rose, and the government kept issuing new long-term bonds to finance its growing needs. The pit began to feel like a rocket launching pad and it seemed like liquid oxygen was seeping out of it. Anticipation filled the air. Inflation marched on, but there was a new structural change coming that changed the markets forever.

On Saturday, October 6, 1979, Paul Volcker, chairman of the Federal Reserve, announced that the central bank would no longer use targeted interest rates to control inflation. The bank's focus would switch instead to money supply, thereby liberating the interest rate market. The event became known as the "Saturday Night Massacre." The rocket took off on Monday, October 8. I was in California that day on a business trip. It had promised to be a quiet time for the markets because it was

[6] Cross-hedge: Hedging a cash market position in a futures or option contract for a different but price-related commodity.

Columbus Day. Although all banks were closed, the exchange had kept its markets open. This was another battle that the financial instruments committee fought. We always wanted the exchange to be open when the spot markets were closed.

We had done this with the opening hour of interest rate futures as well. The U.S. government did not want to issue economic statistics while the market was open. We then opened earlier. That battle stopped when the exchange opened markets at 7:20 A.M. EST.

On Monday, October 8th, the market opened limit up and then closed limit down—the first and only barometer of the impact of the new change in policy. It was later rumored that Salomon Brothers had managed to wrestle a bond underwriting for IBM from its competitors and had hedged it in the market. We never knew how true this story was, but nonetheless the myth helped the markets grow. It reminded me of the quote from the movie, *The Man Who Shot Liberty Valance*: "When the legend becomes fact, print the legend."

From that point forward, the primary dealers in U.S. government debt, large or small, lacked the capital to take on the level of interest rate risk. Hedging became routine. There is another important lesson. The first sign of volatility in any commodity, industrial or financial, often prompts the development of futures to transfer that price risk. However, institutional memories are short, and it often takes a second price shock for hedging to become a more permanent fixture in the financial landscape. One event is random but two events become a trend. This was true of both interest rate futures and energy futures.[7]

The traded volume of interest rate futures continued to expand dramatically in 1980 at both the CBOT and the CME. The CBOT dominated financial futures at this time, but remained eager to explore new opportunities. My connection with the exchange continued to deepen. I was honored to be elected to its board of directors in December 1979, while Les was elected as chairman of the board.

The growth in financial futures required a bigger trading floor. The plan was to move the financial futures to the original trading floor and

---

[7]The first Arab oil embargo of 1973 preceded the launching of heating oil futures. The next oil embargo, in 1979, led to the launch of crude oil futures.

build a new trading floor for the grains. The exchange was running well over budget due to the construction costs, but Les kept costs under control with his leadership. Not only did Les's chairmanship dramatically increase the franchise of the exchange, it also fostered the invention of new financial products. Les cackled that he would make me "chairman of every new products committee." He entrusted me with the responsibility of developing new products, including the 10-year, stock indexes, and options on bond futures. "Let's finish the job we started," he said.

Ten-Year Treasury Note Futures

The bear market that started in 1979 continued, and the supply of 10-year notes issued by the Treasury hit record levels. Ten-year note interest rates had gone from 3.95 percent in 1962 to 13.92 percent by the beginning of 1981. All necessary conditions for starting the market were there: price volatility, homogeneity, competitive pricing, and an active spot market. By this time, I had stopped believing that the failure of alternative means of hedging was a prerequisite. Futures markets provided a cheaper way of going short. If an actor in the financial markets wanted to go short in the spot market, he had to borrow the financial instrument. This was very costly, as credit risk was factored into the price and varied day by day. To go short in the futures market, the actor did not have to put up collateral except for the minimal initial margin, nor sign any legal agreements. He only had to sell a futures contract. This hedging alternative in the futures market provided substantially reduced transaction costs.

In the 1980s, the exchange's role as a central clearer became even more important. The failure of Drysdale Securities had demonstrated that even the borrowing and lending of collateral created credit risk.[8]

---

[8]Drysdale Securities, a New York dealer, was discovered to be involved in fraudulent deals with Chase Manhattan in 1982. Employees from the two firms were caught recording fictitious trades. See Charles R. Geist, *Wall Street: A History* (New York: Oxford University Press, 1997).

This risk had to be minimized by the clearinghouse and margining system. We got kicked by the same mule twice during the 2008 financial crisis and only now seem to be learning from our mistakes.

For the new 10-year note futures contract, the financial instruments committee once again chose a fictional 10-year bond with an 8 percent coupon. This maximized the deliverable supply and could be achieved using any 10-year note with at least seven years remaining. This was once again at odds with the dealer community, which wanted a futures market based on the current coupon. The committee had witnessed this before, but due to the success of the GNMA and bond contracts, had further resolved to stay with the cheapest to deliver.

Then an odd thing happened. Opposition to the new contract started to emerge as usual, but this time it came from within the exchange. Members of the exchange who were physically located in the Treasury bond pit thought that the new contract presented a competitive threat. I found the argument fallacious and believed that the new contract would in fact increase liquidity. Indeed, the two contracts were linked by the activities in the spot market and market participants were already using the yield curve by trading the 10-year note versus the 30-year bond. Given this reasoning, yield curve arbitrage in futures would only provide a cheaper way of doing it. It was not hard to foresee the corresponding development of a spread market for notes over bonds (dubbed the *nob spread*) that later emerged as an informal market on the floor. It subsequently became very active with floor brokers who specialized in executing this transaction.

Research for the contract was completed, and an application was made to the CFTC for the CBOT to be designated as a contract market in 10-year note contracts. Approval was granted on September 23, 1981, and trading began in May 1982. I thought this was my finest hour as an innovator, not knowing that there were other obstacles to come.

I will never forget the opening day for many reasons. The new building had been completed and the grains were moved to the new floor, with the financial instruments moved to the old floor. Bonds were transferred to the old soybean pit, the largest on the floor, and notes were traded in a pit adjacent to it.

We held the opening ceremony on the floor, and I rang the opening bell. Knowing that there would be people there with bids and offers, we did our homework so as to avoid an embarrassment of having no trades. Once again, the market didn't simply start out liquid. To jumpstart the market, the CBOT waived fees. Floor traders were voluntarily recruited from all of the pits, and members of the committee who were in the brokerage business asked their customers for help. Building liquidity for the new market required the dedicated efforts of a group of principals on and off the floor, their agents—FCMs and registered commodity representatives (RCRs)—on the floor of the exchange, and floor brokers. The opening trade was at 71-26/32 points and the total volume traded was an estimated 22,000 contracts.[9]

The structure of forward prices in the 10-year Treasury notes differed from 30-year Treasury bonds in terms of which maturities were deliverable. Some traders expected the 10-year note futures prices to mimic those of the 30-year bonds. Others simply did not study the contract and failed to understand that if delivery occurred, the 10-year note, unlike the 30-year bond, risked losing a lot of value. I knew this because my firm represented one of the principals involved, and arguments over this matter continued throughout the trading day. While trading in the nearby December contract was solid, spread trading dominated the volume. The CBOT reported a trading volume of 35,000 contracts, which turned out to be the largest opening day for any contract in U.S. history. The record was widely reported by the press and stands to this day. The ingenuity of the exchange and the opening day volume became a legend in the industry. There were few mentions, however, in any reports about why it had been achieved.

The success of the contract was very important. The 10-year Treasury note, like the long bonds, was the medium for most foreign governments to borrow, allowing it to become the world benchmark. The international relevance of the 10-year Treasury note futures provided me with the foundation to start new contracts around the world.

---

[9]Chicago Board of Trade, "Ten-Year Treasury Futures Already a Major CBOT Contract," *The Trader* 6, no. 8 (May 1982).

The Treasury bond futures contract had taken off remarkably over the years since its humble beginning in 1977. Beginning in December 1982, the U.S. Treasury even rescheduled a debt auction upon learning that the CBOT would be closed over Christmas.[10] New exchanges continued to form, creating a surprising new geography in interest rate futures.

Innovation by Competition

The Pacific Commodities Exchange fell in 1976 due to the dearth of trading activity and failure to enforce its own rules of government.[11] The latter could have been mitigated had the exchange been electronic. After the fall, Nate Most left PCE to join the American Stock Exchange (AMEX), where he led efforts to launch a competing GNMA contract in 1978. Their contract conformed to the dealers' demand that it be a current coupon contract. The CBOT also decided to list a contract, believing that they would win the competitive battle since the users were already in their store. Ultimately, AMEX's contract failed while the CBOT's prevailed. The success of the Treasury bond contract also inspired imitators. The New York Stock Exchange launched a new exchange, the New York Futures Exchange, which launched a Treasury bond futures contract. Like AMEX, it offered a futures contract on current coupon Treasury bonds. It, too, failed.

The low transaction costs, as measured by the depth and breadth of a market, were almost impossible to replicate. I know of only a few instances when it has been done. In those instances, it was electronic trading versus open outcry or a new product that fit into a family of existing futures. For example, the Comex started a five-year

---

[10]"Treasury Bond Futures Hold Vital Role in Market after 10 Years of Trading," *Investors Daily*, August 21, 1987, 33.

[11]See CFTC Docket no. 17, "In the Matter of Pacific Commodities Exchange, Inc.: Findings and Order Terminating Contract Market Designations and Dismissing Complaint with Prejudice," CTFC Office of Hearing Clerk, May 5, 1977.

contract well after the interest rate complex was established. The CBOT was able to wrest it from them because its customers wanted to trade at an exchange where they had already received approval by their attorneys, and had established relationships with brokers on the floor. They also benefited from reduced margins when trading the yield curve.

Commoditizing Stocks

The ingenuity and widespread success of interest rate futures garnered the attention of the world. There was also another important financial innovation that occurred around a similar time period: the commoditization of stocks, which set the stage for stock index futures.

To give historical context, in the late 1960s the management of equity investments was overseen by seven major banks. Pension funds had only in-house actuaries and relied on these banks to manage their investments. The 1970s gave birth to the pension fund consulting business, which began to evaluate the performance of pension funds and banks.

After the 1970s bear market, pension fund managers and their advisers had to reorient their thought process. There was an implicit agreement between the consultants, pension fund management, and investment managers to invest their assets in such a way as to outperform the S&P 500. The S&P 500 was broader-based than the Dow Jones Industrial Average (DJIA) and was therefore chosen as the benchmark. The S&P 500, which was not well known then, had a readily accessible methodology. Since everyone had performed poorly, they transferred the metric for evaluating funds from absolute returns to relative returns. Investors were primed to see how the funds did relative to a broad-based index such as the S&P, Russell, or Dow Jones. Stocks were poised to be commoditized.

The stage was set for a futures contract in stocks, but there was one regulatory barrier to overcome. Stocks were securities and regulated by the SEC, and stock indexes fell into a grey regulatory area. The Shad-Johnson Accord resolved this dilemma and significantly shaped the futures industry. It sorted out the regulatory jurisdictions of the SEC and the CFTC. Phil Johnson joined the CFTC as chairman on June 8, 1981. That same year, he and the SEC chairman, John Shad, agreed that futures on broad-based indexes should be regulated by the CFTC, and actually banned the delivery on cash-settled futures contracts. Narrow-based indexes would be considered as if they were stocks and could not be traded on a regulated futures exchange. How and why they came to this decision was an interesting tale in and of itself.

Cash-settled futures contracts can be traced back to the Osaka Rice Exchange in the eighteenth century. The first modern use of cash settlement was the iced broiler contract at the CBOT. In 1972, the contract provided buyers with the option to settle the contract at the weekly average price of iced broilers in Chicago, as reported by the USDA. The MidAmerica Exchange followed with mini-Treasury bill futures, the first cash-settled contract. Subsequently, the CME came up with a Eurodollar contract for cash settlement.

Murray Borowitz, regarded as the pioneer of foreign exchange futures, led efforts in 1968 at the New York Produce Exchange to have the SEC allow a futures market on the Dow Jones Industrial Average (DJIA). The contract was presented shortly following the costly Great Salad Oil Scandal set off by Tino DeAngelis, and Borowitz's proposal was turned down.[12] Similarly, the O'Connor brothers in Chicago wanted to trade a futures contract on the DJIA but were advised that the SEC would not approve it. This drove them to pioneer the CBOE, an exchange that was separate from the CBOT. The CBOT did not want to be regulated by the SEC.

The futures industry in 1982 was once again shaped by the CFTC, which permitted the exchanges to trade in an innovation called cash-settled futures contracts—products without physical delivery. The final settlement price was no longer determined by buyers and sellers in the pit, but by what an index provider would publish. For example, a futures contract on the Dow Jones was settled by the reported level of the Dow Jones Index.

---

[12]William Falloon, *Market Maker: A Sesquicentennial Look at the Chicago Board of Trade*, Chicago Board of Trade, January 1, 1998.

The first exchange to commercialize cash-settled futures contracts that prohibited delivery was the Kansas City Board of Trade (KCBT). The CBOT had a cash-settled feature in the iced broiler futures contract. It did not prohibit physical delivery. On February 24, 1982, the KCBT introduced the Value Line Stock Index futures contract. It had the dual distinction of being the first mandatory cash-settled contract and the first stock index futures contract. It didn't attract a lot of volume, however, because of inherent problems in the Value Line Index itself. It had to be rebalanced daily, making it impossible to replicate in the portfolios of investors. In other words, transaction costs were too high to warrant economic success.

Who knows where stock index futures trading would have been centered had they reached out to S&P instead of Value Line? If the KCBT had bought a contract from McGraw-Hill, it could have become as famous as Judy Garland's character from *The Wizard of Oz*. It was a case of the right concept but the wrong contract. While some might find it impossible to believe, the new Better Alternative Trading System (BATS) in Kansas City is now the third-largest stock exchange in the United States.

One takeaway from this occurrence is that a small exchange regulated by the CFTC with an independent clearinghouse could launch a new product. Another is that while the tendency to specialize in certain products allows small exchanges like the KCBT to become first movers, their ability to capitalize on such moves are often constrained by limitations in size and resources. For some perspective, in 2010 the CME had $31 billion in total assets—almost 1,000 times more than the KCBT, which had total assets of $31.5 million. In the same year, the CME had 3 billion contracts in trading volume, over 500 times that of the KCBT, which had 5.5 million contracts.[13]

Although the CBOT and CME were convinced that stock index futures, a concept originated by the KCBT, would be successful, neither of them wanted to engage in a political battle with the CFTC. Instead, they waited for the KCBT, a small exchange aligned with a powerful senator, Robert Dole, to take the political lead. I suggested

[13]CME and KCBT 2010 Annual Reports.

to Les and the committee that we start a futures contract on the DJIA. I went to visit the Dow Jones office in New York but was given a cool reception. I was told that the company's chairman and CEO had said there was no way that he would allow Dow Jones's name to be sullied by speculators in Chicago. I briefed Les and the committee, convinced that there was a case to be made.

Bayer had put out a product called acetylsalicylic acid, first patented on February 27, 1900, and named it aspirin.[14] Even though the new product name was under Bayer's brand, others in the industry had the rights to use it. I thought the same case could be made for the DJIA. There wasn't a patent or trademark, only a brand. I went to Les's office and told him, "We should list the DJIA even though we can't land an agreement with Dow. When I ask anybody what the market did today they would say it was up 20 or down 20 based without referencing the DJIA. The same is true with broadcast journalists. That sure sounds like a generic." Les responded with the old joke, "If it looks like, flies like, and quacks like a duck, then it must be a duck. Let's go to the committee with it." The committee followed suit. We sought advice from our legal counsel, and they thought we had a good case.

Dow Jones sued us when they learned we were moving ahead on listing a futures contract. The CBOT won in local court, and appealed in federal court.[15] Dow was willing to settle if we somehow provided a complicated conversion of their index. Instead of 10 times the index value, it would ideally be some fraction, for example, 7.6, preventing the public from associating the futures price with the DJIA. We wanted a simple conversion so as not to lose the recognition. Les said in his characteristic way, "Let's go for the whole enchilada." The appeals court ruled in Dow's favor, 3 to 2. I was very disappointed.

And thus we failed to list a futures market on the DJIA—in 1982, at least. The CBOT was eventually able to launch futures and options

---

[14]Walter Sneader, "The Discovery of Aspirin: A Reappraisal," *British Medical Journal* 321, no. 7276 (December 2000): 1591–1594.

[15]*The Board of Trade of the City of Chicago v. Dow Jones & Company, Inc.*, Supreme Court of Illinois, October 21, 1983.

on the DJIA in 1997 (see more on this in Chapter 14, "Stock Index Futures: A Postscript").

In the meantime, I had another idea. The stock market had, at any given time, hot sectors such as technology, oil and gas, and retailing. There was another solution. We could develop our own indexes and submit 10 of them for approval to the CFTC. This was a way of legally creating evidence of ownership for sectors of the market. Our reasoning seemed logical, and was even ratified by a number of market players. It came down to a duel with regulators, and it remained for John Shad and Phil Johnson to come to some arrangement. The CFTC prohibited us from launching these contracts.

As an aside, after GNMAs failed at AMEX, Nate Most went on to develop a product called exchange-traded funds (ETFs) based on the S&P 500. It took a very long time before the SEC approved this new concept, but it eventually began trading on AMEX in 1993. Sector-based ETFs, such as energy and industrials, followed. Given that ETFs are today considered one of the greatest financial innovations by both regulators and the public, it is ironic that it was regulatory considerations that almost killed ETFs 30 years ago. Regulatory matters so often shape the nature of invention and innovation in the financial sector. It is a recurring story.

The CME had also failed to get a contract with Dow Jones. Instead they signed an agreement with Standard & Poor's, and began trading futures on the S&P index in 1982.[16] Almost simultaneously, the exchange launched a cash-settled contract on Eurodollars. Fred Arditti deserved the credit he received at the CME for writing the contract and pioneering cash settlement in what would become the contract with the largest open interest in the world.[17] The success of these two contracts would eventually lead to the CME's hegemony in the industry.

[16]"S&P 500 Futures," CME Group, November 14, 2011, www.cmegroup.com/trading/equity-index/us-index/sandp-500_contract_specifications.html.

[17]"Andrew M. Chisholm, *An Introduction to International Capital Markets: Products, Strategies, Participants* (Hoboken, NJ: John Wiley & Sons, 2010), 203.

I worried about what I would be doing in the exchange space after Les left office. We had exhausted the exchange membership with a bevy of new products and memberships. They were tired of change. I knew I had to expand my vistas in the exchange community, but didn't where to do it.

The first part of my journey as a businessman and inventor was over. As a young man, my life cycles lasted about seven years each. I had spent the first seven years in college and graduate school, the next seven as an economist teaching at U.C. Berkeley and working at the CBOT, and the last seven as an inventor running a financial futures business. I had always wanted to learn more about investment banking and the spot markets. The opportunity came sooner than I expected.

Chapter 8

The Decade of the Eighties

Globalizing Markets

Just remember, when you're over the hill, you begin to pick up speed.

—*Charles M. Schulz*

The decade of the 1980s was spent building markets across the globe. In particular, it was a tale of three cities: an international financial hub, a center of cultural and artistic heritage, and the "last truly great American city."[1] London, Paris, and Chicago would soon have something in common. The innovations that began on LaSalle Street were now being replicated globally. Enabling regulation

---

[1]"Chicago is a great American city. Perhaps it is the last of the great American cities." See Norman Mailer, *Miami and the Siege of Chicago: An Informal History of the Republican and Democratic Conventions of 1968* (New York: D. I. Fine, 1969).

in Europe and the United States created new opportunities, allowing new exchanges to grow and new commodity market innovations to proliferate. These shifts did not just emerge fortuitously. Instead, they were the product of entrepreneurial efforts and informed regulation. This is the story.

Exchange-Making in London

One day in 1981, I answered the phone to a plummy English accent, "This is John Berkshire calling from Chicago. We're thinking of starting a financial futures exchange in London. I'd like to meet with you and get your opinions about it."

Half an hour later, John walked into my office. The encounter stood out in my memory because my office was so small that there was literally no place for his luggage. John was not your typical reserved Englishman. He was direct, energetic, and was an entrepreneur. John explained his vision for a financial futures exchange in London. The mainstream UK capital markets possessed the aura of an exclusive club, and he wanted to establish a new club. John was the CEO of a brokerage firm that specialized in foreign exchange and bank deposits. Since the province of the English elite resided in equities and UK Treasury securities known as gilts, John was already marginalized from the typical British financial establishment. Still, I thought his vision could be realized.

The United Kingdom only had one regulator for securities and commodities, the Financial Services Authority (FSA). John needed to convince them of the economic value of the market. The Bank of England also had to be onboard. John had to have the entire UK financial establishment on his side, or else UK regulators would never buy the concept of a futures and options exchange. I gave John's project little thought until Dave Goldberg gave me a call in 1982 and said, "Doc, there's somebody in my office I want you to meet."

Dave Goldberg, a principal of Goldberg Brothers, befriended me when I joined the CBOT. He had supported the Gulf wheat futures contract and taught me about floor trading when I started to frequent the corn pit after work at ContiFinancial. I was teased a lot in the pit whenever I got the hand signals wrong. I bid when I was trying to offer and offered when I was trying to bid. I acquired a nickname when I was trading there. The other locals would yell, "Hey doc, whaddya doin'?" That my trading floor badge spells DOC instead of RLS is a tribute to the merciless, but good-natured teasing by the members in the corn pit. DOC became a nickname that stuck on and off the floor.[2]

Goldberg Brothers was actively involved at the CBOE as a clearing member. They developed personal and business relationships with members of the NYSE because their customers traded stocks and stock options. One of these members asked Dave if he wanted to meet with David Leroy Lewis, the vice chairman of the London Stock Exchange (LSE). At the time, David was also the chairman and CEO of Akroyd and Smithers, the leading broker in the gilt market. He reflected the British financial establishment in accent and demeanor, and reminded me of Charles Laughton's character in the film *Witness for the Prosecution*. Like Mr. Laughton, David was portly, eloquent, intelligent, and spoke with a measured hesitation common in English speech. I learned that Akroyd and Smithers was part of a working group set up by John Berkshire to explore the feasibility of establishing a financial futures exchange in London.

David quickly sensed I was an Anglophile. Growing up with my mother's stories of England and scores of British movies, had made me comfortable in dealing with the English. We quickly got down to a discussion about the potential for a European exchange. The failure to establish an exchange in London might diminish London's role as an international financial center. Chicago, for example, had already started trading a futures contract in Eurodollars—U.S. dollars deposited in European banks that were traded in London. It was just the first opportunity London had missed.

I explained that the gold futures launch in the United States had resulted in the dramatic diminution of London's power in the international gold market. By 1980, the London "gold fix," which had

[2]Intermarket Interview: Richard Sandor, "The Worldwide Futures and Options Report," 1984.

started in 1919, had already become irrelevant. While David was less than enamored with the idea of a futures market, he immediately understood its strategic value for the city of London.

I had developed business in London and Switzerland, and promised to see David on my next trip to the United Kingdom. He arranged an unforgettable luncheon for me with his company's senior management. We gathered at about 11:30 A.M. for cocktails in a room filled with Belgian tapestries on its walls. A dark armoire served as the liquor cabinet. When we sat down, I was bewildered by the silverware set before me. The English seemed to have utensils specific to every course. The three-hour luncheon included a three-course meal interspersed with white and red wines, followed by dessert, port, and cheese. Wines were served clockwise, while port was served counterclockwise. As we discussed history, politics, and the economy, I felt strangely at home. I was subsequently hired by Akroyd and Smithers to advise the firm on its role and strategy in the proposed new futures exchange. I loved the experience, and relished my London trips. My interest in photography took me to Lacock Abbey, where William Henry Fox Talbot invented photography.

John's working party, either by design or by natural evolution, had a clear pecking order and a line of succession. I first met Brian Williamson when the working party came to Chicago. His background and interest in politics, his specific knowledge of discount markets, and his position at Gerard and National made him the ideal successor to John. We built our friendship over the next few years. Brian had me speak to the FSA the next time I was in London, where I explained the economic value of financial futures.

As an adviser to Akroyd and Smithers, I was able to provide input on exchange structure and contract design. I strongly urged the firm to advocate to the working party that the exchange develop a solid base of floor trading members. Our locals in Chicago were mostly neighborhood guys from the West and South Sides of Chicago. "Barrow boys" were their equivalent in London, hailing from the east end of the city. They served as a pool of potential market makers.

When it came to possible contracts, the gilt market offered the largest market potential, but there was also demand from money market participants to start a short-term interest rate market. The members of the Akroyd and Smithers team were quick students but had no prior experience in designing a futures contract. Their initial contract design for short-term interest rates, denoted in sterling, granted the buyer the power to specify some delivery terms. This feature was changed after the team learned that almost all successful futures markets, be it financial instruments or commodities, gave the seller the license to dictate the timing and grade of delivery. The conventional wisdom in having a bias toward the sellers was integral to the liquidity of any market, because sellers alone controlled the supply.

The next step was to convince the Bank of England (dubbed the Bank) of the economic purpose of the market. The Bank assigned a young economist by the name of Pendarell "Pen" Kent to evaluate the benefits that a financial futures market could confer to London's capital markets, and more broadly, the UK economy. I met with Pen in London to share my views and was delighted to discover that we shared a common language as fellow economists.

Pen subsequently visited Chicago. We had dinner at Les Nomades, a French restaurant started by Jovan Trboyevic from Czechoslovakia and a favorite of mine and Ellen's. It was a members' only restaurant with $1 annual membership fees. Upscale but slightly Bohemian, the restaurant fit both of our academic backgrounds and was the perfect setting for our meeting. I gave a lot of thought to how and where to entertain visitors. It was important for business, and I loved watching my guests enjoy themselves. Jovan was a great host but didn't tolerate customers who were impolite to his staff. On one occasion, a customer was abusing the waiter and Jovan promptly asked him to leave. The customer argued that he was a good customer and Jovan's actions were unwarranted, to which Jovan responded, "Good waiters are a lot harder to find than good customers."

Pen was thoughtful and open-minded. I stressed the importance of opening the membership to men and women who had the capital to purchase memberships and were reputable. He understood that the new exchange in London should welcome members that were not part of the financial establishment in London. It was the same argument about "barrow boys" from the east end becoming the backbone of the market. By the end of our evening, Ellen and I were convinced that Pen would support the idea of a London-based exchange. With his backing, the Bank later invited me to discuss the importance of Liffe to the financial community in London.

Liffe opened on September 30, 1982, and became a big success. Brian later suggested that one of my largest contributions may have been in neutralizing the opposition to the London Stock Exchange and the gilt dealers, also known as jobbers. The stock exchange, coupled with the gilt dealers, might have had enough political power to thwart the birth of Liffe. It was yet another example of established interests possibly recoiling from transparent markets, which narrowed their spreads and diminished their profits. Educational efforts and a broad network of friends helped to counter this.

Three Men and a Market—MATIF

LaSalle Street inspired institutional innovation not only in London, but also across the Channel. The launch of the Marché à Terme International de France (MATIF)[3] in Paris was not a product of chance, but the hard-earned fruit of many individual efforts. The efforts of three men in particular stood out—a teacher, a trader, and a senior member of the French government. Yves Simon, Marcel Becker, and Gerard de la Martinière would completely revolutionize the markets in Paris. The push for the exchange, however, could not have begun without one of my former students and a journalist.

In 1974 I taught a group of French students at Kellogg who had been fascinated by futures and options. One day I received a call from Florence Pierre, a former student who was now working at the Chicago office of BNP Paribas. She asked if I wanted to meet Robert Lozada, a journalist from a French magazine called *La Vie Francaise* who was coming to Chicago to do a story on Chicago futures markets. It was an opportunity to start building a network in Paris.

Robert was a quick-witted journalist who asked penetrating questions. He was fascinated by the intellectual revolution in free-market thought

[3]International Futures Market of France.

that was originating from the University of Chicago, and the practical execution of that philosophy at the CBOT. He enjoyed being a provocateur and invited Milton Friedman to lecture in France in 1980,[4] during a time when capitalism was unpopular. I gave him a tour of the CBOT trading floor in Chicago and explained how a futures exchange worked.

I told Robert that Paris too should have a financial futures market. If not, the market for determining French interest rates would migrate to London. I also argued that the mathematical sensibility of the French guaranteed that this project would attract the best and brightest. "I promise to make your ideas about interest rate futures famous in France!" Robert declared. Before he left, he invited me to give a lecture on free markets in France with an emphasis on financial futures. He thought that the central bank, the Banque de France, would support a new French exchange once they understood the U.S. regulatory model and the economic value of the exchange to the French economy.

Even though I was 40 years old and had never been to France, the European influence in my home made me comfortable with French culture. My mother and her sister often spoke French to each other so that others wouldn't understand. French was also one of the languages I read while writing my PhD dissertation.

In the spring of 1980, Robert persuaded the editors of his magazine to hold a seminar on Chicago's experience in financial futures markets, sending out invitations to leading members of the French government and the private sector. It was the first discussion on this topic in Paris, and the lecture was held in a small room with standing room only. On a separate trip, Robert arranged for me to meet representatives from the Banque de France to explain the economic benefits of futures markets. An article by Robert that was published in June 1980 and titled, "Bourses: Oui A L'Innovation!"[5] encouraged public debate on the economic benefits of hedging and price

---

[4]Milton Rose D. Friedman, *Two Lucky People: Memoirs* (Chicago: University of Chicago Press, 1998).

[5]Robert Lozada, "Bourses: Oui A L'Innovation!" *La Vie Francaise*, June 9, 1980.

discovery and its application to French markets. Over the next few years, French academics expressed interest and reached out to me frequently.

During my frequent trips to Paris over the next two years, I met Yves Simon, a quiet but influential economist from the University of Paris, Dauphine with a quintessential thirst for knowledge. Robert and his family hosted a dinner for Yves, Florence Pierre, Ellen, and me. Yves Simon was one of the first academics in France to research and teach about the GNMA futures markets. Tireless in his educational efforts, he trained his students in the formalities of futures markets. They eventually came to Chicago in droves to witness the activities in the trading pits. These individuals were part of a pool of human capital that eventually populated all segments of the financial markets in France: commercial banks, investment banks, and corporations. They traded on the floor of the exchange as well as in locations around "the City of Light."

Professor Simon and his students exemplified the French appreciation of the intricate mathematics behind these markets. His personal role as an advocate sent an important message. The success of futures markets so often depended on the intellectual appreciation of these markets by academics who conferred their knowledge to students, government, and industry. Yves's endorsement gave academic credence to the concept of futures markets in Paris.

Marcel Becker was a trader at Credit Lyonnaise, a skilled professional who picked up the technicalities of the Eurodollar futures market. Realizing that these new markets were inefficient and had high transaction costs, Marcel applied his craft diligently and unselfishly shared these opportunities with other members of the banking community. The success of futures markets ultimately depended on commercial logic. Success bred imitators, and Marcel Becker had his fair share of them. Many traders imitated him out of self-interest, in turn articulating the importance of the markets for risk management to other colleagues and to regulators.

Of course, exchange leadership by members and staff was also vital to the success of any market. Early leadership was characterized by experienced members of the government who were academically trained. Gerard de la Martiniere, who worked for the French Treasury until 1986, provided the leadership and intellectual capacity to lead the MATIF in its early years. His stature in France as a member of the government, along with his intellectual approach to problem solving, were pivotal elements in the success of the MATIF.

I worked tirelessly with the French press and academics until the day the MATIF began trading on February 20, 1986. In addition to doing an interview with *Le Monde*, a leading French newspaper,[6] I accepted Yves' invitation to lecture his students at Dauphine University on the benefits of financial futures and how the Chicago experience could be applied to France when MATIF opens its doors.

I later joined the MATIF's small international advisory board when it was formed in 1995. From the unforgettable advisory board meeting in Nice—where the garden hedges were meticulously crafted into the silhouette of ships—to the meaningful friendships I established in France, my memories of being on the board of the MATIF brimmed with delightful details of dinners and wines and served me well when I later joined the Liffe board. I started to collect French photography, ranging from Paris between the wars, Dada and surrealist works, to creations of Man Ray and Eugène Atget. Most memorable of all was probably the five-year anniversary party of the MATIF, held at Versailles. To this day, I still maintain that it was possibly the best party ever thrown by an exchange.

The importance of the ability to openly debate matters of economic interest should not be overlooked. European socialism was dying in the early 1980s. A free market of ideas promoted free markets for financial instruments and commodities. Human capital, public debate, commercial logic, and exchange leadership all contributed to the success of the MATIF.

The Tale of Two Cities

Liffe and the MATIF became rivals for the next 15 years, only to be ultimately subsumed under the NYSE Euronext. In many ways, Europe's recognition of financial futures markets reminded me of Charles Dickens's *Tale of Two Cities*.

---

[6]"Une Nouvelle Race de Maisons de Courtage," *Le Monde*, February 19, 1986.

English and French exchanges differed not only in the challenges they faced, but in the solutions they found. It was the private sector that led the effort in the United Kingdom, and the public sector that led the effort in France. The core of the difference was cultural. As the United Kingdom championed free markets and commerce, the culture of commodity trading was deeply entrenched in its culture. Free markets were not held in high regard in France, but the French were driven by their interest in the mathematics of futures markets. Leaders in both countries recognized the economic value of good derivatives—futures contracts on transparent, regulated exchanges.

On to Drexel

I met the chairman and CEO of Drexel while convening the International Commodities Conferences in the 1970s. He launched a commodity division at Drexel that dealt in both spot and futures markets, and hired Fred Uhlmann to head the department.

I joined Drexel in April 1982 after being recruited by Fred and the chairman. Charming and mild-mannered, Fred looked like and had the demeanor of Henry Fonda. Fred and his family had a storied legacy at the CBOT. Uhlmann Grain was one of the CBOT's oldest member firms. Fred's father had been chairman of the CBOT and had had a battleship named after him during World War II for his efforts as a patriot. Fred was chairman of the CBOT when GNMA futures were first launched, and he constantly encouraged me.

Financial innovation continued to change the landscape of the capital markets in 1982. The year was marked by the introduction of futures on stock indexes, 10-year Treasury notes, and Eurodollars (launched December 1981). Interest swaps had been born just one year earlier. I could sell these new markets better as an investment banker than as a commodities broker. Investment banks traded stocks and bonds, while commodity brokers didn't. I also wanted to learn more about underwriting and structured finance. Joining Drexel gave me this opportunity.

The transition from ContiCommodity to Drexel wasn't easy. We left behind a well-trained team who serviced clients from the trading floor. The team had grown from a group of inexperienced men and women into seasoned professionals.

Traders who wanted to move their business to Drexel had to complete new account forms, which required approval from the firm's lawyers and board of directors. There was also a myriad of other challenges, which included installing new direct lines from our new booths to the trading desks of dealers, and addressing the possibility that there was no space on the dealers' desks for new direct phone lines. Fred was supportive, but we were not doing well. The chairman was also concerned, and asked the head of marketing to go to Chicago to figure out how to help us out.

Once a Teacher, Always a Teacher

In addition to being a great marketer and salesman, the head of marketing at Drexel boasted a solid academic background. He met with the team and came up with an ingenious idea. Given our academic credentials, he recommended that we set up something like a university that marketed new financial futures and options through executive courses. This would position the financial futures division of Drexel, Burnham as the most knowledgeable people in the futures business. By building relationships as teachers, we could use these courses as our marketing vehicle for recruiting clients. Alongside media coverage and extensive speeches made to industry and trade groups, an executive course would be instrumental in building the human capital in the industry, as well as our own client base.

The Kellogg School of Management at Northwestern University was the natural place to set up our executive course. While the two-day seminars I had run with NYU had been perfectly adequate in length at the time, the proliferation of financial futures and options required more time to be covered in class. We created an on-campus experience with case studies at night to better educate our attendees. The Allen Center on campus was a perfect venue, since the attendees already lived, ate, and attended classes there.

The on-campus program cost $1,650 per participant, including room and board. Our allotted 50 percent of revenue after expenses was donated back to Kellogg. The program was staffed by the Drexel team, Kellogg's finance faculty, exchange officials, and regulators.

The program had to have real educational value and couldn't simply be a sales pitch. We worked on the planning and execution of the program for months. The biggest challenge was getting regulators and elected members of Congress to commit to a certain time and not cancel at the last moment.

The program was launched on November 27, 1983, a Sunday night. After the opening cocktail party, I described the objectives of the program. In addition to helping participants develop a theoretical understanding of interest rate risk and the role of futures and options markets, we hoped to integrate theory with practice through case studies and interactive group projects. We even warned the participants of homework assignments that had to be completed at the end of each lesson. We wanted, after all, for the seminar to resemble a university class. If students did their homework, they would better grasp what we were doing and how to use the markets. Informed customers were our best customers.

During the course, the head of Northwestern's Banking Research Center discussed the need for asset and liability management by depository institutions. It seems so odd today that we had to persuade banks to set up separate units to manage these risks. The head of the banking research center and I were fellow directors at First Federal Savings and Loan Association, appointed by the Federal Savings and Loan Insurance Corporation to serve as transitional directors when it was being bailed out. At the time, it was the largest government bailout of an S&L, with costs exceeding $160 million.[7] We continued to laugh about the disagreements among the management and the board members about how many branches the bank had. That was certainly indicative of the state of management in the thrift industry. It was no wonder that asset and liability management wasn't even on their radar screens.

Clayton Yeutter, president of the CME and former U.S. trade ambassador, described the role of exchanges. His experience as a trade ambassador, his PhD in agriculture, and his training as a farmer meant that he had a completely unique take on the topic. Very few people

[7]Timothy Curry and Lynn Shibut, "The Cost of the Savings and Loan Crisis: Truth and Consequences," *FDIC Banking Review*, December 2000.

had firsthand experiences in dealing such vastly different groups as trade associations, exchanges, and farmers. The program ended with a closing piece by Tom Donovan, president of the CBOT, who had always supported my more controversial ideas at the exchange, and would continue to do so once I moved into the environmental space.

Overall, the presentations emphasized regulatory, legal, tax, and accounting functions. Senator David Boren (D-OK) spoke about pending tax legislation. I had been introduced to David Boren in 1978, and we had since become personal and family friends. We had faculty members and representatives from the big accounting firms speak about the tax and accounting aspects of futures markets. Consulting firms also spoke about the necessity for depository institutions to possess an asset and liability function that measured interest rate risk and pursued policies to minimize them—a novel idea at the time.

Members of the Drexel team gave presentations about the technical aspects of marketing, while depository institutions and corporations provided case studies on their own use of the markets—primarily oriented toward hedging their exposure and the role of futures to that end. The Drexel team covered hedging and trading strategies for interest rate, foreign exchange, and stock index futures.

The program also went into basics, which could not be taken for granted. We were building institutional knowledge from scratch, working to create a critical mass of users who could become fluent in using, accounting for, and regulating these strange new products.

To end, we provided guided tours of the CBOT, the CME, and the Art Institute of Chicago, followed by dinner. All in all, it was a Chicago show. The city's exchanges, museums, and restaurants were all put on stage.

The executive education program succeeded beyond all of our expectations. We forecasted 20 attendees, but had to cut off enrollment at 60. The demand for the program became so large that we even had to host multiple programs each year, as opposed to once a year. We helped to position the exchanges as innovative entities and ourselves as thought leaders in these young and dynamic markets. Although the program originally targeted people who managed interest rate risk at their respective institutions, our "university" drew accountants, lawyers, and compliance personnel from all over corporate America.

The program was modified over the next seven years as the users became more sophisticated. We began to use the platform as a means of developing business friendships. We stopped the large dinners, and instead began hosting smaller groups. Each presenter often had back-to-back dinners, and it became a kind of marathon. We had the dinners themselves down to a science: appetizers and salads at the first dinner followed with entrees at the second, with each dinner accompanied by different traders.

A colleague broke the record one night with three dinners in a row. By the third dinner, his credit card was declined. He called his credit card company, and a skeptical representative told him, "There's no way that someone could have three dinners in one evening." In the end, he had to call me to use my card. That night we had four members of the team hosting 11 dinners. Educating people about financial futures was not always a glamorous affair. Truth be told, I often felt like a lounge act at what were often rubber-chicken dinner events. Table 8.1 is a small sample of other events I spoke at throughout the 1980s.

The reputation we had built didn't require us to sell our expertise. We built off the floor-trading desk as the demand for trading ideas grew. The dealers had made the markets more efficient, but there was still a need to identify opportunities to build relationships that lasted longer than the staccato discussions on the trading floor. Once we had proven our expertise to potential clients, it remained for our business to expand on the shoulders of relationships. Our upstairs sales team explained the cheapest-to-deliver concept, duration slippage in the 10-year note, and identified longer-term arbitrage opportunities.[8] They used the then high-tech and state-of-the-art HP-50 calculators and Apple computers to calculate arbitrage opportunities and call customers. We also added specialists in stock index futures both on and off the floor.

---

[8]*Duration slippage* refers to the fact that the window for delivery of the 10-year contract was 7 to 10 years. The cheapest to deliver was often the 7-year note. The loss of three years was referred to as duration slippage.

Table 8.1 Education and Outreach 1980s

Outreach Event	Date	Type
Presentation on Asset/Liability Management and the use of financial futures One Columbus, Ohio	March 28, 1983	Internal presentation to users
CBOT Financial Futures and Options Trading Strategies Seminar Midland Hotel	April 11, 1983	Educating users
Financial Future Seminar INCAE Central America San Jose, Costa Rica	July 1, 1983	Academic outreach
Institute of Banking and Finance Conference on Financial Future Singapore	July 19, 1983	International outreach
Swiss Commodity Industry Conference Burgenstock	September 2–3, 1983	International outreach
ABA "Management School for Corporate Bankers" Speech, Northwestern University	October 3, 1983	Educating users
Institutional Investor CFO Seminar, "Tools for Managing Financial Risk," Corinthian Room, Biltmore Hotel, Los Angeles	October 6, 1983	Educating users
"Money Talk" Terry Savage, TV Interview	July 1, 1986	Educating the press
Drexel Burnham Lambert Mutual Fund Grand Prix Conference Kona, Hawaii	September 3–7, 1986	Internal seminar
Swiss Options and Futures Exchanges Zurich	October 2–3, 1986	Educating users
Second International Conference Global Risk Management and Investment with Futures and Options London, UK	June 20–22, 1988	International outreach
Mid-Year Conference on Futures Money Management Chicago, IL	June 22, 1988	Educating users
Dewey Daane Conference on International Finance and Financial Policy Vanderbilt University	April 13–14, 1988	Academic outreach

(continued)

Table 8.1 (*Continued*)

Outreach Event	Date	Type
Advanced Futures and Options Strategies for Professional Financial Managers Northwestern University, Chicago, IL	June 17–20, 1989	Educating users
CFTC Financial Product Advisory Committee Conference	November 17, 1989	Educating regulators

Drexel Grows

Drexel's success in Chicago was driven by quick access to the team on the floor and a self-or formally educated sales force. We were also extremely disciplined. Our morning meetings began at 6:30 A.M. since the markets opened at 7:20 A.M., and the door to the meeting room was locked as soon as the meeting began. The intended message was clear: "If you're late, don't bother coming in." During meetings, we discussed the economic news of the day and trading ideas from research and sales. Despite the austerity of our discipline, we never lost our sense of humor. Walking by a salesman's trading desk one day and upon seeing that he was doing nothing, I joked, "Pick up the phone and give yourself a raise." The salesmen were paid on commissions.

Drexel had an office in London and I asked one of our team members who had begun as a runner to go to London and serve as the manager on an interim basis. He recommended that we hire Rosalyn "Ros" Wilton as the head of the London division. Ros wasn't exactly your typical English wallflower. She worked on the floor, where she fought toe to toe with the men. Well educated and tenacious as she was, Ros was still a controversial choice to head the new office. It was London in the early 1980s and women were often subject to a glass ceiling. Against societal expectations, Ros led the office and ran a very successful operation that replicated the business model we had in Chicago. She was elected a director of Liffe, thereby becoming the first woman to be on the Liffe board and the first woman ever to serve on the board of any European exchange. She hadn't just pushed the glass ceiling, but crashed through it.

I interviewed Horace Payne, an African American youth who had offered to help a colleague when his tire went flat on the road. It didn't take me long to realize that Horace was a well-balanced and ambitious young man, and I immediately offered him a job as a runner. Aware of the matriarchal nature of the African American community, I asked to speak to Horace's mother. "I'll call her if you ever mess up!" I teased. He didn't. Horace became one of the first African-American members at the CME and later attended graduate school.

Either by design or by necessity, I often chose outsiders—individuals who were willing to make career choices in an unproven field. One of my hires used to sell life insurance, while another sold crystal drinking glasses door to door. If they weren't professionally trained in economics or finance, they learned it on the job. Through our efforts, we built the human capital needed to help the markets grow in the coming decades. We produced a great team, which ultimately provided 30 percent of CEOs in the top 10 FCMs. Some of the entrepreneurs and independent traders from our team became illustrious. Rick Santelli, for instance, went on to become a leading financial journalist at CNBC. After a short tenure at Drexel, Michael Spencer went on to found ICAP, one of the biggest brokerage firms in the world.

Drexel Becomes More International

Our success in London had opened our eyes to other opportunities around the world. The Singapore International Monetary Exchange (SIMEX) was launched in 1984, and we made a dangerous mistake there that taught me an important lesson.

We hired an American fluent in Mandarin to run our Singapore office. Before long, friction arose between SIMEX and our manager, who had an imperial attitude. This was akin to picking a fight with the government of Singapore, and I knew the issue had to be resolved immediately. I asked Rick Ferina, who was then only in his twenties, to leave for Singapore and sort it out right away. Six weeks later, Rick had repaired the tensions with the Singaporean government and had hired someone else to run our operations there—a Singaporean this time. I trusted Rick, and he performed flawlessly.

I saw a movie called *A Message to Garcia*, starring Wallace Beery and Barbara Stanwyck, in high school that was based on an article by Elbert Hubbard published in 1899. During the Spanish-American War, President McKinley wanted to make contact with one of the Cuban rebels who was sympathetic to America. He was advised that a certain Captain Rowan could get it done, and sent him an order. The details of Captain Rowan's perilous journey were unimportant. What mattered was that he successfully delivered the letter to Garcia in the Cuban mountains three weeks after the president's order. At no point in this process did Captain Rowan ask, "Where is he at?" or "What is the purpose of the message?" or "Is this really urgent and necessary?" Instead, Captain Rowan merely received an order, gathered his resources, and executed. Rick Ferina essentially did in Singapore what Captain Rowan did in Cuba. "The Message to Garcia" became mandatory reading for new employees when I later founded the Chicago Climate Exchange. The message was essentially to be resourceful in doing what you were asked to do.

Rick was more than just reliable. He had a nimble mind, understood risk, liked to read history, and had a great sense of humor. Like me, he loved food and movies. He once told me about an order to buy Swiss francs he received on the floor. He was on the phone with David Albertson about the order when David's wife called on the other line. David put her on hold and spoke on the phone about the market for another five minutes. Rick got nervous and said, "David, your wife is still on hold. Let me transfer her." David responded with a great smile in his voice, "Rick, I can always get another wife but I won't be able to buy the Swiss franc at these levels again."

The lesson of Singapore would not be lost. We opened an office in Paris and staffed it with French salesmen. We later opened a Japanese office and staffed it with Japanese nationals. As we expanded, we located ourselves in cities where new exchanges were opening. With offices in Chicago, New York, London, Paris, Singapore, and Tokyo, we strove to become a global leader in the business. We knew how to make new markets grow. We positioned ourselves more as educators than as salesmen, and it had the desired effect. New good derivatives, traded on transparent, regulated exchanges, were providing economic value all around the world.

Eurodollar and Stock Index Futures Contracts

In 1983 and 1984, Drexel continued to develop new businesses in Eurodollar and S&P futures contracts. I continued to give speeches, write articles, and solicit business. The Eurodollar futures market was successful because there was a latent and overt need for banks and corporations to hedge short-term interest rates, and there were large arbitrage opportunities. One of our largest customers was a French bank. We explained that the bank could lend money at a fixed rate for one year, simultaneously invest it through a 90-day investment, then hedge the next three 90-day periods to make substantial profits. The bank's head of U.S. operations immediately recognized the opportunities in the market.

Treasury bill futures, on the other hand, did not fulfill this hedging need because the cross-hedging risk was too high.[9] It was often the case that government borrowing rates were not sufficiently correlated with the borrowing rates for banks and corporations. This was because government debt was considered a safe haven for investors from a risk standpoint.

Liquidity in the Eurodollar futures market was built the same way as with the earlier interest rate futures, using a combination of market makers, exchange members, arbitrageurs, and smaller dealers. The same methodology was used to determine if the contract was below or above fair value. It is possible to create a synthetic six-month deposit by investing for three months at the three-month Eurodollar rate and then hedging the next three months in the Eurodollar futures market. In effect, two consecutive three-month investments are the same as one six-month investment. This becomes an arbitrage opportunity if the cost of borrowing for six months is lower than the average rate from a three-month investment and a long hedge in the futures market for the next three months. On the other side, what about the person,

[9]Cross-hedging: hedging with a futures contract different from the underlying being hedged.

that is, the arbitrageur, who is selling the three-month Eurodollar future? It is cost-effective to short a futures position, since the cost of borrowing and selling the deposits or other negotiable instrument is more expensive in comparison. In effect, the short hedger was paying the arbitrageur his profit to provide a more efficient way to hedge against higher interest rates.

There were several important differences between this contract and other interest rate futures. Eurodollars were cash-settled so delivery was not possible. Eurodollar deposits were not financial instruments and could not be shorted. It was, however, possible to arbitrage them against a new financial instrument called an interest rate swap, a contract where parties agreed to swap their short-term interest rate exposure for long-term interest rate exposure.

The S&P stock index futures contract began trading on the CME on April 21, 1982. It was yet another example of market makers, arbitrageurs, and traders interacting to develop liquidity. The contract was unusual because it was cash-settled but forbade delivery. It was very expensive to borrow individual stocks and short them separately. The need for a more cost-effective way to transact and hedge contributed to the success of the stock index futures market. The existence of the stock index futures market created a new incentive to short stocks. The increase in the size of the demand ultimately drove costs down. Differential transaction costs created the initial liquidity needed for the S&P futures market at the outset. Market direction was fortuitous.

Stock index futures were introduced at a time when stocks were at their lowest in almost a decade. President Reagan's policies and the actions of the central bank were just beginning to pay off. The economy was on a path to recovery. What followed was a major bull market resulting in enormous success for these innovations. As of December 1, 1982, the S&P stock index was traded at $139.90. It proceeded to rise from $108.40 on July 6, 1982, to $310.20 five years later on July 6, 1987, mostly trading above fair value throughout. For market timers[10]

[10]Market timers are investors who predict future market directions based on trends, and invests accordingly.

and investors wanting to participate in the generally increasing stock market, buying these futures was an alternative to buying a basket of stocks that mirrored the market. The S&P futures contract specifications included a 250 multiple of the index, or the equivalent of $250. The minimum tick was 0.1 point, or $25 per contract. The cost of buying and selling one S&P futures contract is about $50.00 ($25.00 for commissions to a discount futures broker plus another $25.00 for the one-tick bid-offer spread in the futures market), while the cost of buying and selling a representative stock is about $1,300.[11] Once again, the arbitrageur would provide the liquidity by buying the shares in the spot market and selling the futures above fair value. The opposite would take place in a bear market when the futures might sell below fair value. Differential transaction costs created the initial liquidity needed for the S&P futures market at the outset. Everyone was better off.

I continued to work on new contracts at the CBOT throughout 1982. Les's term as chairman was coming to an end. We were like a lame duck Congress and wanted to get as much done as possible. We were intent on designing new contracts when we still had the chance. Hoping to fill out the yield curve, the CBOT started markets in the five-year note and the two-year note. Unfortunately, we didn't spend enough time marketing the new contracts or educating their users. As a result, these contracts died early. The CBOT later relaunched a five-year contract after the Comex started one—more as a defensive strategy than anything else. The five-year note, launched in 1988, turned out to be one of the largest futures in the complex. A two-year note followed, emerging in 1990.[12]

The CBOT Options on Bond Futures

Despite our hit-and-miss record, we did manage to launch one more successful product. The Commodity Exchange Act of 1936 banned

---

[11]William L. Silber, *The Economic Role of Financial Futures* (Washington, DC: American Enterprise Institute for Public Policy Research, 1985).

[12]"Eventually the CME Group further filled out the yield curve with products like three-year Treasury note futures in 2009 and ultra Treasury bond futures in 2010.

the trading of agricultural options because they were thought to facilitate price manipulation.[13] Decades later, the CBOT and other exchanges advocated the introduction of options on futures contracts. We believed that with the appropriate regulatory framework, options on futures would not be abused but would be of value to hedgers. The CBOT formed an options committee in 1981. Les nominated me as chairman and the board approved. This was done when it became public that the CFTC was considering reauthorizing options on futures. Now that we had regulatory authorization from the CFTC, we had to design the contract.

Options on bond futures are contracts in which the underlying asset is a Treasury bond futures contract. An option gives the holder or buyer of the option the right, but not the obligation, to buy or sell an underlying asset at a previously agreed price, called the *strike price*, at a given point in the future. This means that the seller has the right, but not the obligation, as per the contract. This design marked a drastic departure from the design of a futures or forward contract, in which both parties had the right *and* the obligation to fulfill the contract if not offset prior to delivery. The CBOT options on bond futures contracts incorporated calls—the right but not the obligation to buy a futures contract at a price determined today—and puts—the right but not the obligation to sell one futures contract at a price determined today. The costs of these rights were known as premiums. The price at which the option could be exercised was termed the strike price. The options contract could be exercised at any time between the date of purchase and the expiry date. The current price was referred to as *at the money*, and every two points above (for a call option) and below (for a put option) the market price of the underlying asset were referred to as *out of the money*.

We wanted deep out-of-the-money options. To be deemed deep out-of-the-money, an option's strike price had to be at least one strike price above or below the market price of the underlying asset. For

[13]John P. Satrom, Alfred K. Chan, and William W. Wilson, "Commercial and Producer Applications Using Options on Grain Futures," Agricultural Economics Report no. 200, Department of Agricultural Economics, North Dakota State University, May 1985.

example, if the current price of the underlying stock is $10, a put option with a strike price of $5 is considered deep out-of-the-money. Since the strike prices of these options were very far from the market value of the underlying securities, they were likely to be worthless by the time the contract expired. Such options had very low premiums, however, which made them desirable for speculation because profits could be enormous if the price of the underlying securities happened to jump sharply. The CFTC unfortunately overruled our request for deep out-of-the-money options under the pretext that they were too speculative. To this day, I have never quite grasped the reasoning.

The final options on bond futures contracts were American-style,[14] exercisable at any time after the date of purchase and before the contract expiration date of the underlying bond futures. We chose to set the expiration of the options prior to delivery in order to avoid price manipulation. Any individual who owned bond futures or bond call options could theoretically control more of the deliverable supply by exercising the option. There was no way to determine whether the option would be exercised since it depended on the price of the future. But if all parties were required to exercise before the delivery month, the long positions of individuals were in the futures contracts only. They were therefore transparent and could easily be regulated.

Having designed the contract, we now needed market makers. As part of a comprehensive program, seats were offered in commodity options as well as in index and energy products. We distributed partial ownerships in these new seats in order to garner support from the existing seat holders. In essence, it was a dividend to existing seat owners, which helped to placate the potential opposition to the plan.

Nonetheless, the expansion of seats was still highly controversial. An exchange member once told me, "The first thing you learn when you come to America is English. The second thing is to keep the foreigners out." The same mentality seemed true of the CBOT membership. Les, as chairman, exhausted all of his political energy to get the expansion policy passed. A trader I knew was at O'Hare

[14]This refers to the expiration style. European style options occurs only at expiration while American style options may occur at any time up to and including expiration.

International Airport, ready to go on vacation, when he received an urgent call from an owner of a clearing firm at the exchange. "We need every vote we can get," he pleaded. "Get right back here." The trader promptly canceled his vacation just so he could come back to vote. Other traders who were loyal to Les also postponed their vacations. The new seats were authorized by a mere two votes, the closest vote yet I had seen at the exchange. It always made me smile to think that the history of the exchange was forever altered by a few members who changed their vacation plans.

The CBOT options on bond futures contract went on to be extraordinarily successful and served as a paradigm for other options contracts, not only on the CBOT but at other exchanges as well. As of 2010, the annual volume of options on bond futures was 78.2 million contracts and the year-end open interest was 2.2 million contracts.[15]

The options contract marked the termination of my directorship at the CBOT. I was invited to join the CME's board of directors in 1983. It was a welcome opportunity to learn about the exchange's culture and its new markets. There was a bitter rivalry between the CBOT and the CME, and some members of my alma mater thought me a turncoat. In spite of my sentimental attachment to the CBOT, I considered myself a member of the community of exchanges. The familiar hunger to learn that spurred me to participate in the establishment of Liffe now drove me to the CME.

---

[15]"CME Group Volume and Open Interest Report 8:00 A.M. Final Report for Business," CME Group, October 7, 2011.

Chapter 9

Globalizing Chicago Exchanges

To every action there is always opposed an equal reaction.

—*Isaac Newton*

The second half of the Eighties was characterized by great optimism for and growth of financial innovations. The child of the Seventies was healthy, making friends and learning fast. New innovations in the form of index futures proved to be a big success. With increasing maturity of financial futures contracts, a whole new field of asset management thrived. Banks were reinventing their roles with new financial products and services. Triggered by structural economic shifts in the Far East, financial innovations were also becoming increasingly prevalent in Asia. The first hint of a global market for financial futures seemed to be on the horizon.

Keeping pace with these changes, the CME was emerging as a major force in the futures industry. The CBOT made a courageous foray into 24-hour trading. Drexel, an obscure investment bank, was embracing innovative ways to finance entrepreneurs. I remained cautiously optimistic about all of this change and continued to expound on the value of good derivatives. Soon, the world would witness a series of disconcerting events that exposed the major shortcomings in the financial industry. This is that story—one of global expansion of the Chicago Brand.

The Secret Ingredient of the CME

I joined the CME board in 1983. With the introduction of the currency futures and later S&P index futures, the CME was transforming itself from an eggs and butter exchange to a major player in financial futures. Always a student, I was eager to learn about the institutional setup within CME and the reasons for its growing success. I quickly learned that the CME had a completely different culture from the CBOT. The exchange had suffered a near deathblow with the demise of the onion market. Market abuses in the 1950s had resulted in an act of Congress banning futures trading in onions.[1] In fact, onions enjoy the distinction of being the first market ever banned by the U.S. Congress. The second was futures contracts on box office receipts for movies. At the dawn of the 1960s, the CME had a blank slate, which turned out to be a big competitive advantage for decades.

In 1961, the exchange launched a pork belly futures contract, which later gave them some gravitas and left them hungry for more. The exchange had no franchise to rely on so it became far more aggressive in competing for business and appealing to the public speculator. Any public inquiries about hedging or speculating opportunities were given to member firms at the CME—a tradition that was lacking at the CBOT.

Unlike the CBOT, the CME chairman was elected by the board members. By tradition, the CME chairmanship was passed on from one member of the executive committee to another, which meant that the drama of elections for chairman was avoided. More importantly, all the candidates for chairmanship had already been groomed

[1]The Commodity Exchange Authority issued a complaint charging farmers Vincent Kosuga and Sam Siegel with manipulating onion futures contract months, which had resulted in heavy fluctuations in onion prices. Following hearings, Congress enacted a law to ban futures trading in onions.

by years of service on the executive committee of the exchange. Governance was the secret ingredient. This was contrary to any governance procedure at the CBOT. Even though the CME was a mutual organization, it managed to avoid fractious public debates that would result in divisiveness. It was focused on building market share, which was a refreshing experience for me.

There is no doubt in my mind that the continuity of the most respected chairman-and-management team, Leo Melamed and Jack Sandner, helped to push the CME to where it is today. Leo provided the political skills to revitalize the exchange after the onion debacle and started it on the road to becoming the world's largest exchange. Jack Sandner held the position of chairman at 17 years, longer than any other person. Jack was chairman when the exchange introduced the most important products in its history—Eurodollar and S&P stock index futures. Bill Brodsky was president of the CME during the great years of growth. He went on to become chairman and CEO of the CBOE. Bill's management of the relationship of the CBOT and the CBOE was a masterpiece of politics. The fact that the CBOE is a publicly traded company is a testimony to his leadership. Partisans of Leo, Jack, Clayton, and Bill might disagree about the best politicians in the industry, but I would argue that Les had a more politically difficult job as the CBOT chairman, and ranks at or above all of these great leaders. He managed to balance his way through the political intrigue and infighting among 1,402 diverse members. When the CBOT was later merged with the CME in 2006, the interest rate futures and options constituted 79 percent of the annual volume and represented $8.9 billion of the $11.3 billion purchase price.[2]

In addition to having an exemplary management team, which included Clayton Yeutter (1978–1985), the CME made sure that economists played a key role at the exchange. Unlike the CBOT, the CME had a tradition of putting its economists on a pedestal. Mark J. Powers was appointed the CME's first chief economist. Not only did Mark come up with the concept of 90-day Treasury bill futures (see Chapter 7), he also advised Everett "Ev" Harris, CME president from

---

[2]Chicago Board of Trade Annual Reports 2006–2007.

1953 to 1978 and previously CBOT secretary, to start currency and T-bill futures.

During the early 1970s, Ev and I had met with a mutual friend at the Sign of the Trader. It was an odd choice because Ev did not drink. He was a great storyteller and described his trip to the New York Produce Exchange (NYPE) in 1970, the year that currency futures trading began. Murray Borowitz, whose idea to launch a futures market on the Dow Jones Industrial Average (DJIA) was rejected by the SEC, recognized that the fall of Bretton Woods in 1971 presented an opportunity to start currency futures. The NYPE embraced Borowitz's idea and made him the non-executive chairman of the exchange, which was eventually renamed the International Commercial Exchange.

As Ev walked through the NYPE's dingy courtyard and unsuccessfully dodged some pigeon droppings, he was gradually convinced that the CME could do it much better. Ev then persuaded the CME to start these new contracts. The CME established the International Monetary Market and launched trading in seven currency futures on May 16, 1972. Trading volume was modest in the beginning. By 1975, total trading volume on the currency futures contract was modest. The New York Mercantile Exchange (NYMEX) also traded currency futures.

The only way to break into the large market was to find market makers who would make markets that were more profitable than the interbank market. At the time, banks refused to execute directly on the exchanges because they did not want the risk of financing the forward positions of traders and market makers who had less than desirable credit.

The Class B arbitrageur program, also created by Mark Powers from the CME, demonstrated a way for exchanges to circumvent this problem. By segregating all the forward and futures positions of designated member firms in a special account that the exchange was willing to monitor themselves, the banks were willing to open up direct lines of credit. The Class B arbitrageur transacted on the CME using arbitrages that set their bids and offers wider—bidding lower and offering higher than the bank. Whatever they transacted on the exchange could be flipped around for an immediate profit at the bank, given the pricing differential. For example, in the case that a bank forward price that was one bid at two offered, a Class B member would post a market of one bid at three offered. Once the program gained critical mass and the banks recognized the amount of money that Class B members were making, the banks began to arbitrage themselves. Everyone was now dealing with the same set of prices, thereby negating arbitrage opportunities. The CME had succeeded in delivering a valuable product to people who wanted to trade currencies but were not creditworthy to the banks. In doing so, they effectively reduced transaction costs for the public.

The CME's expertise in marketing was working with great effect. It had the same professional research and committee structure that fostered intelligent contract design and member marketing to locals, as well as nonmember hedgers and speculators.

When Mark Powers left the CME to join the CFTC, Frank Jones succeeded him as chief economist. Frank was a mild-mannered man with a bushy mustache. I had met him once before, when he was working for San Jose State and consulting for the Stanford Research Institute. He had arranged a meeting with me in 1976 when he first read about interest rate futures, and I gave him a walking tour of the CBOT trading floor during its busiest hour. He was enthralled by my vision of launching a futures market for long-term Treasury bonds.

Frank led the efforts to write the S&P and Eurodollar contracts. He left right before the contracts were listed when he received an offer to become the president of the New York Futures Exchange, a new subsidiary of the New York Stock Exchange. Rick Kilcollin succeeded Frank as Chief Economist. Chicago-centric staff and members took this as a great slight and in Frank's own words, he had been "ridden out of town on a rail car." Although Frank's name has been written out of the history of the exchange, his service to Chicago's markets remains unquestionable. Frank told me recently that the NYFE was doomed to failure, as the stock traders in New York didn't have the spirit or knowledge of their Chicago counterparts.

My friend Fred Arditti joined the CME as an economist in 1980, and left a legacy of creative innovation at the exchange.[3] He picked

[3] As chief economist of the CME from 1980 to 1982, Arditti pioneered the IMM Index upon which the CME Eurodollar futures contract was founded.

up where Frank left off. The public relations department had convinced the leading broadcast journalist on equities, Lou Rukeyser, to run a television show from the floor of the exchange in the S&P pit, where Fred and I made appearances as representatives of the exchange. Neither of us ever thought we would be there together.

I ended the year on the CME board having thoroughly experienced the culture of a different exchange. I also gained a fuller understanding of why the exchange's existing futures contracts were successful, as well as observed its efforts at promoting new products like Eurodollar and stock index futures.

Financing Entrepreneurs

In tandem with the continued growth in financial futures, there were interesting innovations being unleashed in the world of investment banking. Shortly after reestablishing the financial futures division at Drexel in April 1982, Fred Uhlmann and I went to New York to meet the Drexel management team. It was my first inside look at investment banking, fixed income, and stocks. I was a student again and enjoyed this thoroughly. Although I had been more focused on building financial futures as a marketer in the period from 1983 to 1989, I was also a student of all aspects of investment banking. Over the next few years, I attended and spoke about hedging interest rates at high-yield conferences organized by Michael "Mike" Milken. His intelligence, creativity, and energy were boundless.

Mike was a pioneer in commoditizing bank credit. The nature of fixed income markets, whereby investors were required to sell bonds if they fell below investment grade—pejoratively named junk bonds—coupled with an overreliance of creditworthiness in the sovereign and real estate markets, led to inefficiencies in the pricing of high-yield debt. To this day, there are too few who realize that without this type of financing, we would not enjoy many of the goods and services that we take for granted such as cell phones, cable TV, and competition among telephone companies.

At the conferences, I watched folks advocating an alternative to network broadcasting—Bill Malone promoted cable TV, media mogul

Ted Turner championed CNN as a 24-hour international network, Terry McGraw pushed cellular telephones, and Bill McGowan described MCI Communications as a new company that was competing with AT&T. The entertainment matched the themes of the conferences. Diana Ross not only sang, but offered us her career as a metaphor for how to excel and change with the times. Diana Ross started out with the Motown rock and roll group the Supremes, in the 1960s. After leaving the Supremes in the 1970s, she went on to win an Academy Award nomination and a Golden Globe award for her portrayal of Billie Holliday in *Lady Sings the Blues*. I later bought a photograph by Robert Frank of Billie Holiday performing at Independence Hall in Philadelphia.

The high-yield conferences emphasized that financial capital wasn't the scarce good. It was human capital and entrepreneurship that were scarce. I realized later that many conference attendees weren't simply trying to outperform a stock or bond index which was the trend at the time. They were simply trying to generate high absolute rates of return. Drexel was repackaging existing financial instruments and originating new ones. Convertible bonds were inefficient so Drexel issued bonds with warrants. Unbundling the equity and fixed income components of these bonds resulted in more efficient pricing. There were also some legal innovations. Drexel became the first investment bank to underwrite public debt for a private company. I also witnessed the fact that any type of financial arrangement could be turned into a bond. Payment-in-kind (PIK) bonds were one such example, where coupon payments came in the form of more bonds, as opposed to cash. The poison pill was first used by Drexel in a novel financing. Drexel issued zero-coupon bonds for one of its clients. There was one hitch. If the company was acquired, then the purchaser would have to pay the bondholders at par. That effectively ruled out any takeovers. Poison pills were then made routine by the legal profession. I learned an incredible amount about finance during these conferences and applied these lessons later on.

Above everything else perhaps, there was the idea that a market required a willing buyer and a willing seller, both of whom had to be found and nurtured. New financial markets are sold, not bought. They are not widely anticipated like the updated versions of the iPad.

Financial markets run on a limited number of professionals compared to the retail sector—in 2008, there were only 155,400 securities commodity contracts dealers, compared to the 4,489,200 retail salespersons—and like many new inventions, are rejected by those who benefit from the status quo.

New markets, whether financial futures or high-yield junk bonds, had an easy side and a difficult side when they first began. The easy side of financial futures was finding those who wanted protection against rising interest rates—the hedgers. The harder side was to find those who provided that protection—the speculators and those investors that wanted to hedge against lower interest rates. The magic lay in developing a contract that would induce both parties to transact with one another.

Mike Milken later pleaded guilty to violations of security laws and was punished accordingly. He subsequently went on to establish global conferences focusing on health, education, jobs and the environment. The conference ranks with Davos. The Milken Institute is a leading think tank and Fastcures is setting the pace on finding quicker cures for major diseases. There's an important lesson here. Financial skills and innovation can be extended to furthering social objectives.

Catering to a Global Market with Night Trading

Expanding Drexel's financial futures division across Europe and Japan led me to realize how financial and derivatives markets had become global. Going electronic meant 24-hour trading. I thought perhaps that the CBOT could be a first mover. In 1987, I helped push the CBOT into a new venture that failed. Earlier in 1984, when I was serving on the CME Board, an initiative called that mutual offset system was made, linking the CME and Singapore Exchange. This effort allowed market participants to open positions in one exchange and liquidate them on another. This linkage mechanism again was an indicator of the increasingly global nature of market participants and the universal appetite for financial innovation.

In the late 1980s, I thought adapting to this change of 24-hour trading could be a big opportunity for the CBOT. If interest rate futures traded during the nighttime in Chicago, which corresponded to daytime in Asia, business would expand dramatically.[4] There were fundamental shifts taking place in the U.S. Treasury market driven by larger structural changes in economies of the Far East. In particular, Japan had steadily emerged from an economy in shambles post-World War II into a major economic powerhouse. Its economy had transformed itself by relying on high-value auto and electronics exports. U.S. debt had become the global bellwether for interest rates. Japan had accumulated holdings in 26 percent of U.S. Treasury debt and was now exporting capital along with South Korea and Taiwan, affecting U.S. interest rates. Some Asian firms had even become primary dealers in U.S. government securities. The volatility of the government bond market had increased. The overnight risk of fixed income portfolios now matched daytime risk.[5] I believed the CBOT had no option but to adapt to these changes. The market might welcome a hedging and speculative medium in Treasury debt during its daytime hours.

The CBOT made its foray into night trading on April 30, 1987, launching a three-hour session that corresponded with the opening of the next trading day in Tokyo. The session was initially limited to trading the board's popular futures and options on Treasury bonds and notes. Expanded hours not only drew in new business from East Asia, but provided traders access to liquid overseas capital markets. Investors could now react immediately to news bulletins from Europe and Asia instead of catching up on news the morning after. The move to 24/7 trading on financial futures was an insomniac's dream come true.[6] Interest rate and currency risk existed 24 hours a day, and there should be a way to manage it cost-effectively.

Opening night reached an impressive volume of 42,953 contracts.[7] The night session ran Monday through Thursday, from 6 to 9 P.M. It

---

[4]J. J. Tindall, "Night Trading Heats Up," *Intermarkets*, September 1987, 41–43.

[5]Chicago Board of Trade, "Evening Hours," *Financial Futures Professional* 2, no. 5 (May 1987): 4.

[6]"Chicago: The New Mecca for Global Money Traders," *BusinessWeek,* April 30, 1984.

[7]Chicago Board of Trade, "Evening Hours," *Financial Futures Professional* 2, no. 5 (May 1987): 4.

did not run on Sunday. I strongly favored opening on Sunday night, which was Monday morning in Tokyo, but my arguments fell on deaf ears. I thought, "This is like opening a shoe store and not inviting Imelda Marcos!"[8] Some worried that locals would not be able to—or have any incentive to—adapt to late-night trading. However, I believed that there were plenty of people who wanted the opportunity to become floor traders—not to mention the prospects of making more money. Night trading volume was averaging 14,350 contracts when the CBOT launched its first Sunday night session on September 13, 1987.[9]

Despite some modest success, the night session still suffered from political resistance and was closed down. We would have to wait for electronic trading to ensure Chicago's preeminence as the center of futures trading.

The Attack on Equity Derivatives—Wet Sidewalks Cause Rain

The 1980s ended on a less than optimistic note for Chicago and financial futures. When the stock market crashed in October 1987, Chicago futures markets became the scapegoat. Program trading and arbitrageurs of the futures and stock markets were widely blamed for the decline in the futures market, as every time the futures went down, arbitrageurs bought futures contracts and sold the actual stocks, exacerbating the decline in futures markets. Portfolio insurance,[10] a technical term for the creation of synthetic puts, only exacerbated the decline. In both instances, prices were jointly determined on the stock

[8] Wife of the tenth Philippine president, Ferdinand Marcos, rumored to have had 2,700 pairs of shoes.

[9] Jane Goldenberg, "A New Era for Investors," *Money Maker*, December 1987–January 1988.

[10] "Portfolio insurance: a trading strategy that uses stock index futures or stock index options to protect stock portfolios against market declines."—CFTC Glossary.

and futures exchanges. When futures traded above or below fair value, arbitrageurs provided the link between the spot and futures markets. It was often the same investment banks and investors operating simultaneously in both markets. These were technical arguments that failed to get the resonance that they deserved in the press and in Washington. It was essentially a situation in which the tail was wagging the dog.[11] In fact, the dog had just moved to Chicago. Spot and futures markets were jointly determined and should never be thought of as unlinked.

Chicago's aura of nobility came to a grinding halt in 1988. The FBI had planted agents in the trading pits at both the CBOT and the CME, and had discovered widespread abuses. Dozens of traders were indicted. These traders failed to follow the principles that these markets were based on, which was competition and not collusion. It was a tragic time for the city of Chicago.

Exchanges learned their lesson and tightened their internal compliance procedures. It seemed odd, given the fact that all of this could have been prevented had trading been done electronically. With an electronic audit trail, one could monitor the positions of every single trader. In fact, this is one of the most powerful arguments in favor of electronic trading.

The Demise of Drexel

Financial futures business continued to grow at Drexel in 1989, despite serious allegations of insider trading in the investment banking and high-yield departments. Allegations were often given widespread press coverage. Some of this was probably fed by the "outsider" nature of the bank. The firm had a shroud over its head. Customers were defecting and employees were resigning. John Shad, former SEC chairman, was ushered in as chairman by the U.S. Department of Justice. John was a man of impeccable integrity, and I was optimistic that his appointment would help steady the firm.

In the midst of the crisis, one of my colleagues quipped to me that he wanted to be the last person out of the firm. When I asked him why,

---

[11]A case in which a subordinate part controls the whole.

he answered, "The first people would be crushed in the revolving door by the stampede of people leaving." It was time for gallows humor.

It was the Memorial Day weekend of 1989 when the head of the fixed income and international division asked if I wanted to replace him. I knew it was going to be a big job. Fixed income included governments bonds, mortgage-backed bonds, municipal bonds, high-grade corporate bonds, derivatives, and international fixed income. The current head was consumed by the crisis and needed someone else to manage sales and trading.

I took the job. The fixed income division was hemorrhaging money. Our lines of credit were tightened, and there were limits placed on our trading. In many ways, it was emotionally wrenching. I had to ask for hundreds of resignations. The traders would joke with the punch line, "Here comes Freddie," out of the movie *Nightmare on Elm Street*.

Some of the firm's leadership was living in a fantasy world. My colleagues offered a barrage of tactics during the crisis, whether it meant contacting our elected representatives or advertising about the 10,000 honest and hard-working people in the firm. I was feeling a lot better by the beginning of February 1990. We had turned the corner in fixed income. We went from losing $20 million a month to an $8 million profit that January. With a reduced headcount and a refocus of the business to high-margin business, better days were ahead of us.

The CEO asked me to take a trip to our main offices around the world to share the good news of our profitability. I went to our main offices in Europe and then to Japan. I arrived back in Chicago one late Saturday morning. The phone rang. It was the CEO. He wanted me to come to New York that afternoon. I explained that my close friend Les Rosenthal's son was getting married that night, and asked if I could come first thing Sunday morning.

I went to the wedding that night with a sense of impending doom. At one point, Les got up on stage, holding a black sheep in tribute to his son who had proclaimed himself the black sheep of the family. Not more than a few seconds later, a stream of urine spattered from the frightened animal. The crowd burst into hysterics. I was back in Chicago among friends, and all would be well.

I flew to New York and went to the offices of our lawyers at around 1 P.M. I began looking at all of the financial statements, inventories, and bank lines. People had been discussing these since Friday night. Our banks had either eliminated or reduced all credit lines. I reached the inevitable conclusion that we had to declare bankruptcy at the holding company, so that there would be an orderly process of liquidation. It was the only thing to do in order to avoid losses for the clients of the firm. We had about $1 billion in equity, but like all financial institutions, were leveraged at about 10 or 15 to 1. This was conservative by today's standards. Our inventory was highly illiquid given the concentration of inventory in the high-yield department.

That night shaped my understanding of the 2008 financial crisis. Financial institutions go bankrupt, not from negative equity, but from having illiquid assets. Our goal as a management team, and my personal goal, from now on was simple. Protect the customers and debt holders, and maximize the remaining shareholder value.

At around 6 P.M., a colleague asked me, "Where does the food chain begin?" I turned to him and said, "Divorce lawyers." As the door opened, four of the dourest men I had ever seen walked toward the table, and my colleague said, "No, it starts with bankruptcy lawyers." He had predicted the bankruptcy would end when we ran out of money to pay the lawyers. This was close to true. Seventy-five percent of the equity was eliminated over the next six years. A lot of it belonged to me and the senior management team.

The good will from my work in Paris on the MATIF and a decade of developing good relationships helped me land the position of head of North American Capital Markets at Banque Indosuez in Chicago. It took about two hellish months for me to find new homes for my original team. I finally found homes for over 100 people in my combined team of listed derivatives, swaps, and structured finance. To ensure that none of our clients at Drexel lost any money, all long-term interest rate swap agreements were terminated on mutually agreeable terms. The swaps group at Drexel held one of the largest positions in the Eurodollar futures contract. I worked with Bill Brodsky at the CME in the following month to ensure that our positions were liquidated in an orderly fashion. This was no trivial feat. As a result of our careful maneuver, all our clients were grateful and followed us to

Banque Indosuez, where we were able to found a successful futures and swaps business. Trust and individual relationships were an integral part of markets.

I lived a two-city life, commuting back and forth between Chicago and New York, until our new business at Banque Indosuez took off. The Banque Indosuez office was located right near Radio City Music Hall. The area brought back memories from my childhood. When I was nine years old, my father announced that we were going to the Radio City Christmas Spectacular in Radio City Music Hall. It was a memorable day. Radio City Music Hall was an art deco building designed by architect Edward Durrell Stone, completed in 1932. I could hardly believe my eyes when I saw the 6,000-seat theatre. As a small boy, everything seemed to be strangely magnified. The extravaganza was a musical revue that featured a precision dance team known as the Rockettes. I remember my father being so happy. It was the epitome of upscale, modernized vaudeville.

Shortly after arriving at my new office one day, I got a visit that would change the course of my career for the next 20 years.

Chapter 10

Environmental Finance

My salad days, when I was green in judgement.

—*William Shakespeare,* Anthony and Cleopatra

Phil Senechal was a member of the Coalition for Acid Rain Equity (CARE), a not-for-profit public interest group advocating cap-and-trade. He wanted cap-and-trade to be included in the proposed Clean Air Act and its amendments (CAAA) that were being drafted by Congress in 1990. Phil was politically savvy and very likeable. He owned a business that sold lime, a critical mineral in the chemical process known as scrubbing, the process that removes sulfur from the power plant emissions, thereby preventing it from escaping into the atmosphere. When sulfur enters the atmosphere, it combines with the oxygen to produce SO_2, and the SO_2 then combines with clouds and rain to produce acid rain.

Phil came to the Banque Indosuez office one day and asked, "I know you've commoditized interest rates. Can you do it for air?"

The Acid Rain Problem in the United States

As a result of the significant increase in coal-fired electricity in the post–World War II period, the United States had reached annual SO_2 emissions of about 18 million tons. Most of it was concentrated in the Midwest and Northeast, where environmental and health effects were acute. Lung disease was increasing, rivers were being acidified which threatened the marine ecosystem, and forests were being defoliated. Not surprisingly, the public had begun clamoring for a reduction in emissions.

There were two policy options to reduce acid rain: command and control (CAC) or flexible mechanisms. CAC in its simplest form required every utility to reduce emissions by a certain amount, for example, 20 percent. In a more complex form, it might require different types of remediation at each and every power plant, that is, installation of scrubbers at one plant, and switching from high sulfur coal to low sulfur coal at another plant. In either case, it would take a significant amount of time and resources to formulate and implement these regulations, significantly increasing costs associated with SO_2 reductions. These costs in turn would be passed on to consumers in the form of higher electricity prices.

The other option, flexible mechanisms, consisted of taxes and/or subsidies, or something more dynamic like emissions trading, that is, cap-and-trade. The concept of emissions trading was especially intriguing to me because it had its roots in Ronald Coase's theory of social cost[1] (fully articulated by J. H. Dales).[2] Social costs are costs not borne by the company producing the good/service. For example, the wheels of a train running through a corn field throw off sparks, which causes damage to the corn crops. This constitutes a social cost, that is, a cost not paid for by the train operator. Water pollution is another example, be it a refinery discharging toxic chemicals in a lake, or a wastewater

[1]Coase argued that legal rules are justified in the real world where there are costs of bargaining and information gathering, to the extent that these rules can allocate rights to the most efficient right-bearer. By extension, an emissions trading scheme permits emissions to first be reduced in areas where the marginal costs are the least or by those who can most afford to reduce their emissions.

[2]J. H. Dales, *Pollution, Property and Prices* (Toronto, Canada: University of Toronto Press, 1968).

The Problem of Social Costs: Trading as a Solution

The case of a train running through corn fields illustrates the concept of externalities. The train operator's profit from the economic activity is the total revenues minus operating costs such as fuel and wages. The numeric example illustrates the revenue and costs associated with each run. To maximize profits, the train operator will make three runs. Economists refer to this point as the private optimum.

There are other costs associated with the train running through the corn field. For example, the noise may be considered a nuisance or it may tarnish the scenic farm setting. Sparks from the train tracks may be a fire hazard to the corn crop. Economists refer to these consequences as "externalities." They pose additional societal costs. The presence of externalities suggests that the social optimum may be different from the private optimum.

To illustrate, let us further assume the cost of the externality with each incremental train run as shown in Table 10.1. The social optimum, the point where society maximizes its profit is two runs, different from the private optimum of three runs. The column titled "Societal Gain" in Table 10.1 represents the net gain/loss to society by taking into account the private profit of the train operator and the social cost to the farmer.

In the absence of a legal requirement or mandate, the train operator has no incentive to stop at the social optimum but to

Table 10.1 Examining the Revenue of Train Owner versus Farmer

Train Runs/Day	Revenues/ Run	Costs/ Run	Profits	Cost to Farmer (externalities)/ Run	Societal Gain
1	350	$100	$250	$200	$50
2	350	$100	$250	$200	**$50
3	350	$200	*$150	$200	($50)

*Private Optimum
**Social Optimum

(*continued*)

The Problem of Social Costs: Trading as a Solution (*Continued*)

proceed to operate at his private optimum. One solution to this problem is for a regulator, say the government, restricting the train operator to two runs. This is relatively simple if the regulator can easily measure the damage the trains are causing to the farm. They could theoretically rely on the corn farmer to give reliable loss estimates, but what is to stop the corn farmer from over-reporting the actual costs? The regulator frequently faces the problem of insufficient and asymmetric information, as well as moral hazard.

Suppose bargaining or trading was permitted. The farmers will pay for the train not to make the third run, as the cost to the farmer from third run, \$200, exceeds the profits made by the train owner, \$150. Trading allows prices, and therefore, true costs, to reveal themselves through private market forces and therefore eliminates the problem of asymmetric information.

One easy way to think about social optimum is by viewing the farmer and operator as one person with profit-maximizing behavior. If one owned both enterprises then the optimum number of runs would be two runs.

treatment plant pumping nitrogen into rivers. Trading, or bargaining, was a way to achieve the right social objective.

With cap-and-trade, companies are given predetermined rights to emit, called allowances. If the plant emitted less pollutants than afforded by its rights, the excess rights could be sold to another plant that has insufficient rights to emit. A systematic cap ensures that targeted pollution levels are achieved. The cap is reduced over time, for example, every year fewer allowances are issued. Cap-and-trade incentivizes the low-cost producer of reductions to cut more than is required and thereby sell the benefits to the high-cost producer of benefits. As a result, both emitter utilities will be better off. Since economy-wide reductions occur at the lowest cost, the economy as a whole will also be better off.

Cap-and-Trade

A utility is given a predetermined number of allowances to emit called allowances, that is, one allowance is equal to one ton of SO_2. These rights to emit are annually distributed by the Environmental Protection Agency (EPA). If a utility emits less than the amount allotted to it, it can sell its surplus allowances to another utility that has emitted more than the allowances it has, or bank them for later use. As long as the cost of achieving an additional unit of reduction differs among utilities, there will be gains from trade.

Let's take a simple numerical example. Suppose there are two utilities that each emit 100,000 tons of SO_2 annually. The law requires that they reduce emissions by 10 percent, or 10,000 tons each. Let us further assume that Utility A can reduce emissions at a cost of $200 per ton, and Utility B at a cost of $600 per ton. Under a command and control option, the cost of compliance for Utility A would be $2 million (10,000 × $200), and the cost to Utility B would be $6 million (10,000 × $600). The total cost to the economy would then be $8 million ($2 million + $6 million).

Now, suppose that trading were allowed. If the utilities agree to trade at price somewhere above $200 but below $600, both would be better off, and there would be a reduced cost to the economy. For example, if the utilities agree to a price of $400, then Utility A would reduce emissions by 20,000 tons, instead of required 10,000 tons, and sell the extra 10,000 tons to Utility B. Utility A would be in compliance at no cost—revenue of $4 million less costs of $4 million. Utility B, on the other hand, incurs costs of $4 million. As noted earlier, had Utility B made the cuts themselves, their costs would have been $6 million. Thus, Utility B is better off as well. What about the cost to the economy? It would be $4 million instead of the $8 million under command and control. In a scenario in which Utility A can do this quickly and Utility B would have to wait years to change the technology, trading makes everybody better off.

The Clean Air Act Amendment of 1990

Lime producers like Phil favored emissions reduction legislation because they believed it would increase their business and cost-effectively reduce acid rain. He asked me to author a paper on the subject. I wasn't an environmentalist, but was intrigued in using whatever skills I had to find a market-based solution to environmental problems. After the meeting, I immediately called Jon Goldstein, my former colleague at the University of Minnesota, who for years had been urging me to pursue environmental economics. "This is very important," Jon said. "You have to get involved."

I read about the first-ever application of cap-and-trade. It was the phasing out of lead-based gasoline in 1982.[3] The program was successful and I suspected that it could be implemented on a larger scale for SO_2.

I wrote the paper and made several trips to Washington with Phil to advocate passage of the bill. My experience at the CBOT working on the Act that enabled the CFTC was very valuable. Our task was made easier by the fact that the environmental community had already worked on getting cap-and-trade into the clean air legislation and had explained the concept to many congressmen, senators, and their staffers. The congressman and senators in the environmental committees were heartened by the interest of the CBOT. I also spoke to members of the Senate Agriculture committees about my belief in cap-and-trade. If we drew up a futures contract, it would fall under their regulatory auspices. They too, were very receptive to the idea of emissions trading.

---

[3]The EPA launched a trading scheme for lead use across refineries in 1982. The "cap" was set at 1.1. gram of lead per gallon. Companies were able to sell and buy lead rights to meet their needs. This trading scheme also included the banking feature so that refineries that reduced more than they needed to could store the lead rights for later use. EPA analysis showed that the program resulted in an estimated savings of about $250 million per year. See Joel Schwartz, Hugh Pitcher, Ronnie Levin, Bart Ostro, and Albert L. Nichols, "Costs and Benefits of Reducing Lead in Gasoline: Final Regulatory Impact Analysis, Economic Analysis Division," U.S. EPA, February 1985.

The Clean Air Act Amendment, passed in 1990, sought to reduce SO_2 emissions by 10 million tons from 1980 levels. The reduction program was divided into two phases. The first phase began in 1995, and the second phase in 2000. What was notable about this program was its inclusion of trading of emissions allowances. The affected units could emit SO_2 only if they have enough permits to cover these emissions. Although one can definitely infer a cap-and-trade scheme from the descriptions in the law, the word *trade* was never mentioned.

Although the law explicitly stated that emission allowances did not constitute property rights—they were only recognized as "quasi property rights"—and could be confiscated by the state at any time, the ambiguity did not really affect trading in the beginning. It would later turn into a financial disaster for utilities in the country.

Separately, the accounting and tax treatment of allowances was not specified in the Act.

A lot of the congressional debate centered on whether allowances should be distributed on the basis of historical or current emissions. The latter was chosen. In addition, bonus allowances were granted to entities who installed clean technology. The debate on the distribution of allowances was important from the standpoint of equity. It wasn't important for its efficacy. Economists believed that the initial allocation of resources was irrelevant to achieving the economic goal—that of reducing emissions of SO_2 at the lowest cost to the economy—provided that transaction costs were low.

The bill enjoyed wide support in both the Senate and the House. It passed by 89-11, and 401-21, respectively, and was ratified by President George H. W. Bush on November 15, 1990.

Starting Over

Business was terrific back at Banque Indosuez. Although the structured finance, swaps, and financial futures team consisted of only 100 of 17,000 people at the firm, we were making about 15 percent of the bank's worldwide profits. The year 1990 ended far better than it had started. I had avoided a near-death career experience at Drexel and was starting to explore new markets. New York was treating me well professionally. I didn't realize at first, but it also enriched my personal life considerably.

My younger daughter, Penya, had contracted mononucleosis shortly after beginning her freshman year at the University of Wisconsin. Much to my chagrin, she dropped out of college and moved to New York. However, Penya was very resourceful and landed a job as a writer of an internal newsletter at a large New York law firm. She went back to study history at New York University. When I moved to New York, she gave up her apartment and became my roommate.

I had always worked 10 to 12 hours a day and traveled incessantly. I regretted missing a lot of my daughter's childhood. Fortunately, now as adults, Penya and I had a chance to get to know each other. We frequented restaurants and movies. I also got to really know the man she eventually married, Eric Taub.

Eric grew up in New York and attended Tufts University. Penya and he met in France on a summer program and fell in love. Eric was a deeply empathetic man who enjoyed sports, books, and movies. Penya's passion for poetry introduced him to a whole new world. Penya went on to Sarah Lawrence to get an MFA and become a published poet, while Eric went NYU to get an MBA, and went on to work in the capital markets. I had a lot of fun spending time with both of them. Eric and Penya eventually settled in Atlanta, where Eric works for a hedge fund and Penya started an online Poetry Journal called the Redneck Review of Literature.

Ellen joined us in New York on weekends when I didn't go back to Chicago. We all loved those times. But that wasn't all. My older daughter, Julie, studied for her master's in cinema studies at NYU and moved in with me too. What a hoot to go to movies with her. She was living a dream of mine. Jack Ludden, her boyfriend from Northwestern, was studying for his MFA at the Art Institute of Chicago in Art and Technology. I consider myself lucky to have a son-in-law who shares my passion for art, and another who I can discuss capital markets with. Jack often came to visit Julie in New York. She moved back to Northwestern and received a PhD there. Together, they moved to Los Angeles where they were able to seamlessly fuse art with technology—she produced movies and games and he became the producer of the website at the Getty Museum. It couldn't have been better—Ellen, my two daughters, and their prospective husbands enjoying New York together.

I never enjoyed fatherhood as much.

On the business front, I was continually negotiating my contract with my boss at Banque Indosuez. We had negotiated a deal that gave me and my team a fixed percentage of the bottom line of our operations. It wasn't too long before many in my team were making more money than the CEO. This was not sustainable.

In 1990, I received a call from a search firm asking if I was interested in being the head of fixed income for Kidder, Peabody & Company. Kidder wouldn't hire my team of more than 100 people, so I declined the offer. About a year later, they called again. This time the offer was different. I would be responsible for swaps, structured products, energy trading, and service on the firm's five-man executive committee. The CEO of Kidder thought we might be able to set up an AAA-rated swaps subsidiary under the General Electric flag. I couldn't pull the trigger a year before but knew that the time was ripe now.

Since I would be starting at a very senior level, the CEO wanted me to meet Jack Welch. I was both excited and nervous about meeting a man who, even in those days, was considered to be the top CEO in the world.

Jack Welch and Kidder, Peabody

I went to Fairfield, Connecticut to meet with Jack Welch. Within seconds of our introduction, Jack said matter-of-factly, "With all the success you've had, why haven't you retired?" I responded, "I love to compete, but hate to lose." It was a trait I discovered while playing chess. This answer seemed to satisfy Jack, for he went on to ask me more questions about my background. As we talked about my experience running the fixed income department at Drexel, he asked, "What is the most money your unit ever lost in a day?" I told him that one day when the markets had gone wild over some news event, the losses were just under $5 million. I explained that I had attempted to keep the risk profile at about $2 to $3 million in a day. It wasn't my approach to speculate with the firm's capital. I was there to service customers' needs, whether current or anticipated, and build inventories accordingly. Jack liked my approach to business.

As the interview came to a close, I asked Jack if there would be opportunities to work with other parts of the company. He told me that Kidder was just a small part of the company, and that it would be great if I could help GE in other ways.

As the meeting concluded and we got up to leave, Jack looked me squarely in the eyes before saying something like, "Don't you ever come in this office and tell me you've lost $10 or $20 million in a day." His actual language was laced with profanities. I took his admonitions seriously.

I joined Kidder, Peabody on May 13, 1991. The organized corporate culture at Kidder, Peabody was very different from the less structured entrepreneurial cultures I was accustomed to. Kidder held regular executive committee meetings as well as corporate events. I was invited to an annual meeting of the 300 top people in the General Electric company. It was fascinating to meet and speak with the CEOs of GE Capital and the head of the divisions that produced jet engines, medical equipment, and appliances divisions, among others. My career so far had allowed me to learn about inventive activity at exchanges. Through GE, I hoped to learn more about inventive activity in a corporate environment.

The CBOT's Role in the EPA Acid Rain Program

When William F. "Billy" O'Connor was elected as chairman of the CBOT in 1990, I knew the time was ripe to once again get involved with the exchange. Billy was an innovator who encouraged new ideas.

I was elected to the CBOT board of directors at the end of 1990, under Billy's chairmanship. When the Clean Air Act Amendment of 1990 passed, I asked Billy to form what I termed the Clean Air Committee. My research had suggested that a futures market in SO_2 allowances was potentially as big as wheat futures. It had the potential to benefit America, and Billy thought that a market solution to acid rain was a great idea.

When he brought up the idea at the first meeting of the new board, a number of former chairmen and independent directors such as Governor Jim Thompson of Illinois volunteered to serve on the committee.

While at Kidder, I worked on the SO_2 allowance market on the CBOT's behalf. Clean air emission allowance regulations were being formulated, and I saw a big opportunity for the CBOT and Kidder, Peabody. The Clean Air Act Amendment of 1990 merely played the role of enabling cap-and-trade, just as the CFTC Act of 1974 had enabled the creation of an independent federal regulatory agency with exclusive jurisdiction over commodity futures transactions. It remained up to the EPA to come up with the specific regulations.

I was on the Acid Rain Advisory Committee of the EPA at the time, and it did not take me long to realize that there was a paucity of knowledge about capital markets on the committee. I had to explain some of the basics of capital markets, such as CUSIP numbers[4] and the need for a registry.

The EPA had been publishing emissions on an annual rather than quarterly basis. The emissions were measured using Continuous Emissions Monitors (CEMs), which were installed at the smokestacks. The implementation of the Act called for annual reporting of emissions. I respectfully suggested that infrequent reporting would lead to the problem of asymmetric information, whereby the hedgers—utilities in this case—had easy access to how much they emitted while the speculators did not, giving the utilities an unfair advantage. This issue was of utmost importance as it contributed to the transparency of the market. I spoke to Billy O'Connor about this and he shared my feelings. "I won't trade anything without information about supply," he said, "it's hard enough to trade when you do have information."

I asked Governor Jim Thompson if he could arrange a meeting with Bill Reilly, the head of the EPA. Jim not only arranged but also accompanied me to the meeting, where Bill and one of his staff, Nancy Kete, waited for us. Smart and unconventional, Nancy was a member of a band composed of engineers and scientists while in

[4]A CUSIP number is a unique nine-character code, containing both letters and numbers, used to identify securities.

graduate school. She became an ally in the years to come in a very significant way. Nancy too, felt that the mandated requirement to report emissions on an annual basis should be changed. She sought technical opinion on the matter and our views regarding the quarterly reporting of CEMs eventually prevailed. Enabled by today's newer technology, emissions are reported on an hourly basis.

At Jim's suggestion, we went to visit the head of the Council of Economic Advisors. He was conversant with the concept of cap-and-trade and was a big supporter of this policy tool. To this day, I reflect on the top to bottom Republican support of emissions trading and wonder where all the flowers have gone.

GE manufactured scrubbers and there was an opportunity to learn more and help the parent company too. It was exciting to see great opportunities for synergies for everyone. I recommended that the CBOT submit a proposal to the U.S. Environmental Protection Agency (EPA) asking that the exchange be appointed administrator for the emission allowance auctions.

Under the Clean Air Act Amendment of 1990, the EPA was required to withhold 2.8 percent of total SO_2 emission allowances and auction them annually. These auctions served a dual purpose. They provided a source of allowances for new entrants and sent a price signal to the market. The proceeds from the auctions were distributed back to the utilities.

The EPA awarded the right to conduct the annual SO_2 auction to the CBOT. The EPA had chosen the CBOT over the New York Mercantile Exchange and a brokerage firm, Cantor Fitzgerald, which also sought to administer the auction. By awarding the auction to the private sector, the EPA could concentrate on ensuring that the required pollution cuts occurred on time. It was an intelligent division of labor. The auctions were a terrific idea and helped the market develop.

The First EPA Annual SO_2 Auction

The first annual auction was held in March 1993. I acted as the spokesperson at the event, while Mike Walsh announced the results of the auction. When we formed the auction committee, I asked the CEO if he would assign Mike Walsh to work with us. Mike had received his PhD from Michigan State, worked at the Treasury department, and then taught at Notre Dame. I first saw him give a speech in Washington at a CBOT event. Persuasive and witty, Mike was terrific on the podium. I made a mental note to try to work with him in the future.

I invited Professor Coase to speak at the event and he graciously accepted. Most of the bids in the 1993 auction came from major U.S. utilities, who were the largest SO_2 polluters. Illinois Power, for example, was a utility that released about 240,000 tons of SO_2 annually and was unable to operate on the 171,000 permits allocated to them by the EPA under the Acid Rain Program. Convinced that the cost of abatement was greater than the expected outlay to purchase permits, they submitted bids for 5,000 permits.

Although the bidding process was dominated by utilities, there was one not-for-profit group called National Healthy Air License Exchange (NHALE). According to the group's president, any permits bought in the auction would be retired and kept off the market. They submitted bids for 1,100 permits but came away with only one, for which it paid $350. This is an example of how emissions trading enables private citizens to influence environmental policy—a lesson that is often lost among later environmentalists.

Overall, rights to emit the 150,000 tons of SO_2 were purchased by utilities, brokers, and environmentalists for a total of $21 million. Permit prices ranged from $122 to $450. The largest single purchase was Carolina Power & Light Company, a utility that bid for, and won, over 85,000 permits.[5]

We were all pleased about the results of the auction and the amount of press coverage the exchange received. As expected, almost every victory was accompanied by some frustration. Successful auctions were often derided by headlines such as "Smut Traders" or "Dirt Traders." At the corner of Jackson and LaSalle, marchers from Greenpeace chanted, "Trading pollution is not the solution!" Some environmentalists prefer

[5]Facts about the bidders were adapted from Scott J. Callan and Janet M. Thomas, *Environmental Economics and Management: Theory, Policy, and Applications*, 4th ed. (Mason, OH: Thomson South-Western, 2007).

command-and-control methods and were arguably more interested in punishing polluters than in reducing pollution. In my opinion, moral arguments like that were better left to church on Sunday. I was more interested in achieving the environmental objective at the lowest cost to the economy.

I continued to attend or chair the CBOT and EPA annual allowance auction. The years 1995 and 1996 turned out to be extraordinary. Among the winning bidders in the auction was a fifth-grade class from Glens Falls, New York, whose class assignment was to learn as much as possible about the prevalent acid rain problem in their state. Students studied the impact of sulfur emissions on lung disease, and the effects of acid rain on forests, rivers, and streams. Their teacher posed the question, "What would you like to do to help solve the problem of acid rain?" The class responded creatively. They wanted to buy SO_2 allowances at the CBOT auction and then give them to the American Lung Association to be permanently retired. The problem that the class faced was how to raise the money.

Their solution was a stroke of genius. They decided to have a cap-and-trade market for chewing gum allowances. Students were given a fixed amount of chewing gum allowances. If they did not use their allotments, they could sell them to fellow students. If students wanted to chew more than their allotment, then they purchased more allowances in the market. They had proved savvy in what were the basic elements of emissions trading.

If 10-year-olds in a fifth-grade class could understand the power of markets and successfully implement one, then surely no CEO or congressman could ever say they didn't get it. Sadly, I was wrong.

Shortly after the first auction, the exchange proposed that the CBOT and its clearing corporation, the Board of Trade Clearing Corporation (BOTCC), establish an electronic depository for emission allowances. The exchange was also advised to set up an allowance tracking system that could be used to evaluate the early action metric (EAM), which was designed to reward firms that had taken initiatives to reduce emissions before the start of, or during, Phase I of the Acid Rain Program. Moreover, the CBOT built a network-based cash trading facility that provided order-matching, and developed a bulletin board system for the dissemination of SO_2 prices. The facility would permit trading of standardized and customized spot and forward transactions. The BOTCC also provided a pay-and-collect system[6] and allowance transfer services for such trades.

As the chairman of BOTCC, Bill O'Connor was not only profoundly interested in extending the role of BOTCC, but also in enhancing the CBOT's competitive position by developing an electronic trading platform. Had the CBOT been more persistent in these efforts, electronic trading might have made an earlier foray into OTC markets. I often mused to my colleagues, "If Billy had his way, then the damage caused by the 2008 financial crisis might have been mitigated, if not eliminated altogether!" In fact, a centrally cleared electronic platform for OTC markets is now a requirement under the Dodd-Frank Wall Street Reform and Consumer Protection Act, also known simply as the "Dodd-Frank," for which the broad objective is to restore responsibility and accountability in the U.S. financial system.

When the CBOT researchers finally submitted a futures contract proposal on SO_2 allowances to the CFTC, the stage had already been set. The appropriate monitoring and verification program that guaranteed the standardization of the SO_2 allowance were already instituted. The BOTCC registry provided an easy method for transferring ownership, contributing to the liquidity of the market. Price volatility—another determinant of a successful futures market that amplified the need to hedge—also appeared to be present. Cold winters required utilities to burn more coal and therefore emit more sulfur, while hot summers ensured the opposite. The levels of coal burned also varied according to general economic conditions. A strong economy meant higher levels of output, greater use of electricity, and therefore more burning of coal. Additionally, the cost of scrubbing technology was estimated to fluctuate between $400 and $800 per ton. The following lists the salient features of the final contract.[7]

---

[6]A pay-and-collect system handled the payment and collection of funds after futures positions were marked to market between clearing members and clearinghouses.

[7]Richard L. Sandor, "CBOT Proposes Clean Air Futures for Emission Allowance Risk Management," *Financial Exchange*, September–October 1991.

Salient Features CBOT Clean Air Allowance Futures

Units of Trading: The contract unit shall be 25 one-ton SO_2 emissions allowances.

Standards: Deliverable allowances shall be issued by the United States Environmental Protection Agency (EPA) and registered by the Board of Trade Clearing Corporation (BOTCC). Deliverable allowances shall be applicable against emissions in the current and future years.

Months Traded In: Trading in SO_2 allowance futures may be conducted in the current month and the next 11 months plus quarterly listings in the March, June, September, and December cycle for up to three years from the current month.

Price Basis: Minimum price fluctuations shall be in multiples of $1.00 per allowance.

Hours of Trading: Hours of trading shall be 8:50 A.M. to 2:10 P.M. Central Time.

Trading Limits: Daily trading limits shall be $100 per allowance, or $2,500 per contract. Variable limits shall be $150 per allowance, or $3,750 per contract. No limits shall be in effect for the current month.

Last Day of Trading: No trades in SO_2 allowance futures deliverable in the current month shall be made during the last three business days of the month.

Delivery: Delivery shall be by book entry on the ownership records of the BOTCC Corporation SO_2 Allowance Depository.

Position Limits: Speculative position limits shall be 2,000 contracts in the current month and 5,000 contracts overall.

Since the contract was eventually approved by the CFTC, it may come as a surprise that the the CBOT decided not to list a SO_2 contract after all. Partly due to the failure of the CBOT to list a futures contract on SO_2, the SO_2 market gradually became a brokered OTC market whose user base became increasingly dominated by utilities that had established relationships with the SO_2 allowance brokers. The story of how it came to the decision not to capitalize on all that was already in place to facilitate the SO_2 market—the monitoring and verification programs, the BOTCC registry, the success of the SO_2 auction, and the proof of SO_2 price fluctuation—is a sad one. After Billy left, nobody emerged as a champion for the environment.

Chapter 11

Blame It on Rio

The day it arrives, it will arrive. It could be today or 50 years later. The only sure thing is that it will arrive.

—*Ayrton Senna*

In November 1991, the CBOT research department received a call from the United Nations Committee on Trade and Development (UNCTAD), which was planning a meeting in December at its headquarters in Geneva. UNCTAD wanted to take an active role in climate change and was interested in the CBOT's experience with SO_2 emission trading, and its implications for market-based solution to global warming. The organization wanted somebody from the exchange to explain emissions trading and describe how markets are created. Given my experience in creating markets, they thought I could contribute to their efforts.

The meeting was held in a small, spartan room at the UNCTAD headquarters. The modest location did not foretell the intellectual heft of the meeting, and I soon found myself engaged as a serious group of scholars animatedly discussed the role of markets in addressing global warming.

During the meeting, I spoke with Tom Tietenberg and Michael Grubb, who were experts in environmental economics.[1] They were especially interested in the practical process of creating the market architecture for an emissions market. I was told that there was already a broad base of scientists who believed in the imminent dangers of global warming and saw a cap-and-trade program for CO_2 as the solution. However, many did not realize that this required a market architecture that was much more complex than the one created for SO_2, which had been merely a regional pollutant. My practical experience was a useful complement to the research of the other economists at the meeting.

After a long session of meetings, the UNCTAD officer told me that the group wanted me to deliver a paper at the Earth Summit in Rio de Janeiro in June 1992. At that meeting in Geneva, I realized that there was another commodity far more important than any physical commodity or regional pollutant—the atmosphere. The atmospheric balance could be restored if only we could price the right to emit CO_2. The amount of CO_2 allowances would be capped, and the cap would also be lowered over time. This produced scarcity and price would be determined by factors such as weather, prices of competing fossil fuels, and levels of economic activity.

The United Nations Conference on Environment and Development (UNCED) was scheduled to take place from June 3 to June 14 in Rio de Janeiro, Brazil. I worked on my paper for the next six months. In fact, I was still putting the finishing touches on it as we landed in Rio. This was my first experience at a UN meeting and I didn't know what to expect.

---

[1]Thomas H. Tietenberg has authored multiple books on environmental economics and emissions trading. In addition to serving as an environmental policy consultant to the World Bank, he has served as a director at the U.S. Federal Energy Administration.

Michael Grubb is a professor of climate change and energy policy at Imperial College London, whose research and publications center around the economics of climate change. He is a member of the UK's Committee on Climate Change and an adviser to the United National Programme.

Biographies adapted from "About the Authors," in Richard L. Sandor, "In Search of the Trees: Market Architecture and Tradeable Entitlements for CO_2 Abatement," United Nations Conference on Trade and Development, 1993.

I remember being very excited about visiting South America in general and Brazil in particular. Movies had helped me form a romantic image of the continent: Charlton Heston as a plantation owner in Peru fighting to save his land from ants after taming the Amazon, Glenn Ford as an American cattleman, and most recently, Michael Caine in a frivolous comedy about romance in Rio. My father had once told me to become a civil engineer and work in Brazil. However, the long commute on the subway to CCNY killed the dream and whatever interest I had in that profession. I began to think that there was another way I could contribute to the country, not as a civil engineer but as a financial engineer.

In fact, this was not the first time I had tried to develop new markets in Brazil. I had been invited to Rio in 1985 to give the keynote address for the opening of the first financial futures contract in Brazil. My goal was to spark the interests of Brazil's financial community and to argue that a mature financial sector, with futures markets on interest rates and stock indexes, was a necessary companion to industrial growth. I remember the local branch manager of Drexel taking Ellen and me to a yacht club for lunch. I was struck by the phonetic name of the club—Iate Club—and the never-ending small cups of espresso.

The Earth Summit became the popular name for the UNCED. The event attracted about 20,000 people—2,400 representatives from governments around the world and about 17,500 from nongovernmental organizations (NGOs) like the United Nations, not-for-profit environmental groups, businesses, academics, and students. The size and breadth of the conference was well beyond any previous UN events. I had spoken briefly with Maurice Strong, the conference undersecretary general, at an event, but did not realize how our paths would intertwine in the future. Suave and well-spoken, Maurice fit the picture of the consummate diplomat.

The weeklong meetings produced a number of important documents that would be read and reported on worldwide. These documents included the UN Convention on Biological Diversity,[2] the Statement

[2]The Convention on Biological Diversity is a legally binding treaty that aims to conserve and sustain the use of components of biological diversity.

of Forest Principles,[3] the United Nations Framework Convention on Climate Change,[4] Agenda 21,[5] and the Rio Declaration on Environment and Development.[6]

In a small, tent-filled area, far from the governmental negotiations, UNCTAD was sponsoring the actual panel that been organized six months earlier in Geneva. I delivered my paper at this sideshow, one of many held by NGOs in parallel to the governmental negotiations. Multilateralism was falling out of favor in 1986 when the Secretary General of UNCTAD tried to revive it with environmentalism. I did not know it then, but my future involvement in climate change often landed me in similar sideshows, and even more rubber-chicken events.

The panel was titled "Combating Global Warming," and discussed the challenges presented by global warming and the policy tools available to deal with them. One policy tool was emissions trading. Being the only practitioner in a sea of academics, my assignment was to discuss implementation issues and market architecture for a global CO_2 market. I used the term *market architecture* to denote what had to be in place for a market to be initiated. This included everything from the appropriate regulatory institutions to the salient features of the futures contract itself—like the architectural blueprint for a skyscraper.

---

[3]The Statement of Forest Principles was the first, non-legally binding, global agreement on sustainable forest management. It requires signatories to follow principles of reforestation and forest conservation, and invest resources in seeking alternatives to forestry.

[4]UNFCCC aims to stabilize greenhouse gas concentrations in the atmosphere. The treaty provides for protocols like the Kyoto Protocol that set mandatory emissions limits.

[5]Agenda 21 is a plan of action adopted by UN organizations, governments, and major groups to combat environmental degradation, among other agendas.

[6]The Rio Declaration is a short document consisting of 27 principles intended to guide future sustainable development around the world.

In Search of Trees—Commoditizing CO_2

I anticipated some skepticism in the audience regarding the commoditization of CO_2 allowances. I had witnessed this in the past with interest rate and SO_2 futures and knew how to address the skeptics. While it was important to evaluate the feasibility and potential of carbon markets against the current economic and legislative climate, it was equally important to look to history and learn from its lessons. Not doing so would be tantamount to losing sight of the trees for the forest. Thus I titled my paper, "In Search of the Trees."[7]

The conference coincided with a heightened recognition of the increasing concentration of CO_2 in the atmosphere.[8] I am not a scientist, but the experts convinced me that climate change was anthropogenic, or manmade. Even if there was uncertainty, a student of markets knows never to bet against a ruinous outcome, regardless of the odds. I was reminded of the countless members of the CBOT and the CBOE who did very well shorting deep out-of-the-money options. It was a great short term trading strategy but bankrupted a lot of traders in the long run. This adheres to the principles of Gambler's Ruin and Pascal's Wager.[9] There was sufficient evidence on the irreversibility of climate change, and insurance would be cheap if we could reduce GHGs at the lowest cost.

In my presentation, I traced the histories of spot and futures markets. The first active markets with specific rules and regulations made

---

[7]Richard L. Sandor, "In Search of the Trees: Market Architecture and Tradable Entitlements for CO_2 Abatement," United Nations Conference on Trade and Development, 1993.

[8]For an overview of climate model projections of anthropogenic climate change at the time, see C.-D. Schönwiese, "Recent Developments in Scientific Knowledge on Climate Change," *Energy Conversion and Management* 33, nos. 5–8 (May–August 1992): 297–303.

[9]Pascal's Wager states that even if the existence of God cannot be proven, a rational person should still avoid betting against it. Living life as if God exists has everything to gain and nothing to lose. See Blaise Pascal, *Pensées* (trans. W. F. Trotter), 1670.

their appearance in ancient Rome under the name of *fora vendalie.*[10] The same concept resurfaced in 1200 B.C. Egypt, China, and India in more sophisticated forms.[11] A series of fairs in Europe during the twelfth through the fourteenth centuries further refined the contractual elements of agreement, transfer, payment, and warranty, which implicitly define the essential features of a commodity: standard or grade, unit of trading, price basis, and delivery mechanism.

History also suggested that spot markets evolved into forward and then futures markets. Osaka rice trading in the seventeenth and eighteenth centuries, trading in highly leveraged shares in Amsterdam in the seventeenth century, and Chicago wheat trading in the nineteenth century were all evidence of this. Guided by history and my recent experience, I argued that it would be possible to create a new commodity in tradable CO_2 allowances.

The first step would be to define or standardize the commodity being traded—the CO_2 emission allowance. The Clean Air Act Amendment of 1990 set the precedent by defining SO_2 emission allowances.

Since there was some controversy regarding the status of these allowances as property rights,[12] I strongly encouraged the potential drafters of a global CO_2 treaty to thoroughly study the Clean Air Act in order to glean knowledge from its provisions and its interpretational uncertainties. I further cautioned against improvements and novelties when embarking on a transformational innovation like creating the market architecture for the CO_2 market, and advised them to adhere as closely to the CAAA 1990 so as to avoid confusing market participants.

---

[10]Henry H. Bakken, "Futures Trading—Origin, Development and Present Economic Status in Futures Trading Seminar" 3 (Chicago Board of Trade of the City of Chicago, 1966), 5–7.

[11]Stanley Kroll and Irwin Shishko, *The Commodity Futures Guide* (New York: Harper & Row, 1973).

[12]There is some dissension about the status of emission permits as property rights. Under Title IV of the CAA Amendments, it is stated that "Such allowance does not constitute a property right. Nothing in this subchapter or in any other provision of law shall be construed to limit the authority of the United States to terminate or limit such authorization." There have been no instances, however, of the state confiscating emission allowances.

In addition to using the CAAA 1990 as a prototype, the new CO_2 market would ideally draw on existing pools of human capital, such as the knowledge of economists, traders, scientists, and lawyers, and utilize existing information systems, operations, contract markets, and software expertise. The first step would be to draft a global warming treaty and to create a UN agency as the equivalent of the EPA in the United States to govern and enforce the treaty provisions and assign CO_2 property rights or allowances.

A bonus program similar to that in the Acid Rain Program could also be used to incentivize energy conservation.[13] The granting of allowances would be best based on existing and future acceptable levels of national and global emissions and the baseline level should be estimated from a prior year, for example, 1990. This was to be determined with consideration to factors like fuel type, level of consumption, and age of facilities. Once the baseline year and the emission quantities were estimated, the percentage reduction target and time frame would be determined based on elements like available fuel or technology modification solution and time required for regulatory approval. Furthermore, emissions should be carefully monitored by continuous emissions monitoring (CEM) equipment, which had been successful in the Acid Rain Program.

After discussing the spot markets, I proceeded with a brief description of the set of conditions necessary for a successful futures market:[14] homogeneity, existence of a spot market, competitive markets, price volatility, presence of an inefficient hedging alternative, and contract design. The CO_2 allowance market met all these criteria. What remained were CO_2 allowance contract specifications. These specifications should be borrowed from the outline used by the CBOT in tradable SO_2 allowances.

---

[13]Under the Acid Rain Program, the EPA grants bonus allowances if power plants install clean coal technology that reduces SO_2 releases, use renewable energy sources, or encourage customers to conserve energy.

[14]Richard L. Sandor and Michael J. Walsh, "Environmental Futures: Preliminary Thoughts on the Market for SO_2 Emission Allowances," *Advanced Strategies in Financial Risk Management*, 1993.

Engineering the Market Architecture for a Carbon Market
I used the four features of a commodity to describe the carbon market:

1. Standardization (including grade specifications), whereby the proposed UN agency would also be the sole issuer of permits in order to avoid market segmentation and increase liquidity;
2. Unit of trading, whereby all contract units would be equal to the same amount of emissions;
3. Price basis, whereby minimum price fluctuations should be in multiples of one dollar per ton; and
4. Delivery, whereby the UN agency should maintain all CO_2 allowance tracking systems and act as a clearinghouse for all allowances.

The contract grade was easy. All six greenhouse gases had different Global Warming Potential (GWP). Carbon was the numeraire, the basis on which everything else was measured, and was assigned the number of one ton. Methane has a GWP of 25. Therefore, one ton of methane has 25 tons of CO_2 equivalent (CO_2e).

Delivery should be by book entry on the records of the administrator and issuance information should be maintained by each contract market and exchange. A minimum of 10 different nations, emitting at least 20 percent of total global emissions would need to participate in order for the market to be successful. Moreover, I suggested that a spot market for CO_2 allowances could be modeled after the foreign exchange market, in that it could operate in many locations, and trade both electronically as well as on the floor for 24 hours a day. Auctions should also be held by or on behalf of the UN agency to ensure the availability of tradable permits and give price signals.

Consequently, I argued that there were two major advantages in delegating the organization of the CO_2 spot market to the private sector, just as the EPA had delegated the management of SO_2 allowances auctions to the CBOT under the Acid Rain Program. First, the private sector already had the knowledge and

(*Continued*)

Engineering the Market Architecture for a Carbon Market (*Continued*)

technology to run the spot market. Secondly, it had already implemented a number of credit, legal, and operational mechanisms to ensure the integrity of the market.

Proposed exchanges would ideally enter into information-sharing agreements such as those that existed between the CFTC and the SEC. This was necessary in order to avoid abuses like market manipulation or fraud. The development of a standardized level agreement similar to the International Swap Dealers Associations (ISDA) Master Swap Agreement would also help facilitate the development of a forward market. This was because the enforcement of the provisions could be severely hindered by differences in national laws, making it absolutely crucial for there to be a common agreement between participating countries to ensure that provisions would be upheld for all nations involved.

Most importantly, I believed that the infrastructure used for tradable CO_2 allowances could have positive spillover effects on other commodities and equities in developing countries, such as coffee and cocoa. This would help accelerate economic development in these countries. In order to achieve this, however, the global warming treaty would need to be given enabling language to ensure that developing countries would be subsidized to start spot and futures markets in tradable entitlements.

Finally, I pointed out that contract specifications should be developed by a consensus building process, involving all market participants. The audience was supportive based on the Q&A session.

Caipirinhas and Climate Change

Following the sideshow, I made another more formal presentation to the Rio de Janeiro Chamber of Commerce on the same subject. It had been an exhausting flight and the two presentations finally took their toll on me. I decided it was time to sit on the beach, eat some barbecued shrimp purchased from a man with a small Hitachi stove, and drink a *caipirinha* [kay-pee-ree-na]. I felt the sense of calm that came to me only after hard work and the sharing of new ideas. The guilt that accompanied me during times of idleness and inactivity was absent.

Since I had hurried to the panel and was preoccupied with my presentation, I had not had a chance to look around until now. It was a vibrant setting, and reminded me of my teaching days at Berkeley in the 1960s. There was more tie-dye there than at Grateful Dead concerts. I thought, "This is just like Berkeley in the Sixties. These young climate change activists will succeed like those in the civil rights movement, the women's movement, and the anti–Vietnam War movement." I was only partially right.

It became clear to me at that moment that identifying the problem of global warming and delivering the bad news was only the first step. There had to be the hope of a solution, and the markets would provide the answer. Fortunately, I knew how to pioneer new markets. I had done it with interest rate futures when others thought that interest rates didn't fluctuate and there was no need to hedge. Past experiences assured me that I could weather the torrent of emotions that greeted all new ideas. Arthur Schopenhauer, the German philosopher, had made the observation centuries ago, "Every truth passes through three stages before it is recognized. In the first, it is ridiculed; in the second, it is opposed; in the third, it is regarded as self-evident." I had witnessed these three stages firsthand and figured I was prepared for the ridicule and the opposition. But I underestimated the enormity of the task and the extent of ridicule and opposition.

Although I didn't get to attend some parts of the conference, I was interested in their outcomes. A common source of friction between countries was the benchmarking of emission reductions. Developed countries were able to reduce excess emissions at a lower cost than developing countries, which favored cheaper, higher emitting methods of energy production and transportation. The UNFCC reached a compromise by aiming to stabilize greenhouse gas emissions in 2000 to 1990 levels only among developed countries.

I was similarly interested in the negotiations of the Statement of Forestry Principles. Many developing countries felt that forest preservation could hinder their economic growth and desired funding to compensate for preserving forest reserves. This controversy continues to this day.

After the conference, I flew back to the United States and made a stop at Norman, Oklahoma, home to the University of Oklahoma. Senator David Boren had arranged for me to deliver a speech there about my experiences at Rio. The positive reception I received from the students in a conservative energy-based state bolstered my confidence, and I was convinced that there would be a futures market in CO_2 emissions at some point in the future. It was the first step of a long educational process for the academic community, and reminded me of the premarketing phase for interest rate futures.

I was only halfway through 1992, and the opportunities seemed endless. Once again, I turned to teaching to organize my ideas. The academic world, both professors and students, were always the foundation of my work in pioneering new markets.

A New Academic Field

Meyer Feldberg, a friend from Chicago, became the dean at Columbia Business School. As I meandered through the campus to the dean's office at Columbia in the spring of 1992, I thought of my grandfather, father, and brother, and how they had all attended Columbia University. I was excited about continuing the family tradition—not as a student but as a professor.

The purpose of the meeting was to brief Meyer on emissions markets, and see if he supported a course in an unheard-of area that I described as environmental finance. I told him that we were about to witness a vast change in the public attitude toward global warming, and that this was an enormous opportunity for Columbia to be on the leading edge of the most important issue of our time. To capitalize on this rare opportunity, the university should begin educating its students about the imminent changes in climate and how best to develop policy to deal with them.

I was appointed Distinguished Adjunct Professor of Finance and began teaching a course titled Environmental Finance at Columbia in the fall of 1992. A new field was born. *Environmental Finance* eventually became the title of a new magazine that began publication in 1999, and I was its guest columnist for the first five years of its publication. Looking back, I should have coined the term "environmental finance," as I had already missed my previous chance to coin the term "derivatives."

The course at Columbia covered a wide variety of topics, including the role of emissions markets in combating pollution, environmental regulations, sustainability as business strategy, project finance and the environment,[15] endangered species, derivative markets, and global warming. The syllabus incorporated a mixture of academic papers, books, case studies, and articles from the popular press.

Classroom lectures were supplemented with presentations by experts in the relevant fields. The Commissioner from the Ohio Public Utility Commission spoke about regulation. He supported the markets and led the efforts to ensure a proper balance between stakeholders and stockholders for Ohio utilities. The stakeholders benefited from a reduction in acid rain and the stockholders benefited from a rapid reduction of emissions, and at a lower cost, than required and selling their excess reductions.

A representative from Allegheny Power talked about sulfur emissions and the economics of installing scrubbers. He made some very compelling points about global warming that were, unfortunately, lost in later debates. Many cap-and-trade advocates were concerned that although utilities could comply with the CAAA 1990 emission requirements by buying allowances at current prices for the next five years, they would only buy allowances when the price of allowances was lower than the marginal cost of the technology, and install the technology when the cost of doing so was lower than the price of buying allowances. The Allegheny Power representative argued rightly that it

[15]A major component of business strategy is financing the equipment needed to comply with environmental standards. This part of the class focused on alternative financing decisions, combined with prior readings on environmental disputes.

was the expectation of prices, and not current prices, that drove investments in pollution abatement technology. He also added that Allegheny was already installing scrubbers. To this day, some advocates of emissions trading in CO_2 still miss this simple point. Instead, they argue erroneously that prices have to be very high at the outset of emissions trading, and that the early reductions have to be drastic and achieved in a very short time in order to force firms to change their behavior.

My friend Jon Goldstein came up from Washington, DC to give a lecture on endangered species in general and the spotted owl in particular. Jon was then the chief economist of the Endangered Species Committee at the White House and had done a major study on preserving the spotted owl. He gave some great insight and a somewhat humorous take on an otherwise sober issue. Apparently, spotted owls had bad eyesight and required a lot of land to find each other for mating.

After class, Jon and I went out for a drink. He said happily, "After all my cajoling, you have finally committed to the environment!" I replied, "Jon, I feel like Patty Hearst did. I have Stockholm Syndrome. The environmentalists have captured me and I am in love with their cause."[16]

Since my class attracted students from business, international studies, and environmental sciences, I thought it would be a good idea to divide the class into three sections and have each present a paper in the final class. All three were fascinating.

One group dealt with grey water—wastewater from domestic activities like dishwashing that could be recycled—and how incentives could be used to ensure that New York City's supply of fresh water would not be threatened. Another group dealt with socially responsible investing, which didn't yet exist at the time. The group accurately predicted the growth of what is now termed sustainable investing.

The final presentation was on an options market for spotted owls. In their paper, the students devised a simulation to test the feasibility

[16]Patricia Hearst is an American newspaper heiress who was kidnapped and imprisoned by the Symbionese Liberation Army, only to be reborn as "Tania" and ironically begin performing operations for the army as a devoted soldier.

of a market-based solution to the endangerment of spotted owls. In the simulation, individuals held shares that corresponded to the ownership rights of a tract of land large enough to support a spotted owl. Players were free to trade their shares according to their predictions on factors like timber market movements that pertained to the survival of the spotted owl. To influence players' decisions, the students simulated market news loosely based on real-world events that could potentially affect timber prices. The two main goals of the project were to see if market solutions could be applied to the problem of endangered species, and determine whether it was possible for market forces to preserve a species.

Although I taught the course only once, others soon picked up where I left off. Environmental Finance became a part of the permanent curriculum of Columbia University, which became a thought leader in a field imitated by many. Environmental finance had evolved from a course into a magazine, and eventually into a graduate degree program at many universities. I was proudly reminded of Northwestern's lead in the finance curriculum when it introduced a financial futures course.

In retrospect, 1992 was a banner year. The future of emission markets seemed bright after the Earth Summit. Kidder had also brokered the first registered trade of 30-year options on SO_2 with a New England utility through which we were able to gain experience in trading, clearing, and settling SO_2 allowances trades.

In spite of these exciting developments, I began to see some threatening signs.

Early in 1992, I started to get a little uncomfortable about Kidder, Peabody, even though it had been a good year, thanks to the performance of the fixed income department. 1992 was witnessing a continuation of this trend, and I had been told that both the mortgage market and governments were being run by competent people with MBAs from prestigious universities. Nonetheless, it didn't matter how smart the individuals were or and how good their credentials were. If a market were efficient, it was very difficult to make above-average rates of return. I knew something about bonds and mortgages and thought that some above-average returns could be made on the basis of good analytics. What puzzled me was the discussion about the amount of money that can be made by basis trading and *stripping*—the separation of the stream of interest rate payments from the principal, that is, the amount of money received by the bondholder at maturity.

When I took over fixed income at Drexel, we had a solid business of buying Treasury bonds and selling their component parts if the parts were worth more than the whole. The opposite was done if the parts were cheaper than the whole. The margins were good but not great, and could be enhanced by using futures. When I mentioned this to a colleague on the executive committee, I was told I did not understand the potential for profits in this market—a criticism that triggered an important memory for me.

Sometime after the great bull market of 1973 and 1974, I was told a story about a trader who was the complete opposite of a stereotypical commodity trader—conservative, serious, somewhat dour, with no flash. He traded the only commodity that did not have price controls on it in World War II: rye. One day, a fellow trader came running to him exclaiming, "Tom Jones is going crazy! He just lost his entire fortune in the bean pit and he doesn't understand why it happened."[17] Peering over his half-moon glasses, the first trader said calmly, "Tommy never understood why he made his money, so why should he understand why he lost it?" There was a simple but profound lesson for me. If you didn't understand why you were making profits, it was likely that you would incur significant losses at some point in the future.

Two years later, Joseph Jett committed the largest fraud in the history of the securities industry, and Kidder went out of business.[18] The fraud reflected a trend I had seen before, and one that I would see again. Just as you couldn't completely eradicate drunk driving without banning driving itself, you couldn't completely regulate human folly. You could, however, strive to have institutions in place that minimize systemic damages.

Separately, I had been working on developing catastrophe futures at the CBOT. There was a natural link between climate change and the insurance industry. It was now time to expand my interest in the commoditization of insurance.

---

[17]The real name of the trader has been changed.

[18]The former bond trader used Kidder's computer system to exchange securities with the U.S. government and fabricate $350 million in profits.

Chapter 12

The Beginning of the Entrepreneurial Years

Insurance

You don't need to pray to God any more when there are storms in the sky, but you do have to be insured.

—*Bertolt Brecht*

Berkeley in the 1960s ushered in a dramatic transformation felt throughout the rest of the country. It was the epicenter of free love, free speech, drugs, and radicalism. To many it was a period of catastrophic social change. At the time, however, I had a very different notion of catastrophic change.

My interest in insurance began when Robert "Bob" Goshay, a gregarious colleague at Berkeley and an insurance expert, asked one day, "Do you think catastrophic risks could be transferred using futures markets?"

Bob believed the idea was transformational and I thought it was feasible. It was that conversation, and a subsequent one in 1970 when we discussed the 1966 earthquake in Parkfield, California,[1] which inspired our research. We collaborated on a paper that explored the feasibility of a reinsurance futures market, published in *The Journal of Business Finance* in 1972.[2]

In 1973, Bob took a year's sabbatical at Lloyd's of London, attempting to convince its management and membership that these new insurance risk transfer mechanisms would enhance underwriting profits and reduce risk. Primary insurance firms at the time hedged themselves using reinsurance companies, which insured insurance companies that had too much risk in their books. Post sabbatical, Bob reported, "Lloyd's is living in the nineteenth century. There's no way we can get this cozy club to embrace our new alternative to reinsurance."

I had always harbored a romantic image of the group of insurance syndicates, mainly because of the 1936 movie *Lloyd's of London*.[3] The movie painted the members of Lloyd's as innovative risk takers who insured the British merchant fleet during the Napoleonic wars. Lloyd's had been instrumental in helping Lord Nelson win the battle of Trafalgar. I was crestfallen and disillusioned when Bob described to me the actual lack of imagination of many of the syndicates. I found it paradoxical that those who were willing to underwrite nontraditional risks would not consider new risk management tools.

I had mentioned my interest in catastrophe futures to Henry Hall Wilson when first interviewed at the CBOT. However, insurance futures took a backseat when it became evident that interest rate futures would become a reality. The idea lay dormant for more than a decade before Les Rosenthal brought it to light again in the late 1980s. Les was

---

[1]The Parkfield Earthquake of 1966 was the last of six earthquakes of moderate magnitude that occurred in the Parkfield, California section of the San Andreas Fault in the years 1857, 1881, 1901, 1922, 1934, and 1966. The first earthquake occurred before the major seismic event that ruptured the San Andreas Fault. According to data, all of the six earthquakes occurred in the same area of the fault, on regular intervals of time.

[2]Robert C. Goshay and Richard L. Sandor, "An Inquiry into the Feasibility of a Reinsurance Futures Market," *Journal of Business Finance* 5, no. 2 (1973).

[3]*Lloyd's of London* (1936) was directed by Henry King, and starred Tyrone Power and Madeleine Carroll.

adventurous and liked change. Anxious to get back into developing new products, he called and asked, "Whatever happened to your idea on insurance derivatives?" I explained that my former colleague's sabbatical at Lloyd's had not been positive, and told him that I still believed the industry could use alternative ways to hedge. Les proceeded to champion the idea at the CBOT, urging the exchange to rekindle my early efforts.

Commoditizing Catastrophes

After Billy O'Connor became chairman of the CBOT board in 1990, he formed an insurance futures committee. Les was appointed chairman of the committee, and I was named vice chairman.

I was at Kidder and organized a meeting of industry leaders at the office headquarters in Hanover Square, a triangular park located in the financial district in lower Manhattan. It became clear from industry meetings that the CBOT should focus on catastrophic events like hurricanes and earthquakes instead of the conventional kinds of insurance like medical and auto initially recommended by the staff of the exchange.

In the late 1980s and 1990s, the United States was experiencing a high incidence of catastrophes that should have been, according to executives in the industry, once-in-a-century events. After three consecutive events of this nature, one CEO we talked to still insisted matter-of-factly that the probability of such events occurring was one in a hundred and that there was really no need for the insurance industry to hedge. I never understood how you could have three one-in-a-hundred events in five years.

The more recent losses incurred by the insurance industry were attributed to the increased frequency and severity of natural calamities, but also to the fact that the U.S. population had been migrating toward coastal regions, where the threat of natural disasters posed much greater damage risks. Nearly 70 percent of the U.S. population was now concentrated in these areas. In effect, these coastal regions became hothouses for the development of infrastructure, expensive dwellings, and human capital.

In 1989, Hurricane Hugo caused $5.9 billion in damages in the Carolinas.[4] Furthermore, California's burgeoning population was hit by the Loma Prieta earthquake in 1989, resulting in property losses of up to $6 billion.[5] The populations in the Gulf Coast spanning from Texas to Florida, along with the entire East Coast, continued to grow. In 1938, a major hurricane struck Long Island, causing $306 million in damages, an amount equal to $4.77 billion today, to the potato farms and small number of dwellings that existed at the time.[6] It was appropriately dubbed the "Long Island Express." Today, given the development of the Hamptons and other expensive resorts in the area, a similar event could easily result in a record level of damages. We had a close call in 2011 when Hurricane Irene hit the East Coast.

The insurance industry was and still is undercapitalized for catastrophic events. The arithmetic simply did not add up. In 1997, U.S. primary insurance companies had a total capital of $239 billion, while reinsurance companies had another $52 billion.[7] This was supplemented by another $10 billion to $15 billion[8] in the retrocessional market.[9] All of this was supposed to underpin an economy of $8.3 trillion[10] once including all products and service liabilities, such as toxic spills, director's and officer's liabilities, medical malpractices, legal malpractices, and personal injuries. It also needed to support $12 trillion to $15 trillion

[4]George J. Bullwinkel Jr., *The SCE&G Hugo Experience—Damage Assessment and Lessons Learned* (Montreal, Quebec: North American Electric Reliability Council, 1990).

[5]"Comparison of the Bay Area Earthquakes: 1906 and 1989," in *San Andreas Fault*, ch. 1, p. 5 (Reston, VA: U.S. Geological Survey, August 31, 2009).

[6]"The Great Hurricane of 1938," *Boston Globe*, July 19, 2005.

[7]Reinsurance Association America.

[8]Richard L. Sandor, *Distributing Risk—Seeking New Sources of Capital* (Schaumburg, IL: Zurich Insurance, 1995).

[9]Reinsurance companies could also be insured by other reinsurance companies in what was called the retrocession market.

[10]Ann M. Lawson, Kurt S. Bersani, Mahnaz Fahim-Nader, and Jiemin Guo, "Benchmark Input-Output Accounts of the United States, 1997," December 2002.

in property.[11] The potential for catastrophic losses was $20 trillion, and any single catastrophic event in areas like Miami, Florida or Orange County and Los Angeles, California, could have resulted in insured losses totaling $50 billion to $100 billion.[12] In fact, it was the catastrophes of the late 1980s and early 1990s that generated support for the idea of a futures contract in hurricanes, tornados, and earthquakes. In 1992, Hurricane Andrew struck well south of Miami and left a trail of insured damages totaling $15.5 billion, or $20 billion today.[13] At the time, it was the greatest single cost of any catastrophic event in U.S. history. While the U.S. insurance markets seemed vulnerable to phenomenal losses, the worldwide capital markets, with equities and fixed income totaling more than $30 trillion, could easily absorb a hefty portion of risk from the insurance markets.

Les and I turned our attention to natural disasters in 1990. We spent the rest of the year developing the terms for a catastrophe contract, along with marketing materials. In writing articles and developing marketing materials for Kidder, I applied the same formula for sales brochures, speeches, and seminars that we had used in financial futures, and worked closely with CBOT staff.

Selling Catastrophe Futures

Selling insurance derivatives was more difficult than selling interest rate futures. Although a series of catastrophes had provided the structural change needed to catalyze the development of insurance derivatives, we now had to standardize the product.

Insurance policies were contracts of indemnification, where an insurance company paid the insured for any incurred damages. It was a

---

[11]Richard L. Sandor, *Distributing Risk—Seeking New Sources of Capital* (Schaumburg, IL: Zurich Insurance, 1995).

[12]Richard L. Sandor, "The Convergence of the Insurance and Capital Markets," *Journal of Reinsurance* 6, no. 3 (April 1999): 48.

[13]"At $22 Billion, Insured Losses from Four Florida Hurricanes Will Exceed Andrew's Record," *Insurance Journal*, October 1, 2004.

costly process. It was also a business that required negotiations after the policy was written. I was struck by ads in the trade press that described how the claims department of an insurance company should be run as if it were a profit center instead of cost center. Not only did this seem like a violation of the insurance contract, it was incredibly inefficient.

However, if an insurance policy were a contract for differences instead of indemnification, the insurance payments could be easily determined. The claims department would no longer be incentivized to maximize profits and be at odds with customers. For example, a reinsurance company could offer a policy that was event-based. An earthquake in the City of San Francisco with a magnitude of 7.0 on the Richter scale would trigger the policy payment. The payment would be based on the premium to be paid by the insurance company. Assuming the San Francisco scenario described above, the reinsurance policy would simply state a $200,000 premium for $10 million in coverage. The $10 million would be paid if a previously approved verifier reported an earthquake in a predetermined geographical area of 7.0 or higher magnitude.

I didn't realize it at first, but we even had standardization: a small market had emerged in London for industry loss warranties (ILWs). ILWs were a type of reinsurance or derivatives contract through which one party purchased protection based on the total loss arising from an event incurred by the entire insurance industry rather than by the party itself. For example, the buyer of a $100 million U.S. Wind ILW pays a premium and receives $100 million in coverage if total losses to the insurance industry from a single U.S. hurricane exceed $20 billion. The industry loss, $20 billion in this case, is often referred to as the *trigger.* The $100 million, the amount of protection offered by the contract, is referred to as the *limit.*[14] ILWs were contracts for differences and not for indemnities.[15] The industry's loss might not

[14]Lawrence A. Cunningham, "Securitizing Audit Failure Risk: An Alternative to Damages Caps," *William and Mary Law Review*, 2007.

[15]The pay-off of a contract for differences is based on an event, for example, a change in the market price of an asset. In the case of an ILW, when the market price rises, the buyer is rewarded. The pay-off of a contract of indemnity is based on the damage done to a tangible asset.

correlate with an individual company's losses, thereby triggering basis risk for the reinsured. This risk was higher for companies whose exposure concentration was further away from the industry averages. ILW covers were therefore typically bought by companies whose portfolios closely followed the market.[16]

In the meetings I had organized for industry members, there also seemed to be a demand from the primary insurance companies in the United States. Chicago-based property and casualty companies enthusiastically supported our efforts, as did others. The reception by the reinsurance companies, however, was less than enthusiastic. A transparent market that offered a hedging alternative to reinsurance was not welcome. It was particularly threatening to companies with very strong balance sheets. A cleared hedging vehicle with no counterparty risk was a nightmare. It was the same old story.

In spite of the primary insurance industry's support for the concept, we still met internal opposition. One director at the exchange mounted a campaign to kill the concept. He thought the new contracts posed too much of a financial risk for the clearinghouse. Billy O'Connor and Les Rosenthal convinced the board that this wasn't true and gave the contract its final push. New markets required champions. Leaders willing to take personal risks were indispensable in organized markets, particularly at the CBOT where the political process determined the outcome of research and development. After significant debate, the board of directors finally voted to launch the new insurance futures contract.

Our timing could not have been better. There were rumors that Allstate would violate insurance capital requirements if it failed to hedge the disastrous consequences of another major catastrophe. Industry buzz alleged that Berkshire Hathaway had written Allstate a catastrophe cover of $500 million for another Hurricane Andrew at a 40 percent rate on line,[17] and in doing so received $200 million in premiums. If the rumors were true, this was a great deal for Berkshire Hathaway. If another Hurricane Andrew occurred in the short balance of the hurricane

[16]Ali Ishaq, "Reinsuring for Catastrophes through ILW—A Practical Approach," paper presented at Casualty Actuarial Society Forum, Arlington, VA, Spring 2005.

[17]This refers to the payment of insurance as a percentage of the coverage.

season, the maximum loss for the firm was $500 million. Since the firm had received $200 million in premiums, its exposure was only $300 million. It was an unbelievable risk-reward ratio. I was convinced that there was enough capital available to underwrite risk at this price.

Insurance catastrophe futures contracts commenced trading at the CBOT on December 11, 1992. I felt buoyed with excitement as the opening bell rang, and was reminded of creating the first interest rate futures contract. Like the GNMA futures, insurance futures were a whole new field and asset class. The first trade was made between Les Rosenthal and Billy O'Connor, who sought to set an example for the membership.

The new futures contracts were based on the loss ratios of the catastrophe insurance industry—quarterly insured catastrophic losses nationwide and in three U.S regions: Eastern, Midwestern, and Western. The price of these futures contracts at any given time reflected the market's expectation of the quarter's catastrophe loss incurred by a sample of companies.

The basis of these futures was an index tracking the losses of almost 25 property and casualty insurers, who reported their loss data quarterly to Insurance Services Office, Inc. Unfortunately, the CBOT insurance contracts were not without problems. As argued by Bouriaux and Himick (1998), first, the loss development period of six months was insufficient in capturing the true losses experienced by the industry. Second, the ISO-issued reports were only updated twice during each contract period, preventing them from achieving the continuous pricing that was the hallmark of exchange markets. Finally, we learned that the index was flawed and did not reflect the true industry loss ratios when a catastrophe occurred.[18] The reason was that large industry players such as Allstate and State Farm did not report to the ISO. Consequently, ISO used to have to make adjustments to account for these major players. The inaccuracy of these adjustments became clear after the 1994 Northridge earthquake,[19] when the ISO index severely underestimated the loss index ratio. The contract failed, and we tried another approach.

---

[18] Sylvie Bouriaux and Michael Himick, "Exchange-Traded Insurance Derivatives: Catastrophe Options and Swaps," in *Securitized Insurance Risk: Strategic Opportunities for Insurers and Investors*, ed. Michael Himick (Chicago: Glenlake Publishing Co. Ltd.).

[19] The Northridge earthquake was a 6.7 magnitude earthquake that hit Los Angeles, California, on January 17, 1994.

ISO

The ISO index tracks the losses on a pool of domestic catastrophe policies. The index itself captures the dollar loss on $25,000 of catastrophe premiums. For example, if the loss experienced is $20,000 (the loss ratio in this case is 80 percent), then the index will be valued at $20,000.* Due to reporting lags, the ISO also considered the actual losses at the end of each quarter and adjusted its estimates based on the most recent statutory annual statements of sampled companies. The estimated premiums were made public prior to the commencement of trading. Since the premium was known and constant through the contract, any change in futures prices was caused by unexpected catastrophe losses incurred by the sample. The price of the catastrophe futures, therefore, rose with catastrophe expectations, which varied according to the gravity and frequency of catastrophes. The contracts were settled by cash since the underlying instrument, the index value, could not be physically delivered.

*Part of this box is adapted from Russ Ray, "Catastrophe Derivatives: Insuring the Insurer Against Catastrophic Losses," CBS Business Network, October 1, 1993.

The CBOT catastrophe insurance futures didn't mimic reinsurance. Option call spreads better simulated the reinsurance layers that the insurance industry was accustomed to.[20] Consequently, the exchange redesigned the contracts and began trading options contracts on September 29, 1995, using the Property Claims Services' (PCS) loss estimates instead of those reported by the ISO. The PCS reported cumulative insurance industry losses in a timelier and more accurate fashion, providing additional liquidity. Furthermore, the contract design was simplified and the

[20]A company that wanted to insure itself for damages between $20 and $50 billion bought a reinsurance layer of losses in excess of $20 billion but limited to a maximum of $50 billion. In capital market terms, this was equivalent to being long a call at $20 billion and short a call at $50 billion.

PCS Loss Estimates

The PCS estimates the aggregate amount of insured losses and property damage by asking a wide range of insurers the dollar amount of claim they expect to receive. The risk period of the PCS index denotes the time over which losses are aggregated, for example, the index of seasonal catastrophes are quarterly and the index of nonseasonal ones are yearly. Each index is zero in the beginning and increases by one point for every $100 million insured loss in the risk period.

The owner of a PCS option had the right, but not the obligation, to exercise his option at a prespecified strike price upon the option's expiration for a cash settlement. PCS options could be traded as small cap (for losses up to $20 billion) or large cap (for losses from $20 to $50 billion). This limited the amount of losses included under each contract, and therefore turned the seller of an uncovered call into a call spread seller. While these caps were of theoretical importance, they ultimately did not provide enough protection against large losses in practice. For this reason, market participants traded mostly call spreads. Buying or selling a call was equivalent to buying or selling reinsurance. The buyers also didn't have credit risk because of the clearing corporation. For example, a reinsurance company may become more geographically diversified by selling call spreads to areas where it does not write traditional reinsurance. The firm can also use a combination of traditional reinsurance and call spreads to reach its desired retention level/risk hedging strategy. Furthermore, insurance derivatives may help primary insurance companies manage credit risk by allowing them to mitigate the risk of default with a reinsurance company, and shifting the risk to the capital market.*

*Reprinted from: Michael S. Canter, Joseph B. Cole, and Richard L. Sandor, "Insurance Derivatives: A New Asset Class for the Capital Markets and a New Hedging Tool for the Insurance Industry," *Journal of Applied Corporate Finance* 10, no. 3 (1997): 69–81.

development period was extended to 12 months. Later on, due to the lack of industry demand, PCS-indexed insurance futures were dropped entirely. Only cash options on PCS industry estimates were offered for trading.[21]

Entering the Insurance Space as an Entrepreneur

Despite the many benefits associated with PCS options, initial trading in PCS options was not very liquid. One reason was the steep learning curve associated with this financial product. Both insurance and reinsurance companies needed to be comfortable with the language of derivatives and basis risk, the risk that the loss incurred by insurers or reinsurers may not be correlated with the losses of the industry as a whole. The issue of liquidity was more of an issue for capital market professionals, who were accustomed to being able to enter and reverse a trade at a moment's notice. Insurance and reinsurance companies did not put as much emphasis on easily getting in and out of a trade as their capital market counterparts did. Once these companies bought catastrophe coverage, they intended, for the most part, to keep that position for its duration. At the end of the third quarter of 1997, there were a total of 494 trades for an average of 25 call spreads per trade. We had hoped to have tens of thousands of trades. It was an uphill battle to build exchange volume.

Although Kidder, Peabody welcomed my efforts, the firm was after all an investment bank, and I needed an insurance company to champion the idea. General Electric's insurance company was similarly uninterested in pioneering these new products.

In 1992, a friend called me after reading an article about the CBOT's plan to launch catastrophe futures contracts. He was founding a reinsurance company. I told him about the business opportunities in the catastrophe space because of the recent resurgence of natural calamities, changes in demographic trends, and the increase in property values in high-risk coastal areas. It was a good time to enter the business, and a recent spate of catastrophes had driven reinsurance rates to very high levels. I ratified his business plans, and his enthusiasm added to my own. I wanted to get more involved in the industry and wondered how I could participate.

---

[21]See note 18 for bibliographic information.

My friend referred me to Michael Palm. Michael was one of the brightest people I had met in the business world, and immediately understood my logic about structural changes and standardization occurring in the insurance markets. In fact, he himself was in the middle of his own financial innovation at the time. Michael had, along with a partner, cofounded Centre Reinsurance, a subsidiary of Zurich Insurance that specialized in a new product called finite risk reinsurance, a way to spread the premiums and risks over a particular time period. The losses paid were capped, or in other words, finite.

Michael and I tried to figure out how to work together. Initially, we thought about having me become an employee at Centre Re. Negotiating and renegotiating the specific terms of my employment was an arduous process, and I began to get frustrated. I called my friend to ask for his advice, and received a response that profoundly changed my life. He said, "Why are you negotiating as if you're applying for a job? You're thinking of yourself as an employee when you really want to be an entrepreneur." He was dead right.

I decided to put up all the working capital, negotiate the right to use Centre's name and balance sheet, and give them a share of profits. As soon as I changed my approach, we quickly came to a mutually satisfactory agreement.

On March 1, 1993, I resigned from Kidder and founded Centre Financial Products (CFP). My dreams of becoming an entrepreneur had finally become a reality. I was both nervous and giddy with excitement. For the first time in 25 years, I was no longer part of a large organization.

SO_2 Emissions Trading at Centre Financial Products

CFP's core business was developing products that focused on the intersection between the capital markets and the insurance industry. There was a robust connection between insurance and the environmental space. In the event of a climate change–induced catastrophe, insurance companies would be one of the first to take the brunt. What was happening in the environment therefore mattered a great deal to insurance and reinsurance companies.

For example, one possible effect of climate change was a reduction of snowfall. This could cause a dramatic change in the landscape of the country. It could also threaten the Swiss way of life and the country's vibrant tourism industry. A reduction in snowfall would negatively impact the income of ski resorts, which was an indispensable part of Switzerland's GDP. These concerns were what drove the country's growing involvement in climate change initiatives—in particular, through Swiss Re, Switzerland's predominant insurance provider.

Anticipating the likely convergence of insurance and climate change in the future, I continued to pursue emissions trading as part of our activities at CFP. We started with SO_2 allowances, anticipating CO_2 allowances. I went to different power companies, soliciting their SO_2 allowance business. Thanks to the large size of our balance sheet, we were able to serve as a principal and not just a broker.

SO_2 allowances could also be used as a financing instrument. Priced at $50 million or more, scrubbers were expensive and had to be financed. Utilities could borrow the money required to install a scrubber and pay for the scrubber using proceeds from a future sale of emission allowances. The first trade registered by the EPA was actually a financing that allowed the utility to bypass the assumption of debt.

In 1993, Henderson Municipal Power & Light in Kentucky sold 150,000 tons of sulfur dioxide pollution allowances to CentreFinancial Products for $26.8 million. The sale of allowances represented the third largest SO_2 trade at the time.[22] This was a unique sale, as the revenue from the sale was used to finance and install scrubbers in the Station Two plant of Henderson Municipal Power, planned in April 1993. The scrubbers were estimated to have cost $41 million, yet by installing these scrubbers, Henderson Municipal was able to decrease its sulfur emissions by 95 percent.[23] At the market price, the proceeds from the sale of allowances were enough to finance the scrubbers.

[22]The two larger SO_2 trades were executed by Georgia Southern Company for 320,850 tons and 637,430 tons. See Renee Rico, "The U.S. Allowance Trading System for Sulfur Dioxide: An Update on Market Experience," *Environmental and Resource Economics* 5, no. 2 (1995): 115–129.

[23]SO_2 emissions 5,739 (kg/h) × 8,760 (h/yr)/1,000 (kg/mt) × 0.95 removal rate = 47,760 metric tons of SO_2 removed per year.

In September 1993, CFP in turn sold the original 150,000 allowances to Carolina Power and Light (CP&L). CP&L used very low sulfur coal in its generators. Thus, the marginal cost of removing remaining sulfur by scrubbers in their plants was higher than the industry average. In 1993, CP&L estimated this cost to be approximately $500 per ton of SO_2. Comparatively, in March 1993, the EPA auctioned 150,010 allowances at the CBOT at an average price of $143 per ton. CP&L had little interest in installing scrubbing equipment at the time due to the high cost of scrubbing and the still-evolving scrubbing technology.[24]

Nonetheless, CP&L expected to exceed its EPA sulfur allotment even while introducing fuel switching and demand side management to reduce emissions. Between 2000 and 2009, the EPA allocated 143,968 allowances to CP&L per year. By CP&L estimates, if it failed to make any changes in the way it operated its system, it would emit approximately 230,000 tons of sulfur dioxide in the year 2000, creating a deficit of 86,000 tons. As a result, CP&L would have to either reduce its sulfur dioxide emissions or purchase additional allowances.

CP&L first purchased 85,103 allowance credits at the 1993 EPA auction for $11,490,000 at an average price of $135. They required additional credits and entered into a formal agreement with CFP in 2000 for the purchase of 150,000 SO_2 emission allowances at $47,250,000.[25] Using an 8 percent market interest rate over eight years, the present discounted value of that payment in 1993 was $27,560,000.

CP&L needed to raise additional capital or borrow money to pay for the SO_2 allowances, which posed an additional problem for CFP. Not only did we have to guarantee the interest rate for CP&L's capital raise, we also had to guarantee the price and quantity of the allowances. To solve the first problem, we agreed to lend money to CP&L vis-à-vis Zurich Insurance, which CFP had direct access to under the terms of our contract with Centre Re. Solving the second problem was more challenging. Since the EPA registry wasn't operational at the time that the deal was consummated, CFP wrote the contract such that it closed when the registry was inaugurated.

---

[24]"State of North Carolina Utilities Commission–Raleigh," Docket No. E-2, Sub 642.

[25]"Execution of Proprietary Title IV Sulfur Dioxide Emission Allowances purchase agreement, together with note and security agreement," signed by Robert M. Williams.

Although the price and quantity of allowances were fixed through a forward purchase agreement with another utility, CFP still had to hedge against the interest rate risk. As there was no futures market on corporate bonds, we had to use the CBOT Treasury bond futures contract, which created basis risk. To mitigate this risk, CFP decided to buy puts on the Treasury bond futures contract as well.

The former risk manager at Kidder joined me at CFP. He had come from Salomon Brothers, and his expertise in futures markets proved to be invaluable in managing the hedge at CFP. This was critical because we bought and sold the allowances at the same price. The profit came from the price at which we bought the debt from CP&L and then sold it to an insurance company. Interest rates fell during the time we signed the contract and when we closed the deal. The structured transaction turned out to be very profitable, in spite of the fact that we made little money from the purchase and sale of the allowances.

In the end, CP&L secured their future allowances at favorable prices and financed the transaction at attractive interest rates. The seller of the allowances also fared well. The sale and purchase was done at a higher price than the OTC bid, and at a lower price than the OTC offer.

While this seemed like a simple transaction, a closer examination revealed that the allowance market not only enabled a low-cost compliance tool, but a financing vehicle as well. I later said to the trader that managed the hedge, "I never realized that interest rate futures would enable the first SO_2 allowance trade. Talk about unintended consequences."

Partly due to the failure of the CBOT to list a futures contract on SO_2, the SO_2 market gradually became a brokered OTC market. This diminished profit opportunities for principals like us, so we decided to turn our full attention to insurance and CO_2 emissions.

Creating New Insurance Products

At CFP, we wrote reinsurance policies on catastrophic risks that were contract for differences, which could then be hedged in the futures markets. For certain risks without a corresponding futures market, we hedged indirectly in a related futures market. We did this with crop damage risks using agricultural futures contracts. Other risks, such as airline crashes and oil spills, could be standardized but couldn't be hedged directly or indirectly with existing futures markets. There was no way to hedge these risks except through diversification. We built a quantitative model based on portfolio theory for these risks.

To assume catastrophic risk directly, Centre Re formed a reinsurance company in Bermuda, a major reinsurance center, shortly after we joined. This left little appetite to underwrite more catastrophic risk. CFP therefore had to find more industry warranty contracts to hedge. However, because the futures markets for ILWs were already so transparent, profit opportunities on arbitrage in this were limited. Paradoxically, the transparency in futures market fostered by the CBOT contracts actually hindered the ability to write insurance policies that exploited the differences between reinsurance prices and futures prices.

In addition, there were other barriers that limited the use of futures by reinsurance companies. Key among them was the fact that futures and options positions were never officially recognized as reinsurance, and therefore couldn't be treated as capital. This by default increased transaction costs. Reinsurance companies justifiably viewed insurance futures as a competitive threat. Even if insurance companies didn't use the CBOT, the transparency was putting some pressures on reinsurance rates. Reinsurance companies were not amused by this.

Left with no choice, we sought out reinsurance companies to turn these futures contracts into reinsurance policies that would be recognized by the insurance regulators. We traveled to London to find companies that were willing to hedge by buying insurance policies based on ILWs. The natural place to start was with members and brokers of Lloyd's of London. We had very limited success.

We also tried to find reinsurance companies willing to hedge their exposures in noncatastrophic risks using insurance policies based on contracts for differences, which were termed index-linked or event-based insurance policies. Index-linked insurance, as demonstrated by the CBOT ISO and PCS indexed options and futures, was a financial product in which the payout, or the level of payout, depended on prespecified levels of the index as opposed to the actual losses.

Theoretically, this should reduce the moral hazard of having increased losses be in the financial interests of insured. I worked to persuade some brokers in London to originate this type of risk.

Most brokers wanted to stick to the traditional way of conducting business and found no reason to switch from their existing model, especially because it was profitable. We did, however, find two smaller brokerage companies that were enthusiastic about standardizing the process: Willis Faber and Benfield. I got to know Neil Eckert, a partner and broker at Benfield, who immediately understood the concept of index-linked insurance policies. Neil was creative and a great salesman.

The two of us flew to Germany to discuss the concept with Klaus Gierstner, an entrepreneur who didn't fit the mold of a stereotypical German reinsurer. He was an out-of-the-box thinker, as evidenced by his ponytail. We met at a quaint restaurant in a suburb of Berlin and discussed how index-linked insurance could diversify his risk at Francona, where Klaus was the underwriter. Neil suggested that for the purpose of standardization, we could divide risks into different buckets: hurricanes, typhoons, European windstorms, earthquakes in the United States, earthquakes in Japan, aviation insurance, environmental risks, and so on. We could then write index-linked reinsurance policies based on these risk buckets. Three hours later, we had a deal in principle. Neil and I followed up by writing the index-linked reinsurance policies for a pilot program. Instead of insuring the damage from a specific oil spill, we defined the event in terms of the number of barrels spilled. We also defined the damage to hulls from airline crashes based on the manufacturer and type of aircraft. As we began to model the associated risks, we recognized that the risks varied between airlines run by developed and developing countries. If the same aircraft were under the U.S. and European banner, there would be a specific dollar loss specified in the insurance policy. If the same aircraft flew out of Russia, where maintenance procedures were different, the claims paid would be lower for the same type of aircraft.

I built the team at CFP with former colleagues from Drexel and Kidder. We also hired a number of inexperienced youths from diverse backgrounds ranging from naval officers and to economists who knew nothing about insurance to a nuclear engineer. We continued to build a portfolio of market index-linked reinsurance contracts, which included a policy indexed to the medical component of the Consumer Price Index (CPI).[26]

Crop Insurance

We also entered the crop reinsurance business. The business was very cyclical. Major European reinsurance companies entered and exited the business routinely, because of the significant amount of volatility and the limited profitability of the business. CFP wanted to position itself competitively as a stable, long-term provider of crop reinsurance.

We started to write crop insurance, and hedged in the corn, wheat, and soybeans futures markets. Prices and yields were becoming uncoupled, and therefore net farm income couldn't be hedged without a futures market in yield. We advocated a yield futures contract. It was listed on the CBOT, but died due to the lack of a champion.

In addition to the difficulties in my new business, I experienced a devastating personal loss in 1996.

Charlie O. Finley's Death

The last time I saw Charlie was sometime in 1995 when he visited me in New York. We went to the Jockey Club, where he showed me a glow-in-the-dark football he had patented for use in small towns that wanted to be able to play at night without stadium lights. It was wonderful to see him.

Charlie died on February 19, 1996. He was 77 years old. Ellen heard about it on the evening news when I was still in London. Penya told Ellen not to wake me in the middle of the night with the bad news, so Ellen called me early in the morning, London time. I canceled the rest of my appointments and flew back to the United States

[26]The Consumer Price Index (CPI) is calculated by averaging the prices paid by consumers on a representative basket of goods and services.

immediately. Charlie's funeral service was held three days later in Merrillville, Indiana. I gave the eulogy alongside Charlie's old baseball players, Catfish Hunter and Reggie Jackson.

Catfish shared with us the story of his earliest encounter with Charlie. Back when Catfish had yet to join the Oakland A's, Charlie had sent his scout to Catfish's home in North Carolina in a dogged attempt to recruit him. Charlie called the house, and Al Hunter, Sr. picked up the phone: "Do you want to speak to your scout?" he asked. Charlie replied, "Not unless he signed your son." Al Hunter, Jr. was then ushered to the phone to hear him out. Charlie offered the baseball player a $65,000 salary. The young man bartered it up to $70,000. Charlie agreed to the raise. Feeling empowered, Al Hunter, Jr. decided to push his luck and suggested that Charlie also throw in a red Corvette. Charlie retorted, "I gave you a damn raise. Buy it yourself."

It didn't take long for Charlie to address the next important topic: "Son, do you have a nickname or a hobby?" "No," said Al Hunter, Jr. "Then listen carefully," said Charlie. "When you were a kid you used to catch catfish with a passion, and once landed a whole lot of them. You and your friends were caught by a truant officer. Ever since then you've been called Catfish. Now repeat the story after me." And so Catfish was born. At the eulogy, he reflected to us, "If it hadn't been for Charlie, I'd still be Al Hunter, Jr. Nobody would remember that name, but everyone remembers the Catfish."

Reggie Jackson was the last to speak. He recalled his feelings before joining the New York Yankees. While Reggie made it in Oakland, there were widespread press reports about how tough it was to make it in the Big Apple. Reggie said that he was undaunted by New York because of the high standards set by Charlie. Charlie had always insisted his players to live up to their god-given talents, and Reggie went on to become a superstar in New York. Discipline, training, and determination complemented his natural abilities. I would have to use that same discipline and determination in the next couple of years and beyond.

I thought about my mother after Charlie's funeral. She died a year after my dad did, in a hospital while being cared for by my brother. I think she lost her will to live after my father had passed. I flew in to see her the day before she died. She was in bad form. She said sadly, "Richard, look at what a mess I am." I replied, "No, Mom. You look great." I felt her pain for not being the woman she wanted to be. Nonetheless, I left the hospital after about an hour of very pleasant stories and laughs.

I remember her visiting us in Chicago after my dad died. She stayed with us in Lake Point Tower, and I invited Charlie to come up to meet her. Charlie's mom was strong-willed, too, and he recognized that trait in my own mother. It was funny to see him, the famous Charlie O. Finley, so cautious and tentative around my mother. I was sorry my father couldn't be there, as it would have been a perfect moment.

Exiting the Insurance Space

Sometime after the mid-1990s, the incidence of catastrophes diminished, causing a decline in reinsurance rates and a demand for hedging in the index-linked markets. Premiums had fallen as a result, and we were in what insurance professionals called a soft market. We were also seeing a limited demand for our other index-linked reinsurance policies. Zurich Insurance was trying to make the most out of the declining demand for catastrophic risk, while reducing their involvement in the business.

It became clear that we would have to start our own insurance company. We hired an investment banker to draw up the prospectus. The chairman and CEO of Zurich Insurance had been a big supporter of mine from the outset and agreed to be a seed investor. He said, "This is the perfect solution to our dilemma of avoiding taking more catastrophic risk on our balance sheet, yet still betting on insurance derivatives." He committed to invest $50 million in a new insurance company called Hedge Re.

I thought we would be able to raise $200 million for Hedge Re, but soon realized that I was wrong. There were no catastrophes happening, and reinsurance rates had dropped dramatically.

The bloom had left the rose on the capital raise for Centre Financial Products (CFP), and I was forced to sell the company. Fortunately, I had met the CEO of CNA, an insurance company based in Chicago, during the research phase for the relaunch of PCS-based catastrophe futures, and asked if he was interested in buying CFP or its assets. We finally reached an agreement. There was one hitch. CNA wanted me to become the executive chairman of Hedge Re, the renamed CFP. It was a turning point in my life. I enjoyed being an entrepreneur and did not want to become a full-time employee. It was a tough decision. On one hand, the security of being an executive at a prestigious company appealed to me. I was interested in insurance derivatives, and believed that I could expand the research laboratory of Hedge Re to include new capital markets products. On the other hand, I would lose my independence and would not be able to devote significant effort to emissions markets, which was my real passion. However, its chances at commercial success were limited at that time. We found a compromise that worked for both of us. My colleagues would run the business at Hedge Re, while I agreed to serve as nonexecutive chairman of Hedge Re. I pursued the environmental business separately.

Meanwhile, open interest in catastrophe insurance options at the CBOT continued to grow in 1997 and reached over 18,000 contracts by the end of the year. Hedge Re continued to focus on crop insurance during the following year, but I was unfortunately unable to persuade the CBOT to put more resources into a crop insurance contract. CNA decided to exit the business and closed Hedge Re in the second quarter of 1999.

An analysis of the failure of the CBOT catastrophe insurance options contract yielded some interesting implications for financial innovation. The original hypothesis that structural changes—in this case, the trend of U.S. migration to coastal regions and the increasing frequency and severity of natural calamities—require new capital to be channeled into the insurance markets still rings valid. However, this new capital would come from an influx of Bermuda-based reinsurance companies because of the ease of entry and favorable tax treatments for reinsurance companies, rather than from futures and options. In the years following Hurricane Andrew, nearly $3 billion in new capital flooded into the market and eight different reinsurance companies were formed. Furthermore, Lloyd's of London permitted corporate membership to attract additional capital into their business.

The other source of new capital came from catastrophe-based bonds, also known as cat bonds. A cat bond is an exchange of principal for periodic coupon payments wherein the payment of the coupon or the return of the principal of the bond or both is linked to the occurrence of a specified catastrophic event. Before an insurance company can issue a cat bond, it must establish an offshore special purpose vehicle (SPV) reinsurer from which it will buy a reinsurance contract. The risk premium is therefore passed onto the SPV, who in turn passes this on to the investors in the form of a coupon. Investors will post the notional amount of the bond in a trust and all the funds in the trust are then invested in U.S. Treasuries. This will collateralize the risk of the investors and eliminate credit risk.

Cat bonds were considered more attractive than PCS options because of their inherent flexibility. In a cat bond, a reinsurance company can customize its hedge to be indexed on its own losses, as is done in traditional reinsurance, or it can be indexed on PCS. Moreover, they can be structured to resemble a traditional excess-of-loss reinsurance contract or a quota-share contract, whereby investors share proportionately in the gains and losses of the reinsurer. Cat bonds and the SPV structure also provide the issuing insurance company with access to a broader set of investors than PCS options. Some investors, such as pension funds and mutual funds, are restricted from transacting in derivatives such as PCS options, but are allowed to invest in securities, such as bonds or notes. The ability to offer principal-protected tranches of a note increases the investor base even further because there are some investors who can invest only in AAA-rated securities. This larger set of potential investors may be especially important for companies seeking to transfer large amounts of risk to the capital markets.

In 1996, the United Services Automobile Association (USAA) issued its first cat bond of $477 million, with limited success. It was priced at 575 basis points over the London Interbank Offered Rate (Libor) and had coverage of 2.5:1. This was followed by Goldman Sachs, who successfully marketed a $68.5 million reinsurance securitization deal for St. Paul Re in 1997. From 1996 to 1998, there were a total of 18 separate issues. By the end of 2007, there were 116 separate issuances at an average of $188 million per deal. This totaled approximately $25 billion in new capital, or $2.5 billion per year. Between the new Bermudian reinsurance companies and cat bonds, the shortfall in capital in the insurance market was filled.

Although the CBOT continued to market insurance futures, there was a very big difference between marketing and selling. For products to be truly successful, one had to sell a product by assessing the customer's specific needs and finding solutions tailored to meet those needs, as opposed to more general marketing through conferences and presentations.

On the regulatory front, catastrophe insurance futures and option positions were never qualified as reinsurance, which by default increased the transaction costs. Since there were no internal champions for the product, there was no budget to try to change the rules. Furthermore, futures markets require a constant flow of information in order to prompt hedging and speculating. This was difficult to achieve with earthquakes, which were often hard to predict, limiting the price information available. On the other hand, the method used to forecast hurricanes was more reliable, therefore supplying enough data to warrant trading. Even so, a quiet hurricane season presented little change in risk and therefore a limited need to hedge.

Successful futures markets benefit largely from the participation of primary dealers who need to transfer interest risk, and commodity market participants like grain merchants who need to hedge their price risk. The structure of the insurance industry differs significantly from those of the grain and bond industries. Insurance and reinsurance brokers act as agents who control the flow of business. In fact, the market capitalizations of these brokerage entities were very large compared to the amount of risk capital in the insurance business. In 1994, insurance services comprised 55 percent of revenue for Marsh & McLennan, making the market cap attributable to insurance services \$3.2 billion versus its total market cap of \$5.8 billion.[27] It seemed uncanny that brokers had more capital than the insurance professionals who were underwriting their risk, especially given that the insurance products being sold were practically homogenous. Selling insurance was akin to selling white paint, and should not have required such a large brokerage force to back it up. The fact that most insurance sales are

[27]These values were extracted from the 10K that Marsh & McLennan Companies Inc. filed to the SEC in 1994.

beginning to be done online now through automated systems suggests the obsolescence of the old model.

It was a tradition for those who bought reinsurance to be compensated by premiums rebated to them in the case that there was no catastrophic event. This practice was abused by brokers who attempted to capture some of the reduction themselves. It didn't help when the Marsh & McLennan brokerage was almost ruined as a result of these payments.[28] The lack of volatility in the catastrophe insurance futures didn't inspire speculation either. From the point of view of minimizing the bid-offer spreads, there were permits sold at the CBOT but no dedicated market makers.

The design of the insurance futures contract was imperfect for three separate reasons. First, the ILWs traded in the reinsurance market were based on a fixed level of losses as the trigger, the event that resulted in payment, that is, an earthquake with a Richter scale reading of 6.0 at specified data stations. The futures contract only hedged a layer of losses, that is, $5 billion to $10 billion. This implied a less-than-perfect hedge and thereby increased transaction costs. Second, the presence of basis risk was a big issue among the insurance industry, as it was possible that the insurer or reinsurer's losses would not correlate perfectly with the total industry losses, as well as with the development time for the losses. Basis risk in financial markets was well known, and generally well understood by commodity or financial futures market participants who could easily adjust their hedging strategy to account for such risk. The issue here was that it was much more difficult to quantify basis risk in insurance markets.

The lack of an internal champion for the product ultimately resulted in the demise of catastrophic insurance futures. Although we were active as principals at CNA, the exchange would have had to actively market to FCMs and hedge funds to bring in speculative capital. Furthermore, the exchange never put resources into having the insurance regulators treat hedges like reinsurance. Since hedges on the exchange were not treated as reinsurance, they fell inferior to reinsurance, according to calculations based on regulatory capital.

---

[28]In January 2005, a Marsh & McLennan senior vice president, Robert Stearn, pleaded guilty for instructing insurance companies to submit noncompetitive bids to obtain business contracts, a process known as bid rigging.

In the 1990s, the leadership of the CBOT devoted a significant amount of time and energy toward building a new trading floor. Les and I fought against it. We thought that building a single purpose building for $200 million had no economic logic. Les jested bitterly, "I think it will become the largest McDonald's in the country." Phil Johnson predicted that it would become a food court.[29] The building was completed just as electronic trading was about to become a reality in the United States. It was a perfect example of Parkinson's Law—"work expands so as to fill the time available for its completion."[30]

Postmortem

At the end of the day, insurance futures failed at the CBOT, only to be reborn at the Insurance Futures Exchange (IFEX), an entity affiliated with the Chicago Climate Futures Exchange (CCFE). Insurance futures had a very modest beginning in 2007. In 2005, Hurricane Katrina struck New Orleans, with insured damages estimated at $70 to $150 billion.[31] The earthquakes in New Zealand and Japan have indicated that the industry will continue to need substantial capital. Perhaps it will end up as a centrally cleared product on some exchange. Counterparty risk is ever-present in the reinsurance sector.

There are reasons to be alarmed. In effect, many insurance and reinsurance companies believe that the state or the federal government will bail out companies, when in fact, I am not sure that states like Florida will have the money to do so. The insurance business essentially enjoys a "free put," whereby the government will always bail them out in the event of default. I also worry about the contingent liabilities on the U.S. government.

---

[29]Philip McBride Johnson, "The Food Court," *Risk* 10, no. 5 (May 1997): 16–17.

[30]C. Northcote Parkinson, *Parkinson's Law* (Cutchogue, NY: Buccaneer Books, 1996).

[31]"Gulf Coast Rebuilding: Observations on Federal Financial Implications." General Accountability Office, August 2, 2007.

Insurance derivatives are sleeping, or in a coma. It's still too early to pronounce their death as there was still an immense amount of risk relative to capital in the industry. The jury is still out.

Despite the apparent failure of insurance futures, the experience enabled me to develop key relationships within the insurance sector. In light of my later endeavors in the environmental market, these relationships became critical.

The "Brooklyn farmer" (left) and Max Naylor. *The Jefferson Bee*, Jefferson, Iowa, May 6, 1974.

Her name was Ginnie Mae. First GNMA ad, 1975.

Opening ceremony of CCX, September 30, 2003. From left to right: Former Secretary of Energy Spencer Abraham; myself; Mayor Richard M. Daley; and John McCarter, President and CEO of The Field Museum.

Dr. Michael Walsh of CCX at the CCX Opening Ceremony.

Press conference at the CCX offices announcing that the House of Representatives joined CCX. From left to right: Myself, Rahm Emanuel, Congressman Dan Lipinski, Senator Mark Kirk, and former Chief Adminstrative Officer of the House, Dan Beard.

Preston Martin (left) at the 30th Anniversary of the Launch of GNMA futures contracts and 28th Anniversary of the Launch of Treasury Bond futures contracts (Chicago, 2005).

PHOTO CREDIT: Gregg Schmitz.

Tony Frank at the 30th Anniversary of the Launch of GNMA futures contracts and 28th Anniversary of the launch of Treasury Bond futures contracts. (Chicago, 2005).

PHOTO CREDIT: Gregg Schmitz.

AEP Board after its merger with Central & South West: (from left) Morris Tanenbaum, Kathryn D. Sullivan, John P. DesBarres, Lester A. Hudson (1st row); William R. Howell, James L. Powell, myself, Robert W. Fri, E. Linn Draper Jr. (2nd row); Donald G. Smith, E. R. Brooks, Donald M. Carlton, Leonard J. Kujawa, Linda Gillespie Stuntz, Thomas V. Shockley, III (3rd row).
PHOTO PROVIDED BY AMERICAN ELECTRIC POWER.

IntercontinentalExchange's board: (from left to right) Myself, Judith Sprieser, Vincent Tese, Jeff Sprecher, Sir Robert Reid, Frederic V. Salerno, Charles R. Crisp, and Jean-Marc Forneri.

Climate Exchange plc's Board: (from left to right) Sir Laurie Magnus, Klaus Gierstner, the Hon. Carole Brookins, myself, Matthew Whittell, Sir Brian Williamson and Neil Eckert.

First check handed to the Kerala Biogas Project, India.

Opening of the Tianjin Climate Exchange, September 25, 2008. From left to right: Mr. Dai Xiansheng, Vice Mayor Cui Jin Du, and CNPC's CFO Mr. Wang Guoliang.

Les Rosenthal—under his leadership and political skills as chairman of the financial products committee, financial futures became a reality in 1975. As Chairman of the Board of the CBOT his political support helped the launch of the 10 year futures and Treasury Bonds options.
Used by Permission of Les Rosenthal and Rosenthal Collins Group, LLP.

Jack Sandner—Jack was the CME's longest serving Chairman (17 years). I had the privilege of serving under Jack when he was Chairman of the Board of the CME in the 1990s.

Bill Brodsky—Bill served as president of the CME from 1985 to 1997. He now heads the Chicago Board Options Exchange (CBOE), which launched the VIX Futures and Options contracts, the most successful new product in modern times. I served on the board of the CME when Bill was its president during the 1990s.
Photo Credit: Brian Kersey, *Fow Magazine*.

Chapter 13

You're Gonna Trade What?

Imagination is more important than knowledge.

—*Albert Einstein*

The mid-1990s had provided commercial opportunities in commoditizing insurance. In spite of good business prospects, I wasn't as excited about insurance as I was about the environment. The Rio Summit had become a distant memory by the middle of the decade. However, in 1995, two of its attendees, the Vice President of the Cousteau Society and the Under-Secretary-General of the summit profoundly changed my career. Paula DiPerna, Maurice Strong, and I spent the next 15 years working toward a common goal of combating climate change.

The G-77 Meeting at Glen Cove

In January 1995, the UN head of greenhouse gas emissions trading at UNCTAD invited me to speak on emissions trading to the Group of 77 (G-77),[1] at a meeting held in Glen Cove, New York. The objective of the meeting was to determine the necessary follow-up actions to implement Agenda 21, also known as the Rio Declaration on Environment and Development from 1992.

Knowing that my younger daughter, Penya, had participated in a Model United Nations at the Latin School and loved history, I brought her to the conference with me. We had previously taken a father-daughter trip to Cuba. The two of us always had fun together.

Animated groups of men and women dotted the main area of the conference center like magnets, deep in conversation. An air of diplomacy hung over the room. My daughter and I grabbed our meeting materials and badges and headed to the room where the session was being held.

Several speeches were given on economic development and forestry. I gave a presentation similar to the one I gave in Rio in 1992, as there had not been much development since the summit. I explained the cap-and-trade model and described the successful experience of SO_2 emissions trading in the United States. Emissions trading could be used to achieve the objectives of Agenda 21, but we couldn't be certain unless we actually tried it.

I was greeted by utter silence in the ensuing Q&A session.

Then, one by one, the attendees began to ask their questions. It was the typical official government meeting where attendees came with prepared remarks that barely reflected what the speakers said or the directions provided by the chair. The verbal baton was passed from one attendee speaker to another, and each delivered their prepared remarks as if alone in the room.

[1]The Group of 77 was established by the UNCTAD in 1964 and included 77 developing countries. It aims to promote the collective economic interests of the signatory nations and increase their negotiating power within the United Nations.

After the session concluded, I was approached by a short, salt-and-pepper-haired woman with a determined gait. "I'm Paula DiPerna," she said, "Vice President of the Cousteau Society." She expressed her disbelief that no one in the room had ventured anything about my suggestion for a cap-and-trade program. Nobody asked, "Is it possible?" "Has anything like this ever been done?" or "What makes you think it would work?" Despite the cold reception, my speech had resonated strongly with Paula, who later remarked, "Yours is the only practical idea to emerge in several years' worth of meetings after Rio."

I drove back to Manhattan with my daughter, who looked pleased and told me, "This was just like the Model UN!" Unbeknownst to me, the Glen Cove meeting not only played a decisive role for me personally, but for emissions trading around the world.

The Global Warming Emissions Trading Program (GETS)

After Centre Financial Products stopped trading SO_2 emission allowances, I continued working on insurance derivatives and promoting a market-based solution to the global warming problem. The insurance and climate change markets were related. Insurance companies bore the brunt of climate change, and the potential to bridge the gap between insurance and climate change using financial products was promising. I delivered numerous speeches to maintain CFP's visibility in the space and build my network.

I had first met Maurice Strong at the 1992 Earth Summit, then again at the CFP offices in New York, where we spoke about our shared interest in combating climate change. I related my involvement in the exchange space, SO_2 emissions trading, and CFP's experience in using allowances to finance scrubbers. Maurice had established the Earth Council, a not-for-profit foundation in Costa Rica, after the Rio Summit. It supported local sustainability efforts, and we mused about working together.

The opportunity presented itself three years later. I was in Toronto in June 1995 for a conference on derivatives and met Maurice for dinner. Maurice expressed his frustration at the lack of progress on climate change, and suggested that we form a private company to organize a multinational cap-and-trade regime. It was a bold idea and I loved it. He followed up with a letter that outlined his thoughts on the Global Warming Emissions Trading System (GETS), a proposed pilot program for reducing greenhouse gas emissions by trading allowances. Maurice and I reconvened later that month and agreed on the program's two primary objectives: one, reducing the emissions of participating countries, and two, demonstrating the viability of an international market in emissions trading. We were very ambitious. I thought about recruiting companies, while Maurice thought in terms of recruiting countries.

We attempted to recruit emitters from 5 to 10 different countries, and employed a top-down approach by engaging official multilateral organizations such as the UN Conference on Trade and Development, the UN Environmental Program, the UN Development Program, and the World Bank. As Secretary General of the Rio Summit and chairman of the Earth Council, Maurice had the stature to reach all of these organizations. To complement his governmental contacts, our CFP team at the time had the core competence to build the market. The project was to be divided into three stages: a development phase, the pilot program, and full-scale implementation. GETS would be incorporated as a for-profit corporation. We agreed to reserve 10 percent of the profits for grassroots sustainable development projects in emerging economies.

In February 1996, CFP delivered a preliminary business plan for our pilot global warming emissions trading program.[2] We distributed the plan to the UNCTAD, World Bank, and other potential partners. The secretary general of UNCTAD said he was happy to be associated with the effort. The rest of the responses were either negative or noncommittal. By the end of the year, we had agreed to write a more extensive business plan that laid the groundwork for developing a private placement memorandum to raise

[2]"Preliminary Development Plan for a Pilot Global Warming Emissions Trading Program," Centre Financial Products, February 1996.

$6.5 million. Although the proposal had garnered a tepid response, I was still hopeful that we would be successful in the financing and founding of GETS.

Preserving Rainforests through Markets

When we were unable to raise $200 million for Hedge Re, I sold the insurance part of Centre Financial Product to CNA. The remaining part of the CFP dealt solely with environmental finance. Doing this enabled me to separate the environmental business from the insurance business. The environmental business required little capital and was more of a boutique consulting firm for the development of new financial products and markets.

I now had no way out of my commitment to environmental markets, for I had just risked my capital and reputation on this new venture. As I was always teased, there was the front door, the back door, and the Sandor. There was no Sandor this time. There were no hedges left. This was both exhilarating and frightening as I had, once again, taken on significant personal risk in order to be part of an innovative process.

Sometime in the spring of 1997, I asked Mike Walsh rhetorically, "What do you think of CFP being the first U.S. company to voluntarily buy carbon offsets?" Offsets were credits generated from specific projects that reduced greenhouse gas emissions. These projects included investments in renewable energy (solar, wind, etc.) or carbon-capturing technologies such as reforestation and rainforest preservation. The credits generated were then used to offset, or compensate, for emissions made elsewhere. There was an opportunity to purchase rain forest preservation offsets from the Republic of Costa Rica. This would convey to the world that carbon was a tradable commodity and the purchase of offsets was commensurate with the objectives of a profit-maximizing company.[3]

[3]Casey Bukro, "Free-Market Plan to Cut Pollution Goes Global," *Chicago Tribune*, May 15, 1997.

In 1997, Maurice Strong invited the CFP team to a ribbon-cutting ceremony that was to take place announcing the preservation of a rainforest in Costa Rica. We planned to announce our scheduled purchase of carbon offsets after the ceremony, thinking it was an effective way to land publicity for our fledgling company. Costa Rica's innovative environmental policies, especially with regards to protection of its national parks, were later copied by other countries as potential avenues to incentivize forest preservation. It acted as a catalyst for what would later be called Reducing Emissions from Deforestation and Forest Degradation in Developing Countries (REDD).

We flew down to Costa Rica for the ribbon cutting. Our car was stopped by a roadblock as we drove toward the event. The clear blue sky was now a veil of gentle mist—a wondrous natural phenomenon. We got out of our car and proceeded to the ceremony on foot, where we were given ponchos to shield us from the misty rain. The lush green canopy was dotted with colored birds.

Our involvement in Costa Rica gave us insight into issues of forest carbon accounting methodology, monitoring, and verification that would later be critical to our work. CFP worked hand-in-hand with the Earth Council and the Costa Rican Office for Joint Implementation in the multistep process of purchasing Costa Rican offsets. The offsets were termed Certified Tradable Offsets ("CTOs") to create a brand for a global carbon "currency."

President Figueres personally thanked us at the ceremony for our purchase of the carbon offsets. I was glad that he knew about it and understood the power of markets. We left the event reinvigorated and rushed to a television studio for a news broadcast to discuss our purchase. The dean of INCAE Business School acted as my translator. I had spent a number of summers teaching hedging to farmers in Guatemala, El Salvador, and Panama as a part of weeklong programs organized by INCAE in the 1970s. The school had been established in 1963 by President John F. Kennedy under the Alliance for Progress. Originally located in Managua, Nicaragua, the campus was moved to San José, Guatemala after the Sandinistas overthrew the President. I will never forget the Sandinistas, who came to the hedging seminars with colorful bandanas on their heads and machine guns in their arms.

We signed the purchase agreement for the carbon offsets with the Minister of the Environment and went to the official dinner hosted by President Figueres. President Clinton was the keynote speaker.

I was delighted to be seated next to Tom Lovejoy, who was a chief scientist at the Smithsonian. In the 1980s, Tom was one of the first scientists to alert the world about the disappearing rainforests. Later, Tom marched with Chico Mendes, the main Brazilian advocate for rainforest preservation prior to his murder.[4] Tom and I had a stimulating conversation that lasted for several hours. After a long day, I felt both rejuvenated and tired and looked forward to the Policy Forum scheduled for the following month.

The Policy Forum on Greenhouse Gas Emissions Trading

We made several visits to major U.S. corporations after our purchase to urge companies to join us in buying these offsets, but there was no appetite. This all happened before the Kyoto Protocol even set the guidelines that would enable the carbon markets to begin. Oscar Wilde was right when he said punctuality was a waste of time. You had to be early.

Maurice and I had decided to start a policy forum as part of GETS and in preparation for the United Nations Framework Convention on Climate Change (UNFCCC) in Kyoto, Japan, in December 1997. The first Policy Forum on Greenhouse Gas Emissions Trading was scheduled for June 19, 1997 in Chicago.[5] The forum provided a gathering place and institutional support for governments and private sectors interested in designing and implementing an international greenhouse gas emissions trading system. The inaugural meeting laid

[4]Chico Mendes was a famous Brazilian environmental activist and union leader.

[5]Official program for the "Policy Forum on Greenhouse Gas Emissions Trading" sponsored by UNCTAD and the Earth Council.

out the long-term direction and goals of the Policy Forum. It also identified critical issues and practical next steps for the early operation of a greenhouse gas emissions trading system.[6]

It wasn't appropriate for CFP, a for-profit company, to act as the convener of the conference. We therefore served as the forum host. We organized the event by drawing upon our past experiences at the International Commodities Conferences and the Kellogg executive education programs. The attendees represented four continents and came from 14 different countries, including New Zealand and Australia—the furthest geographically.

The conference was followed by a cocktail party at our home. Ellen and I had been collecting photography and other fine art for about 20 years. Our library contained a wall devoted to portraits of famous politicians like Truman, Eisenhower, Mao, and Churchill. The head of a think tank from India was surprised by how multicultural the art was. He appreciated the irony of Margaret Bourke White's photograph of Ghandi hung next to Karsh's photo of Churchill. The head of the Brazilian Space Agency reveled in NASA's photographs of space and Richard Avedon's portraits of famous astronauts Alan Shepard and John Glenn. The cocktail reception for the Policy Forum began a new tradition of art, business, and diplomacy that Ellen and I continued to this day.

Maurice and I played the role of conference chairmen at the forum. Ronald Coase gave the keynote address, humbly professing that he knew nothing about the subject and did not understand why I had invited him to give a talk. He went on to deliver an inspiring lecture on the battle to auction radio spectrums, inviting the audience to think about other areas, aside from the atmosphere, where property rights could be assigned. He reflected that the absence of property rights contributed to women being like beasts of burden in developing countries. This stunned the audience. They were even more stunned when the 87-year-old Nobel

---

[6]The first forum was designed for governmental experts. It focused on specific technical issues such as allocation of allowances, monitoring, and compliance. The second forum was designed for experts from the private sector. It focused on market issues such as internal regulation, administering trading markets, and data services.

Prize–winning economist literally ran off to catch a bus back to the University of Chicago.

The White House sent a member of their Climate Change Task Force, who spoke about the administration's policy. The head of the EPA's acid rain division discussed the success of the SO_2 allowance trading program. The morning finished with a presentation from a U.S. power company, Detroit Edison, as well as one from the ministers of environment from Poland and New Zealand. Excitement was building for the luncheon speaker.

I had met Bill Daley in the 1970s when his brother Richard was running for the state senate. Bill had not been back to Chicago since he became Secretary of Commerce under President Clinton, and I thought the Forum would be a great venue for him. I extended an invitation to him to be our luncheon speaker. Bill accepted and gave his first speech back in Chicago, welcoming the move toward an international greenhouse gas emissions market as both timely and appropriate, especially given the successful precedent set by the acid rain program.[7]

The rest of the conference was filled by presentations from officials representing the governments of the United Kingdom, Brazil, the Netherlands, Germany, and Russia. Speeches were also given by delegations from the Organization for European Co-operation and Development (OECD), the World Bank, and the U.S. Department of Energy. The impressive array of speakers and attendees served to strengthen our network and build a group of stout-hearted men and women who now believed it feasible to start an international carbon market. We took the mystery out of emissions trading and lifelong friendships began.

It was important to keep the media involved, and the day ended with a press conference involving Maurice, the undersecretary of UNCTAD, and me. This was followed by a private tour of the Art Institute, a dinner at a local Italian restaurant, and revelry until late the

---

[7]Stephanie Foster, Frank Joshua, and Michael Walsh, "UNCTAD and Earth Council launched Greenhouse Gas Emissions Trading Policy Forum in Chicago," *Global Greenhouse Emissions Trader*, September 2, 1997.

following morning at blues and jazz clubs in Chicago. I was having an animated conversation with Michael Zammit Cutajar, the chairman of the UNFCCC and Elizabeth Dowdeswell, the former head of UNEP, when I looked down at my watch and realized it was almost 12:30 A.M. They both became avid supporters of the Chicago Climate Exchange. The party continued until just before 3:00 A.M. I vividly remember humming Frank Sinatra's "My Kind of Town" on the cab ride home and was often reminded of how impressed the attendees had been with Chicago.

Policy Forum Programme

Thursday, June 19, 1997

Evening Programme

7:00–10:00 Official Reception

Hosted by

Maurice Strong, Chairman, Earth Council

Rubens Ricupero, Secretary General of UNCTAD

Richard L. Sandor, President & CEO, Centre Financial Products Limited

Venue: Chicago Home of Dr. Richard L. Sandor

1303 North Astor, Chicago 60610

Friday, June 20, 1997

8:30–8:50 Opening Session

Chairman: *Mr. Maurice Strong* and *Dr. Richard L. Sandor*

Addresses by: *Maurice Strong,* Chairman, Earth Council

Michael Zammit Cutajar, Executive Secretary, UNFCCC Secretariat

Policy Forum Programme (*Continued*)

8:50–9:10	Keynote Address
	By ***Professor Ronald Coase,*** Nobel Laureate, Economics, 1991
9:10–10:30	International Greenhouse Gas Emissions Trading
	Benefits of an Initial-Phase Cap & Trade Market
9:10–9:30	***Richard L. Sandor,*** President & CEO, Centre Financial Products Limited
9:30–10:00	Panel
	Dirk Forrister, Chairman, White House Climate Change Task Force, USA
	Ambassador Ole Kristian Holthe, Royal Ministry of Foreign Affairs, Norway
	Ambassador John Fraser, Ambassador for the Environment, Canada
10:00–10:30	Discussion
10:30–10:45	Coffee Break
10:45–12:00	The U.S. Sulphur Dioxide Allowance Trading Programme: Are There Lessons for GHG Emissions Trading?
10:45–11:05	***Brian McLean,*** Director, Acid Rain Division, USEPA
11:05–11:30	Panel
	Michael Shields, Detroit Edison, USA
	Grzegorz Peszko, Advisor, Ministry of Environment, Poland
	Stuart Calman, Ministry for the Environment, New Zealand
11:30–12:00	Discussion
12:00–12:20	Departure for Chicago Board of Trade
12:20–1:00	Guided tour of the Trading Floor, Chicago Board of Trade

(*continued*)

Policy Forum Programme (*Continued*)

1:00–2:30	Official Lunch—Venue: Union League Club
	Hosted by
	Maurice Strong, Chairman, Earth Council
	Rubens Ricupero, Secretary-General of UNCTAD
	Elizabeth Dowdeswell, Executive Director, UNEP
	James Woffensohn, President, World Bank
	Richard L. Sandor, President & CEO, Centre Financial Products Limited
2:30–4:00	Round-Table Discussion
	Perspectives on an Initial-Phase Cap & Trade International Greenhouse Gas Emissions Trading Program
	Views of Governments
	Franz Tattenbach, National Coordinator, Costa Rican Office of Joint Implementation, Costa Rica
	Panel:
	Lulz Gylvan Meira Filho, President, Brazilian Space Agency, Brazil
	Gerard J. R. Wolters, Deputy Director-General, Ministry of Housing, Spatial Planning and the Environment, The Netherlands
	Franzjosef Schafhausen, Head of Division, German Federal Ministry for the Environment, Germany
	Abraham E. Haspel, Deputy Assistant Secretary, Department of Energy, USA
	Ian Pickard, Chairman, OECD/IEA Annex I Expert Group, Department of the Environment, UK
	Vladimir Berdin, Chief, Climate Change Division, Russian Federal Service for Hydrometeorology (Roshdromet), Russian Federation

The White House Conference on Climate Change

The Policy Forum had set the stage for an even more exciting second half of 1997. The White House had sent the Secretary of Commerce, an adviser to the Vice President, the head of the acid rain division, and others. We also attracted officials from the United Nations and other countries. This convinced me that the upcoming meetings in Kyoto would result in something tangible.

On September 30, 1997, I was invited to make a presentation before the hearing of the Committee on Energy and Natural Resources of the U.S. Senate of the 105th Congress. Our reputation was growing. It was hard to believe how we were reinventing CFP into an environmental company. I discussed the rationale for a voluntary international greenhouse gas emissions trading program, and its possible impacts on U.S. labor, electricity supply, manufacturing, and the broader economy.

We continued to gather momentum. One week later, I presented at another critical event—the White House Conference on Climate Change hosted by President Clinton. On the way over, I ran into Tom Lovejoy, who was with the president of the Carnegie Endowment for Peace. I subsequently delivered a lecture on emissions trading to them. Each of my personal relationships seemed to lead to another connection or speech. I was going through the required steps to build the case for emissions trading.

I entered the conference room and experienced the same humbling disbelief of my first board of directors meeting at the CBOT. Present at the meeting were some of the most important environmental leaders in the country. Among them were President Clinton, Vice President Al Gore, and a score of elected Senate and House members.

I sat in the audience and listened to a number of panels. The current chairman of American Electric Power spoke about AEP's preservation project with British Petroleum in Bolivia. What stands out in my memory is how little it cost to participate in avoided deforestation—less than $1.00 per ton of carbon. The chairman of my panel, Vice President Gore, invited me to give my presentation as the last speaker of his panel. The other panelists before me had spoken primarily about the difficulties and challenges of developing an international greenhouse gas market. I had a different outlook.

I began by saying that I felt like Tom Hanks in *Big*, a movie about a little boy who wished to be older. While his wish was granted, he became a boy magically trapped in a man's body and landed a job at a toy company, where attending dull marketing presentations on new toys was an unfortunate necessity. One day, the man-boy raised his hand and said, "I don't get it. This toy is no fun." This seemingly childish remark ultimately won the day, spurring passions long forgotten in the toy company. I felt the same optimism about developing an emissions trading market. Just as a child would know, perhaps better than any adult, that the purpose of a toy is to be "fun," I knew that markets needed to be built. Contrary to what some may have thought, this optimism did not stem from sheer naiveté, but years of experience.

This refreshing perspective seemed to enliven the President and stir the audience from their lethargic silence. When the panel ended, the Vice President leaned over to me and said with a smile, "Put an incentive in front of the traders in Chicago and watch how quickly they react." He understood the power of markets.

I was invited to a private meeting hosted by Timothy Wirth, who was in charge of negotiations for the upcoming Kyoto Protocol. Behind Tim sat Jane Fonda. Her husband, the media mogul Ted Turner, was also in the audience that afternoon. Ted Turner and Jane Fonda were both interested in climate change. They went on to found the United Nations Foundation in 1998 and Tim Wirth became its first president. Tim later invited Jane to join us at the table. Jane responded with humility, "That's for the experts. I don't belong there." When Tim's continual persuasion came to no avail, he said, "Jane, women are underrepresented at the table." That did the trick.

The day's ceremonies were followed by a cocktail party hosted by Al Gore. I made the mandatory appearance and left to catch a plane back to Chicago. I was always uncomfortable with staying around after a well-received presentation. Perhaps I feared that further conversation would dilute the strength of the arguments made on the podium, or maybe I secretly believed that "familiarity breeds contempt." I was later told that the Vice President had acknowledged my presentation and recognized me personally. It became apparent that I wasn't there. I felt a deep sense of regret whenever I thought about how ungracious I must have appeared. It was a mistake I would never make again.

A lot more happened that year. Molly Boren, wife of Senator David Boren, served on the board of Central and South West Corporation, a Dallas-based utility. There was an opening on the board of directors at CSW, and I had always been curious about how utilities functioned. I met with Dick Brooks, the CEO, and the management team at the Union League club. The chemistry was terrific and I joined the board. It turned out to be one of the most important educations I received. I learned something at every board meeting. It became more important as CSW soon merged with AEP, the largest coal-burning utility in the United States. I finally got to learn from the inside how the utilities made decisions about fuel choices and the environment.

The Kyoto Protocol

CFP was invited to Kyoto as part of the Earth Council team. I served on both the official program and a sideshow on GETS. The atmosphere of the UNFCCC conference at Kyoto on December 5, 1997 was electric. What was taking place in Kyoto felt like a movement, just as Rio had. Young environmentalists from Europe had taken the Trans-Siberian Railway to Vladivostok before making their way to Kyoto. It was obvious from their ruffled clothing and bloodshot eyes that they had been partying for at least a week before they arrived. The energy from the civil rights movement, the sexual revolution, and other passionate causes had somehow morphed into the environmental movement. It would be hard to stop these young people.

Mike and I participated in a sideshow sponsored by the Earth Council and we pitched the GETS idea. In addition, I presented at another sideshow sponsored by the Union of Concerned Scientists and separately was on an official panel with Maurice and others. We were trying to get exposure for GETS since the ratification of the Kyoto Protocol was not yet a foregone conclusion.

Everywhere we turned were old friends from the Nature Conservancy, Greenpeace, and the administration. It felt like we were part of the environmental crusade.

As President Clinton was unable to make the meetings, he sent Vice President Al Gore to take his place. The participation of the Vice President signaled the administration's commitment to the environmental cause. The case for action was further substantiated.

A couple of evenings before the Kyoto Protocol vote, I found myself having drinks with some of the representatives from France and Germany when the conversation drifted to the topic of carbon offsets. Both representatives were strongly opposed to the inclusion of domestic offsets in any emissions trading mechanism. They agreed it would be a cheap way for industrial companies to achieve reductions without taking any actions to mitigate emissions themselves. I pointed out that the entire purpose of emissions trading was to achieve reductions at the lowest cost to the economy—an argument that fell on deaf ears. Some slips of the tongue led me to infer that part of their vehement opposition seemed to have been driven by political reasons. The European Union would be put at a competitive disadvantage if international agricultural offsets were allowed as a compliance tool. The vast size of the United States provided ample opportunity to produce a significant amount of low-cost offset credits, whether through soil sequestration or avoided methane emissions from animal waste or reforestation. These offsets could then be used to flood the U.S. and European markets. Canada, Australia, and other nations could exacerbate the situation by also producing offsets. It seemed irrelevant to these men that global warming was reduced in the process. I was surprised but gained some insights into treaty negotiations. National interest was always a primary driver.

I had to return to Chicago before the final vote. Mike returned to the United States later and relayed the drama of incorporating emissions trading into the Protocol. It had been done at the insistence of the United States, despite the European opposition, and was gaveled into the treaty at 3:00 A.M.[8] The irony of this only really comes out in

---

[8]Kyoto Protocol to the United Nations Framework Convention on Climate Change, Article 17, United Nations, 1998.

retrospect, with the success of the EU Emission Trading Scheme and the death of cap-and-trade in the United States.

The Kyoto Protocol was an agreement that followed the principles approved in Rio. There was one major exception. While the Earth Summit only urged industrial countries to make nonbinding agreements to stabilize their greenhouse gas emissions, the Kyoto Protocol required its signatories to make formal commitments to reduce emissions from 1990 levels by an average of 5.2 percent. Specifically, the European Union would have to reduce their emissions by 8 percent, the United States by 7 percent, Japan by 6 percent, and Russia unchanged. As part of the agreement, some countries like Australia and Iceland were granted concessions and permitted to increase emissions by 8 percent and 10 percent respectively.[9] All these allocations were the result of political negotiations and not economic reasoning.

Moreover, the Kyoto Protocol called for three different mechanisms: emissions trading, a clean development mechanism (CDM), and joint implementation (JI). Emissions trading would be used primarily by Annex B countries to meet their reduction requirements.[10] The CDM and JI were project-based credits. CDMs would allow developed, Annex B countries to implement emission-reduction projects in developing countries. These projects could be exchanged for certified emission reduction credits (CERs), used to meet the emission targets set by the Kyoto Protocol. For example, a CDM project might involve a rural electrification project using solar panels. China and India became the largest providers of offsets.[11] JIs were bilateral

---

[9]Ibid., Annex B.

[10]Annex B countries are countries with emissions reduction commitments under the Protocol. These include mostly industrialized countries.

[11]A joint CDM project by China's Zhejiang Juhua Limited and Japan's JMD company was launched in March 2007. This project facilitated factories' transition from coal burning to alternative energy sources. (*China Daily*, October 28, 2006). India's first reforestation project was approved by the CDM Committee on August 21, 2010 ("India's First CDM-Approved Wasteland Restoration Project Launched," UNFCCC Project Database, August 2010).

emission reduction projects between developed countries.[12] These could be exchanged for emission reduction units (ERUs), used to comply with the mandated targets. One of the major advantages of project-based credits was that it would allow the host country to benefit from foreign investment and technology transfer.

The Kyoto Protocol was signed by 84 countries and ratified by 141 countries, coming into force on February 16, 2005, after the required number of signatories and ratifiers was achieved.[13] Signing indicated an intention to ratify, while ratifying meant that a country had agreed to cap emissions in compliance with the Protocol. Ironically, the United States signed the treaty but the Protocol was never ratified by the Senate. The Europeans, on the other hand, were the first to implement emissions trading.

The year ended on a wonderful note. Ellen and I were invited to Vice President Al Gore's Christmas party. While there were many political fundraisers present, there were even more intellectual supporters of the Vice President. On our way home, we spoke about the journey we had made from our humble beginnings in Brooklyn to this extravagant evening. Chicago had given Ellen the opportunity to be an artist and me, a place to create markets.

Since the remaining part of the CFP dealt solely with environmental finance, I renamed it Environmental Financial Products (EFP). EFP began humbly in May 1997 with me, Mike, and my secretary, Marilyn Grace. Mike's passion and specialty had been in the environmental part of the business, so the transition from insurance derivatives was easy. We were joined by Rafael Marques later that year, a doctoral graduate student in economics at the University of Illinois who had come to the United States from Brazil. He soon moved from his role as part-time research assistant to full-time employee. Rafael was

[12]The installation of three combined cycle gas turbines at GTES "Kolomenskoe," Moscow, was a JI effort between Russia and the Netherlands (*Global Carbon*, March 2011).

[13]Status of Ratification of the Kyoto Protocol, United Nations Framework Convention on Climate Change, accessed November 2011, http://unfccc.int/kyoto_protocol/status_of_ratification/items/2613.php.

extremely affable, intelligent, and a true diplomat at heart. I told him, half joking and half serious, that the job was all in preparation for his future role as the minister of state in Brazil.

Mike, Rafael, and I single-handedly sustained EFP in the early years. We would later go on to found the Chicago Climate Exchange (CCX).

The Demise of GETS

Unfortunately, our business prospect did not look as rosy after 1997. EFP attempted to get a consulting contract for the European Union. In collaboration with Deutsche Terminbörse (DTB), we submitted a proposal titled, "Designing Options for Implementing an Emissions Trading Regime for Greenhouse Gases in the European Community" to the Ministry of the Environment in Brussels in February 2000. I had become acquainted with the head of business development at DTB, and he agreed to work with us. I flew to Berlin to inform the Ministry of the Environment about our efforts. It seemed like an ideal partnership for the European Union. DTB was the leading European exchange, and EFP had both practical experience and valuable networks in the environmental market.

I was wrong. A European consulting firm ultimately won the contract. We learned from the experience that fundraising from governments was a full-time job. You had to know how to prepare the response and which boxes to check, an area in which EFP had no previous experience.

Undaunted by our first failure, we teamed up with the Irish Energy Centre to persuade the Irish government to start a pilot program for an emissions trading scheme. We were again unsuccessful. I learned the difficulty of persuading individual governments to implement pilot programs when there was no mandate for such programs, and abandoned the effort altogether. My disappointment was reinforced by the little progress we were making on the GETS initiative. Surely, if individual national efforts were futile, then any attempt at a multinational level would also be in vain. The GETS project effectively became moribund in early 1999. However, a lot could be learned from a post mortem.

GETS was a transformational idea that required the cooperation of governments, multilateral institutions, and environmental groups. Since GETS had begun before the Kyoto Protocol, it had no framework to rely on. Although it received some support from UNCTAD, the Earth Council, and CFP, GETS was not championed by any individual nation, a condition that was necessary for its success. Similarly, GETS was unable to attract sufficient support from NGOs, as most found GETS too comprehensive to fit their missions. Many of them simply distrusted markets. For all these reasons, GETS had been unable to build the institutions necessary for it to take flight. The legal and accounting framework was never built, and academic support never materialized. The intellectual climate at the time contributed to the project's demise. Academic work on the subject had thus far been limited to proving that global warming was a threat and alerting the world to the problem.[14] Concurrently, economists were more focused on modeling the impact of climate change than building the actual market institutions that would help reverse it.[15] As was the custom, the media was also taking their lead in identifying the problems rather than evaluating the solutions. There were also too many vested interests that would be damaged if GETS were to succeed.

In some small way, GETS had gathered momentum for emissions trading as a policy tool. It may have indirectly contributed to the latter's inclusion in the Kyoto Protocol, but we would never know with certainty. We were certain, however, that GETS had enriched the debate regarding flexible mechanisms. GETS had left a significant footprint in the White House and among senators and congressmen. EFP, on behalf of GETS, had reached out to the governments of countries like the United Kingdom, Germany, Brazil, and Costa Rica, and had built an expansive network in the process. In addition

---

[14]Gian-Reto Walther et al., "Ecological Responses to Recent Climate Change," *Nature*, March 28, 2002, 389–395; Camille Parmesan and Gary Yohe, "A Globally Coherent Fingerprint of Climate Change Impacts Across Natural Systems," *Nature*, January 2, 2003, 37–42.

[15]Anthony Patt, "Economists and Ecologists: Modeling Global Climate Change to Different Conclusions," *International Journal of Sustainable Development* 2, no. 2 (1999): 245–262.

to this, EFP had also conducted the first trade as a private sector entity for avoiding deforestation, which we believed supported GETS. Through dozens of speeches, published articles, and media coverage, EFP achieved widespread name recognition. We had a great reputation but no business.

We held two more Policy Forum meetings over the next two years, one in Toronto and one in London. Although the Kyoto Protocol had diminished the enthusiasm for GETS, I agreed with Maurice that the momentum built by the Forum should not be wasted. Mike went down to Argentina in 2000 for the Conferences of the Parties (COP)[16] meeting and had dinner with Maurice and one of his acolytes. The Policy Forum would be used to create the International Emissions Trading Association (IETA), and Maurice's student became president and CEO. To this day, the IETA remains a potent force in education and advocacy. Mike and I worked with the association in the years to come.

As Alexander Graham Bell, inventor of the telephone said, "When one door closes another door opens; but we so often look so long and so regretfully upon the closed door, that we do not see the ones which open for us." We would not dwell very long on GETS's closed door. Table 13.1 provides a list of some of the events that we participated in from 1995 to 1999. The web of relationships and the competence we had built up were about to pay off.

---

[16]The parties to the UNFCCC met annually in Conferences of the Parties (COP) to assess progress made on the climate change issue, largely reflecting the emissions reduction commitments made in the 1997 Kyoto Protocol. "Climate Leader: What Is the UNFCCC & the COP?," Lead International, accessed November 2011, http://www.climate-leaders.org/climate-change-resources/india-at-cop-15/unfccc-cop.

Table 13.1 Educational Outreach: Speaking Engagements

Date	Location	Description
January 14, 1995	Prague, Czech Republic	Richard L. Sandor, "Statement to the Prague Meeting on Sustainable Development"
September 24, 1996	Columbia University, NY	"Global Warming: Market-Based Solutions for the Environment" Columbia University, Center for Environment, Business, and Renewable Resources
September 15, 1997	University of Oklahoma	Institute of International Affairs—University of Oklahoma; "United States's Role in Environmental Policy," Keynote Speech
September 30, 1997	Washington, DC	Testimony to the United States Senate Energy and Natural Resources Committee: "Getting Started with a Pilot: The rationale for a limited-scale voluntary international greenhouse gas emissions trading program"
October 6, 1997	Kyoto, Japan	IUCN Conference on Innovative Instruments for Protection of Biodiversity
December 8, 1997	Kyoto, Japan	UNFCC/COP3 Sideshow presentation with Dr. Michael Walsh
March 13, 1998	Washington, DC	White House Climate Change Task Force—Roundtable Presentation
March 17, 1998	Vancouver, BC, Canada	Toward Innovative Solutions: Canada–United States GHG Emissions Trading Forum Keynote Speech

March 19, 1998	New York City, NY	The Energy Forum, "Solutions to Kyoto: Emissions Trading" Conference sponsored by the Graduate School and University Center of the City University of New York and the Weissman Center for International Business, Baruch College/CUNY in cooperation with the International Association for Energy Economics, NY
April 7–8, 1998	New York City, NY	"Kyoto: You Will Be Affected" Conference sponsored by the International Environment Forum of the World Environment Center Keynote Speech: "Kyoto: Why Should Industry Care?"
April 22, 1998	Washington, DC	Carnegie Endowment for International Peace Global Climate Change Meeting Session Title: "What Can Be done?"
April 27, 1998	Zurich, Switzerland	Board Meeting and Workshop Sustainable Performance Group–Sustainable Asset Management (SAM) Keynote Speech
May 11–12, 1998	London, UK	Emerging Markets for Emissions Trading: Opportunities from the Kyoto Protocol and the Implications for Business International Conference sponsored by the United Nations Conference on Trade and Development (UNCTAD), Department of Trade and Industry and Environment Transport Regions "Getting Started: Early Beginnings, Small Steps," sponsored by the Commonwealth Institute, Kensington
May 13, 1998	London, UK	Emissions Trading Meeting, Presentation to Officials of the Corporation of the City of London

(*continued*)

Table 13.1 (*Continued*)

Date	Location	Description
May 13–15, 1998	London, UK	Greenhouse Gases Emissions Trading Policy Forum Sponsored by the United Nations Conference on Trade and Development (UNCTAD) and the Earth Council
June 10, 1998	Washington, DC	The National Press Club Eighth Annual Energy Efficiency Forum—"Energy Efficiency in Restructured Markets," Session Title: Energy Efficiency: "The Fastest, Least Expensive Way to Reduce Greenhouse Gas Emissions"
June 19, 1998	Chicago, IL	University of Illinois at Chicago and MacArthur Foundation Conference, "Emissions Trading: Lessons from Experience. A Close Look at the Sulfur Dioxide Cap-and-Trade Market" Co-sponsored by the Federal Reserve Bank of Chicago Keynote Speech
July 13, 1998	Harvard University, Cambridge, MA	Harvard Institute for International Development, Executive Program on Climate Change and Development Presentation: Perspectives on international CO_2 emissions trading
September 22, 1998	The World Bank, Washington, DC	World Bank Seminar "Financial Risk Management of High Severity Risks," and "Convergence of the Insurance/Reinsurance and the Capital Markets" Keynote Speech
October 7, 1998	Washington, DC	Address to the board of directors, Resources for the Future, "Climate Policy Approaching Buenos Aires"

October 10, 1998	Chattanooga, Tennessee	Eighth National Conference of the Society of Environmental Journalists (SEJ) Sponsored and hosted by the University of Tennessee at Chattanooga and the *Chattanooga Times* Event: "Emissions Trading: Lowering Pollution or Red Herring?"
October 16, 1998	University of Kentucky, Lexington, KY	Gamma Sigma Delta Fall Seminar, College of Agriculture Keynote Address: "Using Markets to Motivate Environmental Improvement: The Role of Agriculture"
October 19, 1998	Chicago, IL	Delegation of Latin American Policy Makers Visit sponsored by USIA, State Department Organized by the International Visitors Center, City of Chicago "Market-Based Solutions to Environmental Problems"
October 29, 1998	Dublin, Ireland	Irish Energy Centre Conference—"Kyoto: Opportunity or Threat?" Keynote Address: "Market Mechanisms to Address Climate Change"
November 2, 1998	Northwestern University, Kellogg School, Evanston, IL	A Senior-Level Dialogue on Climate Change Policy Kellogg Environmental Research Center, Kellogg Graduate School of Management Northwestern University Session Title: "Critical Policy Issues Regarding Climate Change"
November 20, 1998	Washington, DC	University of California, Berkeley, Center for Sustainable Resource Development Conference on Carbon Trading and Sequestration, sponsored by the USEPA and Farm Foundation "Creating a Market for Carbon Emissions: Opportunities for U.S. Agriculture" Luncheon Keynote Address

(*continued*)

Table 13.1 (*Continued*)

Date	Location	Description
January 31, 1999	San Diego, CA	National Association of Conservation Districts 53rd Annual Meeting Town and Country Hotel "Agriculture's Potential to Store Carbon and Reduce Carbon Dioxide, the Major Greenhouse Gas" Keynote Address
February 5, 1999	Houston, TX	Energy Conference 1999 Keynote Address
March 15, 1999	Missoula, MT	Montana Carbon Coalition "Creating a Market for Carbon Emissions: Opportunities for U.S. Farmers" Keynote Speech
March 18, 1999	Chicago, IL	Environmental Protection Agency National Global Climate Change Meeting Keynote Address
March 27, 1999	Lyon, France	International Life Sciences Forum—BioVision Improving the Quality of Life and Protecting the Environment "Market of certificates for carbon dioxide and pollutants" Keynote Address
April 26, 1999	Zurich, Switzerland	Annual Meeting of the Sustainable Performance Group Presentation: "Recent Developments in Greenhouse Gases Emissions Trading"

Chapter 14

From the Pit to the Box

The Ascent of Electronic, Publicly Traded Exchanges

> We are no longer the knights who say ni! We are now the knights who say ekki-ekki-ekki-pitang-zoom-boing!
>
> —*Monty Python*

The decade of the 1990s ushered in the era of the next major revolution in U.S. futures markets—electronic trading. This in turn led to demutualization and initial public offerings (IPOs) of all major U.S. futures exchanges. There was no plan etched in stone by any single exchange to make all of this happen. Instead, a series of loosely related, and often arbitrary, events in Europe and the United States drove the trend. I was a witness to those events and played some small part in the transformation.

A Civilization Gone with the Wind

Exciting developments were taking place in the exchange world, and floor trading was on the way to becoming "a civilization gone with the wind."[1] I wanted to be part of the new world of electronic trading.

In Frankfurt, Deutsche Terminbörse (DTB) began an aggressive campaign to dislodge Liffe in London as the leader in Bund futures. To start off, DTB had a market share of about 35 percent, thanks to support from German banks. The first step of its campaign was to provide electronic access to their market for nonresident investors from London.[2] This move signaled the beginning of the end for floor trading in Europe. Electronic exchanges were simply more cost-effective than open outcry. I erroneously thought that U.S. exchanges, in particular the CBOT, would follow suit. I was not only interested in pushing for the CBOT to go electronic, but recognized my potential role to bolster the exchange's marketing of insurance derivatives and promotion of other new products. I also believed that the exchange could possibly become a platform for the electronic CO_2 emissions envisaged by GETS. The interests of the exchange had become perfectly aligned with my own.

My opportunity to transform the exchange emerged when Les Rosenthal and Billy O'Connor encouraged me to run for the position of second vice chairman of strategy. With Les and Billy as my allies, I figured there was little chance of losing. However, I was worried that my running could be misconstrued at the CME, where I served on the board of directors. I called Jack Sandner and Bill Brodsky, president of the CME, to give them a heads up. They wished me well. "I'll keep your resignation in the draw just in case you lose," Bill bantered good-humoredly. I landed the nomination for the position.

CBOT politics remained unchanged. Exchange rules allowed candidates to run on petition. Two candidates ran against me. I went back and forth between Chicago and New York to campaign, while Fred Uhlmann and other friends held events in support of my candidacy. I also went before the exchange members to promote Ceres,

[1]Margaret Mitchell, *Gone with the Wind* (New York: Macmillan, 1936).

[2]By November 1997, 65 percent of DTB's 171 members were remote traders. See Asani Sarkar and Michelle Tozzi, "Electronic Trading on Futures Exchanges," *Current Issues in Economic and Finance* 4, no. 1 (January 1998).

a member-owned corporation that would promote for-profit activities and electronic trading. It was only enjoying limited success at the time and I hoped to change this. I pledged to work toward the development of new products and electronic trading and boldly predicted that membership seat costs would reach unprecedented levels of more than $1 million if the exchange were to develop the appropriate strategy.

Ellen and I were at a charity dinner in New York on the day of the election. After dinner, I called the number given to me to find out the results, but it was the wrong number. I started to get anxious.

The next morning I received a congratulatory call from Les. The campaigning had paid off, for I had received more votes than the other two candidates combined. I went back to Chicago to attend Billy O'Connor's Christmas party at the racquet club. I felt like the prodigal son returning home, and thought the New Year would bring changes to the CBOT. I was wrong.

The executive committee meetings discussions often centered on exchange politics and not strategy. I repeatedly advocated promoting new products such as insurance and environmental derivatives, and electronic trading. I had a vested interest in those new products and was careful to disclose it. I had no conflict of interest with regard to electronic trading. I pushed the issue whenever I could. The leadership of the exchange was not accustomed to addressing politically unpopular issues, let alone educating the exchange members about change and its opportunities. The result was inertia. There was no easy segue into electronic trading. I felt nothing but goodwill toward my fellow members on the exchange. I understood that some were not able to deal and profit from oncoming change. The opposition to electronic trading was a function of too few champions and poor governance. It was not due to a lack of intelligence by the members. I became accustomed to being the sole dissenter at most of the executive committee meetings on many strategic matters.

On other matters, I sat quietly and made no comments. The executive committee spent an inordinate amount of time planning an outing for the members at Six Flags of America. After the event, more time was spent regaling the fun that members had. The 150th anniversary party was also discussed to the last detail by the executive committee. They also debated incessantly about the expenditure for a fountain outside the new building. I quickly grew weary and bored.

The most heavily discussed topic was the new trading floor that Phil Johnson predicted would end up being a food court. Members fought vigorously over the design of the trading floor, as one's physical location, and therefore one's ability to see signals (called the *sight lines*) in the trading pit was decisive in getting orders. I was surprised that there was no debate about regulations on the height of women's high heels. High heels made women taller than men, and gave them a physical advantage in the trading pit. I thought it would be interesting to create a market for booth space and where one stood in the pit. This would have been an efficient mechanism for allocating these scarce resources, and put an end to the political infighting. I brought it up to stimulate debate, only to be completely dismissed. The leadership thought I was from the central bank of Mars.

Stock Index Futures—A Postscript

By the 1990s, the S&P 500 had gained a significant edge over Dow Jones Industrial Average (DJIA) among institutional investors as the bellwether for the stock market. Stock index futures were a critical asset class for the exchange. The head of marketing at the CBOT developed a good relationship with an editor of the *Wall Street Journal*, which was published by Dow Jones. This opened the door for the CBOT management team to successfully negotiate a license to trade a futures contract on the index.

The Battle of CME and CBOT

The CBOT launched the DJIA futures and options contracts in October 1997. S&P retained its franchise as the bellwether of indexing, and volume in the contract was modest. The ink was hardly dry on the Dow Jones deal when the CME swung into action. The seesaw battle between the CBOT and the CME would once again foster innovation. In response to the CBOT's new products, the CME launched an electronic mini-version of the S&P futures, dubbed the E-mini S&P, to compete with the CBOT for business from small investors. Because of the increase in the S&P from 122.74 in 1982 to 747.65 in 1997,[3] there was a growing sentiment to split the contract. Jack Sandner, then chairman of the exchange, was in favor of decreasing the size of the contract.[4] The E-mini S&P was a way to accomplish this goal. The original contract for the S&P futures stayed at the same size and was traded in the pit while a smaller sized contract, the E-mini, was traded on an electronic platform. Booths with computers circled the open outcry pit, thereby enabling arbitrage between the two contracts. This move to electronic trading facilitated the transformation of the CME from an open outcry into an electronic exchange.

At the same time, another change was occurring at the CME. There was talk at the CME board about transforming the CME into a for-profit exchange. Jack Sandner, again, wholeheartedly supported the move. Rick Kilcollin, the president of the CME, also thought the move would focus the exchange and limit future political wrangling.

The CME hired McKinsey and Company in 1997 to recommend the best form of governance. On the basis of their report, the exchange submitted a proposal to demutualize the exchange and turn it into a for-profit company. The membership voted in favor of the proposition in 1999.

Although some would argue differently, the CME's decision to list the S&P E-mini on an electronic platform and demutualize the exchange marked the beginning of the exchange's hegemony.

Battery Ventures

The introduction of the E-mini S&P marked the beginning of the CME's evolution into an electronic exchange which, in turn, led to a demutualization and a public offering. However, the exchange needed some more impetus before its transformation could be complete.

[3]The S&P 500 closed at 122.74 on January 4, 1982, and 747.65 on January 6, 1997—each date was the first day that markets were open that year.

[4]Personal conversation with the author.

In 1997, a visit by a venture capital firm prompted me to become more involved in the process of unlocking value in exchanges. Battery Ventures, a venture capital firm that invested in technology-driven firms, had come to visit Les, who introduced them to me. Battery was investing in the business to business (B2B)[5] space and wanted to learn more about markets. I met with them and developed a personal and professional relationship with Scott Tobin. I later served on the board of one of their portfolio companies and helped them evaluate investment opportunities.

I flew to Boston in 1999 and had lunch with the Battery team at a restaurant called Legal Sea Foods. After listening to the progress they were making in their new ventures, I suggested to them, "I think you're missing the biggest opportunity in the space." I proceeded to make the case that the biggest B2B opportunity was to invest in futures exchanges and help them transition from open outcry to electronic trading, starting with the CME. Scott later remarked that the moment reminded him of the old E. F. Hutton television commercials, which featured individuals milling about in quotidian circumstances. At a particular moment, a person would say, "Well, my broker is E. F. Hutton and E. F. Hutton says . . ." and all activity would freeze, accompanied by a deep, solemn voice in the background that stated, "When E. F. Hutton talks, people listen."

I returned to Chicago that night and called Les the next morning. Battery was interested in buying the CME, and I wanted to partner with them and Les in making it happen. Les was incredibly astute about exchange politics, and went off to float a trial balloon at the CME. He called back after making some inquiries. "I think it's worth a shot," he said, but added as a note of caution, "But the politics may kill it."

After informing the Battery team about the economics and politics of the CME, we went off to make our pitch. I had been to many board meetings in the CME's boardroom before, but never as a presenter.

Depending on the assumptions, Battery's offer to the CME ranged from $400 to $800 million. This was worth more than the seats. Members could take all cash, all stock, or a combination of both. Although the CME's E-mini S&P contract had already set them well on their way

[5]This describes the transactions between a business and other companies, as opposed to the transaction that occurs between a business and a consumer.

toward electronic trading, they still lacked the technological expertise and the network of technology providers that Battery could supply. In fact, their expenditure on technology in 1999 was only $50.8 million, compared to the $180 million in 2011. By injecting the element of venture capitalism into the mix, Battery proposed to help unlock the equity in the exchange and help it gradually transition toward a for-profit culture.

Shortly after the presentation, the CME board conveyed that the offer was insufficient. CME's managing director of product development and sales at the time later told me that the CME management actually found the offer decent, but it was the board of directors who thought it subpar. There was a joke circulating in the futures business about traders who put in orders that they didn't expect to get filled. I called these traders CIC, short for "cancel if close." Similarly, any offer by the CME was likely to be rescinded if our bid was close to their offer. Les and I advised Battery that any small improvements in their bid for the exchange would not change anything, as it would require a ridiculous bid to get the board of the CME to agree. In the end, Battery Ventures didn't think there was value for their investors at a substantially higher price. Both the CME and Battery moved on.

Failing to convince the CME, our next choice was to target the CBOT. Les and I informed the Battery team of the personalities at the CBOT, and how the exchange culture differed from that of the CME. I warned them that there was only a small likelihood of success.

Our pitch to the CBOT took place in one of the more modest conference rooms near the boardroom, suggesting a lack of interest by the executive committee. Shortly after our pitch, the first vice chairman of the exchange asked, "Will you and Les personally benefit if the transaction is completed?" "Yes, of course," Les said, somewhat curtly, and turned his attention back to the presentation. As predicted, we were later told that the CBOT was not interested. Les and I advised Battery not to bother putting together a more detailed presentation.

Unlocking Liffe

Les and I met to discuss the next steps and laugh about the course of events. Neither of us wanted to give up. Les suggested that I call Brian Williamson, the chairman of Liffe.

Eurex, the new German financial futures exchange resulting from the merger of DTB and Soffex, was threatening to replace Liffe as the leading European exchange. Liffe had a futures market in 10-year German government bonds called Bunds, as well as shorter-term German government debt, but was losing market share. In 1998, Eurex had a tipping point and had wrested away Liffe's major product—Bund futures. DTB's market share in Bund futures volume had increased from 19 percent in 1991 to about 42 percent in 1997.[6] By October 1998, Eurex's market share exceeded 99.9 percent in Bund futures volume.[7]

I was on an advisory board of the Bank of England, created specifically to combat the potential decline of London as a financial center. Its members included Brian Williamson and Pen Kent from the Bank of England, both of whom I had worked with when Liffe was being established. One of the recommendations that came out of this advisory board was to turn Liffe around, so that it would become an electronic, publicly traded exchange run by professional management.

Liffe was operated as a mutually owned, open-outcry exchange. Eurex, on the other hand, was a for-profit electronic exchange. I had come to know about their electronic platform from my consulting gig with Soffex. They made the strategic choice of going electronic at the start, and DTB merely continued that tradition. Eurex had a blank slate and no legacy of open outcry traders. In its present state, Liffe was no match for Eurex. Liffe was in dire need of help and Battery Ventures had a real value proposition.

Everyone was counting on Brian to reverse the downward spiraling trend of Liffe. He had had a successful career as a pioneer at the exchange. He also had been chairman of Gerrard & National, one of the leading discount houses, and was awarded a Commander of the British Empire for his services to the financial sector, including his role in helping the Hong Kong Futures Exchange after the 1987 crash.

---

[6]Asani Sarkar and Michelle Tozzi, "Electronic Trading on Futures Exchanges," *Current Issues in Economic and Finance* 4, no. 1 (Federal Reserve Bank of New York, January 1998): 2.

[7]Craig Pirrong, "Bund for Glory, or It's a Long Way to Tip a Market," University of Houston, February 27, 2003, 9.

SOFFEX: The World's First and Fully Integrated Electronic Exchange

Ricardo Cordero was a young Swiss academic and financial markets professional who graduated from the University of St. Gallen in Switzerland. He had an interest in the still-developing financial futures sector in the 80s, and had written his thesis on the subject when it didn't have a lot of academic credence. Europe was following the United States with the creation of LIFFE and MATIF. Ricardo thought there was a role for a financial futures exchange in Switzerland and saw the potential offered by electronic trading—even though computers were still a rarity in trading floors. At the time, the UBS trading floor in Zurich held only one computer, and it was left idle most of the time.

He found a mentor and supporter in his boss, Rudi Mueller, an executive at UBS. Rudi encouraged the young academic to write a paper about his views on the creation of a new exchange in Switzerland, which could consolidate the existing seven exchanges operating in the country. Even more revolutionary, he proposed that the exchange be all electronic, with the trading and clearing functions fully integrated. The idea was first met with skepticism by the heads of securities departments at banks in Zurich. He told us that one head of a bank even left him a note saying "Thank you for your interesting presentation. You may want to come back when you have better ideas."

Ricardo came to the United States to learn as much as possible about the futures industry. While in Chicago, he called me up at my Drexel office. He said he wanted to stop by to talk about financial futures. Although I was getting ready to leave for Switzerland that evening, I agreed to meet him right away. Robert DeNiro had said in the epic saga *Once Upon a Time in America*, "You can always tell the winners at the starting gate." I always found this to be true when spotting talent. Ricardo possessed all the qualities of a promising young man—a hunger for knowledge and an inquiring mind. We spent some time together and since

(*continued*)

SOFFEX: The World's First and Fully Integrated Electronic Exchange (*Continued*)

I had to leave, I asked my colleagues to give him a guided tour of the CBOT trading floor. Ricardo later told me that he felt like a kid in a candy store while our staff explained the mechanics of trading Treasury futures.

The rise of London and Paris as financial centers was exerting pressure on the Swiss financial establishment. On top of that, the Swedish OM exchange was also thinking of starting an all-electronic market. The time was ripe for Ricardo's idea. The exchanges and major Swiss banks like UBS and Credit Suisse supported the concept and financed it to the tune of 60 million Swiss francs. The only company that could commit to deliver the software development team was Arthur Andersen, a Chicago-based company that I had worked with on accounting standards for interest rate futures. I wondered if they took on the assignment because they saw a big opportunity based on their experiences with Chicago exchanges. Due to the high demand for office space in downtown Zurich, the project's team had to set up their laboratory in a somewhat seedy area of town. This location didn't undermine the project because the team was young, diverse, and included almost 100 professionals from all over the world. Ricardo called and asked if I would be a consultant. I flew there and saw the size of the project. It didn't take a lot of insight to realize it was a game changer. From its inception in 1986 to the exchange's launch on May 19, 1988, the project took two years to complete.

To this day, the exchange remains one of the major projects of this magnitude undertaken in Switzerland. During the stock market crash of 1987, many people wanted to stop the project out of fear that the financial system would collapse. UBS threatened to take over the entire project and own 100 percent of SOFFEX, forcing other parties to return to the project. It was also during this time that Ricardo called me, once again, to seek my input and approval of the contract specifications that his team

SOFFEX: The World's First and Fully Integrated Electronic Exchange (*Continued*)

had designed. It was heartening to me to see the work that this young man and his team were doing. It reminded me a lot of my own experience trying to develop an all-electronic trading exchange in California in 1969. Unlike the U.S. exchanges that had been around for over a century, the SOFFEX had a blank slate that allowed Switzerland to move forward, a decade ahead of the United States.

SOFFEX later sold its software to Deutsche Terminbörse, and they later merged. The merged entity became known as Eurex. The success of Liffe and MATIF inspired the Germans to start their own exchange. Since they had no political baggage and no vested interests, the decision to set up an electronic exchange was easy. SOFFEX was a success and still retains the title of the world's first electronic exchange to integrate trading with clearing under one system. When writing this book and reminiscing about my work on SOFFEX, I was reminded of Harry Lime, the cynical character played by Orson Welles in the classic British movie *The Third Man*: "In Italy for 30 years under the Borgias, they had warfare, terror, murder, and bloodshed, but they produced Michelangelo, Leonardo da Vinci, and the Renaissance. In Switzerland they had brotherly love—they had 500 years of democracy and peace, and what did that produce? The cuckoo clock." Now, they can also boast of electronic trading.

Brian was driven by both public service and commercial logic. He was uncertain, however, that the loss of the Liffe franchise would be detrimental for the City of London. To him, the loss of Liffe would merely cause a "Wimbledon effect,"[8] meaning that the status of London

---

[8]Although Wimbledon, the famous stadium where the annual British Tennis Open is held, was purchased by foreigners, the status of the event and London's reputation as the tennis capital remain undiminished.

as a financial hub would remain unscathed even if its leading exchange were to be cannibalized by Frankfurt. He argued that "the traders would still stay in London!" While this was probably true, I contended that the financial infrastructure of an exchange is not merely supported by traders, but by a network of technology providers, lawyers, accountants, and so on. If Frankfurt became the hub of electronic trading, then these crucial market players would disappear from the city of London. Therefore, while it was true that "the traders would still stay in London," the status of the city as an international financial center could still be threatened. Brian's argument was valid in the short term, but not necessarily in the long term.

Accordingly, I shared this view with Brian and the advisory board of the Bank of England. They eventually reached the same conclusion, as did Brian. Liffe would fight for its survival. They needed new leadership and Brian was the natural candidate. Prompted by pressures from the UK government, members of London's financial and political community, the Bank of England, and the Financial Services Authority (FSA), Brian decided to take the position.

Shortly after Brian became chairman, I flew to London to have dinner with him at a restaurant called Wilton's, which served traditional English fare with recipes that traced back to 1742. It was small and intimate, with discreet waiters who went about their business like shadows. It hosted a lot of power dinners. Somewhere in between the quail eggs and the bread pudding—a dessert that my mother often cooked—our conversation drifted to the challenges that were facing my friend. The first step was at least clear: Close the floor and migrate all trading to an electronic platform, more easily said than done. The second step involved inventing a product complex that had the potential to be as significant as interest rate futures.

While racking my brain to come up with a new product complex that would give the Liffe a competitive edge, I was reminded of the success that the CBOE had enjoyed with stock options. There had been a profound change in the importance of equity markets relative to bonds. The concept was certainly not a novel one. In fact, it dates back to the Amsterdam Stock Exchange, where futures and options contracts on the ducaton shares of the Dutch East India Company were traded. I also knew that the Shad Johnson Agreement had banned the trading of single stock futures and futures on narrow-based stock indexes in the United States.[9] If Liffe started trading single stock futures, the U.S. regulatory agencies would have a greater incentive to lift the ban, and in doing so, expand the market for single stock futures. As long as Liffe could capitalize on first-mover advantages, its leadership in the world of futures trading would remain untarnished. I said to Brian, "trade futures on individual stocks."

Debt was a 1980s commodity, and the U.S. financial sector provided the paradigm. In 1990, the United States had accumulated $2 trillion in the form of outstanding federal debt. Ten years later, that figure jumped to $3 trillion and the size of the U.S. equity market rose from $3 trillion to $14 trillion. Europe was undergoing a similar transformation.

That evening with Brian marked the beginning of another 12 years of adventure and innovation.

Several weeks later, the Battery team and I made a presentation to the Liffe board. I met with the team before the meeting to discuss strategy and to coach them about English business etiquette. They were slightly apprehensive about how we would be received. Once again, humor came to my aid. "We don't want to be a pair of brown shoes at a black tie event," I said. This remark seemed to ease the tension, and we went off to make our presentation with a much lighter step.

The presentation led to the consummation of the deal. Battery asked Blackstone to become a partner, and the two private equity firms developed a strong relationship. Brian worked with a consulting firm called Cap Gemini to articulate the exchange's strategy. Battery was in favor of closing the floor and making Liffe an all-electronic exchange. Liffe already had an electronic trading platform called Liffe Connect, but had room to make further investments in the system. Battery pushed Liffe to reinvent itself as a technology provider and an operator of exchanges. The proposed exit strategy was either a sale to another exchange or a public reoffering of stock. Liffe had created a public company earlier, and the stock was trading at about £3 to £4. Battery was prepared to invest at a premium to where the stock was now

---

[9]Russell R. Wasendorf and Elizabeth Thompson, *The Complete Guide to Single Stock Futures* (New York: McGraw-Hill Professional, 2003).

trading. The Liffe board approved of the new strategy and the terms and conditions of the offer.

An extraordinary general meeting of the shareholders was held on November 20, 2000. Brian built an incredible case for the offer. The shareholder vote was nearly unanimous. Ten million new shares were to be issued at £6 per share. The exchange would raise £57.4 million net of expenses. Battery and Blackstone acquired 29.4 percent of the exchange at £6 per share, and were issued warrants to buy an additional 11.6 percent of the exchange at a price of £12 per share. The new shareholders were entitled to two board seats. We reasoned that with investors on the board of directors, the corporate culture at Liffe was likely to change into that of a real, rather than nominal, for-profit exchange. I was elected a director of Liffe and represented Blackstone, while Scott represented Battery.

The next year was very exciting. Brian was not only a visionary, but an outstanding chairman. I particularly admired the way he conducted his board meetings. They always took place in the morning, followed by a directors' lunch. This was different from the model Henry Hall Wilson followed. If contentious issues ever arose in the meetings, the luncheon afterward provided a convivial atmosphere to ensure that issues discussed at the meeting did not leave a bad taste with the directors. I later conducted the Chicago Climate Exchange meetings the same way.

In addition to attending Liffe's board meetings, I helped with marketing and gave speeches on single stock futures, now trademarked as "universal stock futures." Brian had worked with the Financial Service Authority (FSA) and the Bank of England for approval to trade these contracts without having to pay the traditional transaction tax for stocks. This was known as the stamp tax. This would have made transaction costs too high. An entrepreneur, who had advised many of the world's leading exchanges on development and strategy, was hired to coordinate the marketing of the product. We proceeded to give presentations in London and throughout the European continent.

Trading began on Monday, January 29, 2001. Universal stock futures turned out to be the most successful new product in a decade and were widely imitated throughout Europe. In 2010, NYSE Liffe traded 289 million single stock futures contracts, more than any other leading exchange in single stock futures such as RTS and Eurex.[10] To protect their franchise as regulators, the United States ultimately lifted the ban on single stock futures with the passage of the Commodity Futures Modernization Act of 2000. This led to the launch of a new futures exchange based in Chicago called OneChicago that specialized explicitly in single stock futures, with minority investments by the CME and CBOT. A former chair of the CFTC became the founding chairman of OneChicago. The total volume traded at the exchange totaled 4,971,160 in 2010. NASDAQ-Liffe Markets (NQLX) also launched single stock futures, this time in New York. Once again, the U.S. derivatives exchanges in the Midwest led the way. This time, they were imitators and not innovators. Universal stock futures were jointly regulated by the SEC and CFTC, creating some difficulties stemming from dual regulation. The biblical edict of not serving two masters held true into the twenty-first century.[11]

The Liffe management team oversaw a smooth transition from open outcry to electronic trading. Short-term interest rate (STIR) contracts continued to be dominated by Liffe. The Eurex threat was stopped. This included contracts on 90-day sterling rates and 90-day Euro interest rates. The latter was called Euribor as opposed to Eurodollars.

Parenthetically, I trademarked Euribor because I did not want a repeat of my experience with the term derivatives, which I had coined but never bothered to trademark. My original intention was for the term to describe the futures and options contracts that were traded on the Chicago exchange, but it was subsequently used to describe not only regulated products on futures transactions, but any customized products traded off the exchange, that is, bilateral OTC transactions. This confusion between OTC derivatives and exchange-traded derivatives has often led to unwarranted criticisms of exchanges and was one of the reasons that led me to write this book.

---

[10]IOMA/IOCA Derivatives Market Survey, World Federation of Exchanges, May 2011.

[11]Luke 16:13: "No servant can serve two masters, for either he will hate the one and love the other, or he will be devoted to the one and despise the other. You cannot serve God and money." English Standard Version Study Bible.

I notified the European Banking Federation (EBF) that it had violated my rights. Eventually, EBF and I arrived at a private settlement. I gifted the rights to Liffe because of my relationship with Brian and the exchange.

A short 10 months after the Battery-Blackstone acquisition of Liffe, the exchange was in a position to either further promote itself as a public company or sell itself to an existing exchange. The Liffe board was in favor of seeking a purchaser. The two likely candidates were the London Stock Exchange (LSE) and Euronext, a holding company that owned exchanges, including the Paris Stock Exchange, Amsterdam Stock Exchange, and the MATIF. There was a preference for LSE among the board members, but LSE was slow to show interest. By the time LSE came to a decision, it was already too late. Euronext had entered the scene to purchase Liffe and rumors circulated throughout the industry about a pending sale, with obsessive speculation over the sale price. Friends in the industry suggested that a price of £11 or £12 per share would change the face of the industry.

The tragedy of the World Trade Center bombing on 9/11 occurred during this time. All negotiations ceased for about a month. The financial world took a big hit that day. So many of us lost friends and colleagues. I went into a period of mild depression for a month after this incident because of the friends I had lost.

I was at a memorial at Holy Name Cathedral sharing my condolences with friends and family when I saw Scott Gordon. Scott was an old friend and the chairman of the CME at the time. Scott, staunch and compact, usually had an illuminating smile on his face. Not on this occasion. We discussed our losses, and as the conversation came to a close, he said in a tone of forced gaiety, "Congratulations on Liffe. I heard it's going to be £12 per share!" I smiled, but couldn't bring myself to comment.

Unbeknownst to me, Scott was leading an internal effort to take the CME public. The success of the E-mini S&P and a majority vote to finally demutualize the exchange served as the catalysts. To this day, I am convinced that it was the unlocking of value by Liffe that pushed the CME to do an initial public offering. It is ironic how the United States had exported to Europe the idea of for-profit electronic exchanges, but imported the governance and proof of concept from

Europe. The same applies to emissions trading. The opposite seemed to be true of the manufacturing world—the United Kingdom had invented the first jet engine and the radar, but it was the United States that ultimately commercialized them.

The Liffe acquisition was completed in December 2001 and finalized in January 2002, with a final purchase price in excess of £18 per share. This was more than three times the price of the offering announced a mere 13 months earlier, and more than six times the price of the shares when negotiations had begun for the Battery-Blackstone acquisition. The high price was the result of a bidding war between the London Stock Exchange and Euronext.

The valuation of the exchange reverberated throughout the futures industry, hastening IPOs not only in the United States but across the globe, and forever changing the way futures exchanges were governed. Every major exchange in the United States went public within the next three years. The CME did so in December 2002, CBOT in October 2005, NYSE in March 2006, and NYMEX in November 2006. Table 14.1 illustrates the trends of exchanges in listing IPOs, demutualizing, and becoming electronic.

The Wagner Patent—Good Ideas Never Die

The first exchange in the United States to file for an IPO was the CME, which began trading publicly as of January 1, 2003. I started to take a more personal interest in their filings when I realized that it was a follow-up on the work I had done 30 years earlier on CCARP.

E-Speed and its chairman, Howard Lutnick, had sensed the intellectual property of electronic trading and bought a patent for it. The patent was developed earlier by Susan Wagner and eponymously named the "Wagner Patent." After working at the CFTC, Wagner joined the World Energy Exchange and applied for the patent in 1983. The exchange was a commercial failure and the patent was inherited by a Dallas firm controlled by the principals of the World Energy Exchange. When the CME began its transformation into an electronic exchange, in preparation for an IPO, it was sued by Howard Lutnick for patent infringement. After the lawsuit became public, Ellen asked me, "Didn't you originate the idea for electronic trading at Berkeley?"

Table 14.1 Trends in Global Exchanges: IPO, Demutualization, Electronic

Name	Year IPO Held	Year Demutualized	Year Electronic Trading Installed
North America			
ICE	2006	Incep*	Incep
NYSE	2006	2006	2000
CBOT	2005	2005	1998
CME	2002	2002	1992
NASDAQ	2002	2001	1985
ISE	2005	2002	2000
OMX	Incep	Incep	Incep
TMX	2002	2000	1997
Europe			
Deutsche Börse	2001	2000	1991
Euronext	2001	Incep	Incep
LSE	2000	2001	1997
Asia			
HKEx	2000	2000	1986
OSE	2004	2001	1988
Australia			
SFE	2002	2000	1989
South America			
BM&F Bovespa	2007	2007	1990

*Incep: Since inception.

I called up Berkeley's Institute of Business and Economic Research, the original sponsor of our research, to get a copy of the Project CCARP report. I was dumbfounded to hear that there was neither a copy nor record of the report. Surely, this was a mistake. I made several more calls before reaching the director. He made a special effort to learn the whereabouts of the study. He, too, found nothing.

Ellen suggested that a copy of the study might be in the basement of our home, where we kept some old files. My colleague, Rafael

Marques, and an intern left the office to search the basement. They found nothing. Rafael was in the process of putting back all of the boxes when, 10 minutes later, he called to tell me, "I found it. It fell out of a box I was moving." In fact, the only reason Rafael noticed the report was because of the resemblance the electronic systems flowchart bore to the Wagner patent.

By this time, the CME and the CBOT had entered the final stages of negotiation with E-Speed over a license for the Wagner patent. With pending initial public offerings, they did not want to take the risk of delaying the IPO. They each paid $5 million for the license. NYMEX was the next exchange to go public. I called the Chairman, Vinnie Viola, and arranged to see him. They wanted to use the study to contest the Wagner patent on the grounds that the invention should have never been granted a patent, as the system was in the public realm. Unfortunately, they submitted the evidence too late, so it was ruled inadmissible.

I thought the rights to the CCARP idea should be owned by the University of California at Berkeley, so I called the university's lawyers to see if they had any interest in claiming ownership. Their legal opinion was that they did not own the rights to any subsequent patents. I called Carl Shapiro and informed him of the discussion. He indicated that they would publish the study electronically, a decision that pleased me. The *Financial Times* ran the story.[12] It was quickly picked up by other media.[13] Figure 14.1 shows the system flowcharts of the Wagner Patent and the original CCARP design side by side.

Aside from the CCARP design, there were other efforts to start electronic exchanges in the 1980s. Launched on October 25, 1984, the International Futures Exchange (INTEX) became the first electronic derivatives exchange. A retired Merrill Lynch futures broker who I knew from the CCARP project started an exchange in Bermuda called Intex. Parenthetically, the Merrill Lynch broker happened to be close friends

---

[12]Nikki Tait and Mary Chung, "Companies and Finance: The Americas: Documents Could Unravel Patent Dispute," *Financial Times*, September 5, 2002.

[13]Phillipa Leighton Jones, "Sandor Paper Could Aid Defense," *eFinancial News*, November 4, 2002.

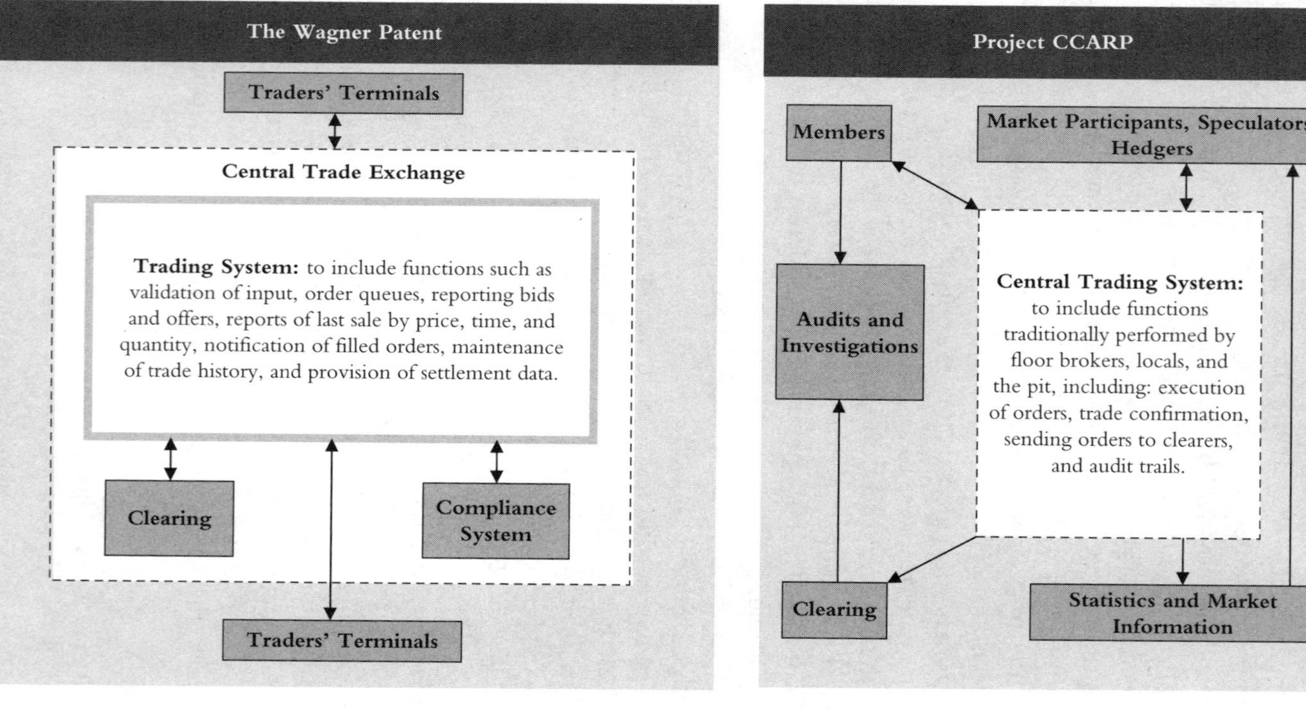

Figure 14.1 Comparing the Wagner Patent with the CCARP Design
Source: U.S. Patent Office and the University of California at Berkeley.

with individuals from the Pacific Commodity Exchange. He embraced our idea of a for-profit, electronic exchange and sought to implement it with some partners. INTEX was able to sell only half the memberships. Their first contract was gold and their marketing effort was insufficient to capture volume from the Comex. In this case, the technology wasn't enough to compensate for the wrong choice of contracts. The same lesson can be inferred from the failure of the World Energy Exchange, the first exchange to use the Wagner Patent. Technology had to be supplemented with the right products and marketing.[14]

For a long time, the Wagner patent was forgotten like the CCARP design had been after the Pacific Commodity Exchange died. The patent was only later invoked during the E-Speed lawsuit once electronic trading was accepted as commercially valuable.

Liffe was never sued, nor was any other exchange for infringement of the patent. To this day, I wonder who had seen the CCARP report of 1970. The legacy of CCARP would continue to have legs in my future.

---

[14]INTEX story adapted from Michael Gorham, "The long, promising evolution of screen-based trading," in *Focus* no. 221, World Federation of Exchanges, July 2011, 3–10.

Chapter 15

Conceiving a New Kind of Exchange

The man with a new idea is a Crank until the idea succeeds.

—*Mark Twain*

The process of going electronic, demutualizing, and going public had reinvented the face of futures exchanges. Unlocking exchange value was its own form of financial innovation. Now that I knew how to both invent new products and unlock value, it was time to use these skills to create a new exchange with new products.

At the beginning of 1999, I found myself in an uncomfortable position with only one ball left in the air—CO_2 emissions trading. I had left the CBOT behind, along with insurance derivatives. In addition, my work on unlocking Liffe would come to fruition and demand less of my time. With my newfound focus, I began a full-time adventure that would occupy me for the next decade.

I worked on two major projects at Environmental Financial Products in 1999, and both had begun two years earlier. The first was brokering a CO_2 offsets trade. I normally eschewed brokering but made an exception in this case because it gave me the opportunity to better understand offsets. The second was writing a feasibility study for a business that sought to monetize the carbon sequestered in trees.

The Largest Voluntary CO_2 Offset Trade in History

In 1997, Mike Walsh from EFP met Bernie Zahren, whose firm, ZAPCO, was in the business of operating landfills. While decomposing, the garbage in these landfills emitted methane—a harmful greenhouse gas. Bernie's business captured this gas by running a pipe approximately 20 to 30 feet down into a landfill's decaying solid waste, somewhat like drilling a well for gas. The gas was then sucked up the pipe by negative pressure, and transferred into an engine that generated electricity. Any excess methane was simply flared. This prevented the excess gas from entering the atmosphere and contributing to global warming. Electricity generated from the methane was sold as renewable energy. Since the methane captured by the landfill process could not enter the atmosphere, Mike and Bernie discussed the possibility of generating carbon offsets from these landfill projects. In fact, such projects had already been envisioned under the Kyoto Protocol. Bernie was confident in the potential of the CO_2 market and wanted to tap into it, creating another source of revenue for his company. Yet his landfill projects were in the United States, where there was no obvious market for greenhouse gas reductions. There was, however, a market for renewable energy. Maybe we could create a market for CO_2 offsets.

EFP signed a contract with ZAPCO to act as its broker for one million tons of CO_2 offsets from landfills. "We can make history together and help scale your business," I told Bernie, suspecting that he loved doing both, given his record as an entrepreneur and a terrific salesman. We decided to make our brokerage fees directly tied to the price of carbon. As the price of carbon increased, Bernie's return on investment would increase. If we succeeded in monetizing the environmental benefits, then landfill projects, which were not particularly profitable to date, could be upgraded into attractive investments. Our deal with

ZAPCO was almost like a joint venture, and was a chance for us to learn if renewable energy and CO_2 offsets from landfills were a scalable businesses.

Between 1997 and 1999, ZAPCO produced its own offsets by capturing methane gas from 20 landfills within the United States. The company was able to capture and destroy 120,000 tons of methane using Bernie's model. We translated this number into 2,520,000 tons of CO_2, or an equivalent of 21 tons of CO_2 per ton of methane, using figures published in 1995 by the Intergovernmental Panel on Climate Change (IPCC).[1] The Canadian government complied with international standards in order to be consistent with the Pilot Emissions Reduction Trading Program (PERT), a Canadian system launched in 1996 which had begun reviewing and registering CO_2 emissions reductions as an alternative to traditional command-and-control.

Although standardization in offsets had been achieved, there was a large regulatory challenge to overcome. If destruction of methane was required by law, then emission reduction credits (ERCs) could not meet PERT standards. This provision was called *additionality*, probably one of the most contentious issues in the CO_2 offsets market. It was first defined in the Kyoto Protocol and was subsequently clarified in 2001 at the seventh Conferences of the Parties (COP) to the UN Framework Convention on Climate Change (UNFCCC). A project qualified as additional if the originator could prove that the reduction of carbon emissions made was above and beyond what would have occurred under normal business conditions. In other words, the project should have reduced greenhouse gases in addition to what would have automatically occurred in the absence of the project. Of course, if there had already been a law in place that mandated methane destruction, then ZAPCO's activities would not be considered additional as they would have had to comply with the law anyway.

We conducted our due diligence on the additionality issue. The 20 landfills ZAPCO had targeted had not been required by law to destroy methane. However, there was one wrinkle. Landfills were

[1]B. Bolin et al. (1995), "IPCC Second Assessment: Climate Change 1995. A Report of the Intergovernmental Panel on Climate Change."

required by federal law to destroy ozone, a gas that caused the buildup of non-methane organic compounds. Since the ZAPCO method did both, we needed to be assured that the EPA would accept these as offsets. Fortunately, the EPA ended up granting this assurance.[2]

There were other legal uncertainties. When it came to signing the contracts, many agreements were silent on whether ZAPCO or the municipalities in which landfills were located would own the offsets. If you don't own it, you cannot legally sell it. We had to get legal proof that ZAPCO owned these rights, and could only proceed once there was legal certainty. This required going through every contract to determine the ownership of the environmental rights. If the contract was silent on the issue, we either sought another landfill or had the municipality send a clarifying amendment regarding the contract.

We still needed to identify a buyer for ZAPCO's offsets. Because EFP didn't have many small clients to buy piecemeal credits, we needed to find a single large buyer. We had built up valuable relationships over the years, so finding a buyer was difficult but not impossible. In 1995, Ontario Power, the predecessor to Ontario Hydro, had committed to cap its emissions of CO_2 at 26 million tons per year, beginning in 2000. Once the company exhausted all internal means of reducing emissions, it planned to buy the reductions achieved at other sources. In December 1997, despite challenges to consummate a transaction, Ontario Power purchased over 1 million tons from the Southern California Edison Company to meet its goals. In light of this activity in the emissions market, we identified Ontario Power as a potential buyer for ZAPCO's offsets.

EFP was active during this time, acting as a consultant to Canadian roundtables and authoring a number of papers. In 1998, I was invited to give a speech at a conference in Canada. It was a wonderful year from a totally different point of view. Our first grandson, Caleb Sandor Taub, was born on March 27, 2008. Penya chose the name Caleb for two reasons. One was sympathy for the character in John Steinbeck's *East of Eden*, and the other was in memory of Charlie. It was an

[2]"Description of ZAPCO-OPG Deal and PERT Registration Procedure," *Environmental Financial Products*, November 9, 1999.

extremely poignant moment for me. Now that I had become a grandfather, my work took on a whole new dimension. Climate change was an intergenerational issue.

Brian Jantze, the manager of market mechanisms at Ontario Power, also happened to be at the conference. A dedicated environmentalist, Brian thought the offset idea was perfect for his company. It took a long time to hammer out the details. Most of Brian's time was devoted to convincing management that purchasing offsets was consistent with the company's policies. Brian pushed the envelope internally, and we managed to sign the deal.

Before the deal could go through, we had to assure Ontario Power, the buyer, that emissions reductions were verified. We contacted PricewaterhouseCoopers (PwC) for an opinion rather than a formal audit, given the prohibitive cost of the latter. The company verified our methodology, and we planned to have ZAPCO, the seller, warrant that it had followed the PwC methodology. The trade between ZAPCO and Ontario Power was consummated in October 1999 for more than 1 million tons—the largest single transaction in emission reductions ever executed.[3] It was the first time that a Big Five accounting firm had provided expertise on an emissions deal of this magnitude across national boundaries.[4] The trade itself had been conducted at substantially below $10.00 per ton[5] and our fees were minimal, given the price. The publicity and revenues from the deal were very important for EFP. There were many committed men and women in the environmental community whose contributions to combating global warming were important but remain unheralded. Brian Jantze from Ontario Power was among them.

---

[3]"World's Largest GHG Trade Sealed," *Environment News Service*, October 29, 1999.

[4]"Ontario Power Generation Purchases Greenhouse Gas Emission Credits from Zahren Alternative Power Corporation," Press Release, OPG, ZAPCO, and EFP, October 26, 1999.

[5]Peter McKay, "U.S. Landfill Concern, Ontario Utility Agree to Swap Gas-Emission Rights," *Wall Street Journal*, October 26, 1999, 16.

We learned a lot from the experience. Legal and accounting fees represented a large amount relative to the value of the trade itself. They constituted about two-thirds of the price of carbon. The transaction costs on bilateral contracts were overwhelming and hampered the development of a carbon market. Had there been a regulated exchange that standardized legal agreements and routinized verification and audits, transaction costs could be minimized. Standardization was critical.

Between trying to figure out who owned the offsets and wading through legal issues, at the end of the day we were seeking to create a solid precedent and infrastructure for emissions trading. Our piecemeal efforts were much like Luigi Pirandello's *Six Characters in Search of an Author*, lost and trying to find a meaningful plot. We were digging in the trenches those few years, building up supply and demand for CO_2 offsets. We encouraged investments in rainforests and renewable energy to fuel supply and create demand for forests as a source of offsets. All the while, we wrote popular and academic articles, spoke with Congress, and educated the press.

The Dow Jones Sustainability Index[6]

Now that we had created a supply of offsets, we had to create a demand for offsets. If investors understood that sustainability and stock prices were correlated, they would embrace companies that participated in market-based solutions to climate change. I wanted to bridge corporate and environmental performance as another way to reduce the impact of climate change.

At the beginning of the 1990s, two apparently unrelated financial developments occurred. The first was the launch of the International Chamber of Commerce (ICC) Sustainable Development Charter in 1990. It marked the first time that a group of industry CEOs recognized the importance of positive social and environmental

---

[6]Parts of this section have been adapted from Richard Sandor and Alois Flatz, "The DJSI—A Story of Financial Innovation," *Environmental Finance*, Dec. 2001–Jan. 2002.

behavior in creating shareholder value. Financial innovation followed, thereby facilitating the flow of billions of dollars into socially responsible investing (SRI) and sustainable investments (SI).[7] The other was the passage of the Clean Air Act Amendment of 1990. The financial and environmental success of these new developments subsequently led to an understanding that these markets would provide profit-making opportunities for companies, thereby increasing shareholder value.

In 1992, the students I was teaching in Columbia University's first environmental finance course prepared a study reporting that the risk-adjusted performance of SRI funds was historically poor compared to the S&P 500. Despite this, they projected that environmental screening criteria and indexes would become better developed and more broadly used. However, this would take time. By 1995, there were 55 socially screened mutual funds in the United States with assets totaling $12 billion. And indeed, 38% of these SRI funds were screened based on environmental performance.

That same year, a Swiss entrepreneur named founded the Sustainable Performance Group (SPG) and Sustainable Asset Management (SAM). The former was a closed-ended equity mutual fund launched and managed by the latter. Launched in September 1995 with over 100 million Swiss Francs to invest worldwide, SPG sought to invest in stocks of companies operating across diversified sectors, typically in energy, water, healthy living, and resource-efficient industries. It was the first departure from SRI to SI, and I agreed to serve on the board of directors, alongside a combination of leading academics and businessmen from Switzerland and Germany. Alexander "Sascha" Zehnder, a scientist and specialist in water resource management, became a life-long friend and colleague. The other professionals on the board later helped me promote the concept of emissions trading in Europe.

---

[7]Socially responsible investment is a strategy that takes into account the social values generated by certain investments. Sustainable investing is similar but focuses more on fine tuning financial returns with social gain. This calls for investing in companies that use their resources more efficiently and in ways that benefit the environment, i.e. companies with better long term prospects.

The SAM fund provided a different type of incentive for corporations to pursue environmental objectives. Under SAM, hopeful and public-spirited companies were supported by stockholders. Even if a company was a big polluter, its stocks would still be bought as long as it was effective in controlling or reducing emissions relative to its peers. This deviated from the SRI model, under which such companies were often shunned.

At SPG's first board meeting, I shared my belief that SPG could quantitatively be measured against a benchmark index. The chairman of SPG thought this was an ingenious idea. Next to speak was Sascha, who went on to become president of both the ETH and the Water Research Institute. He proclaimed with the certainty of a scientist, "I don't think we even have to debate this." By the end of the board meeting, there was no question that the SPG needed a benchmark.

SAM decided to develop its own sustainability index to show that SPG not only outperformed its benchmark, the Morgan Stanley Capital International World index, but was also superior to new competitors entering the sustainable investments field. Alois Flatz from SAM, along with SAM's research team, explored the idea of developing an international sustainability index that tracked the financial performance of the world's most sustainable companies. Industry leaders were to be selected from a ranking of the world's biggest companies based on a relatively simple corporate sustainability assessment system. For example, sustainability was measured by safety (as defined by worker accidents and deaths), gender equality in the work force and board of directors, number of environmental law suits, and other industry specific criteria.

SAM planned to develop the index internally but have it calculated and branded by a third party. The management at SAM contacted the major index companies, but there was little interest. The Swiss Stock Exchange entertained the possibility of branding the index, but the global nature of the index unfortunately didn't fit the exchange's strategy. It subsequently introduced SAM to STOXX, a joint venture between Dow Jones and the Swiss, French, and German stock exchanges. The new managing director at Dow Jones acquainted the SAM team with the Dow Jones management. While initially skeptical, the Dow Jones management team became convinced that a sustainability index could be differentiated from SRI and would be consistent with the mission of Dow Jones Indexes.

The most significant investor in SAM and chairman of the board strongly believed that a strategic relationship with Dow Jones would help legitimize the concept of sustainability and increase the visibility of SAM. Fortuitously, I had previously worked with the president of Dow Jones Indexes in licensing the DJIA to the CBOT. His leadership was decisive in the financial decisions regarding the new venture. He gave the green light to consummate the deal in October 1998.

Next, SAM created a corporate sustainability questionnaire. Questions were created to reflect general and industry-specific criteria for sustainability, based on a series of scenarios. SAM invited the largest 2,000 companies in the Dow Jones Global Index—drawn from 64 industry groups and 36 countries—to participate in the first annual assessment. Some companies welcomed the index and provided SAM with completed questionnaires with boxes of supporting documentation. Others refused to return the questionnaire due to their skepticism about sustainability. All in all, the questionnaires prompted self-assessments among corporations and provided an educational tool for sustainability efforts.

In the spring of 1999, the head of SPG, the founding investor of SAM, and I met with the Dow Jones team to hammer out the final details of the index. The historical performance of the index was determined by "back casting," the opposite of forecasting. There was great uncertainty about how it would perform, but the results were unambiguous. Our calculations showed that the sustainability index outperformed the general Dow Jones Group Index in all three regions, and in eight out of nine sectors.

Commercialization followed. The index was launched on September 8, 1999. At the outset, there were five licenses for the index, though that number has since grown to 31 licenses with more than £2.2 billion under management. This has been accompanied by a dramatic increase in SRI, driven by concerns about stainability and the objective to maximize shareholder value. The DJSI had significantly outperformed all other indexes, with virtually no increase in risk.

I worked with SPG and the DJSI to create demand for emissions trading that was based on increasing the stock price of companies that participated in that activity. If we could bridge the market capitalization of corporations with their environmental stewardship, then combating climate change would obviously be easier.

The original opposition from the Dow Jones management team against stock index futures had evolved into support. The index division cobranded a stock index with SAM in the hope that it would be listed on a futures exchange. In an ironic turn of events, the CME would later buy the Dow Jones Index company in 2010 from Dow Jones.

Sustainable Forestry and Climate Change—A Case Study of Failure

The Swiss Futures and Options Association (SFOA) held an annual meeting in Buergenstock, Switzerland, every year since 1979. I strongly supported the founding of this event and deemed it a great vehicle to educate members of the futures industry in Europe and around the world.

Since the environmental markets were still in their infancy, we followed our usual pattern of speaking and educating the futures industry about its role in combating climate change and the mechanics of such markets. I was often invited to make presentations at the annual SFOA meetings. In 1997, I attended one of the SFOA annual meetings to promote the idea of emissions trading. I bumped into a Chicago born-and-bred attorney who was practicing law as a partner at Mayer Brown & Platt in London. We walked out onto a terrace that overlooked a bucolic pasture with cows. Bells hung from their necks and tinkled gently as the animals roamed. I told him about our work establishing a voluntary emissions trading program and creating an exchange for trading CO_2 credits. "Nothing has really happened since 1992 and now we're trying to work something out with the United Nations and the Earth Council," I said. Apparently, he had been working on environmental issues with a world-renowned scientist and an explorer concerned about rainforest preservation. He suggested that we all collaborate.

I subsequently had dinner with the three principles at the Savoy Hotel in London. We ate in a dark-paneled room with pictures and scores from the original performance of Puccini's *Madame Butterfly*, which had debuted at the Savoy Theater next door. We all expressed interest in marrying our environmental objectives with commercial opportunities that could arise from the upcoming UN meeting in Kyoto, Japan.

We eventually formed a company called Sustainable Forestry Management (SFM), which invested in reforestation projects across the globe. SFM retained EFP to do a feasibility study on assembling a portfolio of forestry projects to supply carbon offsets to emissions trading markets. SFM believed there was a potential business opportunity for CO_2 credits in selective harvesting,[8] reforestation, and avoided deforestation. I had already begun to look at creating demand for emissions credits through SAM and the SPG, and thought the SFM study would provide a great opportunity to stimulate supply.

EFP submitted a feasibility study for SFM in February 2000 which investigated whether carbon mitigation from reforestation could be produced at a cost sufficiently below the market price of credits. If feasible, this could achieve attractive returns on investment while reversing deforestation and climate change. We recommended a number of strategies to exploit new markets that could emerge independently or as a result of the Kyoto Protocol coming into force. These strategies included investment in assisted regeneration of natural forests and the establishment of new forest plantations. Such projects could also protect biological diversity, improve water quality and local climate, and contribute to the sustenance of indigenous cultures.

Our study further examined the financial performance of real and hypothetical reforestation projects under varying prices on carbon, and identified countries with significant prospects for reforestation and low sovereign risk. We evaluated the impacts that selective harvesting of

---

[8]Selective harvesting is the practice of cutting the older trees only in order to let the younger trees thrive. This is considered to be better for the environment than just cutting down all the trees in one area indiscriminately.

high value timber, bioprospecting, and ecotourism facilities could have on the profitability of forest protection and regeneration projects.[9] In addition, we studied market-based risks facing SFM implementers, and introduced proven techniques such as portfolio optimization that were prevalent in the capital markets.[10] Estimates of future pricing for carbon credits were as high as $200 per ton. EFP's 1994 estimate of $20 per ton was conservative, while $70-per-ton pricing from BP Amoco's pilot internal trading program held a middle ground. The price of EUA's at the end of 2010 was not too far off, at about $19.00 per ton. We further hypothesized that there would be about 1 billion tons of carbon credits supplied from various sources. The market value of the CDM carbon was $19.8 billion as of 2010. As of October 2010, forestry projects accounted for only 0.58 percent of registered CDM projects,[11] with another two years before the first compliance period ends.

Working on the study provided us with significant intellectual capital in the field of forestry and helped us with consulting revenues. Most importantly, the knowledge we gleaned from the study would prove to be useful in developing protocols in reforestation and preservation of rainforests.

A Chance Encounter—The Beginning of the Chicago Climate Exchange

I received a call from Paula DiPerna during the first week of July 1999. Though I hadn't seen her in three years, Paula wanted to follow up on our exchange at the Group of 77 meeting in Glen Cove back

[9]Bioprospecting involves looking for organic materials in nature that can be used in commercial products, such as pharmaceutical. Ecotourism facilities attempts to minimize the damage done to local communities.

[10]Modern Porfolio Theory is a strategy that calls for a selective combination of assets in order to optimize the expected returns of the portfolio, given a level of risk exposure.

[11]"Executive Board Annual Report 2010: Clean Development Mechanisms," UNFCCC.

in 1995. She had just assumed the presidency of the Joyce Foundation and moved to Chicago.

We had lunch on July 14 at the University Club in Chicago. After briefly reminiscing about my speech at Glen Cove, Paula said, "I'm running the foundation and we have $1 billion in assets. The next millennium is upon us, and I want to make some special grants that will have inter-generational significance. What would it take to try global emissions trading for greenhouse gases?"

I eagerly proposed a feasibility study on a pilot program in the Midwest that could be scaled globally. The economy of the Midwest rivaled that of several EU countries combined, and was large enough to warrant a large scale pilot program.

Since no papers were allowed at the club, I had to sketch out an outline of the program on the back of a napkin, a gesture that reminded me surreptitiously of the drafting of the first GNMA contract, which was done on a paper napkin at a Chinese restaurant. I estimated that the pilot program would cost about $1.5 million, and could be operational in a couple of years. We shook hands on our mutual commitment. And that was how the idea for the Chicago Climate Exchange was conceived.

The University Club was a relatively short walk back to our office at 111 W. Jackson. Impatient in nature, I normally took taxicabs, even for short distances. This time, I meandered and dreamed about the possible ramifications of the luncheon meeting. The door had finally opened.

The challenge excited me and stirred feelings in me the way interest rate futures did in the 1970s. Although EFP continued to work on sustainable forestry and the landfill trade, we now had a greater and more sustainable project. Timing was everything, and we needed to have a comprehensive proposal ready to be submitted to the Joyce Foundation within eight weeks. This was the biggest ball in the air.

Chapter 16

The Twenty-First-Century Lighthouse

Research is what I'm doing when I don't know what I'm doing.

—*Wernher Von Braun*

The EFP offices were small and cramped. My paltry office was right next to Mike Walsh's even smaller office. The entry area held three desks, two of which were staffed by assistants. Rafael Marques worked at a small desk in the reception area across from the desk of my new assistant, Mary Ann White. Mary Ann was smart, assiduous, and adventurous. After graduating with honors in business from Illinois State, she had gone to live and work in Japan. Somehow, the cramped space didn't matter because we were all so energized about embarking on an epic journey. Something monumental was about to take place.

I was enthusiastic about Paula DiPerna's suggestion to apply for a grant from the Joyce Foundation. They were a renowned, nonprofit foundation that had previously funded environmental projects and enjoyed an untarnished reputation within the environmental and public policy communities. Private funding would have provided cash, but it would not have ratified the intellectual and moral significance of the project. The approval of the president and board of directors of a major foundation, on the other hand, did.

An academic partner would further enhance the credibility of our research. I met with the dean of the Kellogg School to gauge the university's interest in becoming the recipient of the grant and hiring EFP as a subcontractor. EFP was a for-profit company and couldn't accept money from a foundation. The dean welcomed the idea.

Spreading the Light

Paula advised us to give our presentation an educational flavor. We had to start with the basics. We explained why free markets might fail when there were positive or negative spillover effects associated with an economic activity, for example, burning coal. A persuasive case had to be made about why cap-and-trade, one form of flexible mechanism, was superior to other policy measures that dealt with climate change, such as command-and-control. In cap-and-trade, the amount of pollution was capped. Entities that had an excess or shortage of allowances could trade. Trading allowed the aggregate reductions to be made at the lowest cost. We made sure to provide an in-depth discussion of the practical differences between taxes and subsidies and cap-and-trade.

We had to demonstrate that a voluntary mechanism was both feasible and viable, as validation from the success of the Acid Rain Program alone was insufficient. We also had to rationalize that the upper Midwest was the right place to launch a pilot program.

Chicago was a strategic choice geographically, given the Joyce Foundation's focus on the Great Lakes states in the Upper Midwest. Together, Minnesota, Wisconsin, Illinois, Indiana, Michigan, and Ohio make up a gross domestic product of over $2 trillion, comparable to the economy of France. This region also had a diverse mix of utilities and manufacturing companies, with sufficient economic breadth and diversity to facilitate a proof of concept. Utilities such as Alliant in Wisconsin and AEP in Ohio, industrial corporations such as Ford and DuPont, and pharmaceutical companies such as Abbott Labs and Baxter were either headquartered in the Midwest or had significant operations within the six states. The Midwest was also home to a significant agricultural and forestry sector, and a new climate exchange would benefit from the region's human capital in soil science and forestry. The Midwest's proximity with Canada was also advantageous. We envisioned international trading and the possibility of attracting Canadian companies to this pilot program.

Chicago was a natural home for the Climate Exchange, as the city already housed the two largest exchanges in the United States—the CME and the CBOT—and had a critical mass of human capital capable of managing an exchange, along with a large population of market makers and traders. The CBOT also had the experience of conducting annual auctions of SO_2 allowances under the EPA's Acid Rain Program.

Ronald Coase's article on the lighthouse[1] guided me throughout the project. Economists had always assumed that market failure would occur in the case of public goods,[2] for example, with lighthouses, and to a larger extent, air and water. Since people benefited from the existence of a public good and were not easily charged for it, it was unlikely that the private sector would want to provide such a service. The logic stemming from economic theory, however, was historically untrue. Lighthouses did in fact arise as commercial entities, although they ultimately became public entities. Extending this idea, a voluntary pilot program essentially played the role of a commercial lighthouse until public policy would mandate a national cap-and-trade program for greenhouse gas (GHG) emissions.[3]

[1]Ronald H. Coase, "The Lighthouse in Economics," *Journal of Law and Economics* 17, no. 2 (October 1974): 357–376.

[2]A public good in economics is nonexcludable and nonrival. Nonexcludability means that everyone has access to the good. Nonrivalry means that one person using or consuming a good does not prevent another person from using or consuming it.

[3]The paper has been criticized by those who disagreed about nature of the lighthouses as privately run enterprises. They argued that, according to historical records, lighthouses were only able to operate because the government granted them the right to collect dues. See Van Zandt (1993) and Bertrand (2006) for a more in-depth discussion.

Ramping Up

We worked industriously with members of the Joyce Foundation to finalize our proposal, and submitted it on October 6, 1999. Named the "Feasibility and Design of a Voluntary Midwest Greenhouse Gas Reduction and Trading Market," the proposal called for a two-phase implementation period, Phase I and Phase II, and a budget of $346,000 and $760,100 to be allotted to EFP in two separate installments. There was no guarantee of a second grant until we were able to substantiate, with sufficient evidence, the program's likelihood to succeed.[4] From then on, we would have to raise our own money. EFP's budget covered internal staff salaries and allocated funds for consultants, seminars, and travels. The foundation also gave us an additional budget for outside vendors, which was to be used for registry and accounting design, accounting and tax treatment assessment, legal issues, administration, and monitoring and verification methods.

Paula was anxious to keep her board informed of our project. The Millennium Grant was larger than all the previous grants given by the Joyce Foundation, and was in a sense her debut as president of the organization. At Paula's request, we appeared before the board of directors of the foundation on December 6, 1999, to explain the proposal. Overall, the questions and feedback we received were favorable, signaling the enthusiasm and support for our idea.

Parenthetically, a little-known Illinois state senator, Barack Obama, was then also a member of the board. When he became U.S. President in 2009, much ado was made in the press about his being a member of the Joyce board when, in fact, he remained mostly silent during the presentation, occasionally nodding approvingly. Four years after the grant was made, we met again at a social event, where he congenially recalled who I was and what I was doing. After that, I encountered Mr. Obama again at the Commercial Club, where he was making a speech. I told him I was the guest speaker for the following week, and that he was a tough act to follow. He flashed his charismatic smile and said, "You'll do just fine." I saw him one more time after he became President, and took

[4]Eventually, the Joyce Foundation agreed to give us $360,000 for Phase I and $760,000 for Phase II, totaling $1.1 million all together.

the opportunity to ask about the status of U.S. environmental legislation. He smiled and responded, "After health care." To this extent, the press's conspiracy theory about the collusion between the Chicago Climate Exchange (CCX) and President Obama is unfounded and absurd. As a matter of fact, he never mentioned CCX while his opponent Hillary Clinton praised our efforts in her primary battle with Senator Obama. True, President Obama had campaigned on the importance of developing a comprehensive energy and environmental policy for the United States. He had also supported cap-and-trade. However, all the other candidates in the Democratic Party, did so, as well as the Republican nominee, John McCain.

Paula called me to say the presentation was terrific. In a unanimous vote, the board of directors had approved the grant for the pilot program. Mike, Rafael, and I were ecstatic. I went home that night and had a celebratory dinner with Ellen.

Guided by Voltaire's philosophy, "The perfect is the enemy of the good,"[5] we wanted the market architecture to be workable, but did not strive for perfection. Our intention was to underpromise and overdeliver. The CCX feasibility study began in earnest in 2000, with our small but hardworking research team. In the course of completing the study, EFP held a number of group meetings to flesh out the implementation of the proposal. The team was highly disciplined and rarely, if ever, missed a deadline. Our business days ended somewhere between 6 and 7 P.M., and we picked up the where we left off at 8 A.M. the following day. Mike led efforts to develop first drafts for the various elements of the study. Once a draft was near completion, I reviewed it and provided specific comments or criticisms for the next redraft. The collaboration was seamless.

Preliminary Market Architecture

After we were able to demonstrate that the pilot program was feasible, we began to construct the skeleton of the supporting market architecture. The starting point was determining the baseline year and the

[5]Voltaire, *La Bégueule*, 1772.

reductions that would occur until a terminal year in the program, in other words, from what year, by what amounts, and by when. For inspiration, we referred to a paper we had written and presented during the Conference of the Parties (COP) meetings in Bonn in 1999, which called for a simplified approach to the clean development mechanism.[6] We borrowed from its simplicity and its standardized approach and adopted a rules-based rather than project-based approach to market architecture. This reduced transaction costs.

For our architecture, we had to determine a baseline year from which emission targets would be referenced, and outlined a targeted reduction schedule. Although the Kyoto Protocol used 1990 as its baseline year, we realized that companies would possibly find it difficult to have data going back that far. The choice of 1990 was the result of political negotiations, and not sound economic reasoning. The year 1990 was a high point of emissions for Europe, making it a lenient baseline for countries to reduce their emissions from. It was the year that the UK had switched from coal to gas. West Germany was absorbing East Germany and the Russian economy was on the brink of a meltdown. We also wanted to pick a year of high emissions to make cuts easier in the early years of the program. Accordingly, we thought 1998 would be a reasonable baseline. It was a starting point and not gospel. We wanted a reduction schedule that would not only be attainable but would accurately price carbon.

Academics and policy makers were searching for a price level that could effectively change emissions behavior. The debate was not a new one. The prevailing theory set forth that companies would either choose to buy allowances or install emission-reducing technology based on the cost of each option. In other words, if the price of allowances were lower, a firm would purchase allowances instead of install emission-reducing technologies and vice versa. As mentioned previously, this reasoning is flawed. It was the price expectations that mattered and not the current prices themselves. Just as one buys a stock based on its expected price at some point in the future, so too will companies change their purchasing behavior according to the expected

---

[6]Environmental Financial Products, "The Case for the Simplified CDM," presented at COP 5 UN Meeting, Bonn, Germany, October 1999.

price of allowances, and not, contrary to common belief, the current price. Nevertheless, the popular misconception continues. Although obtaining allowances was much cheaper than installing scrubbers under the Acid Rain Program, many utilities chose to buy scrubbers instead of allowances.[7] We sought a reduction schedule that would cause price tension, thereby building in expectations of prices that would change behavior. It was more art than science.

The agreed-upon reduction schedule was 2 percent below 1998 in 2002, 3 percent below 1998 in 2003, 4 percent below 1998 in 2004, and 5 percent below 1998 in 2005—the final year of the pilot.

We also had to identify which greenhouse gases to include in the pilot. We could limit our trading activities to CO_2 exclusively, or we could include some, if not all, of the other five greenhouse gases.[8] Daniel Burnham, the architect and urban planner who helped redesign the City of Chicago, once said, "Make no little plans; they have no magic to stir men's blood."[9] EFP was already in the business of trying to be transformational. If we were going to fail, it should be for some major objective. This was important because we wanted the program to be as broad and to include as many sectors of the economy as possible.

The next challenge was to determine whether we should assign allowances at the point of production or of consumption. There were three basic choices: upstream, downstream, and microlevel. The goal was to achieve our targeted emission reduction levels at the lowest cost possible. The upstream option distributed the allowances to the

---

[7]In 1994, a typical 500 MW coal power plant needed to pay $275 per kW to install an SO_2 scrubber. 275 × 500,000 = $137.5 million. In the same year, the EPA auctioned SO_2 allowances at an average $159. A 500 MW coal power plant emits 10,000 tons of SO_2. If we assume a 40-year lifespan, paying for all emissions with allowances will cost 10,000 × 159 × 40 = $63.6 million—less than half the cost of installing a scrubber.

[8]The six greenhouse gases include carbon dioxide, methane, nitrous oxide, hydrofluorocarbons, perfluorocarbons, and sulphur hexafluoride.

[9]Charles Moore, "Closing in 1911–1912," chap. XXV in *Daniel H. Burnham, Architect, Planner of Cities* vol. 2 (Boston: Houghton Mifflin, 1921).

producers of energy such as coal mining companies and oil producers. There were a limited number of upstream producers and so this approach was easier and cheaper to administer. However, the effectiveness of such a regulatory regime would rely on upstream producers to hike up their prices and influence consumer decisions through the passing on of fuel prices. They may not have had the incentive to do so because it could hurt their profit margins. Alternatively, we could go to the opposite extreme and monitor the micro players, such as individual consumers. This could be cost-prohibitive, as the number of players to monitor and administer were simply too great.

Given these considerations, the most intuitive choices were downstream, or intermediary, market players. The industries and firms we targeted consisted of a combination of downstream activities. This included power generation, refineries, manufacturing, importers, and vehicle fleets. Micro-level activities in the offset area, designed to attract farmers, landfill operators, and the like were also included. Not only was the downstream option ratified by the Acid Rain Program, it allowed us to influence decisions made on the consumer level without having to directly monitor them.

Our choice was based on the assumption that companies responded to price signals to change their behavior. We had to consider the administrative and transaction costs associated with our choices, and the effectiveness of allowance prices in stimulating innovative ways to reduce emissions. We also had to attract enough market players to guarantee that prices would be competitively determined.

The tradable instruments would consist of emission allowances as well as offsets produced by targeted projects. We further specified that targeted offset projects would include methane destruction from landfills and animal waste, renewable energy, and reforestation.

The decision to use an electronic platform and not open outcry was easy. Although the exchanges in the United States had not gone electronic, it was obvious that it was going to happen. The electronic platform had to facilitate continuous trading as well as accommodate bilateral over-the-counter (OTC) contracts. We recommended annual auctions to facilitate price discovery, an idea we borrowed from the EPA auctions in the Acid Rain Program. The indicative market architecture is summarized in Table 16.1.

Table 16.1 Preliminary Market Architecture for the Chicago Climate Exchange

Geographic Coverage	2002: seven Midwest states (IA, IL, IN, MI, MN, OH, WI) 2003–2005: U.S., Canada, and Mexico Offsets accepted from projects in Brazil in all years, other strategic countries to be determined
Greenhouse Gases Covered	Carbon dioxide, methane, and all other targeted gases
Emission Reduction Targets	2% below 1998 baseline by 2002 level and 5% below 1998 by 2005
Industries and Firms Targeted	Combination of downstream and micro participants: power generation, refineries, manufacturing, vehicle fleets; 102 firms targeted based on various criteria
Tradable Instruments	Emission allowances (original issue) and offsets produced by targeted project types
Eligible Offset Categories (projects implemented by entities with emission levels below participation cutoff—250,000 tons)	• Methane destruction (for example, agricultural waste, landfills) • Carbon sequestration through no-till agricultural soils and grass plantings, afforestation, and reforestation • Increased vehicle efficiency in autos, trucks, and buses • Conversion to less GHG-intensive fuels • Wind, solar, hydro, and geothermal power systems • Direct onsite emission reductions from energy efficiency enhancements
Trading Mechanisms	CCX Electronic Trading System and private contracting
Annual Auctions	2% of issues allowances withheld and auction in spot and forward auctions, proceeds returned pro rata

Source: Table ES-1, "Executive Summary First Draft Report," Environmental Financial Products LLC, ES-3.

The exchange system included allowances and offsets and would be compatible with the terms proposed by U.S. legislation regarding the official accreditation of early emission reduction actions. We wanted the exchange rules and procedures to serve as a paradigm for future proposals in early reduction credit and to influence future legislation of the same thread.[10]

Now that we identified the architecture and were thinking about recruiting companies, we needed a name. After throwing around some potential names, we settled on the Chicago Climate Exchange for two reasons. "Chicago" evoked the city's legacy of financial and commodities futures trading. Its name would resonate with investors. We chose the word "Climate" because it reflected not only emissions, but weather-related products, allowing us to expand our horizons.

Once we had the flexibility to establish exchanges in other locations, we could easily substitute "Chicago" with the name of any other region or city. It is funny to think that while others might have hired the services of a professional advertising or branding firm, we did this in about 30 minutes in a small office. Climate Exchange would eventually emerge as a new brand, synonymous with the environmental markets, and be referred to generically around the world.

Educational Outreach

After seeing our interim progress report, Paula exclaimed, "This goes beyond my expectations! We have to start promoting the study right away." She suggested that we present our findings at a sideshow at the Sixth Conference of the Parties for the UNFCCC being held in The Hague, Netherlands. The years that Paula spent by the side of the legendary French explorer, Jacques Cousteau, had taught her to think big.

An officially sanctioned sideshow was the best way to inform interested parties of our progress. Since the Joyce Foundation was a major U.S. foundation, we assumed that there would be no problems in securing an official role in the meeting. In this we were proven

[10]"Executive Summary First Draft Report," Environmental Financial Products LLC, ES-14.

wrong, but the rejection only made us more determined. I suggested to Paula that we hold our own unofficial event. We both knew that it might not attract a lot of the attendees from the UNFCCC but thought it was worth a try. Paula and Rafael handled the logistics for the event, which was scheduled for November 14.

According to UN rules, for-profit organizations could not attend unless they participated as observers under the umbrella of an NGO. For example, a private, for-profit U.S. company could attend as a delegate under the U.S. Chamber of Commerce. Initially, we thought that we could enter under the umbrella of the Joyce Foundation, a nonprofit. However, Joyce was not a UN-registered organization. Rafael worked frantically with the Joyce staff to achieve this. In the end, we managed to secure a table located by the entrance of the main conference hall, which fortuitously gave us good visibility. Paula, her team, and Rafael helped to hang the cardboard CCX logo behind our table and organized the information brochures into neat piles. The traffic was good and we were able to attract a lot of curious minds. We were a motley group compared to the big companies and brokers present. While we had cardboard cutouts, the big corporations threw lavish dinners and disco parties. We only had our ideas. But as Victor Hugo said, "Nothing is as powerful as an idea whose time has come." This was our time.

EFP and the Joyce Foundation co-sponsored our non-sanctioned event in the basement of a hotel in The Hague, quite a distance away from the official UNFCCC meetings. I had just flown in from a World Business Council for Sustainable Development (WBCSD) conference held in Japan and was bleary-eyed and nervous about having enough energy to motivate the attendees. Additionally, I was worried about the turnout because the attendees had to make a special effort to attend this event. Would there be enough attendees to create the perception of a high level of interest in our research?

To my relief, people started to trickle in well before the event started, and very soon only standing room remained. I saw many old friends from the Earth Summit in Rio, and many new faces who would later gain recognition in the international carbon markets. Paula spoke on behalf of the Joyce Foundation, and I spoke on behalf of CCX. We were encouraged by the positive feedback we received. It was a ratification of our belief that CCX could contribute to the international process to address climate change.

The recount for the 2000 presidential election was going on while we were in The Hague. George W. Bush ended up narrowly defeating Al Gore in the elections. But this didn't necessarily translate into the death of cap-and-trade. After all, his father, George H. W. Bush had endorsed the SO_2 emissions trading program. A Republican administration could create a favorable policy atmosphere for CCX. CCX was a voluntary program that the Republicans could embrace and use as a segue into a federal program. I was wrong.

It had been a hectic year for speeches and presentations. I had spoken at events in London, Zurich, Boston, and New York. The team had also made 10 trips of their own, presenting in Paris, Amsterdam, and numerous American cities like Missoula, Houston, and Denver. We steeled ourselves for another end-of-the-year blitz. I told Ellen about the upcoming schedule and she retorted, "What's new?" Till this day, Eric, my son-in-law, still laughs about Penya's first call to me after they had gotten back from their honeymoon. Penya had had to go through my travel agent to find out where I was.

Our reputation grew steadily in the following months, and we used this advantage to educate policy makers. I was invited to testify at a hearing at the U.S. Senate Committee on Agriculture, Nutrition, and Forestry on March 29 of the following year.[11] The American Farm Bureau had been opposed to U.S. participation in the Kyoto Protocol, and expressed concern that a cap-and-trade program would unduly punish the agriculture industry.

I first learned about the power of the farm lobby from a great teacher of mine, Oswald Brownlee. He had joined the Minnesota faculty after writing articles opposing Iowa's ban on coloring margarine in the 1940s. At the time, margarine producers were changing the natural color of their product from gray to yellow in order to make it resemble butter. I was struck by how the government had imposed a ban on colored margarine, instead of allowing the market determine whether there was demand

[11]Proceedings of Hearing on Biomass and Environmental Trading: Opportunities for Agriculture and Forestry, 2001.

for margarine that was processed to look like butter. The farmers had influenced the state legislators, and the ban became law. To succeed, we needed the harness the power of the agricultural sector. Our participation in the hearings would provide a platform for explaining the potential benefits of cap-and-trade to the agricultural and forestry sectors.

One of the benefits attributed to soil sequestration was the additional source of revenue it would provide for farmers. Our research had led us to believe that we could accurately determine the level of carbon sequestered as a result of low-till or no-till practices.[12] There were also standard models for particular species of trees, whereby one could measure the amount of carbon sequestered in the soil by measuring the height and diameter of the tree. While there were some technical questions, our testimony was well received.

Using low-end estimates of $20 to $30 per ton of carbon, paying farmers to sequester 200 million metric tons of carbon equivalents (MMTCE) per year could add $4 billion to $6 billion of gross income to the farm economy—and possibly up to 10 percent of typical net farm income.[13] The increase in net farm income would also increase the value of agricultural land. I told the committee that farmers could grow two crops, one above ground and one below ground.

I didn't read the prepared testimony, and spoke as if I was teaching—a method I was accustomed to. The testimony turned out to be an eye-opener for many of the senators. A fellow director at American Electric Power (AEP) came up to me after the presentation and said, "I try to get all of my clients to speak to the senators the way you did." As I had great respect for her, the compliment buoyed me.

The EFP team continued to publish articles to further educate the public and market the exchange. Several publications were completed throughout 2000. Concurrently, our media outreach continued. We wanted to validate the impression that CCX was a thought leader in the field. There were 27 pieces published in newspapers and magazines across the United States, Europe, and Japan, and six pieces

[12]Tilling exposes organic matter in the soil to the air and emits CO_2. Reduced tilling can therefore decrease agricultural emissions.

[13]Richard L. Sandor and Jerry R. Skees, "Creating a Market for Carbon Emissions: Opportunities for U.S. Farmers," *Choices 1999*, First Quarter, 13.

of electronic media coverage from online news sources such as the Environmental News Service.

Public speaking at conferences and industry-related events were also critical. I was invited to speak at the World Economic Forum in Davos, Switzerland, as well as a panel at the Milken Global Conference that was sponsored by the United Nations Foundation. Additionally, I testified twice before the U.S. Senate and met with Senator Richard "Dick" Lugar from Indiana. I had worked with him many times before on a committee of futures industry professionals that regularly met to discuss issues in the futures market. Dick, too, recognized carbon credits as an important source of farm income.

Table 16.2 provides a list of EFP's media outreach and public speaking efforts during this period.

Our network grew further. The team met with a bipartisan group of senators and staff members from the Senate Agriculture and Environment committees. We also spoke with the senior staff at the White House Council for Environmental Quality (CEQ), and were graciously received by the EPA administrator, Christine Todd Whitman.

Refining the Preliminary Market Architecture

While marketing the CCX concepts throughout the world, we continued to refine the preliminary market architecture of the proposed pilot program. This entailed addressing a number of legal and accounting issues, as well as refining details regarding monitoring and verification, and the industries to be targeted. Our lawyers confirmed that we could use a rulebook, rather than a set of contracts, in order to bind them to their reduction targets. All we needed was a simple letter that stated that said entities that joined the exchange would abide by the rules. PriceWaterhouseCoopers provided the guidelines for companies on the accounting treatment of the allowances that were submitted.

It remained for us to develop the final legal structure and governance of the exchange and write a full-scale rulebook. Finally, we had to identify project verifiers for offset credits generated by offset projects in

Table 16.2 Media Outreach and Public Speaking

Medium	**Description**
Publications by EFP	"Chicago Climate Exchange Moves Toward Launch," Michael Walsh, Rafael Marques, and Scott Baron Forthcoming in *Global Greenhouse Emissions Trader*, Official Newsletter of the Greenhouse Gas Emissions Trading Unit, United Nations Conference on Trade and Development, Geneva "U.S. Carbon Trading Project Wins funding—How I See It," monthly column by Dr. Richard Sandor, *Environmental Finance*
Publication by others	*World Economic Forum 2001*, Annual Meeting Report. Sustaining Growth and Bridging the Divides: A Framework for Our Global Future "Global Warming: The New Climate of Urgency" by Edward Girardet
	"Plan Would Pay Farmers for Pollution-Eating Crops," *Journal Gazette-Fort Wayne, Indiana,* March 30, 2001
	"U.S. Climate Exchange Ready to Start Trading," *Financial Times,* March 29, 2001
	"Carbon Trades in Global Warming," *UPI News*, March 16, 2001
	"GARP Honors William Martin as Risk Manager of the Year and Richard Sandor with the Lifetime Achievement Award," *Environment News Service-E-wire*, February 22, 2001
	"Proposed U.S. Carbon Exchange Sets Targets," *Environmental Finance Magazine*, December 2000-January 2001
	"CTIC Expands to New Markets—Environmental Financial Products Joins as Newest Member," *Partners, CTIC Magazine*, August 2000
	"Portraits: Les 50 qui disent la règle; Richard Sandor, PDG de Environmental Financial Products—Il a inventé le droits de polluer," *Enjeux Les Echos*, France, August 2000
	"A Virgin Forest Market?" *Latin Trade Magazine*, September 2000

(*continued*)

Table 16.2 (*Continued*)

Medium	Description
	"Buying the Right to Warm the Globe," *National Journal*, May 20, 2000
	"Joyce 'Millennium Initiative' Funds Pilot for First U.S. Carbon Trading Market," *Environmental News Service E-Wire*, May 19, 2000
	"Breakfast Briefing Chicago—Grant for Pollution Credit Market," *Chicago Sun-Times*, May 18, 2000
	"The Joyce Foundation Is Funding Work to Design a Voluntary Market for the Trading of Carbon Emissions," *Chicago Tribune*, Business Section, May 18, 2000
	"Broadly Based U.S. Market Proposal," *Financial Times*, May 18, 2000
Electronic Media	Interview of Dr. Michael Walsh on the "Peter Werbe" show, broadcast on the IE American Radio syndicated network, February 2001
	Dr. Richard Sandor, interview with Austrian radio program "Dimensionen" from COP6 at The Hague, aired November 27, 2000
	Dr. Richard Sandor, BBC Radio interview during COP6 at The Hague
	Odyssey Show—WBEZ 91.5 FM, Chicago Public Radio, August 7, 2000
	Interview with Dr. Richard Sandor, Urban Business Review, Channel 26, Chicago
Testimonies	Testimony before U.S. Senate Committee on Commerce, Transportation and Science, Senate Agriculture Committee

the agriculture, forestry, and waste sectors, as well as choose vendors for the registry and electronic trading platform.

EFP had been plagued by difficulties ever since we received the first grant. The whole notion of a private Kyoto Protocol was anathema. The dot-com bubble had burst around the time of our grant application, and the decline of Internet stocks had dragged down the entire stock market. Foundations and other investors suffered major losses. After the crash, President Bush reversed his position on climate change and denied U.S. participation in the Kyoto Protocol. Expectations of a coming U.S. legislative effort to establish a domestic cap-and-trade program was dashed on the rocks. This meant that our efforts to recruit companies to a voluntary pilot program would be a continuous uphill battle.

We had to decide if it was best for EFP to continue the research with no certainty about funding, or simply wait for our second grant. We took the risk and continued our research and recruiting efforts. We didn't stop the countdown. There was really no turning back. It was just like the days of financial futures, when I simply had too much invested in the launch.

Concurrently, there were a lot of exciting events taking place in our family that year. Penya gave birth to Oscar Sandor Taub on March 29, 2001. We were in the midst of preparing the feasibility study for the Joyce Foundation, and it was a wonderful interlude. I now spoke of the impact of climate change in terms of my grandchildren and not my grandchild.

The feasibility study was delivered on April 28, 2001. There was one year, eight months, and six days left until the planned launch of January 3, 2003. Over 200 pages long, the study concluded that a voluntary pilot program to reduce and trade GHG emissions in the Upper Midwest was feasible. Satisfied with our results, the foundation agreed to finance the second phase of the study, which would be focused on producing a more detail-specific plan for a voluntary GHG emissions reduction and trading system.

The payment from Joyce allowed us to continue recruiting companies to join the voluntary, but legally binding, pilot program. But how were we going to persuade companies to make reductions if there wasn't a law in place mandating it? It seemed like a Herculean task back then, and it still does today. Within three weeks of receiving approval of the grant, a terrorist attack destroyed the World Trade Center Towers, and our country lost more people than we had lost on December 7, 1941—the "Day of Infamy."[14] The United States soon went to war in

---

[14]This is the term President Franklin D. Roosevelt used in his presidential address to Congress in 1941 to describe the day Japan attacked Pearl Harbor.

Afghanistan. These two events shocked the country and justifiably put climate change on the back burner. We could not stop the countdown then, but it would be remiss of us not to do it now.

I went into withdrawal for a few months after 9/11 because of the friends I had lost. Rick Ferina, then CEO of Calyon, was scheduled to leave on Sunday, September 10th, but changed plans to fly in the morning of 9/11 only to arrive shortly after the tragedy. I almost lost him. His young secretary had gone to New York earlier to see the city for the first time. Somehow, our limited interaction made it even harder for me to contemplate her death. Calyon's New York office was in the World Trade Center and included a number of my former colleagues from Drexel.

I had hired Steve Goldstein at Centre Financial Products. It turns out that Steve was the son-in-law of my closest friend in college, whom I had lost touch with over the years, This provided an opportunity to renew the friendship. Steve had two small children with my friend's daughter and eventually started an Internet company, which failed. I became close to Steve and tried to look after his best interests. Steve called me at the end of August to say, "I have worked out of my financial difficulties and am tired of being an entrepreneur. I am starting a new job at Cantor Fitzgerald in the first week of September." I could hear the smile in Steve's voice over the telephone and sensed his renewed optimism. He was known in the office for his upbeat attitude. Steve's new position was located at the World Trade Center, and he lost his life on 9/11. It is staggering to imagine how many other people had similar stories about friends and colleagues lost in that tragic event.

Recruiting Members to Design the CCX

The recruiting effort really began in 2001 when EFP started inviting companies from a wide range of industries to participate in the design process of CCX. By April 28, 2001, we had recruited 27 entities to form the design committee. What follows is the list of member companies. The momentum was building. The number of entities involved in the design of the program would increase dramatically by the time we held our first committee meetings in January 2002.

Entities Enrolled in the CCX Design Phase

Electric Power

Alliant Energy
American Electric Power
Cinergy
CMS Generation
DTE
Exelon
FirstEnergy
Manitoba Hydro
Midwest Generation
NiSource
Ontario Power Generation
Pinnacle West Corp. (APS)
PG&E National Energy Group
Texas Utilities Energy Trading
Wisconsin Electric Power

Industry

Baxter
BP
Cemex
DuPont
Ford Motor Company
Grupo IMSA, S.A. de C.V.
ST Microelectronics
Suncor Energy
Waste Management Inc.

Forest Products Companies

International Paper
MeadWestvaco
Stora Enso North America
Temple-Inland

Offset Providers

Agriliance
Cataguazes (Brazil)
Ducks Unlimited
Growmark
Iowa Farm Bureau Federation
National Council of Farmer Cooperatives
Navitas Energy
Ormat
Nuon
The Carbon Fund
The Nature Conservancy
Pronatura Noreste (Mexico)
Conservation Mexico

Service Providers

American Agrisurance
Carr Futures/Crédit Agricole
CEPEA—University of São Paulo
Det Norsk Veritas
Edelman PR Worldwide
IT Group
SCS Engineers
Swiss Re
Winrock International

Municipalities

City of Chicago
Mexico City

While giving public presentations and speeches, we began detailed dialogues with targeted participants. Through these dialogues, we were able to identity 102 firms that were possibly interested in joining CCX. They were chosen based on three well-defined criteria: whether they submitted voluntary reports on their greenhouse gas emissions to the Department of Energy, participated in other voluntary public or not-for-profit programs, or included significant reports on climate change issues on their websites. Many of these companies did not have a significant Midwest presence. However, the 27 companies that did join the design phase represented a cross-section of industries, including power generation, automobile production, forest and paper production, oil exploration, petroleum refining, chemical manufacturing, and technology.

A letter was written, to be signed by officers from all interested parties, that anchored the commitment of each company to participate in the design phase of CCX. The terms of the letter did not bind them to participate in the exchange. This was a soft commitment to join, and a company had the right not to do so if joining the exchange was inconsistent with the company's strategy. Recruiting members to help with the design phase was therefore a way to ensure a member base of founding members when the time was ripe to launch CCX. It was assumed that most companies would want to join a program that they had previously helped to design. We learned later on that this was not necessarily true. AEP, the largest coal-burning utility in the United States, was a leader in public policy. I had met the CEO of AEP at a White House conference on climate change. The company's participation in the design phase of CCX would send a very important signal to the industry and help attract other utilities. Dupont, a U.S.-based chemical company, was very interested in CCX from the outset and would become an important opinion leader. Its representatives had attended many of my speeches, so recruiting them posed no major challenge.

EFP held individual or small group meetings with 26 separate entities in order to get feedback on our initial architecture. For technical expertise, we consulted a group consisting of the World Resources Institute, Gas Research Institute, forestry experts, soil scientists, and civil engineers. We met with potential technology and service providers and interviewed six potential providers of electronic trading platforms. We also needed a clearing entity to guarantee the financial performance of the buyers and sellers for CCX. There seemed to be no insurmountable problems in these two areas.

We wanted to be fully prepared for our first meetings and needed to present a comprehensive term sheet that detailed the market architecture of CCX. Some of our proposed monitoring and verification protocols were theoretically possible but impractical, requiring us to develop alternatives. The exchange could become a reality only if the transaction costs were kept at a minimum.

Finalizing the Preliminary Market Architecture

After about 50 corporate and municipal briefings with members in the design phase, we were able to finalize our preliminary market architecture before we headed into our official design committee meetings. Our original list of advisory committee members underwent a dramatic expansion. Table 16.3 lists the advisory committee members as of December 15, 2001.

Additionally, we modified some of the features of the original term sheet so as to incorporate the interests of the design committee members. For example, we had discovered interest from emitting entities in Canada and Mexico. We experienced geographical creep in offsets as well. We added Brazil because it was a democracy, had a stable economy, and a diverse range of potential mitigation efforts in forestry, clean energy, and renewables. Its time zone was also close to that of Chicago's. Mexico City and the City of Chicago were also added to our list of members. We felt that cities had a great desire to show environmental leadership, and with their buy-in we could more easily recruit companies that operated within their jurisdiction. Between the utility and industrial members, the geographical coverage of the program had the potential to be larger than that of several G-7 countries combined.[15] All the members were excited about the commercial opportunities offered by CCX and the idea of participating in what could be a transformational event.

I completed 2001 with a small sense of satisfaction and a large sense of exhaustion. Our small team of four economists and two assistants had somehow overcome almost all of the political and industrial

---

[15]The G-7 countries consist of France, Germany, Italy, Japan, the United Kingdom, the United States, and Canada.

Table 16.3 Chicago Climate Exchange Advisory Board Members

Richard M. Daley	Honorary Chairman, Mayor, City of Chicago
Warren Batts	Adjunct Professor, University of Chicago Graduate School of Business; former CEO, Tupperware Corporation; Premark International; Mead*
David Boren	President, the University of Oklahoma; former Governor of Oklahoma, former U.S. Senator*
Ernst Brugger	President, Brugger, Hanser & Partner; Director, the International Red Cross
Paula DiPerna	Author and public policy analyst and consultant; former President, the Joyce Foundation*
Elizabeth Dowdeswell	Visiting Professor, University of Toronto; former Executive Director, United Nations Environment Program
Jeffrey Garten	Dean, Yale School of Management
Lucien Bronicki	Chairman, ORMAT International
Donald Jacobs	Dean Emeritus, Kellogg Graduate School of Management, Northwestern University
Jonathan Lash	President, World Resources Institute*
Joseph Kennedy II	Chairman, Citizens Energy Group; former U.S. Representative (MA)
Israel Klabin	President, Brazilian Foundation for Sustainable Development
Bill Kurtis	Journalist and television producer
Thomas Lovejoy	President, Heinz Center; former Chief Biodiversity Adviser, the World Bank
David Moran	Former President, Dow Jones Indexes
R. K. Pachauri	Chairman, Intergovernmental Panel on Climate Change; Director, Tata Energy Institute
Michael Polsky	President and CEO, Invenergy
Les Rosenthal	Principal, Rosenthal Collins; former Chairman, Chicago Board of Trade*
Donna Redel	Former Executive Director, World Economic Forum
Mary Schapiro*	Vice Chairman, NASD; President, Regulatory Policy & Oversight, NASD

Table 16.3 (*Continued*)

Maurice Strong	Chairman, the Earth Council; former United Nations Under-Secretary General*
James Thompson	Chairman, Winston & Strawn; former four-term Governor of Illinois*
Sir Brian Williamson	Former Chairman, London International Financial Futures Exchange
Robert Wilmouth	President and CEO, National Futures Association
Klaus Woltron	Austrian entrepreneur; Vice President of the Vienna Club
Michael Zammit Cutajar	former Executive Secretary, UN Framework Convention on Climate Change

*Denotes members who joined between May 1, 2001, and December 15, 2001.

challenges we faced. We had delivered on time, produced hundreds of pages of term sheets and meeting summaries, and developed a full-scale marketing program. Mike was fantastic as the research leader, and Rafael assumed additional responsibilities conducting research and managing relationships with the press and committee meetings in January 2002. My adrenaline was flowing, but I was also feeling somewhat apprehensive. The countdown clock stood at 11 months and 24 days. We only had 358 days left to meet our internal target and launch the program on January 2, 2003.

Chapter 17

CCX Market Architecture

Daring ideas are the chessmen moved forward; they may be beaten, but they may start a winning game.

—*Johann Wolfgang von Goethe*

Every year seemed to pose a hurdle for CCX. We had just survived 9/11 and the mild recession of 2001. Just when I thought we were through the worst of it, a disturbing event occurred.

Enron, a gas pipeline company with a large presence in energy and emissions trading, was running into severe financial problems and had been targeted for investigation by the SEC and the Justice Department. Their problems could easily sully the reputation and people's perceptions of cap-and-trade. It was an all-too-familiar case of a financial or industrial firm attempting to become the largest or only counterparty to all buyers and sellers. Others had tried it and failed.

Incidents like this incorrectly gave exchanges a bad name. Exchanges abided by a dramatically different business model compared to single companies that were market makers. A central marketplace broadened the market rather than narrowed it. The exchange was the platform for transactions and did not attempt to influence prices. The clearinghouse was simply a financial guarantor of all transactions. Throughout 2002, I found myself having to repeatedly explain how exchanges differed from single or dominant companies that acted as principals.

In spite of the looming problems with Enron, 2002 began with a bang. Our design committee for CCX had grown to 54 members, and in January, we held the very first meetings in Chicago.

"If You're Not at the Table, You're on the Menu"

We held our committee meetings at the Union League Club. The rooms were decorated with military memorabilia, and the organization still carried a bit of the aura of a men's-only club. The gentlemen's bathrooms carried several hair products and colognes that looked like props left over from an episode of the Emmy Award–winning television show, *Mad Men*. The club held special memories of my first lunch during my interview at the CBOT with Henry Hall Wilson, and occupied a sentimental place in my heart.

Although there was a grand, stately dining room, we preferred to book smaller rooms to provide a more intimate environment conducive to discussions. The representatives who came to our meetings needed to know that they belonged to the process and were not simply being lectured to. Mike Walsh and I acted as facilitators. He provided technical expertise as needed while I guided the group through the issues.

Our research had identified six major sectors that constituted a representative core of potential participants. Individual interviews were conducted with representatives from each sector to gather initial input on the draft market rules. We decided that the industry sectors could be aggregated into two main groups: electric utilities and manufacturing. We established a schedule of meetings to be held in person every six weeks to build consensus, figure out what issues were important to the members, and design what would become their own private Kyoto Protocol.

The First Meeting for the Utility Technical Committee

I asked Les Rosenthal to co-chair the first two committee meetings. His experience as an exchange chairman and businessman would come in handy.

There were 12 major utilities represented at the first utility technical committee meeting. The vast majority were Midwest-based, with the exception of one utility from Canada and another from California.

We told the members that the meetings would be run as if this were an exchange that they owned. "We'll start with the noncontroversial parts of the agenda," I added, recalling my experience at the CBOT board meetings.

Monitoring and verification issues were relatively straightforward and noncontroversial, so we began with those. Some suggested annual reporting of emissions. The CCX team argued that markets would perform more efficiently if there were a more continuous flow of information. While power-generating plants that had CEMs installed found it relatively easy to provide quarterly data, others found it more difficult and costly. The final compromise was for units already under Title IV to file quarterly reports, and for all other units to file annual reports. The committee also decided that verification would be provided by the designated Title IV guarantor. There was a lot of humor around this issue. Under the Clean Air Act Amendment of 1990, a designated guarantor of emissions was required to provide support for the risks of emissions project implementation. If the reports were found to be false, the signatory could be personally indicted. We dubbed this person the "designated jailee."

The utilities committee then dealt with the issue of jointly owned facilities. Suppose a utility owned less than 50 percent of a power plant. Should the emissions be prorated based on the percentage owned by the utility? What would happen if ownership constituted exactly 50 percent, but the utility company was not responsible for the operations of the facility and therefore had no control over emission levels? Since there were many possible scenarios, I suggested we form a subcommittee. As was typical of the CBOT, I suggested that the most vocal member of the design committee be appointed as chairman. Borrowing extensively from my experience at exchanges, I suggested balancing the makeup of the committee by including companies most likely to be affected by its decisions. We wanted the committees to have members with vested interests. Neutral parties were generally not welcome unless there was an unambiguous reason to include them.

We anticipated some disagreement over the choice of baselines and targeted reductions. To create a platform for discussion, Mike and I suggested a reduction schedule and baseline. There seemed to be a consensus on our targeted reduction schedule of 1 percent per year in 2003 and a further 1 percent per year thereafter until 2006. However, a lively debate ensued after the following alternatives were presented: using a single-year baseline of 2000; a multiyear baseline of 1998 to 2001; or two years with the highest emissions set as baseline years. Obviously, the latter would have been the most lenient option, as reductions were easier when emissions were already high. We eventually settled on the multiyear baseline of 1998 to 2001 as the preliminary recommendation, pending confirmation with the Industry Technical Committee.

I had learned from Les and Henry Wilson that the most contentious issues should be addressed last on the agenda—in this case, how to handle economic growth. Fast-growing companies would bear a significant compliance burden under the voluntary program. More importantly, these companies faced unknown, unlimited liabilities. The issue seemed insurmountable. Alternatively, if growth were not part of the program, we would not be credible in the eyes of policy makers and the public. We had apparently reached an impasse when Les chimed in. He pointed out that everyone had the same objective and the details could be worked out. The focus of the meeting returned to the larger picture after that.

Overall, the meeting concluded on a very positive note. To keep the momentum, we asked the committee to reach consensus on these important issues within the next 30 days. Our mission was to start the pilot program by the end of the year.

The First Meeting for the Industry Technical Committee

We convened the first meeting of the Industry Technical Committee on January 24, 2002, in Chicago. The group consisted of 15 members representing a broad cross-section of industry. Most of these companies either believed that there were profits to be made from reducing greenhouse gas emissions, or felt that they would gain a competitive advantage from participating in this process. They also wanted to establish themselves as leaders in sustainability.

It took longer to explain the CCX concept to the Industrial Technical Committee than to the utilities, who had been more familiar with cap-and-trade. I peppered my comments throughout with comparisons between the carbon market we were creating and the existing grain markets. To explain the limit placed on the quantity that a firm could sell to minimize the impact on prices, I used the analogy of grain elevators. Grain elevators stored grain that could be released by a spigot during certain times. By the end of a crash course in emissions trading, all of the members seemed excited about the commercial opportunities we were offering and their participation in what could be a transformational event.

Emissions monitoring was addressed next. The Greenhouse Gas Protocol, jointly convened in 1998 by the World Business Council for Sustainable Development and the World Resources Institute, provided a both credible and familiar accounting tool for monitoring emissions from stationary and mobile sources across a number of industries. It included monitoring tools for products such as semiconductors, cements, and refrigerants. The committee members agreed to use this outside source—a logical choice that would minimize costs and lend more credibility to the program. Mike and I endorsed this decision. We chose existing protocols developed by others whenever possible. Too many new microinventions could complicate the macroinvention of a new market.

There was a strong consensus among the committee members that the program should begin in 2003. There also seemed to be a unanimous agreement for CCX to expand beyond the Midwest to the entire United States. After all, if a company reduced emissions anywhere in the country, it should be able to receive credit for it. The committee members also wanted to phase in Canada and Mexico. Within a mere month, the program would go from being a Midwest pilot to a national pilot, with plans to go international. Members of the design committee were moving quicker than we had ever hoped.

The committee dealt with baselines next. The electricity sector technical committee had proposed a multi-year baseline of 1998–2000. The forest products representative pointed out that 2000 had witnessed a slump in the forestry business and to include it would only make reductions more difficult to achieve.

When it came to the emissions reduction schedule, some industry committee members were comfortable with the CCX recommendation of a 1 percent reduction from the baseline in 2003, followed by 1 percent per year in 2004, 2005, and 2006. Others were not. Ford took a leadership role and suggested an even bigger reduction. We formed a subcommittee to iron out any differences with the decisions of its counterparts in the Utility Committee.

Everyone was upbeat and invigorated after the meeting. I was proud of what we had managed to accomplish in just two meetings. Already, there was consensus on a starting date and the establishment of a nationwide program. As always, however, I felt overwhelmed by the amount of technical work left to be done.

We had to form a dozen subcommittees to deal with the more specific issues. The objectives of the subcommittees included setting the baseline year, targeted reductions, eligible offsets to be included in the program, and other key features of the system. See the feature "CCX Utility Subcommittees" for the subcommittee members and their objectives.

Each subcommittee debated the issues and came up with specific recommendations before forwarding them to the main utility or industry committees. The main committees then debated and generated final recommendations on the salient features of the program. In the event of a disagreement between the utility and the industry technical committees, a joint resolutions committee debated the differences. They determined the final salient features, borrowing from the process of joint resolutions in the House and Senate. These features were, in turn, voted on by the two main committees. It was in this fashion that the issues of choosing baseline years and targets were reconciled between the utility and industry committees. Managing the process was a colossal task for a staff of only four economists. It was also exhilarating watching the birth of the exchange.

CCX Utility Subcommittees

Offsets, Supply Constraints, and Early Action Credit Subcommittee
(*Formerly Targets and Baseline Subcommittee*)

Goals:

- Establish program's emission reduction targets.
- Define a backstop mechanism to address growth on existing facilities.
- Approve rules for eligible early action projects.
- Approve list of acceptable early action projects.
- Approve list of acceptable offset project types.
- Develop micro and macro supply constraints.

Members:

- American Electric Power
- Alliant Energy
- Cinergy
- Detroit Edison
- NiSource

Landfill Gas Subcommittee

Goal:

- Develop rules for crediting landfill methane offsets and early action projects undertaken by utility companies.
- Develop standardized monitoring protocol for landfill methane offset projects.

Members:

- Detroit Edison
- Cinergy

Forestry Offset Projects Subcommittee

Goal: Develop eligibility and monitoring rules for CCX forestry offset projects in the United States and Brazil.

(*continued*)

CCX Industry Subcommittees (*Continued*)

Members:

- Cinergy
- Alliant Energy
- American Electric Power
- Winrock International
- International Paper
- Wisconsin Energy

New Plants Subcommittee

Goal: Define rules for accommodating growth on new facilities (completed).

Members:

- NiSource
- Alliant Energy
- Arizona Public Service (Pinnacle West Capital)
- Wisconsin Energy
- American Electric Power
- PG&E National Energy Group

Joint Ownership Subcommittee

Goal: Define treatment of emissions from jointly owned facilities (completed).

Members:

- Exelon
- PG&E National Energy Group
- Cinergy

CCX Industry Subcommittees
Baseline Subcommittee

Goal: Establish program's baseline years (completed).

Members:

- Stora Enso
- International Paper

CCX Industry Subcommittees (*Continued*)

- Mead Westvaco
- Temple-Inland

Oil and Gas Company Monitoring Subcommittee

Goal: Develop standard monitoring protocols for oil and gas companies.

Members:

- BP Amoco Corporation
- Suncor Energy

Unit Size Subcommittee

Goal: Define minimum plant size for estimating emissions from fossil fuel combustion (completed).

Members:

- Temple-Inland
- Stora Enso

Targets and Economic Growth Provision Subcommittee

Goal:

- Establish program's emission reduction targets (completed).
- Define an economic growth mechanism to address growth on existing facilities.
- Establish industry agreement with utility group consensus on targets and economic growth provision.

Members:

- Ford Motor Company
- International Paper
- DuPont
- BP Amoco Corporation
- Cemex
- Temple-Inland

(*continued*)

CCX Industry Subcommittees (*Continued*)

Offsets, Supply Constraints, and Early Action Credit Subcommittee

Goal:

- Define list of eligible project-based offsets and their supply limitations.
- Define supply constraints, or market position limits.
- Develop rules for crediting early action projects.

Members:

- DuPont
- BP Amoco Corporation
- Temple-Inland
- Cemex

Joint Ownership Subcommittee

Goal: Define treatment of emissions from jointly owned facilities.

Members:

- Stora Enso North America
- Suncor Energy
- BP Amoco Corporation
- Cemex

Forest Products Company Sequestration Monitoring Subcommittee

Goal: Develop standardized protocol for estimating and monitoring changes in biomass carbon on lands owned by forest product companies.

Members:

- Temple-Inland
- International Paper
- Mead Westvaco
- Stora Enso North America

The technical details of the program were critical but not more important than building a consensus on the baseline, reduction schedule, and the inclusion of allowances and offsets of the program. Although this was only the first month of meeting, I was very optimistic. The relationships and reputation we had cultivated over a decade gave us credibility when we approached the power and industrial sectors. The soft letter of commitment we required members to sign also provided the impetus for them to give their best efforts in designing the program. We were at a turning point. CCX was more than just a dream.

Over the course of the design phase, we held close to 100 meetings, including phone conferences and in-person meetings. The committees and subcommittees met four or more times formally, and countless times informally. Subcommittees debated the issues and then voted before reporting their recommendations back to the committees. The joint resolutions committee met only at the very end to work out the kinks. It was a complex management process to get everyone in the same place and always have one of our staff present to help mediate meetings.

Consensus Building

As members worked through the technical issues, strong positions emerged and had to be worked out among participants. In our meeting for the landfill gas sector subcommittee, there was an undertow of tension. A member who represented a landfill operator that managed a very large fleet of vehicles started the meeting by stating plainly, "We should only be responsible for landfill operations. We refuse to join if we have to include our emissions from our fleet of garbage trucks." However, since the company's fleet of trucks was very large, it represented a major source of emissions that would not be captured by the program. Furthermore, landfills were already a part of the company's business, so if we agreed to the representative's proposal, the company would essentially become a net seller with no responsibility for its main emissions.

We tried to reason with the member. We explained that this would create a major black eye for the environmental integrity of the program and ultimately harm his company's public image. At first, he was reluctant to budge. I decided to play a different card. "Let's think this through. If your offsets exceed the emissions from the fleet, then your company can both make money from membership in CCX and burnish your reputation for sustainability among your stakeholders." He said that he would have to think about the issue and discuss it with his management. Eventually, the members of his landfill subcommittee persuaded him to change his position. This was a good example of committee members working to reach consensus.

With the help of the subcommittees, we were able to focus on the more contentious aspects of market architecture. Les told the committee that we could work out our differences and we did. Given the voluntary nature of the program, we knew that it would be impossible for fast-growing companies to join, given that they faced potentially unlimited liabilities. The committee entertained a variety of thoughtful proposals on how to address the issue. After considerable debate, the committee eventually reached consensus on what would be called the Economic Growth Provision or EGP. In effect, it placed an upper bound limit on growth providing a degree of certainty as to the potential liabilities of the program for a growing company. In an effort to enhance the environmental credibility of the provision, the committee also placed a lower bound limit on decreases in emissions. This would limit the potential sales of emission from entities that experienced a dramatic decline in emissions. We eventually came up with a plan to keep any extraordinary reductions in a safety box or registry account, which could be used in a later phase of the pilot program. It was similar to the upper bound used to treat over-supply in agricultural markets, which could be stored in elevators until needed later on.

The following box shows gives a sample of some of the other issues dealt by the subcommittees.

Verification Using Continuous Emissions Monitoring

Decisions over which continuous emissions monitoring systems (CEMs) to use differed among the committees. It was relatively straightforward for power plants in the utility committee, most of which had already installed CEMs on their smokestacks in order to comply with the Acid Rain Program, but less so for other types of emitting sources. There were also standardized conversion factors in place for converting quantities of coal, natural gas, heating oil,

Verification Using Continuous Emissions Monitoring (*Continued*)

and other carbon-emitting materials into the volume of carbon emitted. For example, one ton of CO_2 was equal to 102 gallons of gasoline consumed.[1] These conversion factors could be extended to the manufacturing sector. Other types of GHG emissions, for example, from the use of semiconductors and refrigerants, could also be measured and converted into common GHG emissions. For example, one ton of methane was equal to 25 tons of carbon.[2] To avoid completely reinventing the wheel, we ended up proposing monitoring and verification protocols which built upon these in-place methods. The overall consensus was to use CEMs for units already covered by the Acid Rain Program.

Early Action Credits

Early action credits aim to reward early actors while preserving or enhancing the environmental outcomes of the program.[3] If designed and implemented poorly, however, early action credits could risk inflating the emissions cap and reduce the integrity of the program. The committee ultimately decided to adopt this concept for CCX. We planned to conduct reporting on an annual basis, when the financial auditors of participating companies would be required to provide verification. Early action credits were critical in order to avoid penalizing companies for acting early—their CCX reductions would count in the event that a national emissions mandate was eventually passed. Early action would encourage first movers.

---

[1]GHG Equivalencies Calculator, U.S. Environmental Protection Agency.

[2]This is called the carbon equivalent, a metric measure used to compare the emissions from various greenhouse gases based upon their global warming potential (GWP). For example, reducing N_2O emissions by one ton would be equivalent to reducing CO_2 emissions by 298 tons; thus, its carbon equivalent is 298 tons.

[3]Issuing early action credits in addition to the number of allowances that are permitted under the cap could erode the environmental impact of the cap-and-trade regime.

(*continued*)

Verification Using Continuous Emissions Monitoring (*Continued*)

Carbon Sequestration

Carbon sequestration in forests occurred naturally when plants captured CO_2 through photosynthesis and stored it in surrounding soil and biomass. Carbon sequestration would be measured in the first year, with any subsequent changes recorded annually. Since all forestry companies took inventories, this would make things easier. Offset credits generated from carbon storage could then be used to offset emissions from manufacturing activity. Once again, such a scheme would depend on unambiguous property rights. Members suggested treating stored carbon in a fashion similar to mineral rights, which gave landowners the right to examine, extract, and produce all minerals on or below their property. Owners could sell, gift, or lease their rights separately or collectively.

Indirect Emissions

Many member corporations emitted greenhouse gases directly as a result of combustion of fossil fuels or emissions from chemical processes. However, a significant amount of their emissions was produced indirectly, that is, generated from the use of electricity. We all knew that there ought to be incentives in place that could drive reductions in electricity usage, but few were considering this as an element of cap-and-trade. Consequently, we formed a subcommittee on indirect emissions. Ford had rebuilt River Rouge, its state-of-the-art factory in Michigan, which significantly reduced the company's energy consumption.[4] The company was making improvements in energy efficiency that it should have received credit for. DTE argued that as the supplier, it should receive credit for selling power to Ford. We ultimately ended up allotting the credit to the purchaser of electricity—Ford in this instance—because we felt this was the best way to incentivize reduced emissions. The supplier, on the other hand, was not really changing its emissions profile.

---

[4]"Big Generator for Auto Plant Adds to Giant Power," *Popular Mechanics*, September 1937, 374.

I was elated with the committee's back-and-forth. It was a good example of smart people getting together and battling their differences around in a productive way. A representative from a major electric utility articulated this feeling eloquently. He was a Washington veteran of many government and utility association meetings. He told us during a break in the meetings how different the CCX process from his experience in Washington. "You guys get things done," he said. We took it as a compliment. Our design members recognized that they were making a practical contribution to solve a problem to which they were personally and professionally committed. The ability to be part of the creation of an exchange from the ground up provided the glue that kept our design process going.

The End of the Day

To instill a sense of pride and ownership, we celebrated the success of our first technical meetings by handing out coffee mugs, sweaters, and windbreakers as memorabilia. The windbreakers were a big hit, perfect to be worn by the avid golfers in the group. It was more than marketing. It was about building a team mentality. I joked that people should take good care of it because one day these items could be listed on eBay. To close, we held cocktail receptions to allow the design members to let loose and bond. I was proud of what we had managed to accomplish. Already, there was consensus on a launch date in 2003 and the establishment of a nationwide program. We were on a mission and wanted to start the pilot program by the beginning of the following year. The clock was ticking. There were 344 days left before our proposed launch.

In addition to our meetings in January, we had also continued to build capacity in the agricultural sector and other relevant industries by working with experts and authoring relevant papers. We appointed a landfill expert panel drawing from distinguished engineering companies with practical experience in the field. Since agriculture offsets were complex, we also appointed a soil sequestration expert panel that included the top three soil scientists in the country. The panel helped us clarify and validate technical issues to ensure that our ideas would be well informed rather than developed in a vacuum.

It was still early in the game, but the work seemed to be piling up.

The Chicago Accord

We completed the Phase II report in August 2002 and delivered it personally to the Joyce Foundation. Despite EFP's lack of members, the foundation was impressed by the progress we had made. We soon sent in a final report summarizing the features of CCX and drew up a final accord—the Chicago Accord—which codified the details of CCX in what was our private-sector equivalent of an enabling legislation.[5]

Mike and I spent many hours working on the final draft of the Chicago Accord before we could finalize the actual commitment letter. The Accord was critical in outlining the exchange's major objectives. We sought to prove that a significant cross-section of the United States could not only reach consensus on a voluntary commitment to reduce greenhouse gases, but successfully implement a market-based emission reduction program. To establish proof of concept, we needed to demonstrate the viability of a multisector greenhouse gas emissions cap-and-trade program supplemented by project-based offsets. CCX would serve as a cost-effective mechanism for achieving price discovery and developing and disseminating market data in spite of variation in the methods, locations, and timing of emission reductions. We hoped to not only encourage improved emissions management, but also facilitate trading with low transaction costs. We planned to develop a market architecture that rewarded innovative technology and management, and simultaneously encouraged sustainable farming and forestry practices. This required building up the necessary market institutions and human capital needed to facilitate emissions trading. Once this infrastructure was established, the exchange would seek to harmonize and integrate with other international or sovereign trading regimes.

The Chicago Accord was 13 pages in length, compared to the 1,427 pages that went into the American Clean Energy and Security Act of 2009, that is, the Waxman-Markey Bill. The Accord called for similar reductions as other climate change legislation. It reflected the input of more than 30 companies from diverse industrial sectors and had an emissions baseline that ultimately grew to more than 675 million tons. It

[5]"The Chicago Accord," Chicago Climate Exchange, 2004.

also reflected the input of experts from 18 different entities hailing from NGOs, public entities, engineering, forestry and agriculture sectors, and academic institutions. Members of the capital markets also gave input, with an emphasis on the futures and spot markets. See Table 17.1 for a summary of salient features laid out in the Accord.

When we finished the Chicago Accord, our list of tradable instruments included Greenhouse Gas Emissions Allowances (GGEAs), Certified Emissions Offsets (CEOs), and Certified Early Action Credits (CEACs). We were concerned, however, that the different contracts might fragment the market. We decided to combine all the different instruments into a single one, called a carbon financial instrument (CFI), which represented an allowance and offset interchangeably. It was the birth of the CCX currency.

Speaking of which, it turned out that we needed a little currency of our own.

Seeking Investors

We finished the Accord, the members were optimistic, and the reality of financing the venture struck us. The organization was growing, and

Table 17.1 Salient Features of the Chicago Accord (Abridged)

Geographic Coverage	*From early 2003* (outset of program): Emitting sources in the United States and offset providers in both the United States and Brazil *Integrated during 2003*: Emitting sources and offset projects in Canada and Mexico
Pilot Market Time Period	2003 to 2006. Members may choose to extend pilot beyond
Gases Covered	Carbon dioxide (CO_2) Methane (CH_2) Nitrous oxide (N_2O) Hydrofluorocarbons (HFCs) Perfluorocarbons (PFCs) Sulfur hexafluoride (SF_6) All GHG gases converted to CO_2 equivalent using the 100-year global warming potential values established by IPCC

(continued)

Table 17.1 (*Continued*)

Instruments, Vintages, Banking	Greenhouse Gas Emission Allowances (GGEAs) Certified Emission Offsets (CEOs) generated by mitigation projects Certified Early Action Credits (CEACs) Each instrument represents 100 metric tons of CO_2 equivalent, to be designated with a specific serial number and annual vintage. May be used for compliance in their designated vintage year or in later years
Emission Baseline	Each Member's baseline: Annual average emissions from facilities included in baseline during 1998–2001
Emission Reduction Schedule, GHG Allowance Allocations	Members issued Greenhouse Gas Emission Allowances at program inception for four-year period in an amount reflecting the emission reduction schedule: 2003: 1% below Member's baseline 2004: 2% below Member's baseline 2005: 3% below Member's baseline 2006: 4% below Member's baseline
Economic Growth Provision (EGP)	Year/EGP: Maximum amount of net purchases of GHGAs and/or CEOs required for compliance: 2003: 3% of Member's baseline 2004: 4% of Member's baseline 2005: 6% of Member's baseline 2006: 7% of Member's baseline
Annual True-Up	After each compliance year, each Member must surrender any GGEAs, CEOs, and CEACs equal to the CO_2 equivalent emissions from included facilities during compliance year
Registry and Electronic Trading Platform	Internet-accessible CCX Registry managed and administered by CCX, to contain all GGEAs, CEOs, and CEACs. Registry used as official holder of record and transfer mechanism and to be integrated with CCX electronic trading platform
Auctions	CCX-administered auctions to occur regularly
Facilities Included, Emissions Monitoring	Electricity-producing CCX members will use continuous emission monitors (CEM) to record and report emissions data for power-generating facilities producing 25 mW or up. Emissions opt-in is available for all units that generate less than 25 mW, for vehicles operated, and for SF_6 gas

Table 17.1 (*Continued*)

	For non-electricity-producing CCX members, emissions for stationary source fossil fuel combustion, vehicles, and process emissions will be reported according to the protocols of the World Resources Institute/World Business Council for Sustainable Development (WRI/WBCSD) initiative
Emissions Reporting and Verification	CCX members must submit quarterly emission reports. Emissions and offset project reports must be signed by an appropriate representative, and their underlying data will be subject to verification and audits
Certified Emission Offsets (CEOs)	The initial categories of eligible offset project categories are: • Certified landfill offsets in the United States (CLO) • Certified Agricultural Methane Offsets in United States (CAMO) • Certified Forestry Offsets in United States (CFO) • Certified Soil Offsets in United States (CSO) • Certified Emissions Reductions in Brazil (CER)
Certified Early Action Credits (CEACs)	Certified Early Action Credits will be given for: • Reforestation, afforestation, and avoided deforestation • Landfill methane destruction in the United States • Fuel switching and other energy related USIJI projects
Electricity Purchase Opt-In Program (EPOP)	CCX members not primarily engaged in the production of electricity may opt in purchased electricity as a supplemental reduction objective
Renewable Fuels	Emissions associated with combustion of the following renewable fuels will be excluded: • Wood, wood wastes, and wood-derived fuels • Agricultural residues, grasses • Landfill and agricultural methane
Single Firm Sales Limit	Net Greenhouse Gas Emission Allowance Sales limit: Percent of program-wide baseline emissions that can be sold by a single firm 2003: 0.05% 2004: 0.10% 2005: 0.15% 2006: 0.20% Total 0.50% of program-wide baseline emission

(continued)

Table 17.1 (*Continued*)

Use of Certified Emission Offsets and Certified Early Action Credits	Total allowed use for compliance of Certified Emission Offsets plus Certified Early Action Credits as a percentage of program-wide baseline emissions: 2004: 1.0% 2005: 1.5% 2006: 2.0%
Offsets from Owned and Operated Facilities	Total net sales plus use for compliance of CEOs generated from a CCX member's owned and operated facilities: 2003: 0.05% 2004: 0.10% 2005: 0.15% 2006: 0.20% Total 0.50% of program-wide baseline emissions
Exchange Governance	The following lists the currently envisioned committees: Exchange Executive Committee Committee on Certified Emission Offsets Committee on Market Efficiency Committee on Compliance

we were running out of capital. Once we exhausted our foundation grant funds, I continued to finance our operations from my personal savings. By May, however, the need to seek outside investors became inexorable. I suspected there would be natural strategic investors who could supply us with both the technology and capital we needed. The process of seeking investors demanded a lot of work. Hoping to bolster the range of our recruitment efforts, EFP reached out to venture capitalists and foundations for future funding. Without a government mandate, financing proved to be a major challenge going forward. I had to go through countless personal contacts to pitch the idea of CCX. We developed lists of potential targets such as university endowment funds, foundations, family offices, and other individual and institutional investors.

An investment banker at Credit Suisse First Boston suggested NYMEX as a potential investor since it was an energy exchange.[6]

[6]The Intercontinental Exchange (ICE) was not yet around at this point.

I had met Vinnie Viola, chairman of NYMEX, when Cantor Fitzgerald had sued the exchange for infringement of the Wagner patent. I had told Vinnie about Project CCARP and offered my help to him. Although he had disclosed this information in the lawsuit, the revelation had come too late in the legal process and the judge ruled it inadmissible. The chemistry I had with Vinnie was remarkable. He physically resembled the familiar street kid from Brooklyn. Vinnie was intelligent, well read, and grasped ideas quickly. He owned a firm that cleared locals at NYMEX and was very familiar with technology. Like most creative people in the business, Vinnie could work on a dozen different ideas simultaneously and, back to that great analogy, juggle just as many balls in the air. I flew to New York to have lunch with the banker and Vinnie at Tribeca Grill, and explained to them the vision I had for CCX.

I went over the history of SO_2 trading and explained the progress made in enabling emissions trading in CO_2 over the last decade. Together, Americans produced 6.5 billion of the 27.7 billion tons of CO_2 generated annually, and these numbers were growing every year.[7] The top 50 U.S. utilities emitted about 2 billion tons. There were several independent organizations that had estimated the size of a futures market in CO_2 emissions. The World Bank had estimated $10 billion of trading by 2005. Lockwood Consulting predicted $1.2 trillion by 2008 and the U.S. Council on Foreign Relations predicted $2.3 trillion by 2012.[8] The CCX would be a first mover in the United States. Slated to begin as a spot market for GHGs, CCX would be a first mover.

It was the first time I had really focused on the business aspects of the exchange. I valued the business at $10 million, and offered Vinnie a 10 percent stake for $1 million. Vinnie responded quickly and positively, but still needed buy-in from his executive committee at NYMEX. The executive committee subsequently came to Chicago to conduct some due diligence and meet the CCX staff. Unfortunately,

---

[7]Richard A. Felly, Christopher L. Sabine, and Vicotria J. Fabry, "Carbon Dioxide and Our Ocean Legacy," *The Pew Charitable Trust*, April 2006.

[8]"Value at Risk—Climate Change and the Future of Governance," CERES sustainable Future Governance Project Report, April 2002.

the vice chairman wasn't convinced of the opportunity, and there wasn't enough support for the board to approve of the investment. Little did they know, in a mere eight years, the 10 percent stake would be valued at $60 million. Undaunted by this failure, I sent the same business proposal to other exchanges, investment banks, and foundations. I disliked asking for money, however, and quickly became discouraged about our prospects of obtaining funding. We ended up raising our first round of significant capital from the most unlikely source.

I had always had a special place in my heart for my nephew, David Sandor, who had gotten his doctorate in social welfare. Extroverted and fearless when it came to social interactions, David was not an academic in the stereotypical sense. I had kept David apprised of my progress at EFP and CCX, and he ended up calling many of our potential investors. One contact, John Regan, had no capital himself but was interested in combating climate change. He suggested one of his contacts in California to me who shared his passion for the environment—Father Francis Smith of the Jesuit Community of Santa Clara.

From our very first phone call, it was clear that Father Smith was interested in CCX. I followed up with material so he could conduct due diligence. We had never met personally, but he somehow persuaded his board to make an investment of $1.6 million. One day, my secretary walked into the office and whispered, "It's Father Francis on the phone." I picked up the phone and said, "How are you, Father?" "Fine, Richard," he responded. He then asked a question that one never wanted to hear from a man of God, "Richard, how's your burn rate?"[9] "Very high, Father," I said. He asked, "Have you signed up any members to CCX?" "No, Father." "Have there been any positive policy signs from Washington, DC?" he asked. Again, "No, Father." He ended the conversation with a comment I had never heard from any investor on Wall Street, LaSalle Street, or Montgomery Street for that matter. "I pray for you every night, Richard."

Father Francis was public in his support. In a press release, he was quoted to say, "The Jesuit Community is proud to be a part of

[9]The rate at which a start-up uses up its funding before it is able to generate revenue.

the world's only exchange committed to developing a market-based solution to resolve the greatest threat to mankind's existence—the build-up of greenhouse gas emissions." I was profoundly touched.[10]

At the CCX's most recent annual meeting, Father Smith heard me recount this story personally during my speech. He later told me with a big smile that he remembered the conversation in a slightly different way. He quoted and translated, "*Se non è vero, è ben trovato*," a saying in Italian that meant, "If it's not true, it's well told." He said that I sounded like a real stand-up comedian, a compliment that made me think fondly of my father, Henry. In the end, it was showmanship and know-how that resulted in the breakthrough that was CCX.

[10] In a press release of the Jesuit Community at Santa Clara University on April 28, 2003.

Chapter 18

Chicago Climate Exchange

Building the Institution

The more rational an institution is the less it suffers by making concessions to others.

— *George Santayana*

As we embarked on this new journey, I knew it was going to be different. I was somewhat armed by my previous experiences in designing new products in commodity, financial, and insurance markets. I had also played an advisory role in launching and restructuring exchanges and had even helped to shape futures regulation. However, all this was done within an existing institutional framework that carbon as a commodity lacked. I never had to invent a product, start an exchange from scratch, and construct the regulations around it. We had to create the supply and demand of a product that didn't exist, as well as construct the web of institutions to support this new market. The enormity of the task promised to challenge my entire skill set. It was made even more formidable because I had no blueprint to follow. After all, it had been more than a century since anyone had started a successful spot or commodity exchange.

A proof of concept for emissions trading was going to require much more than creating an innovative financial instrument or a new exchange. Since the United States was not a party to the Kyoto Protocol, there was no legal mandate to reduce carbon emissions. Finishing the Chicago Accord, our voluntary mandate, was like finishing the Kyoto Protocol without the force of law. This made recruiting a critical mass of voluntary members a daunting task. A business case had to be made to companies. We also had to build both an environmental and financial regulatory structure, create a registry, monitor and verify emissions, and regulate the market itself. In effect, we had to perform the functions of the EPA and CFTC ourselves, almost as a quasi-governmental entity. The challenge of financing the exchange presented yet another quandary.

To succeed required compressing over a hundred years of commodity market evolution into a few short years. Establishing CCX was counter-Darwinian. I knew that the work of building the exchange had just begun.

Recruiting the First Members—Voluntary Participation versus Legislative Mandate

On January 16, 2003, we held what was surely the mostly unlikely press conference that I had ever been a part of. Assembled in a modest conference room in Chicago's city hall were representatives from some of the most recognizable names in American industry. We had spent the better part of the previous six months cajoling, pleading, groveling, prodding, and otherwise outright begging design phase members and other major corporates into joining the world's first voluntary greenhouse gas emissions reduction and trading program. In the end, 13 brave souls made that leap of faith.

With 13 members confirmed, we finally reached critical mass by the end of 2002. We needed to find a venue for the announcement and to maximize the publicity. We decided to engage a leading public relations firm, Edelman, to manage our announcement.

When Ellen and I first moved into our co-op in 1978, Ruth and Dan Edelman had been the first of our neighbors to reach out to us and help us become part of the Chicago community. Their son, Richard, was attending Harvard at the time, and I helped him with his senior thesis. He was a young man of great expectations. By the time I reached out to him again, Richard was working as a senior manager at Edelman, now the world's largest private PR firm. He eventually succeeded his father as president and CEO. Under his guidance, the firm was named "Top-Ranked PR Firm of the Decade" by *Advertising Age*. You could always tell the winners at the starting gate. He was thrilled about the business opportunity and about working together.

The press conference was jointly hosted by EFP and the City of Chicago. We publicly announced the formation of CCX and its founding members. The commissioner of the Chicago Department of Environment proudly declared the City of Chicago as a founding member, as it was an integral part of the city's goal to make Chicago the greenest city in America. We announced the founding members, included here in Table 18.1.

Table 18.1 Chicago Climate Exchange Founding Members

Automotive	Ford Motor Company
Chemicals	DuPont
Environmental Services	Waste Management, Inc.
Electric Power Generation	American Electric Power; Manitoba Hydro
Electronics	Motorola, Inc.
Forest Products	International Paper; MeadWestvaco Corp.; Stora Enso North America; Temple- Inland, Inc.
Municipalities	City of Chicago
Semiconductors	STMicroelectronics
Pharmaceuticals	Baxter International, Inc.

Among the companies that participated in the press conference were Ford, Motorola, and American Electric Power (AEP). There was even an inspiring telephone presentation by Israel Klabin, a leading Brazilian environmentalist, businessman, and the former mayor of Rio de Janeiro. Israel spoke heartedly about the significance of CCX to international linkages.

Achieving this critical mass was among the most difficult tasks I had faced in corporate life. In the absence of enabling legislation, there was no mandate for corporations or utilities to reduce greenhouse gases. Because of that, we had to recruit the members to voluntarily commit to legally binding reduction in greenhouse gas emissions. In September 2002, we sent out letters inviting members to join the exchange. We targeted design committee members and also recruited Chicago-based companies. Our objective was to recruit 10 companies by the end of 2002 ranging from power to manufacturing, with a baseline of 200 million tons. The pressure was on.

Our first experience was disappointing. We mistakenly thought it was a good sign when an oil company contacted us on its own initiative. The company, which prided itself on sustainability, had sent a representative to every meeting and always engaged in the discussions. On the day of the final decision, the CCX team gathered in my office expecting to high-five each other at the end of the call.

The company representative proceeded by stating succinctly but forcefully that membership was not something they intended to commit to any time soon. It was too early for them, but they still wanted to keep an eye on our progress. Moreover, the oil company had all the people we had dealt with on the call, from their offices in Europe, Texas, and California. They were sending us a very clear message. I was later told by one of the company representatives, "It is our strategy to never do anything unless it is required by law."

Success quickly followed this defeat. Manitoba Hydro sent their commitment letter and became our first member. Mike Walsh was disappointed that the first member was not a major U.S. power generator or industrial company. I told Mike that I saw this as a good omen because my first customer for GNMAs at ContiCommodity had been a Canadian investment bank.

Recruiting proceeded slowly and we needed more recognizable names in order to create momentum. Dupont agreed to join, but said that they would be more comfortable if other major companies joined at the very same time. I knew we would be confronted with the same issue with others and worried about a deadlock. Marty Zimmerman at Ford Motor Company gave me some astute advice, "Why don't you get a group of four or five companies that agree to join simultaneously?" he asked.

Since I was on the board of AEP, I wanted to avoid pitching to AEP directly. Mike called an executive at AEP and informed him of our conversations with Ford and DuPont. I contacted the rest of the targets and made rounds of successive calls. The pressure was on to land our first big five—Dupont, Ford, and AEP, along with International Paper and Baxter. I knew that Dupont and International Paper were driven by both environmental and financial incentives, confident that they could reduce emissions and sell reductions for a profit. They could also benefit enormously from third-party verification of their emissions data, which could be published in annual reports and distributed to their stakeholders. Alternatively, AEP emissions were well over the limit and it would be a significant challenge for the company to achieve its reduction targets. As a leader in public policy and a large beneficiary of the Acid Rain Program, however, AEP saw a much greater benefit in being part of the debate through its involvement with CCX. Baxter Laboratories was a leader in the health-care industry. Although the company's emissions were negligible, its commitment to sustainability and the public relations benefits from joining the exchange were obvious.

Predictably, no one wanted to be the first to take this leap of faith by joining CCX, especially without the assurance that others would follow. We ended up being the mediator, encouraging these companies to hold hands and jump into the pool together. They all did in December 2002.

We continued to target other potential members from the design committees. To reduce the number of rejections, we refused any declinations in the form of a letter and required them to be made in person. Every rejection was personally painful.

I learned an important lesson during the recruiting process. It was very difficult to recruit a company if its CEO was not in favor of CCX membership at the outset. However, if we could seek out champions at a company's middle management level, this might provide the CEO with the right impetus to join. This was not a sufficient condition, but a necessary one.

For example, I was once invited by Chicago's mayor, Richard Daley, to a party for Chicagoland's CEOs at Davos. During the party, I met the CEO of Baxter Labs. Although I did not know it at first, he had been a student of mine at Kellogg in the 1970s. He later admitted that although he never got to use the quantitative techniques I developed in class, these techniques had had a significant impact on his thought process as a businessman. I was moved as a teacher. When he asked me about what I was doing, I took the opportunity to describe CCX and, following the advice given to me by Charlie and Les 25 years earlier. I asked for his help in identifying someone at Baxter who could evaluate CCX membership. Not long after this conversion, Ron Meissen, the senior director of sustainability, health, and safety at Baxter, called us and asked playfully, "Did you meet my boss?" Since the persuasion was coming from the middle management, Baxter's CEO was sympathetic to the idea of joining CCX. Ron became our fearless ambassador, pushing Baxter to become a founding member. Even after his company joined, he missed no opportunity to persuade other colleagues in industry to join CCX. Ron became a lifelong friend and supported me as a guest lecturer when I taught at the University of Chicago Law School many years later.

We routinely researched the directors and officers of all the companies that were considering membership. The relationships and networks I had established throughout my career played an important role in recruiting. One of my colleagues noticed that Tony Frank, a friend from my GNMA days, was on the Temple-Inland board. I called Tony immediately about recruiting Temple Inland, and learned that the chairman of the company was an old friend of ours from the mortgage business. I called the chairman and he said, "We've made money together before. Let's do it again." Temple-Inland participated in the design phase and became a founding member of CCX.

I had become acquainted with the Daley family of Chicago through my former secretary, Marilyn. Mayor Richard M. Daley, who had already agreed to become honorary chairman of the exchange, had introduced me to the head of the city's Department of Environment. We had to convince her that joining CCX was good for the city. She championed the idea, and they joined.

In another instance, a fellow director at the Art Institute introduced me to someone on the board of Motorola. This led to a meeting with the vice president and corporate director at the firm. Motorola, too, became a founding member. Each sale became easier because of the companies that had already signed. Momentum was growing.

Slowly but surely, we were connecting the dots.

Exchange Governance, Structure, and Regulation

It was crucial to develop a board of directors whose names would lend stature to the exchange, and to build the governance of the exchange. In April, we announced that Maurice Strong and Les Rosenthal were joining the board and serve as vice chairmen. I had worked closely with Governor James Thompson during my tenure on the CBOT's board of directors, and he agreed to join the CCX board as well. We subsequently added Governor Christine Todd Whitman, the former governor of New Jersey and head of the EPA. Warren Batts, a retired CEO of Tupperware and a well-regarded philanthropist, rounded out the independent directors. Later on, we included three member directors from Ford, International Paper, and AEP. The rulebook required that these roles be filled by representatives who were no less than two steps down from the position of CEO at their companies. The company structure was starting to approach the one we had envisioned for Project CCARP.

When it came to internal regulation, we designed CCX as a for-profit company. It had a board of directors that consisted of five independent directors and three member directors. An executive committee had jurisdiction over committees on certified emission offsets, forestry, trading and market operations, and environmental compliance. Recommendations from each committee would be forwarded to the executive committee for final approval.

While the exchange was to be independent and self-regulated, I was concerned that CCX would be perceived as a private club that might inaccurately publish the emissions levels of its members. In order to ensure credibility for the exchange, I became convinced that we needed to find an external, third-party regulator. Our experience from the ZAPCO transactions, among others, pushed us to delegate the task of measuring and verifying emissions to a private accounting firm or an engineering firm. The former would be cost-prohibitive, while the latter were experts in technology but not in auditing. There was another less obvious candidate.

Mary Schapiro was the CEO of the National Association of Securities Dealers (NASD). I had known her since her first days of employment at the FIA in the 1980s, when she often asked me to appear and speak at the organization's annual events. Mary and her boss, John Damgard, were spokespeople for the futures industry. I had also known John from the beginning of his tenure at the FIA. A handsome man with graying hair, he represented the political interests of the futures industry. I developed a personal and professional relationship with both of them.

In the summer of 2002, I called Mary and said, "This is probably one of the strangest requests you will ever get." I told her that CCX was exempt from CFTC regulation, but we needed an organization to regulate us even though there were no laws in place.[1] The job of the organization would be to independently monitor and audit our members' emissions. We also needed someone to insure against *congestion*, a formal term for undue influence or manipulation by participants in a market. Mary favored the idea. NASD, which would later become the Financial Industry Regulatory Authority (FINRA), was a candidate.

FINRA and others both submitted proposals for the terms and conditions for this public/private partnership. We selected FINRA as our provider of oversight services. According to the contract, FINRA would assist in the registration, market oversight, and compliance procedures for CCX members. Additional services included auditing emission baselines, providing annual true-ups,[2] and facilitating offset verification

---

[1]CCX operates as an "exempt commercial market," as defined in Section 2(h)(3) of the CFTC regulations.

[2]Annual true-up: After each compliance year, each CCX member would need to surrender any greenhouse gas emission allowances, certified emission offsets, and certified early action credits equal to the CO_2 equivalent emissions from included facilities.

and certification procedures. FINRA would also use its state-of-the-art market surveillance technologies to monitor CCX trading activity for fraud and manipulation, and help translate the Chicago Accord into an exchange rulebook. We all believed that FINRA would provide invaluable assistance in promoting transparency, liquidity, and the highest degree of market integrity to this voluntary pilot program.

By recruiting FINRA to be our self-imposed regulator, we had reinforced our strong belief on how we wanted this market to evolve. It was not a fiscally sound decision for a start-up, but one that reflected our philosophy. Carbon would be a good derivative. It was the right thing to do.

The Electronic Trading Platform

We had to decide whether to build our own electronic platform or to outsource it. Given my previous experience with developing risk management models, I knew that any attempts to build our own trading platform would lead to an enormous time drain on the management team, not to mention a potential loss of speed to market. Accordingly, we persuaded the CCX board to use an outside provider.

In 2002, the Intercontinental Exchange (ICE) was changing its governance from a member-dominated board to one dominated by independent directors. The exchange was laying the groundwork for an IPO and needed to assemble a new board of directors. A former managing director of product development and sales at the CME put my name forward as a board candidate. Richard Spencer, ICE's new CFO, contacted me. I knew ICE by reputation and agreed to meet with Richard. Since ICE was an energy exchange, I thought there could be some synergies with CCX.

Richard came to my office to explain the vision for ICE and the strategy for building the business. He also told me a funny story as a metaphor for the attitude of the exchange's senior management team. He began, "A good friend of mine on Wall Street had an electrophysics PhD from Harvard but rarely led with that moniker. He was salt of the earth and would rather impart his knowledge than dictate.

"After a long summer of working on an endless deal, two associates working for the good doctor were fed up and walked into his office for a two-on-one complaint session about how hard they had been working, working to no avail, and it had to stop. He attentively listened and when they were through, quietly led them out to the lobby and told them both to put their hands on the wall. As soon as they were in position, he told them to push as hard as they could. They did as told. At this point, he got quite excited, actually raising his voice as he encouraged them to push with all their might. They did as told. He then barked, 'Stop! Look down at the floor and the ceiling. Has the wall moved? No! And according to the laws of physics, you've therefore done no work. Now get back to your cubicles and exert more effort into our project. Overworked, you are not.'"

We both laughed. It was the beginning of a long friendship. I knew Richard would help make our vision a reality.

I subsequently joined the board of directors of ICE in November 2002.[3] It was small and functioned like a typical corporate board—a refreshing change from the member-dominated boards I had become accustomed to.

ICE's business model was customer-oriented and had served the exchange well. For products such as natural gas and electricity, ICE employed an OTC platform. I met with Jeffrey C. Sprecher, the founder and CEO of ICE. Jeff was an entrepreneur who executed his vision with great clarity of purpose. His goal was to build a world-class exchange. Having worked in the power sector as an engineer prior to his forming of ICE, Jeff was extraordinarily smart and likeable, and was foremost a pragmatist. He had the vision, but more importantly, possessed the practical acumen necessary to achieve his vision. In line with the business model of ICE, Jeff rewarded the big clients—investment banks, energy companies, and utilities—with equity in the exchange. ICE was like the counter example to mutual exchanges. Jeff was mutualizing ownership, while all the other exchanges were racing to demutualize.

ICE was a technology company as well as an operator of exchanges. I believed that the exchange had set the industry standard in competitively pricing its services. I had a dilemma. If I chose ICE as a provider,

[3]I stayed on until March 2008.

I would be forced to lose my independence as a director and could no longer chair the compensation committee. I made my decision and began serious negotiations with them. We completed our negotiations with ICE and on July 23, 2003, announced that we had contracted with them to provide, design, and service CCX's electronic trading platform. The countdown was at two months, two weeks, and three days before our planned launch on October 10.

The Registry, Clearing, and CCX Rulebook

Unlike conventional physical commodities, our product was an electronic code that conveyed ownership of a carbon emission allowance. This meant that the buyer of the product could not walk into a warehouse to collect it. We had to build an electronic warehouse, called the emissions registry, where buyers and sellers could make and take deliveries. This infrastructure was central to the market, as without it, our market would be no more than a trading simulation exercise. In other regulated emission programs, such as acid rain, the EPA had been tasked with maintaining this central registry. We did not have that comfort, as there was no federal legislation for greenhouse gases. We had to build our own registry.

This was a complex task and we failed to meet our deadline to start continuous trading on October 10 because of the uncompleted registry. I disliked missing deadlines, but the registry was a key piece of our design and we had to get it right. It ended up taking an entire year to build. In hindsight, however, the time we spent on it was justifiable. The European Union Emissions Trading System registry had taken almost two years to complete, and the CDM registry had taken even longer. In fact, we were attempting to do this for greenhouse gases for the very first time.

The registry had to be integrated into the trading platform for a purchase or sale to concomitantly result in the transfer of ownership. The allowances and offsets, now treated homogeneously and named Carbon Financial Instruments (CFIs), would be transferred from seller to buyer through the registry. A screen snapshot of the registry is shown in Figure 18.1.

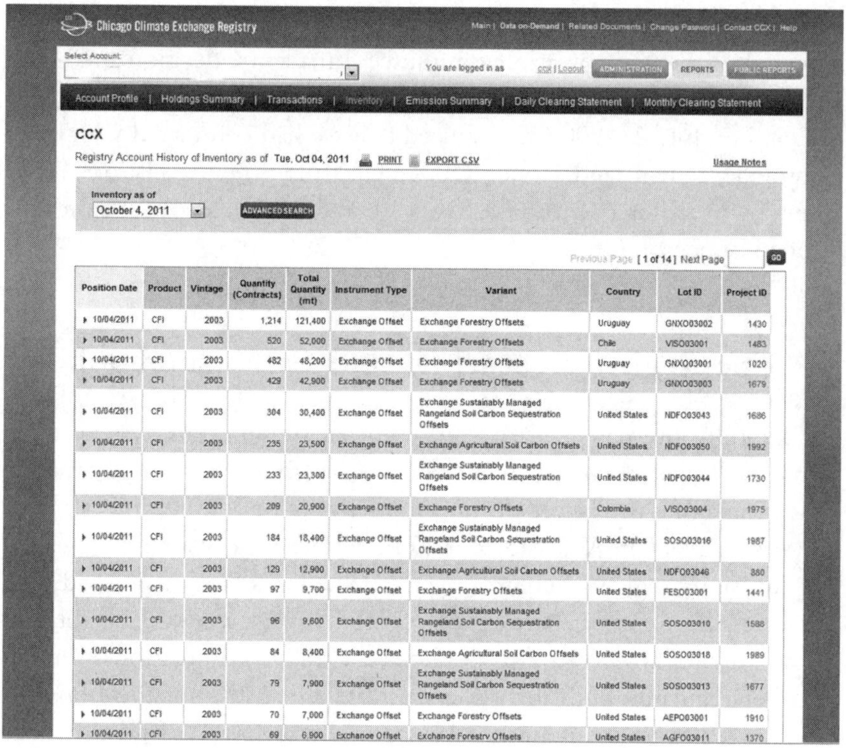

Chicago Climate Exchange Registry

Main | Data on-Demand | Related Documents | Change Password | Contact CCX | Help

Select Account:

You are logged in as ccx | Logout ADMINISTRATION REPORTS PUBLIC REPORTS

Account Profile | Holdings Summary | Transactions | Inventory | Emission Summary | Daily Clearing Statement | Monthly Clearing Statement

CCX

Registry Account History of Inventory as of Tue, Oct 04, 2011 PRINT EXPORT CSV Usage Notes

Inventory as of October 4, 2011 ADVANCED SEARCH

Previous Page [1 of 14] Next Page GO

Position Date	Product	Vintage	Quantity (Contracts)	Total Quantity (mt)	Instrument Type	Variant	Country	Lot ID	Project ID
10/04/2011	CFI	2003	1,214	121,400	Exchange Offset	Exchange Forestry Offsets	Uruguay	GNXO03002	1430
10/04/2011	CFI	2003	520	52,000	Exchange Offset	Exchange Forestry Offsets	Chile	VISO03001	1483
10/04/2011	CFI	2003	482	48,200	Exchange Offset	Exchange Forestry Offsets	Uruguay	GNXO03001	1020
10/04/2011	CFI	2003	429	42,900	Exchange Offset	Exchange Forestry Offsets	Uruguay	GNXO03003	1679
10/04/2011	CFI	2003	304	30,400	Exchange Offset	Exchange Sustainably Managed Rangeland Soil Carbon Sequestration Offsets	United States	NDFO03043	1686
10/04/2011	CFI	2003	235	23,500	Exchange Offset	Exchange Agricultural Soil Carbon Offsets	United States	NDFO03050	1992
10/04/2011	CFI	2003	233	23,300	Exchange Offset	Exchange Sustainably Managed Rangeland Soil Carbon Sequestration Offsets	United States	NDFO03044	1730
10/04/2011	CFI	2003	209	20,900	Exchange Offset	Exchange Forestry Offsets	Colombia	VISO03004	1975
10/04/2011	CFI	2003	184	18,400	Exchange Offset	Exchange Sustainably Managed Rangeland Soil Carbon Sequestration Offsets	United States	SOSO03016	1987
10/04/2011	CFI	2003	129	12,900	Exchange Offset	Exchange Agricultural Soil Carbon Offsets	United States	NDFO03046	880
10/04/2011	CFI	2003	97	9,700	Exchange Offset	Exchange Forestry Offsets	United States	FESO03001	1441
10/04/2011	CFI	2003	96	9,600	Exchange Offset	Exchange Sustainably Managed Rangeland Soil Carbon Sequestration Offsets	United States	SOSO03010	1588
10/04/2011	CFI	2003	84	8,400	Exchange Offset	Exchange Agricultural Soil Carbon Offsets	United States	SOSO03018	1989
10/04/2011	CFI	2003	79	7,900	Exchange Offset	Exchange Sustainably Managed Rangeland Soil Carbon Sequestration Offsets	United States	SOSO03013	1677
10/04/2011	CFI	2003	70	7,000	Exchange Offset	Exchange Forestry Offsets	United States	AEPO03001	1910
10/04/2011	CFI	2003	69	6,900	Exchange Offset	Exchange Forestry Offsets	United States	AGFO03011	1370

Figure 18.1 CCX Emissions Registry
Source: Data from Intercontinental Exchange.

The negotiations with clearinghouses were slow. Services were expensive, and most futures clearinghouses we knew were not really in the business of clearing spot commodities. We decided to self-clear. CCX would act as the guarantor of the financial performance of the trades done by members. We had raised enough capital to become a competent guarantor of the financial risks involved. Through our network, we found an insurance company which was willing to take on overnight counterparty risk. They promised that in the event a buyer refused or was unable to pay for the allowances, the insurance company would backstop any losses to the seller. There was a deductible in the policy, so CCX would have to take the first loss.

On August 6, 2003, we announced the completion of the CCX Rulebook. Mike Walsh and his team had spent countless hours turning the Chicago Accord into a 200-page rulebook that spelled out the rights and obligations of members, exchange governance, and technical details. During the process of recruiting members, there would be times when compliance and legal teams at prospective member companies pored over the rulebook and exchanged multiple letters regarding the detail of the program, rules enforcement by CCX, and potential liability before they pulled the trigger to join. The rulebook provided directions on how to implement the Chicago Accord, which was the enabling legislation for the program.

The Auction

We decided to hold an auction for CCX allowances toward the end of 2003. Bidding would end on September 30 and the results would be announced two days later. It was late in the year, but we planned to beat the lull in markets that generally occurred during the month of December. The purpose of the auction was price discovery before continuous trading began.

I had been making calls to members intermittently, asking them to participate in the auction. Mike and his team led the efforts. We knew that it wasn't enough to announce the auction. This was not a *Field of Dreams* scenario in which simply building the platform would naturally result in participation. If the auction failed to attract buyers at reasonable prices, then further recruitment would be difficult and financing efforts would suffer. Mike and his team prepared a background piece on the auction.

Similar to the SO_2 auctions under the Acid Rain Program, allowances to be auctioned were withheld from the allocations to each member. There were 100,000 metric tons worth of allowances with a 2003 vintage,[4] and 25,000 metric tons' worth of allowances with a 2005 vintage. The design of the CCX auction would be modeled after the discriminating price auction used by the EPA for its SO_2 allowances. To encourage participation, there would be no minimum price.

[4]A vintage refers to the year in which an allowances was issued.

In the case of excess demand, we designed a mechanism that would simply increase the amount of allowances auctioned.

To ensure that the auction would be a significant marketing event, we came up with the idea of announcing the auction results at the Field Museum. The president of the museum had worked with me during the inception of interest rate futures. Since this was a Chicago-based event, Mayor Richard M. Daley also agreed to attend the opening ceremonies.

To our surprise, we received an unsolicited call from the White House, wanting to know if the administration could send someone to speak at the event. Even though the United States had pulled out of Kyoto, CCX was a voluntary, private sector initiative that fitted the administration's approach to climate change. The secretary of energy, Spencer Abraham, agreed to be one of the keynote speakers. It was a nonpartisan event. I chaired the event, the mayor and secretary made opening remarks, and Mike Walsh announced the results.

The auction and the accompanying event was a great success. CCX sold 100,000 allowances from the 2003 vintage at an average of $0.98 per metric ton, and 25,000 allowances from the 2005 vintage at an average of $0.84 per metric ton. Of the 22 bids for the 2003 vintage, 20 were successful, while all 5 bids for the 2005 vintage were successful. Market participants now had a price curve for 2003 to 2005 for the first time.

The Rocket Takes Off

Everything somehow fell into place on December 12, 2003, when the market opened. The much-anticipated rocket finally took off. In traditional exchange fashion, we opened on a Friday in case there were any glitches to fix over the weekend. Fortunately, there were none. On the first day of trading, our head of IT set up a small monitor and the entire staff crowded around it to watch the market activity.

Nathan Clark, an agricultural economist from the University of Kentucky, was a divergent thinker who had spent time in Yugoslavia working on local agricultural problems. On first impression, Nathan was soft-spoken and mild. As we got better acquainted, I found that hidden beneath his gentle manners lay a general skepticism. Nonetheless, I appreciated his universal interests and "doubting Thomas" attitude. He also loved movies. He joined CCX and rose from his research position to become head of the domestic offsets program. I had asked Nathan to fly to Atlanta to occupy the help desk of ICE, which members were supposed to call if they experienced technical difficulties. Although Nathan was miles away on the first day of trading, he shared the vibrations of the rest of the staff through speakerphone. The buyers and sellers remained at different levels. The first trade occurred at 9:02 A.M. CST and the 2005 vintage traded at a price of $0.95. Tradelink was the buyer and Stora Enso the seller. Whenever a trade came in, we cheered and high-fived each other as if we were at a sporting event. We relished this celebratory moment after months of hard work.

Trading was light and intermittent during 2003, and days passed with little or no trading at all. This was inevitable in any new market and we were prepared. The challenge was to add new emitting members and liquidity providers.

I went home thinking about how different this was from my past projects. CCX was a full experience—it involved passing enabling legislation, inventing regulation, inventing commodities and their verification, and monitoring as well as writing the spot contract. It was almost like inventing grain standards and markets for the CBOT back in 1857.

Financing an Exchange

At the beginning of 2003, CCX did not have the capital to launch the exchange. We went back to some of the more proactive members from the design phase and asked if they wanted to become investors in the exchange. They all declined. It was one thing to provide intellectual input, another thing to give financial support.

My anxiety was growing. As I had often done in dire predicaments, I turned to friends. One was acquainted with Sir Evelyn Rothschild, the head of N. M. Rothschild & Sons in London. It was a fortuitous introduction and we eventually retained Rothschild as our investment bank.

All the while, I continued my courtship with investors in the United States. My biggest surprise was the lack of interest from investors with an interest or focus on the environment. Sustainable investing was new at the time, and most portfolio managers preferred safer investments that would yield returns that were comparable to traditional investments. Today, sustainable investing has grown into a significant asset class.

There was no interest from traditional investors such as pension funds and university endowments in the United States. The awareness of climate change and the value of exchanges was not yet part of the conscience of American investors. I was getting very nervous.

Another friend from my insurance days, Neil Eckert, was fascinated by the CCX story and offered to help. I went to London to meet with our second potential investment bank, Collins Stewart. Neil arranged a dinner with two of their salesmen and we met at the Savoy Grill, my restaurant of choice at the time. Its location on the Strand and its proximity to Covent Gardens calmed me. The two salesmen were well-connected in London's financial community, but were outsiders nonetheless. Their unconventional, but successful, recommendations on investments had won them the loyalty of investors. They were intrigued by CCX. Neil suggested that instead of a private placement, we list a fund on the Alternative Investment Market (AIM) division of the London Stock Exchange, a division that specialized in small-cap companies. The fund's first and only investment would be a 25 percent equity stake in CCX. It was a fantastic idea. Valuing CCX at £60 million, we offered to sell 15 million shares at £1 per share. We called the listed company Chicago Environmental PLC in order to promote the brand of the city and bolster its status in the derivatives world.

Our first objective was to land a lead investor. Collins Stewart was very close to Neil Woodford from Invesco Perpetual. If Neil were interested, he would take the maximum position dictated by Invesco's company policy, a 29 percent interest in the total capital raised.

It would be hard to forget that lovely drive from London down to Henley-on-Thames. The small town evoked many stories my mother had told me as a child. It also conjured images of all the English movies I loved. Everything from the quaint pubs to the crews rowing serenely on the river were instilled with a profound sense of history.

Neil Woodford was both an affable man and a contrarian. He invested in stocks that were out of favor or in concepts that he believed in. He also had a small farm and was curious about the role of agriculture in emissions trading. Our story appealed to him. He was particularly interested in the opportunities for methane offsets from dairy farms.

Interest from investors started to emerge, and I could feel the momentum building. Another firm, Moore Capital, seemed to get our story right away and were willing to invest. Almost all of our calls were met with interest. It was clear to me that some of these investors would never invest in CCX, but had agreed to meet because of their interest in climate change.

All the while we were raising capital, we continued to recruit, enhance the registry, arrange for independent monitoring and regulation, draw up the rulebook for the exchange, and finalize agreements with vendors.

I returned to London to make another round of presentations in the summer before the August doldrums. The presentations were getting better with practice, and we were making measurable progress at CCX. Unlike me, Neil showed no anxiety about raising the capital. This was a source of great comfort.

With a blue ribbon list of investors, our financing was completed on September 18, 2003. Although I had made a significant investment in terms of time and capital in the past, I subscribed to 2.1 percent of the shares. This demonstrated my commitment to investors and sent a very important message. Neil did the same. There was a continuous effort to attract even more shareholders after the initial public offering.

For the first time, I was experiencing a sense of anxiety that came from being the chairman of a listed company. I now had to answer to shareholders, the founding members, as well as my staff. As we progressed, the public interest began to grow. As they say on Broadway, it was *showtime*.

Chapter 19

The Rise of the Chicago Climate Exchange

If you intend to take Vienna, take Vienna.

—*Napoleon Bonaparte*

I have always loved December. It is the month when we can reflect on our successes and failures, and plan for the coming year. Contrary to the traditions of the capital markets, we always thought of December as a great time to build on existing business relationships. It was also a time to make new business friends. Financial innovation cannot be explained in a rushed 10-minute call, and people are generally more relaxed as the holiday season approaches, giving us more time to explain our business.

The end of 2003 was no different in this respect. The team worked very hard between Thanksgiving and Christmas, and it paid off. Our Christmas parties moved from a small table of six into a private dining room to accommodate our growing staff.

Recruiting the A-Team

CCX had a truly decentralized business model. We realized early on that our core competence was product innovation and sales, and outsourced almost everything else. It was a unique setup for an exchange. Compliance, technology, legal, and clearing were all outsourced. However, for each function we outsourced, we retained an experienced professional internally to help manage our relationship with the outside service provider and provide strategic vision. Having seasoned professionals on our staff was important, especially in the regulatory and legal departments. We were exempt from regulation by the CFTC but I wanted to have the same standards of any regulated and transparent exchange. Integrity was paramount to our mission.

We hired a president and chief operating officer who had successfully run an FCM. We also added three senior staff with extensive previous experience in the exchange world: a general counsel with extensive knowledge in futures exchanges, an operations executive from the CBOT, and a head of compliance with multiple years of experience at the National Futures Association. Kathy Lynn, who had worked for me over the years heading the back office at ContiFinancial and Drexel, also joined in similar capacity at CCX. Kathy handled all the pays and collects related to trading. She set the standard for long work hours and excellence in operations. Her ability and loyalty were beyond question.

Paula DiPerna left the Joyce Foundation in 2002 after the 9/11 tragedy and moved back to New York. We retained her as a consultant. In 2005, she joined us as a full-time recruiter. Paula's past experience with public policy and the environmental movement were invaluable.

CCX further expanded its staff in 2003. We mainly sought outsiders—a trait that defined the CCX mold. This was particularly true for research, marketing, and sales. Since attracting members was of utmost importance to CCX at this stage, we mainly hired researchers who could double as recruiters. I wanted to build a team of young graduates to do research and sales at CCX. Young people were like blank sheets of paper, harboring few preconceptions and ready to absorb all knowledge conferred on them. Their lack of legacy was treasured in the CCX culture. We interviewed anyone who was persistent.

They had to be bright, enthusiastic, personable, and have impeccable work ethics. For some, this was an opportunity to put to practice the theoretical fundamentals of cap-and-trade that they had excelled in during college. These young minds understood not only the technical details of CCX but were also good problem solvers. It was the same recruiting model we had used in Conti and then again at Drexel. It had its risks. You needed to have a knack for picking the winners at the starting gate.

We needed more professional help in developing soil and forestry offsets. I always had great respect for agricultural economists because of their interest in solving real-world problems. Jerry Skees, an agricultural economics professor at the University of Kentucky, and I had co-authored a paper on the potential benefits of emissions trading to forestry and agriculture.[1] During a speech at the University of Kentucky, I was impressed by the questions fielded by Jerry's students. I immediately thought of them for the new research positions at CCX. Jerry had already recommended Nathan Clark, one of his best graduate students, who we hired in 2002. This time, Jerry recommended Murali Kanakasabai, a native of southern India who had spent time growing up in Iraq.

Murali was a scholarship student who came to Kentucky because they offered him more financial aid than any other university. He was set on becoming a university professor before we convinced him of the opportunities at CCX. Despite his humble background, he was able to attain his situation through sheer intelligence and talent. I immediately identified with his experience as a student on scholarship and his drive.

In 2002, we hired a young Englishman who was an Oxford-trained philosopher. He worked as a professor in a theological seminary after graduate school. His superb writing skills helped us to translate the Chicago Accord into the exchange rulebook.

Our sales staff eventually consisted of an eclectic portfolio of personalities and skills, from English philosophers to former basketball players. The diversity of sales styles was crucial to pitch to a wide array of potential members. Our team was assembled like a chess set: Each member had his or her own unique moves and skills.

---

[1]Richard L. Sandor and Jerry R. Skees, "Creating a Market for Carbon Emissions: Opportunities for U.S. Farmers," *Choices 1999*, First Quarter, 13.

Peer pressure could be felt at all levels of the company because of the competitive office culture. We reinforced this performance-based culture by giving equity and bonuses to teams when we achieved our corporate goals and they achieved their personal targets. In 40 years of business, our professionals were as bright and likable as any I had seen.

The CCX University

By the middle of 2004, our small office was buzzing with a young enthusiastic crew. As a relic of my teaching days, I tried my best to give the new people exposure to new things and events commonly reserved for senior management. Much to everyone's surprise, we often sent young people to educate grey-haired boards and talk at international conferences. Nathan, at the ripe old age of 29, spoke at the UN meetings in Montreal. Similarly, we sent a 24-year-old with a master's in public policy to Iceland to address an international climate conference. I believed this would help our young staff grow and increase their sense of responsibility.

It was important that my young team was learning something new every day. As there were days when we did no business at all, we had to keep everyone focused and enthusiastic. Myself included. I experienced the same sinking feeling from the early days of interest rate futures when trading volumes were low. It was crucial that we continue to look for members, and speak to traders. The burden of keeping the team upbeat fell on Mike Walsh and me.

We repeated a process used during the development of interest rate futures at ContiFinancial and Drexel. We held morning meetings every day at 7 A.M. in my office that everyone—the sales team, the research team, the IT staff, and the communications people—were required to attend. I recall everyone being crammed into my small office space, but the physical proximity meant that all were given an opportunity to update and discuss daily plans. The team sat together and everyone went around rapid fire, sharing progress updates on recruiting and who had eyeballs on the screen. It was a little awkward at times because everyone felt pressured to bring positive updates to the table and there was an element of competition. Who were we going to call? Who had gotten someone to watch the screens? We allowed ourselves as few excuses as possible.

The morning meetings also gave me an opportunity to keep the morale of the team high. I tried to convey my successes and failures, often drawing upon my own experiences and historical facts. I reminded everyone that what we were doing was truly transformational. It somehow worked and most meetings ended with everyone full of enthusiasm for the day ahead. Despite the early hours, all the faces I saw were sanguine and animated.

Educating, Marketing, and Sales

By now, we were honing our skills in education, marketing, and sales. Education included making speeches and publishing articles. Marketing involved recruiting new CCX members, while sales entailed describing the prices on screen, corresponding volumes, and political news in an attempt to stimulate orders. They were very different.

This phase was probably the toughest, and was often characterized by a lot of trench digging. This effort was far more extensive than a conventional product launches at other exchanges. To attract new members, CCX initiated an extensive education and communications effort. This was particularly important as many companies had not even heard of the role of emissions trading in combating climate change. In 2004 alone the media coverage of CCX included 27 print and electronic sources, five radio interviews, and one webcast. We also delivered 27 presentations at industry conferences, congressional hearings, and other events. The talks stretched across six different countries: the United States, Canada, Mexico, Germany, Switzerland, and the United Kingdom. In addition, CCX executives authored four academic articles. In particular, CCX wanted to target high-level officials in the international sphere in order to establish linkages between the exchange and other emerging trading programs. Not only did our publicity efforts reach out to an international audience of financial regulators and academics, they also reinforced ongoing dialogues with technical and policy experts from industry, governments, universities, and NGOs.

Since CCX was a new firm, there weren't clear divisions of responsibility. We stressed a sales and marketing culture throughout the company. Everyone in the company became a de facto recruiter, regardless of their department. I had learned this lesson from Jack Welch. Even the economists themselves did just about anything and everything that needed to be done to get new members in the door. This included researching prospective CCX members, crunching through spreadsheets of energy baselines and emissions trends, writing recruitment memos, cold calling companies, ghostwriting articles for members, digging out statistics, and creating slides at the eleventh hour for a presentation about to be made.

Successful markets depended on years of education, marketing and sales, and a wide network of friends and acquaintances. However, all these years of research, consensus building, and public outreach would mean nothing if we couldn't recruit members and generate orders to buy and sell.

Building Demand

In those days, companies had surprisingly little exposure to the concept of global warming. When we first started, many of the companies we contacted had never considered changing their behavior, and almost none had any idea about how an allowance-based program worked. Some industries simply weren't ready to make the jump. There was a steep learning curve with emissions trading. The first 15 percent of our members—the first adopters and founding members—were relatively easy to recruit because they were already well informed about emissions trading. Recruiting the next 85 percent, however, was truly painstaking. We really had to be around to push and prod them at all times, in fear that they would drop out suddenly. Woody Allen was right when he said, "Eighty percent of success is showing up."

In some instances, we found that companies sent representatives from their environmental, health, and safety departments to deal with us. These departments were sometimes perceived as cost centers by their companies' management rather than potential profit centers, and therefore did not have much persuasive power when it came to selling CCX internally. In other instances, however, the environmental, health, and safety departments took leadership roles and teamed up with the profit centers. The latter often resulted in companies joining CCX.

Our message too often got bogged down in the internal mechanics of the company before it reached top management. Once our efforts were channeled to a profit center of the company, or the trading desk, we had better results.

I always told the potential members, "CCX is like a Doberman Pinscher. If you cut off our front legs, we will walk on our hind legs. If you cut off our hind legs, we will crawl on our stumps and bite you. You will have to drag us along, with our jaws clasped firmly around your ankles." Tenacity was our rallying cry.

We had a breakthrough with the Detroit Edison Company (DTE), a big utility headquartered in Detroit. DTE had been active in the design phase, and despite the good relationships we had with their environmental team, refused to join. Not wanting to burn any bridges, we kept them apprised of our progress. Years later, a young CCX staff member working with utilities trading desks struck a good rapport with a DTE trader. The trader immediately saw the business opportunity given the interrelationship between emissions and the other fuels that DTE traded. This propelled DTE to finally join the exchange. There were similar stories of companies who initially didn't join, only to join four or five years later. The trick was to find the unique angle that made sense for the company. These accounts that we took for dead were dubbed Lazarus accounts. One of the team members said after successfully recruiting a dominant company that this was "the biggest comeback since Lazarus."

When it came to recruiting members who had not been in the design phase, we had to conduct extensive prior research. In instances where we did not do so, we failed to recruit. When it came to determining the most likely recruits, we fortunately weren't just "throwing a fishnet blindly into the ocean." There was a good system in place to research companies and grind the numbers to demonstrate the benefits of membership. The key was to find out as much as we could about a company, including where it was located, what it did, its emissions data, and whether it was involved in any way with the environmental field. In one case, a prospective client commented to its staffers about our analysis, "How come we don't have this information? They know more about our company than we do!" Our internal research demonstrated CCX's expertise and understanding of our clients' challenges. But more importantly, it gave us the opportunity to demonstrate the business upside of engaging in emissions trading.

We continued our key strategy of supplementing approval at the top levels of the organization with champions at the middle management level. Sometimes it was from the top down, and sometimes from the bottom up. The chairman of Roanoke Steel Corp, a Virginia-based maker of specialty steel, was a fellow colleague on the AEP board. Roanoke was an outlier in the predominantly conservative and risk-averse American steel sector. They were a small, innovative, tightly run company that looked for opportunities to advance their environmental credentials while being profitable. The same cannot be said about many of the larger steel companies, which were unwilling to pick up a dollar even if it was delivered to them on a plate. Roanoke had a stellar line-up of companies they supplied, including Wal-Mart. Sustainability was important to them. The chairman introduced us to the sustainability manager in the company. She became our internal champion by embracing the CCX concept and the opportunities it provided. Roanoke eventually joined in the second wave of recruitment, which followed the recruitment of the founding members.

In other cases, we were pleasantly surprised. An IBM staffer reached out to us on its own initiative. It was a sign that the industry was learning. They were not only able to cope with a cap, but desired it as well. Nathan was able to start a dialogue with a member from the firm's middle management. He managed the relationship and sometime later Paula helped close the membership.

Internationally, CCX also broke new ground in unexpected ways. We had picked Brazil as our international country so the concept of cross-border trading could be proven. Brazilian corporations didn't have reduction obligations since they were not required to do so by the Kyoto Protocol. Like their North American counterparts, they were interested in our services for measuring, verifying, and reporting their emissions. These Brazilian companies were truly international and CCX membership gave them visibility among sustainable investors. We ended up recruiting eight South American companies that saw the benefits of a registry, third-party verification, and the disclosure of emissions that CCX provided. One Brazilian company actually joined because membership enabled them to be included in the Dow Jones Sustainability Index, which helped them to engage new clients. This validated my belief that the DJSI would provide that kind of incentive for companies to become more active in emissions trading.

We continued to establish international linkages. Baxter's manufacturing facility in Castlebar, Ireland, was subject to the European Union Emissions Trading Scheme. In Phase I of the program, they accrued a surplus of European Union Allowances (EUAs). Since these allowances couldn't be banked and used later, Baxter expected a downward pressure on EUA prices and a corresponding decrease in the value of their allowance assets. This made no economic sense. I immediately called Ron Meissen and suggested, "Why don't you use your EUAs in Ireland for your U.S. compliance?" Together, we could make these allowances international.

Acting quickly, Baxter's Ireland facility transferred 100 metric tons of its EU allowances to Baxter's Chicago Climate Exchange Carbon Financial Instrument registry account. This transaction was accomplished in two steps. First, Baxter transferred EU allowances to a CCX registry account established in the United Kingdom. Next, CCX canceled those allowances, and in replacement issued 100 tons of greenhouse emission allowances into Baxter's CCX North America emissions account. This transfer effectively linked two international emission markets, demonstrating additional flexibility for companies in meeting legally binding emissions reduction commitments.[2] We wanted to prove the concept that if there was political will, the two systems could be linked eventually.

We learned a lot from firms that declined to join. Some refusals were strange. A large power company that had joined the design phase was steadfast in its refusal to join CCX. When the energy markets took a negative turn and the company was on the edge of bankruptcy, we thought there was an opportunity from which both of us could benefit. CCX had analyzed the company's positions over the years and discovered that it could have been a net seller of carbon

[2] "Global Carbon Emission Markets Linkage Established by Unprecedented Transaction," CCX press release, May 4, 2006.

financial instruments (CFIs), worth many millions of dollars. When we presented the firm with the option of monetizing these hidden assets in the face of bankruptcy, it again turned us down. There was at least a lesson from the experience. If you've found a company that is on the verge of bankruptcy, but won't pick a dollar up off the floor, then they are probably a good shot.

Since Ford had become a member, we had high hopes for another multinational automotive manufacturer. One failure was interesting. In addition to meeting with its head of environmental affairs, our staff had met many times with the company's representatives at the UN meetings. On those occasions, the representatives were always taking copious notes during the environmental panel—something we took as an indication of their interest in addressing climate change. Despite their rejection, we never gave up and felt that trying to make a breakthrough from the financial side of the company might help. I met with the company's senior officer and some of its top traders. They had reduced emissions significantly and had a profit opportunity. Perhaps that part of the company would see the economic benefits of being involved in CCX. Again to no avail. We attributed it to the lack of drive in the company and a crumbling of its corporate culture. In a few years' time, this American industrial echelon went bankrupt and had to be bailed out by the government. We attempted to recruit them after they went bankrupt, but failed again. Corporate structure is sometimes adverse to change.

The stories of recruiting shared a common thread. Every pitch for CCX membership took an enormous amount of time and required tailoring our approach to the listener. It was the job of our recruiting team to educate the clients on the new value proposition. Sometimes this was very complex. New markets are sold, not bought.

The CCX membership turned out to be phenomenal—large, diverse, and dispersed throughout the country. By the end of 2003, we had had 18 members. This number grew to 43 members by end of 2004. By 2008, CCX had over 100 emitting members with an emissions baseline larger than Germany. Our membership covered all 50 states, all major sectors of the U.S. economy, and had an international presence in the EU, China, Canada, India, and Latin America. The CCX membership represented 17 percent of the companies in the Dow Jones

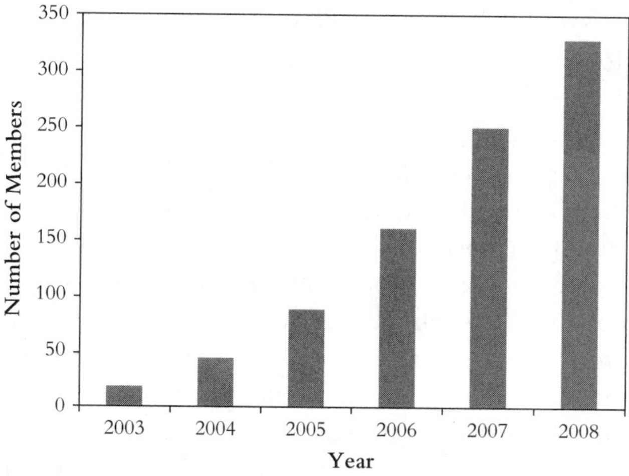

Figure 19.1 CCX Membership Growth (2003–2004)

Industrial Average, 20 percent of the largest CO_2 emitting electrical utilities in the United States, and 11 percent of Fortune 100 companies.[3]

Building Liquidity

We had to continue to recruit industrial companies but also needed more liquidity providers and investors in the market. The hedgers needed counterparties—it was the same pattern for all new markets. I liked to say, "Carbon traders are made, not born." There was not a readily available supply of carbon traders, and carbon as a tradable commodity did not initially fit with energy traders due to the vastly different liquidity profile. By this time, a lot of the CBOT and CME members from the soybean and milk pits joined the exchange. A pool of new locals was born. Keith Bronstein, who supported the Treasury futures contract, was one of the most important new members. He became an original shareholder and the first market maker of Chicago Environmental. Although Keith provided initial liquidity, we still needed other market makers. Joe Gressel, a former local at the CME, also joined. Joe, like Keith, was not only a market maker but one of the few people who viewed carbon as an asset class. He left many other legacies in

[3]"CCX: Cap-and-Trade in the United States," Chicago Climate Exchange, December 2008.

Chicago. Both men represented the heart and soul of Chicago's futures markets. Together they ensured both short and long-term liquidity.

We were selling a brand new asset, so the traditional methods employed by exchanges to introduce new products—such as hosting seminars, giving speeches, and sponsoring trade shows—were not as effective in attracting liquidity providers. Although these methods were helpful for educational purposes, our greatest successes came from extensive prospecting and one-on-one meetings and presentations. It was about tapping into the pool of market makers in Chicago. We often had to give several presentations to the same prospect.

As cap-and-trade could potentially have a pervasive economic impact, carbon was of interest to a broad array of investors looking simply for an undervalued asset, or a hedge to their broader investment portfolio. Two of our larger hedge fund clients saw carbon as a hedge to their distressed asset portfolios of utilities, steel manufacturers, cement, and fuel exploration and refineries. We were often granted meetings just to explain what we knew about potential legislation and its impacts. Our challenge was to turn these information gatherers into clients. It also helped that we were public, because it gave us another avenue to reach and create potential traders. In several instances, we first produced shareholders who later became carbon traders.

As job responsibilities at the exchange became more specialized, Rob McAndrew, a senior vice president of CCX, was made head of carbon trading and focused more on recruiting liquidity providers. He educated potential participants on the advantages of holding carbon emissions and other emissions as an asset class, and was also responsible for generating daily liquidity. Luck played its part in our unwavering commitment to sell the idea. At one point, Rob McAndrew was playing a round of golf with one of his childhood friends, when he mentioned that he was working for CCX. "So what do you guys do? Exchange the weather? Chicago should exchange its weather with California's," his childhood friend taunted him playfully. As a result of this conversation, Rob's friend introduced him to someone at a large, successful hedge fund. Rob had been in equity sales for a long time and knew the language of traders. He personally made the pitch to the hedge fund and explained that carbon was a new asset class that provided boundless opportunities for those involved. The hedge fund joined CCX.

Our success with another prominent hedge fund came about through a sale at Brooks Brothers. One of recruiters had spoken with the manager of the hedge fund over the phone on several occasions about carbon, and he only finally agreed to meet in person because there was a Brooks Brothers sale right across the street from our offices. As he drove home with a backseat full of new dress shirts, the vast potential for carbon as an asset clicked in his head and his focus changed from power trading to global environmental finance.

Building Supply

I had learned a lot about agriculture during my years at the CBOT with my failed efforts on the Gulf wheat contract and from my brief stint in Iowa as a farmhand. From these experiences, I knew that farmers were often excellent businesspeople and that if CCX found a new way for them to earn income, they would become fast adopters. In the long run, farmers could also help us politically.

Sometime in 1999, I was invited to speak at the American Agricultural Economics Association meeting in Nashville. I spoke about soil sequestration and the potential for farmers to harvest carbon, and shared my vision for a carbon market where farmers would be important contributors. I explained how farmers could be selling their soil carbon in a global carbon market, pricing an asset to be stored in the ground. As I looked around, I saw many uncertain smiles greeting this fanciful idea. After my presentation, the academics who had already spent considerable time in the area questioned the practicality of the exercise. People marveled at the vision but seemed skeptical. Nonetheless, the talk stirred the pot.

Three years later, we managed to deliver on the fanciful idea. CCX designed a technical protocol that credited farmers for sequestering carbon in agricultural soils. This effort was not done in isolation but with the expert counsel of a soils technical advisory committee made up of prominent agricultural soils experts from the USDA and the land grant universities. The committee designed a system that monitored farmers' management practices to arrive at conservative estimates of carbon sequestration. This was economically feasible to administer, monitor, and verify and was quickly adopted by producers. Farmers were actually receiving checks for their sustainable practices and were eventually able to trade their offset credits from anywhere with an Internet connection.

The design of the agricultural soils protocol was indicative of the CCX fashion of designing offsets protocols. The offsets program would expand to include protocols for a wide range of greenhouse gas destruction, sequestration, and avoidance activities. Each protocol was built bottom up with a scientific foundation and rigorous technical analysis. Every effort was made simple and easy to implement for the practitioner. In fact, in most cases the entire approval process and project implementation guidelines were so streamlined and clear that there was often no need for external consultants. For the first time, we had managed to commoditize soil carbon.

Our philosophy on designing a standardized, simple, and straightforward offsets system was extended to forestry. Most companies avoided forestry transactions due to the high perceived risks and verification and monitoring costs. Precious Woods, a leading sustainable forestry company, had forest plantations in Nicaragua and Costa Rica. Although they could have sold the offset credits on a nonstandardized bilateral market, they chose to join CCX and sell their credits on the exchange because of our standardized protocols and speed of execution, which reduced transaction costs. Later that year, Precious Woods traded the world's first ever forest carbon through an exchange on CCX.

Armed with a set of standardized offsets rules, we set out to focus on other aspects of making the offsets market viable. The large number of farm participants in scattered locations made the administering of the program cost-prohibitive. To solve this problem, we created another kind of membership—offset aggregators. This innovation introduced an intermediary between numerous farmers and the exchange. The aggregator administered the program by recruiting small farmers to originate soil or animal methane offsets, arrange verification, and trade the offsets on CCX. In return, for its services, the aggregator received a small commission from the proceeds. The business model resulted in a cost-effective way to originate offsets.

Starting with the Iowa Farm Bureau, many farm organizations, including the National Farmers Union, joined CCX as aggregators.

These organizations gave us direct linkage with the rural communities and promulgated the important role that rural America played in solving the climate crisis.

Our offsets program turned out to be an enormous success. For soil sequestration offsets alone, the CCX program had nearly 9,300 farmers, ranchers and forest landowners who registered over 24 million metric tons of GHG offsets from over 18.8 million U.S. acres. This showcased a direct incentive from the global market to practice sustainable agriculture. Furthermore, our offsets portfolio spanned 15 countries and included projects such as renewable energy, dairy methane destruction, and fuel switching. We were quietly making a small difference by promoting a low carbon economy at the grassroots level. A sure sign that the system was credible and functional was that the participants were cashing their checks. One dairy farmer in Minnesota cashed a check for $10,000 for his project, which captured and combusted dairy methane to generate green electricity. Dairy farms could now produce two joint products, milk and renewable energy. This new business model was widely imitated. This is an example of the web of institutions that were required for creating a successful market.

The agricultural offsets protocol, in particular, was a lightning rod for a number of environmentalists.[4] Some argued that farmers did not deserve these offsets because no real change in behavior was being made. The broad name given for this issue was *additionality*. Additionality required that credit be given only for practices that would not have taken place under a business-as-usual scenario. In our view, excluding these few early adopters from participation would have sent the wrong signal on multiple levels. We didn't want to disenfranchise these first movers and were concerned that doing so would lessen the chance of these sustainable farming practices catching on with the masses. We also did not want to risk some actors reversing their environmentally sound practices just so they could restart as "new" practitioners at a later date and qualify for credits. This would be disastrous for the environment.

Offsets were often criticized on a moral basis. Entities that bought offsets in order to achieve reductions were denounced for

---

[4]Jeff Goodell, "Capital Pollution Solution?" *New York Times*, July 30, 2006.

"buying their way out of cutting their own emissions." Although this description was technically accurate, its moral insinuations were unwarranted. After all, the entire purpose of cap-and-trade was to delegate the task of emissions reduction to those who could do it at the least cost. The press often compared the purchase of offset allowances to indulgences—payments made to the Roman Catholic Church in the Middle Ages to ensure one's acceptance into heaven. I was silently amused by the creativity of these arguments but took no heed. Offsets were also considered to be riskier than allowances because they needed to prove the condition of additionality, which could be tricky. However, if there was a clear regulatory framework and effective monitoring and verification tools, then offsets and allowances should be interchangeable.

Corporate Restructuring

As we grew, our staff's roles had become more specialized, and our board composition shifted. At the beginning of 2006, we added the Honorable Carole Brookins, a friend of 35 years, as a director. We had lost touch for a number of years but managed to reconnect while she was the U.S. Executive Director on the World Bank Board. Another vacancy for an independent director was filled by Stu Eisenstadt who was in charge of U.S. negotiations for the Kyoto Protocol. We also added Clayton Yeutter, former president of the CME and the Secretary of Agriculture, as an independent director. Not only did these board members provide me with invaluable guidance over the years, their illustrious reputations also contributed significantly to the pilot program's legitimacy. The lesson to entrepreneurs is very important. It helps to choose independent directors with outstanding reputations, and not "yes" people. My board never simply rubber-stamped recommendations from management.

Halfway through 2006, I called the head of special situations at Goldman Sachs. He was interested in participating in the exchange in a variety of ways, including the possibility of purchasing equity. He wanted to be an owner/user. I spoke to Neil Eckert, and he thought it was a good idea. We eventually agreed to a corporate restructuring, and Neil served as an intermediary for the fund manager.

Subsequently, Climate Exchange bought out all of the CCX shareholders in exchange for its own shares. It was a corporate restructuring that resulted in Climate Exchange PLC becoming an active holding company as opposed to an investment manager. CLE became an operating company with an independent board of directors and its own CEO and chief financial officer.

The restructuring of CLE and CCX and the placement of £12.2 million of new shares with Goldman Sachs occurred simultaneously. We were continuing a model started by Jeff Sprecher, the founder and CEO of ICE, who had made the astute business decision to offer equity not only to exchange members but also to industrial users and commercial banks that were liquidity providers. Since the experience with ICE had been successful, many investment bankers were now looking to participate in the growing opportunities in the exchange business.

Extending the CCX Program

After reorganizing CCX, we turned our attention to extending the pilot program. We had to determine whether there was sufficient demand. The members were informally polled and expressed a strong desire to continue the program. For our Phase II design committee, we appointed a new group of members including a number of founding members. Our new design committee members hailed from AEP, Ford, Amtrak, Baxter, International Paper, and Tradelink.

The design committee was unanimous in its decision to extend the program to 2010 with an additional reduction of 2 percent over the next two years. Responsible for executing the consensus-building process, Mike provided a rundown of the entire process for Phase II.

The CCX board of directors granted approval for the extension. Phase II of the pilot program commenced in April 2006.

Market Highlights

As in any market, CCX carbon price was influenced by the supply and demand dynamics of the underlying commodity. Addition of new members offsets supply and perceptions about whether cap-and-trade would become mandatory in the United States influenced the price. For example, prices increased in April 2004 when Russia signed the Kyoto Protocol. The EU's announcement of a mandatory program the same year had a similar impact. See Figure 19.2 for CFI prices from 2003 to 2008.

Momentum was building for implementing the Kyoto Protocol.

By middle of 2005, prices rose and broke the $2 mark. The offsets program grew from 126,000 registered tons in 2004 to 311,000 tons in 2005. Higher prices helped boost offsets members who looked to the exchange to monetize supply. Total membership also had increased from 43 to 88 members, with 45 emitting members. Corporates and utility members who were long carbon joined the exchange. We had also diversified our membership with liquidity providers.

Post restructuring in 2006, the business soared and the price of CLE shares rose. We were also heading into an election year and many of the

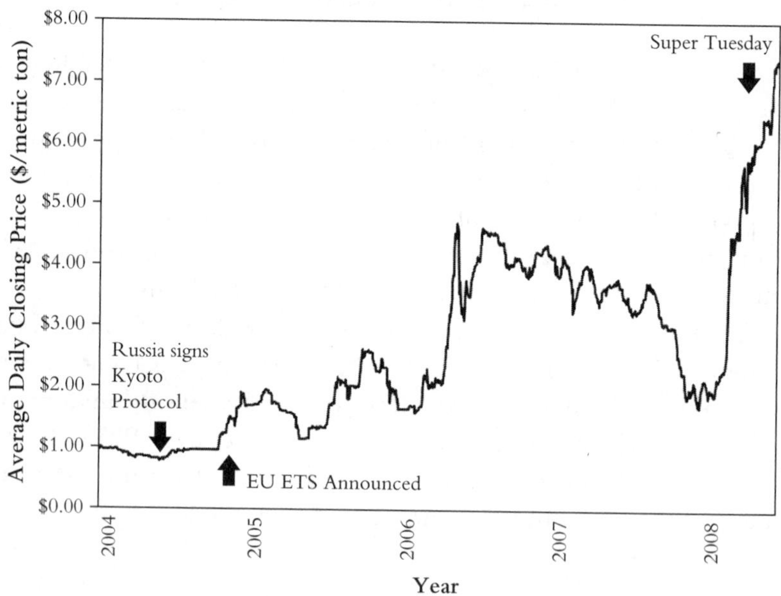

Figure 19.2 Price per Metric Ton of CO_2 (2003–2008)
Note: CFI=100 metric tons of CO_2.
Source: Data from IntercontinentalExchange.

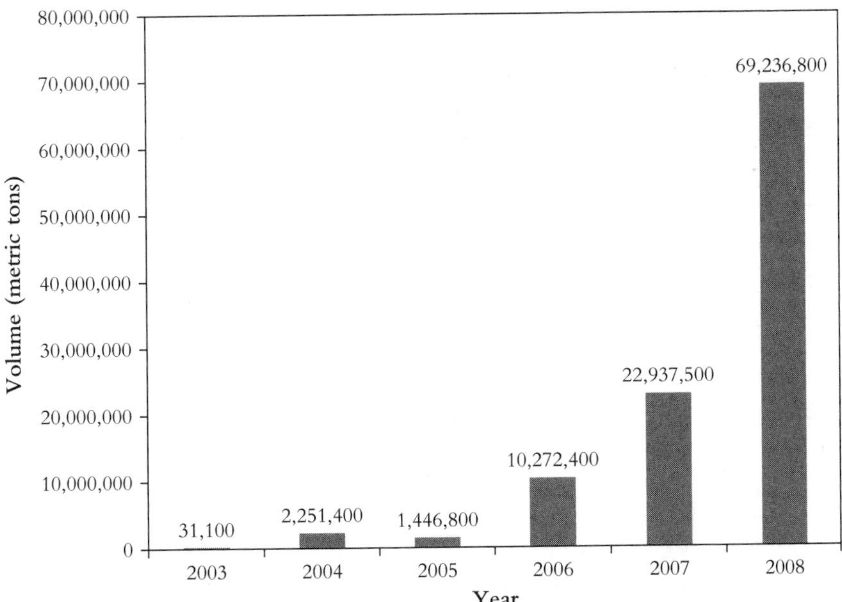

Figure 19.3 CCX CFI Volume Traded (2003–2008)

leading candidates on both sides of the aisle favored cap-and-trade. In 2007, it became clear that all three viable candidates favored a cap-and-trade proposal as a policy tool to address climate change. Prices and volumes leaped to new highs.

We had 328 members by the end of 2008, compared to 88 members at the end of 2005. Volume grew from 1,446,800 metric tons at the end of 2005 to 69,236,800 metric tons by the end of 2008. See Figure 19.3 for the volume traded at CCX between 2003 and 2008.

As we approached the spring of 2008, a combination of strong membership base and change in political winds boosted the market. Carbon prices rose to their highest levels. The increase in prices brought forth new offsets members and emitting members with allowances to sell. The morale of staff and members was at an all time high. I felt an enormous amount of energy. I thought 2008 could be the inflection point.

Chapter 20

The Fall of the Chicago Climate Exchange

The world ends, not with a bang but a whimper.

—*T. S. Eliot*

There was an old adage that traders used: "Buy the rumor and sell the news." The price of a stock, bond, or commodity contained a lot of information, as did the price of emission allowances. In retrospect, the increase in emissions trading volumes could be attributed to the market expectations regarding U.S. climate change policy. Prospects seemed bright for CCX and the carbon markets as we approached 2008. Unfortunately, market expectations were capricious and could swing both ways. I brushed aside the storm warnings. We were at the top of the market, and I forgot the fundamental lesson that "it never looks better than when you're at the top."

Engaging the U.S. Congress

Cap-and-trade legislation began building momentum in Congress, as we began a series of testimonies in 2006 before the House and Senate committees in an attempt to further educate policy makers.

In April, Jeff Bingaman (D-NM), then chairman of the U.S. Senate Energy and Natural Resources Committee, held hearings on climate change. Mike Walsh testified on behalf of CCX. We had a bullpen in our office at the time where most of the recruiting staff worked. The day of the hearing, the entire team crammed in around a monitor to watch Mike's testimony streamed on the web. Mike gave an articulate and engaging presentation on CCX, and answered all questions thoughtfully, like a teacher. His talk made such an impression that Senator Bingaman asked, "What would be wrong with taking what you've come up with by way of requirements for your members and essentially mandating that everybody in the country comply with them?" Back in Chicago, the room erupted in cheers and applause for Mike. Everyone felt that a part of their work had been recognized. Mike Morris, CEO of AEP, testified on the same panel and later called to congratulate me on Mike's performance. I felt a sense of pride, seeing how much Mike had grown in the 15 years we had worked together. As a group, we all felt we were unstoppable. We were doing what we had set out to do—educate policy makers and influence the public debate on the climate change issue.

CCX was eager to share its story with members of Congress. When I testified before the House Energy and Commerce Committee, I cited the number of employees each utility and industrial company had in every congressman's district to demonstrate the size of our constituency. After one of these hearings, Congressman Edward Markey (D-MA) invited us to his office to learn more about CCX. It was refreshing to see how competent his staff was when it came to economics and finance. They were experts in energy and I couldn't have been more pleased about their knowledge of capital markets.

Later in 2007, we were invited to give a presentation to the Senate Foreign Relations Committee chaired by Senator John Kerry. Senator Kerry wanted to discuss what the U.S. stance should be at the upcoming climate meetings in Bali, Indonesia. There was still little federal direction on cap-and-trade, and our testimony sought to raise awareness of the practical experience of CCX in the private sector. At the opening, Senator Kerry mentioned his involvement in the Clean Air Act, an encouraging sign of institutional memory. Senator Richard Lugar, the ranking Republican in the committee, was an offset provider for CCX. In his farm, he had planted walnut trees that were to be sustainably harvested in his "back 40"[1] and held a Senate press conference to announce his membership. The senator had been urging his fellow farmers to take their least productive land, and either grow trees on them or revert them into wetlands to restore natural habitats. His early actions had value because they sent out an intellectual and practical signal to other farmers, encouraging them to take the leap.

Despite the fact that we were fast approaching the date of the Bali meeting, the general atmosphere at the testimony was stale. Many of the other senators seemed uninspired and distracted. The mood in the room seemed to foretell the dismal prospects of cap-and-trade in the United States in the months to follow.

Waxman-Markey—The Beginning of the End

At the start of 2008, we had been optimistic that the United States was going to take a leadership role in dealing with the greatest environmental problem of our time. In February, Super Tuesday presidential primaries took place around the United States and it became clear that Barack Obama and Hillary Clinton were the only two Democratic candidates left. They both supported cap-and-trade and praised CCX. In May, Republican candidate Senator John McCain made a campaign speech at wind turbine manufacturer Vestas, also in favor of cap-and-trade. Carbon prices went from under $2.00 per ton at the end of 2005 to a peak of $7.40 in the middle of 2008 (see Figure 20.1).

Everyone came to work with a heightened sense of pride and accomplishment. What we had worked so hard for the last 15 years was on the verge of becoming the law of the land.

---

[1]Back 40: Phrase that refers to remote, uncultivated acreage on a large plot of land.

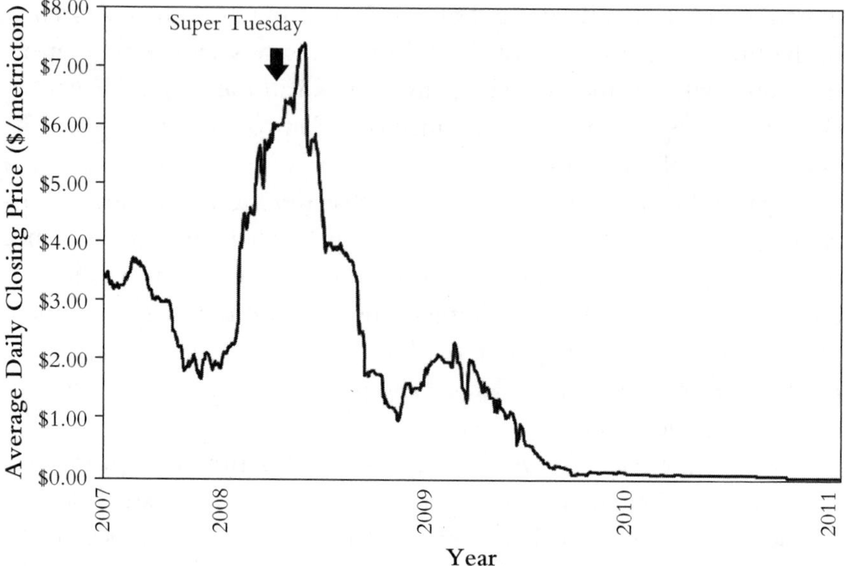

Figure 20.1 CCX CFI Closing Prices (2007–2011)
Source: Data from IntercontinentalExchange.

By the end of 2008, however, we were at $1.64 per ton. A wise futures trader once told me that price changes tell us about the future. We only learn in the future why these price changes occurred. Clearly, the carbon financial instruments (CFI) market was telling us that the greenhouse gas cap-and-trade program was dead on arrival in the United States. In spite of my experiences, I ignored what prices were telling us. I am an unabashed optimist and thought that 2009 began on a good note.

We arranged to have our board of directors attend the presidential inauguration. A bipartisan ball was held at the end of January to celebrate the new president, its attendees ranging from members of the Democratic Party to the most prominent stars in Hollywood. I felt a strong rush of patriotism and a sense of partisanship.

The first sign of the wheels coming off the train was the release of the 2009 budget by the White House in February. The administration factored into its revenue projections $670 billion of proceeds from the sale of allowances in its proposed cap-and-trade bill. It was a total departure from the Acid Rain Program, where a diminishing number of allowances were distributed free based on targeted reductions. If Washington's intention was to tackle global warming, why would they complicate the issue by piling on other objectives, such as revenue raising? Perhaps they were influenced by environmentalists who wanted to punish the polluter, or by economists who thought that cap-and-trade could be combined with taxes in the form of auctioned allowances.

The White House budget made no sense whatsoever to all of us at CCX. The after-tax profit of the U.S. utilities sector in 2008 was $55 billion.[2] Its total CO_2 emissions were 2.4 billion metric tons. Compare these to the figures in the administration's 2009 budget proposal, which expected $634 billion in revenue from selling allowances,[3] with utilities spending $20 per ton on allowances through auctions.[4] The auctioning of allowances would have come close to eliminating a significant part of the entire industry's after-tax profits, thereby causing a political backlash in the private sector. It is ironic that if the program were instituted, there would have been little capital needed to install the technologies to reduce carbon emissions. It was likely another case of sloppy research. These numbers risked losing the potential political support of the power sector and made legislation less likely. Perhaps the strategy was to start the negotiating process with this number and compromise later. If this were the case, it was naïve at best. Furthermore, Senator Harry Reid (D-NV) announced that auction receipts would pay for Obama's health-care bill.[5] This made cap-and-trade resemble "cap-and-tax," and the Republicans leaped at every opportunity to use this jargon.

[2]"Corporate Profits by Industry," GovStats.org, April 29, 2009, www.govstats.org/corporate-profits-by-industry.htm.

[3]"Budget of the U.S. Government, Fiscal Year 2010: Updated Summary Tables," U.S. Office of Management and Budget, May 2009.

[4]William Beach et al., "The Economic Consequences of Waxman-Markey: An Analysis of the American Clean Energy and Security Act of 2009," Center for Data Analysis Report #0904, Heritage Foundation, August 6, 2009.

[5]Brian Faler, "Obama Budget Set for Debate Next Week in U.S. House and Senate," *Bloomberg*, March 27, 2009.

The beginning of this legislative initiative to deal with climate change was really the beginning of the end.

Some other significant changes occurred at the dawn of 2009. On January 8, Congressman Markey (D-MA) replaced Congressman Rick Boucher (D-VA) as chairman of the subcommittee on Energy and Air Quality. I had gotten to know Congressman Boucher over the previous two years. He had been the only elected representative willing to meet with us with no staff present. Although it was typical for elected representatives to have only an abstract understanding of the issues while their staff possessed more detailed knowledge, Rick's knowledge about climate change and cap-and-trade was unsurpassed. In this sense, he was his own chief of staff. We had built good relations with Congressman Edward Markey, and knew that he had an extraordinary staff.

On January 15, 2009, Congressman Waxman, the chairman of the House Energy and Commerce Committee, announced that there would be a Memorial Day deadline for the passage of an energy and climate bill. USCAP, a group of America's leading companies teamed with WRI, held a meeting the very same day.[6] Many USCAP companies were members of CCX. We began outlining our plan to articulate a bill and execute it based on Chairman Waxman's timeframe.

Our next move was clear: to meet with the staff of every member of the House Committee, and as many elected representatives of the committee as possible. Given the impact of local politics, we focused on educating the Illinois delegation on the CCX experience. We prepared a 100-page briefing manual on CCX, which included preliminary explanations of its reduction schedule, membership, monitoring and verification protocols, treatment of offsets, and its results to date.

Secondarily, we thought the legislation should contain credit for early action, as many companies had already begun to make significant reductions in CO_2 emissions. Some of these were CCX members,

[6]The U.S. Climate Action Partnership (USCAP), an alliance of businesses and environmental organizations formed in 2007, encourages the U.S. government to mandate reductions in greenhouse gas emissions.

in which case they had been independently verified and monitored. However, there were many companies that were not CCX members, but had also acted early. We argued that the recognition of these early actions was good public policy, in order to encourage actions performed in the public's interest that were not required by law. Furthermore, the recognition of reductions not used for compliance reduced the costs of achieving targeted reductions. We tried to rally our members to carry this argument forward. They had the political clout that we lacked.

We set up a meeting with Chairman Waxman, who was dedicated to addressing climate change and expressed a sincere interest in learning about the CCX experience. The meeting allowed us to share ideas and stories. During a technical discussion, one of the staff members made an extraordinary statement: "There will never be credit for early action because we don't need it to pass the bill." This gave us tremendous insight into the legislative process in Washington, DC. The bill would only contain provisions that enabled its passage. The rights and wrongs of early action credits, and the question of whether it indeed facilitated the achievement of reducing greenhouse gases at the least cost to the economy, did not matter. This held true for effective verification and monitoring methods as well. In fact, there was little or no interest in design features that helped to meet the environmental objectives in a least-cost manner.

We received the same message repeatedly throughout the year. A powerful staffer who drafted the bill told Mike that they would not meet with us until after the bill was drafted. I, too, received the same comments from staff on the Senate.

Washington had changed dramatically over the past 40 years. When I first visited, there had really been only two fashionable hotels, the Hay-Adams and the Madison. Over the last 20 years, however, dozens of new luxury hotels such as the Four Seasons and the Ritz Carlton had been added. In the past, hotel rooms rates in New York were roughly double that of those in Washington, DC. Now the situation had reversed itself. We were in the midst of the financial crisis, and even a reservation at the Capitol Grille was nearly impossible. My reengagement in Washington politics was a rude awakening to how recession-proof the city had become. Money was everywhere.

Although I read about these changes, personally experiencing them was mind-blowing. One statistic said it all. In 2011, the per capita income of Washington, a city that primarily produced rules and regulations, surpassed that of San Jose, home to Apple, Google, and Facebook—some of our most innovative companies.[7]

Our directors, Stu Eisenstadt and Clayton Yeutter, gave us some astute advice on how to navigate Washington. The legislative process was too Byzantine for us to deal with on our own, so the board welcomed the suggestion of retaining lobbyists. We were also advised to consider registering ourselves as lobbyists, given the amount of time we were spending on Washington outreach. I ruled this out. CCX had neither the connections nor the competence for this to be effective.

We retained three prominent lobbying firms. Mike McLeod from McLeod, Watkinson & Miller was a young staffer I met during my days at the CBOT when he had been working for Senator Talmadge. Mike had been instrumental in drafting the language that enabled financial futures in 1974. He was a Southern gentleman in the truest sense and knew the agriculture business inside and out.

Despite the extensive knowledge of these firms and the sound advice they provided, the murkiness of the Washington process ultimately drowned out our voices. We learned that much of the lobbyists' influence in Washington derived from their ability to raise campaign donations—an eye-opening lesson for our staff. Sadly, we didn't have the resources or the stomach to play this game and therefore our chances to influence the debate were minimal.

We succeeded in personally briefing all 39 members of the staff for the House Energy and Environment committee. The first version of the bill, 648 pages long, was released at the end of March. Only two to three pages were on early action credits and we drafted a document to reflect our interests. Four days of hearings were held from April 21 to 24. Our members provided input to the process by writing to committees and staffers of Congress. On May 15,

---

[7]Frank Bass and Timothy R. Horman, "Beltway Earnings Make U.S. Capital Richer Than Silicon Valley," *Bloomberg*, October 18, 2011.

Waxman-Markey introduced H.R. 2454, with allocations.[8] The bill was now 932 pages. On May 18, yet another version of H.R. 2454 was introduced. The bill had grown to 946 pages in three days. The bill was voted out of the committee on May 21 by a margin of 33 to 25. It was hardly a consensus.

Mike McLeod arranged for a meeting with Congressman Collin Peterson, the chairman of the House Agriculture Committee to discuss passing an amendment that would allow for compensation of early offset credits from 2001 to 2009, based on average historical prices. Otherwise, CCX members were at risk of being disenfranchised, since the vast majority of their offset products would not receive credit under the current legislation. The meeting went well. I had previously met Congressman Peterson after my keynote speech at the National Farmers Union (NFU) annual meeting, and briefed him about CCX. We had support from NFU, and had worked closely with the North Dakota Farmers Union.

On June 22, a new version of H.R. 2454 was reported to the Rules Committee. As the head of an important committee, Congressman Peterson also had jurisdiction over the climate bill. He wanted to make sure that the interests of his constituents were represented on the final draft of the bill. He expressed his concerns to Chairman Waxman. Without his vote, the bill was unlikely to pass. A day later, Waxman and Peterson reached a deal on the inclusion of agricultural offsets. Congressman Peterson supported the bill and brought in as many agricultural constituents as possible. Two days later, the Peterson agricultural amendment on early action was finalized at 2:00 A.M. On June 26, a new managers' amendment that incorporated the Peterson amendment was realized at 1:30 A.M. Section 795 was amended from the June 25 version to open the window for industrial early action, not just early offset projects. Our members had finally made some progress for themselves. The bill was now over 1,400 pages. The last 300 pages were

[8]Under H.R. 2454, the American Clean Energy and Security Act of 2009, regulated industries are required to purchase one credit per ton emitted. The majority of credits are slated to be sold to polluters in return for revenue for the government. The number of carbon credits will decrease while their value will increase, starting in 2012. By 2020, the compliance year allocation pool is estimated at $80 billion.

released a mere three hours before the final vote. I wondered if anyone in the House had read the bill in its entirety.

There was one final procedural matter left—a rehearsed event called a colloquy, approved by the chairman of the committee. Although the concept of early action credit was present in the language of the bill, CCX was not mentioned by name. To make sure that CCX would be on the legislative record, we were advised to have a representative from Illinois engage in a "colloquy" with Chairman Waxman on the floor of the House. We had met with every member of the Illinois delegation to ask for their support. Late in the afternoon but just before the vote, one of the members of the Illinois delegation, Congresswoman Debbie Halvorson, was recognized by the chair. She said that the provisions of the legislation attempted to fairly compensate farmers and others enrolled in voluntary offset programs. To remove the possibility of uncertainty or economic harm to holders of offset credits, she believed that offset credits registered with CCX and other registries were qualified to provide an important source of offset credits in the early years of the program.[9] The chairman responded affirmatively. At 6:30 P.M., the House passed H.R. 2454—known as ACES—by a vote 219 to 212. About one hour later, I received the call from my daughter Penya, and we headed off to the Ernst and Young Entrepreneur of the Year event.

I personally spoke to a lot of congressmen after the vote. They were already getting heat for having voted for ACES. The price of carbon sunk dramatically in the next few months. Perhaps the market was telling us that the bill would not survive its trip through the Senate. Perhaps it was telling us that our efforts to secure early action credit were insufficient.

Falling into a Coma

We witnessed the same behavior in the Senate as we did in the House. Senators Boxer (D-CA) and Kerry (D-MA) introduced S.1733, the Clean Energy Jobs and American Power Act, in September 2009. The bill required a 20 percent reduction in emissions by 2020 from 2005 levels. This was 3 percent more stringent than the House bill. Our

[9]U.S. Representative Deborah L. Halvorson, (D-IL), "American Clean Energy and Security Act of 2009," June 26, 2009.

reduction schedule, if extrapolated, resembled the reductions required by the House bill. In October, Senator Graham (R-SC) joined with Senator Kerry in a call for a climate change bill. It was a potential game changer, and we hoped that bipartisanship would break the ice.

In November 2009, "Climategate" broke when hackers posted stolen data and emails on the Internet from scientists at the University of East Anglia. The integrity of the science was questioned, and opponents of cap-and-trade were having a field day. Despite this, Representative Rick Boucher (D-VA) gave a keynote that month at the Edison Electric Institute's Financial Conference expressing his conviction in the passing of cap-and-trade legislation. I met with him at Starbucks between sessions to compare notes regarding what we saw coming in on the policy end. The timing was ironic given the fact that cap-and-trade was clearly under fire. "I don't think that the passing of carbon legislation is an option. It's going to happen, and you can take that to the bank," he declared at the conference.[10]

In December, the EPA released an endangerment filing recognizing CO_2 and other compounds as air pollutants subject to regulation under the Clean Air Act.[11] This ultimately led to regulation of greenhouse gases from stationary sources such as utilities. The die had been cast. It was going to be command-and-control if no additional legislation was passed.

The year ended with President Obama negotiating the Copenhagen Accord in the waning hours of the fifteenth Conference of Parties (COP). It was viewed as a failure by some, and a very limited success by others. Most were indifferent. We had lost an opportunity to lead the world in meeting the challenge of climate change.

By the end of 2009, carbon prices on CCX had dropped to $0.10. They could trade only a nickel lower. The end was clearly in sight.

---

[10]Representative Rick Boucher (D-VA), chairman of the House Energy and Air Quality Subcommittee, addressing the Edison Electric Institute, November 10, 2008. (Tom Cushing's notes from the Session on November 10, 2008.)

[11]"40 CFR Chapter I—Endangerment and Cause or Contribute Findings for Greenhouse Gases Under Section 202(a) of the Clean Air Act; Final Rule," Federal Registry, EPA, December 15, 2009.

President Obama delivered his State of the Union address in January 2010, proclaiming, "Yes, it means passing a comprehensive energy and climate bill with incentives that will finally make clean energy the profitable kind of energy in America. . . . I am grateful to the House for passing such a bill last year. And this year, I'm eager to help advance the bipartisan effort in the Senate." Unfortunately, the ship had already left the port. Senator Bingaman had issued an energy-only bill that languished for over a year. Senator Graham also would float an energy-only bill. Other separate energy-only bills were being discussed all over Washington, DC.

Without strong White House support, the Kerry-Graham-Lieberman coalition began to fall apart. Graham left in April, stating that partisan politics by the Democrats would kill the bill. Senator Reid mentioned the option of an energy-only bill. In June, Senators Lugar, Graham, and Murkowski introduced S.3464, which promoted energy efficiency and renewable energy.

Finally, in June, President Obama addressed the nation in his first Oval Office televised speech, saying he was open to alternative paths. He didn't mention cap-and-trade or pricing carbon as a requirement.

A Post-Mortem

While opportunities for CCX started to materialize in China and solidify in Europe, in the United States we were still swimming against the tide. It was a different kind of "perfect storm" where everything that could go wrong, went wrong. CCX had generated millions of dollars in value to constituents that Congress ignored. No one believed the upside we had shown was real. Perhaps we made it look too easy, so people suspected there had to be something wrong with our system. Although CCX was the only U.S. company that had practical experience in creating a market for emissions, we were never contacted by Congress. The interest that they had shown in the past had vanished.

With the White House focused on the health-care debate and the growing lack of bipartisanship, the Kerry-Graham-Lieberman coalition fell apart. The environmental movement, which had been key to the passing of the Clean Air Act in 1990, grew overconfident and was not able to form a coalition with businesses, agriculture, and forestry interests to help pass the bill. People that were on the same side in 1990 were now in opposing camps. A representative from a leading environmental group summed this up well, "In the environmental community, we have to be more humble. We can't take the attitude that we have all the answers."[12]

Another factor that hampered our educational efforts in Congress was the lack of institutional memory of the staff of Senators and Representatives. I found myself having to repeatedly explain the basics of cap-and-trade or recite the benefits of the Acid Rain Program from scratch. Many staffers were not familiar with the Clean Air Act of 1990 and didn't know that the most successful emissions trading program in history had been enacted by the United States Congress. I once did an informal survey and found out that 70 percent of members of the 111th Congress (in session during 2009 to 2010) were not in office when the Act was passed. The average age of staffers was around 28 years old. That combination meant that many of the people helping write the climate legislation were in middle school when the Act was passed. This made the learning curve even steeper. We were running out of precious time. Many congressional staff members remained unaware of the history of cap-and-trade and the role of exchanges, while the "tax-and-trade" mantra gained traction. With the financial crisis worsening, many in Washington also turned their backs on market-based solutions. The most important piece of environmental legislation in decades was dead.

We were also witnessing a disturbing trend of attempts to resolve environmental objectives through the courtroom. In 2004, the Bush administration maintained that carbon dioxide was not a pollutant and said the EPA lacked authority to regulate it. In a separate 2007 case brought by some of the same states, the Supreme Court ruled that carbon dioxide met the Clean Air Act's definition for air pollution and fell within the EPA's authority. Under the Obama administration, the EPA has proposed new regulations to settle separate lawsuits filed by

---

[12]"EDF Chief: 'Shrillness' of Greens Contributed to Climate Bill's Failure in Washington," Greenwire, April 5, 2011.

states, cities, and environmental groups. Both the power companies and the administration contend that greenhouse gases are too complicated a problem to be resolved by courts.

The stall in climate change legislation not only signaled a blow to emissions trading, but to CCX as well. Regional emissions trading efforts continued to proliferate, but there was no coherency in the way these programs were implemented. Ad hoc command-and-control programs, such as taxes and subsidies, gradually emerged to take over the void created by the lack of climate change legislation, and the role of CCX became increasingly irrelevant.

The federal legislation that died included more than just credit for early action. The supreme irony was that the last version of the bill looked a lot like the design of CCX.

Looking West

Given the failure of cap-and-trade at the federal level, the country reverted to regional and state-level programs taking place amid the legislative vacuum. This included the Regional Greenhouse Gas Initiative (RGGI) and Assembly Bill 32 (AB 32), the California Global Warming Solutions Act.

On March 17, 2011, the Association of Irritated Residents (AIR) challenged the AB 32 by arguing that it would increase air pollution in some areas of the state. Consequently, a San Francisco Superior Court judge ruled that the California Air Resources Board (ARB) violated a California Environmental Quality Act because it failed to "properly consider alternatives to a cap-and-trade program (such as the carbon tax)." The ARB was forced to present a 500-page document to prove that they had considered the carbon tax, but concluded that cap-and-trade was a better alternative.

The judge's ruling rejected the ARB's rationale for choosing a pollution trading scheme, stating that the law required more than "a discourse on cap-and-trade justification." The decision required ARB to fully analyze alternatives to the cap-and-trade program, and would stop all implementation of the program until ARB complied with the law.

Despite uncertainties surrounding its implementation, AB 32 remains the strongest hope the United States has for the resurgence of cap-and-trade. California tends to lead the nation when it comes to social movements, entertainment and technology. Hopefully it will lead again, this time in the environmental space.

The CCX Legacy

CCX prices continued to fall from $7.4 at its peak in mid-2008 to $0.5 a ton by the end of 2010. Many commentators would opine on how this reflected the death of market-based mechanisms to global warming. For some, this was proof that cap-and-trade was an ineffective tool to combat global warming. The system in fact was working as designed. The market, through CCX pricing, was reflecting the total lack of political will to meaningfully manage global warming. Markets have eyes.

I choose to look at CCX's history differently. The CCX pilot had, for the first time, built the complete infrastructure and practical design for a market-based tool to reduce greenhouse gases. It had built all the institutional capability in terms of verification agencies, regulatory framework, trading systems, technical protocols, and so on required for a global emissions trading. Furthermore, the pilot had built human capacity among hundreds of member firms around the globe on these issues. CCX left a legacy of participants and institutions that have the institutional know-how to combat climate change.

Chapter 21

The Chicago Climate Futures Exchange

Expanding the Brand

Everyone lives by selling something.

—*Robert Louis Stevenson*

It had always been my vision to create markets that covered the entire gamut of environmental products. With the launch of CCX, we had established the very first platform for spot trading carbon. Environmental markets for sulfur dioxide and nitrous oxide allowances, however, were primarily still transacted over the counter as spot and forward contacts through brokerage houses. When brokers entertain lavishly, they must be making lavish profits. In other words, the markets were inefficient. While brokers played an important role in the evolution of markets, their transactions were opaque, and lacked efficient price discovery and clearing. As an entrepreneur and innovator, I was amazed that nearly a decade after launching the Acid Rain Program, existing futures exchanges had yet to launch a futures market for SO_2

and NO_x allowances. My earlier involvement in the Acid Rain Program and conducting SO_2 auctions at the CBOT gave me confidence that a futures market for SO_2 would be well received. In 2004, we began the process of establishing the Chicago Climate Futures Exchange (CCFE).

Setting Up Shop

The CCX model served as a successful blueprint. CCFE outsourced most operational functions to focus on product innovation, marketing, and sales.

Given our solid partnership, the Intercontinental Exchange (ICE) agreed to provide the electronic platform for futures trading. The next step was to arrange for clearing. We considered developing our own clearinghouse but quickly dismissed the idea. It was expensive to set up a new entity, capitalize it, and obtain regulatory approval. Clearing was at the heart of the exchange, so it was important for us to find the right partner.

While searching for a clearing partner, we spoke to the Options Clearing Corporation which cleared for the CBOE, and to the Clearing Corporation (CCORP), which once cleared for the CBOT. The threat of emerging competition played a key role in our choice of clearing partner. The Clearing Corporation could easily connect the ICE trading platform, and also proved competitive on price. We decided to partner with CCORP to provide clearing services for our new futures exchange. We also hired the National Futures Association to provide regulatory oversight to CCFE.

To be eligible to trade futures, CCFE had to be approved by the CFTC as a designated contract market (DCM). Filing for this designation was a complex and arduous process. Obtaining a DCM with the CFTC required complying with eight designation criteria and 18 core principles. The latter included everything from dispute resolution, position limits, or accountability to antitrust considerations. On top of that, we had to produce a self-certification submission, which was basically a legally binding agreement to comply with CFTC rules. The process was iterative and achieved official completion only once consensus was reached between lawyers, compliance and operations personnel, and technology personnel. We had started corresponding with the CFTC several months earlier, sending in applications, and were waiting for feedback, whereupon we had to refile the application. Our seasoned group of veterans proved invaluable. Their knowledge, experience, and thorough research armed us with a 400-page application to the CFTC. On December 9, 2004, the CFTC approved CCFE as a designated contract market—the fastest designation in the history of the agency, and a record unlikely to be surpassed, as a new law requires a minimum of three months before such designation can occur.

In just about a year since the launch of CCX, we managed to open the newest futures exchange in town. With CCFE, Chicago's leadership in environmental derivatives was established.

Launching Sulfur Futures

Parallel to the formation of CCFE, Mike Walsh and the research team were hard at work studying SO_2 market fundamentals. The team's understanding of market size, price trends, trading patterns, and participants' profiles was invaluable to the marketing team as they pitched the new product. As usual we played the role of educators and salesmen.

We had watched the SO_2 market evolve and recognized that the critical ingredients for a futures market were finally in place. In 2003 and 2004, the EPA had allocated 9.5 million SO_2 allowances on an annual basis to targeted companies. With prices above $400 per ton, the market value of registered trades was $4 billion per year, far larger than the existing $176 million oats market. Oats were the smallest grain crop and often used as a benchmark to gauge whether a new market was large enough. If something as small as the oats market could push through, the SO_2 allowance market could stand a fighting chance as well.

Market research suggested about $1 billion worth of private options and forward contracts were being executed each year. Major investment banks well versed in derivative trading were stepping up their investing and trading activities, both in the power sector and emissions trading. Separately, new market dynamics increased price volatility significantly. This escalated the price risk in the SO_2 allowance market and made it ideal for speculators to participate. The high volatility also increased the utilities' need to hedge.

Utilities were concerned about counterparty risks because of downgrades in the sector. Still a brokered market, SO_2 trades were not centrally cleared and suffered from high counterparty credit risk. The lack of transparency resulted in wider bid-offer spreads and higher transaction costs. The opportunity to transact on an exchange, as opposed to over the counter, could address all these problems.

Mandatory NO_x and SO_2 programs, along with other voluntary programs such as CCX, provided the right political and economic climate to launch a futures exchange for emissions allowances. The next step was to design the contract. As economists, we greatly enjoyed this part. The science of it was intellectually stimulating, and the art in it was inspiring.

Designing the Contract

Turning our attention to designing the first contract to be listed on CCFE, we formed an SO_2 advisory committee consisting of utilities, traders, and FCMs. We proposed a contract size of 25 tons, borrowing from the approach used for interest rate futures. At a price of \$500 to \$1,000, the SO_2 contract had a notional value that was competitive with that of wheat.[1] The minimum price increments of \$1 per ton and the exchange fees made the futures contract very competitive with the over-the-counter (OTC) brokered market and facilitated market making. The contract incorporated delivery specifications from the SO_2 allowance registry operated by the EPA. When it came to obtaining contract approval from the CFTC, we found ourselves once again in the educator's seat. The CFTC needed to become familiar with the market fundamentals. It was déjà vu, back to my experience with Treasury contracts.

[1]Wheat contract: 5,000 bushels per contract × \$3.60 price per bushel (2003) = \$18,000. SO_2 contract: 25 tons per contract × \$500 = \$12,500. SO_2 contract: 25 tons per contract × \$1,000 = \$25,000. Notional values: \$12,500 < \$18,000 < \$25,000.

The total supply of allowances allocated in a year was just like the amount of wheat produced in a year. Like wheat, allowances not used for compliance in a given year could be stored for later years. My previous experience in capacity building helped us through the launch of this new product. There were no turf wars with another regulatory agency this time. In fact, the EPA approved of the addition of an organized futures market. It complemented their objectives of price transparency and reduced transaction costs. They provided the registry services that facilitated the delivery process. The CFTC also recognized SO_2 allowances as an intangible commodity. Years of conducting the auction at the CBOT ensured that there were some transparent price signals to lean on. The EPA's leadership in mandating CEMs also ensured the integrity of compliance and monitoring. Unlike our experience with CCX, this time the market had a paradigm.

With the SO_2 contract design, we experienced the same concerns we had heard over the last 35 years—the contract was too small. Typical trades in the spot and forward markets were for 1,000 tons. We prevailed on the users.

On December 10, 2004, 12 years after I had helped write a similar contract for the CBOT, the CCFE SO_2 futures contract was launched. In an attempt to create a brand and trademark, we named the contract SFIs, short for sulfur financial instruments. The day before the launch, we conducted a confidential price survey on the SO_2 market. This was important for purposes of setting price limits for the market launch the next day. We surveyed about 10 brokers and computed a volume weighted price of the SO_2 allowance price. With the launch of CCFE, the first steps for price transparency in the SO_2 market had been laid. The SFI product launch was modest, but we knew that building liquidity would take time. We anticipated a less-than-warm reception from dealers and brokers who disliked competition and transparency, a familiar story.

From the outset, the CCFE SO_2 futures contract floundered. Only 39 contracts were traded in December—slow, but understandable for a new contract. There was sufficient price volatility on SO_2 allowances for the futures market to build liquidity before the summer of 2005. We simply failed to sell the product. Old habits died hard and this was proving to be true for SO_2. The SO_2 allowance market had gradually evolved into an OTC market over the previous decade, and users had already established firm relationships with the major brokers and dealers that dominated the market. Although we published brochures and made calls to educate customers on the product, it was difficult to change the entrenched practices and cut through the web of relationships already established in the market.

We began actively targeting utilities and financial players—a strategy that had proven successful when financial futures had been first launched. Our chief operating officer hung whiteboards on all four walls of his office and filled them with long lists of utility members that he identified as natural clients. Some were already CCX members and others we hoped to cross-market through CCX and CCFE. We believed that if we managed to attract them to CCFE for SO_2 trading, a known and mandated market, we could also try to recruit them for our voluntary CCX program. We were dead wrong. Changing the mindset of utilities was an arduous task. Getting approval from their boards to trade in a new futures market was even harder.

We tried to get major newspapers to begin publishing SO_2 price quotes, arguing that the market was bigger than many of the quoted markets. Our request was denied, due more to entrenched interests than to economic rationale.

Resistance to change was nothing new. Back during my days at the University of Minnesota, Professor Schmookler always used Ignaz Semmelweis as a metaphor when describing inventive activity. Dr. Semmelweis had observed that mortality rates from female bed fever were significantly lower in parts of the hospital that dealt with the poor. He realized that the midwives who treated those patients always washed their hands. In contrast, physicians who dealt with wealthier patients often didn't wash their hands. They were upper-class gentlemen and they didn't have to. Semmelweis believed that many lives could be saved simply through cleanliness, but was ridiculed and opposed for his ideas. He was subsequently dismissed by the hospital and the medical community, and was forced to return to his native Budapest. When he started to denounce his fellow physicians as murderers, his family deemed him insane and committed him to an asylum. The story of Semmelweis indicated that some change could be nearly impossible to bring about. The Semmelweis reflex is usually used as a metaphor for the tendency to reject new knowledge because it does not conform with the standard norms.

My early experience marketing the SO_2 contract plunged me into doubt. Why wouldn't a customer use a product that was cheaper and also had no counterparty risk? Very often, the indifference to change came from the very members who were mostly likely to benefit from it. As the SFI contract continued trading slowly into 2005, we could no longer deny that the SO_2 market was an utter train wreck. We got a good omen on July 26, 2005. Julie gave birth to Justine Sandor Ludden. Ellen and I flew out to California and my heart was filled with joy watching three generations of Sandor women. Ellen was delirious and it felt like change was on the way. And it was.

On August 23, 2005, a seemingly harmless tropical depression formed near the Bahamian Islands. The tropic depression morphed into Hurricane Katrina, striking both Florida and Louisiana and devastating the economy of New Orleans and the Gulf Coast. These regions constituted the hub of natural gas supply to the rest of country. Katrina rattled the energy markets and interrupted the supply of crude oil and natural gas, causing a spike in the prices of these commodities. A secondary effect of the hurricane ended up changing CCFE's future.

The Rise

Hurricanes and sulfur dioxide, two seemingly unrelated concepts, became interconnected. As natural gas prices rose dramatically, utilities began to use more coal to produce electricity. As the use of coal increased, so did SO_2 emissions. This in turn drove up SO_2 allowance prices, which resulted in an increase in volume of SO_2 traded. Over the next four months, the price of SFIs increased from just over \$600 per ton to more than \$1,600 per ton. Implicitly, the SO_2 market prices could theoretically be used as an indirect hedge against hurricanes. Who would have thought that a catastrophic event far out in the sea could be related to smokestack emissions? The team had a great reason to get in touch with customers and build relationships.

Other factors led to the upward pressure on SO_2 prices. Daily weather played an important role. Extremely hot or cold days resulted in higher demand for electricity, which meant more coal burning. This led to higher SO_2 emissions and resultant upward pressure on SO_2 allowance prices. SO_2 prices were again driven upward as freight rail transport from the western to eastern region of the United States experienced delays due to repair and maintenance work on railways. The slowdown in transport of low-sulfur coal from the western power river basin to eastern coal plants forced plants to substitute low-sulfur coal with higher-sulfur Appalachian coal. More generally, gross domestic product (GDP) was also tied to SO_2 prices, insofar as it hinged upon the number of factories running at any given time. Increased price risk in the SO_2 allowance market truly depended on a diverse set of factors and required rigorous analysis just like any other energy product.

However, this whim of nature would not have mattered if we had not already laid the groundwork for the market in the first place. Despite our failure to market the new futures contract, we were determined to push through with a second round of marketing. This time it was different. I called Mac McGregor to my office and gave him a challenge. Mac had joined the team in 2004 and to date had been helping with CCX recruitment tasks. He was an energetic and enthusiastic team player, but I saw in him a competitiveness that left him unsatisfied with his present tasks. I challenged him to take the reins of our CCFE marketing effort. Mac fit the profile of young local traders, spoke their language, and could quickly win their trust and friendship. My belief that young team members would rise to the occasion and outperform when given an important task was again confirmed.

Volume gradually started increasing during the last quarter of 2005. We were now poised to actively sell the value of these markets to hedgers and financial players. At CCFE, we also created a trading privilege holder (TPH) program, which gave the purchaser the right to transact at a discount compared to other users. It was a way to attract liquidity into a new market. Financial players included banks, investment banks, and energy hedge funds. One windfall from the collapse of Enron was the supply of excellent trading talent. Former traders were subsequently employed by utilities, financial institutions, and hedge funds. Many Enron traders left to form their own hedge funds.

We still faced several major challenges. We had a brand new futures exchange and a brand new contract on our hands. To be successful, the only way was to find emissions traders willing to champion the new SFI product. We were well known among the larger utilities that saw the potential benefit of having contracts traded on a regulated exchange with transparent pricing. The OTC transaction costs, which included the bid-offer spread plus OTC broker commissions of 6 percent, were as high as 10 percent of the value of the allowances. We therefore set exchange and FCM fees lower than the OTC fees. If a contract were consummated by delivery, our fees were about $0.20 per ton. The fees for a similar transaction in the spot market ranged from $0.25 to $0.50. Of course, they were only a small part of the transaction costs. The principal benefit came from narrowing the bid-offer spread from hedging and trading.

As was expected, brokers and dealers did not want us to succeed. Market opaqueness was their bread and butter. One dealer said straight to my face, "I'm not interested in supporting you—you're bringing transparency and destroying my margins." I took the comment as a sign that efficient markets were working. While the dealer's attitude was obvious, we ran into more complex cases of opposition to CCFE. We approached a major bank that was a significant market maker in SO_2 allowances to explore if they were interested in buying equity in CCFE. Although the head of the department was intrigued and supported the idea, the deal never went through. The opposition to the deal came from the main trader, who preferred the opaqueness of the brokered market. We later learned that it had to do with the bank's internal incentive structure. The bank had provided equity benefits from the proposed deal to the manager but not to the trader. The trader was therefore better off with the status quo, which provided incentives to participate in the brokered market.

We managed to change some minds. I was particularly interested in changing the attitudes of critics who were especially vocal in their opposition. Open critics often made open supporters. I believed that if we could change their minds, they could turn into ardent supporters and help us push the product with vigor. Mac managed to build a relationship with Amerex, a leading brokerage firm that ended up helping us clear trades and break the broker monopoly. Keith Bronstein once again provided tremendous help by providing liquidity to the market.

The business models of exchanges and FCMs had experienced a profound change since the inception of electronic trading. Volume had increased dramatically, and salesmen had developed a lucrative business from widely traded energy contracts. We had to find individual salesmen in brokerage firms to concentrate on these new emissions products, despite the fact that most had a limited interest in them. There was also a different sales model from the first days of the Treasury contracts, where FCMs and brokers brought in the clients. Not only did we have to invent and launch the contract, we also had to educate the end user and bring these clients to the brokers and FCMs.

To identify and develop champions, we continuously called individual traders and informed them of the prices on the screen. Because there was not yet enough market information to trigger trading, I suggested that we start an SO_2 newsletter and communicate a potential morning marker price. A morning survey of OTC deals with our interpretation of the results was emailed to our clients. There was so much educating to do. One trader joked about taking delivery of SO_2 through gas tanks. In many instances, having traders set up to log in to the CCFE screen was a chore in and of itself.

Although we had garnered interest from utilities that were existing members of CCX, they only provided a limited user base for CCFE. Accounting was another issue. Any trade conducted for allowances within a 30-day period was treated as a simple spot transaction. If the period exceeded 30 days, the trade was subject to mark-to-market accounting. Recall that futures contracts were usually listed in quarterly expirations. Regulated utilities were less likely to use more distant contracts. We met this challenge by listing serial months. For example, for the January 2006 contract, CCFE also listed February, March, and quarterly expirations for 2007 and 2008. We also began listing a new contract as soon as one expired.

Our desire to always be customer-oriented led to some innovations in contract design. The following material is technical, but was important in the success of the contract. Several utilities wanted to trade a futures contract that included delivery of allowances from years beyond the specific contract being traded. Banking was critical to the success of the program, and the contract design needed to reflect the fact that earlier vintages could be used for compliance if they had not been used already. Our contract specified that at the option of the seller, delivery could occur with SO_2 allowances listed in the current year or any prior year. For example, the December 2006 SFI futures contract permitted the delivery of SO_2 allowances in 2006 or any prior year. This practice resembled the cheapest-to-deliver concept in grains and Treasury bonds.

Utilities and financial participants wanted to trade 2007 vintages but have them delivered in December 2006. We therefore added a new delivery feature to the SFI contract. It was a novelty, and we were granted a patent for it.

Sell, Sell, and More Sell

I had always admired Billy Salomon, the founder of Salomon Brothers. He always traveled with new salesmen when pitching to clients. Not only did this heighten the importance of the meeting for clients, it provided a vehicle for him to teach the new salesmen who accompanied him. I adopted this practice during our pitches, deviating once again from the practices of existing exchanges.

Mac McGregor continued to retain his competitive streak from his basketball-playing days and had become a great salesman. His work ethic, knowledge of markets, and likeability led us to offer him the position of manager at CCFE. Mac and I attended a number of meetings held by the Environmental Markets Association, the leading U.S.-based trade association focused on promoting market-based solutions for environmental challenges. Its membership included a diverse crowd, including large utilities, emissions brokers and traders, exchanges, and government agencies. We hosted parties—sometimes on rooftops—and sponsored events at these important annual meetings. I was old enough to be the grandfather of many of the attendees at these events. These meetings combined business savvy and fun but were insufficient in attracting liquidity. Over the next two years, the marketing team at CCFE, including myself, made numerous trips to meet with clients.

In the middle of 2006, we scheduled meetings with various utilities, banks, and hedge funds in Houston, where many energy traders and hedge funds were based. From these meetings, we learned that many traders who traded in SO_2 also traded in NO_x due to the compliance programs faced by utilities. It was then that we decided to launch a NO_x contract.

To launch a new contract, we needed additional staff. Mac suggested that I interview Dan Scarbrough, a teammate from his days of playing college basketball. Increasing our staff allowed us to continue to personally visit new accounts while still retaining at least one professional in the office to service our existing clients. Dan knew nothing about the business but was enthusiastic and willing to learn. He fit the corporate culture, and Mac personally vouched for his integrity and loyalty. Dan became a critical part of the marketing team. While Mac focused on managing relationships, Dan focused on learning and analyzing the details of the ever-changing SO_2 program, NO_x emissions reduction programs, renewable energy certification, and other new cap-and-trade programs. Mac and Dan made a great team and were used as Trojan horses, cross-marketing between CCFE and CCX.

Early one morning during one of our recruitment trips, I received a call from Mac. A sprinkler had accidentally gone off in his hotel room and all his business clothes were soaked. According to the original itinerary, we were supposed to meet in a couple of hours. However, given the incident, Mac asked if he could wait for the clothing store to open so he could buy some new clothing before meeting up. I gently but firmly explained that the CCFE corporate culture did not permit this. "Get creative and meet me up 9 A.M., according to plan," I said with a smile in my voice. I was adhering to the Billy Salomon model. Mac showed up at the meeting in ruffled pants, a T-shirt, and shoes with no socks. Everyone loved the story, and the day was a great success.

During these meetings, Mac and Dan focused on pitching the SO_2 and NO_x contracts, while I pitched everything from the individual contracts to CCFE membership and CCX stocks. We often started with breakfast, had one-on-one meetings throughout the day and ended with a dinner party with 20 to 30 existing or potential users of the exchange's products. These social events furthered the bonding of our team with energy traders, which proved to be extremely useful. Most energy traders in Houston were more comfortable dealing with emissions markets in SO_2 than the newer market in NO_x. However, because of the relationships we had established, our team was able to convince these traders of the opportunities in trading CO_2, which was less common because of the lack of mandatory legislation. We ended up doing a lot of cross-marketing between SO_2, NO_x, and CO_2 on these sales and marketing trips.

Volumes and open interest continued to grow as transaction costs declined. By the second quarter, the bid-offer spread was $2 to $3 per ton. On one particular day during that same quarter, Mac told me that the market was $305 bid and $306 offered. There were 200 contracts on the bid and offer. Ultimately, CCFE cut transactions costs by more than 90 percent.

The RGGI Battle

In 2007, the 10 Northeastern states formed a cap-and-trade program for greenhouse gas emissions known as the Regional Greenhouse Gas Initiative (RGGI). RGGI was a pilot program with modest reduction goals that had the potential to become the first mandated greenhouse gas cap-and-trade program in the United States. RGGI followed the standard model of the SO_2 markets but made some interesting modifications. The program instituted quarterly auctions instead of annual auctions, and auction proceeds went to the states to invest in renewable energy. The program allowed for offsets but had yet to establish firm rules. The RGGI proposal encompassed other political objectives, such as setting aside 20 percent of allowances for an unspecified public benefit fund that included programs to promote renewable energy and energy efficiency, while directly mitigating electricity rate payer impacts. As a student of Professor Coase, I felt that this provision was unnecessary and irrelevant in light of the objective—to reduce emissions at the least cost. It was actually common for cap-and-trade policies to be complemented with other programs and measures, such as a mandated investment in renewable energy. Although such measures could have merit in themselves, they in fact did nothing to change the optimal solution. All we needed to arrive at the optimal solution was a price signal, which would automatically lead to appropriate investments in the appropriate sectors. For example, if the price of emitting carbon exceeded the price of building a low-emitting plant, companies would naturally choose to invest in allowances. Mandating green investments on top of the price signal could be costly and inefficient. It was a problem that plagued many climate change bills, which were burdened by special interests that added little to the ultimate environmental objective.

Regardless, there was an opportunity for a new contract in the RGGI program. We applied the same policies we had used for SO_2 and NO_x markets, and offered to implement whatever program they decided on. Although we shared our experiences with the constituents responsible for drafting the rules and regulations of the program, we sought no direct influence on the drafting process. Ultimately, it was the states, the power sector, and the environmentalists that molded the RGGI program.

By this time, our success had stimulated imitators. The CCFE market had resulted in SO_2 brokers being disintermediated, and the cash market spreads for dealers had been significantly diminished. Ironically, brokers and dealers saw this as a new opportunity. A group of them formed the Green Exchange (GreenX) in March 2008, in order to trade futures in RGGI allowances. The CME became an owner of 25 percent of the equity and provided the trading platform. The new exchange imitated our business model of a virtual exchange. This did not go unnoticed by our investors. Nonetheless, we thought GreenX ratified what we had been doing and provided a strong marketing opportunity for cap-and-trade.

Given that we had already announced a launch date for the RGGI contract at the time, the threat was real. As our trading platform, ICE required us to give them a 90-day notice whenever we wanted to list a new contract. In this case, however, we didn't have the time. If we waited for 90 days, GreenX could become the first mover. We had to be creative. Earlier on, we had listed a futures contract for European Union Allowances, code named EUA US, on the ICE platform but it was never launched. Someone suggested that we replace this dormant contract with the RGGI contract. The EUA futures contract was for 1,000 tons, the price increments were \$0.01 per ton, or \$10.00 per contract—we had no choice but to use the same contract specifications for the RGGI contract, as it would take a long time for ICE to modify the EUA quotes. We decided to label the RGGI contract "EC," short for European carbon, and prepared for launch.

The race was on. We stayed silent about our activities, while GreenX promoted its product through press releases. A stealth launch was a strategic choice. We wanted to avoid announcing our launch and provide the opportunity for GreenX to launch even earlier. However, since we already established friendships with many energy traders, we were able to quietly advise them of our plan, and they helped market the product privately. Our RGGI contract launched two weeks before GreenX launched theirs. By the time they launched their contract, we had already achieved significant liquidity, preventing GreenX from becoming a competitive threat.

CCFE's success with respect to RGGI could be attributed to several factors. We already had the infrastructure in place, the related products, and had members using our markets. Furthermore, no user setups were necessary and all our members had existing brokerage accounts. The success ratified the economies associated with having related markets. It was also a replay of the trend that we had witnessed in the Treasury bond futures market, and in other existing markets over the decade. Competitors have repeatedly failed to seize successful futures markets away from those who started them. In fact, the only historical case where competitors had been successful in doing so was during the shift from electronic trading to open outcry. Electronic trading had helped Eurex wrest the Bund futures market from Liffe. It also enabled ICE to successfully compete with NYMEX on natural gas.

What a difference two years made. By the end of 2005, CCFE's SFI volume was 171 contracts. By 2009, it had grown to 370,503. Open interest growth was comparable. We went from trading only SO_2 allowances to NO_x, RGGI, and renewable energy certificates.[2] Most importantly, however, CCFE became the bellwether for SO_2 and NO_x prices. We had to both follow and lead as government programs emerged—in the case of RGGI we followed, and in the case of CCX and CCFE we led.

Figures 21.1, 21.2, and 21.3 illustrate the volume, open interest, and products offered during that six-year period.

We were not afraid of failure, and launched many products that eventually failed. It was important to experiment and be innovative when establishing new markets.

---

[2]A renewable energy certificate (REC) is rewarded to every 1MWh of electricity produced from renewable energy sources. The condition of additionality applies.

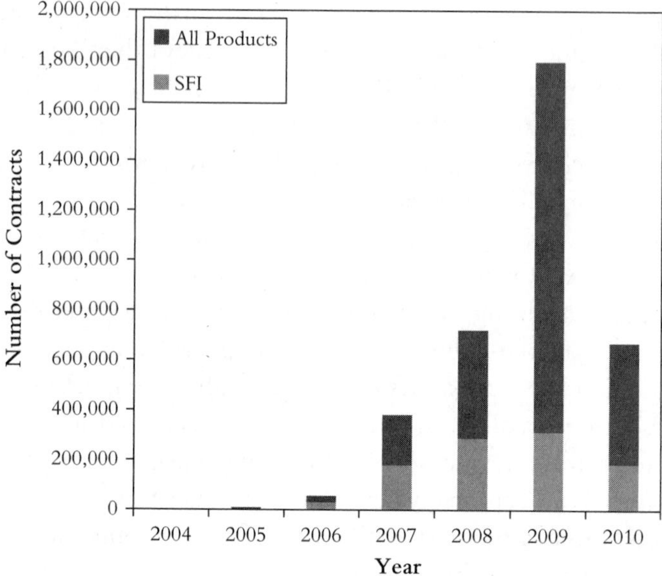

Figure 21.1 CCFE Volume 2004–2010
Source: Data from IntercontinentalExchange.

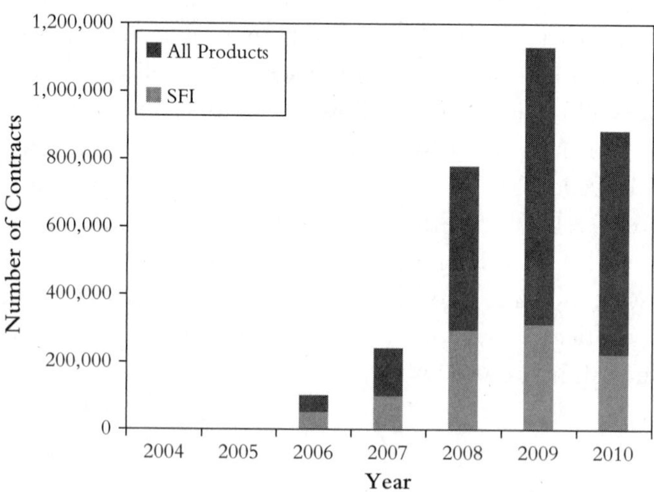

Figure 21.2 CCFE Open Interest 2004–2010
Source: Data from IntercontinentalExchange.

Date	Product
Dec. 10, 2004	Futures contract based on U.S. sulfur dioxide emission allowances (SFI)
Mar. 25, 2005	Sulfur Financial Instrument—Current Vintage Delivery (SFI-CVD)
May 17, 2006	Annual December SFI futures contracts for years 2009 through 2014
Feb. 23, 2007	Nitrogen Financial Instrument—Ozone Season (NFI-OS) futures contract
Apr. 5, 2007	Options on the Sulfur Financial Instrument (SFI) futures contract
July 12, 2007	ECO-Clean Energy Index futures contract (ECO-Index)
Aug. 3, 2007	Carbon Financial Instrument futures contract (CFI-PD)
Aug. 24, 2007	Certified Emission Reduction futures contract (CER)
Sept. 21, 2007	Nitrogen Financial Instrument—Annual (NFI-Annual), European Carbon Financial Instrument (ECFI), IFEX event-linked futures
Nov. 16, 2007	Certified Emission Reduction futures contract (CERC, CERP)
Feb. 28, 2008	Options on the Carbon Financial Instruments futures contract
Mar. 14, 2008	Options on Nitrogen Financial Instruments (Annual) futures contract
July 18, 2008	ELF—Florida Tropical Wind Events and ELF—Gulf Coast Tropical Wind Events
Aug. 15, 2008	Regional Greenhouse Gas Initiative (RGGI) futures and options on futures
Nov. 14, 2008	DJSI World futures contract
Nov. 19, 2008	Carbon Financial Instrument—U.S. Allowance Futures (CFI-US)
Dec. 19, 2008	Options on the CFI futures Jan. 13, Dec. 13, Dec. 14, and Dec. 15 contract months
Feb. 20, 2009	California Climate Action Registry—Climate Reserve Tons CCAR-CRT futures
Mar. 13, 2009	Options on Climate Reserve Tons futures contract (CCAR-CRT)
Apr. 21, 2009	Four Renewable Energy Certificates (REC) futures contracts (REC CT, REC V, REC NJ, REC MA)
July 27, 2009	ELF—Eastern Seaboard Tropical and ELF—Northeast Tropical Wind Events
Nov. 20, 2009	Carbon Financial Instrument United States Offset (CFI-US-O), Carbon Financial Instrument EA (CFI-EA)

Figure 21.3 Timeline of CCFE Products

Benefits of CCFE

Volume and open interest statistics were important determinants of the market capitalization of exchanges. They were also sources of wealth for stockholders. Exchanges themselves provided jobs directly and indirectly. In Chicago, it was estimated that the derivative exchanges provided 100,000 jobs directly and indirectly. These jobs were all worthwhile in themselves but still only told part of the story. The value of regulated futures and options exchanges really extended to other direct and spill-over benefits.

The success of the CCFE futures market gave us a chance to provide insights on how to measure its benefits. It was yet another example of a good derivative. When SO_2 trading began, OTC transaction costs were about 10 percent of the price of allowances, $50 at a price of $500 per ton. As the market matured, this number diminished to $2.00 or less. The reduction caused the cash market spreads to narrow. In 2008, approximately 10 million tons were transferred in the EPA registry.[3] Using a back-of-the-envelope analysis, this suggests that the transaction costs for compliance in the program were reduced from $500 million to $20 million. These savings of close to $500 million have often escaped economists and policy makers, a clarion call for both to do further research to ensure more effective public policy.

There were other direct benefits: hedging, price discovery, and delivery. Additionally, one should take into account the value of price insurance. Keynes suggested it might be 10 percent of the value of the commodity,[4] while others suggested that this might be inaccurate.[5] In either event, this was yet another reason for economists and policy makers to pay closer attention to the value of regulated futures markets. It was easy to blame these exchanges for price volatility and ignore the indirect and direct benefits that they provided to the economy. Volatility in the prices of core commodities such as food and energy was not the fault of the markets. As we say in Chicago, "Thermometers don't cause high fevers."

There were other often-overlooked benefits from pricing emissions and the role of regulated futures and options markets. The price of SO_2, like other prices, sent a critical signal. This signal resulted in the ability of a city to significantly reduce its SO_2 emissions, providing both health benefits and a cleaner environment with more recreational opportunities for residents. There was another very important lesson here. A wide bid-offer spread was associated with higher transaction costs, which could ultimately reduce investments in pollution abatement equipment. Figure 21.4 shows the reduction in SO_2 emissions under the Acid Rain Program over time.

---

[3]A fuller analysis would have to exclude intercompany transfers.

[4]John Maynard Keynes, "Some Aspects of Commodity Markets, Manchester United Commercial European Reconstruction Raw Materials," March 29, 1923.

[5]Lester G. Telser, "Futures Trading and the Storage of Cotton and Wheat," *Journal of Political Economy* 66, no. 3 (June 1958): 233–255.

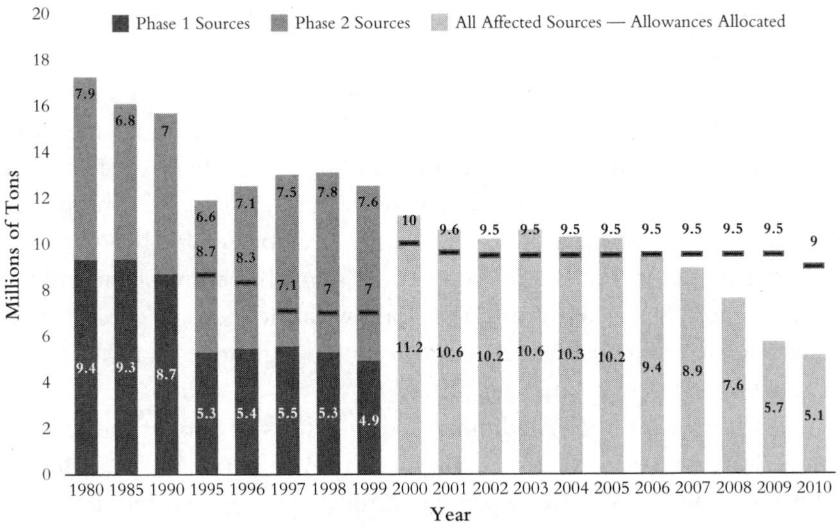

Figure 21.4 SO_2 Emissions under the Acid Rain Program

Source: "SO_2 Emissions from Acid Rain Program Source, 1980–2009," EPA, 2010, www.epa.gov/airmarkets/progress/ARP09_downloads/ARP1_SO2-Emissions-from-Acid-Rain-Program-Sources.gif.

The Fall

Beginning in 2005, the cap-and-trade agenda and the SO_2 legacy forged by the Congress and the EPA began to wither. President Bush had tried to amend the Clean Air Act Amendments (CAAA) of 1990 to attain further reductions, but failed to achieve a bipartisan result in Congress. For reasons well beyond explanation, there was a contentious relationship between the executive and legislative branches of government. The contentious relationship continued into the next administration and contributed to the paralysis of market-based solutions to national pollution.

On March 10, 2005, the EPA finalized the Clean Air Interstate Rule (CAIR). In an attempt to achieve reductions in SO_2 and NO_x emissions that could not otherwise be accomplished through legislative action, the rule sought to provide states with a solution to the issue of power plant pollution that drifted interstate. States had two compliance options. The first achieved the slated emissions reductions with a state emissions budget that required power plants to participate in an EPA-administered interstate cap-and-trade system. The second option invited states to meet emissions requirements using an individual state budget of their own choosing.[6]

On March 25, the state of North Carolina filed a lawsuit against the EPA on the premise that the EPA would be unable to guarantee that individual states met EPA requirements. Therefore, there could be the risk of downwind effect on other states. A group of utilities supported North Carolina, while another set of utilities supported CAIR.

The parties to the lawsuit constituted a small fraction of the utilities in the United States. Most utilities, along with the industry's major trade associations, had actually been in favor of the legislative certainty CAIR would provide—but remained silent.[7]

On May 12, the EPA administered directives of part of the CAAA. States were required to submit their state implementation plans to the EPA for periodical review to prove that they had met their requirements. States were given an emissions budget on their electric generating units. The objective was to reduce SO_2 and NO_x emissions by approximately 70 percent and 60 percent from 2003 levels (SO_2 from 9.4 million tons to 2.5 million tons and NO_x from 3.2 to 1.3 million tons).[8] The three available cap-and-trade programs administered by the EPA covered SO_2, NO_x, and an ozone season emissions cap for NO_x.[9]

Following the promulgation of the final rules back in March, the EPA began receiving a number of petitions. On August 1, the EPA rejected a petition filed by the state of North Carolina.[10] Between

[6]"Clean Air Interstate Rule (CAIR)," U.S. EPA, www.epa.gov/airmarkt/progsregs/cair/index.html.

[7]"Analysis of Potential Quick-Fix Legislative Changes to Address Court Decision," Clean Air Markets Division, EPA, August 28, 2008.

[8]"Clean Air Interstate Rule: Basic Information," U.S. Environmental Protection Agency, July 9, 2010.

[9]CAIR's Seasonal NO_x Budget Trading Program features a tradable permit to emit one ton of NO_x emitted from May 1 to September 30 in a given or subsequent calendar year.

[10]"Clean Air Interstate Rule: Regulatory Actions," U.S. Environmental Protection Agency, July 9, 2010.

November 2006 and March 2007, the EPA received 23 separate petitions. The cat-and-mouse game continued through 2007. On June 22, the EPA received another seven petitions for reconsideration of the federal implementation plan (FIP).[11] The petitions ranged from demanding that the EPA reconsider selected aspects of CAIR and contesting the EPA's authority to place restrictions on Acid Rain Program allowances, to challenging the inclusion of certain states in the program. Petitioners included states, utilities, and environmental groups.

By 2008, the State of North Carolina lawsuit was finally ready to be heard in court. The case was argued in March, and CAIR was vacated in July. The decision of the Washington, DC, circuit court was appealed. In December 2007, the U.S. circuit court sent a revised CAIR back to the EPA, which allowed the rule to remain in effect until it was replaced by yet another rule. The new rule had to be consistent with the court's reasoning and would theoretically preserve the environmental objectives of CAIR. However, it severely limited trading, which undermined whole idea of the CAAA 1990. Laws and regulation were sometimes used by those that couldn't compete in the marketplace. This was another life lesson that I learned firsthand from Charlie O. Finley.

Charlie had been forbidden by the League to sell his three star players—Blue, Rudi, and Fingers—to the New York Yankees for $3.5 million on the basis that this was an unprecedented amount of money for baseball players. Commissioner Bowie Kuhn believed that the sales threatened the competitive balance of baseball as a sport. I told Charlie that not only did the sales not violate existing baseball rules but that similar sales had occurred throughout baseball history. Charlie asked me to meet with his law firm to explain my reasoning, and I was subsequently asked by the law firm to be the expert witness in the trial. I ran an analysis and found that, once adjusted for inflation and taxes, the trades were consistent with those of the great players of the 1920s and 1930s such as Babe Ruth, Jimmy Foxx, and Hank Greenberg.

[11]The FIP served as a stopgap measure for the CAIR while it underwent revisions. Operating under the same principles as the SIPs (state implementation plans), the cap-and-trade program under FIPs was meant to help states achieve emission reductions in CAIR's spirit until SIPs were approved.

Finley's proposed sale had precedents—the former A's owner, Connie Mack, had sold players from his championship teams for over $900,000 in the early 1930s, amounting to $4.5 million in 1977 once accounting for inflation and other economic factors. I also estimated that Bill DeWitt, owner of the St. Louis Browns, had come away with nearly $3 million over the course of his team's breaking up in 1947–1948. This translated to nearly $7.5 million in 1977.[12] We won on this point, but Judge McGarr ultimately ruled against Charlie in *Finley V. Kuhn* on the basis of laws allowing the League to operate in its own way and not be subject to antitrust laws—it was important that the Commissioner retain jurisdiction over attempts to "prevent any conduct destructive of the confidence in the integrity of baseball."[13] The ruling broke the dynasty that Charlie had and prevented him from quickly rebuilding the team. Charlie told me that his fellow owners had all sided with Bowie Kuhn with the sole exception of Augie Bush, the famous owner of Budweiser and the St. Louis Cardinals. They couldn't beat Charlie on the playing field so they changed the rules on him.

We will never know why those utilities took that legal action. This was not only a story about the EPA, petitions, district courts, and federal courts. The process also created an enormous amount of regulatory uncertainty for the public and utilities, dramatically limiting expenditures on pollution abatement. There was an important lesson here. Participating in lawsuits was a dangerous matter. It could often have disastrous unintended consequences, particularly when court practice tended to drop unlawful rules completely instead of let rules remain in place while remanding them to the EPA for correction. In this case, the lawsuit destroyed the most successful environmental policy tool in the history of the United States.

In all fairness, there was some attempt to rectify this in Congress.[14] This was doomed by partisan politics. Needless to say, the markets reflected this uncertainty. The price of SO_2 allowances fell from $430

---

[12]Michael G. Green, *Charlie Finley: The Outrageous Story of Baseball's Super Showman* (New York: Walker & Company, 2010), 262.

[13]Frank J. McGarr, the U.S. District Judge in *Finley v. Kuhn*, March 17, 1977.

[14]See Senator Tom Carper's Clean Air Planning Act of 2007.

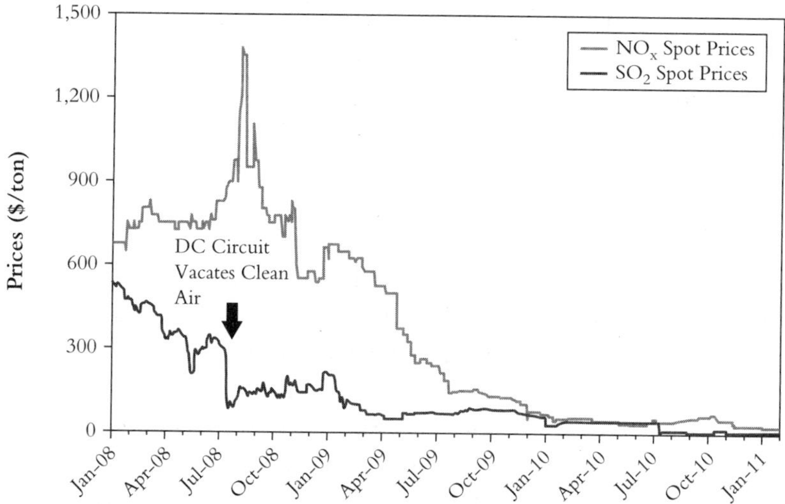

Figure 21.5 SO_2 Allowance Spot Prices and NO_x Seasonal Allowance Spot Prices
Source: Federal Energy Regulatory Commission.

at the beginning of the year to $100 by the end of the year. This uncertainty continued into 2010. On July 6, 2010, the EPA proposed the Clean Air Transport Rule (CATR) as a replacement for CAIR, just as the courts had requested. Trading essentially ceased to be a policy tool in dealing with acid rain. On July 10, prices of SO_2 dropped to $30.00 and NO_x to $62.00. The takeaway was that regulatory uncertainty had more of an impact on the markets than Hurricane Katrina had, and was arguably comparable in terms of economic cost. Figure 21.5 is a chart of SO_2 and NO_x spot prices during this period.

While cap-and-trade was not dead, it was on life support pending the new EPA rule. In July 2011, the EPA published a rule requiring power plants in 28 states to curtail emissions. The Cross-State Air Pollution Rule (CSAPR) replaced the 2005 Clean Air Interstate Rule (CAIR), which the United States Court of Appeals for the DC circuit struck down in 2008.

Closing Thoughts

On March 2, 2010, I came across the final report from the EPA's Office of Air and Radiation, which demonstrated the benefits and costs of the Clean Air Act Amendment from 1990 to 2020.[15] The EPA was required to provide comprehensive up-to-date, peer-reviewed information on the Clean Air Act's social benefits and costs, including improvements in human health, welfare, and ecological resources, as well as the impact of the Act's provisions on the economy. The report estimated the CAAA's costs in 2010 using 2006 dollars, which the current level of inflation rendered conservative. The monetized direct compliance cost in 2010 was $53 billion and the central estimate of direct benefits was $1.3 trillion, implying a benefit-cost ratio of 25/1. Futures traders in Chicago normally considered a 4/1 as a home run.

The report went on to attribute 85 percent of the benefits to reductions in premature mortality. Furthermore, by 2020, the reductions would have prevented 230,000 premature deaths. As of 2010, that number stood at 420,000. These were only direct benefits and did not include benefits associated with the scenic and recreational value of state parks, preservation of ecology, or even benefits associated with the rivers that were no long acidified.

These results invited the inquiring mind to ponder why Congress and the administration could not come to agreement on extending this program. Insofar as our elected representatives were both intelligent and socially concerned, it appeared as if the system was simply dysfunctional. Everyone knew that there was a problem and probably knew the solution. We simply lacked a process that allowed us to achieve the greatest social good at the least cost.

As I later watched the debacle surrounding the debt ceiling negotiations, I couldn't help but think that everything that happened in the Congress during the climate change debate was a harbinger of things to come. The dysfunctional political process and the polarization of views from the left and right had made bipartisanship impossible. The problems CCX and CCFE encountered were minuscule compared to the political turmoil surrounding more important issues such as the deficit reduction program going on at the time.

---

[15]"The Benefits and Costs of the Clean Air Act from 1990 to 2020," Final Report, U.S. EPA Office of Air and Radiation, April 2011.

Chapter 22

The European Climate Exchange

The Jewel in the Crown

Where to elect there is but one, 'tis Hobson's choice—take that, or none.

— *Thomas Ward*[1]

My mother's stories about Europe had always fascinated me as a child. She often spoke of sailing on the *Mauretania* on the one trip she made back home. She regaled my family with the ship's beauty and elegance—its polished mahogany bars, exquisite stairways, and its record time in crossing the Atlantic. I lived and breathed my mother's glories, but it wasn't until I was 33 that I made my first trip to Europe and realized what had inspired her stories. I was determined to visit the great capitals of Europe and walk in my mother's footsteps, not as a tourist but as a businessman and an academic.

[1]Thomas Ward, "England's Reformation," 1688.

Tapping into the European Psyche

I made my first trip to London in 1979. Shortly after landing, I discovered that the baggage handlers were on strike. Since the carousels were not working, we had to pick through piles of luggage that the management brought out by hand. This unlucky incident reminded me of a satirical line from the Peter Sellers movie, *I'm All Right Jack*, a comedy that satirized the trade unions, workers, and their bosses: "We do not and cannot accept the principle that incompetence justifies dismissal. That is victimization." The Brits certainly knew how to make fun of themselves.

The United Kingdom, and London in particular, had changed dramatically during the Thatcher era. Although the economy was still bad, the country felt far more functional. It was also becoming more international. Spirits were buoyed by the successful war in the Falkland Islands. I finally began to find the London of my mother's stories.

Starting new exchanges in Europe, in some instances, was more difficult than in the United States. Futures and options markets had some presence in Amsterdam, London, and Paris, but were absent on the rest of the continent in the early 1980s. The international financial community gradually came to accept them over the next 20 years.

European environmental policy makers and NGOs were skeptical about market-based solutions to climate change, just as they had been skeptical of financial futures during the 1980s. Taxes were the policy tool of choice. However, the public sensibility regarding climate change was already a part of the European psyche, in contrast to the United States. In 1990, the European Commission proposed carbon taxes to help reduce greenhouse gas emissions. Policy makers believed that a tax on carbon caused higher costs of production, and therefore translated into higher prices for consumers. These higher prices would decrease demand for industrial and consumer products and result in lower emissions. The "polluter pays" principle was a policy tool supported by the environmentalists but opposed by large emitters like utilities, energy producers, and manufacturing companies. In particular, the carbon tax targeted heavy industry such as cement and steel.

The success story of SO_2 emissions reductions often fell on deaf ears in Europe. Nonetheless, we remained determined to either start a new exchange in Europe or partner with an existing futures market.

I continued to lecture in London and throughout the European continent between 1990 and 2000. Florence Pierre arranged a keynote address on emissions trading in Paris sponsored by the Ministry of the Environment, and a fellow board member at Sustainable Performance Group arranged a similar conference sponsored by the Club of Vienna. To reiterate, following the approval of Kyoto, attitudes toward markets grew gradually less hostile.

The process of institution-building in Europe began picking up momentum in 2001, with country-level initiatives taken by Denmark, the United Kingdom, the Netherlands, Sweden, and Norway. There was a landmark event two years earlier.

A Brief History of European Cap-and-Trade

The government of Denmark ran a mandatory cap-and-trade pilot program between 2001 and 2003 that was limited to eight electricity generators. The program involved an absolute cap on emissions, initially set at the current level of demand for electricity, to be lowered over time. Domestically, Denmark was disciplined in achieving energy savings. However, because Sweden and Norway depended heavily on hydropower for electricity generation and were experiencing periods of low rainfall, Denmark's reductions in CO_2 emissions were largely offset by exporting electricity to its neighbors.[2] Because of this leakage issue, Danish cap-and-trade essentially became a tax on electricity exports. The fine for noncompliance was £5.4 per tonne of CO_2, and trading was limited.[3]

In April 2002, the United Kingdom began a voluntary cap-and-trade program, the first economy-wide scheme in the world

[2]Adapted from Sigurd Lauge Pedersen, "The Danish CO_2 Emissions Trading System," *Review of European Community and International Environmental Law* 9, no. 3 (Oxford, UK: Blackwell Publishers Ltd., 2000).

[3]Ibid.

(*continued*)

A Brief History of European Cap-and-Trade (*Continued*)

covering all greenhouse gases.[4] The program included sector-based energy intensity targets but excluded utilities. Corporations were encouraged to participate through incentive programs instituted by the government. The government set aside £215 million in incentive payments (£30 million a year after taxes) through a government-subsidized auction for companies that joined the program as direct participants.[5] Companies from the private sector participated, including British Petroleum. In 1997, BP launched an internal trading program across its 150 business units, aiming to reduce greenhouse gas emissions from their operations to 10 percent below 1990 levels by 2010. Each unit was assigned a quote of emissions permits and was given the option of achieving compliance through emissions reduction or purchasing reduction credits from other BP units.[6] There was some price discovery and it was reported that internal prices were $7.60 per ton of CO_2.[7]

In the meantime, the Dutch and Norwegian governments were also studying cap-and-trade pilot programs. The Dutch government had been engaged in discussions with industry since 1997 regarding an emissions trading program for NO_x and launched a market trading simulation in early 2001. Norway had been active in climate policy since the late 1980s and began working on

---

[4]"Framework for the UK Emissions Trading Scheme," UK Department for Environmental, Food and Rural Affairs, 2001.

[5]"Appraisal of Years 1–4 of the UK Emissions Trading Scheme," Report by ENVIROS Consulting commissioned for the UK Department of Environment, Food and Rural Affairs, December 2006.

[6]Gerry Hueston, "Beyond Petroleum—Learning to Achieve Prosperity through Sustainability," West Australian Business Leaders Breakfast, Perth, West Autralia, August 3, 2005.

[7]David G. Victor and Josh C. House, "BP's Emission Trading System," *Energy Policy* 34 (2006): 2100–2112.

A Brief History of European Cap-and-Trade (*Continued*)

plans for a domestic emissions trading scheme to begin in 2005. Once it came to the attention of policy makers that there was a European pilot program in the works, European countries began redirecting their independent efforts in anticipation of eventually converging as member states of the EU ETS.[8]

[8]On the Dutch program, see A. M. Sholtz, B. Van Amburg, and V. K. Wochnick, "An Enhanced Rate-Based Emission Trading Program for NO_X: The Dutch Model," *Scientific World Journal* 1, Suppl 2 (2001): 984–993. On the Norwegian program, see Royal Norwegian Ministry of the Environment, "The Norwegian Emissions Trading System," presentation to ICAO Workshop: Aviation and Carbon Markets, Montreal, June 18, 2008.

Two years earlier, the European Commission had become proactive and urged the Union to develop a specific policy in response to climate change. The Commission published a green paper in 2000 that discussed greenhouse gas emissions trading within the European Union and more or less took the EU's implementation of cap-and-trade for granted.[9]

In the early days of the discussions on the design of the EU ETS, I made frequent visits to Brussels and London to brief policy makers on our experience with voluntary and mandatory emissions markets in the United States. During those visits, I was impressed by the high degree of professionalism and knowledge of people like Peter Vis from the European Union Environment Commission and Henry Derwent, international climate change director for the United Kingdom.

The EU program was named the EU Emissions Trading Scheme. A newly adopted policy allocated free emission allowances, called EU Allowances (EUAs), to EU members, but allowed countries to auction

[9]"Green Paper on Greenhouse Gas Emissions within the European Union," Commission of the European Communities, Brussels, August 3, 2000.

up to 5 percent of their allowances. This was to be increased to 10 percent once the Kyoto compliance period began in 2008. The EU ETS originally included only CO_2, but was later extended to include other greenhouse gases as well in Phase II of the program (2008 to 2012), which coincided with the Kyoto compliance period.

A provision of the EU ETS stated that any unused allowances during Phase I of the program could not be used in the Kyoto compliance period from 2008 to 2012. While the environmental rationale for this provision was clear, it almost caused a disaster in the markets. I remember warning the EU officials in Brussels that this might result in much lower CO_2 prices in 2007, and therefore hurt the credibility of the scheme. The senior staff understood the dangers of no banking, but believed this way to be the only way to obtain a buy-in from the environmentalists. Indeed, given that the total allocation of allowances exceeded actual emissions, prices of CO_2 were driven to close to zero in 2007.

The EU ETS process moved quickly, and a directive was published stating that a three-year pilot program would commence on January 1, 2005.[10] We had just conducted our first auction at CCX when we learned of this new opportunity. "First to market" had been our rallying cry, and time was limited. We had to launch an exchange in Europe if we wanted to maintain our leadership role outside of the United States.

ICE and CCX Collaborate

Our outside counsel advised us that it could take several years to establish a new futures exchange in Europe. It was more expedient to form a joint venture with an existing European exchange to expedite the process. After considering several different partners, we chose ICE to serve as our technology provider and function as the new exchange's regulatory platform. ICE had the trading screens, and a large number of

[10]Directive 2003/87/EC of the European Parliament and of the Council of October 13, 2003: "Establishing a Scheme for GHG Emission Allowance Trading within the Community and Amending Council," Director 96/61/EC, *Official Journal of the European Union*, October 25, 2003.

their users were banks and energy companies. It was their comparative advantage and consequently ours. Many of ICE's members like BP and Shell were already actively trading on the exchange. I was also on ICE's board of directors and on good terms with the exchange's CEO and management team.

While the International Petroleum Exchange, now acquired by ICE and renamed ICE Futures, had floundered in the 1980s with a gas and oil contract, it had since been energized by an odd set of circumstances. When Saddam Hussein invaded Kuwait in 1990, NYMEX was forced to close while IPE, which was owned by ICE, stayed open, a happenstance that enabled IPE to become a force in the world energy markets. This was similar to the CBOT's open doors on Columbus Day, following the Fed's decision to target money supply instead of interest rates in 1979. The lesson to be gleaned from both events was that we would have to lean toward a world that permitted 24-hour trading, irrespective of national holidays. CCX's linkage with ICE prepared us for that eventuality, ensuring a low-cost access to existing energy traders. Such an alliance also made sense from ICE's point of view, insofar as coal and emissions trading would attract new users to the exchange's suite of energy products.

I informed the CFO of ICE of CCX's desire to establish a joint venture with ICE. T he negotiations with ICE took us close to six months, and presented a number of hurdles. For example, would it be possible under UK laws and regulations to operate a new exchange while delegating its compliance and electronic platform to an existing regulated exchange? Fortunately, this turned out to be feasible.

The deal between ICE and CCX was announced in April 12, 2004. Our partnership with ICE resulted in a new entity, which we named the European Climate Exchange (ECX), to be owned by CCX but operating as an independent exchange. In late April, we announced that ICE and CCX would work together to provide a platform for a futures market in European emissions allowances. As part of the agreement, CCX would grant ICE a license to list CCX's EU products on its electronic platform. CCX was responsible for writing the emissions futures and options contracts, ECX was in charge of marketing them, and ICE helped with the marketing efforts and provided all the necessary regulatory services. The final deal called for a revenue share of 75 percent for ECX and 25 percent for ICE, with ECX bearing some technology costs and all product development and marketing expenses. The agreement lasted until 2010, to be renegotiated prior to termination. The contract provided incentives for both parties not to seek new partners for a limited time if the agreement were not renewed in 2010. It also provided a disincentive for CCX to sell ECX to ICE's competitors. We were all very optimistic about the partnership.

In addition to launching a futures exchange in the United States, we now faced the challenge of being able to raise additional capital to fund the new European venture. Fortunately, our agreement with ICE and effective marketing of the pilot program facilitated this capital raise. We had a one-for-one rights offering, whereby the original investors were given the right to buy the same amount of shares that they had initially purchased and at the same price. Once Invesco agreed to buy 29 percent of the offering, it became apparent that the underwriting would be successful. We landed some new subscribers that had passed on the first offering, and were slightly oversubscribed. We sold another 15 million shares at £1 per share, the price of the original offering. The proceeds were used to launch CCFE in addition to ECX. Our bankers and Neil Eckert were superb in their roles.

Establishing ECX

Peter Koster, the CEO of Fortis's FCM, was a former board member at Liffe. He was prudent and spoke infrequently. When he did speak, however, his remarks were intelligent and pithy. Peter was coming to Chicago with a colleague, Albert de Haan, and wanted to meet. Fortis had set up an entity called New Values with Rabobank. The purpose of the new joint venture was to set up a trading platform for spot, forward, and futures contracts on EUAs. New Values was later disbanded because Rabobank wanted to focus on spot and forward transactions, while Fortis wanted to focus on futures.

New Values was interested in buying or entering into a joint agreement with CCX. I kept this in mind, and after the deal between

ICE and CCX was announced, I asked Peter if he was interested in serving as the CEO of ECX. He thought it was a great opportunity. Neil later interviewed Peter and recommended that we hire him. Peter joined the company several months later and hired Albert as commercial director. Albert worked in the power sector and knew many of the players. They were later joined by Sara Stahl, a young chemist who had worked on emissions trading at the European Commission in Brussels. She was an articulate young woman with a no-nonsense attitude, the only original employee who stayed through with the company in its brief history.

In Chicago, the CCX team worked on the research and development of ECX, and have ECX focus on marketing. Mike Walsh managed the CCX research team and they quickly started working on demand and supply fundamentals for the EU ETS. What remained for us to do was to design the contract itself, which was my favorite part. This was straightforward, given our prior experiences. The salient features of the contract, which would be named European Union Allowances (EUAs), are listed in Table 22.1.

There was some dissension regarding the tick size. From the standpoint of reducing transaction costs, I thought it should be €0.01. However, the team in Europe thought it should be higher. I yielded on the issue and we went with €0.05. Determining the launch date was a trickier ordeal. Conventional wisdom suggested that for a futures market to emerge, there had to be a well-developed spot market. In order for a spot market to emerge, there needed to be a location that enabled spot deliveries. In the case of electronic carbon allowances, this location was an emissions registry, an electronic warehouse for EUAs. The EU had proposed building a registry for each of the participating nations. However, there was one small problem. There were no registries operational as of 2004. In their absence, the market consisted of a few forward deals in brokered markets. If we simply let the dealers and brokers develop relationships with the customers, the market could evolve with a bias toward over-the-counter (OTC) deals, making it harder to develop a futures market. To solve this problem, I suggested that we make a bold decision: to go ahead with the futures launch in the absence of a spot market or certain delivery location.

Table 22.1 ICE ECX EUA Futures: Contract Specifications

Unit of Trading	One lot of 1,000 Emissions Allowances. Each emissions allowance being an entitlement to emit one ton of carbon dioxide equivalent gas.
Minimum trading size	1 lot
Quotation	Euro (€) and Euro cent (c) per metric tonne
Tick size	€0.05 per tonne (that is, €10 per lot)
Minimum and maximum price fluctuation	€0.05/no limit
Contract months	March, June, September, December contract months from December 2005 to March 2008; and then December contract months only from December 2008 to December 2012.
Expiry day	Last Monday of the Contract month. However, if the last Monday is a Non-Business Day or there is a Non-Business Day in the 4 days following the last Monday, the last day of trading will be the penultimate Monday of the delivery month. When the penultimate Monday of the delivery month falls on a Non-Business Day, or there is a Non-Business Day in the four days immediately following the penultimate Monday, the last day of trading shall be the antepenultimate Monday of the delivery month. The Exchange shall from time to time confirm, in respect of each contract month, the date upon which trading is expected to cease.
Trading system	Trading will occur on the IPE's electronic trading platform IPE ETS (also known as the ICE Platform), which is accessible through WebICE or through an IPE-confirmed Independent Software Vendor.
Trading hours	08:00 hours to 17:00 hours GMT/BST.
Settlement prices	Trade-weighted average during the daily closing period or Quoted Settlement Prices at the Exchange's discretion.

Table 22.1 (*Continued*)

VAT and taxes	Awaiting confirmation pending discussions with UK's HM Customs & Excise.
Delivery	The Contracts are physically deliverable by the transfer of emission allowances from the Person Holding Account of the Selling Clearing Member at a Registry to the Person Holding Account of LCH.Clearnet at a Registry, and from the Person Holding Account of LCH at that Registry to the Person Holding Account of the Buying Clearing Member at a Registry. Delivery is between Clearing Members and LCH during a Delivery Period. The Delivery Period is the period beginning at 19:00 hours on the business day following the last trading day and ending at 19:30 hours on the third business day following that last trading day. There are provisions for delayed and failed delivery within the Contract Rules.
Clearing and contract security	LCH acts as central counterparty to all trades and guarantees the financial performance of the IPE contracts registered in the name of its Members.
Margin	Margin Variation and initial margin are charged in the usual manner by LCH.

Naturally, there was some uncertainty in drawing the contract specifications. We expected that the UK registry, once established, would have maximum traffic, due to London's financial might and the registry being the one that was closest to completion. Our first deliveries were in December, and we took a bold risk in denoting London to be a delivery point even though there wasn't a registry in place. I knew that the French and the Germans did not have the same institutional capacity and willingness to lead that the British had. Since the flow of allowances across individual European national registries was not feasible at the time, we expected some basis risk based on the delivery point. Mike was already at work designing financial instruments that allowed users to hedge these risks.

Thankfully we never had to use them, as the UK registry was built in May, a month after our launch. The EU eventually designed an elaborate electronic transfer system, which served as a "community independent transaction log" through which EUAs could travel from the registry of one country to that of another, very much like an electronic superhighway. Today, this system provides seamless transfer of allowances within the EU, promoting spot and futures transactions.

Neil and I decided to establish the headquarters of ECX in Amsterdam, a city with a trading heritage dating back to 1602 with the founding of the Amsterdam Stock Exchange.[11] More importantly, the choice of London, Paris, or Frankfurt might have led to adverse political and business consequences, as the three countries saw each other as rivals.

To market the exchange, it was critical to amass enough buyers and sellers on the opening day to send a clear signal that we were the leaders in this new environmental space. Utilities already had trading desks, so they simply had to be educated about the new EU pilot program. Trading was a natural adjunct to the utilities' purchases of coal and sales of power. Energy producers also had trading desks.

ECX held a prelaunch seminar at the ICE offices shortly before the launch of trading. We expected a medium-size turnout, but actual attendance was far beyond modest. People began drifting into the room about 15 minutes before the seminar. By the time we began, only standing room remained. Many major oil companies, even those who refused to join CCX, were present, as were utilities and commercial banks with trading desks. I delivered some brief opening remarks before Peter and Albert discussed the contract details and the opportunities for hedgers and speculators. The groundwork laid by the various pilot programs in Europe played a constructive role in helping this pre-Kyoto pilot program. The years of effort devoted to building our brand throughout Europe, and the extensive prelaunch marketing was finally reaping its fruits.

In order to build the transatlantic bond, showcase the brand, and foster cross-marketing between America and Europe, Mike and Rafael Marques traveled to Europe in late January 2005 to join in our planned

---

[11]Lodewijk Petram, "The World's First Stock Exchange: How the Amsterdam Market for Dutch East India Company Shares Became a Modern Securities Market, 1602–1700" (dissertation, University of Amsterdam, January 28, 2011).

ECX road shows for Paris, London, Frankfurt, Cologne, Madrid, and Amsterdam. We were trying to cover as many people and territories as possible in a short period of time.

During this six-city trip, the CCX team tried to recruit the North American divisions of European corporations while espousing the use of ECX. Bayer, a German chemical and pharmaceutical company, was already a member of CCX. Rafael made a special trip to Bayer's headquarters, which had led the company's membership. The halls at the Bayer factory just outside of Cologne looked like a university hall, with every office name ending with a PhD title. One of the company's representatives made a comment that Rafael would never forget: "In CCX, you asked for industry's input to inform the design of the system. In Europe, the EU designed the system and then asked industry for input."

We began trading on April 22, 2005, and in doing so, became the second exchange to offer futures trading in EUAs. Earlier, Nordpool had started to trade EUAs on February 11, 2005, and had a small but growing volume. The first ECX trade took place between BP and E.ON UK for 10,000 tonnes of CO_2 at €17.05.[12] The trade was cleared by Caylon and ABN AMRO. The first day saw 108,000 tonnes (108 lots) traded, with the price ranging from €16.80 to €17.40. The fact that it was also Earth Day and Ellen's birthday made it even more symbolic for me. A small group of the young crowd in the Chicago office stayed up overnight to witness the first trades.

Following the opening of ECX, carbon spot and futures exchanges proliferated throughout 2005. The European Energy Exchange (EEX) started in Leipzig on March 9, BlueNext in Paris on June 24, Energy Exchange Austria (EXAA) in Vienna on June 28. In February, even the Johannesburg Stock Exchange (JSE) listed a Certificate of Emissions Reduction carbon credit note futures, but it never took off. There was a gush of carbon funds that started to make their appearance in London.

Hedgers were early adopters and ratified the new concept of emissions trading. Many first movers wanted us to succeed and were happy

---

[12]The trade was cleared by Calyon Financial SNC (a subsidiary of Calyon Corporate and Investment Bank) and ABN AMRO Futures Limited. "Trading Starts in First Carbon Futures Contracts," Press Release, ICE, April 22, 2005.

to endorse ECX, thereby allowing us to use their early adoption as a sales tool while educating hundreds of users.

A major marketing effort directed toward the futures industry took place at the Swiss Futures and Options Association's annual conference in Burgenstock in September 2005. It was an opportune moment to market ECX. Since Neil had just left Brit Insurance to join CLE, I figured it was also an excellent opportunity to introduce him to the key players in the worldwide futures industry. I was teased because some of the panels included members who were retiring from the industry. I should have been among them but being a restless soul, I was busy promoting the new EU allowance futures contract.

I ran into Jim Kharouf, a Chicago-based reporter who covered the futures industry. I suggested that we grab a drink. I had an idea that could change his life: "These new markets need a focused newsletter on climate change. Carbon could become one of the biggest commodities in the world." At the outset of financial futures, I shared similar thoughts with the CEO of Telerate and the founder of Bloomberg News. Jim was fascinated by the successes of these companies and hadn't realized that it was the publication of prices and analytics for interest rate futures that drove their initial success. Jim Kharouf eventually went on to publish the *Environmental Markets Newsletter*, while we helped build awareness in other broadcast and print media. ECX picked up attention in European publications such as the *International Herald Tribune, Financial Times*, and *Euromoney*.[13] We still had a lot of other work left to do, however, in order to ensure the success of the markets.

The objective of ECX was to become the dominant allowance market in the EU. In addition to hosting seminars throughout Europe, we also held one-on-one meetings with the companies from the power sector and industrial corporations. Due to his background in the futures

---

[13]Matthew Saltmarsh, "Market for Emissions Picks Up Steam as Kyoto Protocol Takes Hold," *International Herald Tribune*, July 6, 2005, 19; Kevin Morrison, "Climate Exchange in the Black," *Financial Times*, October 1, 2005, 16; Richard Orange, "Tonnes of Trouble for EU on Pollution," *The Business*, January 9, 2005; Deborah Kimbell, "Euro Carbon Trading Graduates to Cash Settlement," *Euromoney*, February 2005, 24.

industry, Peter focused on financial players while Albert and Sara concentrated on the industrial emitters. The list of target companies was easy to determine, as the EU and its member states published lists of the largest emitters. Among the groups ECX marketed to, the industrial companies were the most difficult. For most industrial companies, futures trading was a new concept that had to be explained.

A number of surprises awaited us. Albert and Sara gave a seminar in Warsaw. Language was a barrier so a translator was hired. When the Q&A session began, there wasn't a single question. Some of that could be explained away by Polish culture—it was not in their tradition to ask questions publicly. More important than that, however, was because the translator didn't know how to translate futures into Polish. In another instance, language would become our savior. The ECX office manager in Amsterdam was Czech, and became active in recruiting CEZ, the largest utility in the Czech Republic.

There was no language barrier in Germany. Although EEX in Leipzig was where most utilities traded power, they did not have a tradition in futures trading since they ran a spot market for electricity. RWE, E.ON, and other German utilities made ECX their trading platform of choice, which helped us attract other German industrial companies.

During those years, Peter, Albert, and Sara had made more than 200 flights to and from Europe. They spent more time in planes and hotels than on the ground. In addition to this, ECX had conducted more than 50 group presentations in total, not including innumerous one-on-one meetings in our major cities on the continent. As in any new market, going to where the users were located was critical.

As in the case of CCX, we needed market makers. Although the European banks were there from the outset, Chicago was once again the source of much of the initial liquidity for ECX. Tradelink and other proprietary shops in Chicago provided liquidity for new markets. We also found other liquidity providers in a Manhattan building referred to jokingly as the Hedge Fund Hotel, due to the large number of hedge funds that were located there.

Volume and open interest grew slowly in the opening days, but this was something we were accustomed to. Exponential growth followed. The volume traded reached 94 million tonnes in 2005, 453 million tonnes in 2006, and more than 1 billion tonnes in 2007. Open interest also increased dramatically. Figure 22.1 provides graphs of volume and open interest for those first three years and beyond.

On April 25, 2006, Sara was attending a presentation by the Dutch government when an official casually mentioned that the Netherlands had been allocated more allowances than it needed. Coupled with the fact that none of the allowances issued under Phase I of the Kyoto Protocol could be banked and used in Phase II, which started in 2008, the announcement caused many attendees to leave the room in order to start shorting the futures contract. From that point on, the December 2007 futures began to fall until they finally approached zero at their expiration. Figure 22.2 is a chart of prices of the December 2007 and December 2008 contracts during the pilot program.

Despite the price plunge, the market was able to emerge with only a few small scars. This was largely because it had already been anticipated. There was a flurry of brutal press reports and finger pointing right

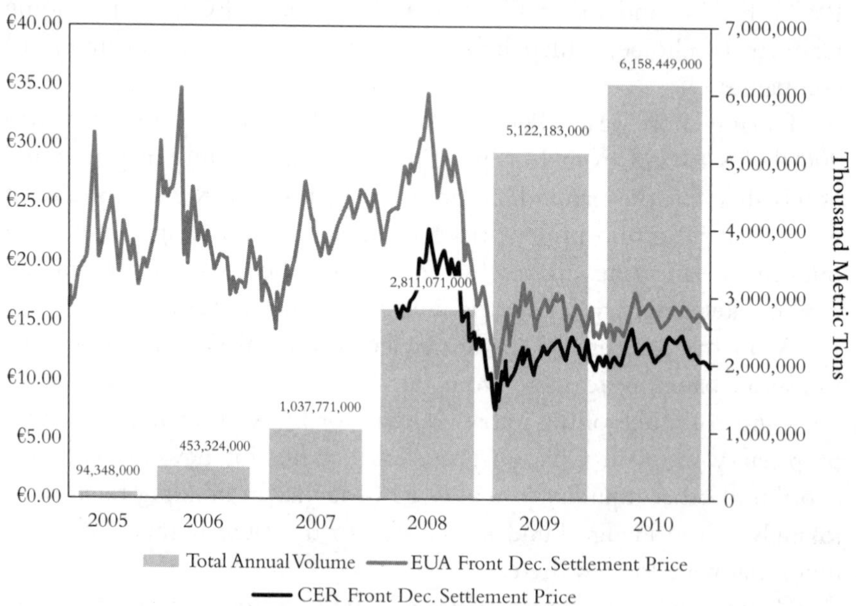

Figure 22.1a ECX Annual Total Volume and Settlement Price
Source: Data from IntercontinentalExchange.

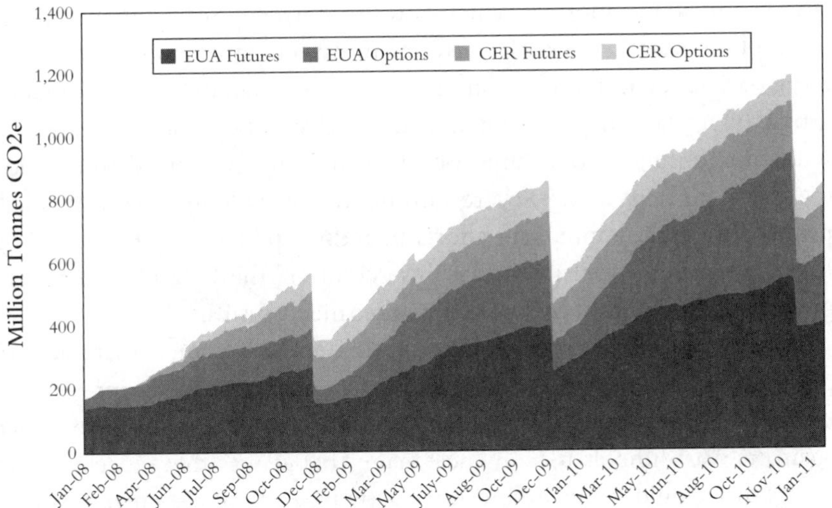

Figure 22.1b Total Open Interest
Source: Data from IntercontinentalExchange.

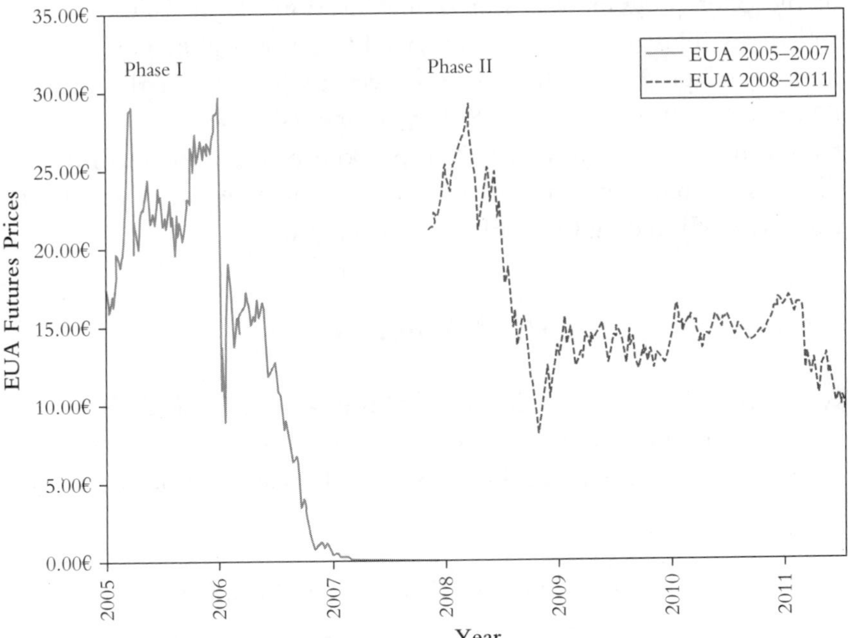

Figure 22.2 EUA Futures Prices
Source: Data from IntercontinentalExchange.

after the incident, most of which was uninformed. Some attributed the price plunge to the lack of emissions measurements before 2005, leading to asymmetric information and initial uncertainty.[14] Environmental groups were fast to point out that the EU had been far too generous with distributing carbon emission allowances in the period from 2005 to 2007, and in doing so, rewarding major polluters with windfall profits and undermining the efforts to reduce pollution.[15] Even leading U.S. newspapers proclaimed that this "colored" the U.S. plan to reduce greenhouse gas emissions through market mechanisms.[16]

Criticisms withered with time, but some still argued that the €15 price of EUAs was not enough to induce a change in behavior—it was estimated that behavior would change at a price of €35 and above. Once again, it was difficult to convince many that it was the expectation of prices that would stimulate inventive activity, and not the current prices. Great caution had to be exercised when making the assumption that current prices and current technology would prevail in the future.

Another criticism was that the €0.05 expiration price at the end of the pilot program was seen as justification of the failure of cap-and-trade. This missed the point that ECX was a pilot rather than a full-fledged program, whose purpose was to prepare for the Phase II (2008 to 2012) of the EU ETS. Environmental benefits were incidental and meant to be just that. The purpose of the pilot was first and foremost to build institutions and human capital. We were still in the early days of building the market infrastructure.

ECX Moves On

At the end of 2008, Peter Koster left his post as CEO at ECX to pursue other opportunities. We reflected on how much had changed around us. Over the preceding two years, London had been gradually

---

[14]"SGI-Orbeo Carbon Credit Index," *Société Générale Index*, February 2008.

[15]"Question Marks over EU CO_2 Trading Scheme," *EurActiv*, June 29, 2007.

[16]Steven Mufson, "Europe's Problems Color U.S. Plans to Curb Carbon Gases," *Washington Post*, April 9, 2007.

transformed into the financial center of emissions trading. In less than three years following our IPO, six UK companies in the emissions trading space were listed on the Alternative Investment Market (AIM): XL Tech, Trading Emissions, AgCert, Ecosecurities, Econoergy, and Camco. The human capital in London also continued to grow. Engineering firms, consultancies, accountants, lawyers, and information technology providers were populating the city. Given these considerations, we made arrangements to close the Amsterdam office and move the ECX headquarters to London.

Patrick Birley had been CEO of an exchange in South Africa, and had recently moved back to London to work for London Clearing House (LCH). When he became available, we offered him the position of CEO at ECX. Patrick's eloquence and charisma made him an excellent salesman. He was very clinical about business and could speak his mind and assert his opinions candidly—a quality that came in extremely handy a short while later. He also continued the tradition of relentless marketing throughout the continent. Patrick and his team were constantly on the road.

Patrick's first challenge came with our intention to launch a CER futures contract. By 2008, the necessary conditions and infrastructure for a CER futures market were in place and we were keen to establish a lead. ECX, however, needed LCH's cooperation as its clearinghouse to list a CER contract. Under our current contract, ICE was our technology and regulatory services provider and we shared LCH as our clearinghouse. However, ICE announced that it was moving the open interest on the exchange to its own clearinghouse, ICE Clear Europe. LCH wasn't amused at the prospect of one of its largest customers forming its own clearinghouse. This led to LCH's refusal to clear any new ICE products, including our allowance futures contract. They didn't want to lavish additional resources on a client who would soon disappear.

By this time, I had already resigned from the ICE board in order to pursue the interests of CLE.[17] Even if I remained, my status as an

---

[17]I was a director at Intercontinental Exchange, Inc. from November 2002 to March 2008.

independent director was eliminated. As a customer, ECX had diminished input in ICE's decision to move its clearing operations. If another exchange were to list the CER contract, CLE's very existence could be threatened if another exchange gained a foothold in the space. After endless personal pleas and letters, LCH refused to budge. Convinced that we had the law on our side, Patrick urged us to take LCH to court—a decision that the ICE board of directors agreed with. The United States was a very litigious country and its lawsuits were often frivolous. The same could not be said about the United Kingdom. We hired a Queen's Counsel[18] to represent us, and a week before the trial, LCH finally relented and agreed to clear the contract. ECX listed the CER contract, and our hegemony of the emissions trading space continued.

Patrick built his team carefully and made sure that our ECX offices were physically separate from the rest of CLE. He wanted to establish the exchange as an entity that was separate from the holding company, and his team appreciated the newfound privacy and identity. It was important for the image of the exchange and helped Patrick market our products. The exchange's trading volume and open interest reflected his hard work. Over the course of the next two years, our volume went from 1,037,000 tons at the end of 2007 to 2,831,000 by the end of 2008. It further climbed to 5,122,183 tons by the end of 2009. By this time, ECX had consistently held more than 85 percent of the EU market share among seven odd exchanges competing in the space. The overall market was maturing as well. Given the total allocation in the EU ETS was about 2 billion tons, ECX volume alone indicated that the market was beginning to turn over multiple times.

Volume continued to grow during the first half of 2010, and ECX became a formidable force in the exchange world. The future was as bright as ever. The open interest of the new allowance contracts eventually exceeded that of Brent Crude oil, and carbon emerged as the single largest commodity in Europe as measured by open interest. As of August 26, 2010, combined open interest in ECX CER and

---

[18]A Queen's Counsel is a lawyer who has been appointed by the Crown in the Commonwealth to wear a silk gown and take precedence over the other lawyers in court. This honor is bestowed only upon on those have practiced law for at least 10 years.

EUA futures and options contracts surpassed one billion tons for the first time and stood at 1,035,091 contracts. This was a large number compared to the 852,971 in open interest for Brent Crude that same day.[19]

There were some minor technical obstacles that had to be overcome. Almost all of the volume was concentrated in the current December contract. There was some trading in the March contract because the compliance of the previous years had to be achieved and reported by April. The June and September contracts hardly traded at all. The companies were able to hedge their compliance needs until 2012. However, the efficacy of the hedges would have been improved if the hedges were more coincidental with the contracts that were listed. Companies faced unnecessary basis risk as a result. Additionally, despite the lack of certainty regarding the continuation of emissions trading in the European Union after 2012, open interest continued to grow.

We continued to innovate, adding CER options and futures contracts with expirations from 2013 to 2020—past the initial Kyoto compliance period—because there was a market demand for it. We believed that the market would welcome these deferred contracts, and it did. The market was sending an implicit message about the expectations and needs of the European industrial community. Policy makers took note of this, and the confidence shown by the markets was widely publicized.

One successful innovation led to a chain reaction of other innovations. We introduced a one-day futures contract to compete with Bluenext, which dominated the spot market for EUAs. We also signed an agreement with XShares to design and market the world's first exchange-traded fund (ETF) for carbon, named the AirShares Carbon Fund, which began trading in December 2008. This was a failure because of regulatory issues and uncertainty regarding the economic value of the product, which was derived from EUAs and CERs.

---

[19]"As of August 26, 2010, combined open interest in the ECX CER and EUA futures and options contracts surpassed 1 billion tonnes for the first time and stood at 1,035,091 contracts. Compare this with 852,971 in open interest for Brent Crude that same day." Data taken from "ICE Daily Volume and Open Interest Records: ECX," *Commodities Now*, August 26, 2010, and "Daily Volumes for ICE Brent Crude Futures," ICE, August 26, 2010.

The Economic Value of an Exchange

I had previously spoken about the value of exchanges in price discovery, hedging, and providing an alternative market for the purchase and sale of allowances. I will leave it to others to determine the value of hedging and the value of price discovery, and focus solely on the *economic* value of the exchange, as demonstrated by ECX. It is also a story of reduced transaction costs.

The same exercise we did for SO_2 allowances can be applied to EUAs as well. The initial bid-offer spread on the exchange was between €0.20 and €0.25. By the end of 2010, it had narrowed to about €0.02. Assuming a €0.20 difference and the fact that 5 billion tonnes were transferred in the spot market, there was approximately a €1 billion value in savings to the participants in 2010 alone in the spot market. ECX witnessed the delivery of 165 million tonnes. Assuming no fees by the exchange and a $20 OTC brokerage fee per contract, or about €0.14 per tonne, the cost savings enabled by the exchange amounted to €30.7 million.[20]

The EUA futures contract, like the SO_2 futures and interest rate futures contracts before it, was an example of a good derivative.

Reflections on the Success of ECX

The EU ETS had been a dramatic success, and so had ECX. According to A. Denny Ellerman from the MIT Sloan School of Management, "The ability to use CERs and ERUs for compliance in the EU ETS has made the price of EUAs the reference price for the world carbon market."[21] ECX had become the benchmark exchange for carbon prices.

[20]1,000 tonnes per contract. Using a 1.18608 exchange rate from December 2005, $20 per contract roughly equals €16.86 per contract. Thus, (€0.20 – €16.86/1000) × (165,000,000) = €30,217,726, or €30.2 million saved. For purposes of simplification, assume no fees by the exchange or other transaction costs.

[21]A. Denny Ellerman, Frank J. Convery, Christian de Perthuis, and Emilie Alberola, *Pricing Carbon: The European Union Emissions Trading Scheme* (New York: Cambridge University Press, 2010).

The reasons behind the success of the scheme can be traced back to public policy in the European Union. Environmental markets work where there is legal and regulatory clarity. In this case, clear and unambiguous property rights were mandated and reinforced by the Kyoto Protocol. The consummation of the Protocol also drove the EU to move forward with a voluntary pilot program. In particular, the program succeeded because it was supported by the consensus that had been built between the EU member states, sovereign governments, and industry sectors. When the United Kingdom and Denmark started their own voluntary pilot programs, most companies felt that the scale of these efforts were too small and did not convey the urgency to learn about emissions trading. With the launch of the mandatory EU ETS, however, these multinational efforts gained more gravitas, and were able to reinforce the validity of voluntary programs like ECX.

Like ECX, CCX was a pilot program that achieved all of its objectives as a proof of concept. It facilitated hedging, price discovery, and created an alternative place to make and take delivery of allowances. Unlike ECX, however, CCX lacked an enabling legislation. Why climate legislation never passed in the United States is a subject of much speculation, and is a tale in and of itself. In the end, the worldwide price of carbon remained determined by the supply and demand for allowances and CERs on ECX.

The Acid Rain Program of 1990, coupled with the implementation skills of the EPA, facilitated the proliferation of an OTC market in SO_2 and NO_x, and subsequently the emergence of a successful and transparent market for both types of emissions. This ultimately dissolved because the government failed to provide legal certainty regarding the extension of the Clean Air Act. Instead of using market-based cap-and-trade, our federal government turned to traditional command-and-control. It is interesting to recall that during the days of negotiating Kyoto, it was the United States that led the efforts to introduce emissions trading as a viable tool. The Europeans were skeptical of the idea and opposed it. How the tables turned. Europe became the leader in market-based policy tools, while the United States became the champion of the reverse. The lessons learned in both Europe and the United States can provide valuable insight when implementing environmental policies in emerging countries like India and China.

Letting Go

I visited London frequently to update shareholders and attend board meetings for the Climate Exchange. In spite of the stellar performance of ECX, our stock had been laboring. We were under some pressure to hold a liquidity event by some of our investors. Some investors had large positions and couldn't sell them easily without driving the price of the stock lower. If the exchange were sold, all of their shares would sell at the same price. ICE was the natural purchaser because it knew our business intimately and because of our original contract with them. In fact, we had considered selling the company just before the financial crisis, but were not successful. Now was the time to actively pursue a sale. I had been in constant contact with Jeff Sprecher over the last few years. ICE had bought a 5 percent stake in CLE at a price of £6.5 in 2009. I consulted with Neil, our CFO Matthew Whittell, and the board, and all favored this decision.

ICE and CLE both retained investment bankers. The last hurdle for CLE was to sell the company at the highest possible price. We formed a board committee to oversee the negotiations. Brian Williamson chaired the committee since he was armed with his prior experience in selling Liffe. Sir Laurie Magnus, an investment banker who specialized in insurance, chaired the audit committee. Detail-oriented and extraordinarily competent, Sir Laurie won my favor the moment I met him. We hired JPMorgan to represent us. We also retained Gavin Kelly, a savvy and tough negotiator who was always up for a fight and had done a great job representing CCX. He became our banker when we sold CCX to the reorganized Climate Exchange PLC in 2006. Gavin was Scottish and reminded me of Hamish Campbell in the 1995 film *Braveheart*—the brave childhood friend who had fought with William Wallace to free Scotland. After a four-month period of negotiations and due diligence, we finally agreed to sell CLE to ICE. There was one condition. CCX members, myself included, would be allowed to help with the transition of ownership. Accordingly, I happily agreed to work with ICE until the end of 2010. The final price of the sale was at £7.5 per share, at a 57 percent premium to where the shares were trading. This equated to a value of $604 million.[22] Much of that value was attributable to ECX. To put this in perspective, the NYSE was valued at $5 billion. This meant that CCX was worth close to one-eighth of the world's largest stock exchange, and this was even without regulatory uncertainty. It was indicative of the value of emissions markets.

I had grown emotionally attached to CCX and emissions trading during the past 20 years. I never intended to sell the company. After all, this was a lifetime bet I had taken. My feelings were obviously mixed, but I had no choice. We called our original investors and thanked them individually for their support. I saved the best for last and made a call to Father Francis. We promised to stay in touch. CLE had literally been a blessing to its stockholders, exchange members, participants, and the management teams on both sides of the Atlantic. ECX had since continued to be the preeminent emissions exchange in the world.

In the meantime, other stories of climate exchanges were unfolding in China and India.

[22]"Intercontinental Exchange Announces Acquisition of Climate Exchange," ICE, Press Release, April 30, 2010.

Chapter 23

India

A Promising Beginning

The earth, the air, the land, and the water
Are not an inheritance from our forefathers
But a loan from our children.

—*Mahatma Gandhi*

Centennial Hall was a nondescript, red-brick building on Delaware Street in Minneapolis. As a graduate student at the University of Minnesota, I used to live on the sixth floor, which was reserved for international graduate students. While unpacking on my first day there, I left the door open and hoped that another graduate student would stumble by and say hello. Nobody did.

The room was small and felt solitary, so I wandered to the dining room in the basement, hoping to enjoy a good meal. The food was served cafeteria-style and was very bland. Another disappointment.

I journeyed back to my room. The sixth floor was now filled with students moving into their rooms and milling around in the hallway. The floor turned out to be an international cornucopia of culture, with students from the United States living alongside others from Europe, Asia, Africa, and South America. It was there that I met my Indian friend, Sanjib Mukherji. He carried himself with great elegance. He was somewhat soft-spoken and shy, but this did not conceal his regal bearing. We quickly became friends, and therein began my real education of the Indian subcontinent.

Brahmins and Katyas

My picture of India had been framed by early childhood memories of American-made movies like the 1942 film adaption of Rudyard Kipling's *Jungle Book*, an action and adventure film about an Indian boy, Mowgli, who was raised by wolves. The vivid prose evoked beautiful imagery and excited my imagination. I was Mowgli. I shared his victories in fighting tigers and taming cobras. I also felt his pain as an outsider when he left the wolves to live among human civilization. I always thought, with childish innocence, "Someday I will go to India." I later saw Richard Attenborough's 1982 film, *Gandhi*, which anchored my desire to see India. Gandhi's public life was also chronicled by the photographer Margaret Bourke White. I discovered the original portrait of Gandhi by her that was used for the cover of *Time* magazine in 1948. It proudly sits in my study to this day.

Sanjib was from Kolkata and proud of his Bengali language and culture. He was a Brahmin but had the common touch. We spent endless entertaining evenings with his friends who were either Brahmins[1] or Katyas. In spite of their upper-class upbringing, they were all sympathetic to the tapestry that was India. They felt empathy for the untouchables, pride for the business class of Banias,[2] affection and understanding for the Muslims living in India, and respect for the Parsees. I learned about prejudice from Sanjib's Anglo-Indian friend, who was often cast out of social circles because of his half-English, half-Indian heritage.

---

[1]India's priestly and scholarly social class.

[2]Bania is an occupational caste of bankers, money lenders, dealers in grains and spices, and in modern times, numerous commercial enterprises.

There were no authentic Indian restaurants in the Twin Cities at that time. To my great delight, Sanjib and his Indian roommates had learned to cook for themselves. They taught Ellen how to make a wicked curried chicken dish that we enjoy to this day. I was amazed that Indian food could be made without prepackaged curry powder. I lost touch with Sanjib after graduate school, but I often wondered how he was doing.

I thought of him as the plane landed in New Delhi, India, in 1991. Arif Inayatullah, one of my colleagues at Banque Indosuez, had invited Ellen and me to his wedding in Lahore, Pakistan. We decided to spend some time in India before heading to the wedding.

It was the start of an exciting time in India. The country had just begun the process of economic liberalization under the leadership of Dr. Manmohan Singh, a PhD economist who was then India's finance minister, and now its prime minister. Many years later, the positive impact of these reforms would hit the commodities market, helping me realize my dream of doing business in India.

The two days we spent there felt more like an appetizer in a seven-course meal. Being in India was like an attack on all our bodily senses. We visually devoured the Taj Mahal, tasted the tantalizing spices of Indian cuisine, heard the constant rhythm of honking in the streets and felt the subtropical heat almost charring our skins.

Riding around Delhi with Ellen in a *phut-phut*,[3] I could feel the energy that was India stirring in the air. Forty-four years after leaving its colonial past, India had the ninth-largest economy in the world by GDP purchasing power parity[4] and was on the verge of economic liberalization.[5] India seemed ready for a change. My thoughts were interrupted when a gust of black soot from a street bus hit Ellen and me straight in the face. Pollution was rampant in India.

Without standards for emissions, waste disposal, or water treatment, heavy pollution took its toll on the health and prosperity of India.

---

[3]A phut-phut is a modified Harley-Davidson with a carriage designed to serve as a rickshaw, prevalent in northern India.

[4]Purchasing power parity (PPP) adjusts the exchange rate for two countries so that an identical good in the two countries has the same price.

[5]*World Economic Outlook Database*, International Monetary Fund.

The World Bank estimated that total environmental damage amounted to $10 billion, or 4.5 percent, of GDP in 1992. Of the total, urban air pollution and water degradation accounted for $7 billion in damages alone.[6] Air pollution caused 500,000 premature deaths and 3 to 4 million new cases of chronic bronchitis in 1992.[7] Of 3,119 towns and cities, only 217 had wastewater treatment facilities.[8] With 70 percent of available water polluted, more than one million children died of gastrointestinal diseases in the 1990s.[9]

There must be something the markets could do to help, I thought.

As we left the country, I entertained the idea that the aspirations of a billion Indians had the power to positively transform the country. I was determined to come back under a different banner. Ellen and I went to Lahore for a magnificent three-day wedding before returning to the United States.

India continued to change dramatically in the following 12 years. Its software industry was booming, and the bureaucracy responsible for hindering economic growth during Sanjib's time was now showing slow signs of decay. Change was also afoot in the financial sector. In 2002, the government of India permitted futures trading on a national basis and relaxed many other rules in its commodities regulatory act. This was highly significant given that, prior to this, there had only been regional spot markets regulated at the state level.

India had a long and checkered history with trading. Its rich agricultural commodity base made it an important stop along the Silk Road. The Portuguese, Dutch, French, and British later landed on its shores with more than just trading in mind. The cotton trade association in Mumbai commenced futures trading in 1875, not long after futures trading began at the CBOT. Bullion, jute, and wheat trading were

---

[6]Donald G. McClelland, Mark Hodges, Vijayan Kannan, and Will Knowland, "Urban and Industrial Pollution Programs, India Case Study," Center for Development Information and Evaluation, Agency for International Development, January 23, 2001.

[7]Ibid.

[8]*Our Planet, Our Health: Report of the WHO Commission on Health and Environment* (Geneva, Switzerland: World Health Organization, 1992).

[9]Central Bureau of Health Intelligence, Health Information of India, Ministry of Health and Family Welfare, Government of India, New Delhi, 1995, 1996.

introduced shortly thereafter.[10] However, years of bureaucracy and fear over speculation and its impact on farmers limited trading to regional spot markets. Following the reforms to the Indian Commodities Act,[11] three new national exchanges were established in 2002 and 2003.[12] As part of its efforts to educate and build relations with Indian futures market policy makers and businessmen, the USAID hosted a trip by an Indian delegation to New York, Washington, DC, and Chicago in 2004 to learn more about the U.S. futures exchanges.

CCX hosted a seminar on emissions trading in our offices for the USAID mission. One of the attendees from the Multi-Commodity Exchange (MCX) came back later that afternoon to discuss a linkage. We agreed to speak in the future. After numerous telephone conversations and e-mails, we agreed to license a mini-size European Union Allowance contract to MCX in 2006.[13] This was done to ensure better local price discovery of carbon credits for the growing Indian CDM market besides helping the participants cover the risks associated with selling and buying of carbon credits. I hoped that it would lead to a CCX-type market in India.

The MCX contract on EUAs failed to attract any speculative interest and was dead on arrival. It was simply too far ahead of its time. The Indian Commodity Exchange Act still did not recognize intangibles, such as carbon permits, as a commodity. I recalled my efforts with Phil Johnson in redefining commodities when interest rate futures were first launched in the United States. History seemed to be repeating itself. After much back and forth with the regulators, we ultimately decided to change the contract to a cash-settled instrument, but it, too, failed to gain any traction. I intended to start a market similar to CCX in India,

---

[10]Bullion was introduced in 1920, jute in 1912, and wheat in 1913.

[11]The Indian Commodities Act of 1957 was modified in 2002.

[12]National Multi-Commodity Exchange of India Limited (NMCE) on November 26, 2002; Multi-Commodity Exchange of India Limited (MCX) November 10, 2003; National Commodity and Derivatives Exchange Limited (NCDEX) on December 15, 2003.

[13]D. G. Prasad, "Carbon Credit: Future Is in Commodity Exchanges," *Hindu Business Line*, December 5, 2006.

but had to be patient. A platform had yet to emerge to promote the activities of CCX, ECX, and the CCFE in India. Thankfully, it arrived quicker than I expected.

Building Interest for Offsets

Rajendra "Pachy" Pachuri, my friend of 10 years, the head of The Energy Research Institute (TERI)[14] and the chairman of the Intergovernmental Panel on Climate Change (IPCC), organized a summit in New Delhi, called the Delhi Sustainable Development Summit (DSDS) in 2006. The event has since become one of the globally preeminent sustainable summits. Pachy and I had met at a number of meetings over the years in New York, Washington, DC, and London. He was a true citizen of the world. His commitment to the environment in general, and India in particular, was inspiring. Very few people could be as passionate about their goals and still be reasonable in their approach, and for that reason, Pachy and I readily understood each other.

On February 1, 2006, Pachy invited me to deliver a keynote speech and participate on a panel for a greenhouse gas forum held by the International Emissions Trading Association (IETA) in New Delhi.[15] There was also a CEO forum the day before the summit that I was asked to participate in. The timing was perfect, but it was a logistical nightmare, as I also accepted an invitation to speak at a two-day Credit Lyonnais Securities Asia (CLSA) conference in Tokyo that was scheduled to start on February 6.

Nevertheless, I decided to give the keynote speech on the morning of February 1, take a 6:50 A.M. flight the next day to Mumbai, and fly back to Delhi that evening to speak at the panel the next morning. The following day, I would fly to Tokyo via Bangkok for the CLSA

[14]New Delhi–based TERI is a leading global think tank and India's premier organization involved in environmental and energy policy.

[15]Delhi GHG Forum 2006, January 31–February 1, 2006, Silver Oak, IHC, New Delhi. Program found at www.teriin.org/index.php?option=com_events&task=details&sid=126.

conference. The planning of the itinerary had to be seamless, as every moment of this trip had to be used effectively.

The key was to remain energized at all times, even after flying for an entire day. I followed a routine that worked for me. My flight from Chicago to India was on a Sunday, and I arrived in Delhi on a Tuesday morning. After checking in at the Taj Mahal hotel, I spent an hour on the treadmill and met Murali Kanakasabai at the hotel lobby. Together, we toured art galleries and museums to relax and learned about the historical and contemporary art scene. I was on the Board of the International Center for Photography and they had referred me to a local artist. Her unavailability disappointed me, but there were so much else to see. At the end of the day, Murali and I went back to the hotel for dinner. The hotel was one of those modern edifices with an opulent lobby. It had very little local color except for its authentic restaurants. The highlight of the day was having chicken chettinad for dinner. It was a fiery spicy southern Indian dish that Murali had recommended. It has since become my favorite.

The next morning, I gave the keynote speech at the Indian Habitat Centre. The Centre was like an academic campus and I felt at home. It was a beautiful brick building, built to promote awareness in environmental issues like energy conservation and water, air, noise, and waste pollution. It was a fitting location for the event. After describing the successes of CCX and ECX, I floated the idea of the India Climate Exchange (ICX). The vision was for ICX to be a voluntary cap-and-trade program for Indians, designed by Indians, and made compatible with India's development needs. I knew that developing economies like India were foremost concerned about economic growth, so my environmental solution had to be fine-tuned to support this important goal.

I stressed that CO_2 emissions would initially grow modestly for some period of time before any reductions could be observed. This was analogous to the emissions targets in Ireland and Portugal under the EU ETS. The initial period of the proposed program allowed for learning by doing and would help the Indian industry adapt by building capacity among Indian corporations.

The CCX offset model also provided guidance for how we might approach a similar program in a developing country like India. The country had a large rural base that depended on agriculture and rural industry for livelihood. Gandhi was absolutely right when he said, "India lives in its villages." A billion people depended on this rural population for their food security, so concerns about agriculture and rural development were high among Indians. I explained that by linking the ICX carbon market with specific offset programs in India, we could create a catalyst for economic development, especially in rural areas. Furthermore, by supporting rural projects, Indian corporations would be able to bring about visible transformations in India's villages. This was my vision and I was anxious to learn how my audience would respond to it. The audience welcomed my ideas and the Q&A session was lively.

Next was a meeting with the chairman and managing director of BASF India, the Indian branch of the largest chemical company in the world. He shared my feelings about the cost of pesticides and their financial and personal impact on India's cotton farmers. Many farmers who could not pay back the loans they took out to buy pesticides committed suicide. As a large producer of pesticides, BASF was concerned about this not just as a business issue but a social issue as well. Since BASF served the agricultural sector, it was interested in our offsets program and wanted to know how it could help India's farming community. BASF units in Europe were participating in the EU ETS program, and he suspected that the firm's senior management in Germany would want the Indian branch to become involved. BASF joined the ICX advisory committee and I was elated. Our next meeting reinforced my beliefs about India's development.

The chairman of Ranbaxy, an Indian pharmaceutical company, had reserved a small conference room in the Oberoi hotel for our scheduled meeting. The room felt more like a study, and the setting was intimate. He explained to me that Ranbaxy was a low-cost manufacturer of generic drugs. The firm's business model entailed using the profits from these generic drugs to develop new drugs.

"We have over 300 PhDs doing research," he said matter-of-factly. "My hope is for us to become a world-class pharmaceutical company that competes with American and European companies. We're already getting FDA approval for some of our drugs, which will gradually be introduced in the U.S. markets. India has the education system in place to achieve this. Our population is also much younger than China's."

India had the potential to become a major economic powerhouse—a country that had transformed from the one that Sanjib lived in. I was convinced that ICX would be the first cap-and-trade market in Asia. To do this, I knew from my previous experience that I had to start with educating and capacity building. Not just with the trading community but with corporations, government, and the general public. For new markets to survive, I knew the complete system of institutional infrastructure had to be activated. The rest of the day was spent networking and attending a dinner addressed by the Minister of Finance. It was the start of a new journey and I knew it was going to be a fun ride.

The next day to be spent in Mumbai was packed with meetings with corporates. We arrived in Mumbai only to find out that the airport workers were on strike. We were welcomed by piles of garbage and placard-carrying workers on the airport premises. We were told that traffic could be blocked and I wondered if we could make all the meetings on time. The meetings had been scheduled after weeks of painstaking preparatory work and late-night telephone calls by Rafael Marques and Murali. I could not miss any of them.

Murali had scheduled eight separate meetings in different areas of Mumbai, so we had to traverse the city twice. The trip from one side of the city to the other took as long as 90 minutes on a normal day, but on that day it took much longer. As we rushed between the city's extremities, I couldn't help but notice the stark contrast around us. Tall skyscrapers, proudly conquering Mumbai's skies, stood side-by-side with tin-roofed slums. The latest luxury cars competed for space with noisy motorized rickshaws and street hawkers. Every available space seemed to be thriving with small retail businesses. There are 210 million people living below the poverty line in India. This exceeds the U.S. population of 309 million.[16] Mumbai represented this duality clearly. Nonetheless, one unmistakable fact was that the city was bustling with energy.

We headed for our last meeting with Mukesh Ambani, CEO of Reliance Industries, one of India's largest conglomerates. The headquarters

---

[16]"100 Million More Indians Now Living in Poverty," *Reuters*, April 18, 2010.

of the company was in the southern end of Mumbai called Nariman Point, a place with some of the highest-valued real estate in the world. Murali and I had not had time to eat any breakfast or lunch and the novelty of trafficking through the streets was gradually wearing off.

Although we could see Maker Chambers, the headquarters of the company, we were told that we would be half an hour late because of the traffic. I suggested that we get out of the car and literally run to be on time. What a sight we must have been, walking across the main thoroughfare and then running through the side streets. We arrived one minute early for our 4 P.M. appointment. I leaned over and said, "Murali, never be late to meet a CEO." He smiled.

The Mumbai monsoon had left visible marks on the building. It looked shabby from the outside, but the inside was another world. The offices were sleek and modern. Mukesh Ambani was a man with a friendly demeanor who didn't wear his success on his shoulders. He had his entire senior management team for the meeting. He listened attentively and when he didn't understand something, he probed us gently for more information.

After my pitch, he said decisively, "Reliance is interested in participating in the CCX offsets program and I want to be part of the ICX design program." He was one of the richest and most powerful businessmen in India and his imprimatur meant a lot to us. I became more convinced that ICX was a reality in the making. Murali and I flew back to Delhi that evening, exhausted but pleased with our productive day.

My vision for CCX in India was beginning to take shape. We would take a threefold approach. First, I believed that the CCX offsets program could be expanded by including projects from India. The fruits of the carbon market had to trickle down to the grassroots. Second, we should develop a framework for a transparent and regulated means of transacting CERs for India. The CDM sector in India was growing but lacked an open market framework. The third approach was my most ambitious one: to develop the India Climate Exchange. ICX would enable Indian corporations to determine the most cost-effective greenhouse gas mitigation measures, and lead to new products, markets, profit centers, and social development opportunities.

I left Delhi that night, laid over in Bangkok, and then proceeded to Tokyo. I was starting to feel like a lounge act by the end of the trip. Meetings and more meetings. Speeches and more speeches. My father would have been proud of me. I was sad that he wasn't at home awaiting my stories of the trip.

ICX Is Conceived

In August 2006, we signed a memorandum of understanding (MOU)[17] with TERI to develop an offset program tailored specifically for India.[18] As part of the arrangement, TERI would lend its technical expertise in building India-specific offset protocols and CCX would link its market to Indian offsets.

At the same time, we decided to develop and trademark the India Climate Exchange (ICX), the first pilot greenhouse gas emissions trading program in India. It was a great opportunity to bolster sustainable development efforts in rural India while expanding the offset market for carbon emissions.

Replicating the framework that worked for us with CCX, we began to actively recruit members for the ICX technical design committee and advisory board. Pachy agreed to serve as honorary chairman of the advisory board.[19] Other board members included Deepak Chopra, chairman of the Chopra Center for Wellbeing, and Jonathan Lash, president of the World Resources Institute. I made two more trips back to India by myself, while the other members of CCX went separately to recruit new members.

---

[17]A memorandum of understanding (MOU) is a nonlegally binding, or soft commitment, between two companies on an agreed-upon course of action.

[18]"CCX and TERI Announce Partnership to Develop Greenhouse Gas Emission Offsets in India," Press Release, Chicago Climate Exchange and the Energy and Resources Institute, August 21, 2006.

[19]India Climate Exchange™ (ICX™) Advisory Board, Chicago Climate Exchange, November 22, 2011, http://prod2.chicagoclimatex.com/content.jsf?id=1602.

The ICX technical advisory committee was the heart and soul of the ICX program. They were charged with designing the emission goals, program time line, sectors to be included, and numerous other criteria that formed the skeleton of the market. We were anxious to have a wide diversity of participants in the committee. This had proved invaluable in the CCX formation process and was critical to our success.

Charged with recruiting members for the ICX technical committee, I relied on Murali, Rafael, and Mike to market the idea. They made numerous trips to India. I knew we had to get the big conglomerates in India to add credibility to the program. Among the big corporations in India were Reliance Industries, Tata Group, Godrej, Bajaj, and the ADAG group. The team was having a roller-coaster ride with recruitment, but I encouraged them to stay persistent.

Despite my excellent meeting with Mr. Mukesh Ambani in Mumbai, Reliance had still not signed on to the ICX committee. This was somewhat understandable, given that Reliance was a huge corporation and everything they did was closely monitored. Their main operations were also centered around petrochemicals and refining, both of which generated high emissions. Getting Reliance on board would be huge, and I urged Murali to focus on them.

The breakthrough came early one morning. Murali had been trying to reach the senior vice president at Reliance all evening but was unable to get through. He finally made the connection at 3 A.M. Chicago time, which was around 1:30 P.M. in Mumbai. Surprised, the senior vice president inquired if Murali was calling from an airport in Europe. When Murali responded negatively he exclaimed, "Why are you calling me at 3 A.M. your time?" Murali politely responded, "Because my CEO has been up all night sending emails requesting the status of Reliance in ICX. Sir, your joining us is very important to make this successful." Reliance's commitment letter came in the next day. Our persistence had paid off once again.

After several other efforts in India, we managed to recruit 24 top Indian companies and universities to be part of the ICX technical committee. It was a diverse group of corporations, similar to the makeup of the CCX technical committees. Members of the ICX technical committee included Tata Motors, Reliance Industries, Lanco

Power, Reliance Power, and Infosys, among others. The committee met on four different occasions to participate in the drafting of what came to be called the Mumbai Accord.

The ICX technical advisory committee held its first meeting in January 2007 at the Hotel Shangri La in New Delhi, coinciding with the 2007 Delhi Sustainable Development Summit, where I gave a keynote speech. After providing some welcoming remarks, I outlined the consensus-building process that the CCX design committee had taken. I gave an overview of the state of environmental markets and stressed

Table 23.1 ICX Preliminary Draft of Term Sheet

Greenhouse gases included	Entity-wide emissions CO_2, methane, nitrous oxide, PFCs, HFCs, SF6 from major emitting activities in India. Members include direct (combustion) emissions plus indirect (from electricity, steam, and cooled-water purchases) emissions from major emitting activities.
Emissions quantification	All emissions to be quantified using agreed-upon standard methods and subject to independent audit.
Annual true-up	Subsequent to each year, each source must surrender instruments in an amount equal to the emissions occurring during that year.
Emission baseline	Annual emissions during the year 2006.
Emission reduction objective	Calendar year 2010: 112% of baseline Calendar year 2011: 115% of baseline Calendar years 2012 to 2020: 118% of baseline
Economic growth provision	Maximum required total purchase of emission allowances and/or offsets is limited to: 3% of an emitter's baseline during 2010 and 2011 4% of baseline in 2012 and 2013 5% of baseline in years 2014 and 2015 6% of baseline in years 2016 through 2020
Eligible project-based offsets	India-specific protocols to be developed
Registry, electronic trading platform	Registry will serve as official holder and transfer mechanism, and is linked with the electronic trading platform on which all trades occur.
Exchange governance	Self-regulatory organization overseen by committees composed of exchange members.

the importance of Indian corporations to participate in the process, particularly given India's role as a leading player supplying offsets under the Clean Development Mechanism protocol.

As we suspected, the big concern was how to handle growth and which emissions to include. At the time, India was growing at an average annual rate of about 4.5 percent and accounting for total greenhouse gas emissions of about 1.8 billion metric tons. Many of the big Indian corporations had started to diversify across multiple sectors. Indeed, Murali joked that you could go through an entire set of daily activities just by using Godrej's products. They made everything from bath soap to storage cabinets to ceiling fans, coolers, and even door locks. Some of these sectors were new and fast growing, which meant that their emissions growth could be enormous in initial years before stabilizing. We were compelled to include all corporate emissions so as to avoid cherry picking the best locations, and knew that we had to design sufficient provisions to manage this. Following the CCX concept, we decided that an economic growth provision would cap the maximum liability for any increases in carbon emissions beyond a certain point. This was designed as a safety valve to avoid hindering economic growth among member companies.

Table 23.1 is the preliminary draft of the ICX term sheet.

The Andhyodaya—A Chain Reaction of Innovation

As we were putting together the bricks to build ICX, our early efforts on the offset side were already bearing fruit. More than 150 offset providers were linked to the CCX markets directly or through their aggregators. By 2008, India was the largest international supplier to offsets in the CCX market.

While this made great business sense, I was always amazed by what the markets could do to help those at the grassroots level. The greatest attribute of the carbon markets was its ability to promote economic development. This was especially true in the poorest parts of the world. The Andhyodaya, the first member of the CCX program from India, demonstrated this point clearly.

I met with the executive director of the Andhyodaya during my first trip to India at Murali's suggestion. An NGO based in the Ernakulam district of Kerala, South India, the Andhyodaya specialized in small-scale biogas, solar energy, and rainwater harvesting.

In January 2007, the organization decided to join CCX as an aggregator of carbon emissions offset credits for small farmers with microdigesters.[20] The credits were generated from sustainable development and renewable energy projects across rural India and sold on the CCX.

We began our collaboration to develop a technical protocol to credit biogas from rural households. The biodigestion process was simple. Animal waste was put in a cylindrical container that resembled a garbage can. The waste was fermented in a sealed container without oxygen. Anaerobic digestion produced methane gas, which rose to the top of the container. Captured gas was transported to a farmhouse by tube, and could be used for cooking purposes.

The small farmers would receive offset credits of about four tons annually per biogas unit, and these were to be sold on CCX for about $4 to $5 per ton. As a result of this offset program, the average farmer made about $20. Since the average family income in this region was less than $1 a day, this was a substantial amount relative to their total income. There were numerous additional benefits to this program. The captured methane gas would replace wood as fuel, allowing young girls the opportunity to go to school instead of foraging for wood every day. The burning of wood indoors caused a number of lung problems that could be reduced if gas was used instead. CCX already had an established protocol for agricultural digesters, which was a useful model for developing protocols for biogas in India.

CCX ended up running into many unexpected complications. The Indian biogas units were tiny compared to North American ones, scattered in remote rural areas that were difficult to access, and were operated by mostly simple farmers. The cost of monitoring and verification many hundreds of units over inaccessible terrain was astronomical, so

[20]"The Andhyodaya Joins Chicago Climate Exchange as an Offset Aggregator, First Indian Offset Credits Approved for Trading in the Exchange," Press Release, Chicago Climate Exchange, January 23, 2007.

we decided to resort to statistical sampling—a technique that was well accepted in industries like semiconductors and airlines but not, at the time, prevalent with the United Nations CDM protocols. The United Nations did eventually come to embrace statistical sampling.

We were met with another obstacle: How could we teach people with little or no education the details of a technical protocol? To succeed, we had to build a protocol that took into consideration the local situation and resources. This required us to work alongside local villagers, NGOs, and technical institutes in India.

The complications were all not external. The CCX offsets committee had never heard of small-scale biogas units, nor did they understand what made sense in rural India. They demanded that we have meters measuring the amount of methane generated at each biogas unit. The cost of doing so would have killed the program. We explained to the committee that the Indian biogas units did not and could not enjoy the economies of scale of their larger U.S. counterparts. To further convince them, we designed a cluster-sampling procedure that took into consideration the geography, size, and number of units. The method grouped the biogas units by their characteristics, and samples were drawn from each of these groups in order to approximate the amount of methane generated by biogas units with similar characteristics. This eliminated the cost of having to measure the amount of methane generated at each biogas unit individually.

After addressing these issues, we finally had a product that was locally relevant and scientifically justifiable. The real work had just begun. When our NGO partner proudly took the program to the people, they were bombarded with all sorts of questions. No one understood what global warming was or what they were supposed to sell. The people laughed at the thought of selling "smelly air" from Kerala all the way to the United States. Local papers branded the program as a big scam. Everyone questioned the motives of the NGO and its new U.S. partners.

In spite of these obstacles, we prevailed through persistence and constant education. The first trade was consummated in 2008, during an event hosted by the Delhi Sustainable Development Summit (DSDS). The small-scale biogas projects had led to cuts equivalent to 40,000 tonnes of carbon dioxide. This represents a market value of approximately €123,000 or $160,000. A huge event was held in Kerala to distribute the first CCX checks. The whole event was decorated like a local wedding, with all the women and children wearing their brightest saris and biggest smiles. After the celebrations, many of the rural participants invited the CCX team to have dinner with them. We did not know their language nor did we know any of them personally, but the program and its success provided the connection. One of them said to Murali, "We've had several organizations that have given checks to us for charity, sometimes bigger than this one. But I am so proud of getting this one because I earned it. We are both partners in solving the sins of industrialization." I was so proud of our team.

The program started with 3,000 families in one state and expanded to more than 100,000 rural poor families in two states. A year or so later, I was told that the carbon program was paying for all the biogas plants to be insured. Not only that, a local bank had started to issue carbon vouchers to the villagers wherein they could exchange the voucher for cash equivalents in any of their bank branches. The seed of innovation we had sown was growing organically. The villagers were now managing their risk and reducing transaction costs through their own resources.

We were successful due to several reasons. Our intervention was bottom up and took due consideration of the local practices. Our technical approach was flexible while ensuring the core principles for offsets. We were also relentless in our education efforts. All of these pointed to a system that was efficient with lowered transaction costs. When there are low transaction costs, emissions trading can bring enormous benefit to the rural poor. I recalled that Sabu from *The Jungle Book* had always dreamed of becoming a forestry officer. This alleviated the disappointment, but I was still determined to find a project that worked.

Holy Cows and Sacred Forests

Doing business in any new country requires great respect and acknowledgment of its culture and social systems. This is even more important in a country such as India, with its rich and complex set of social dynamics and cultural fabric.

Sometime back in 2006, CCX made several attempts to register forest carbon from India to our forest offsets portfolio. We had been very successful in recruiting Brazilian forest companies to CCX and were eager to extend the success to India. Murali traveled to Mathura to discuss this opportunity with the local district forest officer. I recalled Sabu's dream of becoming a forestry officer. Mathura, located about 90 miles from New Delhi, was a holy city famous for its Krishna temple. The city was believed to be the birthplace of the Hindu deity Krishna, and Hindu mythology was filled with tales of a young Krishna herding his cows in its lush forests. Mathura's bustling streets were filled with pilgrims and saffron-robed *sadhus* (Hindu holy men) and hawkers selling trinkets for Hindu rituals. The entire business in the city was somehow tied to the Krishna temple.

The discussion with the forestry department went smoothly. We discussed a pilot to initially demonstrate that the concept could be extended. A new plantation site was identified near the hillock of Govardhan as the pilot location. The site had year-old plantings and could easily be transformed to suit CCX forest carbon requirements. Murali suggested the continued development of the plantation. CCX would revisit the plantation in about six months' time to measure the trees. When Murali returned to Chicago, we initiated the process of introducing Indian forestry tons to CCX. There was much work to be done.

Three months into the process, Murali received a frantic call from the forest officer. His plantation was being destroyed by an army of cows. Apparently, the local *sadhus* were insistent on releasing cattle onto the plantation. The Govardhan hills were part of the area that Krishna was believed to have roamed with his cows, and the *sadhus* would have nothing less than free-roaming cattle in these sacred forests. Of course, the cattle were devouring the young plantation. To add to the destruction, people were releasing monkeys into the forest in an attempt to appease the Hindu monkey god, Hanuman. When the forestry officer tried to disperse the crowds of *sadhus*, they become violent and started blocking the highway. This was something our experience designing carbon markets had not prepared us for. We had planned for many project risks, and had lined up detailed strategies and contingency plans, but had not anticipated being taken over by saffron-robed Hindu holy men. Confronted with that, we ended our first attempt to register forest tons from India.

The Tata Motors Auction

The Tata conglomerate, first set up with a steel company in 1907 by its visionary founder, Jamshedji Tata, had been nation builders in India for more than a century. The group's 90 subsidiary companies had interests in virtually every aspect of everyday life, and had long been associated with promoting education, arts, and other socially responsible endeavors. They had built hospitals, some of India's best educational institutes, and had even started civil aviation in India.

The Tata family were Parsees, a faith based on Zoroastrian tradition. The Parsees immigrated to Gujarat, India, in the tenth century from Iran. I had learned the story of the Tata family from Sanjib, who was a Parsee. We spent hours in my room discussing the bittersweet story of the Parsee religion and its tenets. He had told me, "There is no intermarriage and they don't accept conversion to their religion. Their population in India is doomed to disappear. Today, there are only 100,000 Parsees left in India." The Tatas epitomized all that the Parsees valued. They were highly educated, successful business owners, and very philanthropic.

The Tatas had given Murali, a young student with aspirations to get an education in the United States, a scholarship that paid for his airfare and some tuition at the University of Kentucky. So naturally, when I asked him to name the top five companies that were interested in a nation-building project such as the Indian version of CCX, Murali immediately suggested the Tata group. I was thrilled to finally meet this illustrious family.

I asked Murali to make a pitch to the general manager of government affairs and collaboration at Tata Motors. The Tatas already had some experience in the carbon market through the CDM market. The manager well understood the impact the Tatas could have on the other Indian corporations and the importance of being the first mover, should a mandate for greenhouse gas reductions be introduced to India. In November 2006, Tata Motors signed up to be the first Indian automotive company to join the India Climate Exchange.

Our trading platform for CER futures was another service we could offer, especially to our Indian and international clients, who were the primary sellers in the marketplace. Our focus therefore was to get the Tatas involved with our CER futures marketplace.

Tata had some 165,000 CERs from a wind farm maintained by the company in western India that could be traded using our futures market. The general manager wanted the trade to be done within the next 10 to 15 days, so he could include the revenues in his fourth-quarter financial statements. Unfortunately, our CER futures contract was cash-settled and did not require the physical exchange of the underlying commodity. It was designed as a pure financial hedging tool.

Given this dilemma, we decided to offer a CER spot auction for Tata. Coupled with our advances in China and India, it made perfect sense to offer this service. The CER market was opaque, and transaction costs were high. Sellers of CERs in India often had to shop for the best prices without a central market. The success with the Tatas would showcase to the Indian corporations the power of markets and help with our strategic vision for the country.

I explained the importance of the CBOT SO_2 auctions that Mike and I helped to originate and administer for many years. We wanted to be the first exchange to conduct an auction for CERs. I said to Rafael, who was Brazilian, with a smile, "If we pull this off in time, maybe we can beat your fellow countrymen to it!" The Brazilian Mercantile & Futures Exchange (BM&F), the local futures exchange, had just announced its own plans to conduct the world's first exchange-based CER auction in São Paolo. The expected auction date was September 26, 2007, but there was some uncertainty. Here was our opportunity to be the first exchange in the world to conduct a CER auction. This was another David-versus-Goliath scene, and we were playing David. It was eventually decided that the auction would be conducted on September 24 from the early morning hours until noon.

While the opportunity was tempting, the task at hand was immense. Within a span of the next 10 days, the legal contract for conducting an auction had to be written, an escrow account set up, marketing initiated, auction rules and specifications written, the press informed, and complicated bureaucracy of CDM mastered so the spot tons could be delivered. We had to work closely with the Tatas to carry out these tasks while grappling with the 11-hour time difference. We had a job to be done that spanned all our departments. We set two daily meetings—one in the morning and one to end the day—so we could update each other and take stock of the progress. At night, our job was to coordinate with Tata so they could get their necessary approvals and processes internally and have feedback for us early in the morning. It was kind of like a relay race, only one that was run 8,000 miles apart.

As we approached the auction date, there was a nervous energy from the team. While we had received interest from many companies, no one had confirmed their commitment to participate. We certainly didn't want a scenario in which there were no bids during the auction. A lot of hard work had gone into setting the stage for this auction and we didn't want to let Tata down.

The night before the auction, September 23, Mac McGregor and Kathy Lynn decided to stay overnight in the office. The expectation was that European clients could put in bids overnight and we wanted to make sure there was sufficient operational and marketing support in case they needed it. Morning came and there were still no bids. Anxiety climbed. Unrelentingly, Mac and Rob continued to make calls. Rafael wrote a draft press release to announce the results, despite the fact that we didn't even know if we would have results to share.

Amid all this frenzy, the fax machine started buzzing. We received our first bid for 30,000 tons. This was quickly followed by another. By the end of it, the auction was oversubscribed 13 times for the quantity

Table 23.2 ICX Members as of March 2008

Automotive	**Research and Policy Institutions**	**Sugar**
Tata Motors	Energy Resources Institute	Coramandel Sugars
Ford India	Tamil Nadu Agricultural University	**Technology**
Chemicals	Petroleum Conservation Research Association	IBM India
Tata Chemicals	**Cement**	Motorola India
Dow Corning	Grasim Industries	Infosys Technologies
Rhodia India	**Diversified Manufacturing**	
BASF India	Godrej Industries	
Energy and Power	Reliance Industries	
Sun Group International	ITC	
Reliance Power	**Renewable Energy**	
Lanco Power	Suzlon/Senergy Global	
Tata Power	Indowind Power	
Pharmaceuticals		
Baxter International		
Ranbaxy		

available with 16 bids. More importantly, the power of competitive markets had been proven. Our clearing price of $22.11 per CER was slightly above the prevailing spot price.

Tata was able to monetize its environmental service and include it in its financial report. CCX was now the first exchange to conduct a CER auction, beating BM&F by two days.

After the disbelief wore off, Murali inquired why Tatas had chosen CCX. The general manager responded, "I know all about making the best cars but selling carbon is not my forte. We were approached by many brokers who offered to buy these outright. However, the process of how we go about selling this is important to us. We wanted a regulated, transparent platform where no one could question our intentions. We wanted a credible organization that we knew we could trust." I could not have been prouder of the CCX team. Table 23.2 lists the ICX members as of March 2008.

Moving On

With the level of interest shown by Indian companies and our successes in its offset market, we were convinced that we could help India develop its own voluntary cap-and-trade system. But first, we needed a strategic partner. We found one, and spent about nine months laying out an elaborate business plan and budget. Unfortunately, we entered into an agreement to sell Climate Exchange PLC before we could achieve our objectives in India. While the sale of the company was in the best interests of the shareholders, I deeply regretted our failure to set up the India Climate Exchange. India was an immense educational experience and we have gained a tremendous amount of goodwill among our participants. My mission to help India realize its environmental goals was not yet complete.

There remains significant interest in the Indian private sector with regard to cap-and-trade. India is currently experimenting with a national environmental market for renewable energy credits and a tradable energy efficiency marketplace. This is only the beginning of a bright future for the country. We remain very optimistic about India.

I thought that India would be more promising than China. But fortune favored us in China.

Chapter 24

Opening New Markets in China

A journey of a thousand miles begins with a single step.

—*Lao Tzu*

During my frequent trips to Tokyo to promote stock index futures, my Drexel colleague who headed our Japanese operations inquired if I had interest in traveling to China with a Japanese client. I jumped on the idea. It was a chance to both maintain relationships with an existing client and see China for the first time. One of my favorite movies is Bernardo Bertolucci's *The Last Emperor*, the sweeping historical drama that chronicled the story of Pu Yi, the last emperor of China. It was a timely coincidence that I saw it in 1988, shortly before my first trip to Beijing.

First Encounter with China

After two days of meetings in Tokyo, I prepared for Beijing. My hosts in Japan had the art of travel down to a science. Tokyo's airport was a two-hour drive from the city, and the company arranged for me to stay at a small hotel close to the airport the day before I traveled. The room was tiny and uncomfortable, making me wonder what this augured for the journey. My concerns, however, vanished entirely after my first meeting in China.

My Japanese hosts in China were terrific, their attention to detail unrivaled. Our first meeting was with the U.S. equivalent of an undersecretary of agriculture, who had accompanied Chairman Mao on the Long March. The meeting took place in a stark government building. The minister, a stout man with a round face who spoke with an air of composure, reminded me of the Laughing Buddha. We discussed the possibility of new futures markets in China, agricultural and financial, as the country was growing rapidly and change was in the air. The undersecretary expressed his concerns about implementing a project of this scale, given the limited number of financial institutions in China. He summed up his primary concerns regarding China's economic development with a simple, yet powerful, example: "If every person ate just one egg per day, the country would have to produce over one billion eggs daily." The lack of priority in establishing a futures market was clear.

My interaction with the undersecretary was challenging. When I asked a question or made a statement, it was first translated into Japanese by a bilingual member of our group who spoke Japanese and English, and then into Chinese by the Chinese-speaking Japanese who spoke no English. It reminded me of a game that we played as kids in Brooklyn called Telephone. About seven or eight children sat in a circle. One child whispered a few words to the person to his immediate right, who then repeated what he heard to someone on his immediate right. This continued until the circle was completed. The message that was uttered aloud by the last person in the circle often bore little or no resemblance to the original message.

The language barrier meant that it would take twice as long to do business in China. Additionally, it could potentially pose numerous problems and misunderstandings. However, a curious takeaway of the conversation was that this official seemed to be more interested in free markets than I expected. It became indelibly stamped in my mind that despite the fact that this man had lived as a communist in a dogmatic, centrally planned economy for 35 years, it was ultimately his 5,000-year Chinese commercial and trading heritage that dominated his thoughts and actions.

There were other memorable events during the trip that shaped my understanding of doing business in China. While delivering a lecture on futures markets at Peking University, I was amazed by how crowded the lecture room was and how interested the students were. While the country was nominally a socialist state, the lively Q&A session suggested quite the opposite. After the talk, students flocked around me. Their thirst for knowledge matched or surpassed all that I had seen from previous talks I had given in other countries.

Our trip had been thoughtfully planned, with ample time allocated to sightseeing historical sites such as the Great Wall, the Forbidden City, and the Summer Palace. I told the host about my interest in photography and he arranged for a guide to accompany me as I sought to learn something additional about China's artistic heritage.

Since there were no photography galleries in Beijing, my guide took me to a bookstore where I bought a colossal book called *China*, filled with beautiful photographs from the 1950s that were either tipped in or reproduced. Among them were images of industry and agriculture, traditional Chinese prints, and pictures of Chairman Mao. Apparently, the book can no longer be found in China. This book later became a subject of great curiosity and delight to my visitors from China and marked the beginning of my Chinese art collection. After visiting several other bookstores, my guide began to run out of ideas, so I suggested that we go to the daily newspaper.

When we arrived at the newspaper, my guide asked a staff member if I could visit the archives and look at old photographs. While the newspaper was unwilling to sell the original photographs, it was willing to sell me later prints. I acquired a number of photographs, including portraits of Sun Yat Sen; the Last Emperor, Pu Yi; Empress Dowager Cixi; and one of Nixon with Mao. I found shots of Chinese opium dens and a copy of the iconic photograph of Mao that Warhol appropriated for his paintings and silk-screens. We left the newspaper and returned to the hotel for a final night of karaoke singing.

The trip was memorable, and it was clear that China differed vastly from my expectations. The meeting with the undersecretary and the discussions with faculty and students suggested the advent of monumental change. My initial foray into twentieth-century Chinese history and photography would later prove to be extremely useful. By the end of the trip, I was convinced that it was essential for me to return to China one day. I waited in vain for an invitation that would allow me to work on the promising development of futures markets in grains or financials in China. It took almost 20 years before the right opportunity presented itself.

Satellite Broadcasts

Years after my first trip, I participated in a couple of satellite broadcasts into Hong Kong and mainland China. In 2003, I received a call from Tessa Tenant, the founder of the Association of Sustainable and Responsible Investment in Asia (ASrIA), Asia's first sustainable investment forum. She alerted me to an opportunity to participate as a keynote speaker at a conference on sustainable investing in Hong Kong.[1] Unfortunately, the SARS epidemic broke out so I had to do it by satellite broadcast. The presentation was well received and provided the introduction of the CCX concept to a Chinese audience.

Separately, in April 2004, Christine Todd Whitman asked me to do a satellite broadcast to China on the role of emissions trading in reducing acid rain in the United States. There were 20 to 30 officials from both Hong Kong and Guangdong in the audience. The level of interest displayed by these cities in emissions trading and pollution reduction was uplifting. China had come a long way in the past 15 years.

It became clear to me that these different cities in China were vying to become the home of emissions trading. This competition between Chinese cities became a recurring phenomenon during my experience there for the next six years.

[1]"Prospects for Asia—Emerging Carbon Markets," paper presented at the ASrIA/BEC Energy Market Development Conference, Hong Kong Convention and Exhibition Centre, March 24, 2003.

An Opportunity Arises

During the early part of 2006, I received a call from the United Nations Development Program (UNDP). Maurice Strong had recommended that they ask me to be the keynote speaker at an upcoming event. I was to talk about CCX, the challenge of developing a quantitative measure of the Millennium Development Goals,[2] and the role of emissions trading in reducing the impacts of climate change.

One of the long-term objectives of CCX was to participate in the development of emissions markets in China. I wanted to both attract Chinese participation in CCX and start a voluntary CO_2 market in the country. Given the reverence in China toward the United Nations, the opportunity to speak at the UNDP conference created a visible platform for CCX in China.

There were five major challenges we wanted to address in order to attain these objectives. First, we needed to raise the country's level of awareness of cap-and-trade. Second, we wanted to attract local companies to join CCX as offset providers. Third, we had to find a local strategic partner to provide intellectual and financial capital. Any voluntary or mandatory market had to be designed with Chinese partners in order to ensure that the market's environmental objectives were compatible with the country's regulatory climate and need to grow its economy. Fourth, we needed to sign a joint venture agreement with the strategic partner and choose a city to locate the exchange. Fifth, the city itself had to be a partner in the joint venture, as any local market would be required to obtain a business license and receive regulatory approval from the city.

The two satellite broadcasts had shown us that our timing was opportune—China was finally turning its attention towards sustainability. This was consistent with the observed phenomenon that as nations became more prosperous, they could better afford and were therefore more willing to deal with environmental problems.[3] Despite

[2]The Millennium Development Goals provide a blueprint for the world's countries to achieve eight antipoverty goals by their 2015 target date.

[3]The Environmental Kuznets Curve (EKC) posits that at relatively low levels of income, natural resource use and waste emissions increase with income. Past some turning point, however, they decline with income.

the contradictions in China's political and economic systems and the unhappy state of its per capita wealth, the country was growing rapidly and could not afford to wait any longer to address the environmental repercussions of its growth. I asked our staff to conduct some research on China's pollution and was shocked by how bad the environmental conditions in China had become.

China's Environmental Issues

Every year, more than 400,000 Chinese were dying prematurely from respiratory illnesses.[4] Health-care costs associated with air pollution were estimated at 3.8 percent of GDP, and 4 of the 10 most polluted cities in the world were in China.[5] In 2006, China had also become the world's largest emitter of CO_2 at 8.33 billion tons per year.[6] Furthermore, NASA discovered in 2008 that up to 15 percent of local pollution on the West Coast of the United States was attributable to drifts from China.[7]

There were problems with water scarcity and water quality as well. Approximately 27.3 percent of the country was desertified, and this percentage was only increasing.[8] More than two-thirds of cities had insufficient water and one out of six cities had chronic water shortages. Not only did China have water scarcity problems, it also had water quality issues. There were reports that 700

---

[4]James Reynolds, "Living in China's Coal Heartland," BBC News, Shanxi, January 22, 2007.

[5]Douglas McIntyre, "The 10 Cities with the World's Worst Air," *Daily Finance*, November 29, 2010.

[6]Nina Chestney, "China's CO_2 Emissions Rose 10 Percent in 2010: BP Data," *Reuters*, June 8, 2011.

[7]"Satellite Measures Pollution from East Asia to North America," NASA News Release, March 2008.

[8]He Han, "China's 300-Year Desert Battle," *China Daily*, January 5, 2011.

China's Environmental Issues (*Continued*)

million people in China drank water contaminated by waste on a regular basis, according to the February 2010 issue of *Water in China*. Over half of the water in China is undrinkable and a fourth is too polluted for industrial use.[9] In fact, contaminated drinking water was the leading cause of death in children under five years of age.[10]

Chinese citizens knew about these problems and many were vocal about them. There were an estimated 51,000 local pollution-related protests in 2005 and about 189,000 in 2010.[11] In response to this, the political leadership had begun to take action. The 11th Five-Year Plan called to reduce SO_2 by 10 percent, water pollution by 10 percent, and energy intensity by 20 percent, all below 2005 levels by 2010.[12] As of 2011, much of the quotas were met or exceeded. Water pollution decreased by 12.5 percent, and SO_2 by 14.3 percent.[13]

Given China's heavy reliance on coal as the major source of energy for the production of electricity, committing to the latter would dramatically reduce greenhouse gas emissions in China.[14]

---

[9]David Gutirrez, "Over Half of China's Water Polluted beyond Drinkability," *Natural News*, December 6, 2010.

[10]Igor Rudan, "Causes of Deaths in Children Younger than 5 Years in China in 2008," *The Lancet* 375, no. 9720 (March 27, 2010): 1083–1089.

[11]"Chinese Newspaper Slams Zijin for Its Handling of Copper Mine Waste Leak," *Reuters*, July 15, 2010.

[12]Energy intensity measures the energy efficiency of a country's economy. It takes the ratio of total domestic energy consumption to GDP.

[13]"China Meets Pollution Control Targets for 2006–2010," *Xinhua*, August 29, 2011.

[14]According to the China National Coal Association, China consumed 3.2 billion tons of coal in 2020. This consumption level is projected to grow at a rate of 7.9 percent annually.

Convinced that China was ripe for emissions trading, I asked Paula to accompany me to China. She was an explorer and had the tenacity, credentials, and energy needed for the journey. Possessing an uncanny sense of being in the right place at the right time, Maurice Strong had moved to China in 2005. He encouraged us to come to China and helped organize parts of the trip.

My near-catastrophic hiring experience in Singapore years before had taught me that it would be essential to seek professional help locally. Rick Ferina had employed Jeff Huang, a managing director of ChiSurf Ltd., to assist Calyon in becoming the first foreign entity to have equity in a Chinese-based FCM. Calyon was the minority partner of Citic, the sixth-largest bank in China, and also a subsidiary of Citic Holdings, a major financial and industrial Chinese company. It seemed that this was the only way that a foreign entity could be involved in China. I had previously met Jeff in New York while he was traveling there, and was impressed by his political skills, business acumen, and nuanced sense of language. We retained him as a consultant to help build our network in China.

With the assembly of my advisers, the stage was set for our developing business in China. China was on the track to become the largest emitter of greenhouse gases. I was excited about the possibility of making a difference.

Returning to China

The yarn that started with the UNDP's invitation officially began in Beijing on June 21, 2006. I chose to stay at the Grand Beijing hotel over the standard five-star international chains that were identical in every major capital. The Grand Beijing captured the feel of the royal ancient China in the film *The Last Emperor*. It was directly east of the Forbidden City and only several blocks from the famous Wangfujing shopping street. The hotel had once been a palace until the 1960s, when Chairman Mao ordered for it to be converted into a hotel to showcase China's aptitude in the hospitality business. The hotel boasted spacious bedrooms filled with Chinese-style antique furniture. Everything about the place was authentically Chinese. This suited me, as I intended to fully immerse myself in the local culture.

That night, there was a scheduled dinner with CCX's first Chinese member, one of China's most renowned companies in energy efficiency innovations. Many projects in China were not recognized as certified emission reductions (CERs) under the Kyoto Protocol. These were perfectly viable projects that either could not enter the CER market because of high transaction costs, caused by factors such as rigid bureaucratic rules and uncertainty of approval. I explained the innovativeness and flexibility of the CCX design. China's pending CER projects could be tailored slightly to follow CCX rules and regulations, thus allowing the owners of these projects to sell their offsets through CCX. The company recognized the opportunities provided by the CCX offset program, and volunteered to help expand our network of contacts to other Chinese entrepreneurs.

As I left the dinner meeting, I took stock of our progress. The CCX offsets program was set in motion. However, a significant amount of capacity building and education remained before emissions management and trading could be achieved in China. We also needed to find our strategic partner in China—someone patient who understood our language, knew our business, and was willing to think big. We thought our natural partner would be a Chinese financial futures or commodities exchange. After all, an exchange would understand markets, and have the infrastructure and the regulatory connections. We had succeeded in Europe by partnering with a European exchange, so it seemed like the natural thing to do.

We had a meeting with a senior official from the Dalian Commodity Exchange. Dalian liked to compare itself to Chicago—its exchange traded grain and soybean futures, and hoped one day to trade in interest rate futures as well. The exchange was interested in cooperating with CCX on areas of mutual interest. They also wanted to have me serve as adviser on a report commissioned by the World Bank's Working Group of Market Research, which sought to study the failure of the Chinese bond futures market.

The Chinese government had begun issuing government bonds to raise money for its rapidly growing economy and budget deficit back in 1981.[15] Between late 1990 and early 1991, the Shanghai Stock Exchange

[15]Sanzhu Zhu, *Securities Dispute Resolution in China* (Burlington, VT: Ashgate Publishing Company, 2007), 75.

and the Shenzhen Stock Exchange were established to offer new financing channels for Chinese state-owned enterprises. The government bond futures market was introduced to institutional investors in late 1992, but it wasn't until 1993 that the government bond futures market was opened to the general public. In May 1995, however, following a series of price manipulation and trading irregularities, the bond futures market was suspended.[16]

Although the Chinese government bond market had met the necessary conditions for a successful futures contract, including homogeneity and price variability in a market where price was competitively determined, these were not sufficient. China still lacked an institutional framework that minimized transaction costs and preserved integrity. The country did have the appropriate governmental regulatory authority, the China Securities Regulatory Commission, along with appropriate self-regulatory authorities like exchanges. It did not, however, have a transparent spot market or a well-developed repo market.[17] Futures markets, as well as spot markets, had value if and only if the costs of transactions did not exceed the value from trading. China wasn't there yet.

The folks at Dalian knew about my role in establishing interest rate futures and were anxious for my assistance. I felt a rush of adrenaline at the thought that there was a real opportunity for me to help develop interest rate futures in China. In the bond futures market study, I recommended that a five-year note market could be appropriate if China were to renew its efforts in interest rate futures. However, I cautioned that successful international markets often began with a longer end of the yield curve as seen with Treasury bonds in the United States, gilts in the United Kingdom, and bunds in Germany. The point on the yield curve chosen initially had to have a design that minimized per-unit transaction costs and avoided manipulation.[18]

---

[16]Chao Chen and Zhong-guo Zhou, "The Rise and Fall of the Government Bond Futures Market in China: 1993–1995," *China & World Economy* 17, no. 2 (March–April 2009): 110–124.

[17]In a repo market, a seller exchanges the securities for cash and promises to buy it back at a future date.

[18]Richard L. Sandor, "China Government Bond Futures Market Study: Development and Supervision Report," August 28, 2006.

We later presented the bond paper at a teleconference. I tried to convey the message that financial innovations could not be successful without the support of a web of institutions. By literally copying the contract specifications from the West, the Chinese bonds futures market was doomed to failure. The Chinese were masters at replicating industrial inventions, but perhaps did not realize that, unlike industrial inventions, the blueprint of a financial invention could not be simply copied. Without a developed spot and repo market, futures markets could not succeed. I encountered the same lack of understanding in China when it came to emissions trading. A major educational undertaking was required if China was to establish a world-class futures markets in interest rates and emissions.

After the meeting with the Dalian folks, I retired to my hotel room and carefully reviewed my presentation for the following day. The conference was especially important because it was being convened by the United Nations. I delivered the presentation in a small room. I was pleased with the size of the crowd and the high level of interest in CCX. We also participated in a seminar hosted by the Energy Research Institute (ERI) of the National Development and Reform Commission (NDRC), and had a number of other meetings with corporations and the Chinese press.

Maurice Strong had arranged for C. S. Kiang, dean of the College of Environmental Sciences at Peking University, to host a seminar on CCX at the university. The audience was dominated by undergraduate students in environmental sciences, a few business students, and some faculty members. I had dutifully prepared my slides in Mandarin and expected to have a translator. When I arrived at the podium, Dean Kiang instructed, "You can use the slides but speak in English. There's no need for a translator." A few minutes into the seminar, the dean signaled that I needed to elevate the content of the presentation. My presentation was too basic, and below what he thought the students were able to comprehend. I was flabbergasted, but proceeded as told.

The seminar was well received and the students expressed great familiarity and knowledge of greenhouse gas markets in the European Union and the United States. One student asked, "Why was there a *contango* in European carbon prices?" while another inquired, "Why are the CCX allowances traded at a discount to European allowances?" Their questions were penetrating and revealed an extensive knowledge of the fundamentals. I was approached by a couple of students after my lecture. They were members of what they called the CDM Club, the university's undergraduate emissions trading club. Electrified by everyone's enthusiasm, I became even more determined to help establish an exchange in China.

Given the enormity of CCX's ambitions, every breakfast, lunch, and dinner were a means to increase our exposure and network. I spoke at a lunch hosted by the U.S.–China Business Council with well over 50 attendees, and was approached by a representative from one of the largest steel companies in China after the talk. I was amazed to learn that one of the largest steel mills in China had been moved, bit by bit, to a site 50 miles from Beijing because of the need to reduce pollution for the coming Olympic Games. The swiftness and resolution with which the Chinese government undertook major projects were not lost on me.

The final evening was spent having dinner at the Heaven and Earth Restaurant in the Forbidden City with Dr. Dai Xiansheng, vice director-general of the China National Petroleum Corporation (CNPC) and his wife, Jeff Huang, and the deputy director-general of the CSRC Futures Department. My chemistry with Dr. Dai and his wife was fantastic, and the dinner marked the beginning of a long friendship. Dr. Dai was an intellectual, as well as a successful businessman in charge of CNPC's overseas investments.

The purpose of the dinner was to develop our network in China. Jeff had presciently advised me that CNPC was potentially interested in becoming the first mover in the environmental space. Jeff further suggested that the China Petroleum Exchange (CPE), in which CNPC owned equity, could be a good joint venture partner. CNPC was China's largest oil and gas production and supply company, and among the world's largest companies. Their interests ranged from oil exploration to energy infrastructure and engineering, and had a presence in more than 70 countries. While this choice of partner might have initially seemed counterintuitive, I was open to the idea. It would be good to have CNPC acquainted with

CCX and our efforts in China. Perhaps they were candidates for the CCX offset program.

Another meeting was held in Shanghai with the president of the China Foreign Exchange Trading System, in order to provide him with an education on CCX. It turned out to be as much of an education for me as it was for him. He was a wise man who was very knowledgeable about the foreign exchange markets in particular, and capital markets more broadly. Despite being a government official, he embraced change and welcomed the idea of emissions markets. He wisely remarked that in any crisis, or period of change, there was an opportunity.

The trip appeared to have achieved our objectives. We had raised the profile of CCX and emissions trading. We delivered speeches, university lectures, and UN presentations. We met with exchanges, Chinese government agencies, and more than 20 Chinese companies. Several articles featuring CCX were published in leading Chinese newspapers and journals such as the *Shanghai Daily, Economic Observer*, and the *China Securities Journal*.[19]

In retrospect, the length of the trip itself and its agenda of speeches, lectures, interviews, and one-on-one meetings were truly daunting. Days often began with early breakfasts and ended with dinner running late into the night. The 13-hour flights and 14-hour time difference only dragged out each event and made everything more difficult. My friend Charlie O. Finley had often told his young players, "Sweat plus sacrifice equals success." I kept his advice in mind.

The ambitiousness with which we faced our ordeal reminded me of Charlie's attempt to bring the Beatles to Kansas City, back when he owned the Kansas City Athletics in the early 1960s.

---

[19]See Fu Chenghao, "Greenhouse Gas Trading Rights Loom on Horizon," *Shanghai Daily*, June 30, 2006 (Chinese); Zheng Lifei, "Emissions Trading Could Be Way Forward," *China Daily*, June 28, 2006, 26; Li Xin, "CCX Explores on a New Opportunity for Carbon Trade Market," *Economic Observer*, July 14, 2006 (Chinese); "The Game of Carbon Trading Begins," *China Securities Journal*, May 5, 2007 (Chinese).

Charlie had promised the people of Kansas City a live performance by the Beatles during the group's first tour of North America. He approached Brian Epstein, the group's manager in San Francisco, and offered $100,000 for the Beatles to play in Kansas City. Epstein refused. Undeterred, Charlie followed Epstein to Los Angeles a week later, making a new offer of $150,000. He was again rejected. Being Charlie, he somehow managed to get hold of John Lennon himself and explained his situation. Lennon good-humoredly accepted the offer on behalf of his group. And that was how the Beatles came to Kansas City. Charlie's persistence had paid off. Always the showman, he even had a photo of himself in a Beatles wig printed on the back of all concert tickets. Persistence was the key.

In spite of the obstacles, my trip to China convinced me that emissions markets could be the answer to some of China's problems. Although I knew how to pioneer new markets, having done so with financial futures and emissions trading, I wasn't sure if I was prepared for the challenges that awaited me in China. I realized much later that I underestimated the difficulties of finding the right partner. We were tunneling through unknown territories and ambiguous contexts that we struggled to understand. The path forward was plagued with uncertainty.

In Search of the Perfect Exchange Partner

The CCX team made five more trips to China in the next 18 months, from June 2006 to December 2007, searching for a Chinese exchange partner. In September alone, we visited Beijing, Dalian, Guangdong, and Hong Kong. We went to Dalian to meet senior exchange staff, Guangdong to learn about the local environmental protection agency's attempts to reduce SO_2, and Hong Kong to attend the World Hedge Fund Asia Conference, where we worked to stimulate interest among investors and educate speculators on emissions as an asset class. As the province with the highest GDP in the country, Guangdong was a poster child for China's economic growth. However, with 80,000 factories and 13 million cars, its air pollution was among the worst in the country—1,177,000 metric tons of SO_2

were emitted in Guangdong in 2007 alone, and acid rain accounted for more than 53 percent of Guangdong's total rainfall in the first half of 2010.[20]

While in Hong Kong, Tessa introduced me to her friend Christine Loh. Christine was a former trader, elected political representative, chairman of the Civic Exchange,[21] and a board member of the Hong Kong Stock Exchange (HKEx). She invited us to a dinner that she had organized for major power companies, trading companies, and exchange members. When I stepped into the dining venue, my gaze was arrested by a poster image from the 1955 movie, *Love Is a Many-Splendored Thing.* Tamara, my former piano teacher, had taught me how to play its theme song on the piano. My unpracticed fingers had stumbled over the keys, trying to produce the elegant melody that I had heard at the cinema. Now, standing at the entrance of the dining venue in Hong Kong, I replayed the melody in my head and felt a strong sense of nostalgia. I found out later that Christine's childhood home was actually featured in the movie. Our trip was filled with strange, yet wondrous, surprises.

The event helped CCX reach out to more Chinese firms and offset providers. I thought that perhaps Hong Kong could be an ideal stepping stone to emissions trading in China. The SO_2 emissions problems in Guangdong, coupled with the massive financial trading base in Hong Kong, made Hong Kong an promising prospect for partnership.

I had been looking forward to the meeting with the Hong Kong Exchanges and Clearing (HKEx) staff. There appeared to be a perfect fit for a collaborative relationship. HKEx had an existing platform with well-developed infrastructure, and was forming a study group to consider its strategy in carbon markets. We positioned ourselves as

---

[20]Z. Lu, D. G. Streets, Q. Zhang, G. R. Carmichael, Y. F. Cheng, C. Wei, M. Chin, T. Diehl, and Q. Tan, "Sulfur Dioxide Emissions in China and Sulfur Trends in East Asia since 2000," Atmospheric Chemistry and Physics, July 13, 2010; "News Digest: Guangdong Faces Acid Rain," *The China*, December 26, 2010.

[21]The Civic Exchange is an independent, public policy–oriented think tank based in Hong Kong. It promotes civic education as well as research on social, political, and economic policies.

partners and not consultants. However, HKEx was only interested in our role as consultants, so there wasn't a fit at the time. Nevertheless, we made some good friends with members of the management team that enabled us to work with the exchange in the future.

Our reputation in China continued to grow. I was invited to join the board of the International Advisory Council of the Guanghua School of Management, Peking University. Kellogg's dean emeritus, Don Jacobs, had led an effort to partner with the Guanghua School of Management more than a decade ago and was responsible for creating the international advisory committee there. In addition, I was later appointed a distinguished adjunct professor of finance at Peking University. All this created a very important local network, and CCX's visibility in China experienced another boost.

A Turn of Fortune

We still hadn't found the right partner. Existing futures exchanges in China were interested in the education, but had no interest in a joint venture. As a business, emissions trading was still nascent in China and there was no incentive for existing exchanges to build this new market. The path forward remained unclear. The summer of 2007, however, changed our fortunes in ways we did not anticipate.

It all started with a phone call I received from Jeff Huang one morning. "Dr. Dai has been promoted to head of CNPC Asset Management. CNPC is interested in exploring an MOU with CCX!" Jeff exclaimed. The MOU signaled CNPC's willingness to establish a joint venture in order to explore the feasibility and implementation of an emissions trading platform in China. Perhaps all our efforts—the interminable flights, jet lag, dining marathons, repetitive presentations—were finally paying off. Dr. Dai had delivered a major milestone for CCX. It was the start of a promising journey.

CNPC was the consummate partner. After all, it was the largest company in China and a state-owned enterprise. Moreover, its action on climate change, by being part of our effort, was a huge signal to other companies in China. It showcased the proactive stance of CNPC and the Chinese government. Many years later, at the Futures

Industry Meeting in Boca Raton, Florida, Mr. Wang Guoliang, CFO of CNPC, was asked by a reporter about why he expected the partnership with CCX to be profitable. Mr. Wang observed, "We didn't form the joint venture for short-term profits. We are committed to using emissions markets as a way to achieve China's environmental objectives."

To exploit the favorable turn of events, I arranged to fly to Beijing during the first week of December 2007. The game was now elevated. The trip was highly speculative, and we were uncertain that we could persuade the board of CNPC to sign the MOU. Given the level of publicity the partnership would generate, I suspected that the MOU needed to be reviewed at the highest levels of the company and the Chinese government before it could be signed. In fact, we arrived on a Monday not even knowing if a meeting with CNPC would even occur. Nonetheless, we hoped that our physical presence in Beijing would signal how important the MOU was to us. Doing business in China often made me feel like Tantalus, forever yearning for that succulent fruit that was beyond reach. As I later learned, it was common to be surprised while doing business in China. Meetings with significant government officials would materialize suddenly and we always had to be prepared for the unexpected. Most of our days deviated from the planned itinerary significantly. This constant lack of control was mentally and physically exhausting.

After four uneasy days, Dr. Dai finally arrived unexpectedly on a Friday morning and announced that he had received the consent to proceed with the MOU. The deal was back on track. We spent the morning discussing the outline of the MOU. As we negotiated, the conversation drifted from commercial terms into contemporary Chinese culture. I quoted Sun Tzu's *The Art of War* in English, and Dr. Dai repeated the exact quote in Chinese. We knew at that moment that this agreement would be consummated, at least in principle. The MOU was only the first step. The next step was to consummate a joint venture agreement.

Once we had the outline of the MOU, the time was ripe to meet Minister Xie Zhenhua, vice chairman of the National Development and Reform Commission (NDRC). The NDRC was one the most powerful arms of the Chinese government, responsible for the country's

Five-Year Plans. The meeting took place at the NDRC headquarters, with everyone seated according to Chinese business customs. Minister Xie sat in a large chair at one end of the room. Maurice Strong, his esteemed guest and personal friend, sat to his immediate right. I sat to Maurice's right. The rest of our team was seated one after the other, according to their positions within CCX.

We received many questions about our trading volumes. I shared the story of CCX and covered the history of SO_2 emissions in the United States. We also indicated that CCX had conducted an auction of CERs on behalf of an Indian company—Tata Motors—and had realized higher prices than were available in bilateral contracts. Minister Xie expressed great interest in this activity. The meeting concluded on a very positive note, and we left feeling optimistic.

The signing of the MOU was only the first stage, and additional work remained. Due diligence had to be conducted by both parties. We also had to decide where to locate the exchange and what products to list. A lengthy and unpredictable process was expected before any real partnership could emerge. Paula and I flew back to China during the first week of January to discuss the specifics of the MOU. We hired a Chinese law firm to assist us in drafting the MOU, and were assured by our lawyers that there were no legal impediments to foreigners having equity in a Chinese exchange.

On December 18, 2007, after 18 months of promoting the CCX brand and raising public awareness of emissions trading, the MOU was finally signed with CNPC Asset Management (CNPC AM).

In broad terms, the MOU spelled out our objective of establishing a climate exchange in China that employed market-based mechanisms. We sought to both facilitate China's economic growth and improve its environment—including bolstering the health of the Chinese population. Our intent was to sign a joint venture agreement before the MOU expired. We planned to establish a joint venture and conduct a feasibility study, similar to what we had submitted to the Joyce Foundation in the early years of CCX.

In the past, numerous MOUs had been signed by non-Chinese entities with Chinese companies. My experiences in China had taught me that that these agreements were neither promises to be engaged nor actual engagements. MOUs signed in China were organic and subject to continuous change. I had a difficult time adapting to this, especially because I came from a country where an MOU unequivocally led to a deal. MOUs in the United States were often straightforward and originally tended to be executed as written originally. The experience reminded me of the insurance market, where contracts were somewhat ambiguous and were only settled after there had been a claim for a loss. Nevertheless, after extended negotiations, we signed a joint venture agreement. CNPC emerged as the majority shareholder, and equity was reserved for the city where we would be located.

The Birth of the Tianjin Climate Exchange

The location of our exchange was a trophy that was vied for by various Chinese cities. Although we met with mayors of major cities, it was a lesser known city that emerged as the champion—one that was neither China's capital nor its financial center.

I met Vice Mayor Cui Jin Du of Tianjin during the MOU signing ceremony with CNPC. He expressed an interest in collaboration, and was very specific about the benefits of establishing the climate exchange in Tianjin. The city had established the Tianjin Property Exchange (TPRE), and the People's Republic of China had enabled the formation of the Tianjin Economic Development Area (TEDA). The economic development area designation foretold the city's increasing economic importance. The Pudong area of Shanghai and the City of Shenzhen had also been granted the status of economic development areas and had subsequently become an important part of what might be termed the "Chinese miracle." The Pudong area had been a rice field when I first visited China. It now boasted a skyline that appeared more magnificent than that of Manhattan.

Tianjin had been identified as a location for financial innovation. The city had spent several years building its understanding of emissions trading. It had even assembled an innovation team of 20 individuals, which included practitioners from the exchange world and professionals with diverse backgrounds such as business, engineering, and law.

Vice Mayor Cui led a tour of TPRE and introduced us to some of its personnel. As evidence of the sincerity of the city's interest, he showed us a new building in the young financial square in the TEDA Binhai development area where the exchange could be located. This was followed by a tour of the TEDA. I asked him why Tianjin had chosen CCX as opposed to a Chinese exchange, and received a response that reverberated with my journey as a financial innovator. "To invent, to invent, to invent," he said. In fact, the description of his credentials read more like those of a CEO than that of a vice mayor. I joked with Dr. Dai that perhaps we had found the "third musketeer."

The negotiations continued for the next six months. A typical day for the Chicago and New York staff of CCX began at five or six in the morning and ended after midnight. As with commercial negotiations of any sort, further face-to-face meetings had to be arranged. The team made numerous trips, to and from China, for these negotiations.

The next critical point was the division of equity and the final choice for a partner city. We settled on Tianjin, and decided to name the joint venture the Tianjin Climate Exchange (TCX). After months of negotiating and renegotiating, a two-day due diligence trip from the team at CNPC-AM paid a visit to our offices in Chicago, and capitalized the company with 100 million renminbi (RMB). It also was an opportunity for the CNPC team to meet other members of the CCX staff. We prepared briefings and presentation about all aspects of how CCX and CCFE were run, from the sales division to the role of compliance and technology, and ended each day by showing our partners the great sights of Chicago. Like the Chinese, I was proud of my cultural heritage and took the team to one of my favorite steakhouses.

We reached a final agreement, in which CNPC-AM was the majority shareholder with 53 percent. CCX retained 25 percent, and TPRE received 23 percent.

I returned to China with Ellen for the official signing of the MOU on May 9, 2008, in order to express my personal commitment to the joint venture. Ellen and I attended various lectures together and spent a day with Dr. Dai and his family. In China, family friendships were integral to any business relationship. This was crucial for anyone interested in doing business in China, where business tended to be relationship-oriented rather than transaction-oriented.

Dr. Dai brought his daughter that day and carefully explained to her my teaching credentials. Teachers enjoyed tremendous respect in the Chinese social hierarchy—perhaps a legacy of Confucius himself. Dr. Dai, and other CNPC executives, often introduced me to their children as the "American Professor," so I could give them advice about education and studying in the United States. Education was held in high regard, and this was evident in all areas of Chinese life. The academic ring of CCX helped us build the network and credentials in China that were critical to the successes we had had to date.

The educational efforts continued. I delivered a lecture on emissions trading at the Guanghua School of Management at Peking University on the very same day I landed. We planned to start an environmental finance course at Guanghua just as we had done at Columbia. This helped to lay the groundwork for future TCX activities.

We also briefed the Development Research Center of the State Council, the institution that conducted the research for the national Five-Year Plans. The group was very interested in how China would continue its transition to a market economy. I emphasized the work of Professor Coase and was surprised to learn that almost all of the attendees knew his work. Coase's student, Wang Ning, once remarked, "To my knowledge, no other Western economist, probably with the exception of Karl Marx, has ever been so honored in China."[22] In fact, a conference titled "Coase and China" was also organized in Beijing and Shanghai to celebrate his 100th birthday.

Professor Coase had previously organized a conference in 2008 at the University of Chicago on China's Economic Transformation. It was a eclectic gathering of leading Chinese academics, practitioners,

---

[22]Wang Ning, "Interview with Professor Ronald Coase," paper presented at Coase and China Conference in Beijing, Unirule Institute of China, December 28–29, 2010.

and entrepreneurs. I was honored to be the only non-Chinese speaker. I shared my experiences of starting an environmental exchange in China.[23]

On May 4, after all the details of the joint venture had been agreed to, a dinner was held at the Heaven and Earth Restaurant. We thought that dining again at the location of our original meeting would be propitious. It seemed to be a custom in China that no matter how difficult the business negotiations, they were always followed by a celebratory dinner. This reminded me of my experiences at Liffe, where a casual lunch always followed the board meetings. Business dinners in China, however, were never a casual affair. In China, a great deal of importance was placed on dinner, as it was seen as a bonding experience. I was always delighted by the beautiful presentation of the dishes, and even Ellen thought it was food and art at its best. My CCX colleagues often had great difficulty with chopsticks. Upon seeing Rohan Ma struggling to pick up a piece of bean curd with his chopsticks, the waiter commented, "You are very skillful with your chopsticks. Do they have chopsticks in the United States? You are really quite skilled. . . . Let me get you a fork and knife." Everyone broke into laughter.

All three partners signed the joint venture contract on July 25, to be made public on July 31. We had met the challenge of landing equity in a Chinese exchange.

Raising TCX

Since the signing of the joint venture agreement, enthusiasm levels had been high among the staff of Chicago, Beijing, and Tianjin. The Chinese industry press was filled with CNPC initiatives and successes, and every serious player in the environment market was expanding their offices in China.

The Chicago office, too, seemed to be infected with our recent successes in China. We started to see Chinese art taking over the

---

[23]China's Economic Transformation, July 14–July 18, 2008, conference sponsored by the University of Chicago Law School, University of Chicago Graduate School of Business, and the Coase Foundation.

scarcely available wall space—the result of my avid art collection. For Christmas that year, I presented each employee with a gold coin enclosed in a Chinese *hong bao*, or red envelope, embellished with golden dragons. "The dragon is for good luck and prosperity with all our ventures," I toasted at the end-of-year Christmas party.

Everyone was keen on demonstrating some form of emissions transaction through TCX. This was important to show proof of concept and build trust in the new market. CCX had just completed a very successful CER auction for the Indian corporation, Tata, and I felt that the same formula could be applied in China. If we managed to pull off a Chinese CER auction, the CER price for a Chinese project would be set in Chinese soil for the first time, as opposed to overseas. Not only did this make practical sense, it would also be a source of pride for China given that the Chinese provided about half of the CER volume to the world.

Compared to the CER projects found in other parts of the world, Chinese projects tended to be much larger, the majority of which were generated by a batch of industrial manufacturing processes that had been approved by the UN CDM board. The size of Chinese CER projects was both an advantage and a disadvantage. On one hand, the big industrial companies behind these projects had already sold their tons long-term to European buyers. On the other hand, if we managed to strike a deal with one of them, not only would we be able generate meaningful business volume, but attract the other CER generators on board as well.

CCX delivered technology for auction and trading platforms. To complement this software, the research team wrote a series of manuals to educate our Chinese colleagues on auctions, electronic trading, and offset programs in general. These were all written in English and subsequently translated into Chinese. Even the technology was bilingual, accommodating both Chinese and English speakers.

One source of frustration during this education process was the tendency for management to assume that establishing markets was formulaic. They approached the problem like industrialists, not financiers. Blueprints were simply duplicated and there was little understanding of the need to build human capital and institutions to successfully build markets. We strongly advocated for the appointment of a general manager who had the knowledge and the stature to represent TCX to the CEOs in the international exchange world. The board was not persuaded. We became more determined to educate the exchange management in order to overcome their shortcomings regarding knowledge of capital markets.

Paula and Rohan had set up an office in the Grand Beijing hotel to direct the progress of TCX. Although only 24 years old and a recent college graduate, Rohan had a confidence and business aptitude that was beyond his years and was an invaluable asset throughout the process. On one occasion, he was sent to a high-level meeting with senior government officials. As the meeting began, Rohan was told that he had to say a few words on CCX's behalf. Unprepared for this, he started scribbling down notes frantically. After he made some customary remarks, someone asked, "How does TCX plan to beat out Shanghai and Beijing in this market?" Recalling what I once told him, Rohan responded, "Liquidity is king, because liquidity doesn't move once it settles. If TCX is successful early on in bringing in the important companies, we will be able to maintain our lead because of our liquidity. To win liquidity, you have to sell constantly. It's very important that we market the program 24 hours a day, 7 days a week, and 365 days a year!" What Rohan said won praise as the mayor's assistant openly extolled these ideas in front of the group.

At my request, Murali traveled to Beijing in 2008 to join Paula and Rohan to help educate our CNPC colleagues on emission allowance auctioning procedures. The summer Olympics had just ended in Beijing. The new Beijing airport had been built to coincide with the Olympics—plush monorails extended from the airport gates into an immense main terminal. The sense of pride, patriotism, and accomplishment was felt everywhere.

Murali had the name of his hotel printed out in Chinese for the benefit of his cab driver. As they drove through the highway, the car driver missed no opportunity to point out any visible signs of China's economic success. "Brand new road . . . brand new," he bragged, and added mischievously, "Is Delhi like this?" The Chinese people were proud of their long history and culture. They knew their time had come and were prepared to lead. In a strange way, China and CCX shared the same aspirations.

There were other challenges. We had to win the approval of the Chinese government in order to conduct our proposed auction. To land approval, we needed to make the transaction a completely Chinese-driven process, with our ventures backed by a Chinese identity that reflected the spirit of Chinese people. One productive piece of advice emerged while discussing the name of the auction. It was suggested that instead of calling it an auction, it would be better to call it a bidding market. Our partners felt this sent the nuanced message that we were seeking buyers.

Keen to finally put a face on the Chinese associates they had been working with for so long, the team took the new super-fast trains from Beijing to Tianjin. I recalled marveling at how clean and modern the new stations were. The TCX offices in the Binhai Tianjin complex had rows of glass buildings that playfully resembled rows of mobile cell phones standing upright. Newly appointed staff sat together in the open reception area in the building. It reminded me of the setup that CCX had when it first started, where we all sat around a big table, discussing and learning about the new market. This setup fostered interaction and the sharing of ideas.

A young team from Chicago led the training of the TCX auction platform and trading platform for the TCX staff. It was attended by everyone in the TCX hierarchy, from the IT staff to the CEO. Our partners at TCX were quick to grasp certain elements of the auction platform, but struggled to understand others. Relatively quickly, they were able to design and administer basic auctions, but seemed to be baffled by other concepts like escrow accounts. While our past experiences were helpful, they were at best guideposts in this new territory. Many questions were asked, and procedures had to be fine-tuned to Chinese realities. Everything from the auction specifications to legal contracts had to be understood and reworked to fit the Chinese framework. The CCX team and TCX team had a lot to learn from each other.

When touring the TCX office, Murali's attention fell on a room that had no windows, an ironclad door lined with multiple locks. "The person in this room must be very important," he jested. He was later told that the room was where the exchange intended to keep all their daily revenues from trading. The complete electronic nature of transactions had to be explained. There was much internal education to be done.

By the end of the CCX mission in China, we had managed to create a wide level of discussion on the auction opportunity. The grand opening of TCX was not far away, and we wanted to have a demo to showcase the opening. TCX successfully concluded an auction of SO_2 allowances at the end of 2008, marking its first commercial activity. Finally, after receiving the approval of the Ministry of the Environmental Protection and the Ministry of Finance, TCX conducted an online auction of 50 metric tons of SO_2 emissions allowances in a demonstration project. With seven active bidders competing, the settlement price was 3,100 yuan per ton, with Tianjin Hongpeng Co., Ltd as the winner.

In just over two years, the CCX team had built a vast network and concluded a path-breaking agreement. CCX became the only foreign entity to hold equity in a Chinese exchange. We established an exchange that could implement emissions trading as a policy tool in China. Imitators had emerged during this period in both Beijing and Shanghai and had announced their formation before we did. Unperturbed, we moved on to conduct the first auction of SO_2 emissions at TCX. It was amazing to think that all of this was accomplished with our limited resources.

The trust and respect between the partners continued after we had signed the agreement. The agreement provided that CNPC would designate a chairman, vice chairman, and five directors. Dr. Dai became chairman, I joined the board as vice chairman, and Paula became a director of the exchange.

The Opening of TCX

On August 15, 2008, Tianjin Climate Exchange was granted a business license by the Tianjin Municipal Authority to start a pilot program. Approval was granted by the Ministry of Finance and the Ministry of Environmental Protection in three separate areas: SO_2, chemical oxygen demand (COD), and a measure of water quality and energy efficiency.

TCX opened its doors formally on September 25, 2008. It was vital to send a signal to China and the rest of the world that TCX was an important institution. The partners lavished the opening ceremony with a level of care and attention that was generally reserved for an official visit of the head of state in the United States. Despite the fact that our opening coincided with the summer of 2008 when China was diverting all national resources to Beijing to prepare for the Olympics, no detail was left to chance. The stage was adorned with red velvet, and signs were placed on major highways to direct guests through the maze of construction to the new TCX headquarters. Students from Renmin University even volunteered to direct traffic and handle protocol.

A huge screen at the TCX office displayed the new TCX auction and trading platform, with a demo provided by a CNPC employee. The office included a special exhibit on the history of climate change, complete with taxidermy of extinct species. The walls downstairs were plastered with posters and photos commemorating milestones in the negotiation of the joint venture agreements. Video screens were also set up that displayed the actions each partner in the joint venture had taken to address climate change.

Among the 300 guests in the opening day were friends and dignitaries such as the China director for the World Bank, the managing director of the Davos World Economic Forum, and numerous high-level Chinese and business officials. Dr. Dai invited me to speak on behalf of the partnership, and I presented an overview of the objectives of the new exchange and cited the historic nature of the occasion. Mr. Wang, CFO of CNPC, also spoke about the strategic importance of TCX and noted the high level of attention that the new exchange had received at his firm. He proclaimed that the establishment of the exchange marked a new stage in the development of emission rights trading in China and could provide the country with a long-term mechanism for energy conservation and economic development. He and Vice Mayor Cui proceeded to unveil a beautiful, glistening plaque, complete with a cannon shooting golden confetti. A festive lunch for guests was held at the TEDA International Center, followed by an academic seminar in the afternoon featuring leading Chinese academics discussing climate change and emissions trading.

Immediately following the seminar, Mr. Wang, Dr. Dai, Maurice Strong, Paula DiPerna, Jeff Huang, and I held a private dinner to celebrate and discuss next steps for the partnership.

We had hired photographers and videographers to document the opening ceremony, and our colleague from CNPC eventually sent me an ornate box filled with photos and video footage of the ceremony. On the box, written in gold, were the words "cap and trade."

During my personal experiences in the United States and Europe, individuals seemed more driven by guilt than by shame. My experiences in China demonstrated the reverse. I was growing more conscious of *mian zi*, or face. I met with the CFO of CNPC, Wang Guoliang, only after proving myself to Dr. Dai. Similarly, I only met with the vice president and president of CNPC after I earned the confidence of Wang Guoliang. I had to prove myself at each stage so that none of the men who supported our efforts would lose face. I was later invited to give a lecture at a conference for the top 100 executives at CNPC. The CNPC conference was broadcast on the company's website only after being well received by the 100 top members of their management.

The World Is Getting Flatter!

During my many trips to China and India trying to establish emission markets, I was constantly reminded of the competitive world we lived in. A humorous incident in Mumbai, India, proved insightful into the complex outcomes of this globalizing world.

In their many travels through the congested roads of Mumbai City, Mike Walsh and Murali frequently passed by a traffic-ridden intersection known locally as Prabhu Chowk, which connected southern Mumbai to the city center. Talk about entrepreneurship—the kids from the local slum found the intersection to be the perfect spot to market various wares to the folks caught in traffic. Mike's gaze fell upon a kid holding a pile of recently released books in his arms. There was Al Gore's *An Inconvenient Truth*, Stephen Hawking's *A Brief History of Time*, and, of course, Tom Friedman's *The World Is Flat*. "How much?" Mike asked. "100 rupees," the kid replied in a business-like manner. This was roughly $2. The same book on U.S. shelves sold for $16. Out of curiosity, Mike bought the book. As Mike examined his new possession later on, he noticed that every page of Tom's original book had been photocopied on cheaper paper. It was the same content but delivered at a cheaper cost and manufactured locally. Here was a kid who was telling us the world was indeed flat by selling us *The World Is Flat.* About halfway into the book, the pages were blank.

This funny incident highlighted many lessons for our own adventures. The combination of their long cultural histories and growing economies made China and India formidable forces in the future. Both possessed huge intellectual capital and a growing community of entrepreneurs who were hungry to lead. The world was truly changing. The lower barriers to economic innovation and wealth creation were leading to more efficient ways of production.

However, this transformation was not always smooth or fair, at least in the eyes of some. Corruption remained prevalent in some countries, and the regards for intellectual property rights were scant. Massive infrastructure needed to be built before these economies could advance. Given the right institutional base, India and China had the right ingredients to be major contributors to financial innovation in the future.

The People's Bank of China

As part of our educational and outreach efforts, Jeff Huang arranged a visit to the People's Bank of China, where I met with the head of the Bank's Research Bureau. It was evident that the bank had an interest in the environment and its impact on the Chinese economy. The idea for a potential collaboration between CCX, TCX, and the bank began to germinate.

On one of my next trips, a personal meeting was arranged for me with Dr. Zhou Xiaochuan, head of China's central bank. It was important for central bankers to understand emissions trading. I had already met with Ben Bernanke, his U.S. counterpart, to brief him on CCX, and he had been interested in our progress.

Dr. Zhou was a soft-spoken intellectual with impeccable academic credentials. During our conversation, Dr. Zhou mentioned that he had attended the Nobel Memorial Lecture in Stockholm in 1991 when Ronald Coase had received his Nobel Prize. It was an auspicious coincidence that we both had been influenced by Professor Coase. Equally surprising was Dr. Zhou's outstanding grasp of emissions trading as a policy tool. It was refreshing and humbling to see one of the most powerful central bankers in the world appreciating what we were doing. I also mentioned my interest in establishing a futures market for interest rates in China. This seemed inevitable as China gradually adopted flexible exchange rates and market-determined interest rates. "I hope you will continue to promote this idea in China," Dr. Zhou said sincerely.

Our meeting provided the impetus to formalize the creation of a China–U.S. Low-Carbon Finance Research Center under the auspices of PBC. The center would be housed in Chicago and Beijing, providing a forum where Chinese and American academics and practitioners could share expertise in the development of a low-carbon future for China. We failed to complete this project, unfortunately, because we were focused on selling CLE.

We sold Climate Exchange PLC to ICE in July 2010. I had personally briefed our Chinese partners about the sale one week after it was signed, assured them of ICE's stature, and expressed my willingness to help in the future. I subsequently introduced the CEO and CFO of ICE to Vice Mayor Cui and the head of CNPC AM.

I sometimes look back on those astounding years and wonder how the story will turn out. To this day, I follow it with great interest and anxiously await my next trip.

A Postscript on China

The offices of TCX are now located in the new Bonsai Financial Area, the "Wall Street of Tianjin," connected to Tianjin proper by a fast new bullet train that has turned a formerly nightmarish one-hour car trip into a fast 10-minute train ride. Tianjin itself is now connected to Beijing. A trip from downtown Beijing to the new TCX offices takes 1.5 hours, compared to the three-hour car trip when our joint venture discussions began. When Dr. Dai's daughter first came to the United States, I offered to have someone escort her from the airport to Penn Station. When she entered Penn Station, she remarked, "Oh, this is what China *used* to look like!" How things have changed.

Remarkable changes have also occurred in the Chinese futures market. China established a futures market in equity indexes on April 16, 2010. It has since become the fastest-growing futures market ever to be introduced in the world.[23] When China opened its economy in 1982, futures exchanges started to emerge in the country with astounding speed. By 1994, China had 40 futures exchanges.[24] Market abuse and non-enforcement of contracts, however, were problematic. By 2004, these 40 futures exchanges eventually merged into three exchanges and 188 futures brokerages.[25]

As the Chinese economy grows and becomes even more open, interest rates will become more volatile. As a result, asset liability management may become more desirable to Chinese banks. Another opportunity for China lies in currency futures, given that China's currency, the RMB, will cease to be fixed at some point in the future. There are also prospects for energy markets. Local products like natural gas and power may begin to emerge, and China may begin to seek its own benchmark for crude oil.

TCX has stimulated interest in the role of emissions markets in reducing pollution. There are currently three environmental exchanges in China, not including the ones in Hong Kong,[26] and

---

[23]The futures contracts on the first day of trading reached over $8.86 billion in combined turnover. Zhou Yan and Wang Ying, "Futures Rise on Trading Debut," *China Daily*, April 17, 2010.

[24]Leslie Hook, "China: Rapid Growth but Influence Stunted by Restrictions," *Financial Times*, November 29, 2010.

[25]"China's Securities and Futures Markets," China Securities Regulatory Commission, March 2005.

[26]Shanghai Environment Energy Exchange (SEEE), Beijing Environment Exchange (EBEEX), and Tianjin Climate Exchange (TCX).

seven emissions trading schemes.[27] There has been a growing fondness for markets among the government, industrial sector, and academic circles. The 12th Five-Year Plan has called for a reduction in energy intensity of 40 to 45 percent below 2005 levels by 2020. While this is a voluntary commitment, we should not underestimate the political will underlying this objective. Once a consensus has been reached in the PRC, swift action generally follows. I would not be surprised if China developed a national cap-and-trade program before the United States does.

[27]"China Picks Shenzhen to Host Seventh CO_2 Trading Scheme," *Point Carbon*, November 3, 2011.

Chapter 25

Good Derivatives

The Best Has Yet to Come

> Chicago will give you a chance. The sporting spirit is the spirit of Chicago.
>
> —*Lincoln Steffens*

This book has been a personal story of my past four decades of financial innovation in Chicago, London, Paris, Mumbai, and Beijing. I've learned a lot from these successes, and more from the failures. This story follows my transformation from an academic in a period of social unrest into a practitioner during a time of cataclysmic change in the futures industry. It then chronicles my experience as an entrepreneur. The times changed, and I had to change with them.

The year 1970 serves as the starting point because it marked the beginning of my professional interest in organized futures markets. The natural bookend is 2010, the year I sold the Chicago Climate Exchange PLC. We conclude with a review of the past, lessons learned, and some thoughts about the next 40 years.

The Past 40 Years

This has been a story about LaSalle Street, not Wall Street. Over the last 40 years, the geographic expansion of financial innovation from the Midwest has been astonishing. In a short span of time, financial futures have taken over the reins of commodity trading. We have also witnessed a drastic transformation in the structure of exchanges, geographic expansion, products diversity, trading platforms and futures regulatory framework.

In 1970, futures trading in the United States reached a record level of 13.7 million contracts. Corn, wheat, and soybean futures at the Chicago Board of Trade were the most widely traded products. The CBOT was the world's oldest and largest exchange, followed by a distant second, the Chicago Mercantile Exchange. Derivatives trading was dominated by the United States. Although small markets existed in Canada, the United Kingdom, Australia, and New Zealand in 1975, they constituted less than 7 percent of the world's total volume.[1] Even in the United States, derivatives exchanges constituted a very small part of the financial sector. All of these exchanges were mutually owned at the time, and trading was still conducted physically on exchange floors. One-third of the increase in volume between 1960 and 1970 came from new products. It was just the beginning of financial innovation.

By 2010, there were 22.3 billion contracts traded on more than 78 derivatives exchanges in 36 countries. New derivatives and new exchanges were responsible for almost all of the growth over the past 40 years. The compounded annual growth rate in the volume of futures and options traded was over 18 percent for the 40-year period from 1970 to 2010. The industry doubled every 3.9 years. This far surpassed the growth in number of airline passengers,[2] or the number of automobiles produced,[3] during the same period. Futures and options that didn't

---

[1]"World Market Share of the Futures Industry in 1975, Institutional Financial Futures and Options," Drexel Burnham Lambert Inc., 1989 internal presentation.

[2]The number of air passengers worldwide was 310.4 million in 1970 and 2.274 billion in 2010. This translates to a compounded annual growth rate of 5.1 percent.

[3]Total number of passenger cars in the world was 170 million in 1970 and 622 million in 2010. This translates into a compounded growth rate of 3.2 percent.

exist in 1970 now constitute 79.8 percent of the volume on organized exchanges in the United States.[4] Trading in new commodity complexes such as futures and options on interest rates, stocks, stock indexes, energy, and foreign currencies has bolstered the lightning growth of the industry. Even gold as a commodity was not introduced until this period, as it was illegal for U.S. citizens to own gold before 1975. Since its inception in 2004, the commoditization of air, water, and catastrophic events is no longer a chimera, but a solid reality.

Interest rate, equity index, and energy products have been successfully replicated in Europe and are emerging in Asia. With the changing world economy, Brent Crude, the European grade of crude oil, is already replacing West Texas Intermediate as the world benchmark for oil futures.[5] In fact, the S&P GSCI has recently decided to increase the weighting of Brent Crude relative to West Texas Intermediate. The global listed derivatives markets have changed dramatically, and North America, specifically the United States, seems to be losing its hegemony. The Asia Pacific region is quickly becoming the new world leader in the volume of contracts traded (39.8 percent), followed by North America (32.3 percent), Europe (19.8 percent) and Latin America (6.85 percent).[6] Some of this shift in geography is explained by the smaller contract sizes found on Asian exchanges.

Trading platforms are now predominantly electronic. Those men and women in colorful jackets, frantically signaling and waving their hands in trading pits, have been reduced to a minority. While the shift away from pit trading was faced with much resistance, 85 percent of the entire volume at the CME Group, the largest U.S. futures exchange, is traded electronically today. All new exchanges today are electronic. Furthermore, much of the reference prices in today's world are determined onscreen rather than in the pits. We are seeing an increasing number of high frequency traders (HFTs) who are proving

[4]"Volume of Futures and Options Trading on U.S. Exchanges 2010," Futures Industry Association.

[5]"S&P Move to Increase Brent's Index Weighting Will Cost WTI," *Financial Times*, November 5 and 6, 2011.

[6]Annual Volume Survey 2010, Futures Industry Association. While these statistics are based on the standard used in the futures and options industry, they do not represent notional value.

competitive in a space once dominated by market makers in the pits and by upstairs quants. HFTs, who reap profits from market inefficiencies by using computerized trading strategies characterized by brief holding periods, constitute over 70 percent of trading in equities and a rising share of listed derivatives.[7] Trading is now done through computer code that replicates human market-making behavior. In short, trading has migrated from a pit to a box.

Unlike the 1970s, existing and new exchanges are now run as for-profit enterprises. Derivatives exchanges have transitioned into publicly traded companies in the United States, Europe, Canada, Japan, Australia, New Zealand, and Singapore. The Europeans began this trend, and the Americans later followed. New products were developed on existing exchanges. In other instances, new products demanded the formation of new exchanges like CCX. This required both new laws and regulatory structures.

While we cannot quantify the amount of human and financial capital spent, we can infer the replication costs of "good" derivatives—derivatives that are regulated, transparent and traded on exchanges—from the market capitalization of the exchanges that created them. The total market capitalization of derivatives exchanges in the United States is $33.9 billion. Chicago's major exchanges—the CME Group and the CBOE—had a combined market capitalization of $23.6 billion in December 2010.[8] These figures also indicate that Chicago exchanges account for more than two-thirds of the total market capitalization of all types of exchanges in the United States. A relatively new exchange, Intercontinental Exchange (ICE), had a market capitalization of $10 billion. It would cost about $34 billion to replicate those exchanges. Since 80 percent of the new futures and options contracts were created, we can assume that it would cost about $27 billion to recreate these entities. This may not be totally accurate, but it is good reason for economists not to assume that these exchanges were conjured out of thin air.

---

[7]Hal Weitzman, "Man vs. Machine in the Markets," *Financial Times*, June 29, 2011.

[8]Based on the shares outstanding of the CME and the CBOE as reported in their 10-Ks filed with the SEC on December 31, 2010: (95.754 × 22.86) + (66.495 × 321.75)= $23,583.7 million, or approximately $23.6 billion.

The NYSE Euronext (the parent company of the New York Stock Exchange, the Paris Bourse, the Amsterdam Stock Exchange, the Belgium Stock Exchange, and the derivatives exchange Liffe) had a market capitalization of $7.81 billion as of December 2010. The majority of the valuation for exchanges comes from derivatives, as illustrated by the NYSE family, where as much as 50 percent of the corporate valuation is attributed to its derivatives exchanges.[9] Clearly, the trading landscape has shifted in terms of exchange structure, products traded, and expanded competition.

Another phenomenon that has occurred is the consolidation that followed the surge in new products. Mergers and acquisitions accelerated in the United States after exchanges became publicly traded. By acquiring the CBOT and the NYMEX, the CME emerged as the dominant futures and options exchange not only in the United States, but globally.[10] This trend has not been confined to national borders. Exchange consolidations went international when the German-based Deutsche Börse and Swiss-based SOFFEX merged in 1998 to form Eurex, and Euronext acquired the UK-based Liffe in 2001, fueling a new trend of cross-border mergers. Similarly, Deutsche Börse announced a merger with NYSE-Euronext in February 2011.[11]

Much has been said about the viability of exchanges during tough economic times. Derivatives, along with the broader financial markets, have been accused of causing unnecessary economic risks. Regulated and transparent futures and options, namely good derivatives, have been criticized as if they were subprime mortgages or OTC credit default swaps. Critics and the press have often been sloppy with their generalizations. It is important to note that during the 2008 financial crisis, none of the regulated exchanges required government

[9]Richard Repetto of Sandler O'Neill as quoted in comment by Paul Price on "NYSE Euronext: Finding Gains Thanks to Worldwide Reach and a High Yield," *Seeking Alpha*, January 20, 2010.

[10]The CME consummated its merger with the CBOT on July 12, 2007, for $11.3 billion. On August 22, 2008, the CME Group completed its acquisition of NYMEX for $8.9 billion in cash and CME Group stock.

[11]Ken Sweet, "NYSE, DTB Agree to Merge," *CNNMoney*, February 15, 2011.

bailouts. With regards to financial futures in general, and interest rates in particular, there were no losses associated with these risk management tools. Interest rate futures and options have functioned through thick and thin since 1975. Although interest rate risks had always been present, every bank, be it commercial or investment, had been able to manage these risks effectively through good derivatives. This was very different from the widespread failure of depository institutions in the 1980s. Exchanges were never in danger of creating systemic risk. As a matter of fact, they mitigated it. It would be of great interest to policy makers and the public if economists could quantify the reduction of systemic risk made possible by good derivatives.

Well-regulated and transparent derivatives exchanges provide a number of benefits. Academics and members of the exchange community typically cite three benefits arising from these organized and regulated markets: hedging, price discovery, and in some instances, delivery. These benefits are enormous, and no attempt will be made here to quantify them. The market capitalizations of exchanges only narrowly represent their value, since market capitalization is simply the cost of an exchange replicating itself.

The impact that futures and options markets and centralized clearing have had on the transaction costs in the spot market, be it primary or secondary, has traditionally been overlooked. A back-of-the-envelope analysis suggests that the reduction in transactions costs associated with the 10-year Treasury note, 30-year Treasury bond, and GNMA futures is about $17 billion annually. It's worthwhile to look at where these numbers come from.

The Economic Value of Derivatives Exchanges

Let's look at the most widely traded fixed income futures first—the U.S. 10-year Treasury note futures contract. When the market was started in 1982, the bid-offer spread was 1/8 of a point. Recall that the bid-offer spread can be thought of as the wholesale-retail spread. Shortly after the introduction of the futures contract, the spread was reduced to 1/32. The difference was 3/32, or $93.75 per million. In 2010, the U.S. government issued $265 billion in 10-year notes.

The Economic Value of Derivatives Exchanges (*Continued*)

This is known as the primary market. The arithmetic yields a reduction of $246 million in transaction costs. Informed sources tell us that the secondary spot market trading was 22.64 times the primary issuance, or approximately $6 trillion. At a reduction of $93.75 per million in transaction costs, the total reduction is approximately $5.6 billion. While it is not possible here to determine the exact beneficiaries, it is likely that some significant portion inures to fixed income investors such as pension funds and mutual funds, as well the U.S. government. Arguably, other factors such as the size of the market and the proliferation of transparent electronic spot markets have helped to maintain the current bid-offer spreads. It was the introduction of the 10-year Treasury note futures, however, that narrowed the bid-offer spread in the first place and sustained it at the current level for many years before the other factors emerged.

Similarly, the narrowing of spreads began with the introduction of GNMA futures where the bid-offer spread was reduced from 24/32 to 1/32—equaling a reduction of 23/32. In 2010, the reduced transaction costs translated to $269,843,750 in savings in the primary market, and $9,343,750,000 in savings in the secondary market.

There is another way to look at this. The reduction of $718.75 per $100,000 means that a $200,000 mortgage is reduced by $1,437.50. That is a savings of $109.08 per year per household. Over the 30-year life, this means a total reduction of $3,272.40. Of course, not all of these transaction savings can be passed on to consumers. For now, this figure reflects the amount of savings for borrowers and lenders in the interest rate sector.

In the market for 30-year Treasury bonds, the bid-offer spread went from 1/4 a point to 1/32. This is equal to a $367,500,000 reduction in transaction costs in the direct sale of 30-year Treasury bonds, and another $1,421,875,000 reduction in transaction costs in the secondary market. Using similar reasoning in the market for 10-year Treasury notes, spreads were reduced from 1/8 to 1/32.

(*continued*)

The Economic Value of Derivatives Exchanges (*Continued*)

The reduction in transaction costs were $246,450,000 in primary issuance and $5,625,056,250 in the secondary market. The same story can be applied to SO_2 emission allowances[12] and CO_2 emission allowances. Academic studies have provided more detailed evidence of this.[13]

[12]$500 million in savings (see Chapter 21, "The Benefits of CCFE," for calculations).

[13]Michael Fleming and Asani Sarkar, *Liquidity in the U.S. Treasury Spot and Futures Markets*, Federal Reserve Bank of New York, 1998.

Bruce Mizrach and Christopher J. Neely, "The Microstructure of the U.S. Treasury Market," Working Paper 2007-052B, Research Division of Federal Reserve Bank of St. Louis, April 14, 2008.

Laying Out the Construct for a Good Derivative

I was recently invited to lecture students at a leading American business school. Most of these MBA candidates were surprised to find out that financial futures were not introduced until the 1970s. They believed, as most people did, that these innovations have always existed. This simple example highlights the common misconception that efficient markets materialized spontaneously. Contrary to this, we have demonstrated throughout this book that the evolution of markets is a multi-year, multi-stage process requiring several ingredients. I discuss these under broad categories that roughly follow a seven-stage process of market development. These stages should be viewed as a framework or construct for understanding how markets develop, and need not necessarily occur in the order presented.

1. *Structural Change*: New markets are commonly triggered by an initial structural economic change that spurs new demand. Throughout history, new markets have emerged not as accidental

events but as responses to new economic realities. In sixteenth- and seventeenth-century Europe, the rapid growth in demand for capital to finance maritime explorations and overseas commerce led to the emergence of the world's first stock markets. The commoditization of interest rates in the United States was preceded by a need to hedge interest rates resulting from high inflation in the early 1970s. Similarly, the acid rain problem in the 1980s was the structural change that triggered the emergence of emissions trading.

2. *Emergence of Uniform Standards*: Once the need for a market has been established, the next ingredient is the development of a uniform standard for the new commodity or security. This standardization process involves commoditizing the underlying asset by defining acceptable physical and delivery attributes for the transaction. In the case of grain, the Chicago Board of Trade defined the standards that were later adopted by the U.S. government. In the case of the EU ETS and the Kyoto Protocol, the standardization function has been performed by regulatory agencies or legal treaties. The same applies to the SO_2 emissions market. This is a necessary step for efficient markets to arise. If you can grade it, you can trade it.
3. *Evidence of Ownership*: Standardization alone may not lead to successful markets. If property rights or evidences of ownership cannot be established, then a market cannot function. We trade evidences of ownership of the underlying commodity and not the commodity itself. A legal basis for enabling the transfer ownership is also required. Standardization does not always come before delineation of ownership. Warehouse receipts for grains emerged before grain standards were created, while Global Warming Potential standards were developed before EU ETS allowances. In some cases, the creation of the standard and the ownership is simultaneous, as evidenced by SO_2 under the Acid Rain Program. The earliest organized spot exchange, the Osaka Rice Exchange in 1697, was feasible because warehouse receipts, known as rice tickets, were recognized as legal instruments of ownership. More recently, trading in interest rates, stock indexes,

and emissions futures have required enabling new legislation and regulations from the CFTC and EPA. Legislative clarity, coupled with effective regulation, has been necessary to achieve their success.

4. *Development of Informal Spot and Forward Markets*: After we have property rights, and the legal framework by which market players could transfer these rights, then an informal spot market and forward markets for the commodity may emerge. The presence of a spot market provides the important function of some price discovery.
5. *Emergence of Organized Spot Exchanges*: The development of informal spot and forward markets may lead to the emergence of securities and commodities exchanges, but only if the gains from these market institutions exceed the costs of establishing them.
6. *Emergence of Organized Futures Exchanges*: The existence of organized spot exchanges leads to price discovery and transparency. Price volatility arises in these markets, which results in a demand for a hedging mechanism. Organized futures markets are established when there is a need to hedge, and futures and options offer the least expensive way to achieve that. New futures markets are more likely to be successful when there are a large number of dealers who take temporary ownership of a commodity or financial instrument. This trend was a major driver in the success of the grain markets, which were dominated by grain elevators and international grain merchants. This was also true of dealers in GNMAs and Treasury bonds.
7. *Proliferation of Over-the-Counter Markets*: The emergence of organized futures markets will then pave way for the proliferation of over-the-counter markets.

Table 25.1 shows four historical examples of the seven stages of market development.

Table 25.1 The Seven Stages of Market Development

	MARKET			
STAGE	**Trading of Shares of the Dutch East India Company (1602)**	**Agricultural Commodities Futures Trading at the Chicago Board of Trade (1848)**	**Trading of Mortgage-Backed Securities (1970)**	**Sulfur Dioxide Trading under the Acid Rain Program of the United States (1990)**
1. Structural Change	"Discovery" of America and sea route to India; Expansion in European maritime trade; Rising demand for capital to outfit ships	Removal of restrictions on grain imports into the United Kingdom (1846) and Crimean War (1854–1856) leading to rising demand for imports from America; Population increase in America adds further demand—encouraging new investments and expanding trade	Widening gap between demand for and supply of housing finance in the late 1960s/early 1970s	Rising concerns about the effects of SO_2 emissions on human health and the environment; A tripling of U.S. pollution-control costs between 1972 and 1990; Keen interest in least-cost solution to SO_2 problem
2. Emergence of Uniform Standards	Issuance of standardized shares by the Dutch East India Company (1602–1606)	Standards for measuring and grading grains set by the Chicago Board of Trade (CBOT)	Mortgage-backed pass-through security issued by Ginnie Mae (1970)	SO_2 allowance as defined by the Clean Air Act Amendments (CAAA) of 1990

(*continued*)

Table 25.1 (*Continued*)

	MARKET			
STAGE	**Trading of Shares of the Dutch East India Company (1602)**	**Agricultural Commodities Futures Trading at the Chicago Board of Trade (1848)**	**Trading of Mortgage-Backed Securities (1970)**	**Sulfur Dioxide Trading under the Acid Rain Program of the United States (1990)**
3. Evidence of Ownership	Shares recognized by the Company's clerks as evidence of ownership	Warehouse receipts issued as proof of ownership and made legally enforceable as of 1859	Mortgage-backed securities (pass-throughs and bonds) find growing acceptance as financial products	SO_2 allowance; Registry of U.S. Environmental Protection Agency (EPA)
4. Development of Informal Spot Markets	Emergence of a spot market, linked as of 1611 in an informal way to the Amsterdam commodity exchange, the Amsterdam Bourse	Trading based on warehouse receipts begins	Informal trading between the government-sponsored agencies and Wall Street dealers, mortgage originators and investors	Various trading pilots during 1970s/80s and private sales of allowances in early 1990s; Test auctions in 1993 and 1994
5. Emergence of Organized Spot Exchanges	Amsterdam Stock Exchange formally established (1876)	CBOT Charter (1859)	Secondary Mortgage Market Enhancement Act of 1984 and Tax Reform Act of 1986	Annual auctions conducted by CBOT on behalf of EPA

6. Emergence of Organized Futures Exchanges	Futures and options on single "stocks" were common although not legal according to the Dutch law	Futures contracts being formalized (1865)	Ginnie Mae futures introduced at CBOT (1975); Collateralized mortgage obligations (CMOs) issued by Freddie Mac (1983)	Futures being used but not yet within an official framework
7. Proliferation of Over-the-Counter Markets	Ducaton shares representing one tenth of the value of the earlier shares were issued in the early 1680s, encouraging over-the-counter trading	Options ("privileges") and over-the counter ("bucket shop") trading begins to take off (1879)	Increasing number of private retailers in mortgage-backed securities markets	Informal over-the-counter trades

Lessons Learned

The successes and failures I had in the futures markets during the past 40 years have taught me many valuable lessons. Five stand out.

1. ***Need for Unambiguous Legal and Regulatory Framework***—Legislation and regulation should be enacted so as to minimize transaction costs while achieving public policy objectives. We should have transparency in the legislative process, and the legislation and regulation should be clear and simple. Not only should public policy be guided by unambiguous objectives, it should have a clear regulatory structure. The fact that there are 10 separate agencies responsible for the implementation of Dodd-Frank, for example, will likely result in costly and ineffective regulation. The regulated will game the new structure as they did the old. It's simplicity we need, not complexity.

   As Shakespeare wrote in *Hamlet*, "Brevity is the soul of wit."[14] Legislation and regulation in our story performed best when guided by the principle of Occam's Razor.[15] The original Clean Air Act of 1970 was 50 pages long. The Clean Air Act Amendments of 1990 demanded a hefty 800 pages, while the portion devoted to eliminating acid rain by trading SO_2 allowances was only 15 pages. Similarly, the bill establishing the Federal Reserve Bank was 25 pages long, while the bill creating the CFTC was 148 pages. In contrast, the American Clean Energy and Security Act of 2009 (also known as Waxman-Markey) ran 1,427 pages. Although it narrowly passed in the House of Representatives, no bill emerged from the Senate. A simpler bill with fewer objectives would have been a better starting point for debate in the Senate. Dodd-Frank continues to pose a major challenge at over 2,000 pages—longer than the Old Testament, New Testament, and the Koran combined. It is no surprise that we are already failing to meet deadlines in implementing this

[14]*Hamlet*, Act II, Scene II.

[15]Occam's Razor is the principle that one should always choose the hypothesis that makes the fewest new assumptions. It is thus also known as the law of economy.

legislation. In an effort to comply with these new rules, transactions costs may become higher. This phenomenon could drive innovation to environments with lower transaction costs, such as on regulated derivative exchanges. Unfortunately, increased costs may also drive business away from regulated U.S. markets into less regulated domestic or foreign markets. They could also result in new, but opaque ways to hedge. Lawmakers and regulators alike need to stay alert to these potential unintended consequences.

The clear delineation of a regulator's powers and jurisdiction is crucial to the success of markets. Interest rate futures specifically, and financial futures in general, were enabled by a clear mandate of the CFTC. Similarly, the recognition of emission allowances as property rights by the Clean Air Act Amendments of 1990, the clear definition of EPA's role, and the regulatory purview by the CFTC allowed futures trading in emissions to successfully emerge. Without legislation, regulatory authority may be ambiguous. The failure to extend the Clean Air Act Amendments of 1990 has been the primary cause for the failure of the SO_2 market. There are attempts to rectify this, as gathered by the 2011 EPA Cross-State Air Pollution Rule, or "Casper," which will include a trading program for SO2 allowances.

There are also cases where markets have either failed or are less robust because of uncertainty in regulation or lack of clarity in regulatory oversight. The lack of clear legislation to extend the Clean Air Act Amendments of 1990 has been the primary cause for the breakdown of the SO_2 market. Europe's relative success in single stock futures is arguably the result of its having only one regulator, as opposed to two regulators, as in the case of the United States. Economists may wish to conduct research to quantify the value of regulatory uncertainty.

As efforts to develop new futures markets surface in emerging economies, it is inevitable that the issues of legislation and structures regulation will be encountered time and time again. In fact, we are already witnessing this in India and China. Emerging economies primed to start their own futures markets should be asking these key questions: Are there laws and regulations in place that enable such a market, be it at a federal, state, or local level? Is there a regulatory agency with a clearly defined scope of action?

The absence of clear property rights or legislative clarity frequently means that markets in their infancy will have to deal with judicial risks. This has unfortunately been the case with climate legislation in the United States.

As I pen this conclusion, MF Global, a New York–based brokerage house, announced on October 31, 2011 that it filed for bankruptcy, becoming the eighth largest bankruptcy of a public U.S. company. At this point in time, customer funds are missing. All of the regulators—and there are a lot of them—have to act swiftly to set an example. The case for unambiguous, simple, and clearly defined regulatory powers to defend good derivatives is stronger than ever.

2. ***Exchange Structure and Organization***—Successful markets can only be realized if the gains from trade exceed the costs. The transaction costs associated with creating market architecture generally fall into three buckets: First, legislative and regulatory, for which the CFTC Act and the 200-page application that must be submitted to the CFTC to start an exchange are examples; second, institutional, which involves the creation of exchanges, invention of accounting standards, legal rules, educational efforts, and public outreach to support the market; and third, contractual, or the writing of the actual contracts themselves, which I hope this story has shown is just as much a fastidious science as it is a versatile art.

   Ultimately, successful exchanges emerge and organize themselves when they are able to act as an operator, clearer, and efficient regulator. The evolution from open outcry to electronic trading, the transformation from mutualized to demutualized, the wave of consolidations, and the self-regulatory nature of exchanges in the United States can all be explained through the lens of minimizing transaction costs. From a regulatory standpoint, the key question is whether the exchange structure can enforce regulations at a lowered cost to interested parties. In the case of CCX and CCFE, the trading platform, the compliance function and clearing were all outsourced to minimize transaction costs.

3. ***Research, Contract Design, and Innovation***—The launch of these new markets has required years of rigorous research and a contract carefully designed by existing or new exchanges. Designing a contract is not a simple, mechanical task. Instead, it requires market, regulatory, and sociological insights. A flawed contract can only result in failure, as glimpsed from my experience in launching a futures contract in gold and Gulf wheat. The European emissions market had clarity with separate contracts for emission reductions (EUA) and offsets (CEM). This was a feature that may have contributed to the success of both products. In retrospect, the CCX contract design, which homogenized the market by combining emission reductions and offsets, may have been a mistake.

   Sources of financial innovation have been practitioners working hand in hand with academics. The commercialization of financial products has come from visionary entrepreneurs who were members or employees of exchanges. They also came from the employees of financial institutions or industrial companies. These people recognized the importance of markets and understood how to optimize any profit opportunities that presented themselves.

   As exchanges became large enterprises, their inventive activity diminished, and new opportunities for growth were derived from mergers and acquisitions. As exchanges grew larger, each new product had a smaller impact on their bottom line. Innovation became more difficult as a result. Risk-bearing culture was lost as exchanges demutualized, as no members benefited from the trading of new products. This is not a criticism but an observable fact. New products are costly to develop and unprofitable in the short term. This is also true of inventive activity in the industrial and technological world. Breakthroughs in the world of computers have not always come from the major players. Microsoft, Apple, Google, and Facebook were all new companies at some point. Therefore, we should expect new financial innovations to come from new exchanges and entrepreneurs. This is already happening in China, in spite of the fact that its exchanges are state-owned enterprises. It has also happened in India.
4. ***Market Makers and Speculators***—In retrospect, the Gulf wheat futures launched in 1974 and the five-year Treasury note futures

contract launched in the 1980s might have been successful if there had been more people in the pits. New markets require market makers and speculators who serve to bridge the gap between buyers and sellers and underwrite the price risk of hedgers.

It is easy to attack the latter. Former Spanish dictator Francisco Franco may no longer be around to shoot speculators, but speculation is still often derided by the public and politicians hailing from across the political spectrum. Again, I stress that speculators are not a uniform class of market players. One needs to differentiate among the types of speculators before passing judgment. The value of speculation and investment in futures markets should not be underestimated in mandating public policy. Remember the old adage that the best cure for high prices is high prices and the best cure for low prices is low prices.[16] Institutional restrictions, which prevent the markets from being efficient, should be based on sound economic reasoning rather than on political sentiment.

5. ***New Markets Are Sold and Not Bought***—Education and marketing constitute half the battle when creating a successful new market. Unlike commercial products such as the windshield wiper, the need for a new financial instrument is often not readily apparent. Breakthrough financial innovations with no predecessors, such as interest rate and stock index futures, are even less obvious. Education efforts are not restricted to end users alone but span the entire chain of lawyers, accountants, academics, regulatory bodies, and futures industry service providers. The products have then had to be marketed and sold—a process that can take up to a decade. Marketing has required the building of human capital via hedgers and speculators, and the development of expertise in compliance, legal, and accounting arenas. I like to think of human development as an analogy for market development. There are three distinct phases: Childhood lasts from the birth of the market to its second year, adolescence occurs between its third and fifth year, and the market reaches maturity at its sixth to tenth year.

[16]As prices increase, demand decreases. Low prices, on the other hand, boost demand.

The Next Forty Years

New Geographies

The economic transformations taking place in Asia have the potential to define many of the innovations and shifts in the futures industry that will occur in the next 40 years.

As recent trends in the geographic expansion of listed derivatives suggest, China and India will continue to lead the way. In 2010, China launched stock index futures, the country's first financial futures since the mid-1990s. Volume-wise, it was the most successful new contract in the world. The newly opened Hong Kong Mercantile Exchange launched a gold futures market in May 2011. India's new exchanges, the National Stock Exchange (NSE) and the Multi-Commodity Exchange (MCX), have also been remarkable successes. In 2010, seven of the 14 major derivatives exchanges worldwide were in China, India, Brazil, and Korea. Nearly all of the volume and products traded in these countries didn't exist 20 years ago. Meanwhile, we can also expect new institutions and markets in regions such as Indonesia, Vietnam, and parts of Africa.

In these regions, it is important to note that property rights and the legislative status of markets and regulations are in a state of flux at present. Emerging economies are grappling with the legal architecture that governs markets. There is a lack of exchanges and other institutions required for markets to emerge and grow. There is also a lack of standardization for local commodities. As these markets pass through their teething phase, I remain optimistic about the next wave of financial innovations. As the real economies of emerging countries grow, their financial sector must grow as well. It remains up to policy makers in both the developed and developing world to determine the right balance between the real economy and the financial sector.

New Exchanges

New exchanges will appear in the emerging economies, but timing will depend on legal architecture and the growth of a web of institutions that facilitate their success. Parallel to the emergence of exchanges as large, consolidated, and centralized institutions in emerging markets, I also expect the growth of smaller, more decentralized exchange structures in the developed world. We are already witnessing the emergence of a new business model for exchanges—IP, trading platforms, and clearing arrangements are gradually being outsourced to different organizations. These smaller exchanges will spawn product innovations and niche markets that cannot be supported in a large, institutional framework. Both these exchange models have an important complementary role in the market ecosystem.

Remutualization is another new trend to anticipate, started by ICE. Investment banks, utilities, and energy companies were the biggest shareholders in ICE's early days. Three new exchanges—ELX, Liffe U.S., and Eris—were either started by Chicago market-making firms or had these firms as significant equity owners. There is a certain irony here. These innovations may be driven by new regulations emanating from the Dodd-Frank Act, which will likely result in all interest rate swaps being centrally cleared. If U.S. regulators continue to impose higher costs for corporate and financial users of interest rate swaps, then one would expect to see the invention of new futures contracts. This is happening already. DRW Trading Group has obtained a patent on a futures contract that is more cost-effective when used as a swap-based product rather than as an OTC product. I hope to see a continuation of this trend toward transparency.

In today's electronic world and ease of entry, I expect the proliferation of exchanges. The only reason this might not occur is because governments tend to establish exchanges as monopolies.

New Products

The next 40 years will witness the invention of new asset classes. New products will continue to be driven by latent, unsatisfied demand. Environmental and weather derivatives, volatility indexes, and event-based trading are all examples. Event-based derivatives, which were first introduced with the launch of catastrophic derivatives, offer a vehicle to hedge against a variety of policy risks. Credit derivatives are an inchoate asset class within event-based derivatives and await the invention of a broader credit default swap index. CDS defaults are based on committee decisions. Recent negotiations have suggested that investors agreeing voluntarily will not signal a default and therefore a payoff to buyers of this insurance. As in the case of CERs, we firmly believe that the default decisions should be rules-based and not discretionary. The jury is still out with regard to that asset class.

Another asset class is hedge fund performance. There are a few indexes in existence, but efforts to scale them have not been successful. Volatility has been most successful in the equity area and could easily be extended to commodities, fixed income, foreign exchange, and other asset classes.

I anticipate the commoditization of nonstandardized commodities such as intellectual property. I hope that academics and practitioners will turn technological innovation into an asset class. There should be an innovative way to hedge innovation itself. I never really got a chance to pursue this and regret it deeply. In fact, there are some rumblings with the establishment of Ocean Tomo about developing a product.[17]

There are also opportunities in commodities that have already been standardized but are not yet traded in the futures market. Electricity, a $300 billion market, is one example. Basic agricultural staples such as rice and soybeans could also benefit from new product innovation in places like China, India, and Brazil. Interest rate futures, which have been incredibly successful in the West, have yet to be fully implemented in the East. This presents another exciting prospect. The magnitude of the geographic change in commodity demand and trading means that the pricing reference point and commodity grade specifications could also shift to the East. New futures and options

[17]Ocean Tomo, a leading provider of diversified intellectual property-related services, launched the first equity index based on the value of corporate intellectual property in 2006.

markets in agriculture, energy, and metals may be complementary to, or competitive with, the CME.

I am particularly optimistic about environmental derivatives. It is easy to foresee environmental derivatives being traded in China, India, and Brazil. Even South Korea is planning to launch a carbon emissions trading scheme between 2013 and 2015. We recommended a pilot program before that at the 2011 Busan International Carbon Finance Conference Program. China's next Five-Year Plan from 2011 to 2015 is expected to include a market-based emissions trading program. I will not be surprised if China develops an emissions trading scheme before the United States does. However, there is still a glimmer of hope in U.S. regional programs. Cap-and-trade still lives at the regional levels through programs such as the Regional Greenhouse Gas Initiative (RGGI) and Assembly Bill 32, the California Global Warming Solutions Act. California, for good or bad, has often been a trendsetter in climate change issues, technology, and social networks. The Western Climate Initiative should be closely watched.[18]

Water is an asset class within the environmental sector, and worth a brief digression. Water trading is only at an exploratory stage, and little is known yet about how water can be transported between regions. My good friend, Sascha Zehnder, would argue that there is already a virtual water trade taking place, since grain trading can be viewed as a surrogate for water trading. With regard to water, we are now where we were in the early 1990s with carbon. I talked with others about the idea at the Rio climate summit in 1992, but it took Kyoto and the development of markets in the past decade before global carbon trading matured into what it is today. In fact, water quality and quantity may be exacerbated by climate change. These problems must be addressed before future generations bear the costs of our neglect.

[18]The launch of California's carbon trading program is being postponed until 2013, due to continued opposition. See Margot Roosevelt, "California Delays Its Carbon-Trading program until 2013," *Los Angeles Times,* June 30, 2011.

Starting New Markets with Water

There is no commodity more important than air or water. Both are required for human survival. Water will be the oil of the twenty-first century. Fresh water, which accounts for less than 1 percent of the global water resource, is a scarce resource. Water is needed for food production, energy production, and most manufacturing processes. It is, therefore, not a surprise that water scarcity is becoming a growth limiting factor. Population growth, pollution, rapid urbanization, and climate change only exacerbate the problem. We cannot discount the possibility of conflict over water and other natural resources.

The markets may have a useful role in providing solutions to the water crisis. Just as CCX was the proof of concept for emissions markets, we still need a proof of concept for a water market. Promising signs are already emerging. The Gulf State of Oman had a water exchange system dating back thousands of years. Similarly, Australia has had a system of trading water entitlements for a decade. In June 2011, UK water provider Severn Trent PLC proposed a nationwide water-trading system aimed at balancing domestic supplies, ahead of a government review.[19]

More recently, water research and development efforts conducted by CCX in several regions have reinforced the idea that pricing and market mechanisms can play an important role in fostering better water management, water quality, and conservation. CCX studied the possibility of a water quantity exchange for the State of New Mexico and found it would offer valuable price signals for conservation and new supply management options for water users. An organized exchange can help increase the economic benefits realized from water use in the State, while also offering an efficient tool for assuring that agricultural and ecological goals are achieved. Options for addressing various legal and quantification challenges are now being studied.

In the Great Lakes region, CCX researched the viability of a water market and found pricing water would encourage water use monitoring and pricing which would be critical if major threats to

---

[19]Jacob Bunge, "Carbon Trading Pioneer Dips Toe into Water Markets," *Wall Street Journal*, July 18, 2011.

(*continued*)

Starting New Markets with Water (*Continued*)

the lakes materialize. Currently, water is being pumped out of the Great Lakes at no cost other than the cost of infrastructure required to extract water. Despite various agreements, states and provinces generally do not require measurement of water removals from the lakes. Reliable measurement of water removal remains a key element for any water use management system, market-based or otherwise. Decrease in Great Lakes water will have dire consequences on real estate, recreation, shipping, and water supplies in the region.

Additionally, CCX was engaged by the Alberta Water Research Institute to examine the benefits of implementing a rules-based exchange for water resources in Alberta, Canada. The province has experienced fierce competition between farmers needing water for crops, and oil companies needing water to exploit oil sands, which require far more water than other kinds of oil deposit.[20] It will take additional negotiations with government before a water exchange can be launched.

CCX also helped develop the pilot nutrient trading effort in Pennsylvania.[21] The nitrogen and phosphorus nutrients discharges from factories and farms were polluting the Chesapeake Bay resulting in loss of oxygen in the waters. This is detrimental to marine life. In 2005, the state initiated a nutrient cap-and-trade program that would limit the amount of nutrients flowing into the rivers but issuing "water quality credits" to polluting entities. CCX devised rules, procedures, and educational efforts that enhance use of this system. Various legislative proposals are calling for the system to be expanded to other states. The program could eventually be extended to include fishermen, based on the idea that catches will increase if there are fewer dead zones caused by oxygen depletion.[22]

---

[20]Barbara Lewis, "Water Trade Part of Answer to Feeding World: Nestle," *Reuters*, May 10, 2011.

[21]Pennsylvania Nutrient Trading Executive Summary, Chicago Climate Exchange, November 17, 2009.

[22]"Facts about Nutrient Trading," Chesapeake Bay Foundation, June 11, 2008.

New Regulations

There are other significant ways to use markets creatively for environmental and social objectives. Recalling my students' spotted owl futures project, another area where markets can play a constructive role is in endangered species and ecosystems. Applications in medicine are also possible. Epidemics and pandemics might also be mitigated through market-based mechanisms.

The launch of CCX in 2003 provides evidence that where there are environmental objectives, voluntary markets can emerge. Sometimes the private sector can come up with solutions to social problems, which most economists believe to be the exclusive province of the public sector. We should not underestimate the market's ability for building institutions and providing proof of concept before seeking a solution from the government. Since climate change, water quality and quantity will be enormous challenges in the twenty-first century, we must consider all tools available, public and private, in order to adequately deal with these problems.

There are numerous other asset classes. The opportunities are endless. If past innovation in technology and finance is any guide for the future, then the sources of innovation will be outsider driven—from new geographies and new exchanges.

Chicago, My Kind of Town

Many of the financial innovations have their roots in the streets of Chicago. The city's exchanges, entrepreneurship, and risk-taking ability have allowed it to be the breeding ground for financial innovation. Chicago has not only been home to new markets since 1848, but to generations of members who have proudly made and harnessed the power of markets in grains, meats, interest rates, stock indexes, currencies, and other commodities, whether financial or real. LaSalle Street is the birthplace of the prevalent hedging instruments in today's world. Self-regulation and transparency have been hallmarks of Chicago's exchanges from their inception.

I'd like to put forth a hypothesis that while New York is the center for investment capital and San Francisco is the home of venture capital,

Chicago is the nucleus of market-making capital. Algorithmic trading firms such as DRW, TradeLink, Infinium, and Getco aren't widely recognized, but provide liquidity to many of the world's markets. I was told by informed sources that 40 percent of the trading in German Bunds at one time emanated from Chicago. This didn't surprise me. Some of these algorithmic firms, according to recent interviews with informed members of the Chicago trading community, constitute 30 percent of the volume on all futures exchanges worldwide. These market-making firms may easily evolve into dealers, thereby further lowering the costs for those who use financial markets for stocks and bonds, or even physical commodities like oil and grain. The thousands of employees in these new trading firms may be among the new leaders in financial innovation. They are not alone. Market makers have spread to New York, London, Mumbai, and Shanghai.

Keep in mind that where innovation will take place and where trading will occur are two separate questions. That most trading will occur in China and India does not warrant that most innovations will come from there. In fact, what we are witnessing now in both countries is a constant churning out of imitator contracts—variations of new products that originated elsewhere. Chicago can sustain its niche as the breeding ground of financial innovation if and only if its value-added role exceeds that of its counterparts, based on the human capital of its existing exchanges.

I hope that the lessons learned in my 40 years as a financial innovator will be of some value to future entrepreneurs and innovators. We are at the dawn of a new age where markets can be created to deal with the most important problems facing humankind. They can be used to address environmental and social objectives.

Good derivatives, those that are regulated and transparent, should be encouraged and will flourish for generations if property nurtured. The best has yet to come for my grandchildren and yours.

Appendixes

Appendix A: Commodity Exchange Operating System, 1969

This Appendix describes the operating system of commodity exchanges that existed in 1969. The system is triggered by (1) a decision to buy or sell by a speculator or hedger or (2) customer intention to deliver. The schematic representation indicates that orders from speculators and hedgers are sent to members of the exchange. These orders are then transmitted to the trading floor to be matched in an area called the ring or pit, a name evocative of the unique architecture of trading floors at the Chicago Board of Trade.[1] The diagram also contains a unit labeled "Locals," an alternative term for floor traders. After a trade is consummated by either a

[1]The Chicago Board of Trade featured polygonal pits with steps climbing to a height of four or five feet and then descending by 10 feet into the pit. Due to this architecture, they became known as trading pits. The tradition outside of Chicago was either pits or rings.

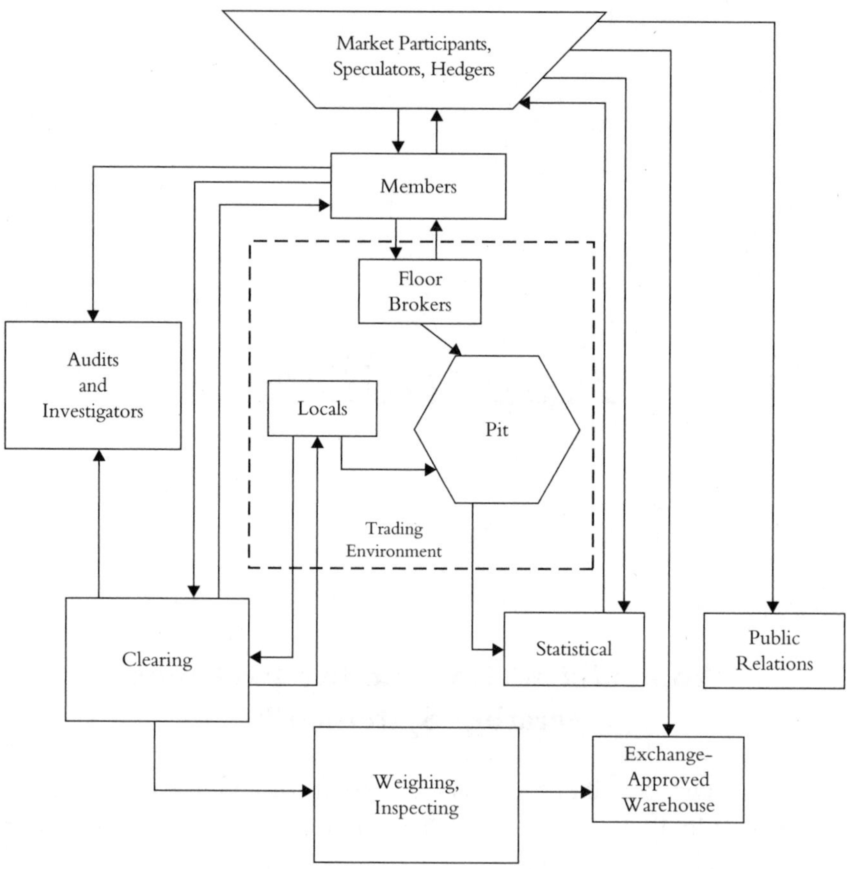

broker or a principal (speculator or hedger) trading for their own account, it is recorded on an order or trading card. Trading cards and orders are put on the computers of the clearing members, who provide the information to the clearinghouse.

Appendix B: GNMA Advisory Committee

Anaheim Savings
Bache & Co.
Bank of America
Brentwood Mortgage Corp.

Citizens Savings & Loan Association
CMI
Engel Mortgage Company
The First Boston Corporation
First Federal Savings and Loan Association of Miami
GNMA
Great Western Savings & Loan Association
Hornblower & Weeks-Hemphill, Noyes
Huntoon, Paige & Co., Inc.
Kaufman and Broad, Inc.
R.H. Lapin & Co.
Mortgage Guaranty Insurance Corporation
Salomon Brothers
F. S. Smithers
Western Mortgage
Dean Witter & Co.

Appendix C: CBOT Financial Instruments Committee, 1975

Leslie Rosenthal, Chairman
Irwin M. Eisen
Walter M. Goldschmidt
Michael E. Green
Michael H. Helberg
William J. Mallers
Ronald Manaster
Marvin Parsoff
Louis M. Skydell
Jerome M. Spielman

Appendix D: CBOT Financial Instruments Committee, 1977

Leslie Rosenthal, Chairman
Donald G. Andrew

Delmar W. Girard
Michael H. Helberg
John R. Kinsella
Ronald Manaster
Lester Mouscher
Richard L. Sandor
Mark Shlaes
Louis M. Skydell
Jeffrey B. Stern
Peter M. Todebrush
Donald L. Van Stone
John R. Wassong

Appendix E: CBOT Financial Instruments Committee, 1982

Ralph Goldenberg, Chairman
Robert Goldberg, Co-Vice Chairman
Paul McGuire, Co-Vice Chairman
Patrick Arbor
Daniel Artmann
John Gilmore Jr.
Michael Helberg
Gerald Macellaio
Ronald Manaster
Monte Monaster
John Ruth
Warren Smith
Robert Witz

Appendix F: CCX Committees

Table A.1 Members of the CCX Utility Committee

Member	Title	Company
James Christensen	Manager, Research & Technology	Alliant Energy
Joe Shefcheck	Corporate Environmental Officer	Alliant Energy
Bruce Braine	VP Strategic Policy Analysis	American Electric Power
John McManus	Manager, Environmental Strategy & Planning	American Electric Power
Dr. C. V. Mathai	Manager for Environmental Policy	Arizona Public Service (Pinnacle West)
Eric Kuhn	Sr. Environmental Analyst	Cinergy
Michael Weber	Director of Environmental Affairs	CMS Generation
Michael Rodenberg	Sr. Technological Specialist, Environmental Strategies	Detroit Edison
Bruce Alexander	Strategy Manager	Exelon
David Cesareo	VP Environmental Health & Safety	Exelon
Mike Jirousek	Consultant	FirstEnergy
Bill Hamlin	Strategic Issues Officer	Manitoba Hydro
Cheryl Corman	Strategic Energy Issues Engineer	Manitoba Hydro
Basil Constantelos	Director, Environmental Health & Safety	Midwest Generation
Art Smith	Sr. Vice President and Environmental Counsel	NiSource
Dave Coates	Senior Trader, Energy Markets	Ontario Power Generation
Gillian Salter	Professional Engineer, Sr. Trader, Logistics Trading/ Portfolio Management	Ontario Power Generation
Robert LaCount	Air Quality Manager	PG&E National Energy Group
Dr. Ed Powell	Governance & Stewardship Manager	TXU Energy Trading
Kris McKinney	Manager, Environmental Strategy	Wisconsin Energy

Table A.2 Members of the CCX Industry Committee

Member	Title	Company
Ron Meissen	Sr. Director, Engineering	Baxter
Randall Farmer	General Manager, HSE Group Resource	BP America
James W. Keating	Air Quality Programs Coordinator	BP Amoco Corporation
Charlos Ward	Emissions Trader	BP Amoco Corporation
Alberto Niño	Environmental Engineering & Ecoefficiency Technology Div.	Cemex
José Ramón Ardavín Ituarte	Environmental Engineer	Cemex
Robert Routliffe	Manager, Emissions Trading	DuPont
Gary Groner	Vice President	Ford Motor Co.
Chad McIntosh	Manager, Facility Environmental Programs	Ford Motor Co.
Enrique González	Chief Executive Officer/ Legal Director	Grupo Imsa
Arturo Garza Zermeño	General Counsel	Grupo Imsa
Craig Lenocker	Manager, Global Forest Strategy, Forest Resources	International Paper
Danny Adams	Environmental Initiatives–Corporate Environment	International Paper
David Bonistall	Senior Environmental Consultant	MeadWestvaco
Mike McClarence	Vice President TQEM & Business Mgmt	STMicroelectronics
Annabeth Reitter	Division Air Programs Manager	Stora Enso
Geoff Johns	Manager, Sustainable Development	Suncor Energy
Gordon Lambert	Corporate Director, Sustainable Development	Suncor Energy
John Orynawka	Director of Energy & Air Programs	Temple-Inland
John Bins	Director of Air Programs	Waste Management

Appendix G: CCX Subcommittees

CCX Utility Subcommittees

Offsets, Supply Constraints and Early Action Credit Subcommittee

(*Formerly Targets and Baseline Subcommittee*)

Goals: Establish program's emission reduction targets **(completed)**
Define a backstop mechanism to address growth on existing facilities **(completed)**
Approve rules for eligible early action projects **(completed)**
Approve list of acceptable early action projects **(completed)**
Approve list of acceptable offset project types **(completed)**
Develop micro and macro supply constraints **(completed)**

Members: Bruce Braine (Chairperson)—American Electric Power
Jim Christensen—Alliant Energy
Joe Shefchek—Alliant Energy
Eric Kuhn—Cinergy
Mike Rodenberg—Detroit Edison
Art Smith—NiSource

Landfill Gas Subcommittee

Goals: Develop rules for crediting landfill methane offsets and early action projects undertaken by utility companies
Develop standardized monitoring protocol for landfill methane offset projects

Members: Mike Rodenberg (Chairperson)—Detroit Edison
Eric Kuhn—Cinergy

Forestry Offset Projects Subcommittee

Goal: Develop eligibility and monitoring rules for CCX forestry off set projects in the United States and Brazil

Members: Eric Kuhn (Chairperson)—Cinergy
Joe Shefchek—Alliant Energy
Gary Kaster—American Electric Power
John Kadyszewski—Winrock International
Danny Adams—International Paper
Noel Cutright—Wisconsin Energy

New Plants Subcommittee

Goal: Define rules for accommodating growth on new facilities **(completed)**

Members: Art Smith (Chairperson)—NiSource
Jim Christensen—Alliant Energy Corporation
Joe Shefchek—Alliant Energy Corporation
C. V. Mathai—Arizona Public Service (Pinnacle West Capital)
Kris McKinney—Wisconsin Energy
John McManus—American Electric Power
Robert LaCount—PG&E National Energy Group

Joint Ownership Subcommittee

Goal: Define treatment of emissions from jointly owned facilities **(completed)**

Members: Bruce Alexander (Chairperson)—Exelon
Dan Chartier—PG&E National Energy Group (substituted by Robert LaCount)
Eric Kuhn—Cinergy

CCX Industry Subcommittees

Baseline Subcommittee

Goal: Establish program's baseline years **(completed)**

Members: Annabeth Reitter (Chairperson)—Stora Enso North America
Danny Adams—International Paper
David Bonistall—Mead Westvaco
John Orynawka—Temple-Inland

Oil & Gas Company Monitoring Subcommittee

Goal: Develop standard monitoring protocols for oil and gas companies

Members: Jim Keating—BP Amoco Corporation
Mike McMahon—BP Amoco Corporation
Geoff Johns—Suncor Energy

Unit Size Subcommittee

Goal: Define minimum plant size for estimating emissions from fossil fuel combustion **(completed)**

Members: John Orynawka (Chairperson)—Temple-Inland
Annabeth Reitter—Stora Enso North America

Targets and Economic Growth Provision Subcommittee

Goals: Establish program's emission reduction targets **(completed)**
Define an economic growth mechanism to address growth on existing facilities

Establish industry agreement with Utility group consensus on targets and economic growth provision

Members: Chad McIntosh (Chairperson)—Ford Motor Company

Danny Adams—International Paper

Rob Routliffe—DuPont

Jim Keating—BP Amoco Corporation

Charlos Ward—BP Amoco Corporation

Alberto Niño—Cemex

John Orynawka—Temple-Inland

Offsets, Supply Constraints, and Early Action Credit Subcommittee

Goals: Define list of eligible project-based offsets and their supply limitations

Define supply constraints or market position limits

Develop rules for crediting early action projects

Members: Rob Routliffe (Co-Chairperson)—DuPont

James Keating (Co-Chairperson)—BP Amoco Corporation

Charlos Ward—BP Amoco Corporation

John Orynawka—Temple-Inland

Alberto Niño—Cemex

Jose Ramon Ardavin—Cemex

Joint Ownership Subcommittee

Goal: Define treatment of emissions from jointly owned facilities

Members: Annabeth Reitter (Chairperson)—Stora Enso North America

Geoff Johns—Suncor Energy

Charlos Ward—BP Amoco Corporation

Jim Keating—BP Amoco Corporation

Alberto Niño—Cemex

Forest Products Company Sequestration Monitoring

Goal: Develop standardized protocol for estimating/monitoring changes in biomass carbon on lands owned by forest product companies

Members: Bill Stansfield (Co-Chairperson)—Temple-Inland

John Paul McTague (Co-Chairperson)—International Paper

John Orynawka—Temple-Inland

Danny Adams—International Paper

Brad Franchi—MeadWestvaco

Tim Tollefson—Stora Enso North America

Appendix H: CCX Members

Members

Aerospace & Equipment
Rolls-Royce
United Technologies Corporation

Automotive
Ford Motor Company

Beverage Manufacturing
New Belgium Brewing Company

Chemicals
Dow Corning★
DuPont
FMC Corporation
Potash Corporation
Rhodia Energy Brasil Ltda
U.S. Salt, LLC

Coal Mining
Jim Walter Resources, Inc.
PinnOak Resources LLC

Commercial Interiors
Knoll, Inc.
Steelcase Inc.

Counties
King County, Washington
Miami-Dade County, Florida
Sacramento County, California

Diversified Manufacturing
Eastman Kodak Company
Robert Bosch LLC

Participant Members

Offset Aggregators
33 Asset Management B.V.
3Degrees Group, Inc.
Ag Carbon Management, LLC (an Environmental Credit Corp. subsidiary)
AgraGate Climate Credits Corporation
Agrinergy Consultancy Pvt. Ltd.
Andhyodaya Green Energy Technologies Pvt. Ltd.
CantorCO2e, L.P.
Carbon Resource Management Ltd.
Carbon-TF B.V.
CARBONyatra
Cargill–Green Hercules Trading
Cargill, Inc.
C-Green Aggregator Ltd.
CP Holdings LLC
Delta P2/E2 Center LLC
ecolutions GmbH & Co. KGaA
Ecoreturn LLP
Ecosecurities Capital Ltd.
Element Markets LLC
Emergent Ventures India Pvt. Ltd.
Environmental Carbon Credit Pool LLC
Environmental Credit Corp.
FC Stone, LLC
First Capitol Risk Management LLC
FORECON EcoMarket Solutions LLC
Foretell Business Solutions Private Limited

Associate Members

Architecture/Planning
Mithun, Inc.
Perkins + Will, Inc.

Consulting
DOMANI LLC
First Environment, Inc.
Global Change Associates★
Natural Capitalism Solutions
RenewSource Partners LLC★
Rocky Mountain Institute★

Consumer Products
Collective Wellbeing LLC

Documentary Production
Cloverland Inc.★

Educational Institutions
Presidio School of Management★
Sidwell Friends School

Embassies
Embassy of Denmark, Washington, DC
Embassy of Finland

Energy Broker
Amerex Energy★

Members

Electric Power Generation
AGL Hydro Partnership
Allegheny Energy Inc.
Alliant Energy
Corporate Services Inc.
American Electric
Power
American Municipal
Power
Associated Electric
Cooperative, Inc.
Avista Corporation
Central Vermont
Public Service
CLECO Corporation
DTE Energy Inc.
Duquesne Light
Company★
Dynegy Holdings Inc.
GenOn Energy
Green Mountain
Power
Hoosier Energy Rural
Electric
Cooperative, Inc.
Manitoba Hydro
NRG Power
Marketing Inc.
Progress Energy
Puget Sound Energy,
Inc.★
PSEG
TECO Energy, Inc.
Electronics
Motorola, Inc.
Sony Electronics Inc.
Square D/Schneider
Electric N.A.★
Environmental Services
Atlantic County
Utilities Authority

Participant Members

Geosyntec Consultants Inc.
Grasim Industries, Ltd.
Greenoxx Global
Environmental Program
Grey K Trading Limited
Guizhou Zhongshui
Hengyuan
Project Management &
Consulting Co. Ltd.
Hudson Technologies
Company
J. Aron & Company
Kentucky Corn Growers
Association
Korea Energy Management
Corporation
LandGas Technology LLC
MF Global Market Services
LLC
MGM International
Mickelson & Company LLC
Mission Climate
Mountain Association for
Community Economic
Development
National Carbon Offset
Coalition
Natural Capital
North Dakota Farmers
Union
Polar Technology, LLC
ProLogis Logistics Services,
Inc.
Rajasthan Renewable Energy
Corporation
Ramakrishna Mission
Ashrama
Reclamation Technologies Inc.
Reliance Industries Limited
Rice Dairy LLC
Rolling Plains Crop Insurance
Agency, Inc.
R.S.J. Ozone Private Limited

Associate Members

Energy Services
Bell Independent
Power Corp.
Orion Energy
Systems Ltd.
Prenova, Inc.
Sieben Energy
Associates

Energy Suppliers
BlueStar Energy
Services Inc.
MXenergy
Holdings Inc.

Engineering
Rumsey
Engineers★
Vanasse Hangen
Brustlin, Inc.

Environmental Services
Resource Recycling
Systems

Financial Services
Access Industries,
Inc.★
G.C. Anderson
Partners LLC
MB Investments
LLC★
Wood Creek
Capital
Management LLC

Financing Agency
Ohio Air Quality
Development
Authority★

Food Services
Big Bowl Asian, LLC

(*continued*)

Members	Participant Members	Associate Members
Lancaster County Solid Waste Management Authority	SunOne Climate Solutions LLC	*Foundation*
Veolia Environmental Services North America Corp.	Tata Motors Limited	Nathan Cummings Foundation
Wasatch Integrated Waste Management Authority	Tatanka Resources LLC	*Information Technology*
Waste Management, Inc.	TerraCarbon LLC	Intercontinental Exchange★
Ethanol Production	TerraPass Inc.	Open Finance LLC
Corn Plus LLP	The Verus Carbon Neutral Partnership	*Legal Services*
Financial Institutions	U.S. Energy Services, Inc.	Foley & Lardner LLP★
Bank of America Corporation	Valley Wood Inc.	Levenfeld Pearl-stein LLC
Food and Agricultural Products & Services	Vayam Technologies Ltd	Sullivan & Cromwell LLP
Agrium U.S. Inc.★	Vision CO2, S.A.	Weil, Gotshal & Manges LLP
Cargill, Incorporated	*Offset Providers*	*Nongovernmental Organizations*
Monsanto Company	Bajaj Finserv Limited	ACORE★
Food Processing	Burnett Ranches, LLC	Delta Institute
Premium Standard Farms★	Cape May County Municipal Utilities Authority	Houston Advanced Research Center★
Smithfield Foods, Inc.	City of Gardner, Massachusetts	Midwest Energy Efficiency Alliance
Forest Products	CNX Gas Corporation	Rainforest Alliance
AbitibiBowater	CO2 Australia	World Resources Institute★
Aracruz Celulose S.A.★	CommonWealth Resource Management Corp.	*Plastics*
Arcelor Mittal Florestas Ltd.	CPI Carbon Asset Management Co., Ltd.	Conwed
Boise Paper Holdings, LLC	Cumberland County Improvement Authority	*Professional Associations*
Cenibra Nipo Brasiliera S.A.★	Dhariwal Industries Ltd.	Confederation of British Industry★
Domtar Corporation	Gazprom Marketing & Trading Ltd	The Professional Risk Managers' International Association★
International Paper	Granger Holdings LLC	
	Lugar Stock Farm	
	Precious Woods Holding, Ltd	
	Public Utility District No. 1 of Chelan County, WA	
	Rivanna Solid Waste Authority	
	Sexton Energy LLC	

Members	Participant Members	Associate Members
Klabin S.A.★	Tata Power Company Limited	*Real Estate*
Masisa S.A.	Trading Emissions PLC	ProLogis Logistics
MeadWestvaco Corp.		Services, Inc.
Neenah Paper	*Liquidity Providers*	
Incorporated	Akeida Environmental	*Religious*
NewPage Corporation	Master Fund Ltd.	*Organization*
Plum Creek Timber	Ameresco, Inc.	Jesuit Community
Company, Inc.	Amerex Energy	of Santa Clara
Suzano Papel E	Apache CR Company	University
Celulose SA	Atrium Carbon Fund LP	
Tembec Industries Inc.	BNP Paribas Energy	*Renewable Energy*
Temple-Inland Inc.★	Trading GP	Airtricity Inc.★
	Brane Strom LLP	American Renew-
Health Care	C-Quest Capital, LLC	able Energy★
Baxter International	CBp Carbon Industries, Inc.	Econergy
Inc.	Cargill Power Markets LLC	International★
Hospira, Inc.	Chapel Street Environmental	Reknewco Ltd.★
	Fund, LP	
Manufacturing	Digilog Global Environmental	*Retiring/Offsets*
Bayer Corporation	Master Fund Ltd	Carbonfund.org
Duratex S.A.	DRW Holdings LLC	Offset Collective,
Honeywell Interna-	Evolution Markets LLC	Inc.
tional Inc.	First Bank and Trust	TerraPass Inc.★
Interface, Inc.	First New York	
Ozinga Bros., Inc.★	Securities LLC	*Social Investment*
Smurfit-Stone	Five Rings Capital LLC	Generation
	Galtere International Master	Investment
Municipalities	Fund LP	Management LLP
City of Aspen	GDF SUEZ Energy Market-	KLD Research &
City of Berkeley★	ing NA	Analytics★
City of Boulder	Grand Slam Trading Inc.	Pax World★
City of Chicago	Green Dragon Fund	
City of Fargo	Green Fund Partners LLC	*Technology*
City of Melbourne,	Grey K Environmental	Millennium Cell★
Australia	Fund LP	
City of Oakland★	Grey K Environmental	*Transportation*
City of Portland★	Offshore Fund Ltd.	*Services*
	Grey K Trading Limited	Valera Global Inc.
Petrochemicals	Haley Capital Management	
LANXESS Elastomeros		
do Brasil S.A.		

(*continued*)

Members	Participant Members	Associate Members
Pharmaceuticals	ICAP Energy LLC	
Abbott	Infinium Capital Management LLC	
	Integrys Energy Services Inc.	
Real Estate Investment	Ironworks Partners LP	
JMB Realty Corporation	J. Aron & Company	
	Jane Street Global Trading LLC	
Recreation	JP Morgan Ventures Energy Corporation	
Aspen Skiing Company	Kellybrooke LLC	
	Koch Supply & Trading	
Retail	Kottke Associates, LLC	
Safeway, Inc.	Lehman Brother Commodity Services Inc.	
	Marquette Partners, LP	
States	Marsus Capital LLC	
State of Illinois	Merrill Lynch Commodities, Inc.	
State of New Mexico★	Newedge USA, LLC	
	Octavian Special Master Fund LP	
Steam Heat	Option Insight Partners	
Concord Steam Corporation	ORBEO	
	Penson GHCo	
Steel	Peregrine Financial Group, Inc.	
Roanoke Electric Steel Corp.★	Rand Financial Services, Inc.	
	Royal Bank of Canada	
Technology	SA Recovery, Inc.	
Freescale Semiconductor	Serrino Trading Company	
IBM	Spectron Energy Services Limited	
Intel Corporation	Stark Investments	
STMicroelectronics	TEP Trading 2 Ltd.	
	The League Corporation	
Transportation	TradeLink LLC	
Amtrak	Tradition Financial Services Ltd.	
San Joaquin Regional Rail Commission★	TransMarket Group LLC	
	Universal Carbon Fund LLC	
Universities	U.S. Energy Savings Corp.	
Michigan State University	Vitol, Inc.	
Tufts University★		

Members	Participant Members	Associate Members
University of California, San Diego		
University of Idaho		
University of Iowa		
University of Minnesota		
University of Oklahoma		

*Member of Phase I (years 2003–2006) program only.

Acronyms

Exchanges

CBOT: Chicago Board of Trade
CCARP: California Commodity Advisory Research Project
CCFE: Chicago Climate Futures Exchange
CCX: Chicago Climate Exchange
CEA: Commodity Exchange Authority
CME: Chicago Mercantile Exchange
ECX: European Climate Exchange
ICE: IntercontinentalExchange
ICX: India Climate Exchange
KCBT: Kansas City Board of Trade
Liffe: London International Financial Futures Exchange
MATIF: Marché à Terme International de France
MCX: Multi Commodity Exchange
NYMEX: New York Mercantile Exchange
NYPE: New York Produce Exchange
NYSE: New York Stock Exchange

SOFFEX: Swiss Options and Financial Futures Exchange
TCX: Tianjin Climate Exchange

Environmental

CER: Certified Emissions Reduction
CFI: Carbon Financial Instrument
CFP: Centre Financial Products
EPA: Environmental Protection Agency
EUA: European Union Allowance
EU ETS: European Union Emissions Trading Scheme
GETS: Global Warming Emissions Trading Program
SAM: Sustainable Asset Management
SFI: Sulfur Financial Instrument
SPG: Sustainable Performance Group
UNCED: United Nations Conference on Environment and Development ("Earth Summit")
UN COP: United Nations Communication on Progress
UNCTAD: United Nations Conference on Trade and Development
UNDP: United Nations Development Programme
UNEP: United Nations Environment Programme
UNFCCC: United Nations Framework Convention on Climate Change

Others

CFTC: Commodity Futures Trading Commission
DJIA: Dow Jones Industrial Average
FHA: Federal Housing Administration
FHLBB: Federal Home Loan Bank Board
FIA: Futures Industry Association
GNMA: Government National Mortgage Association ("Ginnie Mae")
S&P: Standard and Poor's
SEC: Securities and Exchange Commission

Glossary

Unless otherwise specified, financial terms have been taken from the U.S. Commodity Futures Trading Commission Glossary, and environmental terms have been taken from the United Nations Environment Programme Glossary or the United Nations Framework Convention on Climate Change glossary.*

arbitrage A strategy involving the simultaneous purchase and sale of identical or equivalent commodity futures contracts or other instruments across two or more markets in order to benefit from a discrepancy in their price relationship. In a theoretical efficient market, there is a lack of opportunity for profitable arbitrage.

ask The price level of an offer to sell, as in **bid-ask spread**.

basis The difference between the spot or cash price of a commodity and the price of the nearest futures contract for the same or a related commodity (typically calculated as cash minus futures). Basis is usually

* For full glossaries, see www.cftc.gov/ConsumerProtection/EducationCenter/CFTC Glossary/index.htm, www.nyo.unep.org/action/ap1.htm, and http://unfccc.int/essential_background/glossary/items/3666.php.

computed in relation to the futures contract next to expire and may reflect different time periods, product forms, grades, or locations.

basis risk The risk associated with an unexpected widening or narrowing of the basis between the time a hedge position is established and the time it is lifted.

bid An offer to buy a specific quantity of a commodity at a stated price.

bid-ask spread The difference between the bid price and the ask or offer price.

broker A person paid a fee or commission for executing buy or sell orders for a customer. In commodity futures trading, the term may refer to: (1) floor broker, a person who actually executes orders on the trading floor of an exchange; (2) account executive or associated person, the person who deals with customers in the offices of futures commission merchants; or (3) the futures commission merchant.

buyer A market participant who takes a long futures position or buys an option. An option buyer is also called a taker, holder, or owner.

cap-and-trade (or emissions trading) A market-based pollution control system in which total emissions of a pollutant are capped at a specified level. Allowances are issued to firms and can be bought and sold on an organized market or over the counter (OTC).

cash price The price in the marketplace for actual cash or spot commodities to be delivered via customary market channels.

cash settlement A method of settling futuresoptionsand other derivatives whereby the seller (or short) pays the buyer (or long) the cash value of the underlying commodity or a cash amount based on the level of an index or price according to a procedure specified in the contract. Compare to **physical delivery**.

Certified Emission Reduction (CER) unit A Kyoto Protocol unit equal to 1 metric tonne of CO2 equivalent. CERs are issued for emission reductions from clean development mechanism (CDM) project activities. Two special types of CERs, called temporary certified emission reductions (tCERs) and long-term certified emission reductions (lCERs), are issued for emission removals from afforestation and reforestation CDM projects.

cheapest to deliver Usually refers to the selection of a class of bonds or notes deliverable against an expiring bond or note futures contract. The bond or note that has the highest implied repo rate is considered cheapest to deliver.

clearing The procedure through which the clearing organization becomes the buyer to each seller of a futures contract or other derivative and the seller to each buyer for clearing members.

commission (1) The charge made by a futures commission merchant for buying and selling futures contracts; or (2) the fee charged by a futures broker for the execution of an order. (Note: When capitalized, the word Commission usually refers to the Commodity Futures Trading Commission.)

commodity (1) A commodity, as defined in the Commodity Exchange Act, includes the agricultural commodities enumerated in Section 1a(4) of the Commodity Exchange Act, 7 USC 1a(4), and all other goods and articles, except onions as provided in Public Law 85-839 (7 USC 13-1), a 1958 law that banned futures trading in onions, and all services, rights, and interests in which contracts for future delivery are at present or in the future dealt in; (2) a physical commodity such as an agricultural product or a natural resource as opposed to a financial instrument such as a currency or interest rate.

contract (1) A term of reference describing a unit of trading for a commodity future or option or other derivative; (2) an agreement to buy or sell a specified commodity, detailing the amount and grade of the product and the date on which the contract will mature and become deliverable.

contract grades Those grades of a commodity that have been officially approved by an exchange as deliverable in settlement of a futures contract.

contract market A board of trade or exchange designated by the Commodity Futures Trading Commission to trade futures or options under the Commodity Exchange Act. A contract market can allow both institutional and retail participants and can list for trading futures contracts on any commodity, provided that each contract is not readily susceptible to manipulation. Also called designated contract market.

contract size The actual amount of a commodity represented in a contract.

corner Refers to (1) securing such relative control of a commodity that its price can be manipulated, that is, can be controlled by the creator of the corner; or (2) in the extreme situation, obtaining contracts requiring the delivery of more commodities than are available for delivery.

counterparty The opposite party in a bilateral agreement, contract, or transaction, such as a swap. In the retail foreign exchange (forex) context, the party to which a retail customer sends its funds; lawfully, the party must be one of those listed in Section 2(c)(2)(B)(ii)(I)–(VI) of the Commodity Exchange Act.

counterparty risk The risk associated with the financial stability of the party that one has entered into contract with. Forward contracts impose upon each party the risk that the counterparty will default, but futures contracts executed on a designated contract market are guaranteed against default by the clearing organization.

coupon (or coupon rate) A fixed dollar amount of interest payable per annum, stated as a percentage of principal value, usually payable in semiannual installments.

daily price limit The maximum price advance or decline from the previous day's settlement price permitted during one trading session, as fixed by the rules of an exchange. See also **price movement limit**.

dealer An individual or a firm that acts as a market maker in an instrument such as a security or foreign currency.

deliverable supply The total supply of a commodity that meets the delivery specifications of a futures contract.

delivery The tender and receipt of the actual commodity, the cash value of the commodity, or a delivery instrument covering the commodity (e.g., warehouse receipts or shipping certificates), used to settle a futures contract.

delivery instrument A document used to effect delivery on a futures contract, such as a warehouse receipt or shipping certificate.

delivery month The specified month within which a futures contract matures and can be settled by delivery or the specified month in which the delivery period begins.

delivery point A location designated by a commodity exchange where stocks of a commodity represented by a futures contract may be delivered in fulfillment of the contract. Also called location.

demutualization When a company transitions from a member-owned ownership structure to a shareholder-owned ownership structure.

depository receipt A document indicating ownership of a commodity stored in a bank or other depository and frequently used as a delivery instrument in precious metal futures contracts.

derivative A financial instrument, traded on or off an exchange, the price of which is directly dependent upon (i.e., derived from) the value of one or more underlying securities, equity indexes, debt instruments, commodities, or other derivative instruments, or any agreed-upon pricing index or arrangement (e.g., the movement over time of the Consumer Price Index or freight rates). Derivatives are used to hedge risk or to exchange a floating rate of return for fixed rate of return. They include futures, options, and swaps. For example, futures contracts are derivatives of the physical contract, and options on futures are derivatives of futures contracts.

discount (1) The amount a price would be reduced to purchase a commodity of lesser grade; (2) sometimes used to refer to the price differences between futures of different delivery months, as in the phrase "July at a discount to May," indicating that the price for the July futures is lower than that of the May futures.

efficient market In economic theory, an efficient market is one in which market prices adjust rapidly to reflect new information. The degree to which the market is efficient depends on the quality of information reflected in market prices. In an efficient market, profitable arbitrage opportunities do not exist, and traders cannot expect to consistently outperform the market unless they have lower-cost access to information that is reflected in market prices or they have access to information before it is reflected in market prices.

emissions The release of greenhouse gases and/or their precursors into the atmosphere over a specified area and period of time.

emissions allowance A legally defined unit that entitles the holder of the allowance to emit a unit of pollution (i.e., one tonne of CO2e). The European Union Allowance is an example. (Global Carbon Glossary, Point Carbon)

emissions trading See **cap-and-trade**.

exchange A central marketplace with established rules and regulations where buyers and sellers meet to trade futures and options contracts or securities. Exchanges include designated contract markets and derivatives transaction execution facilities.

exchange-traded fund (ETF) An investment vehicle holding a commodity or other asset that issues shares that are traded like a stock on a securities exchange.

exempt commodity The Commodity Exchange Act defines an exempt commodity as any commodity other than an excluded commodity or an agricultural commodity. Examples include energy commodities and metals.

financial commodity Any futures or option contract that is not based on an agricultural commodity, a natural resource such as energy or metals, or any other physical or tangible commodity. It includes currencies, equity securities, fixed income securities, and indexes of various kinds.

financial future A futures contract on a financial commodity.

fixed income security A security whose nominal (or current dollar) yield is fixed or determined with certainty at the time of purchase, typically a debt security.

flexible mechanism Mechanisms defined under the Kyoto Protocol that are intended to lower the overall costs of achieving its emissions targets. These mechanisms enable parties to achieve emission reductions or to remove carbon from the atmosphere cost-effectively in other countries. While the cost of limiting emissions varies considerably from region to region, the benefit for the atmosphere is in principle the same, wherever the action is taken.

floor broker A person with exchange trading privileges who, in any pit, ring, post, or other place provided by an exchange for the meeting of persons similarly engaged, executes for another person any orders for the purchase or sale of any commodity for future delivery.

floor trader A person with exchange trading privileges who executes his or her own trades by being personally present in the pit or ring for futures trading.

forward contract A cash transaction common in many industries, including commodity merchandising, in which a commercial buyer and seller agree on delivery of a specified quality and quantity of goods at a specified future date. Terms may be more personalized than is the case with standardized futures contracts (i.e., delivery time and amount are as determined between seller and buyer). A price may be agreed on in advance, or there may be agreement that the price will be determined at the time of delivery.

futures commission merchant (FCM) An individual, association, partnership, corporation, ortrust that solicits or accepts orders for the purchase or sale of any commodity for future delivery on or subject to the rules of any exchange and that accepts payment from or extends credit to those whose orders are accepted.

futures contract An agreement to purchase or sell a commodity for delivery in the future: (1) at a price that is determined at initiation of the contract; (2) that obligates each party to the contract to fulfill the contract at the specified price; (3) that is used to assume or shift price risk; and (4) that may be satisfied by delivery or offset.

futures option An option on a futures contract.

futures price (1) Commonly held to mean the price of a commodity for future delivery that is traded on a futures exchange; (2) the price of any futures contract.

global warming Strictly speaking, global warming and global cooling refer to the natural warming and cooling trends that the Earth has experienced all through its history. However, the term usually refers to the gradual rise in the Earth's temperatures that could result from the accumulated gases that are trapped in the atmosphere.

grades Various qualities of a commodity.

greenhouse gases Gaseous constituents of the atmosphere, both natural and artificial, that absorb and reemit infrared radiation and that are thought to be responsible for global warming. The most potent greenhouse gas, carbon dioxide, is rapidly accumulating in the atmosphere due to human activities.

hedge To protect oneself against price volatility of a commodity by taking an equal and opposite position in a related securities market (e.g., forward or futures market).

hedge fund A private investment fund or pool that trades and invests in various assets such as securities, commodities, currency, and derivatives on behalf of its clients, typically wealthy individuals. Some commodity pool operators operate hedge funds.

hedger A trader who enters into positions in a futures market opposite to positions held in the cash market to minimize the risk of financial loss from an adverse price change, or who purchases or sells futures as a temporary substitute for a cash transaction that will occur later. One can hedge either a long cash market position (e.g., one owns the cash commodity) or a short cash market position (e.g., one plans on buying the cash commodity in the future).

initial public offering (IPO) When a private company begins to sell its shares to the public.

instrument A tradable asset such as a commodity, security, or derivative, or an index or value that underlies a derivative or could underlie a derivative.

interest rate futures Futures contracts traded on fixed income securities such as U.S. Treasury issues or based on the levels of specified interest rates such as the London Interbank Offered Rate (LIBOR).

Currency is excluded from this category, even though interest rates are a factor in currency values.

liquidation The closing out of a long position. The term is sometimes used to denote closing out a short position, but the latter is more often referred to as covering. See also **offset**.

liquidity In terms of markets, liquidity is the ability to buy and sell an asset quickly and in large volume without substantially affecting the asset's price. In terms of instruments, liquidity refers to those assets that can be converted into cash quickly without a significant loss in value. (Glossary of Statistical Terms, OECD)

liquid market A market in which selling and buying can be accomplished with minimal effect on price.

long (1) One who has bought a futures contract to establish a market position; (2) a market position that obligates the holder to take delivery; (3) one who owns an inventory of commodities. See also **short**.

manipulation Any planned operation, transaction, or practice that causes or maintains an artificial price. Specific types include corners and squeezes as well as unusually large purchases or sales of a commodity or security in a short period of time in order to distort prices, and putting out false information in order to distort prices.

margin The amount of money or collateral deposited by a customer with a broker, by a broker with a clearing member, or by a clearing member with a clearing organization. The margin is not partial payment on a purchase. Also called performance bond.

market maker A professional securities dealer or person with trading privileges on an exchange who has an obligation to buy when there is an excess of sell orders and to sell when there is an excess of buy orders. By maintaining an offering price sufficiently higher than the buying price, these firms are compensated for the risk involved in allowing their inventory of securities to act as a buffer against temporary order imbalances. In the futures industry, this term is sometimes loosely used to refer to a floor trader or local who, in speculating for his or her own account, provides a market for commercial users of the market. Occasionally a futures exchange will compensate a person with exchange trading privileges to take on the obligations of a market maker to enhance liquidity in a newly listed or lightly traded futures contract.

mark-to-market Part of the daily cash flow system used by U.S. futures exchanges to maintain a minimum level of margin equity for a given futures or option contract position by calculating the gain or loss in each contract position resulting from changes in the price of the futures or option contracts at the end of each trading session. These amounts are added to or subtracted fromeach account balance.

maturity Period within which a futures contract can be settled by delivery of the actual commodity.

money market The market for short-term debt instruments.

offer An indication of willingness to sell at a given price; the price level of the offer may be referred to as the ask (i.e., the opposite of the bid).

offset Liquidating a purchase of futures contracts through the sale of an equal number of contracts of the same delivery month, or liquidating a short sale of futures through the purchase of an equal number of contracts of the same delivery month.

open interest The total number of futures contracts long or short in a delivery month or market that have been entered into and not yet liquidated by an offsetting transaction or fulfilled by delivery.

open outcry A method of public auction, common to most U.S. commodity exchanges during the twentieth century, where trading occurs on a trading floor and traders may bid and offer simultaneously either for their own accounts or for the accounts of customers. Transactions may take place simultaneously at different places in the trading pit or ring. At most exchanges open outcry has been replaced or largely replaced by electronic trading platforms.

option A contract that gives the buyer the right, but not the obligation, to buy or sell a specified quantity of a commodity or other instrument at a specific price within a specified period of time, regardless of the market price of that instrument. See also **put**.

out trade A trade that cannot be cleared by a clearing organization because the trade data submitted by the two clearing members or two traders involved in the trade differs in some respect (e.g., price and/or quantity). In such cases, the two clearing members or traders involved must reconcile the discrepancy, if possible, and resubmit the trade for clearing. If an agreement cannot be reached by the two clearing members or traders involved, the dispute would be settled by an appropriate exchange committee.

over-the-counter (OTC) The trading of commodities, contracts, or other instruments not listed on any exchange. OTC transactions can occur electronically or over the telephone.

par (1) Refers to the standard delivery point(s) and/or quality of a commodity that is deliverable on a futures contract at the contract price. Serves as a benchmark on which to base discounts or premiums for varying quality and delivery locations; (2) in bond markets, an index (usually 100) representing the face value of a bond.

physical A contract or derivative that provides for the physical delivery of a commodity rather than cash settlement.

physical commodity A tangible commodity rather than a financial commodity, typically an agricultural commodity, an energy commodity, or a metal. See also **financial commodity**.

physical delivery A provision in a futures contract or other derivative for delivery of the actual commodity to satisfy the contract. Compare to **cash settlement**.

pit A specially constructed area on the trading floor of some exchanges where trading in a futures contract or option is conducted. On other exchanges, the term *ring* designates the trading area for commodity contracts.

position limit The maximum position, either net long or net short, in one commodity future (or option) or in all futures (or options) of one commodity combined that may be held or controlled by one person (other than a person eligible for a hedge exemption) as prescribed by an exchange and/or by the CFTC.

price discovery The process of determining the price level for a commodity based on supply-and-demand conditions. Price discovery may occur in a futures market or cash market.

price movement limit The maximum price advance or decline from the previous day's settlement price permitted during one trading session, as fixed by the rules of an exchange. In some futures contracts, the limit may be expanded or removed during a trading session a specified period of time after the contract is locked limit. See also **daily price limit**.

primary market A market where new issues of stocks and bonds are sold, and where the proceeds go to the issuer. (Glossary of Statistical Terms, OECD)

put An option contract that gives the holder the right but not the obligation to sell a specified quantity of a particular commodity, security, or other asset or to enter into a short futures position at a given price (the strike price) on or prior to a specified expiration date.

runners Messengers or clerks who deliver orders received by phone clerks to brokers for execution in the pit.

savings and loan associations (S&Ls) Historically, depository institutions that accepted deposits mainly from individuals and invested heavily in residential mortgage loans. Although still primarily residential lenders, S&Ls may now offer checking-type deposits and make a wider range of loans. (Glossary of Economic Terms, Federal Reserve Bank of San Francisco)

scalper A speculator, often with exchange trading privileges, who buys and sells rapidly, with small profits or losses, holding positions for only a short time during a trading session. Typically, a scalper will stand ready to buy at a fraction below the last transaction price and to sell at a fraction above (e.g., to buy at the bid and sell at the offer or ask price), with the intent of capturing the spread between the two, thus creating market liquidity.

seat An instrument granting trading privileges on an exchange. A seat may also represent an ownership interest in the exchange.

secondary market The market where securities are bought and sold once they have been issued in the primary markets. The secondary market gives a continuing opportunity for buying and selling and for price discovery, and provides the liquidity that allows the primary market to function.(Financial Glossary, Reuters)

security Generally, a transferable instrument representing an ownership interest in a corporation (equity security or stock) or the debt of a corporation, municipality, or sovereign. Other forms of debt such as mortgages can be converted into securities. Certain derivatives on securities (e.g., options on equity securities) are also considered securities for the purposes of the securities laws. Security futures products are considered to be both securities and futures products. Futures contracts on broad-based securities indexes are not considered securities.

settlement The act of fulfilling the delivery requirements of the futures contract.

settlement price The daily price at which the clearing organization clears all trades and settles all accounts between clearing members of each contract month. Settlement prices are used to determine both margin calls and invoice prices for deliveries. The term also refers to a price established by the exchange to even up positions that may not be able to be liquidated in regular trading.

shipping certificate A negotiable instrument used by several futures exchanges as the futures delivery instrument for several commodities (e.g., soybean meal, plywood, and white wheat). The shipping certificate is issued by exchange-approved facilities and represents a commitment by the facility to deliver the commodity to the holder of the certificate under the terms specified therein. Unlike an issuer of a warehouse receipt, who has physical product in store, the issuer of a shipping certificate may honor its obligation from current production or through-put as well as from inventories.

short (1) The selling side of an open futures contract; (2) a trader whose net position in the futures market shows an excess of open sales over open purchases. See also **long**.

short selling Selling a futures contract or other instrument with the idea of delivering on it or offsetting it at a later date.

speculator In commodity futures, a trader who does not hedge, but who trades with the objective of achieving profits through the successful anticipation of price movements.

spot Market of immediate delivery of and payment for the product. See also **spot market**.

spot commodity (1) The actual commodity as distinguished from a futures contract; (2) sometimes used to refer to cash commodities available for immediate delivery.

spot market The market for the cash commodity (as contrasted to a futures contract) taking the form of: (1) an organized, self-regulated central market (e.g., a commodity exchange); (2) a decentralized over-the-counter market; or (3) a local organization, such as a grain elevator or meat processor, which provides a market for a small region.

tick Refers to a minimum change in price up or down. An uptick means that the last trade was at a higher price than the one preceding it. A downtick means that the last price was lower than the one preceding it.

trader (1) A merchant involved in cash commodities; (2) a professional speculator who trades for his or her own account and who typically holds exchange trading privileges.

trading floor A physical trading facility where traders make bids and offers via open outcry or the specialist system.

transaction The entry or liquidation of a trade.

transaction costs Costs incurred when buying or selling securities. These include brokers' commissions and spreads (the difference between the price the dealer paid for a security and the price at which it can be sold).

Treasury bills (or T-bills) Short-term zero coupon U.S. government obligations, generally issued with various maturities of up to one year.

Treasury bonds (or T-bonds) Long-term (more than 10 years) obligations of the U.S. government that pay interest semiannually until they mature, at which time the principal and the final interest payment are paid to the investor.

Treasury notes Same as Treasury bonds except that Treasury notes are medium-term (more than one year but not more than 10 years).

underlying commodity The cash commodity underlying a futures contract. Also, the commodity or futures contract on which a commodity option is based, and that must be accepted or delivered if the option is exercised.

volatility A statistical measurement (the annualized standard deviation of returns) of the rate of price change of a futures contract, security, or other instrument underlying an option.

volume The number of contracts traded during a specified period of time. Volume is most commonly quoted as the number of contracts traded, but for some physical commodities it may be quoted as the total of physical units, such as bales, bushels, pounds, or dozens of barrels.

warehouse receipt A document certifying possession of a commodity in a licensed warehouse that is recognized for delivery purposes by an exchange.

yield curve A graphic representation of market yield for a fixed income security plotted against the maturity of the security. The yield curve is positive when long-term rates are higher than short-term rates.

Index

ALSO BY JUDY TROY

West of Venus

Mourning Doves

FROM THE BLACK HILLS

FROM THE BLACK HILLS

JUDY TROY

RANDOM HOUSE NEW YORK

This is a work of fiction. The characters and events in it are inventions of the author and do not depict any real persons or events.

Grateful acknowledgment is made to Sony/ATV Music Publishing for permission to reprint an excerpt from "Hello Walls" by Willie Nelson.

Troy, Judy
From the Black Hills / Judy Troy.
p. cm.
ISBN 0-375-50230-0 (alk. paper)
I. Title.
PS3570.R68F76 1999
813'.54—dc21 98-53465

Random House website address: www.atrandom.com
Printed in the United States of America on acid-free paper
2 4 6 8 9 7 5 3
First Edition
Book design by Jo Anne Metsch

FOR MILLER AND HARDY

ACKNOWLEDGMENTS

With gratitude to the Whiting Foundation; to Bob Overturf at the Division of Criminal Investigation in Rapid City, whose help was invaluable; to Frank Walters for his motorcycle wisdom; to Robin Bernstein for his beautiful sentence; and to Georges and Anne Borchardt for, among other things, their faith in me.

I would also like to thank Mark Siegert for his inestimable help and support; Mary D. Kierstead, always; Miller Solomon, for more than I can say; Jeanne Tift; Beth Pearson; Margaret Wimberger; and Daniel Menaker, whose intelligence and talent have now graced my work a second time.

FROM THE BLACK HILLS

PROLOGUE

EARLY Sunday morning in the third week of August, Michael Newlin left Wheatley, South Dakota, for college. His mother stood in the driveway alone, in her church clothes, to see him off. Behind her was the two-story brick house he'd grown up in, which she would live in by herself now. His father had been missing for more than eight weeks. On June 18, without having done a violent thing ever before, he had shot and killed Mary Hise, the young woman who'd worked as receptionist at his small insurance agency. Then he'd disappeared. He'd been seen in Kansas, but that was back in July. By this time he could be anywhere.

"Concentrate on your own life now," Mike's mother said. She was almost as tall as he was, her short hair blown back by the dry wind. She kissed him through the open window of his pickup, and he backed down the driveway, drove down Edge Street, and turned onto the interstate.

South Dakota State University, in Brookings, was over four hundred miles east, not far from the Minnesota state line. It would take him seven hours to get there. He'd brought cassettes to listen to, including one that his girlfriend, Donetta Rush, had made for him.

"Don't listen to it until you're on the highway," she'd asked him the night before. "You have to promise." He'd promised, and then he'd listened to the beginning of it on his way home from her house.

The first thing on the cassette was her voice. "It's three o'clock in the morning," she said. "I can't sleep, I can't dream, and I can't stop thinking of you."

"Miss You," by the Rolling Stones, was the first song.

PART I

WHEATLEY

ONE

IN the spring of Mike's senior year, months before graduation, he was working long hours at Neil Schofield's cattle ranch. He was bored with school, and Josh Mitchell, his closest friend, had moved to Wyoming in February, with his father, after his parents' divorce. Josh's mother was with somebody else now.

Mike had worked at the Schofield ranch every summer since he was fourteen, and this year, in March, he began working mornings before school, getting up in the dark and riding his motorcycle—bought despite his parents' objections—out on Route 8 through the cold dawn. On those days he ate breakfast with the Schofields—with Neil, his wife, Lee-Ann, and their two-year-old daughter, Janna. Often Neil's brother, Ed, who lived in Buffalo Gap, would be there, too, having driven over in his old Corvette. He was an artist; he made pottery that he sold in Rapid City. Two other men, Arthur Strong and Louis Ivy, showed up after breakfast. They looked older than they were, and neither of them could read very well. If they got there early, they waited outside, next to their pickups.

"I can make you breakfast here," Mike's mother had offered. "I'm up early anyway." She taught high school biology and did her class preparations in the mornings before school.

"I don't mind eating with the Schofields," Mike had told her, not saying that he preferred it to being home. The previous summer, when Mike had left home for the ranch before sunrise and not come back before nine at night, he'd said that he liked being alone on the tractor, listening to his father's old rock-and-roll tapes on his Walkman. He'd kept quiet about Neil Schofield, whose first two strikes against him, according to Mike's father, were that he was rich and hadn't had to work for it. Neil's wealthy father had bought the ranch for his retirement. Now he lived in California, and Neil ran the ranch for real, sort of. He could hire as many people as he needed and could afford having bad luck. "Money just doesn't mean that much to me," he'd told Mike.

"Let's see," Mike had said once. "If I work half an hour longer, I can afford to buy Donetta popcorn tonight at the movies." Neil had given him an extra twenty dollars with that week's pay. "I'm bullshitting you," Mike had had to explain.

Neil was fifteen years younger than Mike's father. He was tall, light-haired, and energetic, and in good shape from his work on the ranch. Mike's father, Glenn, was of average height, thin, and dark-haired, and had never been particularly happy. What Mike told himself most often was that his father had gotten lost trying to find what other people already had. Glenn didn't have the key, somehow. Mike felt that his father was always trying to figure out how he'd come into being, and how Mike had come into being, what point there was to it and how you were supposed to get through your life. Once, late one night, when Mike's mother was away, Mike had heard his father cry for almost an hour. In the morning neither of them had mentioned it. His father had never hit Mike—or anyone else, as far as Mike knew—but he got his feelings hurt too easily. And when he got angry it turned into a dark mood that lasted a long time, often weeks. "Mr. Gloom," Mike would refer to him as then, but only to himself. It would be too disloyal to use this kind of nickname, even with Josh and Donetta. Anyway, his father wasn't always like that.

Something else Mike kept quiet about with everyone were his feelings for Lee-Ann Schofield. When he first knew her, when he was fourteen, she had teased him about some things he'd mentioned to Neil, such as getting into trouble with Josh, drunk at the bowling alley, or sneaking out at three in the morning to throw eggs at somebody's window. But over the years she'd teased him less and talked to him more. She was thirteen years older than he was, thirty the year he turned seventeen. Mike was tall by then—not as tall as Neil but taller than his father, and muscular from high school wrestling and working on the ranch. He'd let his dark hair grow as long as he could before his coach objected. He looked more like his mother's side of the family: green eyes, a long face, high cheekbones.

Lee-Ann had small, pretty features. Her brown hair was unevenly cut—collar-length in back, shorter around her face. In the sunlight, Mike noticed, her hair had shades of gold and red. She wore loose clothes and no makeup and seemed to have a private way she felt about herself that was different from what other people thought they knew about her. That was what Mike liked about her. She was secretive, the way he was.

On an October morning of Mike's senior year, he went into the Schofields' house for a Coke just as Lee-Ann was coming into the kitchen after a shower. In the half second before she belted her thin robe, he saw her breasts, her stomach—a fleshiness that the girls he knew didn't have; they dieted and ran and lifted weights. Even Lee-Ann's face was softer, and seemed capable of gentler expressions. After that day, with her wet face and hair, her open robe, and the way she'd looked at him when she saw him looking at her, Mike became more sexual around her. He didn't think about the age difference anymore and hardly thought of her as married. In his mind he separated her from Neil and from his friendship with Neil.

By the time winter came, the moment he saw her was the moment he came to count on most, though he couldn't have said for what, or why. Because, as his advanced-placement English teacher would have said—she was always making them read stories about people who weren't lucky—his life was a lucky one: a nice-enough house, responsible parents, the ability to get good grades. And even that left out something: Donetta having sex with him on weekend nights at Crow Lake. Yet Mike couldn't change the way he felt about Lee-Ann Schofield; it was a fact, to him, rather than something he might question.

Instead, he fantasized about her all winter and spring. She was on his mind as he sat in class, watching snow fall on the field outside the window; as he rode his motorcycle too fast on the first warm days when the trees were budding; as he had sex with Donetta in the backseat of his mother's car. And at night in his house—his mother up late, grading papers in the dining room, his father in front of the television in the den—he lay in bed in the dark and masturbated, imagining that moment in the kitchen with Lee-Ann and picturing her robe coming off. His goal became to masturbate one day in her empty house—the emptiness sexual to him, somehow, as if his own body could fill all that space.

He didn't have the nerve or opportunity to do it until an

afternoon in late May, when Lee-Ann and Janna were in town and Neil had driven over to Ed's house in Buffalo Gap. Mike had walked through the house, noticing two things he'd never noticed before: a photograph of Lee-Ann breast-feeding her daughter, and a white plaster cast of Lee-Ann's hand when she was a child, her name etched into it underneath. He walked upstairs to the bedroom she shared with Neil, with its white curtains and pale carpet. But a pair of Neil's boots were next to a chair in the corner, so Mike settled for the upstairs hallway, in sight of Lee-Ann's robe in the bathroom and the blue comforter on her bed. He leaned against the wall and unzipped his jeans, and afterward, using toilet paper to clean himself up, his legs were shaking. He wanted to do it again, almost immediately. But the house was reassuming its identity, which didn't include him. He felt like an intruder then. He went home that night without coming up to the house to say good-bye the way he usually did, and he didn't come for breakfast the next morning.

On Saturday Lee-Ann came into the barn to find him. "Are you mad at me? Did I do something I don't remember?"

"No," he told her. "It's me. I've been busy with school."

"I miss you," she said, in the sweet voice he'd heard her use only with Neil and Janna; it made tears come to his eyes. "It's all right," Lee-Ann said gently, and they put their arms around each other for the first time. She held him so closely that he had to pull back in order to kiss her.

But she stepped away then, and walked out of the barn. He didn't see her again until that evening, as he was leaving. She was watching him from the front yard.

After that were days at the ranch Mike had to miss because of finals, graduation, and then, on June 18—a hot, bright Thursday afternoon—because of what his father did.

TWO

MARY Hise died before the ambulance arrived. It was Neil who told Mike what had happened. Mike, on the riding lawn mower, circling the pond, with the sun low behind him, saw Neil walking toward him from the house. He looked so serious that for a moment Mike was afraid he was going to say, "I know you want to screw my wife." What he said instead was, "Let's go sit on the porch. I have to tell you something about your father."

Mary Hise was naked. She was lying in the bathroom doorway of room 14 at the Tenderly Motel, in Wausee—a motel Mike had been to twice with Donetta.

"Your mother wanted you to hear this from me," Neil said. "Not from the police. They're already at your house." He was sitting across from Mike on the screened-in porch, Janna's dolls scattered on the floor between them. "Your father and Mary met at the motel. They got there at one o'clock, and they were drinking. Afterward your father called an ambulance, then drove off in Mary's car." Neil looked at his watch. "It's been three hours since he made the call."

"Why her car?" Mike's mouth was so dry that it was hard for him to talk.

"I don't know. Maybe to buy him time. They didn't know who she was for a while. Her purse wasn't there." Neil stood and went into the kitchen; he came back with a glass of water that he handed to Mike. "Your father even left the gun behind," he said. "It was registered to him."

"It was my grandfather's," Mike said slowly. He looked down the hill, toward the pond. He could see the line between what he had mowed and what he hadn't. It looked as sharp and distinct as the edge of a razor.

Neil leaned forward, the chair creaking as he moved. "I know how hard it is to believe. It is for me, too. I thought, somehow they've got your father confused with somebody else. But they don't. It's not a mistake."

"I know," Mike said. But that sounded as if he knew more about his father and Mary Hise than he did. He didn't know anything. That was what he couldn't put into words—what it was like to discover that there were things you almost knew but didn't know. He looked away from Neil. He leaned down and picked up Janna's dolls. He put them one by one in her red toy box.

"Your mother wants me to drive you home," Neil said. "She doesn't want you on your motorcycle tonight."

"I'm all right."

"I'll drive you anyway. I promised her."

Neil turned toward Lee-Ann, whom Mike noticed for the first time. She was standing at the porch door with the baby in her arms. They were like a snapshot of normal life, Mike thought—something he knew he hadn't been a part of even before this happened, something he seemed cut off from now in a permanent way. "I'm sorry, Mike," she said.

FIVE minutes later Neil loaded Mike's motorcycle into the back of his pickup. Lee-Ann had come outside with them. "Call us," she told Mike. She set Janna down, put her arms around Mike, and hugged him. It was nothing like before; he knew it couldn't be. And that scared him almost as much as the news about his father had. What he needed was proof that she wanted to be with him. If he could have that, then he could handle everything else that was happening.

"Don't worry about work," Neil told him on the way home. "Come back when you're ready, or just come over and talk."

"Okay," Mike said.

The sun was sinking behind the Black Hills, which were just a few miles away. It was cooler there, and Mike thought about how you could ride up there and get lost for a while on the winding roads, though they all brought you back to Wheatley or Hill City or one of the other small towns. You could never get lost long enough to see what lost felt like. You could never just disappear.

"I can't believe this happened," Neil said.

He pulled up in front of Mike's house. There were five policemen standing in the yard. There were seven cars parked along the curb.

THREE

THEY asked him questions. Had he seen his father carry anything out to the car last night, or this morning? Some of his father's clothes were gone. Did he know that his father had been transferring savings into his parents' checking account and then withdrawing them? He might have as much as four thousand dollars with him. Why did his father have books about wilderness survival? They'd taken those out of the bookshelf and gone through them, even though Mike's mother, Carolyn, had said, "Glenn hasn't looked at those in fifteen years." Had Mike ever seen his father with another woman? Why did his father have a gun? Had Mike ever been afraid of his father? Did Mike love him?

That last question came from a special agent with the Division of Criminal Investigation in Rapid City. His name was Tom DeWitt; Mike knew him and his mother knew of him. His brother lived in Wheatley and was a teacher, and his nephew had been on Mike's wrestling team. Mike had seen Tom DeWitt at meets and knew that he had a cabin somewhere near Lead. Once, after a wrestling meet in Rapid City, he had treated the team to pizza.

He sat with Mike on the small patio outside the kitchen door. It was not quite dark. Mike's mother was sitting inside at the kitchen table with two of her friends, both female teachers. Mike only had to look to his right, through the window, to see her distressed, anxious face. And so when the special agent asked Mike if he loved his father, Mike glanced at her and said uneasily, "I guess I do. What difference does it make?"

"I'm trying to get a picture of your father. I want to understand him."

"Why?"

"So I can think like him." Tom DeWitt crossed his legs, his left ankle resting on his right knee. His intelligence made Mike nervous. He wasn't expecting it. He'd grown up seeing movies in which even smart policemen were foolish in some ways. He wasn't sure that he could fool this person, which made him wonder why he would think about trying. Fool him about what?

"Am I your enemy or your friend?" he asked Mike.

"Neither."

"If your father contacted you, would you tell me?"

"I don't know."

The agent stood up to take off his suit jacket. He had

brown, thinning hair, narrow eyes, and a wide, relaxed-looking face. Under his jacket he was wearing a short-sleeved shirt. He worked out, Mike saw. He had large biceps and strong forearms. He was big-chested for his height. He lay his jacket across his lap. "I've seen you wrestle," he said. "Are you going to wrestle in college?"

"Not if it gets in the way of school."

"Is that you talking, or your parents?"

"I don't want to be some dumb-ass jock."

He laughed in such a friendly way that for a second Mike was confused about what the agent was there for, why he was talking to Mike. Mike looked through the window at his mother.

"Did your father watch you wrestle?" Tom DeWitt asked.

"Yes. He just didn't come every time."

"Why not?"

"Why should he?"

"I don't know. Some fathers would."

"I didn't expect him to," Mike said.

"Some fathers would go regardless."

"Well, he wasn't one of them."

"What kind was he, then?"

"Why should I describe him to you?" Mike said.

"Why shouldn't you?"

"Because you don't give a shit about him."

"He killed a twenty-four-year-old woman," the agent said.

"He called an ambulance," Mike said. "He wished he hadn't done it. He didn't want her to die."

"But she did die."

In the silence that followed, Mike could hear the cicadas, which sounded to him too harsh and too loud. He wasn't perceiving things right. The backyard seemed larger than it was; his mother, in the kitchen, seemed smaller and older. He had changed, too. He felt that he was looking at himself through unfocused binoculars. Yet the agent remained solid and whole. He seemed casual, even, until he said, "Do you think he's being blamed for something he didn't do?"

"Do you?"

"I'm not his son. I don't know what I'd think if I were."

"Because you know your father could never have done it."

"No. Anybody could do it."

"I couldn't," Mike said, and knew right away that he'd made a mistake. "That's not true," he said then. "I don't know what I could or couldn't do." He moved his hair out of his eyes. His hands were shaking. "I'm tired," he said. "I don't want to talk anymore."

Tom DeWitt stood up slowly, as if he were the tired one. He walked into the kitchen behind Mike, said good night to Mike's mother—one of her friends was leaving as well—and said good-bye to Mike. He looked once more at the pile of survival books before disappearing into the front part of the house. Mike didn't hear the door close, although from his room upstairs, which faced the street, he saw him cross the yard and get into a light-colored car.

Mike wasn't alone for more than a minute before his mother was standing in the doorway in her brown dress. That summer she was teaching part-time at the community college, and she was still in her teaching clothes.

"Ms. Watkins is spending the night with us," she told Mike. Noleen Watkins, who dated Mike's wrestling coach, had been Mike's seventh-grade social studies teacher; she'd taken his class on a field trip to Badlands National Park. His mother sometimes referred to her friends at school by their last names, even younger women like Noleen. "You've spent too much time in school, Carolyn," Mike's father used to tell her. "Everybody is Mr. or Mrs. So-and-So."

"Mr. or Ms.," his mother would say sharply, ignoring the point his father had been making. She was good at that, Mike knew. She never thought that people's responses had anything to do with her, with how she acted or what she said. Mike had seen her do that at school, too. For four years he'd had to see her there in addition to at home. While she'd kept track of his behavior, his grades, and his friends, he'd kept track of her, too—of how she could ignore an unhappy student or snub an entire class that didn't like her. In the end that changed the way Mike felt about her. Before that, she'd been his friend. She'd helped him with his homework. She'd driven him and Josh to Rapid City for baseball games.

Now she shut Mike's door behind her, crossed the room, and stood with him at the open window. "Did Tom De-

Witt tell you anything?" she asked. "Do you think they know where he is?"

"He just asked questions," Mike said. The night had grown windy. Mike could hear it in the chimes that hung from the front porch, below his room. His father had bought them for his mother a long time ago. His father had paid for them, but Mike had picked them out.

"You should eat something," his mother said. "There's meat loaf, and macaroni and cheese." When Mike didn't respond, she touched his arm. "Even if you don't feel hungry."

"I don't."

"Sit down with me." She sat on the bed and waited for Mike to sit next to her. "Your father and Mary Hise were having an affair," she told him. "It started last fall, or in the winter. I'm not sure. I didn't know until three weeks ago." Her voice had become unsteady, and she began to cry. Mike looked down at the brown carpeting, then at the closed door. Finally, he put his arms around her—something he'd never done before unless he was hugging her hello or good-bye. He felt how thin she was, thinner than she looked.

After a few moments she sat up straight and dried her face. "I'm all right," she said. "You know that. I'm not the kind of person who falls apart."

Like Dad, Mike thought. He moved over a little, so that there was a few inches of space between them.

"Mary Hise told Dad she was quitting," his mother

said. "That was toward the end of May, when you weren't home much."

"I wanted to make money for college."

"I know. I'm not criticizing you." She took a deep breath. She looked at Mike's closet and so did he—the door to it open, his jeans and work shirts stacked neatly on the shelves. "Dad was distraught," she said. "He would hardly talk. He couldn't sleep. Finally I called Mary Hise and asked her to meet me for coffee, and she said yes. We met at Shoney's. I said, 'You and Glenn are having an affair,' as if I already knew, because I was sure. And she said, 'We were having an affair, but that's in the past. That's why I'm leaving. He still wants—' " Carolyn stopped and turned her head at a noise in the hallway—Noleen Watkins closing the bathroom door. Mike had already forgotten that she was there, that she was staying overnight. Then his mother said, "I hate telling you these things. I hate for you to know them."

"Well, you know them," Mike said.

"I'm not eighteen. I'm not his child." When Mike started to protest, she said, "You're not a child anymore. I know that." She seemed to focus on the Grateful Dead poster taped to the wall above his bed. Donetta had bought it for him a year ago—what seemed to Mike now like a hundred years ago.

"Dad didn't want Mary Hise to leave," his mother said. "I told her, 'Just stay in the job a little longer, until he gets used to the idea of your leaving. Wait until he calms down.' " She turned toward Mike as if he'd spoken. "What would you expect me to say? I was afraid your father was going to kill himself."

She didn't have to explain why; Mike already knew. His father had tried to kill himself once before, twenty-some years before, during his freshman year at the University of South Dakota. He'd been dating Mike's mother's roommate, and when she had broken up with him he'd taken an overdose of pills—tranquilizers of some kind. "Things were different then," Mike's mother had told Mike once. "Vietnam was going on. People talked about death and suicide. I felt compassionate toward your father. He was more sensitive than the other boys I knew."

Mike had seen an old picture of his parents: the two of them sitting on the grass in front of a classroom building, his mother's hair waist-length and his father's almost to his shoulders. It had been taken the spring of their sophomore year, by which time they were a couple—his father the handsome one and his mother the smart one. It seemed to Mike that they'd stayed the same in that way, except that his father's expression had changed, had become bewildered, Mike thought, or hopeless.

"You know as much as I do about the rest," his mother said. "Mary stayed on. Your father seemed calmer. I didn't know they were still involved. I didn't know she'd lied to me. I thought that she'd quit before long, and then your dad and I would—I don't know. Talk about it." She looked down at her hands. The only ring she wore was her wedding band.

"Did Dad know you knew?"

"No. I don't think so."

"Did you tell the police you knew?"

"Of course. I had to." She got up and closed Mike's curtains. "When you're married a long time . . ." she said. Then, "Dad and I weren't . . ." She turned toward him. "Marriages are complicated. All of them are." Her eyes were teary. "Are you all right?" she asked. "Do you think you can sleep?"

Mike nodded. She stood next to the door for a moment, before opening it, and Mike thought about how many nights she'd done that during his life—not nights like this but ordinary ones, when she'd come in to say good night, then stand there as if she couldn't bring herself to leave. He used to count the seconds to himself until he could be free of her. Although there was a time, when he was much younger, when he hadn't minded it; sometimes he had liked it. That was hard for him to remember now.

"I'll see you in the morning," she said. "Things will seem clearer when we've gotten some sleep."

She opened the door, and he listened to her footsteps in the hall, his heart beating fast. He knew too many private things, and now he knew more. He'd known that his parents weren't happy with each other. He'd known that his father was never going to be happy with anyone. He'd known, even, that there had been something wrong with his father lately, but that hadn't been the only time he'd felt that. If you felt something often enough, you hardly felt it anymore. You were so used to certain things being wrong that you didn't ask questions. You stopped wondering. You just told yourself that everything was the way it always was.

He could hear thunder in the west, over the Black Hills, or even farther away, in Wyoming. He turned off the light, sat on his bed, and thought about Mary Hise. She had been his father's receptionist for a year and a half; she'd had red hair and dark eyes. Mike hadn't known her well. One afternoon in December, at his father's office, he had spoken to her for just a few minutes. They'd talked about her dog, Harrison. "In warm weather I take him out to Little Falls Park after dinner," she'd said. "I ride my bike, and he runs behind me." She showed Mike a picture of herself with the tan dog at her feet. Part cocker spaniel, she had said. She'd put the picture back in her desk drawer. She'd stopped talking when Mike's father walked over.

Mike had seen her once, the previous summer, at the public pool. In a bikini, she'd looked sexier than he would have imagined. She'd had bigger breasts than he would have thought. Mike had been at the pool with Donetta; he'd not spoken to Mary Hise, but he remembered how she looked. He was uncomfortable now—ashamed, even, of recalling so clearly what her body was like. It didn't seem believable that she was dead.

Lightning lit up his room, and rain began to fall. When he looked out the window there was only a minute before the Hylers' house across the street became impossible to see. Their place was a disaster, anyway—an old frame house with peeling paint and a second-floor porch in danger of caving in. In the front yard was an oak tree over a hundred years old. The Hylers were almost that old themselves. It was Donetta's favorite house in Wheatley, and not for its potential to be fixed up, either. She liked it the way it was—almost condemned. "If you lived in it," she'd say, "you'd feel that your life was part of history."

Mike went downstairs and opened the kitchen door. It was after midnight. It was raining so hard that he couldn't see beyond the patio to the neatly mown lawn, which was his job to keep up, or to the garbage cans in the alley, which were his responsibility, too—to take out the garbage and move the cans back up the driveway between pickup days. His mother kept things clean inside, as he did outside. What were his father's jobs? Mike wondered now. There was a workbench in the carport, which Mike had seen him use only a few times. Did something happen to people who didn't have routine, everyday things to do?

Mike hadn't eaten since noon. He closed the back door, opened the refrigerator, and took out the meat loaf, which he ate cold, standing up. Then he put it back and climbed the stairs. The rooms were dark. His mother's door was closed; the door to the guest room wasn't shut completely. He could see the shape of Noleen Watkins in bed. He stood there until his eyes adjusted to the darkness; then he could see that the bedsheet was thrown back, and that she had on a sleeveless nightgown. He wasn't attracted to her; she was a teacher he'd liked but never had a crush on, yet in the dark hallway he couldn't stop looking at her. Because he was a bad person, he thought—capable of any terrible thing.

Back in his room, he sat at his desk. In front of him was a stack of notebooks from his senior year that he hadn't gotten rid of yet; a pencil sketch of himself that Donetta had drawn, which said, on the back, "I love you forever"; and his acceptance letter to the honors program at South Dakota State University. That was all from the life he used to have, which now seemed shallow and unimportant. He hadn't been serious enough. He hadn't been paying enough attention to what was going on around him. He hadn't realized how much of your life could just come apart.

He lay down and tried to sleep. The rain outside hadn't let up. When he did fall asleep he woke twice from dreams in which his father, stranded in a storm, with the police after him, felt desperate enough to kill himself—this time for real. After the second dream Mike sat up and turned on his lamp. All right, he told himself. That's how I would feel. But how would Dad feel?

Misunderstood, Mike thought. He was able to sleep a little then. Years later he would realize how ironic that was, to find that comforting.

FOUR

IN the morning there was an unmarked police car parked across the street. The sky was overcast, and the storm had torn things up. Mike would have to pick up the fallen oak branches and the pieces of his mother's ceramic bird feeder, which he'd heard break in the night. Next door, Clyde Pate, old as he was, was up on his roof with a push broom.

Mike was standing at the window, watching him, when Donetta drove up. She walked across the yard to the back of the house, barefoot, wearing her blue uniform from Andell's Diner. Seeing her, Mike felt more able to go down to the kitchen and face his mother and Noleen Watkins. What ruined it was that when he walked into the kitchen, Donetta said, "Honey"—as if they were married, he thought, as if what his father had done had given her some kind of right to him.

She jumped up and hugged him; then she got him a glass of juice and brought it to where he stood, leaning stiffly against the farthest counter. He knew he was being a jerk; he felt that he was entitled to be anything he wanted to be today.

"Don't you have to be at work in a few minutes?" he asked her. He saw his mother frown at him.

"I am going to work," Donetta said. "I tried to get off, but Mr. Andell said no, he couldn't replace me."

Mr. Asshole, Mike thought, correcting her in his head. That was what Donetta would have called him any other day, even in front of his mother. Andell's Diner was just outside Wheatley, off the interstate—a truck stop, really, though no one in town called it that.

"I even have to work an extra shift," Donetta said in an offended way. She went back to the table and stood behind his mother and Noleen Watkins.

Mike stayed where he was, looking down at his juice glass, knowing that he'd become the center of attention. He couldn't tell if they expected him to do something crazy, or to do some take-control, you're-the-man-now kind of thing.

"I cancelled my classes for today and tomorrow," his mother said to him. She was in her nightgown and robe. "I'll go back Monday. Can Neil Schofield do without you for a few days?"

"I don't think so," Mike said. "I might have to help him out today or tomorrow." He tried to look right at her as he spoke, but it was hard. He was more used to telling half-truths and leaving things out than he was to lying outright. But he had to see Lee-Ann sooner than Monday. Monday was too far away. If he could just see her, he thought, then he could keep her inside his head and keep what was happening outside.

"All right," his mother said. He could see how tired she was then, probably even more tired than he was, and he almost gave in to the impulse to be nicer. What stopped him were his mother, Noleen Watkins, and Donetta lined up there like that at the table—against him, he felt, treating him like all of a sudden he might be a different person.

"It's probably better for Mike to stay busy," Noleen said. She said it so kindly that Mike's anger just left him. He sat down and let Donetta take his hand.

"I just wanted you to have company this morning," Donetta told him shyly, and that made her seem more like herself again to Mike. She understood how he felt—partly because they were alike. She had told him, as early as their first date, that he was the only person who'd ever made her feel less alone. "Alone in what way?" Mike had asked. "Alone as a person," she'd said, and he'd felt that she was talking about him, even though she'd been talking about herself.

They were both more themselves when he walked her outside to her car. "I can't believe this shit," Donetta said. "I can't believe this is real."

They were standing next to her silver Geo, in view of the

policeman parked across the street, looking at the house through his open window. Donetta put her arms around Mike's neck. She was small and small-boned; she had long hair streaked blond at the beauty school her mother owned. She was a year behind Mike in school. "That cop is watching us," Mike told her.

"I know," Donetta said, and she put her hand down the front of his jeans for just an instant as she kissed him. After she left, there was just Mike and the policeman, the empty street between them, and Donetta's silver car speeding away twice as fast as it should have.

"She's late for work," Mike said to the officer as offhandedly as he could before walking across the soaked grass toward the house. He picked up branches from the oak tree his father had planted the year he was born, and he picked up pieces of his mother's bird feeder. He knew that the policeman was probably watching him, and he felt as if he were in a movie, acting the part of a criminal's guilty son, even though he didn't know what he was guilty of.

Inside, he sat at the table with Noleen Watkins and ate a bowl of cereal. He felt uncomfortable alone with her. His mother had gone upstairs to dress. Noleen, in jeans and a pink shirt, her hair pulled back and her glasses hanging from a chain around her neck, was holding her coffee cup with both hands. "I haven't seen you in a long time," she told Mike. "Your mother says that you're going to South Dakota State in the fall."

"I was. I still am, I guess."

"I know how you must feel," she said. "But don't lose sight of your own plans."

"I won't," he said, to be polite. Outside, the sun broke through the clouds and streamed in through the window, filling the kitchen with light.

"It's easy to give advice, isn't it?" Noleen said. "Teachers do that too much. It becomes a habit."

"I guess it would," Mike said. After a small silence he asked, "Do you still take classes to the Badlands?"

"Sure," she said.

"Do they have to go through the nature center?"

"Why? Did you dislike that part?"

"No. But I liked walking around better," Mike said.

"I do, too."

They were quiet, and Mike could hear his mother on the phone, upstairs—the anxious tone of her voice and a few stark words: shock, Glenn, police.

"Donetta and I go out there sometimes," Mike said, to drown out his mother's voice. "We sit on the rocks and watch for mountain goats."

"Do you?"

"I like how empty it is."

"Why?" Noleen asked.

"It's peaceful. It's just you and the rocks."

"And the goats," Noleen said.

"Yeah. And the goats."

They heard something break upstairs, then Mike's

mother saying, "Damn it!" A moment later she came down to the kitchen.

"What was it?" Noleen said. "Let me clean it up."

Carolyn shook her head. She got out a broom and dustpan and went back upstairs. After that, the light in the kitchen seemed hotter, less bearable. Across from Mike, Noleen moved out of the sun, away from the window.

LATER in the morning, when it was just Mike and his mother at home, a police officer came and asked more questions. But only Tom DeWitt, who arrived at noon, spoke to them at any length. Wearing a shirt and tie, he sat formally with them in the living room. "In a situation like this," he said, "you either find the person by now, or you don't find him for quite a while."

"A situation like this?" Carolyn asked.

"Where the susp—person is intelligent and doesn't have a record."

"You can call him whatever you want," Carolyn said. "We know what he did. We're as horrified by it as you are."

"I'm just saying, don't panic each time the phone rings, or when you see a police car out front. We probably won't have any news for some time."

"I don't know whether that's good or bad," she said, looking at Mike; Mike avoided looking at either of them.

"It's bad for us," the agent said. "I don't know which

would be easier for you." He stood up to leave, then turned to Mike's mother apologetically. "That was insensitive," he told her. "Of course it's hard for you either way."

He opened the front door and closed it silently behind him. From the window, Mike watched him observe the house and yard for a few minutes before getting into his car.

HIS mother spent the early part of the afternoon on the phone; then she and Mike tried to sleep. Mike, in his room, shut the curtains against the sun. In his mind were his mother's conversations with her parents, up in Mobridge—his father's parents were no longer alive—and with insurance people and friends. No one could believe what had happened. No one could have predicted it. No one knew what to say. To Mike it seemed as unreal as it did too real. It was like, only worse, the time Donetta's period didn't come and she did a home pregnancy test that came out positive. Facts were the scariest things there were. Anything else you could change in your head, somehow, make less bad, but a fact was as definite as an object. It stayed where it was until something else happened—in Donetta's case, a miscarriage she'd had three weeks later. Mike took her to the doctor himself; no one else ever knew, and Donetta had never wanted to talk about it again, even to Mike. He remembered what those three weeks were like. And they were nothing compared with this.

He gave up on sleep. He walked past his mother's closed

door and went downstairs to the den. He sat in the armchair his father had sat in to watch television. His father, who liked mysteries, tried to figure out the endings in advance. "The brother of the priest did it," he'd say to Mike. "I'll bet you fifty dollars."

"I don't want to bet," Mike would say, meaning, I don't give a shit who did it and I don't see why you do. But now it seemed significant, his father caring so much about complicated plots. It revealed something about him. "If you know enough," Mike's history teacher had said once, "everything means something." They'd been talking about wars and how they got started.

It was too hard for Mike to stay in the house. He went into the backyard and sat on the picnic table they hadn't used in years. It was stained with birdshit and littered with twigs. They used to eat out there on summer nights when Mike was small. The worst thing he ever did to his parents was grow up. He didn't know where that thought came from, but he knew it was true. His parents had been happier when they'd had him to take care of.

He went back inside. His mother was still in her room, and he wrote her a note: "Be back for dinner. Don't worry. I rode out to the Schofields'."

LEE-ANN came outside as soon as Mike rode up. What he'd started feeling about her last fall—that he counted on her for something important—now seemed so true that the muscles in his legs were quivering, as though he'd ridden his bicycle all the way there instead of his motorcycle.

"Come inside," she told him. "I just made coffee." Neil's white truck wasn't around; Ed's old Corvette was parked near the barn.

Mike took off his helmet and followed her into the kitchen. She was wearing shorts and a T-shirt Mike had given her when he'd outgrown it: WHEATLEY WRESTLING, it said on the back. She used to tease him for wearing it so much. "You just want girls to know you've got muscles," she used to say. From the living room he could hear *The Little Mermaid* playing on the VCR.

"Janna's almost asleep," Lee-Ann said. "Sit down. I didn't think you'd come today."

"I know. I can't stay long."

She poured him coffee with a lot of milk—the only way he could drink it and like the taste. She sat next to him at the table, and when he crossed his legs, jiggling his foot up and down, she reached over and touched his boot. "Don't be nervous," she said.

"Okay. I mean, I'm not, really."

"We kept thinking about you last night," she told him. "We wondered if you were all right, if you could sleep."

He hated that she'd said *we.* Before, he thought, she would have said *I.* "I slept some," Mike said, more conscious than he wanted to be of the shape of her breasts under the white T-shirt. He wasn't ashamed of looking, but he didn't want to be too obvious about it. He made himself look away, at the squares of light on the clean kitchen floor. "My father was having an affair with her," he said then. "Big surprise, right?"

"I guess we all figured that, after what he did."

"I should have known before that," Mike said. "I should have known something was going on."

"Why?" Lee-Ann asked.

Mike looked at her, feeling his face get hot. "You know," he said. "You can tell when there is. People act different around each other."

She hesitated, then said gently, "You've got too much on your mind. You can't think about everything at once. You have too many things happening to you."

Mike felt foolish then, and looked out the window at Route 8 and the distant hills.

"I'm glad you came, though," Lee-Ann said. "I wanted you to know that you could come over and talk. I mean, we're friends. We can talk about things, right?"

"We are talking," Mike said.

"I mean, really talk. Like about how you feel and what's going on in your life. You're not the most talkative person in the world."

"I'm better at other things," Mike said, and as soon as he said it he knew that he'd struck the wrong note.

"That's because those other things are easier," Lee-Ann told him quietly. In the next room *The Little Mermaid* ended, and she went in to see if Janna was asleep. Mike could hear the videotape rewinding, and the ticking of the grandfather clock in the hallway. When she returned, she poured herself more coffee. "Did I make yours too strong?" she asked Mike. He hadn't drunk any.

"No," he said. "I forgot about it."

He watched her remove her barrette, which caused her soft hair to fall against her face. "So did your mother know about your father's affair?" she asked him.

"Not for very long." He told her part of his mother's story, leaving out the fact that she'd asked Mary Hise to stay in her job a few weeks longer. That had become a secret the moment Mike had heard it.

"Why do you think your mother just didn't leave him?" Lee-Ann asked.

"Because she thought it was over."

"But she knew that it had happened."

"I know," Mike said. "Maybe she just didn't care about him enough for it to matter."

"Maybe it was the opposite. Maybe she loved him so much that she was willing to forgive him. Or maybe she just understood how it could happen. Maybe she understood that it would be natural, almost, for people who were around each other a lot." Lee-Ann averted her eyes from Mike's then, and looked down at her coffee.

"For people who were attracted to each other, you mean," Mike said softly. Lee-Ann didn't look at him. "I don't think my mother would understand about that," he said then. "I don't think she loved him a whole lot, either."

"It's hard to tell about a marriage from the outside," Lee-Ann said.

"How outside could I have been?"

But Lee-Ann was watching out the window now, as Neil and Ed came up the long driveway in Neil's white truck. There was a wooden structure in the back of it. "That's an old lean-to they bought," she said. "From somebody out near Red Shirt."

She stood up then, and Mike did, too, and there was a moment before he opened the door when Lee-Ann was close enough for him to smell her clean hair and the lotion on her skin. Neither of them moved. Finally Mike said, "Thanks for the coffee," and let his arm brush against hers as if by accident. Then he walked out into the bright afternoon, keeping himself from turning around to see her again.

NEIL and Ed stopped talking to each other when Mike walked up.

"I'm sorry, Mike," Ed said. "I found out this morning."

"Did you hear it on the news?"

"A neighbor told me. He heard it on the radio."

"Has anything else happened?" Neil asked.

"No. I mean, he hasn't been caught yet." It was a weird thing for Mike to hear himself say. "I mean, found."

The three of them stood there, looking at the old, musty-smelling lean-to. Mike had often heard Neil and Ed say that they would have been happier a hundred years ago, when the West was a frontier—at least more than it was now. But it was hard for Mike to imagine that the past could have given them more than the present did.

"I can't stay long," Mike said to Neil. "But I thought we could fix that fence."

"Screw the fence," Neil said. "Ed and I can do that."

"I hate sitting around," Mike told him. "I'd rather do something."

NEIL and Mike drove out to the farthest pasture, beyond which were pine-covered hills and the late-afternoon sun shining through the tops of the trees. Neil asked how Mike's mother was.

"Tired," Mike said. He told him part of what he had told Lee-Ann. He also told him about the police asking questions, and about how Tom DeWitt wanted to think like Mike's father.

"Good luck," Neil said.

"I know."

They were riding along the fence line, with the windows down, the road less dusty after last night's rain. "I shouldn't have said that," Neil said. "Your father usually seemed all right. But I saw him not too long ago at the bar in Hermosa, giving the waitress a bad time."

"About what?" Mike asked.

"Not coming over to the table enough times, or not talking to him enough—something like that."

"He gets strange sometimes," Mike said, which was such an understatement, given the circumstances, that he stopped talking and looked out the window.

"But then I didn't know him well," Neil said.

He parked on the roadside, and he and Mike got out with their tools. They worked without speaking—Neil faster, as usual, and Mike feeling sluggish, as if he were moving through water. He felt "thick," as Donetta would say, explaining a sensation she had once in a while, lying in bed, when her limbs felt as thick and heavy as logs. "You know why I think that happens?" she'd said to Mike. "Because in my mind I'm trying to fly away from myself, and my body is telling me I can't go. I'm stuck here. Extra gravity is making sure I stay."

"Did my father ever talk about me?" Mike said. He listened to himself say it, conscious of the past tense, and thinking that his voice sounded as fake as it did on the answering machine at home: "The Newlins can't come to the phone right now. Please leave a message, and we'll call you back."

"No," Neil said. "Not that I remember."

They kept working. Mike, kneeling down clumsily, snagged his sleeve on a rusty wire and tried to free it too quickly. He cut his arm pretty badly—more like a rip than a cut.

"Let me see it," Neil said. Mike rolled up his torn sleeve, and Neil went back to the truck for antiseptic and a bandage. "Get a tetanus shot tomorrow," he told Mike.

"I got one last fall," Mike said. "Dad makes me get them more often than I need." He said it without thinking, and suddenly he was trying to keep from crying. He walked away from Neil, toward the wide field beyond Neil's ranch, where at dusk there were almost always ten white-tailed deer. He tried to get control of himself by watching for them now. He didn't know why he was crying. No one had died except somebody he hardly knew. And what his father had done he'd done to her.

"Mike?" Neil said, behind him, not coming closer. He finished the fence himself and waited until Mike walked back toward him before he put the tools in the truck. "Just so you know," he told Mike, "we can help out easily enough, if money's a problem."

"Okay," Mike said. "Thanks."

The sun was setting by then, and as they drove the few miles back to the house Mike fell asleep for a second, dreaming that his father had set fire to the lean-to with somebody inside it. Neil woke him. "It's all right, Mike," he said. "It was just a bad dream."

AT the house, in the kitchen, with Lee-Ann in the next room with Janna, Mike called his mother. "I'm leaving now," he told her. "I didn't mean to stay this late."

Still, he took as long as he could to leave. He drove the tractor into the pole barn and checked on five baby rabbits, born the week before, under the Schofields' porch. Finally he put on his helmet and started his motorcycle. It was twelve miles to the Wheatley water tower, then half a mile more to Mike's house. He'd been riding his motorcycle for two years, but tonight was the first time he'd minded the things he'd heard older riders complain of: bugs, wind shears, cars that followed too closely.

By the time he got home, he was like somebody thirty-five or forty, he thought, who couldn't feel the satisfaction of speed anymore, who just rode a motorcycle to get someplace he didn't want to go.

FIVE

At nine o'clock on Saturday morning Mike drove to his father's office to unlock the door for an insurance agent named Stuart Wells, from Rapid City. Mike didn't know anything about his father's business, except that it wasn't very profitable.

The office was on Collier Street and shared a building and parking lot with Anderson Chiropractic Arts. Mike arrived before the insurance agent did and sat in his mother's Buick to wait; his father's car had been impounded by the police. Mike watched people walk into the laundromat across the street.

It was a sunny, warm morning, gusts of wind whipping up dirt from a construction site half a block away, where a new police station was being built to replace the deteriorating building behind the public library. Fewer than four thousand people lived in Wheatley. Mike had lived there all his life. He recognized two of the people driving past, both slowing down when they saw his mother's car, then him. Neither stopped, but both of them—classmates from high school—honked and waved. Mike hadn't ridden his motorcycle because he would have felt that much more conspicuous. He was still conspicuous, but it was better than going inside. He turned the ignition key and listened to the only cassette his mother had that wasn't classical—Keith Whitley. Mike had given it her.

Stuart Wells drove up in a new Chevy. "I thought your mother was supposed to be here," he said when Mike got out of the car. He was a heavy man, younger than Mike's father, with slicked-back, wet-looking hair.

"She didn't feel well," Mike told him. "She asked me to do it." He unlocked the door but didn't go in himself. The insurance agency was a wide room partitioned into two sections—a larger space on the left, for Mike's father, and a smaller space on the right for the receptionist. The spaces were open in front, then separated farther back by a thin, laminated wall. Through the window Mike watched Stuart Wells go straight to his father's computer.

Less than a minute later Tom DeWitt showed up. He had on jeans and cowboy boots—dressed as if he could have been anyone, Mike thought. "I'm glad you're here," he said to Mike. "I wanted to look around a little."

"I thought you came yesterday."

"I wanted to see it again." He put his hand on Mike's

back at the same time that he opened the door to walk inside, so that Mike had no choice but to go in with him. He introduced himself to Stuart Wells. "You're getting his accounts?" he asked.

"The few he had."

"It's a shame it's not quality that matters in business," Tom DeWitt said lightly, and moved into the other part of the office, where Mike was standing.

"My father wanted to be an engineer," Mike said. "It was only when that didn't work out that he settled for insurance."

"Is that right?"

"Yes, sir."

Mike watched him turn on Mary Hise's computer, look through the papers on her desk, and empty out a white plastic container, shaped like a lamb, that held pens and pencils. "Call me Tom," he said to Mike. "I don't like *sir.*"

"It's what I was brought up to say."

"Did your father make you call him sir?"

"No," Mike said. "He didn't make me do anything."

Tom sat in Mary Hise's chair—a cushioned brown office chair that swiveled and could be adjusted up or down. He looked through her desk drawers and filing cabinets. In the back of one drawer, under office stationery, he found the photograph of Mary and her dog that she had shown Mike that day in December. "She had a dog?" Tom said. He stood up, holding the photograph. "Where is it, then?"

"I don't know," Mike said.

"But it was hers."

"I guess."

Tom took the photograph and went outside, motioning for Mike to walk out with him. They stood between their cars. "Do you know anything at all about Mary Hise?" he said.

"Not really."

"Her parents are on a camping trip in Canada. We can't get in touch with them. We've reached a brother in Sioux Falls, who hasn't seen his sister in two years. He wants us to keep the body here until his parents get back." Tom put on his sunglasses. "Does that seem cold to you?"

"I don't know," Mike said. "I hardly knew her."

"Would you like to see where she lived?"

"No," Mike said. "Why would I?" Then he realized how unfeeling that sounded. "Why do you want me to?"

"I thought you might be curious. I'm going there now, anyway." He opened the passenger door of his car. "Get in. I'll give you a ride back here afterward." Mike hesitated, and Tom said, "You don't have to come if it makes you uneasy."

"It doesn't make me uneasy."

"Good," Tom said. "Get in."

They drove past the construction site and the elementary school, and past Saint Ann's, the small Episcopal church Mike's mother attended weekly and Mike attended on Christmas and Easter. His father used to belong to the Lutheran church his parents had attended—they were buried in the cemetery beside it—but Mike couldn't remember his father ever having gone to a service. "I don't believe there's a God," he'd told Mike recently, one Sunday morning. "Not many people are brave enough to say that."

Behind the trailer park on Montana Street, Tom DeWitt parked in front of an older two-story building divided into apartments. Mary Hise's was on the first floor, second from the end. There was a cement walkway that ran the length of the building.

"You shouldn't be here," he told Mike, unlocking the door. "So don't mention it to anyone."

"I can wait outside."

"No. Go ahead and look around." He took off his sunglasses and turned on the kitchen light. "Just walk through the rooms," he said. He stayed behind, in the kitchen.

It was eerie for Mike to be there. He looked at the walls, which were in need of paint, and the green carpeting covering the uneven floors. She hadn't had much furniture, just the basic things, like a couch and coffee table, a television but not a VCR. Mike walked into each room, knowing that what Tom DeWitt wanted was for him to feel worse than he did about Mary Hise's death. And he did think he should feel sorrier. But no one had forced Mary Hise to be with his father.

He stood longest in her bedroom, looking at the radio and lamp on her nightstand and at the yellow curtains on the small window. On top of her bureau he read what was on a slip of paper: "milk," "tomato soup," and "frozen peas." Next to it was a framed picture of herself—her high school graduation picture, Mike guessed, because she looked younger, her smile hesitant or uncertain.

On her double bed was a thick, yellow-flowered comforter. Mike wondered how many times his father had been in that bed with her. It was even more disturbing for him to imagine her in it alone, because he could still envision how she'd looked in a bathing suit. Behind the door—Mike almost didn't see it—was a laundry hamper with pink underwear thrown on top.

In her bathroom he looked at her toothbrush and toothpaste, her comb and brush, and something Mike knew his father had given her: a little porcelain hummingbird on a green base. It used to be in the upstairs bathroom of Mike's house, until his mother had said, "Let's get rid of that thing." She'd forgotten that it had belonged to Mike's grandmother—Glenn's mother—and Mike's father hadn't reminded her.

Mike went back into the kitchen, where Tom DeWitt pointed out to him a bowl of water on the floor. "It was under the edge of the dishwasher," he told Mike. "We missed it somehow."

He had opened all the cabinets; in the back of the second one were three cans of dog food. "How does your father feel about dogs?" he asked Mike, before picking up the phone and dialing. Mike didn't answer. He was looking at the magnets on her refrigerator door, each one a miniature kitchen gadget. Under the teakettle was a reminder of a dental appointment on June 22, two days from then. Mike was thinking that Mary Hise had been only six years older than he was, and that she'd talked to him that day in December as if she might be lonely.

Behind him, on the phone, he heard Tom DeWitt say, "This is our fuck-up. We should have known Thursday."

TOM drove back to the insurance agency by way of the root-beer stand on Laramie Street. "Do you mind?" he asked Mike. "I'm thirsty." He got a root beer for each of them, and they drank them in the car. Across the street was the post office, a square stone building designed a long time ago by somebody famous, whose name Mike couldn't remember. Mike watched as somebody from out of town—Oregon, her license plate read—snapped a picture of it.

Tom turned toward Mike. "Do you know how Mary ended up in Wheatley?" he asked. "She moved here a year and a half ago, to be close to a boyfriend working on that dude ranch south of town. We learned that from a neighbor."

Mike didn't say anything. He didn't want to seem interested.

"According to the neighbor, the boyfriend moved away last October, then came back for a visit. We're trying to find him. Do you know anything about him?"

"No."

Tom looked at Mike in a friendly way. "Did you open Mary's closets or drawers?"

"Of course not."

"Well, you should have, because they're interesting. My sister's a buyer for a department store in Rapid City. I brought her over here last night to look at Mary's clothes. I said, 'Tell me what kind of person she was.' " He put his empty glass down on the seat. "I don't know anything about women's clothes. And neither do the female agents I know. Not like my sister does. It's a specialty, like anything else. To be a good detective, you have to be smart enough to know who the experts are." He smiled at Mike. "That's my ego talking. So now you know I think I'm smart."

"Why do you care about her clothes?"

"I don't, exactly. But you can never predict what things will be important and what things won't."

He took Mike's empty glass from him, picked up his own, and returned them to the person behind the counter. He had an easy walk that Mike didn't trust. He'd seen wrestlers who walked that way, who could move as if they were less muscular than they were. They were so flexible that their strength was disguised, and they fooled you into thinking they couldn't take control.

Tom got back in and put on his seat belt. "What was I saying?" he asked Mike.

"You were talking about your sister."

He pulled back onto Laramie. "She looked through the

closet and dresser and said that Mary probably hadn't bought much since high school. My sister dated the clothes. Just like a coroner figuring out when somebody died."

He drove past Wheatley Western Wear and the Rush School of Beauty, which Donetta's mother owned, and stopped at the red light on the corner of Pearson Street. "My sister said that Mary bought childish-looking clothes," he told Mike. "Things that hid her body, especially her breasts. Mary wanted to look younger, and maybe more carefree than she was. She didn't want to be held responsible. And something major must have happened to her in high school, my sister said, to make her quit shopping. I laughed when she said that, but she was serious. For girls, my sister told me, not shopping anymore is like not sleeping, or not eating. It's a sign of disturbance."

They were back at the insurance agency. Tom pulled in next to Mike's mother's Buick. "What do you think?" he asked Mike, as if they'd been exchanging opinions all along, as if he hadn't done all the talking.

"I don't see why Mary Hise matters so much. It's not her you're trying to find."

"Do you think it's random," Tom DeWitt said, "who people end up with? Don't you think you can define people by who they choose? For example, what kind of wife do you think I'd have?"

"Mary Hise wasn't married to him."

"Sometimes wives and lovers are the same people, and sometimes they're not."

Mike looked at his mother's dark red car. "If a person has a wife and a girlfriend," he said carefully, "which one do you define the person by?"

"Which do you think?"

"I have no idea."

"Well, you get a third defining thing," Tom said, "which is the fact of the girlfriend—the fact that he'd have one."

"So I guess you think that automatically makes somebody a bad person," Mike said. "Like you and people like you are in a special category. You're always faithful, and you're never for one minute attracted to somebody else."

"I don't know," Tom said. "I've never been married."

"But I'm supposed to guess what your wife is like?" Mike opened the car door angrily. "You try to trick people you think aren't as smart as you. You think you know people when you don't know shit about them." He banged his knee on the dashboard as he got out, and shut the door as hard as he could. He was so unnerved that he tried to open his mother's car with the wrong key.

Finally, leaving the parking lot and driving home, he said to the empty car, "Her dog's name is Harrison. And my father would sooner shoot a person than a dog."

He didn't see the humor of it until after he'd said it, and then he understood for the first time something his English teacher had once said, quoting some dead writer: "Humor is almost never about happiness."

SIX

THE fact that Mike knew these small things became more important to him than the things themselves. They wouldn't have given Tom DeWitt much more information than he had figured out on his own. But they made Mike feel more in control. He found himself repeating them in his mind, along with something else that only he and his mother knew: that when Mike was in the fourth grade, and their dog, Lucky, had been killed by a car, Mike's father had been so grief-stricken that he'd walked around the house half the night and had never allowed them to get another pet. His father's reaction had seemed extreme even to Mike, who had loved the dog as much as anyone did. Even more extreme was that a month later, when Mike's parents had driven Mike to summer camp, his father had seemed unable to leave him there. Mike remembered standing in a clearing with his duffel bag, watching his mother help his weeping father into the passenger seat, so that she could drive him home.

Mike didn't tell anyone about going to Mary Hise's apartment. He would have felt like a traitor, not to his father but to his mother. What made him angry was knowing that Tom DeWitt probably counted on that; he and Mike had a secret now. And it was hard for Mike to stop thinking about that apartment, especially about Mary Hise's pink underwear on top of the hamper. It wasn't a perverted thing that he felt, though. It was just too private, and he pictured her in it even though he didn't want to.

HE spent that Saturday afternoon and the rest of the weekend mowing the yard, trimming hedges, and cleaning out the gutters. He didn't know what else to do. He would have worked at the ranch, but his mother had said that they should both stay home. She said that on Monday they would go back to work and try to get back into a regular routine.

They had their meals in the kitchen instead of the dining room; the dining room table was covered with documents his mother was going through—bank statements, insurance policies, and the mortgage information on the house. "We have to act as if he's never coming back," she told Mike. Sometimes she got emotional, but other times she got angry. She snapped at him about tracking grass clippings into the kitchen; she insisted that he come in and eat the second she wanted him to.

On Sunday morning Mike was relieved to see Noleen Watkins come over to have breakfast with them and to attend church with his mother. As they were eating, Noleen listed all the people who had asked about Carolyn and Mike. "Everyone's sympathetic," she said. "People are concerned about you two." Mike's mother had been afraid that she might have trouble at work, but her principal and vice principal had called, asking what they could do to help. Only a few people had called in order to fish for details.

And the phone was tapped. The Division of Criminal Investigation had gotten permission to do it, although even Tom DeWitt had told them to stop thinking that the next call might be from Glenn. Mike didn't think his father would call, anyway. He'd let more time pass, if he called at all. "How could he face talking to us?" Mike's mother said now, to Noleen. But Mike thought of it differently. He thought that his father might be not ready yet to tell them what really happened, why he did what he did. There might be some reason that he couldn't explain yet.

Mike waited for his mother and Noleen to leave for church before calling Josh Mitchell, in Sheridan, Wyoming. He'd been waiting to be alone to do it. Mike and Josh had been best friends almost all of their lives, and Mike hadn't seen him since February, when Josh had moved away. When school was in session they'd E-mailed each other—whatever they could get away with in case their teachers were reading the mail. Josh would quote from a book he'd made up, called *Sexual Guide for Teenagers in the Twenty-first Century.* He'd quote things like, "Girls: Keep in mind that oral sex is a healthy alternative to intercourse."

"I heard about your dad on the news," Josh said now, when Mike called. "I didn't know what the fuck to do. My dad said, 'Let him call you first, when he's ready.' But, then, my dad's a prick."

Mike couldn't let himself laugh.

"Your mom must be freaking out," Josh said. He cleared his throat. He was doing something in the background—making coffee, Mike guessed. Josh had started drinking coffee when he was twelve. "I like the buzz," he used to tell Mike.

"She's at church right now," Mike said. "Ms. Watkins went with her."

"Is Watkins still fucking Coach?" Josh asked. "Wait," he said then. "I'm being an asshole." He was quiet for a moment. Then he spoke in a more serious voice. "It seems crazy. How could he do that? That's what I said when I heard it on the news. My dad said, 'People can do anything.' "

"I know some stuff," Mike said awkwardly. "He was, you know, seeing her." He didn't feel like saying "fucking," or even "sleeping with."

"I figured that," Josh said. He was quiet again. Mike

knew that Josh's mother had had an affair; that was why his parents had split up. Josh had told Mike later who it was—Duane King, who owned King Trucking Company. She was still with him.

"Anyway," Mike said, "we're being listened to. The police are tapping the phone in case he calls."

"Which he won't."

"I don't think so, either."

"Well, shit," Josh said. "Now I feel like saying more about Watkins and Coach."

Mike laughed. It felt good, but unfamiliar, to do it.

AT four o'clock that afternoon, as Mike was wishing he could find an excuse to see Lee-Ann Schofield, or to call her at least, Tom DeWitt came over again. He said that the district attorney would try to go before a grand jury to get an indictment. "You can bypass a preliminary hearing if there's enough evidence," he said.

Mike didn't really know what that meant. The three of them stood in the stuffy living room, his mother not responding either. Earlier, when she'd come home from church, she'd just sat on her bed for almost an hour. Mike had gone upstairs twice and walked past her open door; he'd been afraid to ask if she was all right for fear that she wasn't. Finally, he'd just stood in the hallway between her room and his. He'd told himself that he really wasn't all that frightened. But when she came out of her room he found that his back hurt from standing so rigidly.

Now, in their living room, Tom DeWitt said, "There's the gun with Glenn's fingerprints on it. In addition, the clerk at the motel identified him from a photograph. There are the money transfers, his fingerprints on the phone, and so on." He sat down on the couch without being invited to. "I wouldn't typically tell the suspect's family any of this."

"We want to know," Carolyn said. "Glenn should have to pay for what he did." She turned to Mike for confirmation, but he kept his eye on the window behind her.

"Not all families would feel that way," Tom said.

No one spoke. After a moment Carolyn politely asked, "Would you like coffee?"

"I would," he said. "Thanks." After she left the room he unbuttoned and rolled up his shirtsleeves. The day had been dry and hot; the temperature had reached a hundred. The windows were open, but there was almost no breeze. "Your mom's a nice person," Tom told Mike.

"What do you think is nice about her?"

"She has dignity."

Mike looked out the window at Mr. Hyler, across the street, watering the geraniums on his front porch. "She always does what she's supposed to," he said. "That's not hard to do."

"Some people find it impossible." On Tom's face was

that pleasant expression Mike didn't trust. He seemed relaxed, as if their house had become a familiar place to him.

Mike waited impatiently for his mother to come back in. She shouldn't have left him alone with Tom DeWitt. How did she think he'd feel, sitting there? He concentrated on Lee-Ann and how her breasts had felt against him that Saturday afternoon in the barn, when he'd held her, finally. He needed more moments like that with her. They gave him a way to feel sexual that nobody else knew about. They made the life inside his head count for more than the life outside it.

When his mother did come in, bringing coffee, she and Tom DeWitt talked about ordinary things—about Tom's brother, who taught at the elementary school, and about Tom's nephew, Kyle, who'd wrestled with Mike. In the fall Kyle was going to attend Black Hills State University, in Spearfish. "It's the only place he got accepted," Tom said.

"Maybe he just applied too late," Mike said.

"No. He didn't get the grades you did."

"How do you know what grades I got?"

"Mike," his mother said warningly.

"Kyle told me. He was envious of you, I think."

"Not anymore, probably."

Mike ignored the look his mother gave him and went upstairs to his room. He couldn't stand that his mother and Tom DeWitt were talking as if they'd become friends. Mike's mother was liable to say anything. Like what, he thought then. What did she know? Whose side was she on? That was stupid, he knew. Taking sides was what you did in junior high school, when your friends got pissed-off at each other and you had to make a choice.

He sat at his desk, then stood restlessly in front of the window. After he saw Tom leave, he went downstairs and outside, changed the oil in his motorcycle, and rode around the block. He thought about riding out to the Schofields', then realized that he'd forgotten his helmet. That was something his mother got furious with him about. His father did too, but his father had been unpredictable—like if Mike had driven the car and left it only a quarter full of gas, sometimes his father had gotten mad and sometimes he hadn't. Sometimes he'd even laughed—as if, since he was in a good mood, what difference did it make what Mike did? But it worked the other way, too. There'd never been a way to change his father's mood from bad to good.

Mike, depressed now, put his motorcycle in the carport. He sat in the backyard and looked at the oak tree in the Pates' yard, next door. He remembered the times he'd climbed it—falling, once, fifteen feet, and how even though he'd been all right his father had taken him to the emergency room and woken him up several times that night, to make sure that he wasn't unconscious. It was painful for Mike to think about that. It was easier to think of his father as a bad or fucked-up person.

His mother came to the kitchen door. "Why didn't you wear your helmet?" she asked.

"I forgot it. So I came back."

Reluctantly, he sat with her in the kitchen while she cooked, and they ate without mentioning his father or Tom DeWitt. His mother didn't eat much, not that she'd ever eaten all that much. She was thin by nature, but also she didn't overdo anything. She didn't drink, she never went over the speed limit, and she didn't spend too much money. It seemed to Mike that she turned not overdoing things into a fault.

What she talked about now was that financially they'd be all right. The money they'd saved for his college tuition was safe; his father hadn't touched that. At some point Mike might have to work part-time, but didn't a lot of students work these days? She talked as if his father and whatever happened to him was irrelevant.

Outside, a sparrow perched on the clothesline and a squirrel ran past the shed. The light was gentler, almost golden, and across the grass were long evening shadows.

"What do you think will happen?" Mike said, and felt odd, asking that. He wasn't used to talking to his mother as if they were allies—on the same side of things.

"I don't know. I can't even guess. I didn't know him, apparently."

She carried their plates to the sink. Mike usually washed the dinner dishes—the house had been built before dishwashers were installed, and they'd never bought one—but his mother was already doing them. The kitchen was large and square, with yellow linoleum and white curtains. It was homey, his mother always said. Her parents—Mike's grandparents, who lived upstate in Mobridge—had a house that wasn't homey. It was as upright as they were. They had wanted to come to Wheatley when Mike's mother had told them what happened, but his mother had said no, thank you for offering. To Mike she had said, "As if I could stand for them to see me like this." She was an only child, just as he was.

Mike wiped off the table and told his mother that he didn't want dessert; maybe he'd have pie at Andell's Diner. He was going there to meet Donetta. He would have gone even if his mother had asked him not to. But Noleen Watkins and another teacher were coming over, to keep his mother company, and he left her standing in the kitchen, making sure that he remembered his helmet.

IN the fading light, Mike rode his motorcycle through town and out on the highway to the diner that had been there since before he was born. He sat alone at a back booth, waiting for Donetta to finish her shift. He drank a Coke and ate a piece of cherry pie. It was painful for him to sit there, even though the diner was half empty and he didn't recognize anyone. In fact he thought it might be easier if he did know people; then they'd at least have to keep quiet or treat him the way Mr. Andell had when Mike first walked in—as if Mike had knives stuck in him and Mr. Andell were afraid to mention them or pull them out. As it was, though, Mike overheard a man say, "What I don't understand is why, if he was trying to kill her, the son of a bitch called an ambulance."

Donetta's shift was over at eight. Mike left his motorcycle in the parking lot, and they took her Geo out to Crow Lake, the violet sky in front of them darkening. Mike drove, and once they were on the two-lane county road she changed clothes, taking off her dirty uniform and her underwear, and putting on a pair of cutoff jeans and a tank top.

Mike was almost used to seeing Donetta naked. She was the second girl he had slept with—when he was in the tenth grade and she was in the ninth. Over the past three years they'd broken up twice, seen other people, and come back together. They became a more permanent couple after Donetta's father died, when she was fifteen and a half. Her parents had gotten divorced six years earlier; her father, the manager of a hardware store, had lived in Hot Springs with a woman who was an alcoholic.

"He took care of her," Donetta had explained to Mike. Her father had died suddenly, of a heart attack, and Donetta had said that his heart had always been a problem; he'd always had too many emotions.

Crow Lake was six miles southwest of Wheatley, a large manmade lake on land that once had been a family-owned ranch; now it was owned by the government. There were cottonwood trees along the western edge and an outcropping of limestone on the southern side. To the north and east were fields of prairie grass long enough to disappear in.

Mike parked the Geo under the trees, and he and Donetta spread a blanket next to the water. They were the only people there, on that side; across the lake some teenagers were swimming. They could just barely see them. High school kids often swam there. Every once in a while, maybe once every three or four years, somebody drank too much and drowned.

"I had a sex dream about us last night," Donetta said. "I woke up thinking, you don't know where your father is, or if you'll ever see him again, and all that's on my mind is fucking you."

She lay back on the blanket and pulled up her tank top so that Mike could see her smooth, tan stomach—her mother's beauty school had a tanning booth. "Tell me if I'm getting fat," she said. "I eat french fries at work, and sometimes coconut cream pie."

"You're nowhere near fat," Mike told her.

"Well, I've been running farther," Donetta said. "I wanted to surprise you when I got up to six miles, and it happened this morning. I ran out of town all the way to Lame Johnny Creek, to that tree that leans down over the water."

"You shouldn't run alone that far out of Wheatley," Mike said. "Most people who use that road don't even live around here."

Donetta opened her mouth to speak, then didn't. She put her hand on Mike's hair. "You know what I almost said? That strangers are probably not more dangerous than people you know. I feel like I can't say anything anymore without having it mean too many things."

They lay close to each other and watched the stars appear, with the Milky Way just above them, and no moon. They heard the teenagers drive away.

"I don't care about your father, or what he did," Donetta whispered. "I really don't. I just care about us." She sat up halfway, leaned over Mike, and unbuttoned his shirt. Her long hair was loose, and the ends of it brushed across his neck and chest. She undid his belt and unzipped his jeans. "What do you think?" she said softly. "Don't you think this will feel good?"

He closed his eyes and put his hands on her hair, then under her tank top and under the waistband of her shorts. She didn't wear underwear any more than she had to; she'd said that once to Mike's mother. It was true that she liked to shock people, but at the same time she was honest and almost naïve. For example, she couldn't believe that his mother had later said to him, "A girl like that has no intention of being faithful to anyone."

"What does that have to do with underwear?" Donetta had said. And she was right, because she was completely and sometimes ridiculously loyal. She'd once gone around for months with frizzy, orange hair—and not the stylish kind—because her sister, Margo, had colored and permed it.

She was ten times more faithful than Mike was. Now, for

example, with his hands on her hair and skin, he was thinking about Lee-Ann Schofield. And before he'd become so attracted to Lee-Ann, he'd thought of a dark-haired girl who sat in front of him in eleventh-grade homeroom. It was almost second nature to him, to be thinking of another girl when he was with Donetta, and to sometimes think of Donetta when he was with someone else. He did it so automatically that he didn't question or judge it, but he knew that it influenced what he thought about himself.

"I'm good at being analytical and objective," he wrote in his college application essay. "I think that, more than most people, I'm capable of standing outside a situation. One thing I could improve on, though, is knowing when it might help to do the opposite, and take more part in things."

"What did you mean by that?" his mother had asked him when she proofread it. "I don't know," he'd said. "It was just what I was thinking."

"Did you bring condoms?" Donetta whispered to him. She was sitting up now, taking off her shorts and tank top. It was too dark to see anything except the stars reflected on the water and, up close, Donetta's tan skin, pale in the darkness.

He had sex with her. She called it either fucking or making love, depending on the mood she was in; to him it was a more generic thing. But tonight Mary Hise—the way she would have looked naked—came into his mind for just a second and scared Mike so much that he not only concentrated on Donetta, he even said, "I love you" when he had an orgasm. He didn't usually say that to her unless she said it to him first, and that was what made her cry.

"I love you, too," she said. "But you know I do. It's not like I keep it a secret."

She turned away from him and put on her clothes. He dressed, too, and they got in her car and sat with the windows down, listening to the frogs.

"Don't think you shouldn't use that word again," Donetta said. "My father used to tell me, 'Tears are just salt water.' "

She moved close to Mike, and he kept one arm around her as they drove back to Andell's Diner, where Mike got his motorcycle and followed Donetta to her house. Mrs. Rush had a rule: If Donetta was out with a boy, she needed to be brought home by that boy. "That's civilized behavior," Mrs. Rush had told Mike a long time ago. "The boy comes in and says a proper good night and thank you. That's how I should have been raised."

The lights were on at Donetta's house. She lived half a mile east of Wheatley on Flat Rock Road, at the edge of a small crop of new houses. Her house had been the first one built out there. It was a one-story aluminum-sided home with an attached garage. It looked more expensive than it was. Inside, the walls were not nearly as thick as they were in Mike's house. But there were nice, modern things about it, like a built-in microwave and a bathtub you could turn into a Jacuzzi.

Donetta lived there with her mother, her twenty-eight-year-old sister, Margo, and Margo's sometimes husband, Cory Burris—sometimes because he came and went as he pleased, driving up to Montana on the spur of the moment, or riding his Harley into Sturgis in August, for the Black Hills Biker Rally, and not coming back until September. He worked occasionally as a trucker; mainly it was Margo who supported them, working with her mother at the beauty school in Wheatley and helping her open a second one in Rapid City.

Cory Burris was a weight lifter; he was big and tough-looking but quiet-spoken. He drove Mrs. Rush crazy. Donetta's favorite story was the night her mother had drunk too much and gone after Cory with the B–C volume of the encyclopedia. "Just don't make me read it," Cory had said. Lately, Mrs. Rush, Cory, and Margo had been seeing a Christian therapist in Rapid City.

Tonight they were all in the kitchen, waiting for a pan of brownies to be done. They were sitting at the blue Formica table at the far end of the room, under the dormer window. This was the first time Mike had been over since his father's crime, and he stood self-consciously in the doorway. They were all looking at him.

"Mike!" Mrs. Rush said. "Come and sit down. Get him a chair, Cory."

"I can't stay," Mike told her. "I just wanted to bring Donetta home."

"Just stay for a brownie," Margo said. "We've got five minutes left on the timer."

Cory was bringing in a chair from the dining room, and Mike took it from him and sat down. Donetta sat beside him. Donetta didn't look like her mother or her sister—they were both bigger-boned and bigger-hipped, with dark hair and eyes. Donetta took after her father, who had been slight, with light-brown hair and blue eyes. Mike had seen pictures of him. Donetta's father had had the same interested expression Donetta often had—as if he'd had more questions about life, or himself, than most people had.

"How's your bike running?" Cory asked Mike.

"Okay. A little rough, still."

"I'll take a look at her next time you come over."

"Is your mother all right?" Mrs. Rush said. "I wasn't sure if I should call or not. I knew her teacher friends would be calling."

"She's okay," Mike said. "I'll tell her you asked about her."

Mrs. Rush was wearing a long pink housecoat that zipped up the front. She had unpinned her hair, which was shoulder-length and wavy; now, down around her face, it made her look older but more attractive, Mike thought—like a reminder that even women older than his mother still had sex, though as far as Mike knew, Mrs. Rush wasn't having any these days. "Will you tell me if there's anything

I can do?" she asked Mike. "That way I can help without bothering her."

"Yes, ma'am," Mike said.

The timer went off, and Margo rose to get the brownies out of the oven. She had on a short, silky robe that brushed Mike's arm as she walked past.

"Mrs. Newlin is teaching at the community college this summer," Donetta told her mother.

"I admire someone that educated," Mrs. Rush said to Mike. "A lot of people take that for granted, but I don't."

"High school was enough for me," Cory said.

"Is that why you couldn't be bothered to finish?" Mrs. Rush asked.

"That's a past-history question," Margo told her mother. "Pastor Kelly said we can only talk about things that happen now."

"It would help if certain people were actually doing something now," Mrs. Rush said.

There was a moment of silence. Cory looked at Mike, then up at the ceiling, and Donetta's cat, Sophie, appeared from the hallway and jumped up on Margo's lap.

"Maybe Cory and I can't live here under these circumstances," Margo said. "Maybe we can't even stay here in the same town."

"All I did was ask a question," Mrs. Rush said. "Don't make a federal case out of it."

Donetta took Mike's hand. "Do you want a brownie?" she asked him gently.

Mrs. Rush looked at him. "My goodness," she said. "Take all you want. Wrap them up and take them with you. They'll only make us fatter."

"No, thanks," Mike said. "But I should get going."

He carried his chair back to the dining room, said good night, and walked outside with Donetta. They stood in the driveway and looked at the sprinkling of lights in the houses behind them. "Mom doesn't think about what she says," Donetta told him. "That 'federal case' thing was just an accident."

"I know."

Donetta put her arms around Mike. "You're the only good part of my life," she whispered. "You're the only happy thing I have."

He held her. Across Flat Rock Road was a field that in the darkness looked like water, except that it didn't reflect the stars.

"Me, too," Mike said. He put on his helmet, got on his motorcycle, and rode down the driveway toward Wheatley, and home.

SEVEN

MIKE and his mother went back to work on Monday, though nothing about their lives felt the same. To Mike it was as if they'd woken up in a different house, in another town—almost as if they'd woken up as different people. They were both moodier now, and when Mike heard his mother crying late Monday night, in her room, he didn't know what to do. He felt too awkward and unsettled by it to go in and talk to her; instead, he turned on the radio and listened through his headphones to the all-night rock-and-roll station from Rapid City. He listened to the disc jockey announce who was sending what love song out to whom.

Mike didn't eat breakfast with the Schofields anymore—he felt too guilty now that his mother was alone. She got up early and made him scrambled eggs or waffles, neither of which she would eat. She'd have only cereal or toast, then come outside with her coffee as he got his motorcycle out of the carport.

"Make sure you drink enough water on these hot days," she'd tell him; she didn't seem to want him to leave. She wasn't anxious to go to work herself. "People at the college are being kind," she told Mike one night at supper. "But that just makes me more uncomfortable."

Mike knew what she meant. Neil went out of his way to be nice to him. He paid Mike more per hour than he had been, and when Mike objected Neil said, "We can afford it. And we were underpaying you before." That second part wasn't true.

Ed gave Mike a present for his mother, a large yellow bowl he'd made, which Mike knew would sell for something like sixty or seventy dollars.

The hardest thing for Mike—the change in his life that felt the worst—was that Lee-Ann was never sexy with him anymore. She was friendly and kind, the way that Neil was, and she avoided being alone with him. The only time he saw even a hint of who she used to be with him was one morning when he was working outside the barn without his shirt on. She walked past, holding Janna, and when he caught her watching him she seemed embarrassed to have been caught.

The only people at the ranch who treated him normally were Janna, of course, and Arthur Strong and Louis Ivy. Mike wasn't sure if they knew about his father—although it seemed unlikely that they didn't. "I'm not sure they know your last name," Neil had said to Mike. But Neil underestimated people, the same way he underestimated the importance of money to people who didn't have much. Lately Mike had noticed more negative things about Neil than he had before. He found himself thinking words like "spoiled" and "egotistical"—words Mike's father had used that Mike had objected to. Then he felt guilty. Neil had always been a friend to him, whereas what kind of friend was Mike when it came to the way he felt about Lee-Ann? He'd hate himself for a moment, after which he'd think, I'm only eighteen. She doesn't take me seriously. And we really haven't done anything.

All the time, though, every day since June 18, these thoughts and others were dwarfed by fears about his father: where he might be and what might happen to him. One evening, riding home from the Schofields', he almost ran into a pickup that braked in front of him. His reactions weren't quick anymore. He wasn't focused on what was happening. He was always preoccupied.

ON Friday a rainstorm blew up, and Mike came home from the Schofields' early. He sat in his room, looking through his college brochures at pictures of the campus and of the dorm where he would be living. He had a letter saying who his roommate would be and what his interests were: Raymond Nelson, an honors student from Aberdeen. A computer nerd, he sounded like to Mike. But college seemed too far in the future, and unrealistically carefree. College was where people went before their real lives began, Mike thought; his own life had gotten an early start on real.

From downstairs now, he could hear NPR on the radio, and he went down to the kitchen and cut up potatoes as his mother made pork chops. In her dark skirt and blouse, her short hair combed back from her face, she looked to him like a spinsterish school teacher.

"Slice them thinner," she told Mike, and then, "Would you set the table, please?" It was a relief when the phone rang, until Mike, listening to his mother talk, knew that it was Tom DeWitt. He was calling with the first news about Mike's father: Mary Hise's car, an older-model Chevy Cavalier, had been found in the parking lot of an all-night supermarket in Salt Lake City. Tom DeWitt asked if he could stop over after supper, to talk in person.

THEY had just finished eating when Tom came, too early, and to the kitchen door instead of the front door—as if he wanted to be thought of as a friend, Mike thought, somebody who thought about their interests instead of his own. He stood in the kitchen in a wet windbreaker, saying, "I wonder why Glenn chose Salt Lake City. Why not Denver or Omaha?" He spoke as if he were talking to himself, Mike saw; he was watching for their reactions while pretending not to.

"Isn't that where Dad's friend lives?" Mike said to his

mother. "Didn't Dad say he'd hide Dad if he ever killed anybody?"

His mother stared at him.

"I guess that means you don't know," Tom said.

"Nothing about this is funny," Carolyn said to Mike, and he noticed how quickly she moved their plates out of the way and how politely she asked Tom to sit down. Tom was removing his windbreaker already and putting it over the back of the chair. Under it he had on workout clothes—nylon pants and a stretched-out T-shirt too small for him. He was a gym rat, Mike realized, which was Josh's name for guys they saw in gyms who seemed either shy or dangerous, not usually anything in between.

"We don't know anyone in Salt Lake City," Carolyn told Tom. "We have some friends here, of course. But we're not very social people." She stood at the screen door and looked outside. The sky was gray with rain. "What else have you learned?" she asked. "What was found inside the car?"

"A dress in a dry cleaner's bag" was all Tom DeWitt listed. There must have been more in the car than that, Mike thought. "A short dress," Tom told them. "Denim, I think it was. I can't figure out why Glenn didn't get rid of it. I don't suppose it has any significance for either of you."

"No," Carolyn said.

Mike shook his head, although he was almost sure that that day in December, when they'd talked, Mary Hise had been wearing that dress. He remembered because of the way she'd buttoned and unbuttoned the top two buttons as he was standing there—it was sexy, the way she hadn't seemed to know she was doing it. But he wasn't about to say that he remembered it. That would make him guilty of paying Mary Hise too much attention.

"Why should we know anything about her dress?" Carolyn asked.

"No reason. I just thought I'd ask." Tom crossed his legs and turned to Mike. "Girls and their dresses," he said. "It's a mystery to us, isn't it? Why they put on one and not another."

I thought she wasn't wearing any, Mike almost said.

It was thundering outside, and rain was pouring out of the gutters and pounding the concrete patio outside the screen door. Mike's mother was sitting up very straight, very stiffly. "Mary Hise's parents must know by now," she said. "Do you know when the funeral was?" she asked Tom.

"Three days ago."

"I didn't have the courage to ask. I don't suppose there's anything I could do, by way of apology."

"Apology for what?" Tom said. "What did you do?"

She hesitated. "You know what I did," she said. "I told Mary not to quit yet. I told her to give Glenn some time to get used to . . ." She didn't finish. She got up, filled the sink with soapy water, and stood at the counter with her back to them. She didn't seem able to speak.

Mike stood up quickly and said, "I'll do the dishes, Mom. Go in the other room if you want. I'll make coffee, too." He couldn't normalize his voice, even though he tried, because he could see the way that Tom, and his mother, too, were looking at him.

"All right," his mother said. "Thank you."

After she left, Mike scraped the dishes and put them in the sink, making more noise than he needed to.

"Do you have a dish towel?" Tom asked. "I'll dry."

"I'll do it."

"I'm an old hand at doing dishes."

"So am I," Mike said.

Tom leaned casually against the counter, as if he didn't notice that Mike didn't want him there. "I eat at my brother's house a lot," he said. "Too much, probably. I do the dishes with Kyle, or his sister. My sister-in-law has to rest after dinner."

There was something wrong with Kyle's mother—Mike knew that but couldn't remember what it was. It was one of those background facts you knew about someone. Now he had one of his own: Mike Newlin's father killed somebody. Mike Newlin's father killed a woman he was having an affair with.

"She's in a wheelchair," Tom said. "She has ataxia. It's a disease that affects the nervous system."

"That's too bad," Mike said, sounding friendlier than he meant to.

"She's all right in every other way. Her family compensates for what she can't do. You know. They cover for her."

Mike put down the plate he was washing and looked at him. "Is this out of a psychology textbook?" he asked.

"Are you this suspicious of everything people say to you?"

"No," Mike said. "I'm not. Not with everybody." He got out two coffee mugs, ones his mother liked. They said: KISS THE TEACHER WHO HELPED YOU READ THIS.

"What's going to happen if you meet somebody smarter than you?" Tom asked.

"There are plenty of people smarter than I am."

"I'm not so sure about 'plenty.' "

"Don't bullshit me," Mike said. "That's what I hate. That's what makes me suspicious."

"So you'd be less suspicious if I said you weren't smart."

"You'd be too smart to say that," Mike said.

They stood less than two feet apart, not speaking. Mike poured water into the coffeemaker. Until the coffee began to brew, the only sound in the room was the rain falling outside.

"Mary Hise was smart, too," Tom said then. "Mostly A's in grade school, middle school, and the first two years of high school." He folded the wet dish towel and laid it on the counter. "Because," he said, "she got pregnant at sixteen. And the boyfriend didn't want anything to do with it. Or with her. That's what Mary's mother said."

"So things like that happen sometimes," Mike said.

Tom looked at him with his narrow eyes. "Don't you want to know what happened?"

"No," Mike said. "Or yes. Whatever." He was flustered; he'd been caught off guard. "I don't know. Whatever it is you expect me to say."

"I don't expect you to say anything in particular," Tom said calmly. "Anyway, she put it up for adoption." He shook his head, correcting himself. "I say 'it.' It was a girl, perfectly healthy."

He picked up the coffeepot. "You don't want any?" he asked Mike, and without waiting for an answer, he poured coffee into the two mugs Mike had set out. "You know what makes it so sad?" Tom said then to Mike. "That she'll never get a second chance. She'll never have a child she can keep as her own. That's what changes everything."

He went into the living room, and Mike was left in the kitchen alone, standing with his back against the counter. He felt terrible suddenly—not just terrible in the way that he imagined Tom wanted him to feel, but terrible beyond that, as if he had played a part in every bad thing that ever had happened to Mary Hise.

"Mike?" his mother called out from the next room. "Could you bring the milk and sugar?"

He carried those in and saw that Tom was sitting on the couch, next to her. She'd turned on only the standing lamp in the corner, which threw ghostly shadows onto the ceiling.

"This coffee smells good," Tom said. "I'm usually lazy and make myself instant."

Mike started to go upstairs, but his mother said, "Sit down for a minute."

"I have things to do."

"You can do them later."

He sat on the piano bench, next to a photograph of himself on Halloween. He'd been seven or so. He could remember his father taking it.

"I want to say what I started to say," his mother said, and he then could see how tense she still was. "I shouldn't have asked Mary Hise not to quit. I was afraid that Glenn might hurt himself. I never thought he would hurt Mary Hise. I could see that he loved her." Her voice had become high and distressed-sounding. She put her hands up to her face.

Mike was looking down at the piano keys. He was counting the black ones, hardly aware that he was doing it.

"Glenn had never hurt anyone before," Tom said.

"Everything about this was different from the way he was before," Carolyn said. "Maybe he'd never been in love before."

Mike felt shaky, even dizzy. Next to him was the photograph of himself, at seven, dressed in jeans and boots, with a metal star on his shirt: a sheriff, like in a Western movie. He'd wanted a holster and gun, but his mother had said no. Why not? his father had said. What's wrong with a gun if it's used to help people?

His mother was sitting still, her hands in her lap. She didn't seem to have more to say. Tom had his arm over the back of the couch, close to but not touching her. Outside, rain was still falling.

"I'm going to bed," Mike said, and left the room without looking again at either of them.

. . .

UPSTAIRS, he closed the door and sat on his bed in the dark. He used to do that after losing a wrestling match—just sit, not feeling sorry for himself but trying to believe that losing didn't matter. He wanted to call Donetta but knew that she'd gone to Keystone with her mother and sister. She liked the small shops and the tourists. She liked to drive past Mount Rushmore.

Finally Mike turned on his desk lamp and got out the road atlas his mother had bought him after he was accepted into South Dakota State. He looked up Salt Lake City. There were interstates leading away from it in four directions, but his father would have to be on one of those highways a long time before he'd get anywhere big. The bordering states were Nevada, Colorado, Wyoming, Idaho, Arizona, and New Mexico. He remembered a classmate who had moved to Wheatley from Phoenix. He remembered her saying, "Arizona's got a lot of old people and a lot of criminals."

Outside the thunder grew more distant. Mike's windows were open, and his brown curtains were being sucked in and pushed out by the wind. He turned off his lamp. After a while he heard the front door close and then a car door open and close: Tom DeWitt leaving.

So long, asshole, he thought, though a moment later he just felt sad. It seemed as if every man he knew was like his father—looking for a way to not be alone. It just wiped out whatever bad things men did. Then the next minute he thought about Mary Hise, and about himself not thinking about Donetta even when she was going down on him, and he saw everything from the opposite side—if men were alone, then they shouldn't fuck up so much. They shouldn't be such selfish assholes.

Mike heard his mother come up the stairs and stop outside his door. Don't even think about it, he said silently. He heard her walk down the hall and go into her room. It was after ten.

Mike undressed and got into bed. He used to sleep naked, but he didn't do that anymore. He wore underwear in case his mother should come into his room, or in case something happened and he'd have to get up suddenly. A lot of things were his responsibility now. Also, with underwear on he seemed to dream less about sex. He was too sexual, he thought. It was on his mind all the time, and he wondered about things he'd read, connections there were between male hormones and violence. He didn't feel like a violent person. He'd never done anything violent, except wrestling. He'd never even gone out for football.

He lay in bed, forgetting to put on his headphones so that he wouldn't hear if his mother was crying. He didn't care right now, anyway. But tonight he could hear her opening drawers and moving hangers in the closet. She wasn't doing it loudly. If he'd been asleep he wouldn't have heard it; it wouldn't have woken him up. For just a moment he was afraid that she was leaving, too. Then he understood that she must be getting rid of his father's clothes.

He got up, put on his jeans, and went into her room. "What are you doing?" he said.

She didn't answer. She was piling his father's clothes into storage boxes she kept under the bed. There were more clothes than Mike had expected, even though his father had taken things with him. There were still pants, shirts, sweaters, and shoes.

"I want to think of him as dead," Mike's mother said.

The clothes were blurry now. Mike kept his back to his mother until his vision cleared, by which time she was crying. When he turned around, she was holding his father's blue shirt up to her face.

EIGHT

By the second week of July, there had been no more news about Mike's father, except that the district attorney had gotten an indictment against him, as Tom DeWitt had predicted. The search had intensified and was covering a bigger area. Though he might be in Canada by now, Mike's mother had said, or Mexico. But Mike didn't think so. His father wasn't courageous enough to escape to another country.

Mike and his mother began not to talk about the situation directly. The truth was that Mike and his mother didn't talk much anymore, period. Carolyn started tutoring students in the evening, and Mike started working more hours at the Schofield ranch—six days a week and sometimes seven.

"It wouldn't hurt you to be home more often," his

mother said to him early on a Saturday morning. The temperature had been in the upper nineties, and the kitchen was already hot, flies buzzing against the screen door.

"What about you?" Mike said. "Look at how much you're working."

"I've always been responsible for everything in this family. Maybe you just never noticed before."

"Thanks for reminding me."

"I'm sorry. But I'm not going to lie about it." She shoved her chair back, getting up to make Mike more pancakes, though he hadn't asked for them. "I'm tutoring people who want to improve their lives," she said then. She mentioned an adult student named Jim Reynolds, and how enthusiastic he was about being back in school. "He doesn't just sit there and expect me to do all the work."

Like Dad, Mike thought, noticing how, now that they didn't talk about his father directly, his mother couldn't let a sentence just be a sentence. Everything had to be an indirect reference to something his father had or hadn't done—even before he'd gotten involved with Mary Hise. His father had screwed up in other ways; Mike knew that. More often than not he'd been difficult to be around. He hadn't been successful at his job, and he hadn't helped out much around the house, either, or with Mike, when Mike was young. His parents always had been unequal, Mike knew; they'd been like an unbalanced seesaw. His mother had been the one to keep his father up, keep him going. Without her, his father might have come crashing down. But what about his father's side of things, Mike wondered. What would it feel like if your family didn't have faith in you?

He watched his mother eat. He could tell by looking at her that she wasn't sleeping enough. The skin under her eyes was dark, and she looked exhausted first thing in the morning. She probably didn't feel all that great, either. But he didn't want to think about that. If he did, he'd feel sorry for her, which would be like giving in, somehow. Having it be just the two of them now made the tension between them more obvious. Neither one of them wanted to give in, on anything. They were alike, Mike thought, whereas Mike's father had been a completely different kind of person from either of them—more emotional, less reliable. Mike's father had been in the middle, between Mike and his mother, more than Mike had been in the middle, between his parents. Mike had never understood that before.

"What are you thinking so hard about?" his mother said.

"I don't know. Nothing," he told her. "The heat."

LATER in the day, at the Schofields', Mike felt tired and slow. While standing in the shade with Lee-Ann, who was waiting for a new couch to be delivered, he drank two Cokes to wake himself up. Neil was nearby, showing Janna the baby rabbits.

"She wants to play with them," Lee-Ann said. "She doesn't understand that they're just babies." The wind blew through her brown hair, redder now from the sun,

Mike noticed, though her skin was still white. She was wearing a sleeveless dress so thin and light that he could see her slender legs through the fabric.

They watched the furniture truck turn into the long gravel driveway. "There's nothing wrong with our old couch," Lee-Ann told Mike, "except that we're sick of it. I know how spoiled we must sound to you." It was the "our" and the "we" again that Mike hated.

"It's not like I live in a trailer," he said. "You have the right to get new furniture if you want."

"You're right," she said. "I'm sorry. I didn't mean anything by it." And Mike regretted having said anything.

It was Neil who asked Mike if he'd help Lee-Ann rearrange furniture. "She's always wanting to move things around," he said. "It drives me crazy. So this time it's your turn." Before heading down the hill toward the barn, he kissed Lee-Ann, and Mike thought that Lee-Ann seemed shy, suddenly, knowing that Mike was watching.

Inside, she put Janna down for her nap, then in the living room, with Mike's help, tried every possible furniture combination. "That probably seemed silly to you," she told him afterward.

"Why do you keep worrying about what I think?" Mike said. "It's like you think I'm judging you all the time."

"I care about what you think," Lee-Ann said.

She got him an iced tea, and they sat on the screened-in porch. Lee-Ann asked him how things were at home.

"Okay," he said. "Strange."

He saw the tractor far in the distance, with Louis Ivy on it; in front of the barn Neil and Ed were looking at the engine of Ed's old Corvette. Watching them, Mike felt homesick for the way he used to feel about the Schofields, when he was younger, when he'd looked up to them and wanted to be like them. He was too old to have those kinds of feelings now. And his view of the Schofields had altered, first because of his father's attitude toward Neil, then because of his own attraction to Lee-Ann.

"We packed up my father's stuff," he told Lee-Ann now. "My mom went through the house and packed away everything that was his."

"Did that make her feel better?"

"I'm not sure about better. Different, maybe."

"That must have been hard."

"I guess," Mike said. "I don't know. We just did it."

"You're so cool about it. You don't have to be that way with me."

"I'm not being any way with you," Mike said. He watched her lift her hair and hold it up from her neck. Her skin was damp from the heat. "You're the one who's not the same with me anymore," he said quietly.

She got up and stood with her back to him, looking down the hill toward the pond. "Too many things have changed," she said.

"Okay," Mike said. "But don't tell me I'm the one who should be different." She didn't speak or turn around, and he looked at her dress, the material thin enough for him to know almost exactly what she would look like without it.

"You can change the way you act, you know, without changing the way you feel," Lee-Ann said.

"Why would you want to?"

She turned to look at him. "Because," she said. Then, "I don't know. I think what you need is a friend."

"I have friends," Mike said.

They watched Neil and Ed get into the Corvette and drive it out onto the highway.

"Who besides Josh?" Lee-Ann said. Mike was glad that she didn't mention Donetta.

"I don't know," he said. "Do you want a list?"

"Just give me one name."

"Dave," Mike said.

"Dave who?"

"You mean they have to have last names?"

"Most real people do," Lee-Ann told him.

"You mean they have to be real?"

She smiled a little. "Real is the minimum requirement. Anyway, when was the last time you talked to Josh?"

"Three days ago," Mike lied.

"Really?"

"Why would I lie about it?"

"Well, that's good then." She stood next to the wicker rocker, the breeze stirring her dress. "Don't you think I have a point, though?" she asked in that sweeter, more intimate voice. "Don't you think that what I'm saying makes sense?"

"It's not about sense," Mike said. "I don't think about sense when I look at you."

Her face and neck flushed. She looked toward the inside of the house, as if she'd heard Janna wake. Then she looked at Mike flirtatiously, the way she used to. "What do you think about when you look at me?" she asked him, and Mike got up and reached for her. He felt the dampness of her dress and her cool hands on the back of his neck, and this time she didn't move away from him. She moved closer, and he put his hands on her hips, then under the dress. But when he kissed her, finally, after imagining for a year what it would be like, he was sick and had to push her away and hurry inside, down the hall to the bathroom. He shut the door behind him and sat on the floor, sweaty and cold, too dizzy to stand up. He leaned his forehead against the cool, porcelain bathtub and listened to Lee-Ann's footsteps coming down the hall.

"Mike?" she said. "Are you all right?"

"I'm sick," he said. "I have the flu." Then he lay down on the tile floor, feeling worse about himself than he could ever remember.

When he came out she led him into the kitchen. "Sit down," she said, and placed a glass of 7-Up in front of him. "It's good for your stomach." She sat across from him, her elbows on the table. "That was my fault. I don't know what I was thinking. I wasn't thinking."

"No," he told her. "I was just sick."

"Sick since when?" Lee-Ann said.

"I don't know. Yesterday."

"Thanks for sharing your germs with me." When Mike didn't even smile, she said, "Well, here's my excuse. I missed your paying attention to me."

"You're kidding."

"Do you think I'm too old to care about things like that?"

"Like I think thirty is old?" Mike said.

"Well, some people do. I bet your friends do."

"My friends are smarter than that."

Lee-Ann was watching him from across the table. "Things don't always have to be physical," she said. "You don't always have to do something. You can be close to people without even moving. It can all take place in your head."

"That's not the same kind of close," Mike said.

"It's a good kind, though. Maybe it would be good for you."

"Like medicine."

"See?" Lee-Ann said. "You can't really even picture it." She poured him more 7-Up, her soft hair falling forward against her cheek. "Do you know what I worry about?" she said to him. "That when you're my age you'll look back and wonder what kind of person I must have been."

"No," Mike said. "I'll just know I was lucky."

He finished his drink and left the cool house for the hot afternoon outside. He was already replaying in his mind what had happened and trying to make it different, like maybe he did have the flu—though he felt all right now—or maybe he'd been afraid that Neil and Ed would drive up at that moment and see them together. Lee-Ann shouldn't have taken that chance, he thought. She shouldn't have made him that nervous. She shouldn't have made him wait so long to begin with.

MIKE worked alone after that. Neil and Ed returned, and Mike washed and waxed the Corvette, then cleaned out a dark, clammy corner of the barn, which reminded him, in a depressing way, of the cellar in his grandparents' house—his father's parents, who had died, one after the other, the year Mike was eleven. They'd lived in a one-story frame house on the eastern edge of town; Mike's grandfather had had a small welding business. When Mike thought of their house, he thought of his father going down into the cellar for a box of old toys for Mike to play with. He remembered the ugly way his grandparents had talked to each other, and then the nice way they'd talked to Mike and Mike's parents, as if that niceness were a kind of punishment for each other.

Mike's father had been the only person in the family to attend college. Glenn's brother, Randall, who had enlisted and stayed in the army, was stationed in Germany. They weren't close. Mike hardly knew him, and Mike's mother had waited weeks before contacting him. "I don't have anything to say about it," Randall had said. "There was always something wrong with his personality."

"How helpful," Mike's mother had said afterward. "I'm sorry I called him."

IT was five o'clock by the time Mike finished. He needed to be home earlier than usual—Donetta had invited him to a family barbecue that night. Her grandmother was visiting from Pierre, along with the grandmother's new boyfriend. Before Mike left the Schofields', however, he went up to the house, where Lee-Ann was sitting on the front steps with Janna.

"I've thought about what happened," he said. "I understand it now." In a lower voice he added, "Let's go inside for a minute."

"You don't have to prove it to me. I believe you."

"I'm not trying to prove anything."

She looked at him the way his mother did sometimes—as if she knew more about him than he did, and he said good-bye, turned around, and walked quickly down the hill to his motorcycle. He put on his helmet and rode out of the long driveway too fast, skidding on the gravel, and on the way home he planned how to act the next time he saw her—as if this day hadn't happened. Then he would gradually start flirting with her again, so that before long they could get back to where they used to be with each other, back in May. Then he could kiss her for real. She'd be able to see, then, how much he'd always wanted to. But first he had to act as if it were no big deal. He thought about calling her as soon as he got home, pretending that he'd forgotten to tell Neil something so that she could see that his mind was already on other things. He just needed to think of a reason to call that would make sense.

By the time he was back in Wheatley, though, on Edge Street, he was too tired to think about it any longer. He was tired of having to make things all right all the time, of having to act a certain way so that somebody would think of him a certain way, or so that he could fix something he screwed up. He wished he could just make a mistake once in a while, he thought, as he rode his motorcycle up the driveway and into the carport. Then he saw his father's disorganized workbench and thought, If you let yourself make mistakes, how do you keep them small? How do you keep worse ones from happening?

He took off his helmet and began to organize his father's tools.

NINE

CORY Burris was cooking a pig in a hole in the Rushes' backyard. He'd dug the pit early that morning, without asking for Mrs. Rush's permission, and when Mike rode up the driveway, Mrs. Rush was standing out front near the juniper bushes, talking on her portable phone. Mike cut off his motorcycle engine in time to hear her say, "It's not like he dug it with a spoon, Pastor Kelly. I could bury my mother in that hole."

She gestured for Mike to go into the house. The only person inside was Margo, in the kitchen, drinking a wine cooler as she made potato salad. "Donetta's out back," she said, drying her tears with a paper napkin. "I don't know why there has to be this kind of trouble all the time. I think people should try to be peaceful with each other."

Mike went through the living room and out the sliding

glass door into the early-evening light. Donetta was sitting on a lawn chair next to her grandmother and her grandmother's boyfriend, a short, elderly man with glasses.

"Here's my sweetheart," Donetta said, when Mike appeared. She got up and kissed him. "This is Grandma Sharp and her friend, Wilbert Greenway." Mike shook hands with Mr. Greenway and said hello to Donetta's grandmother, whom he'd been warned about. "She's not mentally ill exactly," Donetta had told him, "but she can be mean enough to make you cry."

"We've heard all about you," Donetta's grandmother said. "We know everything, and Donetta said not to bring it up. But I don't agree with that."

"Thanks a lot," Donetta told her.

"I believe in being straightforward," her grandmother said.

"You're going to college in the fall?" Wilbert asked kindly.

"South Dakota State," Mike told him.

"In the honors program," Donetta said. "He gets better grades than I do."

Cory waved to Mike from the back of the yard, which was already in shadow, and Mike walked across the thick, green grass, watered daily in the summer unless it rained. That was Donetta's job. "Personally I don't care if it turns blue," she'd told Mike more than once.

Cory was standing guard over the pit, in which a pig,

wrapped in heavy tinfoil, was buried in coals. "Isn't this something?" he said. "I've wanted to do this for years." Behind him was a cooler filled with Cokes and beer. He got a beer for Mike and opened one for himself.

"She's pissed off, though," he told Mike, meaning his mother-in-law, Mike knew, whose name was not in Cory's vocabulary. "I can't blame her really—I did fuck up the lawn—but I hate how she makes Margo feel. She tries to come between us that way." He looked across the lush lawn. "There's a thing in the Bible about that," he told Mike. " 'Let no man put asunder.' It means you have to respect your in-laws."

"She's into having a nice house and yard," Mike said. "Donetta said she grew up in a trailer park."

"Well, nice grass is one thing," Cory said. "But a marriage is a lot more important."

Mrs. Rush was coming outside now, followed by Donetta's heavyset aunt, Nancy, and Nancy's daughter, Ellen. They lived in Spearfish, and Mike had met them before. The daughter was four years older than he was and always wore a camouflage army jacket, no matter what the weather. She'd failed junior college and was rejected by the army; now she worked as a security guard at an office building in Rapid City. "They almost gave her a gun," Donetta had told Mike. "Then they came to their senses."

Donetta kissed her aunt and walked toward Mike and Cory. She had on a short yellow dress and sandals with straps that wound around the ankle. When she saw Mike watching her, she smiled the way she had the first time she'd ever seen him—as if she'd never smile that way again for anybody else. Cory got her a Coke.

"I'm sorry about Grandma Sharp," she told Mike. "We didn't tell her anything. Wilbert's hobby is reading newspapers."

"They're leaving tomorrow, right?" Cory said. "Isn't that what they promised?" He waved to Margo, who came outside carrying the bowl of potato salad. "My beautiful baby is finally here," he told Mike. He poked at the coals, peeled back the tinfoil, and inspected the pig's head.

THEY ate outside at a long wooden table Cory had made out of leftover lumber from a Rapid City subdivision. Mike figured he'd gotten the lumber, unknowingly, from somebody who'd stolen it. Cory wasn't smart, but he wasn't a thief, either. He brought over a huge platter of pork.

"This is delicious," Donetta's aunt said.

"There's nothing wrong with pork cooked in the kitchen," Mrs. Rush said.

"What you need is a cook-off," Wilbert told her. "Invite the neighbors and see who likes what best."

"No, thank you," Mrs. Rush said.

"Do you even know the neighbors?" Grandma Sharp asked.

"Of course I know the neighbors."

"The lawns here are so gigantic," Grandma Sharp said. "You'd need a go-cart to get from one house to the next."

"It's a beautiful area," Wilbert said.

"People go up to their ears in debt to live in these houses," Grandma Sharp told him. "They go into debt so that they can clean rooms they never go into."

"That's hardly how we live," Mrs. Rush said. "Our house is too crowded, if anything."

"Is that right?" Margo said. "Well, it doesn't have to be anymore."

Everyone ate in silence. Under the table Donetta had her hand on Mike's leg. All she was eating for dinner was potato salad, bread, and olives. "I'm not going to eat any pork," she'd told Mike earlier. "Pigs remind me of Wilbur, in *Charlotte's Web.*"

For dessert there were berry cobblers that Donetta's aunt had brought. It was nearly dark, and Margo lit candles. Donetta's cousin Ellen ran around the darkening yard, catching fireflies with her hands.

"We had family picnics like this when I was growing up," Wilbert said. "It was during the Depression. My dad would cook hot dogs. Wieners, we called them."

"Were the picnics happy?" Margo asked.

"Sure," Wilbert said.

"Maybe things you remember just seem happy," Margo told him.

"I remember bad things, too, honey."

"Grandma?" Donetta said. "What kinds of things do you remember?"

"I don't like rummaging around in the past," Grandma Sharp said. "It's over and done with."

Mrs. Rush picked up a candle, crossed the pretty lawn, and looked down at the pit. She nudged a little dirt back in with her shoe.

LATER, Mike and Donetta took a walk through the small subdivision and into the field on the other side of Flat Rock Road. The moon was up, so white and shining that they could see deer paths in the long grass.

"I think about this field when I can't get to sleep at night," Donetta said. "I imagine I'm lying in it with you."

"You think about me too much," Mike said.

She let go of his hand. "Who should I think about, then?"

"Well, nobody, really. You should think about yourself and what you want."

"What do you think I want?" Donetta said.

There was silence. Then they could hear, in the distance, firecrackers Cory was setting off in the Rushes' backyard.

"I don't know," Mike said finally. "Me, I guess."

"But I shouldn't say it, right? Because it makes you feel trapped, and you worry about what's going to happen to me when you go away to college."

"Yes," Mike said.

Donetta stood apart from him in the darkness. Mike

knew she was crying, though she wasn't moving or making a sound. When her father had died, she'd cried silently like that, as if she'd not expected to be comforted.

"I'm not trying to be an asshole," he said.

"Then don't be one."

He put his hands on her shoulders, looking down at her wet face.

"Are you breaking up with me?" she asked him.

"No. I don't know what I'm doing."

"You always know what you're doing."

"I used to," Mike said. "I used to think I did." He touched her face and hair, and when she didn't respond, he dropped his hands and lay down in the grass, just as he'd lain down in Lee-Ann's bathroom that afternoon.

"You're going to get chigger bites," Donetta told him.

"I know. I don't care."

He closed his eyes, and after a moment heard her lie down next to him. The firecrackers had stopped, and from across the street they heard voices, then a car leaving. "Aunt Nancy and Ellen," Donetta said sadly.

Mike leaned over and kissed her. It was a test for him, at first—given what had happened earlier with Lee-Ann—until Donetta began to kiss him back. She slid her hands up under his shirt and caressed his shoulders and chest; she stroked his erection. As he unzipped his jeans he watched her lift up her dress and take it off. He positioned her on top of him, so that he could see her body in the moonlight. For the first time Mike was thinking only of her, even from the beginning, and though he didn't say that he loved her, he could have said it without lying.

Afterward he reached up and touched her long hair, and the necklace she always wore—a small gold heart on a gold chain, a present from her father. His hands were trembling, and he felt the edge of something hiding inside him: the fear of what it might be like if Donetta didn't love him.

"Let's get up," he whispered. He stood, tucking in his shirt, and led Donetta through the field. He felt better then, but he wanted to get back to where he could see lights and houses, and the shadowy, familiar outline of the Black Hills in the distance. He and Donetta stopped at the edge of the road, from where they could see Mrs. Rush and her mother in the big, lighted kitchen window. Donetta's grandmother was drying a butcher knife.

"Your family's screwed up," Mike said.

"I know. My father was the only nice one."

"No," Mike told her. "The nice one is standing next to me."

IT was after ten when he rode up Edge Street. He'd expected his house to be dark and his mother asleep, but from a block away he could see lit-up windows and a car out front—Tom DeWitt's, he recognized as he got closer. Something had happened with his father.

He left the motorcycle in the driveway and went into the house wearing his helmet. In the kitchen, standing at the table, his mother and Tom were looking down at a map of Kansas.

"There's been a close call," Carolyn said. "But they don't know where he is."

Mike's father had been seen in a Jeep, with a woman, stopped on the side of Interstate 70 between Denver and Kansas City—a Jeep Cherokee with a Colorado license plate. They had a small dog with them, Tom said. Mary Hise's dog, almost certainly. Ten miles west of Oakley, Kansas, heading toward Kansas City, they'd had car trouble and were looking under the hood—a spark plug had come loose. A Kansas state patrolman had pulled up behind them and asked if they needed help. That was three hours ago now. Routinely, he'd called in the license plate; the car was registered to the woman.

"That's why he didn't check Glenn's identification," Tom said to Mike. "There was no reason to. But afterward, the patrolman had a feeling about it. He said that the man had seemed nervous, and that he'd let the woman do all the talking. By this time half an hour had gone by. He checked with the dispatcher, found out about the ATL—Attempt to Locate—and gave her the license plate and description of the Jeep. But it hasn't been seen since. They must have gotten off the highway. Western Kansas is an empty place, but Glenn was in a vehicle that could go anywhere. We had a chance and messed it up."

He folded up the map and helped himself to a glass of water. It was hot and still outside, and there'd been heat lightning as Mike had ridden home. Mike watched Tom set the glass on the table, then rethink that and place it in the sink. There was nothing he did, Mike thought, that he didn't do deliberately.

"Why are you telling us this?" Mike asked him.

"Don't you want to know?"

"Of course we do," Carolyn said.

"You should keep it to yourselves, though," Tom said. "It's not something you'll see in the newspaper."

"Then you shouldn't have told us," Mike said.

"Don't be so difficult," his mother told him. "Would you rather not know?"

Tom rested his hands, casually, on the back of a chair. "I'll tell you why I told you. I thought you might have the same concern we have. That your father might harm this woman."

"He won't," Mike said.

His mother said, "There's no reason to worry about her. Glenn hates himself for what he's done."

"How do you know that?" Tom said.

"Because he hated himself before he did it."

Mike turned away from them. That was bullshit, he thought. It was the kind of thing people said on talk shows. And it was too personal a thing to say. For the last eighteen years his mother had felt fine being private about private things. But now that his father was hiding, his mother was doing the opposite, revealing things about both herself and

Mike's father. Mike wondered what kinds of things she'd been telling Tom DeWitt about him—Mike.

"I'm putting my motorcycle away," he told them, and went outside. He wheeled his bike into the carport, and as he hung up his helmet he thought about the fact that his father wasn't hiding alone anymore. Mike had been able to imagine what it might feel like to be alone and in trouble. He couldn't picture his father that same way now.

He stood in the dark driveway, watching his mother and Tom DeWitt through the window. They were sitting down, talking, both of them leaning forward in their chairs. Mike's mother's hair was a little longer and less neat than it used to be—a more ordinary length—and her red sleeveless blouse was open at the neck. Sitting there under the kitchen light, they both seemed more substantial to Mike than Mike seemed to himself. They were sharp-edged and vivid, whereas he felt like a shadow. Why couldn't he seem that definite to himself? Why didn't he feel that solid? Why couldn't he see himself as clearly as he could see them?

He stayed outside and walked—down Edge Street to Pine and up Arapahoe, where Josh used to live and where Josh's mother lived now with her boyfriend. If Josh were around, Mike thought, the two of them could take off for a few days, go to a rodeo in Wyoming, or go camping in the Hills. Josh was always up to something adventurous, and often illegal. In the fall he was going to the University of

South Dakota in Sioux Falls, on a football scholarship, and he'd said once to Mike, "I'm trying not to get arrested before that."

And that made Mike think of the university he would be attending, and of the visit he'd made there last fall, with his parents. There had been an away football game that weekend, and everybody in Brookings had seemed to be crowded into bars and restaurants, watching the game on television.

"You'll get caught up in that, too," Mike's father had told him. "Don't think you won't. You'll be shouting along with the rest of the idiots." He'd gotten into a bad mood then, and Mike and his mother had ended up walking around the deserted campus by themselves.

Mike was back on Edge Street, all the houses dark except his own. He waited at a distance, away from the streetlight, until Tom DeWitt drove off.

TEN

WYLENE Moseley was the name of the woman his father had been with, and might be with still. She was a waitress from Central City, Colorado, a town in the mountains west of Denver. She was forty-two years old.

"I can tell you what she looks like," Tom DeWitt told Mike on the phone, Monday morning, during a thunderstorm that had begun at dawn and kept Mike home. "My mother's teaching," Mike had said at first, when Tom had called, and Tom had said, "I know. I thought just you and I could talk."

"Blue eyes and black hair," he said now. "Five seven, a hundred forty pounds. Attractive features. Is that how you pictured her?"

"I didn't picture her."

"But you must have wondered."

Mike knew better than to say he had. All day Sunday, as he and his mother had waited for a phone call telling them that his father had been arrested, or worse, they'd never once mentioned the woman. She'd become unmentionable—like an untouchable in India, Mike thought, which was a bad joke, because he knew that his father would be touching her.

"Have you heard her name before?" Tom asked.

"No."

"Do you think she's somebody your father knew?"

"I don't know," Mike said.

"My guess is that he met her on the road, somehow, and that she knows he's in trouble."

Mike was on the phone in the upstairs hallway, from where he could see his mother's neatly made bed and the window beyond it. "Why would she go with him, then?" he said coolly, as if he didn't care, really.

"Do you know who gets the most letters in prison?" Tom said. "Men who've murdered women." When Mike said nothing, Tom said, "I don't understand it either. But I can tell you what I think she thinks—that your father's been treated unfairly. Also, she likes danger. Adrenaline makes her feel more alive—that kind of thing."

"It makes everybody feel that way."

"Some people feel good and alive the second they wake up in the morning."

"Like you?" Mike said.

"Never. Do you?"

"No."

"We have something in common, then," Tom said. "We have something else in common, too. We don't want to see this woman get hurt."

"So?" Mike said.

"It's just something we share, like the way we wish Mary Hise hadn't died."

"Everybody wishes that."

"You must wish it especially," Tom said. "You knew her."

That was true, which was the meanest thing about it. Mike stood in the dim hallway for a long time after they hung up, looking through his mother's window at the dark sky and falling rain. Finally he got out the vacuum cleaner, as his mother had asked him to, and started downstairs, pushing it hard into the corners, angry at himself for answering the phone to begin with or for not saying: You think you're being clever, making me feel bad about Mary Hise? How could I not feel bad about her?

Upstairs, he did his mother's room, his own room, and the small, oblong guest room, which had a window overlooking the backyard. Then he turned off the vacuum cleaner and sat on the old four-poster bed that had belonged to his great-grandmother. The guest room was where he and Donetta had had sex whenever his parents had been out of town. Often, Mike would walk past the room, look at the bed, and remember exactly how Donetta had looked, naked on the white sheets. An unused room was sexual the way a motel room was, Mike thought.

Never occupied long enough by any one person, it was emptier than empty, like a pool without water, or sleep without dreams.

Mike's father was probably staying in motels with Wylene Moseley—if that was even her name, Mike thought, if Tom DeWitt hadn't made up the name, or even the whole story. But if she was real, Mike knew, his father was sleeping with her, because if he'd slept with Mary Hise, then he'd sleep with other women as well. That was how Mike was himself, in a way, and he felt too depressed right then to imagine that he could be different. He wondered if Wylene Moseley knew about Mike and his mother, or about Mary Hise; he wondered how his father had gotten her to help him. His father acted differently around attractive women. The first few times Donetta had come over for dinner, for example, he'd cleared the table, carried in dessert, and stood when Donetta got up from her chair. He'd been overly friendly and polite around some of Mike's mother's friends, as well. Women had always seemed to like him more than men had, at least at first. Donetta had liked him a lot, until she got to know him better. Then she'd said to Mike, "I get tired of paying attention to him."

Outside, in back, rain was pooling in the low spots under the crab-apple tree. Mike had filled in those hollows with dirt, then peat moss, but they formed themselves again each time it rained. There were things you couldn't change, including things about yourself, Mike thought; he was bad at being faithful, and women—girls—liked him, too. He knew how to make them like him.

He stood at the window, imagining what Wylene Moseley must be like, taking off with his father like that. She was probably an outdoors kind of person—the kind of person Mike was more than his father was, although his father never would have admitted that. Mike had seen pictures of him hiking in national parks, but his father had never backpacked anywhere, or climbed a real mountain, or even stayed in a tent for more than one night.

Mike remembered that when he was five or six, his father had set up a small yellow tent for him and Josh in the backyard. "You boys will have a lot of fun out here," Glenn had told them. "You'll be like cowboys." He'd gotten them sleeping bags and settled them out there after dark. Then later, after a dog barked and an animal got into the trash, he came outside and knelt at the tent's opening. "Are you scared?" he'd asked kindly. "Do you want to come in?"

"No," they'd told him.

"Stay out all night, then," he'd said coldly, and gone inside.

AT noon, Mike's mother came home for lunch, shaking off her umbrella on the patio and bringing into the kitchen the smell of rain. "Were there any calls?" she asked.

"No," he said, lying so that he didn't seem so involved, somehow. Tom DeWitt kept doing that to him, Mike thought—creating secrets between the two of them, and even when Mike could see it coming, he didn't seem able to stop it. It just kept happening.

"That's good, I suppose," his mother said, taking a pot of soup from the refrigerator and heating it up on the stove. She turned around and smiled at Mike. "I had a good class this morning. You know how I judge that? Because when there's ten minutes left I suddenly remember what I have to come home to—the situation, I mean."

"That happens to me sometimes," Mike said, relieved that she was referring to it. "I'll forget about it for a while." He moved aside his mother's books in order to set the table.

"Some of those are for you," she said, "from your list. I got them out of the library." Mike's high school guidance counselor had given book lists to everyone going on to college.

"Just don't make me read them."

"What?" his mother said sharply.

"It's a joke," he told her. "It's what Cory Burris said about a book Mrs. Rush tried to hit him with."

His mother wasn't smiling anymore. "I worry about you spending time over there," she said.

"That's ridiculous."

"I guess it is," she said. "I guess it's Mrs. Rush who should worry about Donetta coming over here. It must seem funny to people now, what a snob I was."

"I didn't say that."

"I know you didn't. But it was implied in what you said."

They ate lunch without speaking further. It was useless to talk to her, Mike thought, even though she'd come home in a good mood. Things he thought were funny she didn't; she was always trying to be the parent. She couldn't sit there and just listen.

He washed the dishes as she got her books together. "I have an afternoon class," she said. "Then a tutoring session with Jim Reynolds and two others. Jim Reynolds is the only one I look forward to." She put a lipstick into her purse and came toward Mike as if she wanted to hug him good-bye. When he kept his hands busy with the dishes, she hesitated, then opened the door. A few minutes later he heard her backing the car down the driveway.

MIKE slept most of the afternoon. He dreamed of a rainy night in which his father was being chased through a cornfield with Lucky, their dog that had been killed so long ago. There was a woman with him. There was a building in the distance, a cross between a silo and a prison, and Lucky was half running, half flying. Close by on a playground, a kid was hanging by one hand from the top of a slide. Mike woke up sweating.

It was five-thirty, and the rain had stopped. The house was silent and empty. He got on his motorcycle and rode through town on the wet streets, past his father's insurance agency, which now had STUART WELLS written on the door, past the apartment where Mary Hise had lived, and north on County Road 51 to Little Falls Park, where Mary used to go with her dog.

The park consisted of hay fields and cottonwoods, and a rocky stream wound through it. Some summers it dried up completely, but now it was shallow with rain. Mike walked along the gravel path. During his freshman year, he'd been a member of the track team, and the coach had driven them out there to run. Mike wasn't fast enough and didn't focus, according to his coach. He'd just run and think. He'd solve math problems in his head. At the end of the season he quit the team but kept on running, and Donetta started running with him. "So I get to spend more time with you," she had said. Even from the beginning she'd made it clear to Mike how much he meant to her.

"You shouldn't do that," he'd told her. "It makes you easy to take advantage of."

"Why would you take advantage of me?" she'd asked.

She didn't understand, still, that you should always hold back, keep part of yourself to yourself. Otherwise, you'd be affected by external things all the time—by what people said and did, by the way they acted toward you. You'd be like a rootless tree, Mike thought, too shallow to live. His father had been like that. That was why his father had cried all night when the dog died. That was why he'd taken an overdose of pills when his college girlfriend broke up with him. Mike thought about that incident now, as he walked along the path. Did his father think that trying to kill himself would bring the girlfriend back? Because why would you want somebody who didn't want you?

The sky began to clear before dusk, the clouds dissipating and the horizon peach-colored and bright. The fields were golden green from the rain. A woman came toward Mike, jogging, her Border collie running behind her.

Mary Hise will never see this park again, he thought. She'll never have another dog. She'll never pose for another picture.

He walked until it was too dark to see across the field. He tried to keep his mind blank, but thoughts about Mary came into it, serious ones: the baby she'd had; how uncertain she'd looked in her high school photograph; the fact that she'd died alone.

Mike kept walking, just looking at the darkness.

ELEVEN

JOSH Mitchell came back to Wheatley on a Sunday at the end of July. He had a court hearing to go to: Duane King had attacked his mother. He'd broken her wrist and bruised her face, and Josh was scheduled to testify. He'd seen him threaten her once. "It was a few weeks before my dad and I moved," he told Mike Sunday night. "I kicked him in the balls."

"Why didn't you tell me?"

"I was too pissed off to talk about it." After a moment he added, "She was nuts to be with him."

It was after dark, and they were at Crow Lake, sitting in Josh's car with the doors open, drinking beer and waiting for Donetta and Josh's ex-girlfriend, Pam, to drive out and meet them. It wasn't certain that Pam would come. She was dating somebody else now, somebody older, from

Spearfish. And she was supposedly still angry at Josh for breaking up with her last winter.

"She expected me to marry her or some bullshit like that," Josh said now. "So I told her to back off and get real, and she punched me."

"You deserved it," Mike said.

"Why?"

"I don't know. I'm just quoting Donetta."

"Donetta hates me," Josh said.

"Hate's a strong word. Detest might be closer." Mike opened another beer and put his bare foot up on the cracked dashboard. Josh's car was an old, beat-up Lincoln his father had traded an ancient Airstream for. Josh's father was a geologist, but he also collected junk that he sold or traded for more junk. Josh's mother had wanted him to get out of that business. They'd fought constantly. It was no surprise to Mike that they got divorced. The surprise was that Josh's mother had been sneaking around with Duane King, who already had three ex-wives. Mike and Josh had gone to school with his son, who everybody figured would end up in prison.

"Do you think Pam'll come?" Josh asked.

"Donetta will. I don't know about Pam."

Josh got out of the car and took off his T-shirt and jeans. He walked in the darkness to the edge of the lake, dove in, and swam underwater until he was out deep.

"This feels so fucking good," he yelled to Mike.

Mike had gone swimming earlier, when they'd first gotten there. He'd worked with Neil and Ed all day, and the temperature had been up to 104. Lee-Ann had come out of the house once, in cutoff jeans and the top of a two-piece bathing suit. Mike had gotten an erection as soon as he saw her. He'd felt like unzipping his jeans right there, in front of her husband and brother-in-law, to prove to her that he was okay again, and as attracted to her as ever. It was such a crazy thought that it scared him. It made him think that anybody could become crazy just by doing a crazy thing. It could happen in a second if you let it.

Mike heard Donetta's car. He got out, stood behind a tree, then jumped out in front of her headlights.

"I knew you'd do that," she said. "I just said that to Pam."

"She did," Pam said.

They had carry-out boxes with them from Andell's Diner—cheeseburgers, onion rings, and Cokes. Donetta spread a blanket on the ground between the cars, and Pam said hello to Mike. She didn't ask where Josh was. She and Mike had been friends in high school; they'd sat next to each other in advanced calculus and worked together on the problems. She was tall and long-legged, with large breasts and a pretty face. She looked older than she was.

"Hey," Josh said. They couldn't see him, but they could hear his footsteps. He went behind the car to put on his jeans.

"So what's going on?" Pam said in a less-than-friendly way.

"Nothing," he told her. "Everything. A lot of shit has happened."

"No kidding," Mike said.

"I don't mean just that," Josh said. "Things seem different, like I've been gone for years. I don't know why. Maybe it's just me. It probably is. It's probably just me being weird like I get sometimes." He was talking rapidly. For as long as Mike had known him, people had thought of Josh as cocky, but to Mike he'd always seemed more nervous than people realized.

"I'm sorry about your mother," Pam said. "I always liked her."

"She's not dead," Josh said. "I mean, it spooks me to hear you say it like that."

"I was just being polite."

"Okay. That's okay then." Josh took a breath, and they sat down on the blanket to eat. "I'm hungry as shit," Josh said. "Thanks, Donetta. I'll pay you for it."

"Forget it." It was the first thing Donetta had said to him. She was leaning back against Mike, her legs outstretched between his. She'd once told Mike that when it came to girls Josh was like dynamite—dangerous at a distance, deadly up close.

"Donetta gets a discount, even for take-out," Mike told Josh.

"It was still nice of her to think of it," Josh said.

"I'm a nice person," Donetta said.

The night was hot and hazy—a few stars but no moon,

and lightning too far in the distance for them to hear thunder.

"My dad said to tell you hi," Pam said to Josh. "Can you believe it? He started liking you the second you stopped liking me."

"What second was that?" Josh said. "Because I must have missed it. I don't remember it happening."

No one spoke. Donetta took Mike's hand. After a minute they got up and left Josh and Pam alone. They found their way down the dark trail to the water, undressed, and swam halfway out into the lake. They were both strong swimmers, but Mike was faster. He got there a minute or so before she did and waited for her to catch up. Then they headed for the bank on their left and pulled themselves up onto a limestone ledge that jutted out over the water. They lay close to each other in the darkness.

"You should give Josh a chance," Mike said.

"Why?"

"Because it's not like you not to."

Donetta was silent. Then she said, "That's a mean thing to say. It's like saying, 'You're proving you're not as good a person as you think you are.' You're not even thinking about the way Josh is. You just make it all about me."

"You're so fucking smart sometimes," Mike said.

Donetta sat up, her long hair dripping. "I hardly ever feel smart," she said. "I worry that you'll end up with somebody a lot smarter than me. And then when I do say something smart, you act like it makes you mad. So I just don't know what person you want me to be."

"Lie back down next to me," Mike said.

"No. You can't just make it all right like that."

He reached up and touched her smooth skin, which seemed to shine in the darkness. He pressed his hand against her back and felt her heart beating; touching her was like holding a bird, he thought, the way she seemed too small to be alive. And suddenly his face was wet. It just came from nowhere—more like rain than tears. He wanted to say that he was sorry for a hundred different things. He felt sorry for things that had nothing to do with her. He'd apologize to Mary Hise if he could. He'd say, My father didn't mean to do what he did.

"Mike?" she said. "What's wrong?"

He couldn't answer, even though he could hear how frightened she was. "Don't be mad at me," he said finally. "I can't stand it right now."

"Okay. It's all right. I'm not mad." She lay down and put her arms around him.

"I didn't mean for that to happen," Mike said. "I don't know what's wrong with me."

"It's okay," Donetta said. "I'm sorry."

She was saying what he should be saying to her. Things had gotten turned around, somehow—as if the responsibility lay with the darkness or the trees or the moonless sky. And whatever had happened to him was disappearing already, or going under the surface, like a rock thrown into water. He was all right again.

He and Donetta kissed. All around them in the black night were the sounds of insects and frogs. The noises just took over the night. It made Mike want to imitate them, leave being a person behind and be this thing that didn't require thought.

"I like the sounds," Donetta said. "I wish I could make them." She'd read his mind like that before. Or maybe he'd read hers, he thought. Maybe he had that backward.

They kissed more deeply. Donetta ran her fingers over his back, along his spine, from his neck down to the small of his back. Her breathing quickened with Mike's, though in the end they didn't let themselves have sex; the condoms were on shore, in the pocket of Mike's jeans. Donetta wouldn't take birth control pills. She'd feel slutty, she had told him; she'd feel like the kind of person who would fuck anybody. The only person she'd ever had sex with was Mike. The first time was just before her fifteenth birthday, in her empty house. She had said, afterward, "Isn't it strange that it hurts the first time? Do you think every good thing is like that?"

They swam back across the lake. Mike swam with her this time. He could see just flashes of her—a white arm, her face as she turned her head to breathe. She reached the shore before he did. He liked watching her—what he could see of her—walk naked out of the water. They didn't know where Josh and Pam were.

They dried off, dressed, and sat on the blanket, sharing a beer. They both heard Pam at the same moment—she cried out Josh's name. She and Josh were in the backseat of Josh's car.

"She's making a mistake," Donetta whispered to Mike.

He didn't answer. He was thinking that Pam's voice would come back to him in bed, that night, and the next time he and Donetta had sex. That was the difference between males and females. It was some ancient, inborn thing; therefore you didn't have to feel bad about it. It kept you separate, which made you strong enough to look out for the females and offspring. That's how they wrote about people in textbooks: males, females, offspring.

Still, he felt bad when Donetta took his hand.

"I wouldn't want anyone besides you to hear me," she whispered.

They got up and walked along the lake, away from the cars, until they couldn't hear anything human anymore.

TWELVE

WYLENE Moseley returned home to Colorado by herself.

"We had her house watched," Tom said to them Thursday night, after dinner. "We knew she was back twenty minutes after she got there."

He had come over to the house this time without calling first—to catch them off guard, Mike thought, to catch *him* off guard, because it was Mike who was the target. Mike knew that, even if his mother didn't. His mother was the one to act too pleased to see Tom. She made him coffee and suggested they go outside on the patio, where it was cooler. It was dusk, and she lit citronella candles to keep the mosquitos away. Tom didn't sit down until she did.

"Wylene met Glenn at a bar," he told them. "A roadside place in the mountains. We knew about that bar earlier.

The bartender remembered Glenn and Wylene leaving together. He said he remembered because he used to go out with a friend of hers." Tom paused. "I figured he used to go out with Wylene. That's the kind of thing people lie about to policemen."

Carolyn smiled, but Mike didn't. His head had begun to hurt. He thought that it was starting to make him sick, seeing Tom DeWitt.

"Why did she trust him?" his mother said.

"They were close in age. He was polite. They liked the same music. She said that Glenn kept playing an old rock-and-roll song they both liked. Something about heaven. I can't remember the name."

Mike knew but kept still.

"It drives me crazy when I can't remember something," Tom said.

"Is it important?" Carolyn asked.

"No. But it's in my mind somewhere. Let me think for a minute." In the silence Mike watched Tom attentively survey the yard.

"I know it had *heaven* in the title," Tom said. "Heaven something or something heaven. Some word like *star.*"

"Mike, you know a lot about music," Carolyn said. "What song is he thinking of?"

They were both watching him; his headache grew worse. " 'Stairway to Heaven,' " he said finally.

"That's it," Tom said. He crossed his legs. Mike recognized his cowboy boots from the day he'd taken Mike to

Mary Hise's apartment. "How did you know it was that song in particular?" he asked Mike.

"It's famous."

"You and your dad must have the same taste in music," Tom said.

"They do," Carolyn said.

"We don't," Mike said.

"So he went home with her," Carolyn said then.

Tom looked from Mike to her. "Sorry," he said. "Yes. He followed her home."

"In what?" Carolyn asked.

"What kind of car did I say he had?"

"You didn't," Mike said.

"Oh. I thought I had. Well, it doesn't matter. It was barely running, and he used it as an excuse to stay with her for a few days. He told her that he was in trouble but couldn't say what kind. He said that he'd left his wife, and that he had a thirteen-year-old son." Tom paused there. He put his hand on the arm of Mike's chair. "He told her that you had leukemia."

Mike could feel, even without looking at her, how shocked his mother was.

"You mean that this made-up son did," Mike said. "If my father said it to begin with. You're only hearing it from her."

"I don't think she was making it up," Tom said. "It made too much of an impression on her. She'd had a sick child once, too."

"You don't know if that's true, either."

"We do," Tom told him. "We looked into it."

"What happened to her child?" Carolyn asked.

"He died."

The moon had come up, turning the grass and patio a milky color. Mike, his head hurting, wished that he were by himself, so that he could think about this without anybody watching him. He needed to think more clearly than he could now.

"There's not much else to tell," Tom said. "Glenn wanted to be driven as far away as she would take him. She said she'd drive him to Topeka, where her mother lived. They started out, then had the car trouble. They took back roads, ending up in Oklahoma, and she let him off at a bus station. She gave him money in exchange for the dog. She liked the dog. Then she drove up to Topeka for a visit. After that she drove straight home. No one stopped her, even though there was an all-points bulletin out."

"Did you tell her what Glenn did?" Carolyn asked.

"She said there must be more to it. That we needed to hear his side."

"Don't you ever think that?" Mike said. "Haven't you wondered about it even once?"

"No," Tom said. "I think I know his side." He took a drink of his coffee and set the cup on the table. "I think he meant to leave town with Mary, and that she didn't want to go."

"But you might be wrong," Mike said.

"Because he thought Mary still loved him," Carolyn said emotionally. "Because Mary hadn't quit yet."

"No," Tom said. "Because that's what he wanted to think."

Mike heard his mother exhale, or sigh. Her shoulders dropped as she leaned back in her chair.

"Do you remember my saying that Mary Hise had a boyfriend?" Tom asked.

"No," Carolyn said.

That was information Tom had given Mike the day they went to Mary Hise's apartment. Mike sat nervously and quietly, afraid that DeWitt would tell his mother that.

"We just found him in Idaho," Tom said. "He used to stop by Glenn's office when Mary was first working there. Glenn would tell her to stay away from him. Mary and the boyfriend fought a lot, apparently. Even Mary's neighbor said that. She said that the fights were pretty bad. You don't remember Glenn saying anything about him?"

"No," Carolyn said.

"He was here in May," Tom said. "He was sixty miles away the afternoon she was killed, but he and Mary had a date that night. The night she died. We just learned that. That was probably what the dress was for."

"That's a sad detail," Carolyn said.

"It is," Tom said, looking at Mike. "It makes you realize the things she'll never have. Children. A wedding and so forth. The boyfriend said he wanted to marry her."

"He was near Wheatley the same day she was killed?"

Mike said, hopeful in spite of himself. He was thinking that it was too big a coincidence not to matter. His father used to say that about mystery movies, that you could figure out who did it as soon as you saw a coincidence.

"We just learned that," Tom said a second time.

"And they fought a lot, right?" Mike said. "What about that? Dad might have been trying to protect her from him."

"Is that something your father would have done?"

Mike knew, then, that he'd let himself be tricked again.

"Yes," his mother said. "That would be just like him."

"Some men feel that very strongly," Tom said. "They exaggerate the harm somebody else could do. They underestimate the harm they themselves could do. They see themselves as heroes."

"How do you know how he sees himself?" Mike said.

"How do you think he saw himself that afternoon?" Tom asked.

"I don't know. I just said that you can never know."

"Take a guess."

"No," Mike said.

"Why not?"

"You know why not."

"I don't," Tom said. "I'm not a mind reader."

"Then don't ask *me* to be one," Mike said.

His mother stood up, suddenly, her chair scraping the concrete. "It doesn't matter," she said. "Nothing changes the fact that he killed her."

The conversation was over, and no one spoke. After a

minute Tom stood up as well. "One thing I feel bad about," he said. "I'm always bringing bad news."

"You can't help that," Carolyn said. "You're just keeping us informed."

"Maybe I shouldn't be."

"No," Carolyn told him. "I'd rather know than not know." She didn't consult or even glance at Mike.

Tom reached in his pocket for his car keys. "I'm heading up to my cabin tonight," he said. "I thought I'd stay there for a few days. I could use some time off." He looked down at Mike. "Do you like to fish?" he asked.

"No," Mike said.

"Well, you'd like it there, anyway. I'd bet on that."

Then he was gone. Mike didn't have enough energy to move, let alone go inside and find aspirin or go upstairs to lie down. And his mother was looking at him seriously, worriedly.

"That was a terrible thing for your father to say," she told him. "About the illness."

"It was just a story," Mike said. "We don't even know if he said it."

"I think he did. Couldn't you see that it bothered Tom to tell us?"

"You're not smart about him," Mike told her. "You don't see what he's up to."

"He wants to find your father," she said sternly. "I don't hold that against him."

"You don't hold anything against him," Mike said.

"What does that mean?"

Mike hesitated. "He wants us to see Dad the way that he does," he said then. "He thinks that we might know things."

"Like what? What could we possibly know?"

"Anything. He probably isn't sure what."

"You read too much into him," Carolyn said. "You're giving him intentions that he doesn't have."

"How do you know?"

"Because I listen to what he says, the same way you do." She stood there for a moment, watching Mike. Then, to his relief, she went into the house.

Mike blew out the candles and sat in the darkness, tired, hurting, and feeling ashamed, as if he'd invented his father's lie himself. It seemed to him that he was connected now to the death of somebody else, somebody he didn't even know—Wylene Moseley's child.

He heard a car pull up then and dreaded that it was DeWitt again, up to something else. But it was Josh, carrying a backpack, who walked up the driveway.

"Can I stay here tonight?" he asked Mike. He dropped his pack and slumped into a chair. "Duane King's been sending my mother flowers and shit. I said, 'You take him to court and then forgive him a week later? Are you crazy?' " In the house, a few minutes later, he said to Mike's mother, "Could you call her sometime and see if she's okay?" Then he went outside alone and sat in the grass under the crab-apple tree.

"Give him a little time out there," Carolyn said to Mike, who would have anyway, who knew Josh better than anyone did. He took two aspirin and watched his mother clean off the counters and the stove and sweep the floor. Finally he got out a Coke and took it out to Josh in the yard.

"Hey," Josh said. Mike sat under the tree with him. After a while Josh said, "I was so pissed at my mom that I felt like hitting her myself. How's that for fucked?"

"But you didn't do it," Mike said.

"I wanted to, though."

"Wanting doesn't count."

Josh drank his Coke as he and Mike watched old Clyde Pate, next door, come out to his back porch and sit down heavily on his porch swing. His wife had died the year before; Mike and his parents had gone to the funeral and brought food over afterward. "I feel so sorry for him," Mike's mother had said. "I feel sorry for anyone that alone."

Now Mike's mother was coming outside, crossing the lawn, bringing Mike and Josh each a bowl of ice cream. "I used to do this when you two were small," she said. "You probably don't remember."

"I do," Josh said.

She surprised Mike by sitting with them in the grass. She started talking about how soon it would be fall, and how they would be in college, leading their own independent lives. She told them about her own freshman year—how hard it was to leave home, yet what a relief it was to be away. "Some girls called their parents every night," she said. "I called once a week because I thought I should. I don't know what I thought would happen if I didn't."

"Why didn't you wait for them to call you?" Josh asked.

She seemed never to have thought of that. "Who knows?" she said. "Who knows why you do anything at that age?"

She picked up their empty bowls and crossed the yard to the kitchen—her old self again, Mike thought, though his mind was not on her but on his father. As the sky grew overcast and the night windy, he told Josh about Wylene Moseley, and about how his father had said he was sick. "Well, not me, exactly," Mike said. "This imaginary kid he made up, who was thirteen."

"Well, you were thirteen once," Josh said.

Mike's mother opened the back door and called to Josh. "Your mother's on the phone," she said. "Mr. King isn't there. She said to tell you that."

Josh went inside. Mike could see him standing in the middle of the kitchen, holding the receiver. Then Josh hung up and didn't come back out. Mike picked up his backpack and went inside. Upstairs, in the guest room, Josh was sitting alone in the dark.

"What's going on?" Mike said.

"Just more of the same shit. My mother thinks people are really sorry when they say they are. That's so fucking dense."

"Does she want you to come home?"

"I said I'd come by in the morning, before I left for Sheridan." He got up to look out the window. His mother's house was not far away; Mike could see the roof of it in the winter, when the trees were bare. "I wonder where old Glenn is right now," Josh said. "Like right at this instant."

"Some motel somewhere."

"Or somebody's house," Josh said. "Some other woman who believes his bullshit." He opened his backpack. "Can I smoke in here?"

Mike closed the door, got a window fan from the closet, and took one of Josh's cigarettes for himself.

"You shouldn't smoke with your illness," Josh said. "Plus, you're only thirteen."

"On the other hand, I already have cancer."

They laughed. After a while Mike went downstairs to smuggle a bottle of Jack Daniels out of the liquor cabinet. His mother was occupied with the news on television, though later she stopped outside the guest room on her way to bed.

"Don't stay up all night," she told them through the closed door.

"We won't," they said.

Mike sat on the bed, listening to Josh talk about Sheridan, Wyoming, and the Big Horn Mountains. "I backpacked up there one weekend," he told Mike. "I didn't want to come down. I thought, fuck everything."

"Fuck Pam," Mike said.

"Definitely fuck Pam."

Over the whir of the fan Mike could hear the wind rising again outside.

"The duplex we live in is at the edge of town," Josh said. "It's near the foot of the mountains. I can look out my window and see deer in the field behind us."

"I'm surprised they come so close."

"They have less to be afraid of there. You can't hunt that close to town."

"Still," Mike said.

Josh lit another cigarette. He was on the floor, leaning back against the closet. "Our duplex is kind of shabby," he told Mike. "The walls are thin. You can hear every sound."

"Like your dad with women?"

"No," Josh said. "Like him talking in his sleep. My mother's name and that."

"He hasn't met anybody else?"

"He has," Josh said, "but nobody he likes much. Nobody he wants to fuck, anyway." He tapped his cigarette ash into his hand. "I don't think he's trying very hard."

A tree branch brushed against the house. From where Mike was sitting he could see the brightness of the moon behind a veil of clouds. "The weather's changing," he said. "Maybe it won't be so hot tomorrow."

"Maybe not," Josh said. Mike handed him the Jack Daniels, and he shook his head. "I'm not feeling it. I only get drunk when I'm trying not to." He put out his cigarette and got a book out of his backpack: *Sheep,* by Archer Gilfillan.

"What's that about?" Mike asked. "I mean, what about sheep?"

"He herded them," Josh said. "That's what he did for eighteen years."

It was after midnight. Mike returned the bottle to the liquor cabinet, made sure the front and back doors were locked, and went up to his room. In bed, too drunk to think clearly about either his father or Tom DeWitt, he thought about Pam—how she'd looked that night at the lake, and how she'd sounded in the backseat of Josh's car. Mike could probably fuck her if he wanted to. She wouldn't tell anyone. She wouldn't want to hurt Donetta. She'd do it because she liked Mike; they liked each other. They'd fuck and then they'd probably stop being friends. But not because she wouldn't have liked it.

He fell asleep, then woke from a bad dream. He'd been in an ambulance, too sick to move or talk. It had seemed so real that Mike got out of bed now just to prove to himself that he could. It was raining outside, and he looked across the street at the Hylers' run-down house. It was haunted-looking in the rain. It was a depressing thing to see. It probably wasn't fixable even anymore. It took Mike three hours to fall back asleep.

THIRTEEN

SCHOOL, suddenly, was only three weeks away. It had crept up on Mike, despite his mother's reminders. He'd stopped thinking about the future. His life had changed too much.

"I think I should stay home this fall," he said to his mother in the kitchen, early Sunday morning. "I'll work at the Schofields' and go to school next semester."

"Absolutely not," his mother said. "There's nothing worse than standing in one place, or going backwards."

"I couldn't go backwards if I tried."

But she refused to talk to him about it further. She left for church, and he went upstairs and stood in the doorway to the guest room, which had become a depository for items he would take to school, things his mother had been buying that Mike hadn't thought of even: a phone machine, a clock radio, a throw rug, a desk lamp. He'd been watching those things accumulate without feeling as if they were his. He closed the door now, so that he could walk down the hall without having to see them.

By the time his mother returned from church, he was down in the basement, cleaning the storm windows with vinegar and water. The temperature had dropped down to fifty during the night, the first sign of autumn. Cleaning and putting up the storm windows had been Mike's job since he was fourteen—his father had only supervised.

His mother came halfway down the rough basement steps in her dress and high heels. She sat down and watched him.

"You'll get dirty sitting there," he said.

"This dress is washable. Don't you want company?"

No, he thought. "Sure. Whatever."

"My students use that word," she told him. "I don't know where they get it from."

"Everybody says it."

"People your age, maybe," she said, no longer looking at Mike but at the boxes of his father's belongings, stacked in the right-hand corner of the basement. "I don't think this will come as a surprise," she told Mike. "But I want you to know. I've talked to a lawyer about divorcing your father."

Mike stopped working. "When?" he said.

"As soon as possible."

"I mean, when did you talk to a lawyer?"

"Two weeks ago."

Mike looked at the storm windows he hadn't washed yet—that probably wouldn't get washed, he thought, if it weren't for him. "Why do I have to learn about things after they happen?" he said. "Why can't you just tell me at the time?"

"Nothing's happened yet. And what should I do, ask your opinion? What kind of parent would I be if I put you in that position?"

"I'd just like to know what's going on," Mike said. "You don't have to get so pissed off."

"Don't use that phrase with me."

"Why not?"

"Because you should show more respect. Who do you think is taking care of you?"

"Nobody's making you do it."

"Who would be if I weren't?" his mother said.

"Me," Mike said. "I do it anyway." He put down his rag and walked past her up the steps. "I can't wait to get out of here," he shouted. He went out the kitchen door, slamming it behind him.

Outside, without his jacket or helmet, he got on his motorcycle and rode through town to Route 8, then out past the Schofield ranch in the direction of Badlands National Park. It was the only place he could think of to go, the only place that was far enough away and uninhabited enough to suit him. It was uninhabited by people, anyway. And it didn't cheer him up to know that he would be leaving

Wheatley in three weeks. Leaving didn't seem as if it would fix what was wrong.

It was a long ride. The wind was cool and the sun hot, and there was the lightness of not wearing a helmet. He rode through the Pine Ridge Indian Reservation, thinking that if he were in a car he could be listening to Indian music broadcast from Pine Ridge or Rosebud. Kids in town made fun of it—not Mike's friends, but assholes who didn't understand that you might want to hear something new or different, or that your own life might not be always what it was now.

Because you had to be ready for your life to change, even if you didn't want it to. The important thing, Mike thought, was being prepared for the next thing that happened—like his mother getting a divorce now that it no longer meant or solved anything, as opposed to a year ago, or six months ago, when it could have saved his father from killing Mary Hise. Mary could have quit work when she'd wanted to. She would not have had to see either one of Mike's parents again. She'd gotten caught between the two of them. Being unhappy made people do dangerous things.

Mike passed an old red Chevy driven at a crawl by an old man. And suddenly he just felt bleak, even though he could see, finally, the Badlands in the distance, the jagged edges of the jagged rocks, rising from the plains like dinosaurs.

He pulled off the road. He looked at the blank, blue sky, pulled back on the road in the opposite direction, and didn't stop until he got to the Schofield ranch.

. . .

LEE-ANN was the only one home. As he walked up to the house, she came to the door in jeans and a sweater. "Neil's out at Ed's," she said. "He didn't say you were working today."

"I'm not here to work. I was just out riding."

She watched him from the doorway. It was hard for him to read her expression. "Come on in," she said.

Mike followed her into the living room, where the shades were drawn. There was an unfolded blanket on the couch.

"Where's Janna?" he asked.

"With Neil," she told him. "Sit down. Do you want a Coke?"

"No. I'm sorry I woke you up."

"It's okay." She sat down and looked at him closely. "What's wrong?" Out of nervousness he picked up the blanket and folded it. "You don't have to do that," she said. "You don't have to be so conscientious all the time."

Mike dropped it on the carpet.

"That's a small first step," she told him.

They sat there without speaking. The house was cold. The last time he'd been inside was when they'd kissed and he'd gotten sick, or whatever it was that had happened to him. He thought about saying, I'm leaving for college in three weeks. He thought about telling her that his mother was getting a divorce. Both things seemed wrong. The house had the same feeling it had had that afternoon in

May, when he'd come in alone and gone upstairs. He felt like he'd become less grown-up, over the summer, less sure of himself. He wanted to tell Lee-Ann what he'd done that day, so that she could see how unafraid he used to be. He reached for her hand.

"Listen," she said. "I'm glad to see you. But one minute it's like you're my son, and the next minute you're like my high school boyfriend or something. It's creepy."

"Thanks," Mike said. "That makes me feel like an asshole." He got up to leave and tripped over the blanket, falling against the couch. It was too clumsy not to be funny, and they both smiled.

"Sit down," Lee-Ann said. "It's my fault, too. It's probably more my fault than yours."

"There is no fault."

"I just want to be a friend to you," Lee-Ann told him. "I know you think you don't need it. But I'm a safe person for you."

"I don't know what you mean by safe," Mike said.

"I want what's best for you. And I'm not in a position to hurt you."

"I know. That's why it would be okay."

"It?" Lee-Ann said.

"You know," Mike said.

"I don't think that's what you need."

"How do you know what I need?"

"Well, I'm older than you."

"I forget that you're so old," Mike said. "You could be my grandmother, right?"

"Not quite."

"Listen," Mike said. "You don't feel the way you used to, I guess. That's okay. I mean, I can't change that."

Lee-Ann fingered the hem of her sweater. "I didn't say that exactly."

"So what are you saying?"

"It's complicated. I think one thing and feel another."

"So you should go with your feeling," Mike said.

"Why?"

"Because it's the same as mine. And because I'm leaving, and I won't see you for a long time."

"I've thought about that," Lee-Ann said pensively.

The grandfather clock in the hallway chimed three times. In the stillness afterward, Mike moved close to her, put his arm around her, and kissed her. That was all he anticipated doing, to make up for last time. But when she didn't pull away, he kept his mouth on hers, and when he put his hand under her sweater she suddenly was responding to him as if she'd been waiting for this as long as he had. She was passionate and in a hurry. She interrupted their kissing only to take off her sweater and undo her bra as Mike pulled off his T-shirt. Her breasts were against his bare chest, and she moved his mouth down to her nipples, to one and then the other. "Take off your jeans," she whispered then, and took off her own while he removed his.

Then they were naked, Mike on top of her on the couch, almost inside of her, when she just stopped.

"Wait," she said. "I can't do this."

"Come on," Mike whispered. "It's okay."

"It's not okay."

"Lee-Ann," Mike said, but she was disentangling herself, then sitting up, looking for her clothes.

"I'm sorry," she told him. She put on her underwear and sweater and stood up to pull on her jeans. Mike still had an erection, and he dressed with his back to her. He stood in the middle of the dim living room, barefoot. He hadn't found his socks.

"I'm really sorry," Lee-Ann said. "You're never going to forgive me, are you?"

"Not anytime soon."

Mike sat in a chair, away from her. There was no way to get her body out of his mind. He watched her search under the couch for his socks. She handed them to him. "Are you okay?" she said.

"Why wouldn't I be?"

She sat down, too, her face still flushed. "When I was in the ninth grade," she told him, "in health class, they warned us about boys and their hormones. They said, 'Never put your hand in a boy's pocket.' I didn't understand why. I thought the boys would think we were trying to steal their money."

"You probably *were* trying to steal their money," Mike

said. He rested his head back against the chair and breathed deeply.

"I'm sorry," Lee-Ann said.

"I know. Stop saying that."

"I want to be good for you," she told him.

"You were doing a great job," Mike said.

"I mean without that. Because what I thought I could do, I can't."

"Okay."

She straightened out the couch cushions and folded the blanket. "It's not just Neil," she told him. "It's you, too."

"That's not a compliment," Mike said.

"You know what I mean. Your whole life got disrupted overnight. You've had this horrible summer."

"You were making it a lot better."

"Not in the long run, though. Even though it was really nice," she added, blushing, which made Mike feel somewhat okay. He tried to stop thinking about her breasts, and how she'd felt underneath him. He'd think about those things later, when he was alone.

They ended up in the kitchen, which was so familiar to Mike, and they sat at the table, looking out at the bright, cool afternoon. "I got pissed off at my mother today," Mike admitted then. "I just took off."

"Without your helmet," Lee-Ann said. "I noticed that. You should call her, tell her you're all right."

"Fuck her," Mike said, but then he got up and did it.

"I'm at the Schofields'," he told her, and, "Okay. I'll wear it next time. I'll see you in a while."

After that, more openly, he told Lee-Ann about his mother seeing a lawyer, and about Tom DeWitt trying to trip him up. "It's me he's always trying to get to. It's like he thinks I know something, like my father contacts me somehow. I can't trust him."

"You don't trust most people."

"I'd be stupid to."

"So you'd be stupid sometimes," Lee-Ann said. "So what?"

"I don't want people to see me that way."

"People are going to see you however they see you," she told him. "You have to separate people you can trust from people you can't. I'm in the first category," she told him. "No matter what."

It was after five. Outside the sun was illuminating the roof of the barn and the white fence along the road, and Lee-Ann began to make dinner. Mike set the table for her and helped her mash potatoes. Then he said, "I guess I should leave before Neil gets home."

They looked at each other.

"Either way is okay," Lee-Ann said. "He won't think anything of your being here." Her face flushed. "I'll remember it, though," which gave Mike another erection.

He stayed a little longer, and before he left they said good-bye without touching. She waved to him, from the window, as he got on his bike. Riding down the driveway, he didn't feel anything extreme—just really relieved that he'd shown her what he could be like sexually. That was the important part. Otherwise he'd be feeling awful about himself.

LATE that night, he had a dream that was four months back in time. It was May, school was in session, and Mike had killed Kyle DeWitt in a wrestling match.

Awake, Mike had trouble remembering what month it was now. It took him a full few minutes to figure it out. The divorce thing had put him over the edge, he decided.

He focused on Lee-Ann. The places she wasn't perfect excited him most—the soft swelling of her stomach, her slightly fallen breasts. And he liked her white skin, which made her seem more naked than naked. Getting an erection made him forget his bad dream. What he liked was to imagine somebody and masturbate, so that how he felt wouldn't depend on anyone except himself.

FOURTEEN

"I remind myself every morning that he's going," Donetta said to Mike's mother one afternoon three days before Mike was to leave for college. He was in his room, packing, and his mother and Donetta were on the stairs, carrying down boxes from the guest room. "If I keep reminding myself, I won't be so dramatic about it when he leaves."

"What do you mean?" Mike's mother asked.

"I'm not sure," Donetta said. "It's what my mother says I do."

Then they were downstairs, and outside, and Mike couldn't hear them anymore. From his window, he saw them standing in the driveway next to his new used pickup—a 1991 dark blue Ford Ranger Mike and his mother had bought the week before, with money Mike had saved and part of his mother's summer salary. He was taking his motorcycle, too, against his mother's wishes. They'd fought about it for a week. "I'm not going without it," Mike had said finally, that morning. "I don't care what you say," and he'd walked out of the room. They'd also fought about whether or not she should go with him to Brookings and help him settle in. She'd wanted to drive there with him, then fly back from Sioux Falls. "Are you kidding?" Mike had said, which had caused more trouble. Later he'd said, "I want to do this on my own." That was the kind of decision she respected.

A warm wind was coming in through Mike's window. Low clouds were moving east—toward Brookings, Mike thought, trying to make college seem more real. From his window he watched Donetta, in jeans and a tank top, lean over to tie her shoe. She had a pretty butt; that's all he was thinking, and suddenly he was looking at her through tears.

On the floor was a suitcase half filled with clothes, and another, empty one. Dust had gathered under his desk and bed; he hadn't cleaned his room lately, despite his mother asking him to. There was disorder in your life and then disorder in yourself; he'd read that somewhere. Anyway, it reminded him of his father, who probably had never in his life done the same thing in the same way two mornings in a row. He always threw a wrench in it somehow—like dropping his toothbrush in the toilet or knocking spices out of a cupboard in his effort to reach a coffee filter. "Why do you keep these shelves so crowded?" he'd yell at Mike's mother, and she'd say, "Grow up, Glenn." Then Mike's father would realize what a fool he looked like, and get in a worse mood. Meanwhile, Mike, sitting at the kitchen table, would keep eating his breakfast.

Outside now, Donetta was across the street, talking to Mrs. Hyler. The Hylers had eight cats. In the mornings Mrs. Hyler would be out on the porch, feeding them. Some were allowed in the house and some weren't; Donetta was always trying to learn which cats were the inside ones and which were the outside ones, and what determined which cats were which. "Do you think they can change categories?" Donetta would say to Mike. "Or do you think the outside cats can never be good enough to get inside?"

He watched her walk back to the street, turn around to wave good-bye, and come across the lawn, the wind lifting her hair. He listened to her running up the stairs. She had to leave, he knew; she was working the dinner shift at the diner.

"Mike?" she said, out of breath. "I have to get there early, to change into my uniform. I always hate for you to see me in it."

"You look good in it," he said. "You look good in everything."

"Do you really think that?" She put her arms around his neck. "Not that it matters, how you look. I know it doesn't."

She kissed him, and he pulled her close. But then they heard his mother come into the house. "I've got to go," Donetta told Mike. "I wish I didn't."

He went with her downstairs and walked her to her car; on the passenger seat of her Geo was a letter addressed to him at his dormitory address in Brookings. "You weren't supposed to see that," Donetta said. "It's so you'll get mail your first day there." Then she was in her car, driving off; he stood in the street until she rounded the corner. Then he walked across the yard, stooping under the low branches of the oak tree.

LATE in the afternoon, he and his mother got into his mother's car, with Mike driving, and left for Tom DeWitt's cabin in the Black Hills. Agreeing to go was Mike's way of compensating for the motorcycle argument. His mother was still angry at him. He could feel it in everything she said and did, even in the way she sat—too stiffly straight and close to the door. She had on new jeans and a light blue shirt and had taken a longer time than usual to get ready. She'd brought a dessert, covered with tinfoil, which she was holding on her lap.

"What's that for?" Mike asked.

"It's polite to bring something."

"What is it?"

"Coffee cake."

Mike stopped trying to make conversation. He took the more interesting way to Lead, through the National Forest, driving through Hill City and Silver City. He and Josh used to come up this way sometimes on Saturdays. They'd go to Deadwood to make fun of the tourists, or else they'd hang out in the cemetery above the town. Josh liked Wild Bill Hickok's grave. "Pard, we will meet again," Josh used to say at school, when he'd pass Mike in the hall. That was part of the sentence on Bill Hickok's gravestone, followed by GOODBYE, in a comma-shaped drawing.

Mike would walk through the highest, steepest section of the cemetery, where children were buried. It seemed spooky to him, how dangerous just being a child used to be. It would make your life a more intense thing, he'd think, as he stood there among the faded headstones, looking down at the strip-mined hills and the town screwed up with small casinos made to look like old-fashioned saloons. Sometimes you'd see a school bus go down that street, full of ordinary kids trying to grow up in a fucked-up place.

"Don't forget to give me whatever clothes you need washed," Mike's mother said. "I don't want to be doing laundry at the last minute."

He nodded, hardly listening.

"Make a list of things you haven't done yet," she told him. "That's the only way you'll remember."

As they got closer, she read him directions: left near a ranger station, then past a log cabin. The sun was getting low, and they were on a winding road with pines on one side and Elk Creek on the other. "Turn here," his mother said at a dirt road that led uphill. A quarter of a mile through the woods was a small frame house with Tom DeWitt's car parked next to it. The door opened, and he came outside.

"I'm sorry we didn't get here earlier," Carolyn said. "We've been getting Mike ready for school."

"That sounds like I'm in the first grade," Mike said.

"No, it doesn't." She turned her back on him, and he heard the way she sucked in her breath. Give it up, Mike wanted to say to her. Stop being an asshole. He walked inside behind her.

"I can show you around in under two minutes," Tom said, and walked them through the main room, which had a rustic kitchen at one end and a living room at the other, with a wood burner in the middle. The walls were pine, stained dark. Down the hall was a small bathroom and bedroom, the bed made up with a red wool blanket. Also in the bedroom were a phone, an answering machine, and a tiny television. "I don't completely rough it," he said, "as you can see."

"When you find my dad," Mike told him, "you'll be able to see yourself on television."

"Why would you say something like that?" his mother said.

"Look," Tom said. "If I wanted a movie career, I'd go to Hollywood. It's not like I haven't had offers." When neither Mike nor Carolyn laughed, he said, "I'm kidding. It's a joke."

He led them into the living room and brought them beers. "I assume it's all right for Mike to have one?" he asked, and handed it to Mike before his mother had a chance to answer.

"I want to look around outside," Mike said abruptly. He walked out on the porch, then down past the cars into the cool, dark shadows of the pines. Behind him, he heard the door open.

"Mike?" his mother said.

He didn't speak or move. After a minute she went inside, and he walked down the hill and along Elk Creek, which was wide and shallow, though its banks were steep. He stood in the gathering dusk, drinking the beer he didn't want much, tired of his mother, tired of whatever attempts Tom DeWitt would make tonight to manipulate him or whatever it was he always did. His mother was a fool where DeWitt was concerned. Mike's father used to say, "Your mother wants to believe that people are better than they are," and he also had been right about how controlling she was, and what it did to you after a while.

Mike watched the creek for muskrats or beaver. The temperature was lower here, as it always was in the Hills. Before long, Mike thought, there would be the first frost—maybe not right here but farther south and higher up, toward Harney Peak. It would snow there then, and you could go from fall to winter just by driving out of Wheatley up to Hill City. It wasn't far, though the roads were twisting and narrow, and coming back down into Wheatley you'd have long views again of long grass, which would seem almost liquid, put in motion by the wind blowing through them.

Those were just his thoughts, and all at once he was overcome with homesickness and uncertainty. He felt lost somehow, even from himself, and it was hard for him to take a breath. The ground under him seemed unsubstantial, and the way he felt was nothing he could find words for; maybe it was like dying, he thought, and for a second he almost believed that he was, though he didn't know of what, or what had made it happen. It was like being caught high in the air, like in a flying dream, except that you couldn't fly. You couldn't even fall. And there were no stars or planets above you, or earth beneath you.

Then, as suddenly as the fears had come, they faded, and within a few minutes Mike found himself paying attention again to the creek, and to the night sounds in the growing darkness. The tightness inside him went away. It went below ground, somehow. Mike stood in the dusk, listening to the creek, and didn't turn around and walk back until he started feeling angry again—at his mother, particularly, for causing him to feel so bad.

When he entered the house, Tom said, "There's more beer in the refrigerator. Help yourself."

"One is plenty," Carolyn said, which was the only reason Mike helped himself to a second one. He stood near the wood burner, while his mother and Tom DeWitt sat at opposite ends of the couch.

"Are you ready for school to start?" Tom asked Carolyn.

"Yes," she said at first. Then, "I don't know. I suppose so."

"You teachers should get paid more," he said. "I don't know how you do it, spending every day with kids who'd rather be someplace else."

"Some of the students want to be there," Carolyn said.

"No, they don't," Mike said. "Not in a class, anyway."

"So now I'm a bad teacher."

"He didn't say that," Tom said.

Carolyn put down her beer and stood up. "Excuse me," she said, and walked down the dark hall to the bathroom.

"You don't have to defend me," Mike said to Tom.

"Sit down."

"Why?"

"Because it hurts my neck to look up. And I want to tell you something." He got a card out of his pocket and handed it to Mike. There were three phone numbers on it. "When your father contacts you at school," he said, "I want you to call me."

Mike's head began to hurt. "How do you know he will?" he said.

"I don't. I just think it's going to happen."

"Then where is he now?" Mike said.

"I'm not sure."

The bathroom door opened, and Tom stood up when Carolyn walked into the room. "I spoke out of turn," he told her. "I'm sorry. I have a tendency to do that."

"That makes two of us," she said. She turned to Mike. "I didn't mean to jump on you, either."

Mike was too distracted to reply. He was thinking about

how he'd get rid of Tom's card later, throwing it away someplace his mother wouldn't find it. Meanwhile, he put it in his pocket.

THEY had dinner at the small kitchen table. Tom had made chili, which Carolyn made a fuss over. "Don't give me too much credit," he told her. "It's mostly out of a can. But I'm glad you like it."

He was smiling at her, helping her to more, and for the first time Mike thought that Tom seemed less sure of himself—maybe even nervous. He did most of the talking. He told them about seeing a mountain lion a few weeks earlier, and about how many more coyotes there were around than people thought, and how much more Mike's mother must know about science than he did, given that she taught biology. Then the phone rang, and he went into the bedroom to answer it.

"That's why he keeps it in the bedroom," Mike said to his mother. "So that he can talk in private."

"Don't be paranoid. How much company do you think he gets?"

"What I'm saying is, he's always working. Even when you think he's not."

"Mike," his mother said hesitantly. "Are you jealous that he seems to like me?"

No, he started to say. Then he realized how useless it could be to tell the truth, to think that you weren't alone, on your own, in every situation. "Maybe I am," he told her. "Maybe that's right."

She smiled at him for the first time in a week. "That's only natural," she said gently.

When Tom DeWitt came back to the table, they finished their chili. They ate the coffee cake.

FIFTEEN

MIKE wasn't sure where to take Donetta for their last night together. If they went to Crow Lake, she'd know he wanted to have sex with her. If he didn't take her there, she might think he didn't care about having sex with her. He was overly preoccupied with it, and with other things as well, especially saying good-bye to Lee-Ann. He wanted to make exactly the right impression—confident but not arrogant, easygoing but not immature. Whatever he was like today would be what she would remember, he thought. He didn't always realize that there was latitude with people, built-up stock, that most people didn't think you were only what you were on any one day.

He drove to the Schofields' early in the morning, the day before he was to leave. The sun had just risen, and there were antelope in the low hills above the Schofields' property. Near the barn, next to the old lean-to Neil had bought, Neil and Ed were at work on a new project: an old jailhouse they had bought and moved there from Montana. "So we can arrest each other," Neil joked to Mike. Then he said, "Shit," and hit himself in the forehead.

"It's okay," Mike said. "I wish everybody would forget about it like that."

Neil and Ed admired his new truck—it was the first time they had seen it—and gave him advice about college.

"Wear condoms," Ed said.

"Only go to class if there's nothing better to do," Neil told him. "I mean it. Have fun sometimes." He put an arm over Mike's shoulders. "Say good-bye to Lee-Ann, or she'll never forgive you. She has something for you."

Lee-Ann was waiting for him at the open kitchen door. Behind her, Janna was in her high chair, eating Cheerios; Mike sat next to her. On the table in front of him were five stamped envelopes, addressed to Lee-Ann. "So you won't have an excuse not to write," she told him. She was barefoot, dressed in shorts and a loose shirt, her soft hair uncombed. She handed him a greeting card, which said, "Good luck in your new life from your friends in your old life." Inside was a check for five hundred dollars.

"I can't take this," Mike said.

"Force yourself. It's for extras, like movies and pizza. Or maybe a trip home some weekend." She got coffee for herself and Mike. "Are you excited about going?" she asked him. "Or are you nervous?"

"Neither. It's just school."

"Four hundred miles away, though."

"It's only a day's drive."

Lee-Ann looked at him thoughtfully.

"What?" Mike said.

"Going away to college is a big deal," she told him.

"Not to me."

"Well, it should be," Lee-Ann said.

"It doesn't seem important," Mike said, "compared to everything else."

"You have to make it important."

"I'd rather stay here," Mike said, and when Lee-Ann looked startled, he explained, "I mean in Wheatley."

They sat silently in the sunny kitchen, Janna smiling between them. Mike looked at the white-tiled floor and the shiny appliances, and the hallway leading to the living room. He could see in his mind exactly how Lee-Ann had looked, naked, on the couch, but equally vivid was the afternoon in the barn when he'd held her. That had grown in significance. He knew that neither of those things would happen again.

"It's going to be lonely, not seeing you," Lee-Ann said.

"I know. It will be for me, too." Mike turned to Janna so that Lee-Ann couldn't see how sad he was. "What about you?" he said. "Are you going to miss me?" Janna took a Cheerio out of her mouth and offered it to Mike. "That's what I thought," he said.

Before he left, he and Lee-Ann hugged, as friends, without kissing and without intensity, and Mike felt fine until Lee-Ann hugged him longer than he'd expected her to. He didn't know why that affected him so strongly, why that, more than anything else, seemed to divide his life in Wheatley so definitively and permanently from the life he would have from tomorrow on.

"You have to come see us whenever you're home," Lee-Ann said, and Mike thought: I feel like I'm never going to come back home.

"You know I will," he said.

She walked him outside into the warm sun. Then he was on his own, waving to Neil and Ed from a distance, starting his truck, and heading down the long driveway. It was when he got to Route 8 that he knew he couldn't face Wheatley. He needed to be alone someplace.

He drove to Hot Springs, then up into the Black Hills all the way to Custer. His windows were down. The road was crisscrossed with strips of sun and shadow, and the hills were green and dark with pines. He felt better now that he was alone in his truck, concentrating on driving.

Still, returning later to Wheatley, he could not think about Lee-Ann Schofield. It was like having a toothache, or a cut too tender to touch. She got to him somehow. She knew him too well. She didn't allow him to keep his defenses up.

• • •

LATER in the day he finished packing: his books, his computer, his school supplies. He mowed the yard one last time and had a steak supper with his mother in the dining room—a celebratory supper, she said. "We're going to leave the past behind," she told him. "That's where it belongs, doesn't it? The past belongs in the past."

"I guess so," Mike said. He wasn't hungry, but he ate to please her.

"If Tom comes by with new information," his mother said to him, "I'll let you know only if it's something significant. I don't want you distracted from school."

"He'll probably let me know himself," Mike said, to see if she knew more than he thought she did.

"Of course he won't. He wouldn't do that without telling me first."

Mike said nothing. On the wall above where she sat was a square blank space where a picture of their family used to hang: Mike at age ten, with his parents standing behind him. He hadn't remembered his mother taking it down. He was noticing only now that it was gone.

His mother cleared the table and brought in, as a surprise, a chocolate bakery cake with GOOD LUCK, MIKE written on it. Mike, cutting them each a big piece, tried to act happy.

HE drove through Wheatley just as the streetlights were coming on. It was a windy night, and the streets were empty except for a group of high school kids fooling around in the Taco John parking lot. Mike went out of his way not to drive past his father's office. He took a route past the hardware store and the community college, and as he turned onto Flat Rock Road the moon, rising behind him over town, looked impossibly big.

When he pulled into Donetta's driveway, he saw that the front door was wide open. Moreover, there was Cory Burris, walking up to it with a baby goat in his arms.

"It's okay," Cory called out. "She's just unconscious. She'll come to in a few hours."

"Not in this house she won't," Mrs. Rush said. Mike could see a tearful Margo behind her.

"Why would somebody give Wild Turkey to a baby?" Cory asked Mike. "Party or no party?"

"I have no idea," Mike said.

"Donetta's in the kitchen," Mrs. Rush told him, stepping aside to let Mike in, and Cory ran in right behind him. He lay the goat down in a cardboard box that Donetta was lining with towels. He and Margo hovered over it.

"She doesn't look good," Margo said.

"That's because she's dead," Mrs. Rush said from the front hall.

"Being negative is harmful," Margo told her mother. "How many times has Pastor Kelly said that?"

"Don't throw Pastor Kelly at me," Mrs. Rush said. "Dead

is dead. Furthermore, the goat isn't my fault. I wouldn't attend a party where people gave liquor to an animal."

"I was just passing by," Cory said defensively.

Next to Mike, Donetta knelt down, patted the goat's head, and burst into tears.

"For Pete's sake," Mrs. Rush said. She came into the room and put her hands on Donetta's shoulders. "Just calm down," she whispered. "Don't be like this on Mike's last night home."

IT was almost nine by the time they left for Crow Lake. It was Donetta's idea to go there. "I want to go someplace that seems like ours," she told him. "Someplace really private."

"We don't have to have sex," Mike said. "It's not like that's the only reason I see you."

Donetta had been sitting close to him, but she moved over now and looked out her window. Then she said, "That's not the only reason you *see* me? That's an egotistical thing to say. It's like you're doing me a favor. Or else it's like you see me and then who else do you see? Who else *will* you see?" she asked, correcting herself. Before Mike had a chance to answer, Donetta said, "I told myself I wouldn't do this. Pastor Kelly said it was self-destructive."

"You saw Pastor Kelly?"

"Just once," Donetta explained. "I went by myself. I didn't tell anyone."

"Why didn't you just talk to me?"

"Because it was about you," Donetta said. "It was about you with me, anyway."

"I guess you don't trust me very much," Mike said indignantly.

"I know," Donetta said. "That's what I talked to him about."

Mike's face reddened. He couldn't think of a response. After a minute he reached for her hand and held it as he drove. She didn't pull it away.

HE parked where they always did, a little distance from the lake, out of sight of the road. Donetta rolled down her window. In the darkness came the sound of wind through the trees. Mike waited for Donetta to say something. When she didn't, he touched her white dress. "Is this new?" he asked awkwardly. She nodded. "I like it," he told her. "It looks good on you."

"I ordered it from a catalogue. I got it for tonight." She turned her face toward the open window. "That's the kind of lovesick thing I do for you."

"That's not lovesick," Mike said. "I don't even know what that means."

"It's what you always say about me. Not that word, exactly, but that I think about you too much. Which is like saying, 'You think about me more than I think about you.' "

"Well, I was wrong," Mike said.

She got out of the car and walked down the dark path to the edge of the water. There was enough moonlight for Mike to see her, but he couldn't tell if she was crying. He felt depressed and defeated. He didn't know, anymore, what she thought, or how he came across to anyone.

He walked down to the water and stood beside her. "I'm not as bad as you think," he said.

"What does that mean? Like, 'I'm bad, but I could be worse'? Well, so could everybody." She crossed her arms. "I'm trying not to be stupid."

"You don't have to try. You're not."

"Stupid is when you love the wrong person," Donetta said.

He stepped back clumsily, and when Donetta saw his face she moved close to him. "I shouldn't have said that," she whispered. "I should have used different words." She put her arms around him. A car drove up on the other side of the lake, and they heard people get out. One of them said, "The water's cold."

"I've fucked up this night," Donetta said.

"No, you haven't."

"I think it started with the goat. I felt okay until then."

They walked back to the truck, holding hands. Mike opened the door for her, and they sat together on the wide front seat. The windows were open to the sounds of frogs and cicadas, wind and water. For Mike everything about Donetta suddenly seemed important—how she felt, what she thought, how this night would seem to her tomorrow.

"I wish I didn't have to go," he said.

"Do you really feel that way?"

"Yes."

She kissed him, and for a while that was all they did. Now that he was leaving so soon, he wasn't in a hurry. He wanted to delay time instead of speeding it up. Donetta was wearing only her dress and sandals, and she took them off while Mike was still dressed. It aroused him to see her naked when he wasn't, to see her smooth skin against the rough fabric of the seat. She unbuttoned his shirt as he undid his belt. She watched him as he took off his jeans.

They had sex on the front seat, Mike trying not to put too much weight on her. He held himself over her carefully and, after he had an orgasm, stayed inside her as long as he could. He looked down at her face and shoulders, aware as always of how small she was. And all at once he realized that if anyone was likely to hurt her, it would be him. Not physically—nothing like what his father had done—but in terms of her feelings, which was exactly what she'd been saying earlier.

Afterward he watched her put on her dress, reach for her purse, and brush her hair. He got out of the truck and looked at the dark woods, beyond which were fields; beyond the fields were the Black Hills, which he'd seen, in the distance, practically every day of his life. Beginning tomorrow he'd see something else—it didn't matter what. It wouldn't be as good or mean as much. It wouldn't make him remember specific moments in his life, such as this one. It wouldn't be home to him.

"What are you thinking about?" Donetta asked.

"You," he said, shivering as he said it.

ON the way home he made her put on her seat belt. "You should always wear it," he told her. "It should be the first thing you do when you get in the car."

"What about you, with your motorcycle helmet?" she said. "You never want to wear it."

"I do, though."

"Not all the time."

"Then I should. I will," he said. "Anyway, you have to be careful, especially because your car's so small. It's not that safe."

"Does that mean you love me?" Donetta asked.

"Yes." He took her hand and held it tightly.

After they turned onto Flat Rock Road, they both, at the same moment, spoke of the goat. Donetta said, "I hope the goat's alive," and Mike said, "The goat might be okay. Cory might have been right."

"He hardly ever is, though," Donetta said.

Mike pulled into her driveway. The house was dark except for the outside porch light and a light on in Donetta's room. Donetta got a tape cassette out of her purse and put it in his hand.

"I made this for you," she told him. "Don't listen to it until tomorrow, when you're on the highway. You have to promise."

"I promise," he said.

They embraced, her wet face against his shirt. "I'll still be in South Dakota," he told her. "I'll just be at the other end of it." He'd intended it to be funny, but it didn't sound funny. He didn't feel humorous. When Donetta moved in order to reach for a Kleenex, he didn't want to let her go.

It was one in the morning when he walked her up to the door. "If you fall in love with somebody," Donetta said, "tell me. Don't make me figure it out."

"I won't."

"Unless it's with me," she said, so softly that he didn't catch the words until she'd opened the door and gone inside. He stood there a minute, under the yellow porch light. Moths fluttered above his head, and from inside the house he heard Donetta's mother call her name.

He opened the door to his truck and could smell her perfume. He backed down the driveway, and on Flat Rock Road, before it curved to the west, he pulled over and got out. He stood on the shoulder of the road, looking back at her house. It was small from this distance, one of three with lights burning. There weren't all that many houses, anyway, and they were far apart, like stars, he thought, in what was mostly dark and vacant space. He knew which light was the light in Donetta's bedroom, and when it went out was when he really understood that he was leaving.

He drove home listening to the tape Donetta had made for him. The first thing on the cassette was her voice. "It's three o'clock in the morning," she said. "I can't sleep, I can't dream, and I can't stop thinking of you."

The first song was "Miss You," by the Rolling Stones.

SIXTEEN

SAYING good-bye to his mother was easier.

She got him up at seven and helped him finish loading his truck; she made him waffles as well as a lunch to take with him. She was dressed for church in a skirt so new it had a price tag hanging from it.

"You might want to take that part off," Mike told her, and she laughed and got out scissors.

"Do you think you'll miss this house?" she asked at breakfast. "It's the only place you've ever lived."

"Maybe," Mike said. He didn't add that he'd miss her.

"Did you sleep all right?" she asked then.

"Yes," he said, though he hadn't. He'd dreamed that somebody his own age was trying to run him down with a truck. Awake, then, he'd become nervous about ordinary sounds: the refrigerator starting up, downstairs; a car speeding down the street. By the time he had fallen back asleep, it was almost dawn.

"I'm going to keep tutoring at the college," his mother told him. "I'm helping Jim Reynolds on Tuesday nights. In fact," she added, "I'll probably see him at church this morning."

"He goes to Saint Ann's?"

"He just joined."

"Well, good for him," Mike said.

"Are you being sarcastic?" his mother asked. When he didn't answer she said, "Never mind. You say what you want." She drank her coffee. "Don't ever skip breakfast," she told him. "You can't think on an empty stomach."

"Who said I was going to think?" Mike said, and his mother smiled. It was probably the nicest moment between them all summer.

She walked out with him into the warm, sunless morning. They spoke for a few minutes, said their good-byes; soon after that he was heading east—driving away from his house, from Wheatley, and from the Black Hills. In front of him the sun emerged briefly, then withdrew into a bank of clouds.

PART II

BROOKINGS

SEVENTEEN

It was drizzling by the time Mike reached Brookings and found his dormitory, Hansen Hall. When he'd come to campus in October, with his parents, he hadn't known where he would live. He'd pictured one of the older, red-brick dorms in the center of campus. But Hansen Hall was at the western edge of the university, on Eleventh Street. It was a newer building, a rectangle four stories high, with a dimly lit lobby in the middle that separated the west wing from the east wing. Males west and females east, the desk clerk told him; she was an older student—older than Mike, anyway—studying an economics textbook. "Is there an elevator?" Mike asked. His room was on the fourth floor.

"No," she said, smiling briefly. She returned to her book.

Mike's room was at the end of a long, plain hall and faced the street. The door was open. A tall, brown-haired boy was sitting next to the window, in front of a computer. "Raymond Nelson," he said, getting up to shake Mike's hand. He had a thin face and wore glasses. His limp hair was collar-length.

"Hi," Mike said, looking at the beds, one on each side, raised up on iron posts more than five feet off the floor. There were rungs at each end.

"It's so that we can use the space underneath," Raymond told him. That was how small the room was. At the foot of each bed was a desk, and above each desk were three small shelves. "I'm on the left side," Raymond said. "Though I can switch if you want."

"No. That's okay," Mike said. "How long have you been here?"

"Since Friday." He was already engrossed again at the computer. Mike could see some kind of drawing on the screen. Raymond's computer was more sophisticated than his was.

Mike went downstairs and unloaded his truck, carrying suitcases and boxes into the lobby. His hair and denim jacket were wet by the time he finished. A boy who'd come down to watch television helped Mike carry things up the four flights of stairs. "Thanks," Mike said.

"No problem."

Raymond looked up, surprised, when Mike came back in, lugging suitcases. "Sorry," he said. "I kind of got into this thing I'm doing."

"What is it?"

"High-tech space warfare." He helped Mike bring in the remaining items and watched him unpack the first box: a striped rug, tan curtains, and a phone machine. "Wow," he said. "You thought of all that stuff?"

"My mom did. She said that if you already had any of it, I could just bring mine back home."

"I don't," Raymond said. He took the rug from Mike and put it on the bare floor, under the beds. "Homey," he said. At first Mike thought he was kidding. But Raymond watched with a lot of interest as Mike unpacked a microwave.

"I have money for a small refrigerator, too," Mike said, "in case you don't have one."

"Shit," Raymond said. "I don't. That's great."

"She memorized every word of everything the school sent me," Mike told him.

"That's lucky."

"That's one way to look at it."

"What's another?" Raymond asked. He was serious.

"I don't know," Mike said. "I was just talking."

For the next two hours he unpacked, putting his clothes in the small dresser and closet at the head of his bed. From down the hall he could hear a television; Raymond didn't have one, and Mike's mother hadn't wanted Mike to have one. Mike hadn't argued with her; he'd worried about hearing or seeing something about his father on the news. It was bad enough that he had brought a radio.

During the seven-hour drive to Brookings he had

planned what he'd say to people who recognized his last name: "He's a relative I hardly knew," or, to people who somehow knew more: "My mother's divorcing him." Mike worried about teachers who might know but not say anything. He hated for anyone to know more about him than he knew they did. Thoughts along those lines had occupied him for the whole seven hours.

"Are you hungry?" Raymond asked, after Mike had set up his computer. "We could walk to Mad Jack's. It's not far."

"Okay," Mike said. He had forgotten that he hadn't eaten.

They went downstairs and through the lobby, empty now except for two girls watching an old black-and-white movie on television. "Don't you wish guys dressed up like that now?" one of the girls said. "And took us dancing?"

Outside the rain had stopped. The night was warm, and so muggy that halos of mist surrounded the streetlights. "It's pretty humid here," Mike said.

"You're West River," Raymond said. "I thought you'd show up in a cowboy hat." West River, Mike knew, meant that you lived west of the Missouri River, and that you spent more time with cows and horses than with people.

"I left it home with my spurs."

Raymond laughed. "A lot of people didn't."

Mad Jack's, across the street from campus, was crowded and noisy. In a back corner was a large group of students who seemed to be getting together for the first time that semester. They were informal and cheerful. At another table were three scornful-looking long-haired guys.

Mike and Raymond sat at a table next to the window and ordered a pizza. Beyond their reflection in the glass, Mike could see the bell tower across the street, lit up from below. It was four or five times as high as the big elm trees around it.

"I've only gotten lost once," Raymond said. "The campus is not that big." He had weak brown eyes and pale bad skin. "I wanted to go to school out of state," he told Mike. "I was interested in an engineering program at Purdue University. Dad said, 'There's nothing in Indiana you won't find here.' "

"Except Hoosiers," Mike said.

"That's good," Raymond said. "I wish I'd said that."

Mike started to ask about his father—if he was some kind of engineer, himself, up in Aberdeen. But he caught himself. He needed to stay focused on college, or the future, so that Raymond—or anyone Mike talked to—wouldn't ask him about his own family and past. "Isn't there some kind of meeting Dr. Boyd is having tomorrow?" he asked instead. Dr. Boyd was the head of the honors program, whom Mike and his parents had met the previous fall.

Raymond nodded. "At ten," he told Mike. "Maybe we can catch breakfast beforehand."

They were finishing their pizza when the group of students in the corner got up to leave. At another table, a pretty, blond-haired girl looked over and smiled at Mike; her smile died when she looked at Raymond. Raymond wasn't paying attention. He'd taken a pencil out of his shirt pocket and was drawing what looked like a space station on his napkin.

"I get these ideas sometimes," he said to Mike. "Suddenly I'll just have a solution to a problem." He folded the napkin and put it in his pocket. On the short walk back to Hansen Hall, he took it out once and looked at it.

In their room the phone machine was flashing. There was a message from Mike's mother: "Did you forget to call when you got in?"

Mike called her back. "Sorry," he said. "Raymond and I went out to eat."

"What is he like?"

"Okay," Mike said. "You know." Raymond was in the room, working at his desk again.

"Where did you eat?"

"Mad Jack's. A pizza place," Mike said. He imagined her shaking her head. "It's just a few blocks away."

"So the drive was all right? I was afraid you'd run into rain."

"It was drizzling when I got here," he told her.

"Well, I'm glad you had a safe trip." She was silent for a moment. "The house feels a little lonely," she said then, "a little too big. But I'll survive it. I'll get used to it."

"I told you I'd stay home," Mike said.

"Don't be silly. I'll be fine. You take care of yourself. Get settled in and buy your books, and I'll talk to you later in the week. Call me if you need anything."

"I will." Mike stayed where he was after he hung up, looking at the concrete-block walls and the ugly, industrial-looking beds. Even the view from the window was poor: just the wide, flat streets and a row of small houses, probably rented to students.

Mike picked up the phone to call Donetta but put it back down. Because she would say that she missed him, and what would Mike say—that what he missed were the fields on either side of Route 8, as he rode out to the Schofields'? Or the antelope you could see early in the morning or just before dusk? He was missing things more than people. He missed how things made him feel.

Though it wasn't even eleven o'clock, he got up into bed, which was narrower and less comfortable than his bed at home. The room was dark except for Raymond's desk lamp, a small circle of light shining down on the keyboard.

Mike listened to the rain start again and to Raymond at his computer. He wasn't used to having somebody in the room with him. He'd always slept alone except for the nights, in childhood, when Josh had slept over. Mike hadn't liked it even then. As he'd gotten older he'd tried to hide that fact about himself, because on TV, weirdos were always described as antisocial, or loners. They turned into serial killers when they grew up.

Raymond turned off his computer, left the room for a few minutes, and came back in. He got into bed.

"Did you finish what you were doing?" Mike asked him.

"Almost. I thought you were asleep."

"Not yet."

"That was your mom who called before?"

"I was supposed to call when I got here," Mike said.

"I do E-mail. It's easier."

"Your parents have a hookup at home?"

"Dad does," Raymond said. Then, "It's not parents, exactly. I have a stepmother and a stepbrother. My mother died four years ago."

"Oh," Mike said.

"She had cancer."

Mike didn't speak, afraid that anything he said wouldn't sound serious or sincere enough.

"You can get E-mail here easily. I can show you."

"Thanks."

After a small pause, Raymond said, "People get freaked out when you say your mother's dead. I just like to say it and get it over with."

"I know," Mike said. "I mean, I don't know, but I know what you mean." He wished he could say: I know because my father's dead, so that whatever his father had done might be erased. Finally he said, "It doesn't freak me out. I just think it's sad."

"Okay."

Only a few minutes passed before Mike could tell, by Raymond's breathing, that he was asleep. Mike never fell asleep that quickly, not since he'd been eleven or twelve. He'd always thought of it as a sexual thing, as if puberty had gotten in the way of sleep. Nights were when you thought about girls and sex. He got an erection now, thinking about the girl at Mad Jack's who had smiled at him. She'd been wearing a tight little top and no bra. He'd caught her looking at him a few more times. But he had trouble now keeping her in his head. Other things intruded—worries about school, thoughts about home—and his erection disappeared.

The problem was being in a new place, in a new phase of his life, while feeling, somehow, that he hadn't come to terms with the old phase. He couldn't catch up with the things that had happened to him. Worse, there was an acceleration to it now, sending him at a faster rate further and further behind.

He closed his eyes and tried to lie exactly in the center of the bed, as if he were in a boat in danger of capsizing.

EIGHTEEN

THERE were 1,294 freshmen at South Dakota State, including Mike. There were something like 5,000 undergraduates in all. Nonetheless, late Friday afternoon in the University Union, he almost ran into a girl he knew from high school. He managed to escape into a rest room before she saw him.

Afterward he went to Hansen Hall to pick up his mail—a letter from his mother and one from Donetta—and retreated to the privacy of McCrory Gardens, on the opposite side of campus. He found a bench half hidden by dogwood trees.

He opened Donetta's letter first. He'd already received two from her, including the letter he'd seen sealed, in her car, before he left for school. The one he opened now said,

"Guess what? The goat *was* alive, and she and Sophie are becoming friends. They sleep together in the cardboard box."

Toward the end of the letter she wrote, "You know what I have on right now? A white T-shirt you can almost see through. I want to take it off for you and do things you've never done with anyone else and never will." That excited him, then upset him a moment later. It implied that he'd been unfaithful in the past and predicted that he'd be unfaithful in the future. Why would she want to think of him that way?

Also in the envelope was a little watercolor she'd done: a painting of the cottonwood tree whose limbs bent down low over Lame Johnny Creek. In the bottom right-hand corner were her uncapitalized initials: *dsr.* What was the *s* for? Mike knew but couldn't remember. He went through every *S* name he could think of. He repeated "Donetta something Rush" to himself over and over again. Finally, giving up, just looking at red poppies planted along the gravel path, the name Senn came into his head—a family name on her mother's side. Donetta Senn Rush. He felt relieved to remember it, as if he were afraid of losing his memory or even his mind.

His mother's letter was short. She'd run into Lee-Ann Schofield, who'd said to tell Mike that Janna kept asking for him, and that the rabbits were healthy and growing.

His mother also wrote, "There's no news on any front," by which Mike knew that she meant his father. "Tom De-

Witt stopped by, just to be friendly," she wrote. "He wanted to know how you were doing at school." She still didn't seem to know about DeWitt's idea that Glenn would try to contact Mike in Brookings, and her not knowing made it seem less possible. Mike had to remind himself that it could happen, that he needed to be on guard in case it did. Tom wouldn't have given him those phone numbers if he didn't think Glenn would show up. Or would he? Mike didn't trust DeWitt to be honest or straightforward about anything.

His mother ended her letter with, "I try not to look at your empty room when I walk past it." That had a strong effect on Mike. His room now seemed almost human. He imagined the room missing him as if it were a person. Mike had left his room behind, which made him feel as if he'd left himself behind.

Leaving McCrory Gardens, walking back across the hot campus, Mike threw his mother's letter into a Dumpster behind the Union. He kept Donetta's and, back in his room, tacked up her watercolor above his desk. He could hear Raymond next door, talking with their neighbors, Terry Linder and John Watts. The three of them had chemistry together. In a few minutes they'd probably come and ask Mike if he wanted to walk to Medary Commons for dinner. They were the only people Mike had met so far, except for a girl named Heather Coates, in his honors writing seminar, who also lived in Hansen Hall. She was tall and friendly and had spoken to him after class the day before.

The class was subtitled: "Writing about Crises of Faith and Ethics," and she had said, "I like Professor Jakes, but I've never had what you'd call a real crisis."

"Me either," Mike had lied, but a difference had established itself between them, separating him from her. His father's crime had given him less in common with almost everybody. And he never had felt that he was much like other people to start with.

Outside now the sun was low. Mike couldn't see it from his window, which faced south, but he could see the sky becoming paler, and the walls of his room changing from white to pale yellow.

He left before Raymond and the others could find him. He walked all the way to Larson Commons, near Sixteenth Avenue, where he was unlikely to know anyone. He got his tray of food and carried it to the far back corner. Three people at a nearby table looked up, then returned to their conversation. Most people were in groups or couples, but even the students sitting alone, like him, didn't seem particularly lonely. Mike felt the solitary way he usually did; it was just more noticeable to him now. It was like clouds parting so that you could see the moon, when you already knew the moon was there.

HE'D forgotten there was a party that night at his dorm. When he walked into the lobby, after supper, there were at least fifty people there, a table with punch and pizza rolls, and Dwight Yoakum playing on a boom box. Heather Coates was standing next to the front desk with her roommate, Morgan Gault—the pretty girl who had smiled at Mike at Mad Jack's. Heather waylaid Mike and introduced him to Morgan. Both girls were from Chamberlain.

"We've been best friends since the seventh grade," Morgan said. She had on a short skirt and a blouse that tied under her breasts, leaving her stomach bare. "I'm not an honors student, though," she told Mike. "Heather's the smart one."

"What one are you, then?" he asked.

She looked at Heather and they both laughed. "I'm the fun one," Morgan said. "I'm the one who goes on a date the night before I have a test."

John Watts came over to talk to Heather, and Morgan put her hand on Mike's arm. "Will you sneak outside with me so that I can smoke?"

"Why do we have to sneak?"

"We don't. I'm just used to it, from high school."

He left with her through the back door; she led him across the lit-up parking lot to the dark field on the other side. It was a clear night, with stars beginning to appear. She walked into the middle of the field before sitting down.

"Do you want one?" she asked, lighting a cigarette.

"No," he said. "Thanks."

"So you don't smoke."

"Not usually."

"What do you do usually?"

"Heroin."

"Not really."

"No," Mike said. "Not really."

It was deserted where they were—on the northern edge of campus, beyond which were only flat pastures owned by the university.

"I saw you at Mad Jack's Sunday night," Morgan said.

"I remember."

"I have a boyfriend at school in Sioux Falls," she told him. "But I'm not serious about him. I don't expect to marry him or anything like that." She put out her cigarette. She leaned back on her elbows, brushing her arm against Mike's. "I'm free to date other people."

"I don't like that word, *date,*" Mike said. "It's a fruit, for one thing."

"How about 'fuck around with'?" Morgan said. "Do you like that better?"

It was something Donetta would have said, but only to him, and only after they had been dating for a long time. It was sexy, but weird, coming from somebody he hardly knew. He turned toward her and they kissed. She pressed herself against him. Her breasts were larger than Donetta's; she had wider shoulders and stronger arms, and as they kissed more deeply she reached down and put her hand on the crotch of his jeans.

"I want to jerk you off," she said, which startled him even more. She undid his jeans and slipped her hand into his underwear, and it was clear that she was practiced at doing it. After just a few minutes he was ready to come but didn't let himself. He reached up under her skirt and encountered thong-bikini panties—something he'd never seen on a girl except in magazines. He felt overstimulated and slightly crazy. When he couldn't help but come, she acted as if she did, too. Mike couldn't tell. Nothing about her seemed genuine.

He lay on the grass, breathing hard, looking up at the stars and moon. It was Lee-Ann who came into his mind, almost as if she were watching what he was doing. What would she say right now? he wondered. But he already knew. She'd say, "I don't think that's what you need." She'd say, "You have to separate people you can trust from people you can't."

Morgan smiled at him. "Next time we'll bring Kleenex," she said. She stood up and brushed off her clothes, then brushed off Mike's when he stood up.

"Get rid of the evidence, right?"

"There's nothing wrong with what we did," Morgan said coldly.

"I didn't mean that."

"All right," she said. "It's just that some guys are hypocritical about sex."

He walked her back to the party. They didn't talk, and once inside the lobby she moved away from him. He was both glad and hurt. He stood near Raymond, who was talking to a plain-looking girl named Carla Beeker. Mike recognized her from his writing seminar. She'd read aloud a journal entry about her brother, who had cystic fibrosis. She was, in fact, the only person in the class Mike could relate to, because she was thoughtful, and she didn't smile unless there was a reason to. You could tell by looking at her that she had serious things on her mind.

She and Raymond were talking about the valedictory speeches they'd given at their respective high schools. Conversations like that, Mike knew, were the kinds of things people made fun of straight-A students for. It made them seem like nerdy overachievers. But the people who made fun of them were idiots with inferiority complexes. Mike's problem was that he saw both groups critically. He could never be part of any group unself-consciously.

He went upstairs, turned on the light, and stood next to the phone. He hadn't written to Donetta yet, and he called her now.

"Hey," he said when she answered. "I thought you'd be on a date with some hotshot football player."

"Why would I be on a date with anyone?" she said.

"You wouldn't. I was just kidding."

"Why?" Donetta asked.

Mike didn't have an answer. He looked at his small room—the window too narrow to let in enough air, the beds suffocatingly close to the ceiling.

"Mike?" she said.

"Listen," he told her. "I just wanted to say thanks for the

letters. And for the drawing of the tree. I put it up over my desk." He stopped, listening to her breathe. "I don't know why I was joking like that," he said then. "I don't."

Raymond came in holding a box of pizza rolls. "They had them left over," he said, before seeing that Mike was on the phone.

"Your roommate?" Donetta asked.

"Yes."

"And there's no girl waiting for you?"

"Of course not."

"It's really hard," she told him, "being far from you. I knew it would be. But it's worse than I thought."

"For me, too," Mike said.

"Is it?"

"Sure."

After getting off the phone he stood at the window, looking at the flatness of the streets and the scattered lights of campus. Raymond, behind him, was sitting in front of a blank computer screen. "Is there a definite way to know if a girl likes you?" he asked Mike.

"I don't know about definite," Mike said. "You have to go with what it feels like. You have to trust your instincts."

Raymond laughed a little. "Then I'm really in trouble," he said.

They both settled down to study. Mike got out his honors writing anthology and read his assignment, "The Allegory of the Cave," by Plato, about how most people don't see the world but see only shadows of the world, and about how we should ascend into the light of intelligence and truth and see things as they really are.

What would that mean, Mike thought—that how things seemed were never how they really were? And that you couldn't believe that what you saw was what other people saw? And how could you stand to be objective anyway? For example, he knew what a creep he would look like to himself, right now, if he could see tonight objectively. Fortunately, he thought, there was no danger of that.

He gave up on reading and took refuge in daydreaming—imagining himself in the Badlands, high up, sitting still, waiting to see mountain goats. He'd never seen just one. They were always in pairs or groups of three. They had ways of communicating that were impossible for human beings to discover. They were mysterious to humans, and humans were mysterious to them. In that way Mike was safe from them. It was also a given that they were safe from him.

NINETEEN

MIKE'S life assumed a routine. He ate breakfast alone, unless he couldn't avoid Raymond; he attended his classes; and he had most of his other meals at the far end of campus. On the few occasions he went to dinner with Raymond and their neighbors, Terry and John, he listened more than he talked, especially when the subject was where each of them was from, or what their families were like. If they asked Mike a question, he answered in as few words as possible. On a Saturday night two weeks into the semester, he did talk a little about his job at the Schofields', as a way to describe his summer.

"That sounds great," Raymond said. "I spent all summer taking care of my stepbrother."

"I worked for my dad," John said. "It wasn't as bad as I thought it would be."

"I'd end up killing my dad if I had to work for him," Terry said. "Or he'd kill me."

They all laughed about that, Mike forcing himself to smile.

On that night he left the cafeteria earlier than they did and went to the library with his books. In terms of school he wasn't as on top of things as he might have been. "Learn your professors' names," Dr. Boyd had said. "Stay one class ahead with your reading and homework." Mike found the second part difficult to do.

Right now, in the library, he took a seat next to an open window, from where he could hear people playing soccer, in the dusk, in Sexauer Field. It was a warm night. The library was mostly empty. Mike opened his calculus book but became interested instead in the gray patterned carpeting and vacant carrels, then in the sound of the voices outside. He got up to get a drink of water and use the rest room. After that he made himself solve one problem before closing his book and returning to Hansen Hall.

On the fourth floor, in the hallway, Raymond, John, and two other honors students were trying to play hockey with umbrellas and a bar of soap. Raymond called a time-out, following Mike into their room. "Morgan Gault called," he told him. "She said for you to call her."

"Thanks."

"To call when you got back."

"Okay," Mike said. He put down his books, opened his

closet, and stuffed dirty clothes into a pillowcase. Laundry was something else that he hadn't stayed on top of.

Raymond was watching him. "She's really good-looking," he said.

"I guess so."

"But not very smart?"

"Smart enough."

"Her number's on the pad by the phone," Raymond told him.

Mike picked up his keys and opened the door.

"What should I tell her if she calls back?"

"Ask her out yourself," Mike said. He'd meant it to be funny, but it came out sarcastic and mean. "It doesn't matter," he told Raymond. "Say you haven't seen me."

DOWNSTAIRS, Mike had the laundry room to himself. He had brought along his calculus and world-history textbooks, which had been a mistake, he realized. Both books together made him feel overwhelmed. He should have brought one or the other. What he read instead were two *Sports Illustrated* magazines somebody had left behind.

When a Chinese student came in to collect her clothes from a dryer, Mike talked to her a little. She was small and slender, and her shiny hair reached almost to her waist. She said she was from Beijing. "What's it like to be so far from home?" he asked her.

"Not so bad. I get lots of letters from my family. And from my fiancé as well," she added shyly.

"Do you talk to them on the phone?"

"Almost never," she said. "It costs too much. You're lucky to attend school in your own country."

She finished folding her clothes and smiled at him. After she left he thought first about the letters from Donetta and his mother that he hadn't answered, and then about the Chinese girl. He got an erection imagining how, if she were undressed, her long hair would look against her skin. He considered masturbating, taking the risk of somebody walking in. It at least would differentiate how he spent a Saturday night from how he spent a weekday night. When two girls walked in a few minutes later, he wondered how he'd turned into such a pervert.

LATER, he went downstairs and outside, where streaks of clouds were blowing past a white moon. He wanted to get away from Raymond and the other people on the fourth floor. He walked down Seventh Avenue, past the rental houses close to the university, then past houses that were larger and nicer: older, two-story homes with cared-for lawns and big trees.

He could see into lighted living rooms and kitchens, and he imagined himself older, out of school, living alone in one of those houses. He'd put up a wooden fence people couldn't see through and get a dog; he wouldn't talk to anyone he didn't feel like talking to.

It was warm outside, not yet fall, not even at night. Donetta would like that, he thought. She hated the cold. For the previous Christmas, he'd bought her a down comforter with money he'd saved from the summer. She'd told him that on cold nights she'd get into bed early and look at the photo album her father had given her before he died—photographs he'd taken the year he was eighteen, hitchhiking cross-country by himself.

The pictures had titles like "Snowed-in in Greybull, Wyoming," or "Brush Mountain near Altoona, Pennsylvania." "It's like a diary," Donetta had said. She'd started one of her own, with a photograph of herself and Mike, at the lake, which she called, "In Love, at Crow Lake, South Dakota." Mike had had a copy of it once. He'd lost it, or thrown it out—he couldn't remember anymore. Early senility, he thought. Lose your mind at college.

When Mike got to Sixth Street he walked west, downtown, where the post office and restaurants were, small stores, and a bar called Ray's Corner, which had poker and blackjack machines. The streets were full of people. Mike didn't feel a part of the university or the town.

At the end of the wide street was Sexauer Feeds, a granary so big that Mike could see it all the way from his dorm window. That's where he could work, he thought, if he lived in one of those houses on Seventh Avenue. He could have a simple job, some repetitive thing he could do without thinking; then he could go home at night to his dog and his own peaceful house. He wouldn't have to lead a complicated life. His life could be as simple and quiet as that sheepherder's life in the book Josh had been reading. He could settle somewhere, draw a small circle around himself, as if with a compass, and live inside it.

Mike walked past the black, reflective glass of Mac's Retro-Rock-It Diner, where he hadn't eaten yet, though Raymond had asked him to several times. "They have good milk shakes," he'd told Mike. Mike pictured Raymond alone at a table, working on his space drawings, hardly looking up when the waitress came by.

Mike walked farther west, toward the railroad tracks and the airport. Away from the lights of Brookings, the moon was more distinct, but the clouds were increasing, and by the time Mike turned back toward the university there was no moon.

Most of the houses he'd walked past before were dark now; they weren't so inviting anymore. They could have been the houses in Mike's neighborhood in Wheatley—inhabited by people who were more screwed up than you wanted to know. Or else just boring.

A car drove by under the speed limit. Mike hardly noticed until it came around a second time. It was an Oldsmobile or a Buick, he thought, either brown or gray, and driven by a man, not a student. Mike kept walking, watching it inch toward the corner, then turn left and speed up slightly.

Don't be paranoid, he told himself. Someone was probably lost, or else maybe the driver thought Mike was somebody else. There were a lot of possibilities, except that none of them seemed likely. What seemed likely was that it was either the police or somebody connected to his father.

And the next moment Mike felt as lost and overcome with fear as he had that night standing next to Elk Creek. He stood rigidly, trying to remember that the sidewalk under him was solid, as was the earth, and that if he were dying, the earth would not be dying with him; it would stay whole and in place no matter what his heart did.

The fear faded by degrees, but this time more of it was left behind, and what went underground only went to some purgatorylike place. So that while he felt less afraid, he also knew that he wasn't the same anymore. He probably hadn't been for a while.

Hansen Hall was in front of him now, and he stood back from the lighted street, under an oak tree, waiting to see if the car came around a third time. He was across the street from the girls' side of the building; there were ten or twelve lighted windows with open curtains. He saw one girl in a nightgown, brushing her hair, another wearing only a sweatshirt and panties. If somebody was watching him, he thought, then they were watching him watch that.

He waited only a few seconds longer. Then he crossed the street, went inside and up the stairs.

. . .

EARLY Monday morning, by accident, and without wanting to, he ate breakfast with Heather Coates. He was sitting alone at Medary Commons; she came through the cafeteria line, saw him, then came over. "I don't know if I should sit with you or not," she said. "You didn't call Morgan back."

"I meant to."

She took her juice and plate off her tray and sat down, smoothing back her dark hair. "I guess I'll talk to you. But not about that."

"About what then?" Mike said guardedly.

"I don't know. Anything. I don't have anything specific in mind."

"Good."

"What do you mean?"

"Nothing," Mike said. "Just good." He watched her butter her toast. His own plate of food was in front of him, most of which he hadn't eaten.

"Aren't you hungry?" she said.

"Not really."

Heather ate all of her scrambled eggs before putting down her fork. "Just tell me why you didn't call her back," she said.

"I thought you weren't going to talk about her."

"I know. I can't help it."

"Well, it was late," Mike said.

"What about all day yesterday, or last night?"

"So that makes me what?" Mike said. "An asshole?"

"I was thinking that you weren't one."

"So now I am."

"What do you think?"

"I might sound like one," Mike told her. "But that doesn't mean I am one. Like maybe I just have a lot on my mind."

"A lot of girls, you mean."

"Not quite," Mike said.

They sat in silence. Heather drank her juice.

"Did you read 'Fern Hill' yet?" she asked. It was a poem by Dylan Thomas, and was the next day's assignment for their writing class.

"I had to memorize it in tenth grade."

"You were lucky."

"Why?"

"Because it's like the best poem ever written."

"Who told you that?" Mike said.

"Nobody. I just like it."

"I'll read it again tonight."

"Before or after you call Morgan?" Heather said, and stood up to leave.

Fuck you, Mike said silently. He wasn't sorry for Morgan, but he was sorry he'd screwed around with her. It made him feel desperate for sex. Or just really, really depressed. He sat in the cafeteria a while longer, through his first class, in fact.

TWENTY

THE nights and mornings grew chilly. The leaves weren't changing yet, but in western South Dakota the temperature dropped into the thirties one night. Mike's mother called one morning just to say that. She called him often, reminding him to get the oil changed in his truck, to eat three meals a day, to get involved in extracurricular activities. He hadn't gone out for wrestling. Why would he have cared whether he won or lost a match?

"Aren't there clubs you can join?" his mother said one night on the phone. He'd fallen asleep at his desk; the telephone had woken him up. "Why not ask Dr. Boyd about it?" The head of the honors program, an agronomy professor, was boyish-looking and slight. All Mike knew about him was that he'd been on the rodeo circuit when he was young. Mike's mother seemed to believe that Boyd was the head/teacher/father/priest of the university—somebody Mike could go to for anything.

Mike's mother only mentioned his father once; she told Mike that the divorce would be final soon. Mike had not told her about the car following him. It had not happened again, as far as he knew, and he had been paying careful attention, both when he was walking and when he was driving. He'd told himself, finally, that there was no point in worrying. Mike didn't know anything. His father had never called him. Tom DeWitt had been wrong.

A sentence or two later, his mother told him that she'd been on a date. "I wasn't sure I should mention it," she said. "But I want you to know. I want to be honest with you. And I thought it might make you feel better, knowing that I had some company."

"Okay," Mike said. He didn't bother asking who it was. It was one more way Tom DeWitt was staying in their lives.

"All right, then," his mother said brightly. "So. How are your grades? What subject are you best in?"

"Physical education," Mike said.

His mother laughed. "I've missed your jokes," she told him.

Me, too, he thought.

When he got off the phone he became aware of voices next door—Terry's, John's, and Raymond's. They were talking seriously, it sounded like, and Mike thought he heard his name mentioned. He sat as still as he could, listening. But he didn't hear it again, and soon they began talking more casually.

THE following day, after Mike's classes were over and he was back at his dorm, checking his mail, a girl standing next to him said, "It's not here yet. It's late today." But there was an unstamped envelope in his mailbox. Morgan, he told himself, but it wasn't from Morgan, and his head started hurting the second he saw the name. He went out to the parking lot so that he could read the letter alone, in his truck. It was handwritten on plain white paper.

"We think that your father was on a bus in Illinois," Tom had written, "traveling north. He might be working his way up to you. If he is, and if he contacts you, you're going to have to make a decision. Think about it beforehand. He might not be that far away."

Enclosed, in case Mike had lost or thrown out the one he had, was a card with three phone numbers on it. At the bottom of the card Tom had written, "Don't forget what your father did," and, "Don't put yourself in the middle."

Two girls were getting into the car next to Mike's. The one who sat in the passenger seat smiled at him. He looked at her blankly, not recognizing her from one of his classes. He realized who she was as the car was backing out, and found himself raising his hand to wave at the empty space between his truck and a Pontiac.

. . .

HE read the letter several times, locked it in his glove compartment, and started driving slowly and nervously through campus and then through town, looking for Tom DeWitt's car.

It was a cool afternoon. Students were playing Frisbee under the elms near the bell tower, and a group of girls was jogging through campus. Mike drove through every university parking lot and in and out of the parking lots of every motel and restaurant in Brookings. He saw two state police cars near the stadium, on North Campus Drive—he never had seen any on campus before.

For all Mike knew, his father was already in Brookings, and Mike was being used as bait. Or else maybe DeWitt was testing him somehow, trying to figure out, in advance, what Mike would do. All Mike was sure of was that none of this was about him. Mike, as an individual, didn't matter to Tom DeWitt—not that Mike needed to, or expected to. But it was important for him to remember, because the thing that could fool you, Mike thought—or make a fool of you—was believing that people were thinking about you when they weren't, caring about you when they didn't.

He drove through campus a second time, and through Brookings again, ending up near the Best Western and the Wal-Mart as the streetlights were coming on. The line along the horizon was blue gray, the color of storm clouds over the Black Hills. But there were no hills in Brookings.

There was no place from where he could have seen far enough.

He drove back toward campus, the northern edge of which was barren-looking and unkempt. There was grass growing up through the tennis courts. There was the shiplike sports complex looking alien among the other buildings. There was no car he recognized, nobody following him or waiting for him at his dorm—just a note from Raymond, which said: "Went to dinner. Waited for you then gave up." He'd left the same note three times before.

LATER in the evening, while Raymond studied diligently and Mike lay in bed, doing nothing, Donetta called. "I'm failing precalculus," she said. "I don't ever want to hear the word *exponential* again. And what the hell is an imaginary number?

"Never mind," she said, when he started to answer. "I don't want to waste a phone call on it."

"Me either," Mike said. "Anyway, I can't remember what it means."

"Why not? What do you mean?"

Mike looked at Raymond, who looked back at Mike, picked up his book, and left the room. As soon as he was gone Mike turned off the light and stretched the telephone cord so that he could keep watch out the window for Tom DeWitt's car—for any suspicious-looking car. "I'm not doing too well in calculus," he told Donetta. "It's like I'm senile. Or stupid."

"Your mother says that you've been hard to talk to."

"Why are you talking to my mother about me?"

"I'm not," Donetta said. "But how can I help seeing her at school?"

"You could walk the other way." She was quiet, and Mike could hear Cory and Mrs. Rush arguing in the background.

"They've been doing that since breakfast," Donetta said. "I don't even know what about. I just stay in my room. I've been working part-time at Andell's to earn enough money to visit."

"No wonder you want to come here."

"No," she said. "I want to see you."

Mike was silent.

"I don't even know if you've kept your promise," Donetta said.

"About what?"

"About loving somebody else. And not making me figure it out."

"I don't love anybody else," Mike told her.

"What's wrong, then?"

"Who says anything is wrong?"

"You did," Donetta said. "About calculus."

"Well, that's just school," Mike said.

"It seems like more than that."

"Nothing that's wrong is about you," Mike told her. "Or

about you and me. Some things I have to handle on my own." Donetta was quietly listening. In the background he heard a door slam.

"Will you call me when you feel bad?" she asked him.

"I don't feel bad."

"But if you do," she said, "tell yourself what I do. That it's not a fact. It's just a feeling."

Mike watched a dark car go past the dorm and turn down Seventh Avenue.

"Mike?" Donetta said.

"Okay," he told her.

"But are you really listening to what I'm saying?"

"Yes. I heard you." Outside, the car kept going.

"It can really help," Donetta said. "Even though it might sound silly now."

"Listen," Mike told her. "I have to go. I have a lot of work to do. I'll talk to you soon, okay?"

Afterward, Mike made up his mind not to call her for a while, not to call anyone, or check his phone messages. Because it was too stressful to talk to people. They didn't understand how he felt. He was different now. The person they were talking to was not the person they had known in the summer. Maybe he hadn't been that person ever.

The door opened. It was Raymond, making sure that Mike was off the phone. "I understand about privacy," he told Mike. "Just tell me when you need it."

Mike nodded. He sat at his desk, which was piled up with books and assignments, all the work he didn't have the energy to do. He glanced out the window every few minutes. Then he searched through his desk for the five self-addressed envelopes Lee-Ann had given him. He thought that she might be the only person who could understand what he was going through.

"Dear Lee-Ann," he wrote. "I just wanted to say hello. I was wondering what was going on there and what Neil and Ed were up to. And you. Because I really haven't made any friends here."

He crossed out that last sentence. But there was nothing he could think of to replace it with.

TWENTY-ONE

OVER the next few weeks Mike got D's on two tests and F's on three quizzes. He was too tired, for one thing, and got winded climbing one flight of stairs, let alone the four to his room. And he'd begun waking at four-thirty in the morning and not falling back asleep. He'd hear the first birds sing and lie with his eyes closed as the darkness turned to light. His dreams stayed vividly in his mind. A few days earlier, after receiving a letter from the Schofields—with Janna's scribbling at the bottom of the page—he dreamed that the rabbits born under their porch had been born dead. In a more recent dream he was a child, and his father was teaching him how to swim in the deep end of a pool. "See how long you can hold your breath," his father told him.

He'd stopped answering the phone or checking his messages, though he still read his letters. Donetta wrote him almost every day, and his mother wrote often as well. In his mother's most recent letter she asked him to make sure his answering machine was working. She also told him that she'd been on two more dates, and he read that part of her letter closely.

"I had a good time," she wrote. "What I mean is that it's somebody I'd like to keep on seeing. And I'd like you to meet him, Mike. It doesn't have to be anytime soon. I don't mean that. But Jim has heard a lot about you."

It was the student she was tutoring, and not Tom DeWitt. Instead of relief Mike felt that he'd fallen backward again, that he was falling behind at the same speed that his life, and the lives of the people around him, were moving forward.

ON the third Thursday of October, a mild morning, the sun shining down on the autumn trees, Mike was late—again—for his Honors Writing Seminar. He took a seat in the back of the room; Professor Jakes looked up but said nothing. They were discussing *Spiritual Autobiography,* by Simone Weil. Mike had read it twice, trying to understand it, and unlike his other homework, it remained in his head.

"Why did she think so much about God?" one person asked.

"Because she thought so much about dying," Heather Coates said.

" 'If only I knew how to disappear,' " Professor Jakes read, " 'there would be a perfect union of love between God and the earth I tread, the sea I hear. . . . I disturb the silence of heaven and earth by my breathing and the beating of my heart.' That's from a journal she kept," he told the class. "What do you think she's saying?"

"That she hated herself," somebody said. "That she thought the world would be a better place if she died."

"Except that she believed in love," said Carla Beeker.

"If she lived now," a boy asked, "wouldn't we think she was crazy?"

"Don't you ever think about who you are?" Carla said. "Or about God? Or about the kind of life you should lead?"

"No more than I have to."

People laughed. Mike looked at the phrases he'd underlined in his book: *I always believed that the instant of death is the center and object of life. If I am sad, it comes primarily from the permanent sadness that destiny has imprinted on my emotions . . . ; Ideas come and settle in my mind by mistake, then realizing their mistake, they absolutely insist on coming out. . . .*

"What do you think, Mr. Newlin?" Professor Jakes asked.

Mike looked up. "I don't know," he said slowly. "There's something personal about the way she says things. You feel like you know her when you read this."

"Because she feels things so strongly," Carla said. "Like how she read that one poem over and over."

"Did anyone look up the poem?" Professor Jakes asked.

Carla held up a thick volume of poetry, and everyone laughed, including her. Professor Jakes asked her to read it.

In a soft voice she read: " 'Love bade me welcome: yet my soul drew back, Guiltie of dust and sinne. . . .' " And Mike's eyes filled with tears, though he wasn't sure what, exactly, the poem was about. He sat low in his chair, holding his book up in front of him, trying to focus on something else. But everything hurt to think about: his father, his mother at home, Donetta alone at night in her room, writing letters to Mike that he didn't answer.

Behind his thoughts Carla was gently saying, " 'Love took my hand, and smiling did reply,/Who made the eyes but I?' " And Mike, closing his own eyes, thought of the moon rising over the Black Hills into the wide dark sky. " 'And know you not, sayes Love, who bore the blame?' " And Mike was thinking of the long shadows on the backyard grass, and antelope coming into the fields at dusk, and himself, always watching, always distant, always far away.

" 'You must sit down, sayes Love, and taste my meat:/So I did sit and eat.' " That was the last line of the poem. The class was over. Mike left first, hurrying out into the hall, down the stairs, and into the sunlight.

HE didn't attend his other classes. Instead, he went back to Hansen Hall, put his books in his truck, and unloaded his motorcycle from the back of it. He hadn't ridden it since he'd come to Brookings. He'd been too distracted, or even somehow too afraid. But now the only thing on his mind was getting away from Brookings and from his life there.

He rode east on Highway 14, stopping first to buy gas. Inside, as he paid, the girl behind the counter said, "Are you a student?" She had on a South Dakota State sweatshirt. He nodded. "Me, too," she said. "I study between customers." She was freckled and overweight, with long, braided hair. "It's a different world in here," she told him. "It's like what I read about." She held up a psychology textbook.

"I bet," Mike said. Outside, two hunters in a mud-splattered pickup were pulling up to the air hose.

"I hate hunters the most," the girl said. "I hate when they drive in with deer strapped to their cars."

"Well, I don't hunt," Mike said.

"That's what I thought. I try to figure out things about the people who come in here. Only usually I never know if I'm right." Mike stood there, waiting for his change. "Do you want to know what I think about you?"

He didn't. But he said, "I guess."

"That you're skipping class. And you're not very happy."

"I'm just worried about something," he said.

She gave him his change, and as he turned to leave she handed him two candy bars. "In case you're worried because you're hungry," she told him.

Outside he straddled his motorcycle, watching the highway and watching the hunters. He'd lied inside. He'd gone hunting with Josh and Josh's father a few times, and twice with Neil and Ed Schofield. He'd shot a pheasant. His father had hunted from the age of ten, or so he'd said, but he'd never suggested doing it with Mike. He was scornful of people who did it in groups. "You have to hunt alone," he used to say. "It's a solitary activity."

That's what Mike was thinking about when he saw, or thought he saw, Tom DeWitt's car, traveling west. It wasn't a distinctive car, and it wasn't close enough for him to be sure. Mike's hands were shaking, though, and he pulled onto the highway in the direction he'd just come from and rode, fast, through Brookings and all the way past Highway 81 without seeing Tom's car or one like it again. It must not have been DeWitt, Mike thought, but he rode through town and through campus before deciding to just say fuck it. What would he do anyway, if he did see him?

He headed east again, riding past the gas station and into the country. The road was bright with sun, and on either side were cow pastures and hay fields. He hadn't brought his helmet and felt nothing but sun and wind, heard nothing but the noise of the engine. Instead of campus buildings and students he saw farmhouses and grazing cows and horses. The road unfolded in front of him as endlessly as the way he used to imagine the future.

He turned onto a smaller highway marked SCENIC and accelerated, following the center line closely and leaning far in on the curves. In his head was a sentence from the essay they'd discussed in his writing seminar, the first sentence he'd underlined: "I always believed that the instant of death was the center and object of life." Mike kept saying that to himself, even though he'd never believed in heaven, not even as a kid. He wished there was something he felt that sure of, that he'd always known, always understood.

He accelerated again and felt the candy bars fall out of his pocket. He hadn't wanted them anyway, and it was none of that girl's business whether he was happy or not, hungry or not. She'd wanted him to respond to her in some way, and he was tired of people wanting reactions from him. The more detached you were, the more people wanted to get attached to you. You were the center and object for them, but you didn't have a center for yourself; you were too busy being theirs.

A pickup rushed toward him, then past him, and then a white car. Tom DeWitt will probably come along next, Mike thought, or else Mike's father, in a car belonging to some new woman gullible or dumb enough to help him, and as Mike downshifted on the next curve his rear wheel locked and he didn't pull the clutch in fast enough.

He lost control, the bike just going out from under him. It seemed prolonged, and there was a second when it felt more like being super alive than having an accident. He stayed with the bike as long as he could—too long—then jumped clear of it as it slid down into a dry ditch. He landed facedown in the grass.

The world was suddenly still and suddenly silent. Would death feel like this? Mike wondered. But the complications of his mind and heart were already flooding in, and so was the pain he felt—in his right shoulder, and leg, and particularly in his grass-burned hands, which he must have put down first, trying to break his fall. He sat up and took stock of himself. His jeans and jacket were torn, but none of his bones seemed broken. It took him a minute to stand up. Then shakily and gingerly he slid down into the ditch to check his bike, which was less damaged than he was, and rideable.

He slowly climbed up the other side of the embankment. The barbed-wire fence was stretched enough, in one spot, for him to get through, and he carefully lay down in the field grass, looking up at hawks gliding in the blue sky. It took a long time for his heart to stop racing. He told himself that he wouldn't have to move until he felt like it. He could stay there all day, if he wanted to, and even into the night. He could stay there forever. After a while he fell asleep, dreaming that a car he was in, driven by his father, was speeding out of control. Mike jerked awake. Just watch the hawks, he told himself—the way they rise and fall with the air currents, the way they dip and climb.

HE rode back to Brookings. He'd come farther than he'd realized, and now he hardly noticed the straw-colored fields or the farmhouses. He had the glare of the sun in his eyes until the sun dropped below the horizon; then the air turned substantially colder.

At Hansen Hall he left his bike next to his truck, and up in his room he got into bed without undressing. He pretended to be asleep when Raymond came in an hour later, followed by Terry Linder, who said, "Want some dinner?"

They left, and Mike heard Raymond say, in the hallway, "It's like I don't have a roommate."

Then Mike was left alone with his imagination: himself on his bike on that scenic road—except that this time, when he lost control, he skidded into the other lane where there was a truck, and when he collided with the truck his body was mangled like in a horror movie. The truck driver called the police, who called Mike's mother, and though she was sad for a while she at least didn't have to worry about him anymore; and when his father found out—assuming he ever went to that trouble—he felt bad that he'd given Mike leukemia, a deadly disease even if Mike was recovering from it, and maybe his father tried to kill himself, probably without success.

The main thing was that Mike finally would be able to fuck up, fuck himself up, and in that instant be through with everything. Any other way you fucked up, you had to pay the consequences afterward. Fucking up just partway meant that you were still trying to hold things together. It was even worse, because the more you fucked up, the more pieces there were to hold together. So the only real freedom was to completely let it go—fuck your family, fuck your life, fuck yourself.

Ideas come and settle in my mind by mistake. . . . He was like that writer. He thought he understood what she was saying.

TWENTY-TWO

IN the morning Mike stayed in bed until he was sure he would have the bathroom to himself. He hurt more today. He was better after his shower, though so tired that he sat in his desk chair for twenty minutes before getting dressed. He ate cold cereal in his room, then went to the classes he hadn't missed already.

In his biology class he sat in a back corner and tried writing a letter to Donetta, getting as far as, "I know I haven't written much" and "I don't have much to say," before giving up and looking out the window. There was a strong wind blowing, and torn-looking clouds were moving fast from the west. The temperature was twenty degrees colder than it had been the day before.

While the professor at the lectern talked about Darwin, Mike drew pictures in the margins of his notebook—nothing you could recognize, he knew, nothing as good as Donetta's drawings, which always had a feeling to them; you could tell what she felt by what she drew. The high school art teacher had told her, "Be disciplined. Use your brain." Mike thought that he was wrong. Donetta had her own way of being intelligent. He looked down at his letter, thinking that if he never saw her again, how would she know that he'd finally understood that?

He reread his sentences and crossed out the three *I*'s. They said and meant nothing, and drew too much attention to themselves. They were like black lines of paint on a white wall. As long as he had to use that word, he thought, there was no point in writing letters to anyone.

IT was four o'clock when he returned to his room and discovered a note on his desk from Raymond: "Dr. Boyd called. He wants you to come by Solberg Hall. He said it was important."

As Mike hurried across campus, he told himself what must have happened: Either his father had shown up in Brookings and been arrested, or worse; or Tom DeWitt was setting a trap for Mike's father right now, one that he was involving Mike and Dr. Boyd in as well. Mike should have stayed home in Wheatley, as he'd wanted to, no matter what his mother had said. His father's belongings were already out of her way, in the basement. She'd never have to see Glenn again unless she wanted to. For Mike it was different.

Dr. Boyd's door was open, but he was with a student. He looked up and said, "Give me five minutes."

Too jittery to wait in the hall, Mike walked outside and stood on the top step, shifting from one foot to the other. The wind in the elms was shaking loose the leaves, and dark clouds sailed past overhead. Students were walking along the sidewalks and cutting across the grass. The gap between himself and them had grown too wide for Mike to cross.

"Mike?" Dr. Boyd was holding open the door for him.

"What's wrong?" Mike said.

"Come on in first." He led Mike down the hall and into his office. The building was old and the room was large, with a casement window that overlooked the street. He closed the door and asked Mike to sit down. "It's not an emergency," he told him then. "I just thought we could talk."

Mike took a deep breath, tried to calm down. "About what?" he said.

"I thought we could talk about a few things," Dr. Boyd said again. He sat at his desk, looking down at an open folder. "Grades, for one thing."

"They'll get better," Mike said. "I got off to a slow start."

"It's not just that. You've missed classes. You've been late to the ones you do attend. I'm concerned about how you're doing in general."

"I'm all right," Mike said.

Dr. Boyd closed the folder and rested his arms on it. "Your mother phoned me before the semester started," he told Mike. "But I already knew. I'd read about it in the paper."

"When?" Mike said.

"When it happened. Not lately. I haven't seen anything about it since then."

Mike was too upset to speak. He looked out the window at traffic passing by in the street. "I don't want people to know," he said finally. "It's private."

"I can understand that," Dr. Boyd said. "But maybe you and I could talk about it. About the effect it's having on your schoolwork."

"It's not having an effect," Mike said.

"Have you discussed your grades with your professors?"

Mike shook his head, feeling tears rising. He put his hand over his mouth, pretending to cough, and remembered too late about the bruises.

"How did you hurt yourself?" Dr. Boyd asked.

"A bike accident," Mike said. "No big deal." He looked away again, this time at a filing cabinet, on which there was a framed photograph: a woman and two boys on the front porch of a two-story house.

"My family," Dr. Boyd said kindly.

"Your house reminds me of ours," Mike said, humiliated to hear his voice catch on the "ours."

"We've lived in it since our sons were born," Dr. Boyd

said. "Fourteen years." He smiled at Mike. "Time goes by faster as you get older. It helps you put things in perspective."

From the hallway came the sound of doors closing, and footsteps. "Friday," somebody said. "Time to party." The cheerfulness of the voice sounded alien to Mike, almost inconceivable. The room was growing dim, the light outside less bright. Dr. Boyd reached toward his desk lamp, then seemed to reconsider.

"You should talk with your professors, Mike," he said. "Or I could, with your permission."

"No. Thanks."

"You can come over here anytime, just to talk."

"Okay."

"Or I could refer you to someone—a psychologist, for example. I don't mean right now. But if you ever think it might be useful."

Mike shook his head, keeping it down, keeping Dr. Boyd from seeing his eyes. "Is that it, then?" he asked.

"I'd like to help."

"I don't need help."

"Maybe there's something else I could do that I haven't thought of."

"No," Mike told him. "I'm okay."

Dr. Boyd looked at him, not speaking. Mike concentrated on the window, then the office floor, which was clean and wavy with wax—like the kitchen floor at home. Then Dr. Boyd rose, walked to the door, and opened it. He said good-bye to Mike, and Mike felt himself being watched as he walked down the hallway toward the double glass doors and went outside.

The sun was down, and the wind was blowing carpets of leaves into the street. Mike's shoulder and leg were sore; he hadn't worn his jacket, and he was cold. He walked past couples holding hands, past small groups of talkative girls. Unexpectedly, pieces of "Fern Hill" came into his mind: "rivers of the windfall light," and "nightly under the simple stars." He didn't know what came before, in between, or after, but the poem was about time, he knew—how it kept you captive, because you were always dying, even from the beginning, even before you realized it.

IN Mike's dorm room, Raymond was sitting on the rug beneath the beds, with three books open in front of him, working on a paper. "Do you want to get dinner?" he asked Mike.

"I don't think so. I'm not hungry." Mike walked around him.

Raymond said, "You know, you should eat sometimes. You should call people back, too. You've got five messages."

"I'll listen to them later."

Raymond pushed back his limp hair. "Look," he said. "People are worried about you."

"Like who?" Mike said.

"I don't know. Your mom. Your girlfriend, if that's who she is." He gestured to the phone machine with his pen, which flew out of his hand. He didn't move to retrieve it.

"I have things on my mind," Mike said.

"What things?"

"Just some private things."

"Well, I can't make you tell me," Raymond said. "But I know what it's like to feel bad. I didn't talk about it either. I just waited for it to get better."

Mike nodded.

"It takes a long time that way," Raymond said.

Mike retrieved Raymond's pen. "Okay," he said. "I know."

"So let's go eat," Raymond said insistently. "We'll just go to Medary Commons." He stood up and got his jacket. He opened the door without giving Mike a chance to say no.

The night had grown wintry. They walked down Eleventh Street with their hands in their pockets, into the wind, which blew in gusts. "It's supposed to snow tonight or tomorrow," Raymond told Mike. "Can you believe that? It's a good thing we don't have to go anywhere."

At Medary Commons they got their food and chose a table against the far wall. Mike, not hungry to start with, was too tired to eat. He tried hard to act normal. "How are your classes?" he asked Raymond.

"Pretty good except chemistry. At this point I'm hoping for a B."

"Everybody says that honors chemistry is a bitch."

"How are yours?"

"I've screwed up some tests," Mike said, with difficulty. "I think I can make up for them later."

Raymond focused on people coming through the cafeteria line, then said, "I asked Carla Beeker out. We went to eat one night."

"How was it?"

"Tense," Raymond said. "I mean for me. But she's easy to talk to," he told Mike. "She thinks I'm smart. And she knows what sad is."

Tears came to Mike's eyes immediately. He put down his fork, drank his water, and told himself: It's only a feeling. It's not a fact. That helped, but barely.

After Raymond finished eating he looked at Mike's plate—chicken, mashed potatoes, and green beans, mostly untouched. "Clean-plate club," he said. "You're not a member."

"What?"

"How my mother used to get me to eat."

They returned their trays, crossed the emptying room, and walked back to Hansen Hall through the windy night.

LATER, while Raymond worked on his paper, Mike read history—the fall of the Roman Empire. Out the window two girls were walking down Eleventh Street toward the dorm; as they passed under a streetlight, he saw that they were Heather Coates and Morgan Gault. The person Mike used to be would have had more sex, by now, with at least one of them. Not that he liked either of them much. But that wasn't as important as people thought. What was important was that you kept doing things in the world, making things happen. That's what history was about. You couldn't stop just because you didn't feel like waking up or talking to people, or because nothing seemed to matter to you anymore.

Mike shut his book and turned off his desk lamp.

"You're done?" Raymond said.

"Not exactly. I'm resting." He got into bed.

"I can turn off the light, go to the library."

"No," Mike said. "Study for both of us." He lay in his clothes on top of the covers. There seemed to be nothing ahead for him except cold weather, poor grades, and conversations that left him upset. He listened to Raymond leafing through the pages of his books. Raymond seemed pathetic to Mike, despite the fact that he did well in school and had friends and now might have a girlfriend. Raymond couldn't see the sorrowfulness of his life the way that Mike could. Raymond couldn't see the pointlessness of college.

Mike tried to concentrate on things that once had made him feel good. But swimming naked with Donetta or drinking whiskey with Josh belonged to some past life that didn't seem to be his anymore. He didn't fantasize about Lee-Ann anymore, and she probably didn't about him, and when Mike thought about sex it didn't drive away his other thoughts, the way it used to. If Raymond weren't there, he could masturbate. But maybe he wouldn't. Maybe he wouldn't even bother.

He got out of bed to get another blanket just as the phone rang.

"Mike?" his father said. "Drive on out! Did you forget about us, man? Come on! We're waiting for you!"

TWENTY-THREE

OUTSIDE, nothing was different—just the lit-up parking lot and the dark field behind it. Raymond had said, "Who was that?" and Mike had said, "My friend Josh. He's at the campgrounds with some friends. I'm driving out there."

Mike stood now at the back door of Hansen Hall, thinking: Maybe that hadn't been his father on the phone. Maybe Mike's own paranoia had changed one person's voice into another. But he wasn't that crazy.

He tried to think coherently. He had Tom DeWitt's card in his wallet, but there was no way he was going to call him. He didn't have any specific information, anyway. He didn't know where his father was or even where he, himself, was supposed to go. Still, he didn't want to be in this alone. He needed somebody to know. If he called Donetta, she'd freak out and call his mother. Josh would keep it to himself, but it was a weekend night and it was unlikely that he'd be home. Mike went to the pay phone in the lobby and called him anyway. There was no answer, not even an answering machine. He called again with the same result.

Behind him, three girls were laughing at something on television. The student working the desk had his head down, studying. Mike stood again at the back door, concentrating on the night outside. He waited. Then he walked out, unlocked his truck, and got in. If his father drove up now, he thought, they could talk right there, in the parking lot. Mike could find out exactly what had happened with Mary Hise, and what it was, if anything, his father wanted from him now. He could learn what the truth was without having to get too involved.

He sat for a long time, looking out, starting the engine when he got too cold. The wind was blowing hard enough, at moments, to rock the truck. Nobody drove up or walked past.

Then, across the wide field that separated Hansen Hall from its neighbor, Berg Hall, a car flashed its lights twice. Mike tensed up and watched. He hardly breathed. A minute passed, and the lights flashed twice again.

Okay, Mike thought. He would drive over there. His father, if it was his father, was afraid, probably, to come to Hansen Hall itself. They could talk there, then, in that parking lot. And if that car had no connection to his father, which was what Mike hoped, Mike would come back, go up to his room, and wait for his father to call again. Then if his father wanted to talk to him, he'd have to do it on Mike's terms, either on the phone or in the lobby, or in the parking lot of Hansen Hall. If talking to Mike was important enough, his father would have to take one of those options.

But as Mike drove toward Berg Hall, the car, flashing its lights only once this time, pulled out in front of him on Eleventh Street and kept going. When Mike got closer he saw that the only visible occupant was the driver, who was small and female. The car was a two-door, hatchback Toyota. It had an Illinois license plate, and Mike memorized it. He repeated it out loud while following the car through town, up one street and down another—a circuitous route, Mike thought, like in a detective movie. He was the private detective on the trail of the criminal's girlfriend. It felt a lot less fictional when he followed the car into the parking lot of a Taco Bell and saw his father run out of the restaurant. It stopped seeming like a game then. His father had a beard now, looked thinner, and was wearing a dark nylon jacket. He was holding a take-out sack and didn't look in Mike's direction. He opened the passenger door of the Toyota, and the driver accelerated the second he closed it.

Then they were on the entrance ramp to the interstate, heading south, and Mike, behind them, knew that he'd gone too far. He'd get off at the next exit, he told himself, but the car his father was in was not getting off; it was going exactly sixty-seven miles per hour, and if Mike didn't follow it, the space between himself and his father would widen to infinity.

He drove past the exit. In his rearview mirror he saw the lights of Brookings grow distant; in front of him he saw what he didn't know grow closer.

Halfway to Sioux Falls the Toyota left the interstate, heading east on a two-lane road and crossing the state line into Minnesota. That made it much worse, Mike knew, whatever crime this was that he was committing. But he couldn't stop. It was one thing to be afraid, he thought, but another thing to be a coward, and in addition it was his father he was following, not some maniac or stranger, and his father was the only person who could tell Mike what really had happened with Mary Hise. Mike was the only one who could find out. He could accomplish what no one else could.

He followed them through forty miles of countryside and one-stoplight towns, turning, finally, onto a long dirt road that ended at a semicircle of concrete-block cabins called the Twilight Lake Motel. There seemed to be no one staying there except them.

Mike's father jumped out of the car and ran back to Mike's truck. "Turn off your headlights and pull around behind the motel," he said. "As far back under the trees as you can. I'll meet you there."

He pointed to a rutted, overgrown trail that led through pine trees and ended an eighth of a mile into the woods. Without headlights Mike had to inch down it, and when he got out of his truck he knew the lake was close by: He heard water rippling and smelled the wetness. The night was absolutely black and cold. Then his father appeared, carrying a flashlight, a wrench, and a Minnesota license plate. "Here we are," he said, and grasped Mike's shoulders in an awkward hug. Mike didn't step away, but he kept his own arms at his sides. Then his father eyed the truck. "This is nice," he said. "Looks dependable. And it doesn't stand out." Then he stooped down behind the truck and loosened the bolts.

"Wait," Mike said. "I'm not staying. I'm going back to school tonight."

His father didn't move or lift his head. "No," he said. "I've got enough on my hands as it is."

"I'm just saying that I can't stay."

His father stood up. "Are you wearing a watch?" Pointlessly, because it was too dark for Mike to read it, he showed Mike his. "We won't have time to talk tonight," he said. "I won't be able to tell you what happened. We'll talk in the morning, then you'll go back first thing."

"Then I don't need a different license plate."

"Here's where I know more than you do," he told Mike. "A minute's work can save you heartache." He handed Mike the flashlight. "Hold it still," he said. "Keep it steady." He replaced Mike's South Dakota plate with the Minnesota one. "Welcome to the North Star State," he said. "Here. Put yours under the seat. We'll replace it when you leave."

"In the morning," Mike said.

"Fine. Whatever." Glenn stood up and took the flashlight from Mike. He turned it off and walked toward the motel. Mike hung back under the trees. "Mike!" his father said. Then he was walking again, with Mike behind him, trying to find his way in the darkness.

Ahead of them then was a bright rectangle of an open door and the sound of a radio, and then Mike was inside, facing a woman who looked as old as his father but was the size of a ten-year-old. She was so skinny that the outline of her shoulder blades was visible through her flowered top. "This is Inez," his father said, shutting and locking the door behind him.

She touched Mike's arm. "I guess you're real!" she said, then sat down in a dilapidated armchair. Then she was up again, moving into the adjoining kitchenette. She took a cigarette from her purse and lit it at the gas stove. "You two go on and talk," she said. "Just pretend I'm not here." She slid herself up on the counter and let her high-heeled sandals drop. Her toenails were painted pink. Her feet were so pale that Mike could see the blue of her veins.

The cabin was shabby, small, and old. There was only one bed, and Glenn, sitting down on the side that was farthest from the kitchenette, motioned for Mike to sit next to him. The heater came on noisily.

"Tell me what's going on at home," he said softly. "Keep your voice down. Inez doesn't know the details."

"Mom's okay," Mike said.

"Fine. Good. But I mean, as far as I'm concerned." He was leaning forward, his eyes intense and excited. His face was thin. He looked older, and his beard was more gray than brown. His left eye was bloodshot.

"Well," Mike said, "people know what you did."

"I didn't have to see you to find that out." He put his hand on Mike's knee. "It wasn't what they think, though. They're after me for the wrong thing."

The heater turned off. Glenn swiftly reached for the transistor radio and turned it up.

"You mean you didn't kill her?" Mike whispered.

His father jerked back around. "Listen," he said quietly. "She died, and I was there. But *kill* is the wrong word."

Behind them Inez jumped off the counter and opened the refrigerator. "How about eggs?" she said with her back to them.

"What?" Glenn said.

"Eggs," Inez said loudly.

"Where are the tacos?" Glenn said. "What happened to the Mexican food?"

"How should I know?"

"What's the right word, then?" Mike said in a low voice. "What word would you use?"

"I'd just as soon not use a word," his father said. "A word can mean one thing when you mean another."

"Did you shoot her or not?" Mike whispered.

"It's not that simple. You're asking the wrong questions. I can see already that you have bad information." Mike watched him rub the back of his neck, then move his head back and forth. "I get stiff," he told Mike. "It's tension. You'll find out about it when you get older."

"I find out about it every day," Mike said.

His father stared at him.

"I can do scrambled," Inez called out. "I can do over easy."

"What?" his father said.

"Scrambled, then," she said. "People who don't answer don't get what they want." After a moment she sang, along with the radio, "It hurts as much in Texas as it did in Tennessee."

"Tell her how good the meal is," Mike's father said. "Don't forget. Say it a couple of times."

TWENTY-FOUR

THEY ate at the Formica table in the kitchenette: eggs, toast, and milk on the verge of going sour. "Drink it anyway," Glenn told Mike. "It won't kill you."

"It's yogurt," Inez said happily. She crossed her thin legs, and Mike saw her slide a bare foot along Glenn's calf. "I have the coldest feet. So did my dad. We had that in common."

"Put on socks," Glenn said.

"Your dad's not a good listener," Inez told Mike. "But I guess you already know that. You have a whole history, you and your dad." With her toast she moved her eggs from one side of the plate to the other.

"This is good, isn't it, Mike?" Glenn said. He was eating with intensity. "It's delicious, isn't it?"

"Yes," Mike said. "Thank you."

"Then finish it," Inez said.

"I'm not all that hungry," Mike told her.

"Eat it anyway," his father said tersely.

Inez inched her own plate toward the center of the table. "I like history more than your dad does," she told Mike. "I'm interested in facts, like where somebody comes from, and who his people are."

"We have all day tomorrow to talk," Glenn said. "Let's just relax right now. Mike's tired."

"Why aren't those words coming out of Mike's mouth?" Inez said.

"Because it's full of your good food!" Glenn said with fake cheeriness.

Inez studied his face, then Mike's. "All right then," she said. Her eyes moved back and forth between them as they ate. Then she cleared the dishes while Glenn unrolled a sleeping bag at the foot of the bed. "It's where our dog would sleep if we had one!" Inez joked to Mike, who hadn't moved, who felt stunned and exhausted.

"You don't even like dogs!" Glenn said, steering her away from the kitchenette sink. It was apparent to Mike that he was moving fast to get her out of the kitchenette, then in and out of the bathroom. He did the same thing with Mike.

"How about this?" his father said to him, pointing with the toe of his shoe to the sleeping bag, which Mike got into—automatically and obediently, he realized, as if he were a dog—without undressing. Within a few minutes the light was off and the room was quiet. His father and

Inez, in the double bed, above him, seemed to fall asleep within minutes.

The situation was really wrong, really off kilter. It was so much crazier than Mike had expected that he couldn't keep up with it, especially because he was so tired. What had he expected? he thought then. Nothing. He hadn't had time to expect anything. But all he had to do was sleep, he thought. He would be out of there in the morning.

Except that he was almost too tired to sleep. The floor was cold; the sleeping bag was a cheap one, just thin polyester, and if Mike could have been anywhere right then, it would have been with Donetta under the comforter he'd given her—though not at her house, he thought—someplace else, someplace alone. Mike was the only person who had ever made Donetta feel less alone. Why did that mean so much to him? It came back to him often, how she'd said that on their first date, how she'd trusted him that much, as opposed to now, when she didn't anymore, when she'd gotten smart enough, he thought, not to.

He was lying on his back, tears making a path out of the corners of his eyes and wetting his hair. There were tears in everything, he thought, if you looked around you, if you saw the truth behind your situation and the sadness that was always behind the truth. Because underneath, you were tied to the world and to yourself, and who you were had already been decided beforehand, and without you.

In his sleep, Mike's father said, "Forget it," then, awake, he got out of bed. Mike heard the floor creak under his weight, then heard water running in the kitchenette sink. His father had always gotten up at night—to use the bathroom, to get a drink, to wander through the house in a lost way. He'd done it all Mike's life. Sometimes Mike had woken at two or three in the morning to the sound of his parents talking—his mother's voice more frequent, somewhat comforting, his father's hollow and depressed.

His father came to the foot of the sleeping bag. "Mike," he whispered; Mike kept his eyes closed. His father knelt down and shook him. "Mike," he whispered more loudly, and Mike was forced to open his eyes, to get up and follow his father into the kitchenette. "Keep an eye on Inez," his father said. "Though she sleeps soundly. She takes something."

"Where did she come from?"

His father hesitated. "I don't want to be cruel. I'll just say, she's helping me and I'm helping her." He put his hand on Mike's arm. "Did you tell anyone you were leaving?"

"My roommate."

"Who did you say I was?"

"Josh."

"When did you say you'd be back?"

"Last night," Mike lied.

"Call tomorrow and say Sunday."

"I can't."

"I'm asking you to, if it's not a risk to me."

"I don't want to," Mike said.

"Are you afraid of the police? Do you think that anyone

would fault a son for wanting to see his father?" He tightened his hand on Mike's arm. "I go from place to place," he said. "I hide by moving. You don't know how hard it is." He broke into tears.

Mike looked away from him, at the cold, dark room.

"Just stay until Sunday," his father said.

"Glenn?" Inez said. She got out of bed. She stood, shivering, in a long, white sweatshirt, her thin legs bare.

"It's okay, honey. Everything's fine. No problem of any kind." Glenn squeezed Mike's arm. "Sleep on it," he whispered, and followed Inez back to bed.

"Warm up my icy feet," Mike heard her say.

Mike lay back down. The wind outside had increased. There was no light yet, but he knew that it wasn't far away. The room was growing shadowy. It was the time of morning he'd been waking up at school, in his small, bare dorm room. But that room didn't seem so bare to him now, nor did his life at school: walking to his classes, returning to Hansen Hall afterward, and opening his mailbox, hoping to find what he almost always did—an envelope addressed to him in Donetta's small, back-slanted handwriting. Even the nights there seemed less lonely now.

It didn't matter anymore how unhappy he'd been in Brookings. That had been his life, and now he felt on the verge of losing it. He was missing it as if it had been lost.

TWENTY-FIVE

MIKE woke alone, after ten. The day outside was overcast and blustery, and there was a note for him on the unmade bed: "Don't leave. Dad." Inez's car was gone. The first thing Mike did was check his jacket to make sure that his father had not taken his truck keys.

In the kitchenette he ate two doughnuts from a package on the counter and was in the bathroom, throwing up, a minute later. Then, not feeling much better, he got into the shower, standing under the hot water until it ran cold. He dressed and walked out to his truck. He was unlocking the door to get aspirin from his glove compartment when he heard a car at the edge of the woods and saw his father get out and run toward him. "Didn't you see my note?" he shouted at Mike.

"Yes."

"What did it say?"

"I just told you I saw it."

"It said don't leave, didn't it?"

Mike got the aspirin from his glove compartment while his father stood under the trees, his face white and tense. "All right," Glenn said. "I made a mistake. Good." He shook his head. "Don't scare me like that again." He hurried away, stopped to wait for Mike, then sped up again, toward the motel.

"You said we would talk," Mike said, right behind him. "Just stop and talk to me. Tell me what happened. Then I need to go."

"Fine," his father said. "As soon as we eat. Inez wants us to have a real meal together."

"Why?"

"Who knows?"

And already his father, then Mike, were turning the corner of the motel, with Inez less than ten feet away, unloading plastic grocery sacks from the car. She looked younger in the daylight, and her face was scarred, as if she'd had acne or something worse. "So your dad brought you back," she said cheerfully to Mike. "Good for him. I like company."

"Inez thinks this is a vacation," Glenn said.

"You'd think so, too, if you had my life," Inez said.

Glenn maneuvered both of them into the stale, gloomy cabin, and within just a few minutes there was the sound of a car out front. It didn't occur to Mike to be afraid until he saw his father's reaction. "Inez!" Glenn said. "Go to the window and tell me what you see. Don't stand too close."

"You've got it," Inez said. She moved briskly and watched for almost a minute without speaking.

"Come on!" Glenn said.

"A fat red-haired woman with a little dog, in a beat-up station wagon with Indiana plates. She's checking in."

"Where?"

"Here."

"Which unit, damn it?"

"Don't talk to me like I'm retarded," Inez told him. "The one at the other end."

Glenn looked out the window himself, pulled the curtain closed, and turned toward Mike. "I'm taking a chance, being this close to you. They think I'm dumb enough to be here, and here I am."

"Leave, then," Mike said coldly.

"Don't talk to me like that."

"I hate fighting," Inez said. "It makes me nervous."

"Me, too," Glenn said at once. "I agree with you." He checked the window again. "I'm under a lot of pressure," he told Mike. "I'm asking you to understand that."

"Fine," Mike said. He sat in the armchair and closed his eyes. He repeated to himself the contents of Tom DeWitt's letter. Mike knew more about what the police knew than his father knew he did. That was how he would get through this, he thought. He would stay in control by remembering the knowledge he had.

When he opened his eyes, his father was standing with his arms around Inez. She was so small that she made him look bigger than he was.

"See?" Glenn said. "Everything's fine."

"It's not," Inez said.

"It is. Mike?" he said. "Come tell Inez that everything is okay."

Inez was breathing rapidly, like a panicked animal. Her small eyes were fixed on Mike's face.

"Everything is okay," Mike said. "It's no big deal. I just got mad for a minute."

"See?" Glenn said again.

"No," Inez said.

"Let's eat lunch," Glenn said energetically. "How about it? Anybody hungry?"

"Nobody's hungry," Inez said.

Mike looked at her restless, angry eyes, and at the tension in his father's face. He said that he was hungry.

"Good," Glenn said. "That's what I thought." He patted Inez's arm and filled a pot with water. He put the pot on the stove and turned on the burner. "Simple as could be," he said. "Over and done with." When the water boiled he poured it into three bowls.

"You forgot the ramen noodles!" Inez said.

Glenn laughed loudly. "For Pete's sake," he said. "I did, didn't I? What was I thinking?"

"Get out of here," Inez said in a normal voice. "You men. You don't belong in a kitchen."

Mike and his father grabbed their jackets and went outside. Glenn led Mike around to the back of the motel, from where, on a small rise, they could see through the pines to the stirred-up lake. The clouds were low and dark. The temperature was dropping, and the wind was loud. "Do you understand now what I mean about pressure?" Glenn said to Mike. "There's something wrong with her."

"What?"

"I have no idea." He looked at his footprints in the sandy dirt and slid his feet around, erasing them. "I'll have to leave before too long anyway. She and I have been seen together enough."

"Leave for where?"

"I don't know yet. I can't say."

Inez's intense face appeared around the corner of the building. "Lunch," she said, then disappeared.

"Listen," Mike said. "I want to talk to you. I want to know what happened. But then I have to go back."

"Why?"

"I said I would. And I have studying to do."

"Studying?" Glenn said. "Are you kidding me?"

"It's more than that. What if my roommate tells people I'm missing?"

"Okay, then," Glenn said. "I see what you mean." He checked his watch. "Inez will drive you to a pay phone. You'll call your roommate then."

"No," Mike said.

From inside came the sound of Inez knocking loudly on the wall.

"Let's go," Glenn said. "We have three minutes before she explodes." He was already moving, and Mike, too tired to think quickly enough, too slow to keep up with how fast things were happening, followed at a distance.

INSIDE, they were trapped again at the tiny kitchenette table.

"The soup got cold," Inez said. "While you were out back, telling secrets."

"What secrets?" Glenn said.

"How would I know? You're keeping them from me!" She was laughing, though, and Glenn joined in. Then she turned toward Mike, whose stomach was knotted and tight. "I thought you said you were hungry!"

"I am. It's good." He made himself eat and shook his head when she asked if he wanted more.

"How about cards after lunch?" Glenn said. "Inez is good at cards."

"I specialize in hearts," Inez told Mike.

"Then later on," Glenn said firmly to Mike, "Inez will drive you to a pay phone so that you can call your roommate. How's that, Inez?"

"I like to drive," Inez said.

"You know what we'll do after that?" Glenn said animatedly. "We'll open a bottle of wine. I'll cook the steaks we bought this morning. It's not safe for us to go anywhere as a group. I'm taking a big enough risk staying here one more night."

"Listen," Mike said as politely as he could. "I'll go back to school right after lunch. I don't mind. That way, you and Inez can go someplace safer."

"No," Glenn said. "Seeing you is worth the risk."

"That's more like it," Inez said. "That's how families should be."

TWENTY-SIX

THEY sat on the unmade bed and played hearts. The room was cold, and there had not been more than a minute, since lunch, when Mike and his father had been alone. Inez never sat still. She was like a bird, Mike thought, or like an insect—buzzing from one spot to the next, flinging herself in and out of the bathroom, darting into the kitchenette to light a cigarette at the stove. Mike planned to wait an hour, then tell his father to walk him out to his truck—to talk to him seriously, so that Mike would know exactly what happened. Then Mike would leave.

Meanwhile, a winter storm was moving in. Three inches of snow, they heard on the radio. "Not enough to worry about," Mike's father said, each time Mike got up to look at the threatening sky. "We're lucky. It will keep the police busy."

"No kidding," Inez said, exhaling cigarette smoke. "Imagine no indoor toilet," she told Glenn. "Alton did all the plumbing himself. Can you picture that? As big and crazy as he was?"

"Isn't that something," Glenn said.

She put down her cards and shot into the bathroom. Glenn waited until she closed the door. "Alton was a relative of some kind," he whispered to Mike.

Mike watched the bathroom door. Quietly, he said, "I'm leaving soon. Just so you know. I'm not changing my mind. Whatever you want me to know you can tell me then."

"What do you mean by soon?" Glenn said.

The door flung open. "What's happening soon?" Inez asked.

Glenn hesitated. "Snow," he said then. "I have a feeling. I'm good at predicting things."

"You think you're good at everything," Inez said, and perched on the bed, cross-legged.

They played one more game, then Mike put down his cards. "That's it for me," he said.

"Because you lost," Glenn said. "That's bad strategy. The time to quit is when you're ahead." His eyes were on Inez, who had stood up and was taking small steps from one end of the room to the other.

"I don't like the end of things," she said. "I don't care if it's a card game or a movie. I like things to keep going."

"Get back here and play another hand then," Glenn said with strained lightheartedness. "How about canasta?"

"No," she said. "I don't mean that. You don't get what I mean."

"Sure we do," Glenn said.

"*We* is a lie," Inez said. "It's almost always a lie."

"*I* know what you mean," Glenn said. "That's what I meant to say."

"You can't fix it afterward. I don't know who told you that was fair."

Glenn looked at Mike nervously. He went up to Inez and put his hand on her rough hair, smoothing it back from her small face.

"You don't need to worry about me," Inez said. "You have your loved one here."

"Don't you think I love you?" Glenn whispered. Mike was too close not to hear.

"Of course not. And wouldn't I be in trouble if I did!" She seemed to pull herself together then. She went into the bathroom and came back a moment later, wearing red lipstick. She put on her coat and got her keys. "Who has quarters?" she said matter-of-factly.

It took Mike a second to understand. "I don't need to make a phone call," he said.

"Sure you do," Glenn said.

"I'll go alone then," Mike said. "I mean, I have to get going anyway."

"Make the call," his father said authoritatively. "That way, you can still leave later, if you want to. There's nothing wrong with showing up early. There's only something wrong with showing up late." He took a handful of quarters from his pocket. "Isn't that right?" he said to Inez, who was standing at the door, glowering at Mike.

"Inez?" Glenn said. "What's wrong, honey? Mike didn't mean that he'd rather go alone, did you, Mike? Didn't it come out different than you meant?"

They were both watching him—Inez with fury and his father with desperation or suspicion, Mike didn't know which. He felt unsteady and hot, even in the cold room. The situation had gotten beyond him. "I'm not sure," he said. "I don't know what I meant."

"I told you," Glenn said to Inez. "He's just confused. We've got too much going on here." He picked up Mike's jacket and handed it to him. "Inez loves to drive. I don't know why, but there it is. She wants to take you."

He put an arm around Mike and walked him outside. "You and I will talk when you get back," he said very softly. "Then you can leave. I promise. You're the only person I can tell the truth to." He steered Mike into the passenger seat of the car. In his regular voice he said, "Don't go any farther than you have to. And make the conversation short. People suspect something's wrong when you talk too much."

"Get in," Inez told Mike.

Glenn closed Mike's door and hurried inside. When Mike looked back, the road was empty except for the station wagon at the far end. Mike hadn't seen either the woman or the dog go in or out.

All right, Mike thought, as Inez started driving. He'd

been manipulated into this car ride because he hadn't been smart enough to avoid it; he hadn't been smart enough because he was overtired, plus whatever it was that was wrong with his stomach. As things were now, he thought, it was easier just to make the call—to go along with most of what his father wanted—then leave afterward.

Inez lit a cigarette. "Are you okay then with your dad?" she asked. "Children should never be angry at their parents. Your father's not responsible for what he does."

"Why not?"

"He's a man," Inez said. "He's no more responsible than you are."

Snow was beginning to fall. Inez reduced her speed, driving with exaggerated care. Along the road were flat brown fields and fenced pastures. There were few cars on the road besides theirs.

"I was in a terrible accident once," Inez said. "I almost lost someone I love."

"Who?"

"Me," she said. "Inez."

"Why do you like to drive, then?"

"That's a good question," Inez said. "I'm going to give that some thought."

They drove for fifteen silent minutes before approaching a small town—a boarded-up elementary school and a closed gas station. "Hicksville," Inez said. Further on was a grain elevator, a diner, and a stretch of modest houses. Inez stopped at a Handy-Mart that had a pay phone out front.

She got out with Mike and stood next to him at the phone. "I like fresh air," she said. "I'm not like your dad, the way he holes himself up." She opened her purse and took out three dollars' worth of quarters.

"I have a calling card," Mike said.

Inez laughed. "And you're in college!" She pressed the change into his hand. "Go ahead and call. It's cold out here."

Mike dialed his phone number and put in the quarters. Nobody answered. When the phone machine came on, he said, "Raymond? It's Mike. I might not come back tonight. I might come back tomorrow."

"Right," Inez whispered. She lit a fresh cigarette and peered into the store window as Mike hung up the phone. "Is there anything you need?" she asked. "Any personal grooming items?"

"No."

"Magazines? A *Playboy*?"

"No, thanks."

She seemed reluctant to leave.

"Is there something you want?" Mike asked.

"Not really. Not anything they have."

She stood there a moment longer, her face close to the glass, her breath creating small foggy circles. Then she and Mike got back in the car and she pulled onto the windswept road, the houses and patchy grass alongside it dusted with snow. "Do you like malls?" Inez asked.

"Not much."

"I knew you'd say that." Her voice was sad. "I like walking through them. I like the way they smell. I like the way the lights look." She glanced over at him. She touched his knee with her fingers. "Do you know what I mean?"

"Not exactly."

"Well," she said. "At least you're honest. That's more than I can say for you-know-who." She turned on the radio and found only static. She turned it off and sang, " 'Hello, window. Is that a tear I see in the corner of your pane?' "

"Willie Nelson," Mike said.

"That's right. Score one for you."

There was more snow on the road now, and she was sitting forward in the seat, driving intently. When they were close to the turnoff for the motel, she said, "Why didn't you want to go with me? What's wrong with my company?"

Mike's stomach hurt again. "Nothing," he said. "It just seemed easier that way."

"Easier for you," Inez said. "Isn't that a surprise."

TWENTY-SEVEN

THE cabin door opened as soon as Mike and Inez got out of the car. "How did it go?" Glenn said. He came toward them in the snow. It was dusk by then; there was a light on in the cabin and one at the far end of the motel.

"Fine," Inez stated. She slammed the car door and stomped past him.

"Everything went smoothly?" Glenn said, talking fast.

"What did I just say?" Inez said.

"Isn't she a good driver, Mike? I told you that. She's nice and careful."

Mike was standing in the road, halfway between the car and the motel, waiting for his father to walk toward him and for Inez to go inside. But she didn't go inside. She stopped in the open doorway. "Get the wine out," she told Glenn.

"Okay. Great," Glenn said. "Come on," he said to Mike. "Come in out of the snow."

Mike spoke as cautiously and judiciously as he could, for Inez's benefit, not for his father's. He understood now that everything depended on her reactions. "I thought I would leave now," he said. "That way I won't get home too late. I thought we could talk for a minute. Then I'll take off."

Inez scowled at Mike. "He doesn't want to be around me," she told Glenn.

"That's not true," Glenn said. "That doesn't sound like Mike."

"Who does it sound like then?" Inez said icily.

"Nobody," Glenn said. "That doesn't sound like anybody I know. Right, Mike?"

Mike looked toward the far end of the motel, where the station wagon was parked. What if he walked down there? he thought suddenly. Would it scare his father into doing what he wanted? What if it didn't? But Mike was too worn-out to think beyond that. Meanwhile, Inez's small eyes were fastened on his face.

"Mike?" his father said. "Let's have one glass of wine and eat dinner. Are you a drinker these days? Then you can be on your way. A glass of wine won't hurt you as long as you eat."

"He doesn't want to be here!" Inez shouted, and Mike's father flinched.

"Let's talk inside, Mike," he said urgently, looking up and down the road. "Look at us, standing in the cold like fools."

"Don't call me names!" Inez said. "Call yourself whatever you want, but leave me out of it!"

"Mike, please," his father said, moving toward him. "Just to get her inside," he whispered. "Please. So she doesn't leave with the car."

"What?" Inez said loudly.

"Just one more hour," his father pleaded.

INSIDE, Glenn poured wine into three plastic glasses. He clinked his own glass against Inez's without making a toast, and he and Inez drank theirs quickly. "So everything went smoothly," he said to her. "I knew it would. I knew I could count on you."

"You don't know anything," Inez said. But with her next drink the anger went out of her voice; she poured Glenn a second glass, and topped off Mike's, where he stood next to the window, wearing his jacket. "Take that thing off," she said. "Can't you tell it's warmed up in here?"

"I fixed the heater while you were gone," Glenn told her, his voice no longer sounding so lively. Mike watched the two of them—the way Inez moved rapidly and his father navigated warily around her. Mike told himself that all he had to do was be careful around Inez, to make sure she stayed. That was one thing his father was right about. Otherwise the only person there with a vehicle would be Mike. That would have occurred to him sooner if he'd had more sleep, if he'd felt healthy the way he used to, a long time ago. He looked out the window at the snow, and at dusk turning into night.

In the kitchenette Inez was pouring herself a third glass of wine. "Go for it," his father said, and she reached out and put her hand on his crotch. He jumped away. "Oh," she said, laughing. "You didn't mean that?"

Glenn turned back to the stove. He stopped smiling. He looked so intense that Mike was afraid something was happening to him—a stroke or a heart attack.

"Dad?" he said, using that word for the first time since he'd gotten there.

"What?"

"Nothing. Never mind."

Then dinner was ready, and though Mike had stopped drinking, his father and Inez hadn't. "I'm glad you're here," Glenn told Mike at the table. "Inez understands that you have to leave soon, and I know this has been tough on you. But now you can see how it's been for me. I wanted you to see it from my perspective."

"What's this 'it' you're talking about?" Inez said. She gestured with her arm and knocked Glenn's wineglass off the table.

"Goddamn it," he said angrily. "Can't we have one meal where nobody spills anything?"

Mike hadn't heard his father say that in years. It was what he'd said whenever Mike had spilled anything as a child. How often could that have happened? Mike thought now. How irritating could it have been?

Inez had stopped eating. "Who the hell spilled anything at lunch?" she said, her voice cold and dangerous-sounding.

"I don't know," Glenn said. "Somebody."

"Nobody," Inez said.

"Mike did, didn't he?"

"No." She got up from the table and stood in front of the small stove. She lit a cigarette from the gas burner.

"Don't smoke while we're eating," Glenn said. "I've told you that before. I hate that."

"I don't care what you hate."

Mike stood up, sick and dizzy. "Just back off," he said to his father.

"I've been backing off," Glenn said. "I think that's obvious."

"I think that's obvious," Inez said. She walked up behind him and stubbed out her cigarette in his food.

Mike's father crossed the room and opened the front door. He shut it hard behind him.

"There he goes," Inez said. "Into the cold without a jacket. If that isn't crazy." She lit another cigarette and sat down at the table. "You haven't eaten a thing," she said to Mike. "That's a good steak you're wasting."

Mike, the cigarette smoke in his face, hurried into the bathroom, vomited, then sat on the floor with his head down, his hands cold with sweat. He tried to picture himself four hundred miles away, in Wheatley. He imagined driving out to Crow Lake, lying down on the front seat of his truck, and letting himself sleep.

"Mike?" Inez said. She pounded on the bathroom door. "I don't see him. I don't know what happened to him." She banged on the door until he opened it and came out.

"It's too dark to see anything," he told her.

"No. That's wrong. I can see the car." She opened the front door. "Glenn?" she called. She waited a moment. "He's not answering. Maybe he's too far away."

"That's probably it," Mike said. Inez looked at him hatefully. "I'm agreeing with you," he said. "I'm saying you're probably right."

She opened the door again. "Glenn!" she shouted into the night.

"Listen," Mike said. "Don't yell like that. Come inside." He touched her arm; when she stepped back in he pulled the door shut. "It's okay," he told her. "He'll come back. He'll walk in here in just a few minutes."

"He was done with his food!" she said in a high-pitched voice. "I was just putting garbage into garbage!"

"Maybe he wasn't done," Mike said. "Maybe he had a little steak left on his plate."

"That was your plate, with that nice steak left over! I don't know why you don't eat what's put in front of you!" She opened the door again. "Glenn?" she called tenderly. "Come back in, honey. Warm yourself up." She crossed her arms. She turned around and faced Mike. "Why does he want to make me so unhappy? What is he punishing me for?"

"The cigarette," Mike said softly. He watched her face

change from distraught to hopeless. She closed the door and sat down on the thin, worn carpeting. It's all right, Mike wanted to tell her. People get over being mad. People walk out and then they come back. But he couldn't say anything. Like her, he watched the door.

TWENTY-EIGHT

THE room was too warm now, and there seemed to be no way to adjust the heat. The kitchenette was cluttered with dirty dishes and pots, the bed had not been made nor the sleeping bag rolled up. Inez had not moved. She was sitting with her knees pulled up, making small, moaning sounds, and Mike thought that he should try to comfort her. But he was afraid that she'd use it as a reason to get crazier, even. He stayed where he was, his stomach hurting, looking at the wallpaper behind her. It was yellowed and old. Everything in the cabin was discolored. Probably nothing had ever been nice. If you weren't depressed when you walked in, you'd want to kill yourself by the time you left.

"Look," Mike said. "I'll see if I can find him."

The snow was falling less heavily, and Mike walked far into the field across the road, then back and behind the motel, where he and his father had stood earlier. He felt better being outside in the cold darkness. The wind was decreasing, and an owl was calling from somewhere behind him. The pine boughs were blanketed lightly with snow.

"Glenn," he said softly, as an experiment, to see how strange it felt to say the name. But it seemed even stranger to say "Dad"—because his father never had been one, really, he knew, not the kind they showed in movies and Father's Day commercials. And even if those were phony, his father still hadn't been one in Mike's own mind.

He stood in back of the motel, breathing the cold air, knowing that he didn't want to find him. Because he'd gotten where he was on his own. He'd managed this far without him.

In the next moment there were footsteps and voices, and his father and Inez were hurrying toward him. "I didn't know where you were," Glenn said, panting. "Inez wouldn't tell me."

"Fuck you," Inez said.

"Come on now. Don't be like that. I'm here now."

She gave him a black look, then vanished; Glenn—with Mike following only because he was sick again suddenly—ran after her to the front of the cabin and inside, where she was furiously throwing her belongings into a small flowered bag.

"I was at fault," Glenn said. "I know that. I made a mistake." He pursued her into the kitchenette. "Tell me what you want me to say!"

"How about nothing?" Inez said. "How does that sound?" She zipped up her overnight bag and put on her coat. She was out the door, with Glenn running after her, when Mike got past them to the bathroom.

By the time he came out, his father was standing at the open door, alone. The car was gone. Mike thought he saw movement at the other end of the motel, near the station wagon, but whatever he thought he saw was gone when he looked again.

Behind him now, his father was packing. "She'll be back in a few minutes," he said. "But I won't wait more than ten. Then we'll have to get in your truck and leave." He was throwing things into the duffel bag Mike had taken to summer camp ten years earlier. For a second Mike could think only of standing in that clearing, watching his mother help his weeping father into the car. Inside the duffel bag his mother had left a note: "Try not to be homesick. We'll be back for you in two weeks."

"Where are your keys?" his father said. "Let me have them just in case."

"In case what?" Mike said.

"In case anything happens." He got out a plastic trash bag and threw everything in the kitchenette into it: dirty dishes, leftover food, the contents of the refrigerator. Then he put on a pair of gloves and cleaned off every surface in the room with a wet towel. "Isn't this something?" he said to Mike. "Doesn't this remind you of the movies we used to watch?"

Mike shook his head.

"Get your things together. What did you bring?"

"Nothing."

"Then watch the window for me."

Mike put his cold hands against the cold glass, watching for Inez's car. If she would just come back, he thought, he could walk out the minute he saw her headlights. He could walk out and be in his truck, driving away, in less than five minutes. He could leave, even if he didn't find out anything from his father, as long as his father had somebody else to turn to.

Glenn put the duffel bag and trash bag next to the door. "Do you have any money?" he asked Mike.

Mike gave him thirty dollars—all but five of what he had.

"Good," Glenn said. "Where are your keys?"

"I have them."

"Give them to me. I'll drive. I don't mind. It will look less suspicious than you driving me."

"Driving you where?" Mike said.

"I'm not sure yet. Maybe Cleveland." He switched off the light and came toward Mike. He held out his hand.

"Give her more time," Mike said. "You said she'd come back. You said you were helping her."

"She's crazy."

"But not completely!"

"Okay," his father said. "Forget Cleveland. I can make do with Minneapolis. We can be there in two hours."

"She'll be back before then!"

"Just give me the keys. I'm only asking this one thing. After Minneapolis, you can turn around and drive back to school." His thin face was tightly pale. "If you didn't want to help me," he said, "you shouldn't have come."

Mike stepped back from his father then. He looked at the hand he held out—first for money, and now for this, which Mike should have realized from the beginning.

"I want to know what happened," Mike said. "I want to know why you did what you did."

His father glared at him. "She grabbed my arm," he said. "I never intended to shoot her. It was at least sixty percent her fault. Because she was like you are now," he told Mike fiercely. "She was going to leave me when I needed her."

LEAVING, and leaving his father in the cabin, alone, wasn't as hard to do as Mike had thought. He just opened the door. But behind him his father was crying. His shoulders were hunched and his arms were loose at his sides. Tears were streaming down his face into his collar.

Mike went into the bathroom for Kleenex. Standing in front of the sink, in the harsh brightness of the overhead light, he stared at his own face in the mirror. It was just a sound, he told himself, and after a while it would stop. It wasn't going to kill him to hear it, no matter how bad it made him feel.

He delivered the Kleenex to his father, who followed

Mike outside and down the dirt road to the rutted path leading into the woods. Mike wanted to stop and explain that there were things you couldn't make people do—even people who loved you. But he kept walking instead, and by the time he unlocked his truck, his father was twenty feet behind him, standing without a jacket in the middle of the snow-covered trail. Mike drove out slowly, watching his father move aside, finally, letting him go.

MIKE drove for thirty minutes before stopping to call Tom DeWitt from a pay phone outside a closed gas station. He dialed the third number, the one that was cellular, and hoped that it would just keep ringing. He was willing to stand all night in the cold, listening to it ring. But Tom answered. "We know," he said. "Don't say anything. We're at the motel now."

Mike held the receiver, looking at the road and snow and at his blue truck, parked safely in the darkness.

"Where are you?" Tom said, and Mike told him the name of the gas station, and the town it was close to. "Stay there," he told Mike. "Just sit in your truck until I get there."

Mike, waiting in the darkness, already knew most of what Tom would tell him later: that the red-haired woman at the motel was a police officer, and that there were more police with her; that they had listened in on Glenn's call to Mike at school and had followed Mike before that, in Brookings; and that Tom had been in Brookings, too, more than once. And, most important of all, that Tom's letter had correctly predicted that Glenn would contact Mike, would try to involve him.

Mike had been too worried about himself—that was what he thought now. He should have been smarter about that letter. He should have believed it more, and he should have trusted his father less. He should have said no when he called. He should have done nothing. Because Tom De-Witt would have caught his father soon enough anyway, without him.

TWENTY minutes later Mike saw headlights, coming fast. Then Tom was getting into Mike's truck, his heavy jacket swinging open to reveal a shoulder holster and gun. His face was chapped from the wind. "Are you all right?" he asked.

"Tell me what happened."

"Your father's under arrest. He's all right, not injured in any way." He settled himself into the seat and pulled his jacket closed, over the gun. "You're in the clear," he told Mike. "The important thing is that you didn't help him. All that matters in the end is what you do."

Mike watched him brush snow from his hair and jacket—as if he'd been out hunting just deer, Mike thought. "Does that go for you, too?" he said bitterly. "Is that why you feel so good now?"

"Who said I felt good?"

"Don't you?"

"It's not that simple," Tom said. "Sometimes you regret things you have to do. Sometimes you can't find another way to do them."

"So you screw people over."

Three state police cars went by, heading west, one after the other, the headlights shining in sequence into the cab of Mike's truck. "My dad?" Mike said, and Tom nodded. They both watched the cars for as long as they could see them.

"Sometimes you screw yourself, too," Tom said, in a less certain voice. "Not usually, but when you want to stay in touch with people afterward."

"My mother?"

"You *and* your mother."

Mike looked at the dark, empty highway. For the first time he knew something significant that Tom didn't: It wasn't Tom DeWitt Mike's mother cared for. But Mike didn't feel even glad. He looked at Tom's weathered face and his thinning hair, and felt bad for him.

"I haven't called your mother yet," Tom said. "I wanted to wait until you were away from here. But I'll be honest with her. I'm not asking you to keep our surveillance of you secret."

"But you'd like to."

"Would it do any good if I did?" He smiled at Mike without looking happy. "Yes. I would like to. But I won't."

"What was the point of the dog, at the motel?" Mike asked quietly. "Whose dog was that?"

"It was just a prop," Tom said. "Your dad likes dogs. He doesn't think of them suspiciously."

"Do you plan everything you do?" Mike said. "Don't you ever do anything by accident? I mean, just by chance?"

Tom thought before he spoke. "Yes," he said. Then, "No. Probably not. Not for a long time." He zipped up his jacket and said, "I'll call you in a few days. I'll tell you whatever I can. Meanwhile, go back to school. Go to your classes. The worst has already happened."

"Because of us," Mike said.

"No. Because of what your father did." Tom looked at Mike for a few seconds. Then, hesitantly, as if he weren't sure what Mike might do, he rested a strong hand on his shoulder. "Be careful driving back to Brookings," he told him, then opened the door and stepped out into the cold.

TWENTY-NINE

MIKE stayed there for a long time after Tom left. He noticed, without thinking about it, that the snow had stopped and that a quarter moon was visible. And he noticed that now, because of the moon, he could see farther into the pasture across the road than he'd been able to before. But he didn't feel much of anything. The part of him that had been preoccupied with his father was now vacant, just emptied out. There was nothing else inside of him, he thought. Next to him on the seat was the card with Tom's phone numbers on it, and Mike picked it up and put it in the glove compartment, out of sight.

Finally he just started driving. Two miles east of the state line, remembering about the license plate, he turned into a parking lot next to a church. He drove to the back of it, where the snow was untouched, and as he replaced the

Minnesota plate with his South Dakota one, he remembered his father saying, "I don't believe there's a God. Not many people are brave enough to say that."

That struck Mike now as a foolish thing to say. But what did he, himself, believe in? He didn't know. He looked at the small cemetery next to the church, a layer of snow as thin as paper on top of the gray stones. He put on his seat belt when he got back in his truck.

He drove mile after mile through the darkness. Then, his stomach still queasy, he stopped near the interstate and bought a 7-Up at an all-night convenience store.

"I guess the snow's stopped," said the short, older woman behind the counter. "That was the earliest snow I can remember in a lot of years."

"Me, too," Mike said.

"You're too young to know what a lot of years means," she told him.

A man in a cowboy hat came in just before Mike left. "I guess the snow's stopped," the woman said to him. "That was the earliest snow I can remember in a lot of years."

That should have made Mike smile, at least, but he barely registered it. He walked to his truck, got in, and pulled onto the flat, straight highway that would take him into Brookings. He drove automatically and not very carefully. He realized that there was something wrong with the way he felt. He should have been having some specific reaction, he thought, like relief, if nothing else. But he couldn't say that he felt relieved. What he did know was that he was tired and cold. He never, maybe, had been that tired.

He turned on the radio and listened to a country station: songs about love of one kind or another. There was a commercial for the Corn Palace, in Mitchell. Mike had been there with his parents, but Donetta had never seen it. "My father was going to take me," she'd told Mike more than once. "It was on his 'things-to-do-next-summer' list."

Unexpectedly, the sadness of that affected him, and made him see what he hadn't seen before. There were too many things on that list. Donetta had named nine or ten over the years since her father had died. He never would have done any of them, Mike understood now. Summers would have come and gone, and all he would have done was kept writing them down.

Close to Brookings now, watching the highway, Mike started to cry. Tears, unaccompanied at first by emotion, ran down his face, and when he no longer could see the road he pulled off to the side of the highway and wept. It was the only time he ever had. Hearing that word Mike would have thought that he knew what it meant, but he wouldn't have known that it was like this. Tears were only salt water, Donetta's father had said, but he had been wrong about that, too. What they were made of, Mike knew now, didn't tell you what they did. They brought up to the surface what you had pushed down to the bottom. They let you know how much of you there was.

It was a while before they stopped. Then he wiped his

face with the sleeve of his jacket and looked out at the flat, open land along the highway. He was homesick for the fields near Wheatley. He was homesick for the Black Hills, from where he had taken the high, narrow roads that led down to the outskirts of Wheatley. From the Black Hills he had seen, sort of, himself. He didn't know yet how he would get that back.

IN Brookings, he drove down the empty streets to Hansen Hall and parked behind it, next to his motorcycle. The lobby was deserted except for a couple making out on a couch in a dark corner. Mike tiredly climbed the stairs. Raymond was asleep, though he woke up when Mike came in. "I thought you weren't coming back until tomorrow," he said.

"I changed my mind."

"Why?"

"No reason," Mike said. Then he said, painfully, "No. There is one. But it's too much to explain. I'll tell you tomorrow."

He went down to the rest room, returned, and locked the door behind him. He undressed and got into bed. For the most part, the dorm was quiet. He heard a door slam, then the sighing sound of the heat coming on, which stirred the curtains. He could see the outline of his desk and chair, and the shapes of his books—the familiarity of things that belonged to him.

Across from him Raymond yawned and turned over. "Your girlfriend called," he said.

"Did she?"

"Twice."

Mike lay on his back in the darkness, picturing his father's face, and the three state police cars going past, one after the other, after the other. Too many things had happened. Too many of them had revolved around Mike. But that was over now.

And gradually, without effort, as Mike let himself move toward sleep, he realized that whatever happened to his father was not connected to him. There weren't unbreakable strings between people in families. Mike had thought there were, but when his father had pulled on them too hard, had counted on them unfairly, they'd broken.

He closed his eyes. He thought about driving up into the Black Hills on the curving roads; about his bedroom at home, with its view of the Hylers' house across the street; and about the Hylers' cats—the outside ones—waiting patiently on the broken-down porch for their dinners.

And finally he reached for his Walkman and headphones and listened to the tape Donetta had made for him. The first thing on the cassette was her voice. "It's three o'clock in the morning," she said. "I can't sleep, I can't dream, and I can't stop thinking of you."

He rewound and rewound it, listening to her voice until he fell asleep.

ABOUT THE AUTHOR

Judy Troy was born in northern Indiana. She has taught writing at an alternative high school, Indiana University, and the University of Missouri. Her collection of stories, *Mourning Doves,* was nominated for a *Los Angeles Times* Book Award, and she received the 1996 Whiting Writers' Award. She is now Alumni-Writer-in-Residence at Auburn University.

ABOUT THE TYPE

This book was set in Garamond No. 3, a variation of the classic Garamond typeface originally designed by the Parisian type cutter Claude Garamond (1480–1561).

Claude Garamond's distinguished romans and italics first appeared in *Opera Ciceronis* in 1543–44. The Garamond types are clear, open, and elegant.